ST. MARY'S COLLEGE OF EDUCATION
LIBRARY

Date Due	Date Due	Date Due

THE LIFE OF FRIEDRICH ENGELS

Other Works on Friedrich Engels by W. O. Henderson:

Engels: Selected Writings, edited by W. O. Henderson (Penguin Books, 1967)

Die Lage der arbeitenden Klasse in England, by Friedrich Engels, with an introduction by W. O. Henderson (Verlag J. H. W. Dietz, Hanover, 1965)

"Friedrich Engels in Manchester", by W. O. Henderson, in *Friedrich Engels 1820–1970* (Schriftenreihe des Forschungsinstituts der Friedrich-Ebert-Stiftung, 1971)

"The Firm of Ermen and Engels in Manchester", by W. O. Henderson in *Internationale Wissenschaftliche Korrespondez*, Heft 11/12, pp. 1–10, April, 1971

Books and Articles by Friedrich Engels translated and edited by W. O. Henderson and W. H. Chaloner:

Condition of the Working Class in England, by Friedrich Engels (Basil Blackwell, 1958; new edition 1970; Stanford University Press, 1968)

Friedrich Engels as Military Critic (Manchester University Press, 1959)

By W. O. Henderson and W. H. Chaloner:

"Friedrich Engels in Manchester" (*Memoirs and Proceedings of the Manchester Literary and Philosophical Society*, Vol. 98, Session 1956–7)

The Life of
Friedrich Engels

W. O. Henderson

In two volumes

VOLUME II

FRANK CASS: LONDON

First published 1976 *in Great Britain by*
FRANK CASS AND COMPANY LIMITED
67 Great Russell Street, London WC1B 3BT, England

and in United States of America by
FRANK CASS AND COMPANY LIMITED
c/o International Scholarly Book Services, Inc.
P.O. Box 4347, Portland, Oregon 97208

ISBN 0 7146 3040 3 (Case)
ISBN 0 7146 4003 4 (Paper)

Library of Congress Catalog Card No. 72–92963

Printed in Great Britain by
Clarke, Doble & Brendon Ltd.
Plymouth

Contents

Documents

Illustrations

* From *Reminiscences of Marx and Engels*, Foreign Languages Publishing House, Moscow.

6

ENGELS AND *DAS KAPITAL*

In whatever literary projects they were engaged Marx and Engels were accustomed to work in close co-operation. Engels gave his friend every possible assistance when he was writing his major work on the capitalist system.[1] Marx often consulted Engels on theoretical and practical problems. Engels had studied economics and had written an essay on "Outlines of a Critique of Political Economy" in the *Deutsch-Französische Jahrbücher* in 1844.[2] His wide reading and practical knowledge of business enabled him to offer valuable comments upon Marx's criticisms of the classical economists as well as upon Marx's own economic doctrines. Engels also gave Marx considerable help by supplying him with information concerning the cotton industry. Marx had no experience of the business world and he relied upon Engels for information concerning the running of an office or a factory. Sometimes Engels passed Marx's queries on to others. On Engels's advice Marx wrote to Henry Ermen for data concerning cotton spinning as practised in the Bridgewater Mill at Pendlebury.[3] The information that he received appeared in Marx's discussion of the rate of surplus value in the third part of the first volume of *Das Kapital*.[4]

In January 1851 Engels discussed Ricardo's theory of rent with Marx. Ricardo held that farm rents represented the difference between the value of the produce of a piece of land and the costs of production on that land. Rent also represented the difference between the yields of a fertile piece of land and of the least fertile land worth cultivating. Rent could be increased only in conjunction with a rise in the price of the produce of the land. Marx declared that Ricardo's theory was "everywhere contradicted by history". He argued that if – by scientific farming – the yield of land rose, the general level of rents might rise even if the price of particular products (such as cereals) fell. Engels reminded Marx that in his article of 1844 he had shown that improved agricultural techniques would counteract the decline in the fertility of farm land which had been brought about by excessive cultivation. Engels accepted Marx's theory of rent as "correct in every respect".[5] Eleven years later Marx returned to the problem. In June 1862 he claimed that he had at last solved the problem of the "swindle" of Ricardo's "ground rent shit".[6] On August 2, 1862 he discussed his new theory of rent at some length[7] and a few days later he argued that "even if one accepts the possibility of establishing the existence of an 'absolute' theory of ground rent, it certainly does not follow that in all circumstances the least fertile land or the least productive mine must pay rent".[8]

In February 1851 Marx and Engels examined the theory of the "currency school" that the economy should be protected against inflation (through the overissue of banknotes) by making paper money behave in the same way as a metallic currency. Marx argued that the volume, the expansion, or the contraction of the supply of money – coins or banknotes – were not affected by the import or export of bullion, or by the balance of trade, or by foreign exchange rates. Engels congratulated Marx on having elucidated satisfactorily "the simple, clear, fundamental facts of the mad theory of monetary circulation".[9] Subsequently Marx sent Engels a copy of Proudhon's latest work[10] with a vigorous criticism of the writer's views. He asked Engels for his comments. After reading half of the book Engels replied that he agreed with Marx's criticisms.[11]

In 1853 Marx and Engels corresponded on the question of landownership in the Orient. Engels declared that the absence of landed property there was "the key to whole history" of the region and he argued that this could be explained by such factors as the climate and the poor soil.[12] In January 1858 Marx wrote to Engels that his studies had reached a stage at which he wanted some practical information on matters about which the writers of books on the theory of economics were silent. In particular he asked for details of the circulation of capital and its effects upon profits and prices.[13] Shortly afterwards Marx asked how often the firm of Ermen & Engels renewed its machinery. He thought that Babbage had been "not quite trustworthy" when he wrote that machinery in Manchester was replaced after five years.[14] Engels agreed that Babbage had been "quite wrong". Lancashire manufacturers generally wrote off $7\frac{1}{2}$ per cent of the value of their machinery every year to cover repairs and depreciation. This meant that machinery was expected to last for 13 years and four months. But Engels added that one could find cotton mills in Manchester operating machinery that was twenty – even thirty – years old.[15] Marx returned to the problem some years later when he argued that the profits from the sale of goods made by machinery was "a progressive return on fixed capital, enabling a manufacturer to build up what is in effect a fund on which he can draw to replace his machinery when it has worn out."[16]

On another occasion Marx asked Engels what proportion of a manufacturer's circulating capital was normally laid out in raw materials and wages and what proportion was kept in a bank. He considered that the theoretical laws on the subject were self-evident "but it is useful to know what happens in practice".[17] In March 1862 Marx asked Engels to let him have a description of "feeders on circular frames" and to suggest a German translation for the word "gigs".[18] He also enquired as to the structure of the labour force employed by the firm of Ermen & Engels. He wanted information concerning the nature of the tasks performed by various types of operatives. "I need an example for my book to show that the division of labour, as described by Adam Smith as the basis of manufacturing (in workshops without power-driven machinery) does not exist (in modern factories). Andrew Ure has already drawn attention to this fact. All I want is an example."[19]

In January 1863 Marx asked Engels about self-acting spinning machines. "My question is: What rôle did the so-called spinning operative play in machine spinning *before* the self-actor was invented? I can understand the self-actor but I cannot understand the situation as it existed before the self-actor was introduced."[20] In 1865 Marx wrote to Engels asking him to obtain from the manufacturer Alfred Knowles some information concerning the wages of cotton spinners in Lancashire and the price of raw cotton and yarn.[21]

In 1868 when Marx was working on the second volume of *Das Kapital* he asked Engels to find out from Carl Schorlemmer the title of "the most recent and best German book on agricultural chemistry". "I should also like to know the present state of the controversy between the supporters of mineral and nitrogen fertilisers." "And does Schorlemmer know anything about German scholars who have criticised Liebig's theory of the exhaustion of the soil? I must at least know, to some extent, the most recent state of the question when I am working on my chapter on ground rent."[22] In April 1868 Marx asked Engels for his opinion on the theory of the rate of profit that he had worked out. Marx was trying to explain "how it can happen that when the value of money (or gold) declines, the rate of profit rises and vice versa". Engels replied that Marx's theory was very clear.[23] In 1868 Marx asked Engels to describe the financial transactions between the firm of Ermen & Engels and its bankers. He wanted to know "the monetary way of doing things" when buying raw cotton. He also wished to know "your relationship with your customers with regard to bills of exchange".[24]

There were occasions when Marx asked for help of a different kind in his researches. In 1858 he needed a copy of J. Maclaren's recently published *A Sketch of the History of the Currency* which cost 9/6d. This was more money than he had in the house and so he asked Engels to send him a postal order. Engels did so.[25] In 1866 Marx wrote: "At this moment I have not got a farthing to spend on books." So he asked Engels to buy for him a copy of Thorold Rogers's *A History of Agriculture*.[26]

Since Engels spent some of the best years of his life in a far from congenial office in Manchester to earn enough money to enable Marx to write his book on the capitalist system it was natural that he should anxiously await the appearance of his friend's major work. Engels believed that it was essential for the future triumph of Marxian socialism that a full account of Marx's doctrines should be written by Marx himself. But Engels had to wait for many years before even the first volume of *Das Kapital* appeared and his patience was sometimes sorely tried. He repeatedly appealed to Marx to hasten the publication of the results of his researches. Marx, however, refused to be hurried and it took him over twenty years to produce the first volume of *Das Kapital*.

The saga of the writing of *Das Kapital* began in 1844 when Marx began to study economics and compiled some notes to form the basis of a draft of a book on *Criticism of Politics and National Economy*. In the following year Engels urged Marx to produce the book quickly. "Strike while the iron is hot," he wrote. The situation was favourable since – in his view – communist ideas were spreading rapidly in Germany at that time.[27] In August 1846 Marx assured the publisher Leske – who had paid him an advance on royalties – that the first part would be ready in November and the second would follow soon afterwards.[28] But at the end of 1846 Marx told Annenkov that he could not publish his book in Germany because of censorship difficulties.[29] The book was not published in Marx's lifetime. Eventually some of his notes were published under the title: *Economic and Philosophic Manuscripts of 1844*.[30]

Marx suspended his studies on economics in 1847 to write a pamphlet on *Misère de la Philosophie* – an attack upon Proudhon – and to engage in political activities which culminated in the production of the Communist Manifesto (1848). Then his editorial work on the *Neue Rheinische Zeitung* kept him busy in 1848 and the early months of 1849. His only writings on economics in those years were five leading articles on wages and capital which appeared in the *Neue Rheinische Zeitung* in April 1849. Engels declared that these articles were "a clear indication of the social aspects of our policy".[31]

In exile in London in 1850, after the failure of the revolution,

Marx returned to his researches in economics and embarked upon a study of Ricardo's theory of rent and the doctrine of the "currency school". In January 1851 Engels congratulated Marx on his new theory of rent and urged him to complete his book on economics as soon as possible.[32] Two months passed and then Marx told Engels that he hoped "to finish the whole economic shit" in five weeks.[33] Engels replied: "I am delighted that you have at last finished your book on economics. The whole business has taken too long."[34] Another two months passed and then Marx wrote to Weydemeyer: "I am usually at the British Museum from 9 o'clock in the morning to 7 o'clock at night. My subject has so many damned ramifications that I will not be able to finish it for another six to eight weeks, in spite of all my efforts. Then there are always practical interruptions, unavoidable in the miserable conditions under which one vegetates here. Nevertheless the job is rapidly approaching completion. One must break off somewhere or other by main force."[35] In August Marx wrote that his time was fully occupied with his book.[36] In October Marx declared that he was still working on his book but that much of his time was taken up with the study of technology and agricultural science.[37] Marx's notes and comments upon Ricardo's *On the Principles of Political Economy and Taxation*, compiled in the spring of 1851, show how conscientiously he was studying the works of the classical economists at this time.[38]

Marx does not seem to have made much progress with his book on economics in 1852 or in 1853. Much of his time was devoted to writing a pamphlet denouncing the methods used by the Prussian police and judicial authorities to secure the conviction of the German communists who had been brought to trial at Cologne.[39] In December 1852 Marx told his friend Adolph Cluss that the Cologne trial had "totally estranged the German booksellers with whom I had hoped to sign a contract for my *Political Economy*"[40] Nearly a year later, in a letter to Cluss, Marx confidently predicted that there would be a commercial crisis in the following spring. "I still hope that – before this occurs – I shall be able to retire quietly for a few months to finish my *Political Economy*. But I doubt if I shall be able to manage it."[41] For the next four years Marx appears to have done little work on his collection of notebooks on economics. He was too busy writing articles for the press and composing a brilliant denunciation of Louis Napoleon's coup d'état of December 2, 1851,[42] which Engels described as "a work of genius".[43]

It was only towards the end of 1857 that Karl Marx resumed his researches on economics. He told Lassalle that he had been "spurred on by the present commercial crisis to turn again seriously to my work on the *Principles of Economics*". "I have to work throughout the day to earn a living and so only the nights are left for *real* work. And I am also delayed by illness."[44] To Engels he wrote that he was working until four in the morning – and consuming "an immense quantity of tobacco" – on two projects. The first was his *Principles of Economics* and the second was a pamphlet on the commercial crisis of 1857.[45] The pamphlet was never written. In February 1858 Marx informed Lassalle that he had been working for several months on the "final version" of his book on economics.[46] He explained that he planned to write six volumes on (1) capital, (2) landed property, (3) wage labour, (4) the state, (5) international trade, and (6) the world market.[47] By this time Marx had written a rough draft (*Rohentwurf*) of the first of his six volumes. This consisted of two long chapters on money and capital. The second was divided into three sections: (i) how capital is formed, (ii) how capital circulates, and (iii) how surplus value is turned into profit. This first draft of what eventually became the first volume of *Das Kapital* was published in Russia in 1939–41 and in Germany in 1953.[48] Marx described this "rough draft" as a series of monographs written for "self-understanding" and not for publication.[49]

Marx now decided to rewrite the "rough draft" and to publish it in parts. Lassalle found a publisher for him – F. G. Duncker of Berlin – who agreed that the book should appear in serial form. In March 1858 Lassalle urged Marx to let Duncker have the first part as soon as possible.[50] But in April Marx told Engels that his liver complaint made it impossible for him to start on the manuscript.[51] And it was not until September that he wrote to Engels that the manuscript would be ready in a fortnight.[52] But two months later Jenny Marx was still making a fair copy of the manuscript.[53] Marx told Lassalle that the delay had been caused because of his determination to improve his style. "I owe it to the Party that my book should not be spoiled by being written in a stolid, wooden style and that is how I write when my liver is out of order."[54]

On January 21, 1859 Marx was at last able to report to Engels that "the wretched manuscript is ready but I cannot post it as I have not got a farthing for postage or insurance".[55] So Engels sent Marx £2 and the manuscript was sent to Duncker on January 25.[56] The preface followed on February 23. Published as *Zur Kritik der politischen Ökonomie* the little book consisted of two thirds of the first part of Volume I of the six volumes that Marx had hoped to write. It was only a fragment of a vast project which was never realised. By the middle of 1862 Marx had abandoned his grandiose plan. What was originally planned to be the third chapter of Part I of Volume I of *Zur Kritik der politischen Ökonomie* eventually became the book on capital which made Marx famous.

In January 1860 Engels urged Marx to complete the third chapter of *Zur Kritik der politischen Ökonomie* – the one on capital – without delay. He wrote: "I do wish that at long last you would be a little less conscientious in passing judgment upon your own work. What you write is far too good for the lousy public anyhow. What really matters is that your work should be written and published. The silly asses will not tumble to the weaknesses in it that you can see. And suppose that the revolution breaks out. How would you feel then if you had allowed your researches to be interrupted and if you had not even published the chapter on 'capital in general'?" Engels warned Marx not to be deflected from writing his chapter on capital by his natural anger at Karl Vogt's recent pamphlet attacking him.[57] But Engels's appeal fell upon deaf ears. Marx was determined that Vogt should not be allowed to get away with allegations that he was living on the fat of the land at the expense of the workers. He believed – and he was later proved to be correct – that Vogt, once a member of the Frankfurt Parliament, was now a paid agent of Napoleon III. So Marx laid aside his work on economics to write a lengthy and abusive pamphlet attacking Karl Vogt.[58]

Marx resumed work on his chapter on capital in the autumn of 1860. In September he told Lassalle that he hoped to let Duncker have the manuscript by Easter 1861.[59] But eighteen months passed and still the chapter had not been completed. By June 1862 what had been planned as a "chapter" had grown into a "book". Marx wrote to Engels: "Despite all the miseries with which I am afflicted my brain box is working better than it has done for years." He claimed that he was working hard and explained that he was writing at greater length on capital than he had originally planned "because the German dogs judge a book by its weight".[60] Six months later – at the end of 1862 – Marx reverted for a moment to his original plan. He told Dr Kugelmann that his chapter on capital was finished "apart from making a fair copy and giving it a final polish for the press." He proposed to find a new publisher since Duncker had taken too long to get *Zur Kritik der politischen Ökonomie* into print. Marx explained to Dr Kugelmann that his new chapter covered what was known in England as "the principles of political economy".[61]

In 1862 and in the first half of 1863 Marx worked on his theory of surplus value. But he failed to rewrite his notes in a form suitable for publication. After Marx's death – when Engels had brought out the second and third volumes of *Das Kapital* – Engels planned to edit Marx's manuscript on surplus value and to publish it as the fourth and final volume of *Das Kapital*. But Engels did not carry out the project. It was not until 1905–10 that Kautsky edited part of Marx's manuscript of 1862–3 and published it under the title: *Theorien über den Mehrwert*.[62]

Marx made only slow progress with *Das Kapital* in the second half of 1863 and in 1864. The Polish rising of January 1863 fired Marx and Engels with enthusiasm, for they hoped that it would be a signal for revolutions all over the Continent. Marx declared that "the era of revolution is now again fairly opened in Europe"[63] and Engels replied that if only the Poles could hold out, the conflagration would soon spread through the length and breadth of Russia.[64] In the spring of 1863 and again in the autumn of 1864 Marx turned aside from his studies of economics to plunge into a detailed examination of the history of the Polish question.[65]

Although *Das Kapital* was delayed, it was not forgotten. In May 1863 when Engels impatiently declared that it was high time that the book was finished,[66] Marx replied: "If only I could retire quietly somewhere I could soon complete the manuscript."[67] Several months passed and in August 1863 Marx assured Engels that *Das Kapital* was making satisfactory progress.[68] In 1864 Marx was busy with private and political affairs. He received two legacies and moved to a new house. In the autumn of that year, when the First International was established, Marx devoted much of his time to the affairs of this organisation. Consequently little work was done on *Das Kapital* in 1864. In October Marx blamed his boils and carbuncles for his slow progress.[69] And then in November he told Dr Kugelmann that his book would be ready for the press in 1865.[70]

In February 1865 Marx was in touch with a new publisher – Otto Meissner of Hamburg[71] – who in that year had brought out a pamphlet by Engels on the military controversy in Prussia. In May Marx claimed that he was "working like a horse".[72] In June he interrupted his work on his book so that he could prepare a lecture – an attack upon John Weston – on "Wages, Prices and Profit" for the Central Council of the First International. In July Marx wrote that his book was nearing completion. All that remained to be written were three chapters of "the theoretical part" and the "historical literary section". "I cannot bring myself to send off any part of the manuscript until the whole of it is ready. Whatever my failings as a writer may be I can claim the merit of producing something which is an artistic unity." "And this can be achieved only by never letting anything get into print until the entire work has been completed."[73] Marx declared that his "damned book" had been "*finished* at the end of December (1865)".[74] What Marx meant was that a first draft had been completed. He still had to polish the style, to make some revisions, and to write out a fair copy. What had first been intended to be a chapter and then a book was now being planned as a work in three volumes.[75] The first volume would cover "the process of capitalist production" the second would be "the continuation and conclusion of the theories", and the third would examine "the history of political economy from the middle of the seventeenth century".[76] The original section on rent had been greatly expanded.[77] Marx began to make his fair copy on January 1, 1866 "working twelve hours a day"[78] but in February he fell ill[79] and in April he told Dr Kugelmann that over two months had been lost.[80]

In the summer of 1866 the completion of Marx's manuscript was delayed not only by illness[81] but by his work for the International Working Men's Association – particularly the preparations for its first conference in Geneva and the publication of its journal, *The Commonwealth*. Marx now decided to issue the first volume of *Das Kapital* separately and not, as originally planned, at the same time as the second volume. He wrote to Engels that he hoped to complete the first volume by August.[82] But in August Engels was told that the manuscript was not yet finished and that Marx had no money with which to buy writing paper.[83] In October Marx assured Dr Kugelmann that the manuscript would be sent to Meissner by November.[84] This time he kept his word. On November 10 he told Engels that the first pages of the manuscript would go to Meissner "next week".[85] Engels was delighted at this good news which, he declared, had lifted a great weight from his mind.[86]

In January 1867 Marx told Engels that Meissner had suggested that the first two volumes of *Das Kapital* should be published together. Marx declared that he could not complete the second volume at the same time as the first. Owing to his poor health he would need to recuperate when the first volume was finished. Moreover Marx proposed to go to the Continent as soon as possible to try to borrow some money.[87] In February Marx assured Engels that if only his creditors would leave him alone – his grocer was pestering him for £5 – he could soon complete his manuscript.[88] In the middle of March Engels enquired if the book was now ready for the printer.[89] At last, on March 27, Marx wrote that his first volume was complete and that he would take the manuscript to the publisher himself if Engels would pay his fare.[90] Engels was delighted. He wrote: "Hurrah! I could not repress this exclamation when I at last read in black and white that your first volume is finished and that you propose to take it yourself to Hamburg."[91] On April 13, 1867 Marx wrote from Hamburg that the precious manuscript had been deposited in Meissner's safe.[92] A few days later Marx wrote from Hanover – where he was the guest of Dr Kugelmann – that Meissner had sent his manuscript to Otto Wigand of Leipzig to be printed.[93]

On April 30, 1867 Marx wrote to his friend Siegfried Meyer to explain his recent silence. "It is because I have continually had one foot in the grave. I have had to use *every* minute – when I have been fit to work – to complete the book for which I have sacrificed my health, my fortune, and my family . . . I laugh at so-called 'practical' men and their wisdom. Anyone who wants to behave like an ox can, of course turn his back upon the misfortunes of humanity and look after his own skin. But I would really have regarded myself as 'impractical' if I had pegged out before I had at least finished the manuscript of my book." "In a few weeks the first volume will be published in Hamburg by Otto Meissner."[94]

Marx wrote to Engels on May 7 from Hanover: "That damned fellow Wigand did not start to print my book until April 29, so that I did not receive the first proofs until the day before yesterday. . . ." Meissner had asked for the manuscripts of the second and third volumes by the following spring. Marx thanked Engels for his help. "Without you I could never have finished my book. I assure you that it has lain heavily upon my conscience that your wonderful powers should have gone to rust in the world of business mainly on my account." "And you have had to share my *petites misères* into the bargain."[95]

In the summer of 1867 Engels helped Marx to correct the proofs of the first volume of *Das Kapital*. He praised the book, for which he had waited so long, but offered two criticisms. First, Engels thought that, in comparison with *Zur Kritik der politischen Ökonomie*, the theoretical argument was clearer in *Das Kapital* but the narrative was not so vivid. Secondly, he urged Marx to insert subheadings to help the reader to follow the more abstract arguments. "The general reader – even the scholarly reader – is no longer accustomed to this type of (dialectical) thinking and it is therefore necessary to help him as much as possible."[96] Marx replied: "Your satisfaction at what you have read so far is more important to me than anything that the rest of the world may say. Anyhow I hope that as long as they live, the bourgeoisie will have cause to remember my carbuncles!"[97] Meanwhile Marx and Engels were trying to find translators and publishers for French and English editions of *Das Kapital*. Marx asked Ludwig Büchner to recommend a French translator.[98] Engels persuaded his friend

Samuel Moore to undertake the English translation.[99] Marx arranged that George Eccarius should approach Harrison & Co who might be prepared to publish an English translation of *Das Kapital*. If the negotiations were successful Marx promised Engels that "Mrs Lizzy" should have a new "London dress".[100] But Lizzie Burns did not get her dress since twenty years elapsed before the English translation was published.

On August 15, 1867 Engels wrote to Marx that he had finished reading the proofs of the first volume of *Das Kapital*. "I consider that it is *essential* to get the second volume out – and the sooner the better."[101] On the following day Marx wrote that he had sent the last of the proofs to Meissner. "I have you – and you alone – to thank that this has been possible. Without your sacrifice on my behalf, I could not possibly have undertaken the immense researches required to write the three volumes. I embrace you, full of thanks. . . ."[102] In his reply Engels again urged Marx to insert more subheadings in his book. The fourth chapter was nearly 200 pages long but had only four subheadings which were difficult to find.[103] In September 1867 the first volume of *Das Kapital* was published. A few weeks earlier Marx had written that he was working on the second volume.[104] It was not until many years later – after Marx's death – that Engels discovered that the manuscripts of the second and third volumes had never been prepared for publication. When the manuscripts came into his possession he found that they were "written in a slovenly stlyle", that the technical expressions were in English or French, and that whole pages were in English. "Marx's thoughts appeared on paper exactly as they had first been formed in his brain."[105]

Why did it take Marx so long to write the first volume of *Das Kapital* and why did he never publish the later volumes? Marx gave various explanations for this which, however, did not tell the whole story. His main excuse was that long periods of ill health prevented him from writing. It is true that for many weeks at a time Marx was incapacitated by carbuncles, boils and digestive troubles. Moreover his illness was aggravated by nervous strain brought about by continual financial worries. But it is also true that Marx brought ill health upon himself. There were times when he worked for ridiculously long hours. Engels declared in 1866 that "the book has been largely responsible for your poor health".[106] Moreover Marx frequently ignored his doctor's advice to reduce smoking and to eat less highly spiced foods.

Another reason advanced by Marx for his slow progress was that – to earn his living – he had to devote much of his time to journalism. Marx spent many hours preparing and writing a single article. He would sometimes go to the reading room of the British Museum for several days to gather material for a single article. "To write continually for a newspaper, tires me out," he complained in 1853.[107] Marx was a compulsive reader. He studied subjects which lay only on the fringe of his main theme. He once complained to Weydemeyer that his subject had "so many damned ramifications".[108] He admitted that his researches had led him to investigate "apparently quite remote disciplines."[109] In 1851 Engels wrote to Marx: "The trouble with you is that you will not get down to writing anything so long as there is a single important book on the subject that you have not read."[110] And a few months later he reminded Marx that their first book – *The Holy Family* – had been planned as a pamphlet but had ended up as a book.[111]

These were by no means the only reasons for Marx's failure to finish *Das Kapital* more quickly. His study of economics was supposed to be his main work since his elucidation of the nature of capital was intended to pave the way for the triumph of socialism. But he allowed himself to be diverted from his main task by his political activities. Much time was taken up by writing pamphlets attacking his enemies – such as Proudhon, Karl Vogt, Louis Napoleon and the Prussian government. And when the First International was founded in 1864 Marx plunged into active political propaganda again. All these activities took up time which might have been devoted to writing *Das Kapital*.

Perhaps none of these explanations really account for Marx's inability to finish his life's work. It has been argued that he was incapable of finishing the task which he had undertaken. In his imagination Marx saw the six volumes which he had planned in 1858 as something much more than a standard work on economics. They were to give the world a new materialist philosophy which would inspire the communist social and political order of the future. The ideal work which Marx planned would be more accurate and more comprehensive than any ordinary book on economics. It has been argued that Marx never finished *Das Kapital* because he was always searching for new facts to confirm his theories. Twelve years after the appearance of the first volume of *Das Kapital* Marx told Danielson that he could not complete the second volume because he was studying "the bulk of materials I have had not only from Russia but from the United States etc". Moreover he considered that it was essential for him to await the outcome of "the present English industrial crisis".[112]

Another possible reason for the slow progress of *Das Kapital* was the fact that Marx's methods of research were, in certain respects, different from those of other scholars. Research normally involves posing a problem, ascertaining the facts, and then propounding a solution. Marx, however, began by propounding a solution to a problem and then proceeded to find facts which would support his conclusion. He claimed that his theories were revealed to him in a flash of inspiration. He subsequently devoted years of research to proving that he was right. Treitschke wrote that "Marx completely lacked a scholar's conscience which is the hallmark of a genuine man of learning. In his works there is no trace of the humility of the true researcher who, aware of his own ignorance, approaches his material with an open mind in order to learn. For Marx what has to be proved is known before the research starts."[113] And it has been argued that Marx dared not complete his great work in case the day after publication some new book might appear containing facts that did not accord with Marx's grand design.

Arnold Künzli argues that Marx was "a master of non-fulfilment". "There is hardly any other thinker in his class who has been so incapable of moulding his life's work into a proper form". "The whole of Marx's work is a single fragment. Or rather it is largely a collection of fragments many of which have been put together with great difficulty after his death. It is a Greek torso without arms or legs stuck together by more or less skilled disciples and researchers."[114]

Marx was a perfectionist. Paul Lafargue wrote that he was never satisfied with what he wrote. "He was always making some improvements and he always found his rendering inferior to the idea he wished to convey."[115] Engels complained that Marx was too conscientious in passing judgment on his own writings. And so the philosopher, who hoped to influence mankind for hundreds of years to come, published only a fragment of his main work.

In 1867, when the first volume of *Das Kapital* appeared, Engels – though anxious that the completion of the later volumes should not be delayed – was more concerned that the first volume should be adequately publicised. Some years previously Marx had complained to Dr Kugelmann about "the conspiracy of silence with which I am honoured by the German literary rogues".[116] Now he dreaded "the conspiracy of silence of the experts and newspaper crowd".[117] In November 1867 Marx declared that the lack of reviews of his book was making him feel "fidgety"[118] while Engels wrote to Dr Kugelmann that "the German press is still silent about *Das Kapital*."[119] And the year after Marx's death Engels complained that the first volume of *Das Kapital* had been for many years "both zealously plagiarised and obstinately hushed up by official German economists."[120]

Engels was determined to make the first volume of *Das Kapital* known in Germany and elsewhere. To do this he resorted to an unscrupulous strategem. Through his German friends – Siebel, Kugelmann, and Liebknecht – he foisted ten reviews of his own upon the unsuspecting editors of various newspapers and periodicals. He skilfully changed his style of writing and his attitude towards the book to suit the different types of readers of the journals whose editors he deceived. The review written for the *Barmen-Zeitung* in his home town (a paper with middle class readers) was couched in very different language from the article written for the *Demo-kratisches Wochenblatt* (which was read mainly by workers). On one occasion Marx gave Engels detailed instructions on how to write an article on *Das Kapital* for the *Beobachter*.[121] A book is normally reviewed by an impartial writer who is not connected with the author. But Engels's articles on *Das Kapital* came from the pen of Marx's closest friend and this was not known either by the editors of the periodicals and newspapers or by their readers.

In September 1867 Engels asked Marx if he should plant an article on *Das Kapital* in a German paper – through Meissner or Siebel – "attacking the book from a middle class point of view". This would help to bring Marx's work to the attention of the public.[122] Marx agreed that "the best way to wage war would be to attack the book from a bourgeois standpoint". And Dr Kugelmann should be told how to write some reviews himself.[123] In October Engels – at Marx's urgent request[124] – sent some articles to Dr Kugelmann and to Siebel.[125] On October 18 he appealed to Siegfried Meyer to do everything in his power to publicise Marx's book in the German-American press.[126] On the same day Engels wrote to Marx: "I can write four or five articles about your book from different points of view but I do not know where to send them".[127] Marx replied: "Send me your reviews for German papers and I will have them copied and sent to the most suitable papers." He also asked Engels to write an article on *Das Kapital* for the *Fortnightly Review*. Professor Beesly would get it published.[128] Engels wrote that he was preparing two articles for Siebel who had promised to place them in German journals.[129] On November 8 Engels reported that Siebel, whom he had met in Liverpool, had promised to place three more of Engels's articles in German papers.[130]

By January 1868 Marx was able to tell Dr Kugelmann: "You probably know that Engels and Siebel have got articles about my book published in the *Barmen-Zeitung*, the *Elberfelder-Zeitung*, the *Frankfurter Börsen-Zeitung* and . . . in the *Düsseldorfer-Zeitung*".[131] In that year Engels wrote two articles on *Das Kapital* which were submitted to the *Fortnightly Review* but – despite Beesly's efforts to get them accepted – they were rejected by the editor John Morley.[132] Engels declared that Morley was a bourgeois who had "every reason in the world to stop your ideas from getting any publicity".[133] Marx subsequently discussed the matter with Beesly who said that Engels's articles were "too dry".[134]

Even to some of his own friends Marx kept silent about the true authorship of the articles on his book written by Engels. In July 1868, for example, he wrote to Siegfried Meyer that several favourable reviews of *Das Kapital* had appeared in the German press but he failed to mention that some of them had been written by Engels.[135]

Among Marx's disciples few did more than Wilhelm Liebknecht to make *Das Kapital* known in Germany. He told Engels in January 1868 that he had reprinted Marx's introduction to *Das Kapital* in the Leipzig *Demokratisches Wochenblatt* (which he edited) and had sent copies of the introduction to several papers in Switzerland. He had written to many "influential people" about *Das Kapital*. He had "bombarded" the Vienna *Presse* and the Berlin *Volkszeitung* with information about the book. And he had spoken about *Das Kapital* in his recent speeches to working class audiences.[136] In March 1868 Liebknecht thanked Engels for an article on *Das Kapital* suitable for publication in the *Demokratisches Wochenblatt* and other papers. He mentioned that Marx's book was selling well in Germany and declared that the best way to publicise it would be to refer to it in a speech in the North German Reichstag. "I will certainly do my duty in that respect".[137]

In two articles on *Das Kapital* which appeared in Liebknecht's *Demokratisches Wochenblatt*[138] Engels declared that "as long as capitalists and workers have existed no book has appeared which is of such importance for the workers as *Das Kapital*. The relation between capital and labour, the hinge on which our entire present system of society turns, is here treated scientifically for the first time and with a thoroughness and acuteness of which only a German is capable." Engels summarised Marx's doctrine of "surplus value". According to Marx "every worker employed by the capitalist performs a two-fold labour". "During one part of his working time he replaces the wages advanced to him by the capitalist. This part of his labour Marx calls 'necessary labour'. But afterwards the worker has to go on working and during that time he produces 'surplus labour' for the capitalist, a significant portion of which constitutes profit." Engels explained that the longer the working day the greater was the "surplus value" pocketed by the capitalist. Hence it was in the interest of the workers to reduce the length of the working day. In England the factory workers had secured a ten-hour day. Legal restrictions on the length of the working day applied only to women, children and young persons but – in practice – the men also enjoyed the benefits of the law. "The English factory workers have won this law after years of endurance and after a long stubborn struggle with the factory owners." Engels observed that by 1867 the law had been extended to nearly all branches of industry in which women and children were employed. He urged his German readers to press for similar legislation in the North German Federation when the Reichstag met. "We hope that none of the deputies elected by German workers will discuss this bill without previously making themselves thoroughly conversant with Marx's book." "Marx's book gives the representatives of the workers in ready form all the material that they require." Engels concluded his review by asserting that capital "is continually increased and multiplied". "And the power of capital over the workers who own no property is also continually increased. Just as capital itself is reproduced on an ever greater scale so the modern capitalist method reproduces the class of workers (who own no property) on an ever increasing scale." Engels believed that Marx had scientifically proved "the main laws of the modern capitalist social system and the official economists have been careful not even to attempt to refute them." Marx had shown that capitalism creates not only wealth but also "the social class of oppressed workers which is more and more compelled to claim the utilisation of this wealth and productive forces for the whole of society." Engels's "little manoeuvres" to publicise the first volume of *Das Kapital* were not very successful. There was no quick sale for the book. It was not until 1872 that the first edition was sold out – earning a mere £60 for the author in royalties. But Marx's book was by that time at last becoming more widely known. Not only was a new German edition published in 1872 but French and Russian translations also appeared.

In September 1868 Engels proposed to Marx that a short popular version of *Das Kapital* should be prepared for the workers.[139] Marx agreed and suggested that Engels should write a pamphlet summarising the main points of *Das Kapital*.[140] Engels prepared a brief conspectus of *Das Kapital*[141] but it was not published. It was not until the 1880s that a pamphlet by Engels entitled *Socialism – Utopian and Scientific*[142] – three chapters from his *Anti-Dühring* – served as a popular introduction to Marx's doctrines and achieved a wide circulation among the workers in many countries.

NOTES

1 The correspondence between Marx and Engels on *Das Kapital* has been printed in Marx-Engels, *Briefe über "Das Kapital"* (1954). See also L. E. Mins (ed.), *Engels on "Capital"* (1937).

2 English translation in W. O. Henderson (ed.), *Engels: Selected Writings* (Penguin Books, 1967), pp. 148–77.

3 F. Engels to Karl Marx, May 10, 1868 in *Gesamtausgabe*, Part III, Vol. 4, p. 53.

4 Karl Marx, *Capital* (English translation by Eden and Cedar Paul, Everyman Edition, 1930), Vol. 1, pp. 216–17.

5 Karl Marx to F. Engels, January 7 and February 3, 1851 and F. Engels to Karl Marx, January 29, 1851 in *Gesamtausgabe*, Part III, Vol. 1, pp. 124–36.

6 Karl Marx to F. Engels, June 18, 1862 in *Gesamtausgabe*, Part III, Vol. 3, p. 77.

7 Karl Marx to F. Engels, August 2, 1862 in *Gesamtausgabe*, Part III, Vol. 3, pp. 86–91.

8 Karl Marx to F. Engels, August 9, 1862 in *Gesamtausgabe*, Part III, Vol. 3, pp. 94–5.

9 Karl Marx to F. Engels, February 3, 1851 and F. Engels to Karl Marx, February 25, 1851 in *Gesamtausgabe*, Part III, Vol. 1, pp. 136–40.

10 P. J. Proudhon, *Idée générale de la révolution au dix-neuvième siècle* (1851).

11 Karl Marx to F. Engels, August 14 and October 13, 1851 and F. Engels to Karl Marx, August 21, 1851 in *Gesamtausgabe*, Part III, Vol. 1, pp. 239–44 and p. 275.

12 F. Engels to Karl Marx, June 6, 1853 in *Gesamtausgabe*, Part III, Vol. 1, pp. 480–2.

13 Karl Marx to F. Engels, January 29, 1858 in *Gesamtausgabe*, Part III, Vol. 2, p. 280.

14 Karl Marx to F. Engels, March 2, 1858 in *Gesamtausgabe*, Part III, Vol. 2, p. 295.

15 F. Engels to Karl Marx, March 4, 1858 in *Gesamtausgabe*, Part III, Vol. 2, pp. 295–9.

16 Karl Marx to F. Engels, August 20, 1862 and August 24, 1867 in *Gesamtausgabe*, Part III, Vol. 3, pp. 98–9 and p. 410. In letters of August 26 and 27, 1867 (*ibid.*, pp. 411–14) Engels stated that machinery was written off at $7\frac{1}{2}$ per cent (depreciation only) or at 10 per cent (depreciation and repairs). In 1868 Engels wrote to Marx that he (Marx) had been misled by Henry Ermen concerning the depreciation of steam engines in cotton mills (*ibid.*, Vol. 4, p. 54).

17 Karl Marx to F. Engels, March 5, 1858 in *Gesamtausgabe*, Part III, Vol. 2, pp. 297–300.

18 On July 7, 1866 Marx asked Engels how to translate "put stretches upon the mule", "picks" (in weaving), and "flyer" on a spinning mule (Karl Marx to F. Engels, July 7, 1866 in *Gesamtausgabe*, Part III, Vol. 3, p. 343).

19 Karl Marx to F. Engels, March 6, 1862 (postscript) in *Gesamtausgabe*, Part III, Vol. 3, p. 61. In *Das Kapital* Marx quoted in a footnote the following sentence from Andrew Ure, *Philosophy of Manufacture* (1835), p. 20: "The principle of the factory system, then, is to substitute . . . the partition of a process into its essential constituents,

for the division or gradation of labour among many artisans." See Karl Marx, *Capital* (Everyman Edition, 1930), Vol. 1, p. 402.

20 Karl Marx to F. Engels, January 28, 1863 in *Gesamtausgabe*, Part III, Vol. 3, p. 123. See also his previous letter of January 24 (*ibid.*, p. 120). The self-actor, invented by Richard Roberts, was a spinning machine which made the mules run in and out at the proper speed by means of an automatic device.

21 Karl Marx to F. Engels, November 20, 1865 in *Gesamtausgabe*, Part III, Vol. 3, p. 287. Alfred Knowles (of H. Knowles & Sons) was a cotton spinner. His address in 1869 was 53 Hyde Grove, Plymouth Grove, Manchester.

22 Karl Marx to F. Engels, January 3, 1868 in *Gesamtausgabe*, Part III, Vol. 4, p. 2.

23 Karl Marx to F. Engels, April 22, 26 and 30, 1868 and F. Engels to Karl Marx, April 26 and May 6, 1868 in *Gesamtausgabe*, Part III, Vol. 4, pp. 41–51.

24 Karl Marx to F. Engels, November 14, 1868 in *Gesamtausgabe*, Part III, Vol. 4, p. 125 (second letter of that date).

25 Karl Marx to F. Engels, May 31 and June 7, 1858 in *Gesamtausgabe*, Part III, Vol. 2, pp. 320–1.

26 Karl Marx to F. Engels, December 17, 1866 and January 19, 1867 in *Gesamtausgabe*, Part III, Vol. 3, p. 370 and p. 374.

27 F. Engels to Karl Marx, January 20, 1845 in *Gesamtausgabe*, Part III, Vol. 1, p. 10.

28 Karl Marx to K. W. Leske, August 1, 1846 in Karl Marx and Friedrich Engels, *Briefe über "Das Kapital"* (1954), pp. 13–15.

29 Karl Marx to P. W. Annenhow, December 28, 1846 in Karl Marx and F. Engels, *Briefe über "Das Kapital"* (1954), p. 27.

30 Karl Marx, *Economic and Philosophic Manuscripts of 1844* (Foreign Languages Publishing House, Moscow, 1961): first published in Russia in 1927 and in Germany in 1932.

31 F. Engels, "Marx und die *Neue Rheinische Zeitung*" in the *Sozialdemokrat*, March 13, 1884: reprinted in Karl Marx – Friedrich Engels, *Die Revolution von 1848 . . .* (1955), p. 37.

32 F. Engels to Karl Marx, January 29, 1851 in *Gesamtausgabe*, Part III, Vol. 1, p. 135.

33 Karl Marx to F. Engels, April 2, 1851 in *Gesamtausgabe*, Part III, Vol. 1, p. 180.

34 F. Engels to Karl Marx, April 3, 1851 in *Gesamtausgabe*, Part III, Vol. 1, p. 184.

35 Karl Marx to J. Weydemeyer, June 27, 1851 in Karl Marx and F. Engels, *Letters to Americans 1848–95* (1963), p. 23.

36 Karl Marx to F. Engels, August 14, 1851 in *Gesamtausgabe*, Part III, Vol. 1, p. 241.

37 Karl Marx to F. Engels, October 15, 1851 in *Gesamtausgabe*, Part III, Vol. 1, p. 275.

38 See appendix to Karl Marx, *Grundrisse der Kritik der politischen Ökonomie* (Rohentwurf) (1857–8) (Europäische Verlagsanstalt, 1953), pp. 781–839.

39 Karl Marx, *Enthüllungen über den Kommunisten-Prozess zu Köln* (1852: new edition with introduction by F. Engels, 1885). The first edition, printed in Switzerland, was seized by the German police. The pamphlet then appeared in the *New England Zeitung* (Boston) and 440 offprints were purchased by Engels for distribution in Germany.

40 Karl Marx to Adolph Cluss, December 7, 1852 in Karl Marx and F. Engels, *Letters to Americans 1848–95* (1963), p. 51.

41 Karl Marx to Adolph Cluss, September 15, 1853 in Karl Marx and F. Engels, *Briefe über "Das Kapital"* (1954), p. 67.

42 Karl Marx, *Der 18te Brumaire des Louis Napoleon* (1852). The first edition was published in New York by J. Weydemeyer in the journal *Die Revolution (eine Zeitschrift in zwanglosen Heften)*. The second edition was printed in Hamburg in 1869; the third in 1885).

43 F. Engels's preface to the third edition of Karl Marx, *Der 18te Brumaire des Louis Napoleon* (1885): English translation – Karl Marx, *The Eighteenth Brumaire of Louis Bonaparte* (Foreign Languages Publishing House, Moscow).

44 Karl Marx to F. Lassalle, December 21, 1857 in Karl Marx and F. Engels, *Briefe über "Das Kapital"* (1954), p. 78.

45 Karl Marx to F. Engels, December 18, 1857 and January 14, 1858 in *Gesamtausgabe*, Part III, Vol. 2, p. 258 and p. 274.

46 Karl Marx to F. Lassalle, February 22, 1858 in Karl Marx and F. Engels, *Briefe über "Das Kapital"* (1954), pp. 80–1. See also Karl Marx to F. Engels, April 2, 1858 in *Gesamtausgabe*, Part III, Vol. 2, pp. 307–12 and Karl Marx to J. Weydemeyer, February 1, 1859 in Karl Marx and F. Engels, *Letters to Americans 1848–95* (1963), pp. 60–2.

47 Plan of Karl Marx's book in six volumes (1858–62):
    Volume   I   On Capital

1. Capital in general
   (a) Goods
   (b) Money

   (c) Capital
      { (i) How capital is produced
        (ii) How capital circulates
        (iii) Capital, profit, and interest }

(a) How money becomes capital
(b) Absolute surplus value
(c) Relative surplus value
(d) Combination of absolute and relative surplus value
(e) Theories of surplus value

2. Competition
3. Credit

    Volume II   Ownership of Land
    Volume III   Wage–Labour
    Volume IV   The State
    Volume V   Foreign Trade
    Volume VI   The World Market

48 Karl Marx, *Grundrisse der Kritik der politischen Ökonomie* (Rohentwurf) (Europäische Verlagsanstalt, 1953): for an abridged English translation see D. McLellan (ed.), *Marx's Grundrisse* (1971).

49 Introduction to Karl Marx, *Zur Kritik der politischen Ökonomie* (1859).

50 F. Lassalle to Karl Marx, March 26, 1858 in A. Künzli, *Karl Marx* (1966), p. 271.

51 F. Engels to Karl Marx, April 2, 1858 in *Gesamtausgabe*, Part III, Vol. 2, p. 308. Jenny Marx wrote to Lassalle at this time to explain that her husband's illness would delay the completion of the manuscript (A. Künzli, *Karl Marx* (1966), p. 271).

52 Karl Marx to F. Engels, September 21, 1858 in *Gesamtausgabe*, Part III, Vol. 2, p. 338.

53 Karl Marx to F. Engels, November 29, 1858 in *Gesamtausgabe*, Part III, Vol. 2, p. 349.
54 Karl Marx to F. Lassalle, November 12, 1858 in Karl Marx and F. Engels, *Briefe über "Das Kapital"* (1954), p. 93.
55 Karl Marx to F. Engels, January 21, 1859 in *Gesamtausgabe*, Part III, Vol. 2, p. 357.
56 Karl Marx to F. Engels, January 26, 1859 in *Gesamtausgabe*, Part III, Vol. 2, p. 358. Marx was mistaken when he told Dr Kugelmann that he had sent the manuscript to Duncker in December 1858 (see Karl Marx, *Letters to Dr Kugelmann*, p. 24).
57 F. Engels to Karl Marx, January 31, 1860 in *Gesamtausgabe*, Part III, Vol. 2, p. 459.
58 Karl Marx, *Herr Vogt* (London, 1860: new edition Berlin, 1953).
59 Karl Marx to F. Lassalle, September 15, 1860 in Karl Marx and F. Engels, *Briefe über "Das Kapital"* (1954), p. 102.
60 Karl Marx to F. Engels, June 18, 1862 in *Gesamtausgabe*, Part III, Vol. 3, p. 77.
61 Karl Marx to L. Kugelmann, December 28, 1862 in Karl Marx, *Letters to Dr Kugelmann*, p. 23.
62 A new and better edition of Karl Marx's manuscript of 1862–3 on surplus value was published in 1965 as Volume 26 of *Karl Marx – F. Engels Werke*.
63 Karl Marx to F. Engels, February 13, 1863 in *Gesamtausgabe*, Part III, Vol. 3, p. 126.
64 F. Engels to Karl Marx, February 17, 1863 in *Gesamtausgabe*, Part III, Vol. 3, p. 128.
65 Karl Marx, *Manuskripte über die polnische Frage*, 1863–4 (The Hague, 1961: edited by Werner Conze and D. Hertz-Eichenrode). In 1863 the Workers Educational Society in London passed a resolution (inspired by Marx) supporting the Poles in their struggle for freedom. See F. Lassalle, *Gesammelte Reden und Schriften*, Vol. 4 (1919), pp. 304–5.
66 F. Engels to Karl Marx, May 20, 1863 in *Gesamtausgabe*, Part III, Vol. 3, p. 140.
67 Karl Marx to F. Engels, May 29, 1863 in *Gesamtausgabe*, Part III, Vol. 3, p. 141.
68 Karl Marx to F. Engels, August 15, 1863 in *Gesamtausgabe*, Part III, Vol. 3, p. 152.
69 Karl Marx to Karl Klings, October 4, 1864 in Karl Marx and F. Engels, *Briefe über "Das Kapital"* (1954), p. 124.
70 Karl Marx to L. Kugelmann, November 29, 1864 in Karl Marx, *Letters to Dr Kugelmann*, p. 26.
71 F. Engels to Karl Marx, February 5, 1865 in *Gesamtausgabe*, Part III, Vol. 3, p. 225.
72 Karl Marx to F. Engels, May 20, 1865 in *Gesamtausgabe*, Part III, Vol. 3, p. 272.
73 Karl Marx to F. Engels, July 31, 1865 in *Gesamtausgabe*, Part III, Vol. 3, p. 279.
74 Karl Marx to F. Engels, February 13, 1866 in *Gesamtausgabe*, Part III, Vol. 3, p. 308.
75 Karl Marx to L. Kugelmann, October 13, 1866 in Karl Marx, *Letters to Dr Kugelmann*, p. 43.
76 Karl Marx to S. Meyer, April 30, 1867 in Karl Marx and F. Engels, *Letters to Americans 1848–95* (1963), p. 73. See also Karl Marx to

L. Kugelmann, October 13, 1866 in Karl Marx, *Letters to Dr Kugelmann*, pp. 42–3.

77 Karl Marx to F. Engels, February 13, 1866 in *Gesamtausgabe*, Part III, Vol. 3, p. 308.

78 Karl Marx to L. Kugelmann, January 15, 1866 in Karl Marx, *Letters to Dr Kugelmann*, p. 33.

79 Karl Marx to F. Engels, February 10, 1866 in *Gesamtausgabe*, Part III, Vol. 3, p. 305.

80 Karl Marx to L. Kugelmann, April 6, 1866 in Karl Marx, *Letters to Dr Kugelmann*, p. 35.

81 Karl Marx to F. Engels, June 9, 1866 in *Gesamtausgabe*, Part III, Vol. 3, p. 338.

82 Karl Marx to F. Engels, July 7 and 21, 1866 in *Gesamtausgabe*, Part III, Vol. 3, p. 343 and p. 348.

83 Karl Marx to F. Engels, August 7, 1866 and F. Engels to Karl Marx, August 10, 1866 in *Gesamtausgabe*, Part III, Vol. 3, p. 354 and p. 356.

84 Karl Marx to L. Kugelmann, October 13, 1866 in Karl Marx, *Letters to Dr Kugelmann*, p. 42.

85 Karl Marx to F. Engels, November 10, 1866 in *Gesamtausgabe*, Part III, Vol. 3, p. 365.

86 F. Engels to Karl Marx, November 11, 1866 in *Gesamtausgabe*, Part III, Vol. 3, p. 366.

87 Karl Marx to F. Engels, January 19, 1867 in *Gesamtausgabe*, Part III, Vol. 3, p. 373.

88 Karl Marx to F. Engels, February 21, 1867 in *Gesamtausgabe*, Part III, Vol. 3, p. 375.

89 F. Engels to Karl Marx, March 13, 1867 in *Gesamtausgabe*, Part III, Vol. 3, p. 376.

90 Karl Marx to F. Engels, March 27, 1867 in *Gesamtausgabe*, Part III, Vol. 3, p. 378.

91 F. Engels to Karl Marx, April 4, 1867 in *Gesamtausgabe*, Part III, Vol. 3, p. 379.

92 Karl Marx to F. Engels, April 13, 1867 in *Gesamtausgabe*, Part III, Vol. 3, pp. 380–2.

93 Karl Marx to F. Engels, April 24, 1867 in *Gesamtausgabe*, Part III, Vol. 3, pp. 382–3.

94 Karl Marx to Siegfried Meyer, April 30, 1867 in Karl Marx and F. Engels, *Briefe über "Das Kapital"* (1954), p. 133. English translation in Karl Marx and F. Engels, *Letters to Americans 1848–95* 1963), pp. 73–4. Siegfried Meyer, a mining engineer, emigrated to the United States in 1867 and was one of the founders of the New York branch of the First International.

95 Karl Marx to F. Engels, May 7, 1867 in *Gesamtausgabe*, Part III, Vol. 3, pp. 388–9.

96 F. Engels to Karl Marx, June 16, 1867 in *Gesamtausgabe*, Part III, Vol. 3, p. 393.

97 Karl Marx to F. Engels, June 22, 1867 in *Gesamtausgabe*, Part III, Vol. 3, p. 395.

98 Karl Marx to L. Büchner, May 1, 1867 in Karl Marx and F. Engels, *Briefe über "Das Kapital"* (1954), pp. 134–5.

99 F. Engels to Karl Marx, June 24, 1867 in *Gesamtausgabe*, Part III, Vol. 3, p. 397.

100 Karl Marx to F. Engels, June 27, 1867 in *Gesamtausgabe*, Part III, Vol. 3, p. 402. On October 15, 1867 Marx wrote to Dr Kugelmann

that "a certain Natzmer in New York has offered himself as English translator. *Quod non*" (Karl Marx, *Letters to Dr Kugelmann*, p. 53).

101 F. Engels to Karl Marx, August 15, 1867 in *Gesamtausgabe*, Part III, Vol. 3, p. 407.

102 Karl Marx to F. Engels, August 16, 1867 in *Gesamtausgabe*, Part III, Vol. 3, p. 408.

103 F. Engels to Karl Marx, August 23, 1867 in *Gesamtausgabe*, Part III, Vol. 3, p. 408.

104 Karl Marx to F. Engels, August 24, 1867 in *Gesamtausgabe*, Part III, Vol. 3, pp. 409–11.

105 Engels's introduction of 1893 to Karl Marx, *Das Kapital*, Vol. II (edition of 1957), p. 3.

106 F. Engels to Karl Marx, November 11, 1866 in *Gesamtausgabe*, Part III, Vol. 3, p. 365.

107 Karl Marx to Adolph Cluss, September 15, 1853 in Karl Marx and F. Engels, *Briefe über "Das Kapital"* (1954), p. 67.

108 Karl Marx to J. Weydemeyer, June 27, 1851 in Karl Marx and F. Engels, *Letters to Americans 1848–95* (1963), p. 23.

109 Introduction to Karl Marx, *Zur Kritik der politischen Ökonomie* (1859).

110 F. Engels to Karl Marx, April 3, 1851 in *Gesamtausgabe*, Part III, Vol. 1, p. 184.

111 F. Engels to Karl Marx, November 27, 1851 in *Gesamtausgabe*, Part III, Vol. 1, p. 289.

112 Karl Marx to N. F. Danielson, April 10, 1879 in Karl Marx – F. Engels, *Briefe über "Das Kapital"* (1954), pp. 241–3. Marx's correspondence with Danielson is held in the Department of Manuscripts (add. Mss. 38075) of the British Museum.

113 Quoted in Hans Blum, *Das Deutsche Reich zur Zeit Bismarcks* (1893), p. 253.

114 Arnold Künzli, *Karl Marx* (1966), p. 282.

115 Paul Lafargue in *Reminiscences of Marx and Engels* Foreign Languages Publishing House, Moscow), p. 78.

116 Karl Marx to Dr Kugelmann, December 28, 1862 in Karl Marx, *Letters to Dr Kugelmann*, p. 23.

117 Karl Marx to Dr Kugelmann, December 7, 1867 in Karl Marx, *Letters to Dr Kugelmann*, p. 55.

118 Karl Marx to F. Engels, November 2, 1867 in *Gesamtausgabe*, Part III, Vol. 3, p. 440.

119 F. Engels to Dr Kugelmann, 8(–20) November, 1867 in Karl Marx and F. Engels, *Briefe über "Das Kapital"* (1954), p. 151

120 Engels's introduction to the first edition of *Der Ursprung der Familie, des Privateigentums und des Staates* (Hottingen–Zürich, 1884) (edition of 1952), p. 7. English translation: *The Origin of the Family, Private Property and the State* (Foreign Languages Publishing House, Moscow).

121 Karl Marx to F. Engels, December 7, 1867 in *Gesamtausgabe*, Part III, Vol. 3, pp. 459–61. An article by Engels, written on the lines suggested by Marx appeared in the *Beobachter* on December 27, 1867.

122 F. Engels to Karl Marx, September 11, 1867 in *Gesamtausgabe*, Part III, Vol. 3, p. 422.

123 Karl Marx to F. Engels, September 12, 1867 in *Gesamtausgabe*, Part III, Vol. 3, p. 423.

124 Karl Marx to F. Engels, October 10, 1867 in *Gesamtausgabe*, Part III, Vol. 3, p. 431.
125 F. Engels to Karl Marx, October 11, 1867 in *Gesamtausgabe*, Part III, Vol. 3, p. 431.
126 F. Engels to S. Meyer, October 18, 1867 in Karl Marx and F. Engels, *Briefe über "Das Kapital"* (1954), p. 151.
127 F. Engels to Karl Marx, October 18, 1867 in *Gesamtausgabe*, Part III, Vol. 3, p. 435.
128 Karl Marx to F. Engels, October 19, 1867 in *Gesamtausgabe*, Part III, Vol. 3, p. 437.
129 F. Engels to Karl Marx, October 22, 1867 in *Gesamtausgabe*, Part III, Vol. 3, p. 438.
130 F. Engels to Karl Marx, November 8, 1867 in *Gesamtausgabe*, Part III, Vol. 3, pp. 445–6.
131 Karl Marx to Dr Kugelmann, January 30, 1868 in Karl Marx, *Letters to Dr Kugelmann*, pp. 60–1. Articles written (or inspired) by Engels on *Das Kapital* appeared in the following German papers: *Die Zukunft* (Berlin), *Rheinische Zeitung* (Düsseldorf: edited by Heinrich Bürgers), *Düsseldorfer Zeitung* (reprinted in H. Hirsch (ed.), *Friedrich Engels: Profile* (1970), pp. 171–2), *Der Beobachter* (Stuttgart: edited by Karl Mayer), *Staats-Anzeiger für Württemberg, Neue Badische Landeszeitung, Demokratisches Wochenblatt* (Leipzig: edited by W. Liebknecht). The articles are printed in *Marx-Engels Werke*, Vol. 16, pp. 207–35.
132 Karl Marx to F. Engels, August 10, 1868 in *Gesamtausgabe*, Part III, Vol. 4, p. 82. The articles are printed in *Marx-Engels Werke*, Vol. XVI, p. 288.
133 F. Engels to Karl Marx, August 12, 1868 in *Gesamtausgabe*, Part III, Vol. 4, pp. 82–83.
134 Karl Marx to F. Engels, October 15, 1868 in *Gesamtausgabe*, Part III, Vol. 4, p. 113.
135 Karl Marx to S. Meyer, July 4, 1868 in Karl Marx and F. Engels, *Letters to Americans 1848–95* (1963), pp. 74–5.
136 Wilhelm Liebknecht to F. Engels, January 20, 1868 in Wilhelm Liebknecht, *Briefwechsel mit Karl Marx und Friedrich Engels* (edited by G. Eckert, The Hague, 1963), p. 88.
137 Wilhelm Liebknecht to F. Engels, March 29, 1868 in Wilhelm Liebknecht, *Briefwechsel mit Karl Marx und Friedrich Engels* (edited by G. Eckert, The Hague, 1963), p. 90.
138 *Demokratisches Wochenblatt* (Leipzig), March 21 and 28, 1868: English translation in W. O. Henderson (ed.), *Engels: Selected Writings* (Penguin Books, 1967), pp. 177–84.
139 F. Engels to Karl Marx, September 16, 1868 in *Gesamtausgabe*, Part III, Vol. 4, p. 90.
140 Karl Marx to F. Engels, September 16, 1868 in *Gesamtausgabe*, Part III, Vol. 4, pp. 92–3.
141 F. Engels, "Konspekt über 'Das Kapital' von Karl Marx. Erster Band" in *Marx-Engels Werke*, Vol. 16.
142 French edition 1880, German edition 1882, English edition 1892.

7

THE GENERAL

On one occasion Karl Marx wrote to Engels that he would await instructions from "the War Office in Manchester". He was referring to Engels's reputation as an expert on military affairs. Engels was one of the few civilians in the middle of the nineteenth century who became an acknowledged master of the theory of warfare and an authority on the technique of armed insurrection. Between 1850 and 1870 he established for himself a reputation as a military critic and his friends called him "General". In his later years he was actually consulted on military matters by Major Wachs of the General Staff in Berlin. Engels's articles on military affairs appeared in newspapers and journals in the United States, England, and Germany.[1]

After his death Engels's military writings were, to some extent, neglected, though they appear to have influenced Lenin's thinking concerning revolutionary warfare. In 1923 Engels's articles on the Franco-Prussian war were reprinted. Then Engels's achievements as a military critic were discussed in the Soviet encyclopaedia. In 1958–64 a selection of Engels's military writings was published by the East German Ministry of Defence, while in 1961 a new edition of his essays on the English volunteer movement was published.

Engels's letters to his sister Marie which were written when he served with the Guards Artillery in Berlin in 1841–2 do not suggest that his interest in military affairs was aroused at this time. He was too busy discussing philosophy, religion, and politics with the Young Hegelians to have much time for military studies. The only lasting impression that he took with him, when his year with the forces was over, was a passionate hatred of the Prussian military system and of the Prussian officer class.[2]

There are only a few references to military affairs and armed insurrections in Engels's writings and correspondence between 1844 and 1848. In his book on the English workers he observed that the Plug Plot riots of 1842 had shown that "unarmed crowds, who had no clear common objective in view, were easily held in check by a handful of dragoons and police in enclosed market places".[3] He also described a riot in Manchester in 1843 when Pauling and

Henfrey's brickworkers went on strike and displayed "all the courage needed by revolutionaries".[4] But Engels believed that courage was not enough and that the workers would have to master the art of revolutionary warfare if they were to face trained troops with any prospect of success.

In a speech at Elberfeld in 1845 Engels discussed the rôle of war in a communist society, arguing that armies would be superfluous in a communist world. But since communism would first be established in industrialised countries, communist and capitalist societies would exist side by side for a time – a period during which communist states would need to be armed in self-defence. This could be achieved by conscription. Engels believed that the morale of a communist army would be very high because the soldiers would be fighting for "a *real* fatherland and a *real* fireside".[5]

During the revolution of 1848–9 Engels began to take a serious interest in military affairs. Two aspects of warfare which appeared to him to be of particular significance from the point of view of the revolutionary workers were the wars of independence waged by subject peoples – the Italians, Poles and Magyars – and the popular risings which occurred in many towns and country districts on the Continent. Engels served in the town militia in Cologne in 1848. For a few days in 1849 he was in charge of the barricades in Elberfeld. Later he took part in the rising in Baden.

Engels wrote several articles on the popular revolts of 1848–9. The first was an account of the rising in Paris in February 1848 which led to Louis Philippe's abdication. Engels was not an eye witness of the revolt since he had recently been expelled from France, but he had lived in Paris for some months and had been in touch with some of the men who played a leading part in the rising. In an article written soon after the events which he described, Engels accused the middle-class opponents of the July Monarchy of gross cowardice. He denounced the "loud-mouthed heroes" who had cancelled a banquet planned as a demonstration against Guizot. The workers of Paris, however, had shown more courage and had risen in revolt. They had erected barricades, seized key points in the city, and had torn up railway lines to prevent the government from bringing reinforcements to Paris. Deserted by the National Guard, Louis Philippe had fled to England and Second Republic had been proclaimed.

One of the members of the new republican Provisional Government was a worker – "the first time that this has happened in any country in the world". "By this glorious rising the French workers have again become the leaders of the European revolutionary movement." "The victory of the republic in France is a victory for democracy throughout Europe." "Everywhere the power of the middle classes will crumble or will be overthrown." "If the Germans can summon up enough pride, energy and courage we shall only have to wait for four weeks before we too can exclaim: 'Long live the German republic!'"[6] But events were to take a very different course.

In the summer of 1848, shortly after becoming one of the editors of the *Neue Rheinische Zeitung*, Engels wrote five articles on the June rising of the workers in Paris, which was ruthlessly put down by General Cavaignac. Engels declared that the savage street fighting was a civil war between former allies who, only a few months previously, had fought together to overthrow Louis Philippe. It was a clear example of class war – a fight to the death between the workers of the eastern districts of Paris and the middle classes who lived in the western suburbs. Engels showed how four columns of armed workers had marched from their barricades to converge upon the Town Hall only to be outnumbered and overwhelmed by Cavaignac's well-armed troops. Engels was confident that the workers of Paris would rise in revolt once more. "If 40,000 workers in Paris can achieve so much when outnumbered four to one, what can all the workers of Paris achieve if they act in unison!"[7] In 1851 he still thought that there might be a successful revolt in Paris but by the following year Engels had revised his views. He now admitted that "the proletarians of Paris were defeated, decimated, crushed with such an effect that even now they have not recovered from the blow".[8] Many years elapsed before Paris was again the scene of bitter street fighting in the days of the Commune.

In 1848 Engels joined the town militia (*Bürgerwehr*) in Cologne. His propaganda among its members led to the formation of a "red company" composed of men who shared his political views. Since Cologne was a garrison town the militia was in no position to rise in revolt. In September 1848 the city was placed under martial law and the publication of the *Neue Rheinische Zeitung* was suspended. Engels fled first to France and then to Switzerland. There he received a letter from Marx suggesting that since he had a sound knowledge of geography, he should contribute some articles on the recent campaign in Hungary to their newspaper.[9] Engels studied the operations with the aid of maps and Austrian reports and submitted his first article in January 1849.[10] Engels believed that the campaign which had driven the Austrians out of Hungary was a striking illustration of the ability of an oppressed people to gain its freedom by successful military action. In the spring of 1849 he wrote that "an unruly mob without proper leadership" had been "suddenly transformed into a well-organised, numerous, concentrated, and brilliantly led army".[11] Engels's last article on the war in Hungary appeared on May 19, 1849 when Russia's intervention opened a new – and, for the Magyars, a disastrous – phase of the campaign.[12]

Engels later claimed that his articles on Hungary had been "plagiarised in almost every subsequent book upon the subject, the works of native Hungarians and 'eye-witnesses' not excepted".[13] And he boasted to Marx: "In the *Neue Rheinische Zeitung* . . . we followed the events of the war in Hungary with remarkable accuracy, although we relied for our information entirely upon the Austrian communiqués." "We made some cautious – but brilliantly correct – prophecies."[14] Already the high quality of Engels's military criticism was being recognised. Wilhelm Liebknecht declared that Engels's articles had been "attributed to a high-ranking officer in the Hungarian army because they always proved to be correct".[15] And a writer in the *Deutsche Monatshefte* complimented the "very able reporter" who had covered the Hungarian campaign for the *Neue Rheinische Zeitung*.[16]

Just before Engels's last article on the war in Hungary appeared, he went to Elbergeld where an insurrection against the Prussian authorities had broken out. He described his brief intervention in this rising in the *Neue Rheinische Zeitung* on May 17, 1849. Two days later the last number of the newspaper appeared and Engels's duties as an editor came to an end. He joined Willich's corps in Baden and fought with the revolutionaries who were supporting the German constitution drawn up by the Frankfurt National Assembly. This was the only occasion on which Engels was under fire. Mathilde Anneke wrote in her diary that all the members of Willich's corps whom she met praised Engels for his "zeal and courage". Eleanor Marx, writing many years later, stated that Engels's companions in this campaign recalled his courage and reckless disregard of danger.[17] His observations during the Baden rising of the conduct of both officers and men convinced Engels that if any future revolution were to succeed it would be essential for the workers themselves to have some knowledge of the art of war and for them to be led by competent officers.[18]

The campaign was over in four weeks. The Prussians and their allies had no difficulty in driving the insurgents out of Baden. Since Engels had served in the Prussian army in 1841–2 his action in joining the rebels in Baden rendered him liable to a court martial as a deserter. But he escaped to Switzerland. It was not until 1860 that he was drummed out of the Prussian army.[19] When he was in Switzerland he began – at Marx's request[20] – to write an account of the "glorious campaign" in which he had taken part. He asked

Weydemeyer to find a German publisher for him.[21] Engels's description of the "Reich Constitution Campaign" appeared as a series of articles in Marx's *Neue Rheinische Zeitung. Politisch-Ökonomische Revue*. Unlike his later writings on military affairs these articles dealt with a campaign in which he had taken part himself. They were one of his finest pieces of descriptive prose. He criticised the irresolute and inefficient leadership of bourgeois professional soldiers like Franz Sigel. He denounced the "stupidity and treachery" of commanders whose irresponsible behaviour ruined any slim chance of success that the rising might have had. In his view most of the officers were "ignorant and incompetent".[22] Many years later Engels wrote that Johann Philipp Becker was one of the few leaders of the revolutionary army who was free from these faults. In the rising in Baden, Becker "undoubtedly achieved more than anyone else".[23]

In March 1850 Marx and Engels offered some advice to the workers on the strategy of revolution.

> "The workers must be organised and they must be armed. They will have to get hold of flintlocks, fowling pieces, cannon and ammunition. They must, if possible, prevent the revival of the old middle class national guard which would oppose the proletariat. If this cannot be done, the workers should try to set up their own militia under elected officers and an elected general staff. This militia should not obey a bourgeois government but should take its orders from revolutionary workers councils. Those workers who are employed by the government should be organised in a special corps, under elected officers, or they should form part of the workers' militia. This militia should in no circumstances surrender its arms or its ammunition. If the government should try to do this it should, if necessary, be resisted by force".[24]

Early in 1851 Engels began to study Napier's *History of the War in the Peninsula*, which was "by far the best military history" that he had read.[25] Napier had "an enormous amount of common sense" and showed sound judgment in assessing the genius of Napoleon.[26] One reason why Engels studied the art of war was the fact that the Willich-Schapper faction which had broken away from the Communist League included several former officers such as Willich, Krieger, Schimmelpfennig and Sigel. Engels was determined that the members of the League who remained faithful to Marx should have the benefit of the advice of a military expert. Moreover Engels hoped to take part in the next revolution not merely as a military adviser but also as an officer in the field. He regarded horsemanship as "the material basis" of his military studies and he devoted some of his leisure time in the 1850s to riding with the Cheshire

Hunt. He boasted that if he ever saw action again in Germany he would give the gentlemen of the Prussian cavalry a lesson in horsemanship.[27] For many years Engels devoted much of his spare time to his military studies. In 1859 he told Lassalle that, since settling in Manchester, he had "concentrated upon the study of military science".[28]

In April 1850 Marx suggested that Engels should write a history of the campaigns in Hungary in 1848–9. Engels replied that the materials at his disposal were inadequate. "If one writes a military history," he wrote, "it is all too easy to make a fool of oneself by venturing to pass judgment without being in full possession of all the facts concerning the numbers, the armaments, and the provisions of the opposing armies."[29]

In June 1851 Engels asked his friend Weydemeyer – formerly a lieutenant in the Prussian army – for advice on books to read on military science and the history of modern warfare. He wrote:

"Since I arrived in Manchester I have begun to study military affairs, on which I have found fairly good material here – for a beginning at any rate. The enormous importance that the military aspect will have in the next movement, an old inclination of mine, my articles on the Hungarian war in the *Neue Rheinische Zeitung*, and finally my glorious adventures in Baden, have all impelled me to this study, and I want to work in this field at least enough to be able to express a theoretical opinion without disgracing myself too much.

"The material available here – dealing with the Napoleonic and, to some extent, with the Revolutionary campaigns – presupposes the knowledge of a mass of detail, which I do not know at all, or know only very superficially, and about which one can obtain only very superficial information, laboriously unearthed, or no information at all. Self-instruction is always nonsense, and unless one follows up a thing systematically, one won't achieve anything worth while. You will get a better idea of what I really need, if I remind you that – aside from my promotion in Baden – I never got further than a Royal Prussian Landwehr bombardier; thus, to understand the campaigns, I lack the intermediate schooling, which is provided in Prussia by the examination for promotion to lieutenant, in the various branches of the service.

". . . What I need is a general survey of the elementary knowledge required for an understanding and a correct evaluation of historical facts of a military nature. Thus, for example: elementary tactics; theory of fortifications, more or less historically, covering the various systems from Vauban down to the modern system of detached forts, together with a study of field fortifications and other matters within the province of the engineers, such as the various types of bridges etc; as well as a general history of military science and the changes produced by the evolution and perfection of arms and the methods of using them. Then something thorough on artillery, as I've forgotten a lot and many things I don't know at all, as well as other requirements that don't come to mind at the moment, but that you must certainly know. . . . As soon as I have made some more progress I shall study the campaigns of 1848–9 thoroughly, especially the Italian and the Hungarian campaigns. . . ."[30]

At the same time that he was writing to Weydemeyer about his military studies, Engels was examining the situation that would arise if war should break out on the Continent in 1852. In April 1851 he told Marx that "if a revolution should occur in France next year the Holy Alliance would undoubtedly advance *at least* as far as the gates of Paris".[31] In September Marx summarised for Engels's benefit a manifesto by G. A. Techow which had appeared in New York. Techow had served as an officer in the Prussian army and as a staff officer in the revolutionary army in Baden. His manifesto of August 3, 1851 suggested that a revolution (directed against Louis Napoleon's government) might break out in France in 1852. In that event the reactionary Powers – Russia, Austria and Prussia – would attack France as they did in 1792. Marx told Engels that (according to Techow) "the question of the next revolution is also the question of the next war in Europe". "The conflict will decide if Europe is to be republican or cossack." Marx asked Engels for his views on Techow's estimates of the strength of the armies of the revolution and the reaction if war should break out.[32] Engels replied that Techow's views were sometimes superficial and sometimes erroneous. He gave Marx his own estimate of the probable size of the contending forces in the event of a war between revolutionary France and the "Holy Alliance".[33]

Engels followed up this letter by a memorandum in which he discussed the question of a future war on the Continent at greater length.[34] His views on the size of the armies which the leading Powers could put into the field are no longer of interest but in two sections of his memorandum Engels discussed problems of greater significance. His third section included some general observations on the art of war in the middle of the nineteenth century. Engels argued that in any age the way in which wars are fought is the military aspect of the structure of society and the nature of the economy. The art of warfare represents the military thinking of the dominant class in society. Engels considered that warfare, as practised in the middle of the nineteenth century, originated in the campaigns of the French revolution and Napoleon. When the revolution of 1789 freed the craftsmen from the authority of the gilds and when the serfs were emancipated from their feudal obligations, a new type of middle class society was created which raised armies and fought wars in a new way.

According to Engels, the main feature of this new type of warfare was the raising of very large armies capable of much greater mobility than earlier armies. The small armies of the seventeenth and eighteenth centuries had to live off the land and were able to manoeuvre – or go into winter quarters – in a small area. The larger armies of the nineteenth century could not do this. When the food and fodder available on the spot had been consumed these armies had to move on since the supplies that they carried with them had to be saved for emergencies. As Napoleon had discovered in Spain, the armies of the nineteenth century had great difficulty in operating in "poor thinly-populated semi-barbarous countries."

Engels argued that success in war now depended upon recruiting both officers and men who were more intelligent and better educated than their forefathers who had fought in the campaigns of the eighteenth century. As armies increased in size, more men were needed to operate in advance and on the flanks of the main force. They acted as scouts or they searched for food and fodder. Scouts, snipers and sharpshooters had to take quick decisions on their own initiative.

The armies of the nineteenth century were appropriate to the bourgeois society and the capitalist economy that had developed as a result of the revolution of 1789 in France and the industrial revolution in England. Engels predicted that when the workers had overthrown the middle classes and the capitalist system, a new classless communist society would be established, and a new type of warfare would emerge. Population growth would make it possible to raise even larger armies, while improvements in transport and communications – railways, steamships and telegraphs – would increase their mobility. But, in Engels's view, these armies would never have to go into action because in a communist world they would never find an "adequate enemy." In his utopia, brotherly love would take the place of national rivalries so that war would no longer occur.

In the last section of his memorandum Engels examined the situation that would arise if – after a successful revolution in France – the reactionary Powers (Russia, Austria and Prussia) were to attack France. The invaders would try to capture Paris since France would collapse if the capital fell. Engels argued that the first French line of defence was a semi-circle drawn about 320 miles around Paris to the north and east. Any point on this semi-circle would be about 14 days march from the capital. On the other hand the invading armies would start from various points on this semi-circle in order to converge upon Paris. Engels considered that if the first line of defence were breached, the French could fall back upon a number of natural defensive positions closer to Paris, such as the Jura mountains, the Vosges, the hills between the Yonne and the Loire, or the highlands between the Seine and the Meuse. Engels observed that it was by the brilliant use of these natural defences that Napoleon "with a mere handful of soldiers" had been able to hold a great coalition at bay for two months in 1814. Here the memorandum broke off, but Engels returned to the problem of the defence of Paris a few years later in his pamphlet on *Po und Rhein*.

Engels did not need to finish his memorandum. There was no revolution in France in 1852 and no invasion by the "Holy Alliance". By his coup d'état of December 2, 1851 Louis Napoleon abolished the republican constitution of France and imprisoned or exiled his opponents. Engels dismissed the coup d'état as a "complete comedy"[35] but later had to admit that it was no joke for Louis Napoleon's enemies. In January 1852 he wrote that "they are still hunting down insurgents like wild beasts in the southern departments".[36] In February Engels contributed an article to Ernest Jones's *Notes to the People* on the "Real Causes why the French Proletarians remained comparatively inactive in December last".[37] Marx declared that he was "quite bewildered" by the events in Paris on December 2, 1851 but he rejoiced at the discomfiture of Techow who had regarded the French army as "the apostle of the trinity of democracy – liberty, equality and fraternity".[38]

One consequence of Louis Napoleon's coup d'état was a war scare in England. There were those who believed that Louis Napoleon – like his uncle – would embark upon a career of aggression, which might include a plan to invade England. Joseph Weydemeyer asked Engels for his views on this question. Engels replied on January 23, 1852 that an army which landed west of Portsmouth might be driven into Cornwall, while forces which landed near Dover might be cornered between the Thames and the sea. The first aim of an invading force would be to seize London and this would require an army of 90,000 men. The next objectives would be Birmingham and Manchester to secure England south of the Mersey and the Humber. The first line which could be permanently held would run between Carlisle and Newcastle upon Tyne but the defending army would still control Scotland. Eventually the invaders would have to advance to the Clyde and the Firth of Forth. Engels added that "the difficulties of maintaining the position begin after the conquest, since communications with France will certainly be cut off". "How many men would be required, under these conditions, to set up a decent front on the Clyde?" "I think 400,000 would not be too high a figure."[39]

But on the previous day – in a letter to Marx – Engels had expressed different views on a French invasion of England. He considered that the French would be deceiving themselves if they imagined that they could seize London very quickly. England's southern ports – except Brighton – lay in deep bays, which could be entered only at high tide, with the aid of local pilots. "Piratical raids" by 20,000 or 30,000 men would not achieve very much. Only a coalition of the major European Powers could seriously contemplate an invasion of England. This would take a year to prepare, but Britain needed only six months to strengthen her coastal defences, bring home some ships of the line, strengthen the yeomanry, and raise a new militia.[40]

Speculations on a possible invasion of France by the "Holy Alliance" or of Britain by Louis Napoleon were not Engels's only writings on military affairs in 1851–2. He also contributed several articles to the *New York Daily Tribune* on the German revolution of 1848. He wrote on political rather than military events but he did discuss how revolutionaries should face trained troops. Engels views on the art of armed insurrection were as follows:

"1. Never play with insurrection unless you are fully prepared to face the consequences of your play. Insurrection is a calculus with very indefinite magnitudes, the value of which may change every day; the forces opposed to you have all the advantages of organisation, discipline, and habitual authority, unless you bring strong odds against them, you are defeated and ruined.

2. The insurrectionary career once entered upon, act with the greatest determination, and on the offensive. The defensive is the death of every armed rising; it is lost before it measures itself with its enemies. Surprise your antagonists while their forces are scattering, prepare new successes, however small, but daily; keep up the moral ascendancy which the first successful rising has given you; rally those vacillating elements to your side which always follow the strongest impulse, and which always look out for the safer side; force your enemies to a retreat before they can collect their strength against you; in the words of Danton, the greatest master of revolutionary policy yet known, 'de l'audace, de l'audace, encore de l'audace'.[41]

3. In war, and particularly in revolutionary warfare, rapidity of action until some decided advantage is gained, is the first rule, and we have no hesitation in saying that upon merely military grounds.[42]

4. In revolution, as in war, it is always necessary to show a strong front, and he who attacks is in the advantage; and in revolution, as in war, it is of the highest necessity to stake everything on the decisive moment, whatever the odds may be.

5. In a revolution he who commands a decisive position and surrenders it, instead of forcing the enemy to try his hand at an assault, invariably deserves to be treated as a traitor.

6. A well contested defeat is a fact of as much revolutionary importance as an easily won victory. (Defeated insurgents leave behind) in the minds of the survivors, a wish for revenge, which in revolutionary times, is one of the highest incentives to energetic and passionate action.[43]

7. It is an established fact that the dissolution of armies and the complete breakdown of discipline is both a cause and a consequence of every successful revolution in the past".[44]

In 1852 Engels bought the library of a retired German artillery officer.[45] His purchases included a book by a Swiss officer, Gustav Hofstetter, on the Italian campaign of 1848; an account of the Russian campaign in Poland in 1831 by the Prussian General Karl Wilhelm von Willisen; and H. Küntzel's study of modern fortifications, which Engels found particularly useful.[46] Looking back on his studies in later years, he remarked that military thinking in Prussia – after producing "a star of the first brilliance in Clausewitz" – had long been in a state of decline in the 1850s.[47] At this time Engels was still planning to write a history of the war in Hungary in 1848 which might be extended to include a survey of all the campaigns in 1848 and 1849. "Give me another year to study military science and the democratic lieutenants will get the devil of a surprise.[48] Marx had already warned Engels that democratic "military fellows" like Techow were jealous of his growing reputation as a military expert.[49] In August 1852 Marx sent Engels a list of books on the campaign in Hungary in 1848[50] and Engels asked Marx whether certain military periodicals were available in the British Museum reading room.[51]

The Russian invasion of the Turkish principalities of Moldavia and Wallachia in the autumn of 1853 was the first of a series of wars on the Continent in the 1850s and 1860s. As a military expert Engels wrote for various newspapers on all the campaigns from the Crimean war to the Franco-Prussian war. He never left Manchester to visit the front but derived his information from official communiqués and from the reports of war correspondents. His knowledge of military history and his skilful use of maps – Lassalle gave him "a fine military atlas" in 1861[52] – made up for his failure to gather information on the spot. The fact that some of his essays appeared as leading articles – and not as military reports – shows that the editors of the *New York Daily Tribune* and the *Pall Mall Gazette* recognised that Engels's contributions contained more than a description of a battle or a campaign.

In September 1853 Marx received an article on the Turkish army from Engels[53] and assured his friend that "if any military movement takes place, I will rely upon immediate instructions from the War Office in Manchester".[54] The essay appeared in the *New York Daily Tribune*.[55] In December 1853 Marx thanked Engels for a "beautiful article" which would secure for Dana the reputation of a Field Marshal, and in January 1854 he wrote: "Your *militaria* have aroused great interest." "In New York it is rumoured that they have been written by General Scott."[56] Shortly afterwards Marx suggested that Engels should write on the campaign in the Balkans for the London *Daily News*. If he became the military correspondent of this newspaper he would find it easier to secure an English publisher for his projected study of the Hungarian campaign of 1848.[57]

In March 1854 Engels tried to escape from his Manchester office by securing work as a free-lance journalist in London. Armed with a letter of recommendation from Dr John Watts, he offered his services as a military critic to H. J. Lincoln, the editor of the *Daily News*. He wrote to Mr Lincoln that he had been trained in the Prussian artillery and had seen "some active service during the insurrectionary war in south Germany in 1849". He claimed that for many years the study of military science had been one of his chief occupations. He had access to "the best sources of information" on the campaigns on the Danube and in the Crimea since he could read Russian and Serbian. He enclosed an article on the fortress of Kronstadt as a sample of his work. He also offered to review books on military subjects.[58] But the editor of the *Daily News* declined Engels's offer, stating that Engels's articles were "too professional" and more suitable for a "military paper".[59] Marx warned Engels a few years later against writing military articles for the *New York Daily Tribune* above the heads of his readers. He wrote: "You must colour your war-articles a little more since you are writing for a general newspaper and not for a professional military journal."[60] A year after he had failed to join the *Daily News* as a war correspondent Engels was in touch with the editor of the *Manchester Guardian* and hoped to become a contributor either to this paper or to the *Manchester Examiner and Times*. But some years elapsed before any of his military articles were accepted by the *Manchester Guardian*.[61]

Meanwhile in June 1854, Engels had assured Marx that he would write an account of the Hungarian campaign of 1848 in the following winter[62] but the book was never written. At the same time Marx wrote that recent events in the Balkans had "brilliantly justified" Engels's predictions concerning the Russo-Turkish campaign in Moldavia and Wallachia.[63] Marx declared: "You have written a wonderful article on Silistria."[64]

Engels contributed several articles on the Crimean war to the *New York Daily Tribune* between October 1853 and December 1854 and to the *Neue Oder Zeitung* (Breslau) between January and October 1855.[65] The merit of Engels's articles was that while most writers at that time confined their attention to the campaign in the Crimea, Engels discussed six theatres of military or naval operations – the Baltic, the White Sea, Moldavia and Wallachia, the Caucasus, Armenia, and the Crimea – and insisted that the war should be viewed as a whole. In one essay he shrewdly observed that the siege of Sebastopol was "a striking proof of the fact that in the same proportion as the *materiel* of warfare has, by industrial progress, advanced during the long peace, in the same proportion has the *art* of war degenerated."[66] In another article Engels rightly criticised the allies for dissipating their war effort on widely separated fronts on the periphery of Russia. Strong Russian resistance was forcing France and Britain to commit large forces to flanking operations which had no common focus. But Engels's attempt in 1854 to forecast future military and political developments was not successful. He argued that when France had been drained of troops, Austria and Prussia would unite to march on Paris. This would lead to a rising in France against Napoleon III, to the fall of the Second Empire, and to the repulse of the invaders by a revolutionary army.[67] This line of thought – reminiscent of the argument in Engels's unfinished memorandum of 1851 – was no more than wishful thinking. It was a curious notion that Austria – which opposed the Czar's territorial ambitions in the Balkans – would be likely to join Prussia and to attack France. In fact Austria and Prussia remained neutral throughout the Crimean war. They attacked neither Russia nor France. Far from being threatened by a rising in France, Napoleon III was more firmly in the saddle than ever when Sebastopol fell and he was able to act as host to the plenipotentiaries who negotiated the peace treaty that concluded the war.

During the Crimean war Engels also contributed several articles to *Putnam's Monthly Magazine* on the armies of Europe.[68] In his first article[69] he observed that the impartial scientific study of military affairs was still in its infancy. He asserted that many accounts of past campaigns were far from objective. They were frequently written by generals who had sheathed the sword only to continue the struggle with the pen. In Engels's view impartial military histories were few and far between. Yet the materials for examining the organisation of the various armies in Europe were readily available. Governments were surprisingly generous in publishing information concerning their military forces and they regularly invited foreign observers to attend their manoeuvres. In the circumstances it was possible for Engels – writing largely from official publications – to describe the size, recruitment, training, organisation and armaments of the principal European armies.

Engels enjoyed writing on military topics and when the Crimean war ended, he complained that "la paix allait me démoraliser."[70] So he assented with alacrity to Marx's suggestion in April 1857 that he should contribute some articles on military affairs to the *New American Cyclopaedia* which was edited by Charles Dana and George Ripley.[71] Engels looked forward to "a regular occupation in the evening" and observed that the two dollars a page which Dana was offering would be a welcome addition to Marx's income.[72]

Marx considered that, however useful Engels's military studies might be from a financial point of view, their real significance lay in the way in which they helped to elucidate an important aspect of economics. He wrote:

"Nowhere is the relationship between factors of production and the structure of society more clearly illustrated than in the history of the army. Economic expansion is greatly influenced by the army. In ancient times, for example, the payment of wages in money was first fully developed in the army. In Roman law the *peculium castrense* was the first legal recognition of the principle that property could be owned by anyone other than the head of a family. The same applies to the gild activities of the corporation of blacksmiths (in Roman times). And after what Grimm calls the Stone Age the special value given to metals and their use as money appears to rest upon their importance in time of war. Moreover the division of labour within a single sphere of human activity was first seen in military forces. The whole history of the structure of middle-class society is clearly summarised in the history of armies."[73]

Between July 1857 and November 1860 Engels contributed about 50 articles on military topics to the *New American Cyclopaedia* and a few more were written jointly by Marx and Engels.[74] The work was interrupted from time to time by Engels's illness and by the extra work at the office brought about by the "general crash" of 1857.[75] The articles included general surveys,[76] accounts of campaigns and battles,[77] descriptions of weapons,[78] and military biographies.[79] These essays show the high quality of his military writings. They exhibited a detailed knowledge of the history of warfare and of the geographical factors which had influenced military campaigns. Engels was familiar with the various methods of raising and training armies and with technical advances in such weapons as artillery and rifles. He quickly appreciated the changes that were taking place in the art of war owing to recent improvements in communications – particularly new highways and railways. He showed that he was familiar with the complex problems of the commisariat and the provision of medical aid for the wounded. Engels's articles gave an excellent survey of the art of warfare as practised in the middle of the nineteenth century.

At the same time as he was contributing military articles to the *New American Cyclopaedia*, Engels was paying close attention to the Indian Mutiny. His illness in 1857 prevented him from giving Marx much help with regard to military articles on the mutiny. Marx wrote: "I have had to deputise for you as military expert on the *Tribune*."[80] But Engels did write some articles on the Indian Mutiny, one of which was described by Marx as being "splendid in style and manner and reminiscent of the best days of the *Neue Rheinische Zeitung*".[81]

Engels wrote on the capture of Delhi[82] and Lucknow[83] and on General Windham's defeat at Cawnpore.[84] He regarded Sir Henry Havelock as the best of the English commanders in India. He wrote to Marx that it had been "an enormous achievement to march 126 miles in that climate in eight days and to fight five or six engagements on the way".[85] Engels regarded the war as a national revolt rather than a mutiny. When the sepoys were defeated, Engels speculated on the possibility of the insurgents harassing British troops by guerilla tactics. In July 1858 he wrote that a large region of northern India

"was swarming with active insurgent bands, organised to a certain degree by the experience of a twelve months' war, and encouraged, amid a number of defeats, by the indecisive character of each, and by the small advantages gained by the British. It is true, all their strongholds and centres of operations have been taken from them; the greater portion of their stores and artillery are lost; the important towns are all in the hands of their enemies. But, on the other hand, the British, in all this vast district, hold nothing but the towns, and of the open country, nothing but the spot where their moveable columns happen to stand; they are compelled to chase their nimble enemies without any hope of attaining them; and they are under the necessity of entering upon this harassing mode of warfare at the very deadliest season of the year. The native Indian can stand the midday heat of his summer with comparative comfort, while mere exposure to the rays of the sun is almost certain death to the European; he can march 40 miles in such a season; where 10 break down his northern opponent; to him even the hot rains and swampy jungles are comparatively innocuous, while dysentery, cholera, and ague follow every exertion made by Europeans in the rainy season or in swampy neighbourhoods."[86]

By this time – as Marx wrote to Lassalle – the study of military science had become Engels's main field of research.[87] In the 1850s most of Engels's military criticism had appeared anonymously in the American press. In 1859, however, events on the Continent encouraged Engels to write for the German public once more. Early in that year it became clear that the question of Italian unification would lead to hostilities between France and Austria. The attitude of the German states – particularly Prussia – was of vital importance to the outcome of the conflict.

Engels discussed this problem in a pamphlet entitled *Po und Rhein* which was published in April 1859.[88] Austria's supporters in the German press – such as Hermann Orges in the *Augsburger Allgemeine Zeitung* – were urging Prussia to come to Austria's aid so as to maintain Habsburg rule in Lombardy and Venetia. They asserted that Germany would be secure from attack from Italy only if a German state held the valley of the River Po. It was argued that this was Germany's "natural frontier" in the south. Engels wrote: "The question, expressed in strictly military terms, is this: Does Germany need to hold the Etsch (Adige), the Mincio, and the lower Po – with the bridgeheads of Peschiera and Mantua – to defend her southern frontier?"[89]

Engels categorically denied that the valley of the Po must be in German hands to ensure the safety of the German states from the south. He argued that if Lombardy and Venetia were under Italian instead of Austrian rule they could quickly be occupied by German forces if this should be necessary in time of war. The Alps had never barred the Germans – or the French – from occupying northern Italy. French armies under Napoleon and Austrian armies after 1815 had successfully crossed the Alps to occupy the valley of the Po. In Engels's view a study of past campaigns showed conclusively that certain Alpine passes could be used, even in winter, to move troops from Germany, Austria or France into Italy. New Alpine roads and railways were facilitating the movement of armies from the north or west into the valley of the Po. There was no need for any German state to hold the Quadrilateral fortresses – Mantua, Lugnano, Peschiera and Verona – because they could quickly be occupied in time of war. Engels held that, from the point of view of Germany's security, there was no need for a

German state to hold the northern provinces of Italy. German security was adequately served by holding the Alpine passes that led to the plain of the River Po. Engels supported his case with a wealth of historical arguments and by a detailed examination of the geography of the main passes across the Alps.

The Austrian occupation of northern Italy was, according to Engels, a mistake not merely from a military but also from a political point of view. The movement in favour of Italian unification was making rapid headway and it was obvious that one day Lombardy and Venetia must form part of a united Italy. Since 1849 an Austrian army of occupation of 70,000 men had been needed to maintain order in Lombardy and Venetia.[90] Through his business contacts with Italy, Engels possessed reliable information concerning the oppressive nature of Austrian rule in Lombardy and Venetia.[91] The Italians hated not merely the Austrians but all Germans as well, although German states, other than Austria, had no responsibility for the occupation of Lombardy and Venetia by a foreign power. "But is it in our interest", asked Engels, "to hold on to fortresses of the Quadrilateral when we know that this earns us the hatred of 25 million Italians, who have been thrown into alliance with France?"[92] He believed that a united Italy would be no danger to Germany and would be more likely to fall under German than French influence.

Finally, Engels observed that if Germany insisted upon holding the Po and the Mincio for her own security as a "natural frontier" then France had just as strong a claim to the Rhine as her "natural frontier". He repeated the arguments that he had advanced in his memorandum of 1851. Any invasion of France must be aimed at Paris since the fall of the capital would inevitably be followed by the fall of France. The first line of defence of the French capital lay along a semi-circle around Paris to the north and east of 320 miles distant from Paris. This was virtually the line of the River Rhine. No defensive positions closer to Paris would be as effective as the "natural frontier" of the Rhine. Incidentally Engels had little confidence that the neutrality of Belgium would prevent a German army from attacking France through Belgium. The treaty which guaranteed Belgian neutrality was only a "piece of paper".[93] Engels argued that what was sauce for the goose was sauce for the gander. If Germany retained the Po as her "natural frontier" then France could claim the Rhine, Denmark the Eider, and Russia the Vistula or the Oder. Marx repeated this argument in 1871 when he refuted Germany's demand for Alsace-Lorraine to secure the "natural frontier of the Vosges". Marx asserted that it was "altogether an absurdity and an anachronism to make military considerations the principles by which the boundaries of nations are to be fixed". "If this rule were to prevail, Austria would still be entitled to Venetia and the line of the Mincio and France to the line of the Rhine in order to protect Paris".[94] Engels's pamphlet was well received in Germany, being favourably reviewed in a leading military journal. Marx declared that Engels's reputation in Germany as a military critic was assured.[95] In army circles in Berlin the pamphlet was attributed to a senior Prussian officer. Lassalle, too, wrote in enthusiastic terms about *Po und Rhein*.[96]

A year later, in a pamphlet on *Savoyen, Nizza und der Rhein*,[97] Engels examined the effects of the Italian war upon Germany. Prussia had mobilised and France had withdrawn from the war without liberating Italy "right to the Adriatic". The Habsburgs surrendered Lombardy but not Venetia. Then France regained her frontier of 1801 by annexing Savoy and Nice in return for agreeing that the duchies of central Italy should join Piedmont. The French claimed Savoy and Nice on grounds of military security since the Alps were France's "natural frontier". In *Po und Rhein* Engels had criticised the doctrine of "natural frontiers" as applied to the Austrian occupation of northern Italy. Now he criticised the doctrine as applied to Napoleon III's annexation of Savoy and Nice. Engels argued that these territories were not necessary for the defence of France but they did give France an advantage if ever she wished to invade Italy. Engels declared that "when Victor Emmanuel looks from the Villa Della Regina in Turin at the magnificent view of the Alps and realises that not a single peak belongs to him, he will appreciate the situation very clearly".[98]

Moreover the French-speaking districts of Switzerland were now open to attack from France. French troops could occupy Geneva in 24 hours. Engels asserted – quite erroneously – that having seized Savoy and Nice, Louis Napoleon would proceed to annex the French speaking parts of Switzerland.

Engels concluded that since France had advanced the doctrine of "natural frontiers" to justify her annexation of Savoy and Nice she would soon use the same argument to defend the acquisition of the Rhine frontier by annexing German and Belgian territories on the left bank of the river. Engels was correct in assuming that Louis Napoleon had designs upon various territories on the left bank of the Rhine but he was wrong in supposing that France would conclude an alliance with Russia to attain her ends.[99] No Franco-Russian alliance was formed in the 1860s.

The annexation of Savoy and Nice had repercussions in England as well as in Germany for – as after Louis Napoleon's coup d'état of December 1851 – it sparked off an invasion panic. There was a widespread fear that Louis Napoleon would follow up his seizure of two Italian provinces by embarking upon a career of aggression. For the second time in a decade it was thought that France might attempt to invade England. In articles which appeared in the *New York Daily Tribune* in August 1860 Engels discussed the measures taken by the government to strengthen England's coastal defences against a French attack. He criticised the government for spending large sums on fortifying the major naval dockyards and argued that – since it was impossible to defend every harbour – it would be more sensible to protect London by building 20 forts in a ring round the capital at a distance of six (possibly 10) miles from Charing Cross. He asserted that his plan would give Britain security against a French invasion.[100]

Meanwhile in the spring of 1859 the British government had authorised the establishment of local volunteer corps under an Act passed during the Napoleonic wars. Units were generally raised by the landed gentry in the country districts and by manufacturers in industrial towns. In August 1860 Engels attended a review of the local volunteers held at Newton-le-Willows race-course in Lancashire. He described the review in the *Allgemeine Militärzeitung* (Darmstadt)[101] and in the *Volunteer Journal for Lancashire and Cheshire* (Manchester). The *Volunteer Journal* was edited by Isaac Hall and was published by W. H. Smith & Sons.[102] Extracts from Engels's article on the review appeared in leading English newspapers and Marx wrote to him: "Your rifle article has made the rounds of the entire London press and has also been reviewed in the *Observer*, which reflects the views of the government. It is sensational."[103] Engels reported that the volunteers had carried out their exercises "steadily and without confusion". "The advance in line, this chief and cardinal movement of British tactics, was good beyond all expectation." Engels's chief criticism was that many volunteer officers were not yet adequately trained. "Officers cannot be manufactured in the time and with the same means as privates". He urged the government to insist that companies should be joined together to form permanent battalions and that an adjutant from the regular army should be attached to each battalion. "These adjutants should be bound to give all the officers of their respective battalions a regular course of instruction in elementary tactics, light infantry service in all its branches, and the regulations affecting the internal routine of service in a battalion."[104] And in a later article Engels emphasised the fact that the volunteers had been fortunate to have "a numerous well-disciplined and experienced army to take them under its wing".[105]

Engels's contributions to the *Volunteer Journal for Lancashire and Cheshire* included discussions of various aspects of the volunteer movement (such as the general, the officers, the engineers, and the artillery), nine articles on the history of the rifle, and eight on the French army.[106] Isaac Hall wrote to Engels that his article on the French light infantry was "very good and very instructive". "It is highly appreciated by the proprietors and has been most favourably spoken of by many people."[107] When some of Engels's essays in the *Volunteer Journal* were reprinted as a pamphlet a reviewer wrote:

> "We read the 'History of the Rifle' with much pleasure and certify to its accuracy in all important particulars. 'The French Light Infantry' we did not like quite so well, as the tone indicates that the writer is, to a considerable extent, bitten with that new-fangled admiration for French soldiering which we, after long and intimate knowledge, hold to be an utter delusion. The paper, however, is valuable. . . . The question of Volunteer Artillery is well handled, and . . . the whole brochure . . . is modestly and carefully written."[108]

The American civil war was the next conflict which attracted Engels's attention.[109] Although he wrote little for publication on this war he discussed the campaigns in his letters to Marx who incorporated extracts from them in articles written for *Die Presse*. In December 1861, in the *Volunteer Journal*, Engels declared that "the kind of warfare which is now carried on in America is really without precedent." Armies had faced each other – marching and counter-marching – in Missouri, Kentucky and West Virginia and on the Potomac without any decisive action taking place. Engels believed that this state of affairs was inevitable since the armies consisted of volunteers rather than professional troops. He discussed the difficulties of training a citizen army. There were not enough officers or sergeants to teach recruits even the rudiments of the military skills that had to be learned. Even greater difficulties faced those responsible for training the cavalry and the artillery. Moreover the problem of feeding and providing ammunition to large forces operating over long distances in thinly populated regions still had to be solved.[110]

In March 1862 Engels (in an article written jointly with Marx) again emphasised the unusual features of the conflict.

> "From whatever standpoint one regards it, the American civil war presents a spectacle without parallel in the annals of military history. The vast extent of the disputed territory; the far-flung front of the lines of operation; the numerical strength of the hostile armies, the creation of which drew barely any support from a prior organizational basis; the fabulous cost of these armies; the manner of leading

them and the general tactical and strategical principles in accordance with which the war is waged – all are new in the eyes of the European observer."[111]

A few months later Engels argued that, despite early failures, the North was not taking the war seriously enough. He wrote that

"the defeats do not stir these Yankees up; they make them slack. . . . They are afraid of conscription, afraid of resolute financial action, afraid of attacks on slavery, afraid of everything that is urgently necessary. . . . In addition, the total lack of talent. One general more stupid than the other. Not one that would be capable of the least initiative or of independent decision."

On the other hand the South was taking the war very seriously indeed.

"That we get no cotton is already one proof. The guerillas in the border states are a second. But what, in my opinion, is decisive, is that after being shut off from the world, an agricultural people can sustain such a war, and after severe defeats and losses in resources, men and territory, can nevertheless now stand forth as the victor and threaten to carry its offensive right into the North."[112]

Marx did not agree with Engels's assessment of the situation at this time. He wrote: "I do not altogether share your views on the American civil war. I do not think that all is up. . . . In the end the North will make war seriously, adopt revolutionary methods and throw over the domination of the border slave statesmen. . . ."[113] Engels was not convinced. In September 1862 he asked Marx if he still thought that "the gentlemen of the North" would win the war.[114] Marx replied that he was confident that they would eventually do so, while the South – despite Stonewall Jackson – would "come off second best". He warned Engels not to let himself be unduly influenced "by the military aspect of things".[115]

Engels continued to doubt the ability of the North to win the war. On November 5, 1862 he declared that the North still refused to treat the struggle as "a real question of national existence". "I cannot work up any enthusiasm for a people which, in such a colossal issue, allows itself to be continually beaten by a fourth of its own population, and which, after eighteen months of war, has achieved nothing more than the discovery that all its generals are idiots, and all its officials rascals and traitors."[116] In his reply Marx again warned Engels against "looking too much at only one side of the American quarrel".[117]

In the end Marx was proved to be right. Superiority of territory, population, wealth, and industrial resources eventually gave the

North an overwhelming advantage over the South. As the war progressed, Engels accepted Marx's view that the ultimate victory of the Northern armies was inevitable. When the South capitulated, Engels declared that he had won a bet made two months previously "that on May 1 (1865) the Southerners would no longer have any army".[118]

The decisive stroke which finally defeated the South – Sherman's march through Georgia in 1864 – was one which Marx and Engels had recommended in *Die Presse* two years earlier. In March 1862 they observed that "in well populated and more or less centralised states there is always a centre, with the occupation of which by the foe the national resistance would be broken. Paris is a shining example. The slave states, however, possess no such centre." The military centre of the Confederacy lay in Georgia and if Georgia fell the South "would be cut into two sections which would have lost all connection with one another". It would not be necessary to seize all Georgia. "In a land where communication, particularly between distant points, depends more on railways than on highways, the seizure of the railways is sufficient. The southernmost railway line between the states on the Gulf of Mexico and the Atlantic coast goes through Macon and Gordon near Milledgeville. The occupation of these two points would accordingly cut *Secessia* in two and enable the Unionists to beat one part after another." Later events proved that Marx and Engels had been right.[119]

In 1865 Engels wrote a pamphlet on the constitutional crisis in Prussia, which followed the refusal of the Landtag to vote the funds needed to expand and reorganise the army. Bismarck defied the Landtag and raised taxes without parliamentary authority. The main purpose of Engels's pamphlet was to show the German workers how their interests were affected by the constitutional crisis but he also examined the proposed army reforms in some detail. In his opinion a reorganisation of the army was urgently necessary. In the past the need to economise had led to a decline in the efficiency of the army and the mobilisations of 1850 and 1859 had demonstrated that Prussia no longer possessed military forces adequate to maintain her position as a great Power. Engels doubted whether the reforms planned by Roon and Moltke would provide Prussia with the army that she needed. He advocated universal conscription, a short period of training, and a relatively long period of service in the reserve. He believed that two – not three – years service would be sufficient, provided that intensive methods of training recruits were adopted. He also put forward the novel suggestion that some preliminary training should be given to schoolboys to prepare them for future military service. In every district a retired non-commissioned officer should be appointed to give schoolboys lessons in gymnastics and military drill.[120]

Since Engels had had grave doubts in 1865 concerning the efficiency of the Prussian army it is not surprising that a year later – when hostilities broke out between Prussia and Austria – he should have thought that the Austrians would win the war. He contributed five articles on the Seven Weeks War to the *Manchester Guardian*[121] for which he received two guineas for each article.[122] On June 20 he wrote that the Austrians had the advantage of superior numbers both in infantry and cavalry. The Prussians, on the other hand, were led by a monarch of "very mediocre capacities" and were reluctant to fight. All that he could say in favour of the Prussians was that they had breech-loading rifles and better provisions. When the Prussians invaded Bohemia, Moltke admitted that the army was in an "unfavourable but inevitable" situation.[123] Engels vigorously criticised the strategy of the Prussian high command. The Prussian forces were split into two armies, one of which advanced into Bohemia to the east of the Riesengebirge while the other advanced to the west of the Riesengebirge. Engels (writing on July 3) declared that the Austrians could crush the two Prussian armies separately before they could unite. He attributed the gross error of the Prussians to the fact that the King of Prussia was in supreme command.[124] Three days later came news of the decisive Prussian victory at Königgrätz and Engels had to try to explain away his rash prophecy. He wrote that "the campaign which the Prussians opened with a signal strategic blunder, has been since carried on by them with such terrible tactical energy that it was brought to a victorious close in exactly eight days."[125] The articles on the Königgrätz campaign are among those which Engels's admirers would prefer to forget.

When he discussed the German invasion of France in 1870 Engels did not repeat the mistake that he had made in 1866. This time he acknowledged the skill of the Prussian generals and the efficiency of the forces under their command.[126] In July 1870 Marx told Engels that a correspondent of the *Pall Mall Gazette*, who was covering the campaign in France, had asked him to act as a war correspondent in Germany. Marx passed the invitation on to Engels.[127] Marx praised the *Pall Mall Gazette* as "the gentlemen's paper *par excellence* and one which sets the tone in all the clubs, including the military clubs".[128] George Smith, the owner of the *Pall Mall Gazette*, declared that his paper was "written by gentlemen for gentlemen". "To a very unusual extent our contributors were not professional writers in the ordinary sense and were in a higher social class than most newspaper men."[129]

Engels had retired from business and was now able to devote more time to journalism. He offered to write two articles a week if he were "well paid" for his trouble. By "well paid" he meant three or four guineas for each article.[130] Engels was anxious to earn some more money as he was "rather short of cash" at this time.[131] But in the end he had to be satisfied with two and a half guineas for each article.[132] Engels preferred to write his articles at home rather than at the Prussian headquarters where he feared that Wilhelm Stieber (head of the Prussian intelligence service) might make life difficult for him. Stieber – described by Marx as a "notorious Prussian police spy"[133] – was a declared enemy of all communists. Twenty years before he had achieved some notoriety at the trial of the Communist leaders in Cologne and his unscrupulous methods of securing evidence against the accused had been vigorously denounced by Marx.[134]

Marx sent one of Engels's articles to Frederick Greenwood, the editor of the *Pall Mall Gazette*, without mentioning the author's name and it was published on July 29, 1870.[135] Two days later Engels sent Marx an article on the Prussian plan of campaign and asked him to take a cab and deliver it at once to the newspaper office. Engels hoped to achieve an "enormous reputation" as a military critic from this essay in which he revealed the Prussian plan to invade France. When he heard that a cousin of his friend Dr Gumpert had left Aachen for Trier with the advance guard of the seventh Prussian army corps the nature of the Prussian plan of operations was revealed to him in a flash.[136] Engels believed that the plan would be a success and that the Prussians would win the war. On August 1, 1870 Marx complimented Engels on his recent articles. Greenwood had now been given the name of his new military correspondent[137] and he sent Engels a "very polite" letter inviting him to submit military articles as often as he pleased.[138]

Between July 1870 and March 1871 Engels contributed 60 articles on the Franco-Prussian war to the *Pall Mall Gazette*. The article on "The Prussian Victories" (August 8, 1870)[139] was the first of several to appear as leading articles. Engels's reports on the military situation in France soon attracted attention. The *Spectator* declared that "somebody makes on the middle page of the *Pall Mall Gazette* suggestions of noteworthy acuteness – suggestions rarely wrong – but he is too chary of both words and facts, and his rivals tell their readers very little indeed".[140] Marx declared that Engels would "soon be recognised as the leading military expert in London"[141] and that he had given a masterly description of the fortifications of Paris.[142] Engels attributed his success to good luck as well as to good management. He wrote to Jenny Marx that since his "little prophecies" appeared in the evening they were quickly confirmed in the press on the next morning. "This was sheer good luck and it greatly impressed the philistines."[143]

Engels complained that some of his articles were being reprinted in other papers without permission. A leading article in the *Times* had been copied from two of his articles.[144] Marx wrote that his wife and daughters were furious that Engels's contributions were being "plundered by all the London newspapers without acknowledgement".[145] Engels was also annoyed that "that fool" Greenwood, the editor of the *Pall Mall Gazette*, had made alterations in his manuscripts and had cut out some of his attacks upon newspapers which had copied his articles.[146] But it was a quarrel between Marx and Greenwood which caused the final breach between Engels and the *Pall Mall Gazette*. Marx called Greenwood "a libeller" and in July 1871 Engels told the General Council of the Working Men's International Association that he had "resigned his connection with the *Pall Mall Gazette*".[147] At the same time Engels – who in June was still hoping "to keep a footing" in the paper – wrote to Wilhelm Liebknecht that he and Marx had "definitely broken off relations with the *Pall Mall Gazette*".[148]

In his articles Engels traced the advance of the German forces into France. In his pamphlet on *Po und Rhein* he had suggested that it was likely that German armies invading France would march through Belgium. In fact Belgian neutrality was not violated in 1870. On August 26, 1870 – when most English war correspondents were discussing the progress of the Crown Prince's army towards Paris – Engels asserted that the outcome of the campaign depended upon the fate of MacMahon's army which was so situated that, if it were defeated, it would have to retreat "through a narrow strip of territory leading towards neutral territory or the sea". "MacMahon's troops may have to surrender in that little strip of French territory jutting out into Belgium between Mézières and Charlemont-Givet."[149] This was a correct forecast of the German victory at Sedan which occurred a week later and it was Engels's most brilliant analysis of a military situation.

After the battle of Sedan the war entered upon a new phase since few regular French troops capable of resisting the invader survived. The Germans occupied one-sixth of France and besieged Paris and Metz. When Metz fell the war was still not over because Paris held out and a resistance movement sprang up. Moltke complained that although nearly all the regular French troops had been interned, more Frenchmen were under arms than when war broke out.[150] Engels had long been interested in popular risings and guerrilla warfare. He hoped that the methods employed by armed

French resistance fighters to harass the German army of occupation might be used on some future occasion by workers fighting their bourgeois oppressors. Engels criticised the German reaction to the activities of the *francs tireurs*. He denounced the Germans for operating "a code of warfare as antiquated as it is barbarous".[151] If civilians fired upon their troops the Germans burned down the village concerned and shot every man carrying arms who was not a regular soldier. Engels argued that popular resistance by civilians was a legitimate method of warfare sanctioned by long usage. In the American war of independence, in the Peninsular war, and in the risings of 1848 in Hungary and Italy, civilians had fought professional soldiers. In Prussia in 1813 Scharnhorst had organised a volunteer militia to fight the French invaders in a "spirit of uncompromising national resistance". The French in 1870 were simply doing what the Prussians had done in 1813.[152]

In assessing the military situation after Bazaine's capitulation at Metz, Engels did not display the same acumen that he had shown in his earlier articles on the first phase of the war. He believed that the French would stage an effective counter-attack either by their own efforts or with foreign aid. In November 1870 he contemplated the possibility of 30,000 British troops being landed at Cherbourg or Brest to support the French forces operating against the Germans.[153] But at the end of January 1871 he admitted that "the military intervention of England in favour of France . . . could have been of any use whatever at a certain moment only, which has long since passed away".[154] Marx on the other hand still thought in February 1871 that the Liberal government would probably be "kicked out of office and supplanted by a ministry declaring war against Prussia".[155] In fact there was no question of Britain becoming involved in the Franco-Prussian war. In November 1870 Engels thought that the prospects of France had "much improved"[156] since the French Army of the Loire had become an efficient force capable of giving a good account of itself. If the capital could hold out for another month "France may possibly have an army large enough, with the aid of popular resistance, to raise the investment by a successful attack upon the Prussian communications".[157]

Although Engels had to admit on December 2, 1870 that the attempt to relieve Paris had failed, he still believed that the French could continue to offer effective resistance to the Germans. He wrote:

"We make bold to say that, if the spirit of resistance among the people does not flag, the position of the French, even after their recent defeats, is a very strong one. With the command of the sea to import arms, with plenty of men to make soldiers of, with three months – the first and worst three months – of the work of organisation behind them, and with a fair chance of having one month more, if not two, of breath-time allowed them – and that at a time when the Prussians show signs of exhaustion – with all that, to give in now would be rank treason, and who knows what accidents may happen, what further European complications may occur. in the meantime? Let them fight on, by all means."[158]

On December 17, 1870 Engels asserted that

"everywhere the forces appear to be nearly balanced. It is now a race of reinforcements, but a race in which the chances are immensely more favourable to France than they were three months ago. If we could say with safety that Paris will hold out till the end of February, we might almost believe that France would win the race."[159]

Even after the fall of Paris and the signing of an armistice Engels still refused to accept the fact that France had been defeated and could not resume the struggle. On February 8, 1871 he declared that there was still a compact block of territory in the south of France – as well as the ports of Brest, Le Havre and Cherbourg – which had not been occupied by the Germans. He wrote:

"By using the fleet to advantage, the French might move their men in the West and North, so as to compel the Germans to keep largely superior forces in that neighbourhood, and to weaken the forces sent out for the conquest of the South, which it would be their chief object to prevent. By concentrating their armies more than they have hitherto done, and, on the other hand, by sending out more numerous small partisan bands, they might increase the effect to be obtained by the forces on hand. There appear to have been many more troops at Cherbourg and Havre than were necessary for the defence; and the well-executed destruction of the bridge of Fontenoy, near Toul, in the centre of the country occupied by the conquerors, shows what may be done by bold partisans. For, if the war is to be resumed at all after the 19th of February, it must be in reality a war to the knife, a war like that of Spain against Napoleon; a war in which no amount of shootings and burnings will prove sufficient to break the spirit of resistance."[160]

These extracts from articles which Engels wrote between December 1870 and February 1871 show that he completely misjudged the military situation at that time. He greatly exaggerated the ability of France to recover from the crushing defeats of Sedan and Metz. Engels was also mistaken in supposing that the collapse of the Second Empire in France would herald an era of revolution

in western Europe. In August 1870, when he was making arrangements to move from Manchester to London, Engels wrote to Jenny
Marx: "In view of the present state of affairs in France, where
everything can collapse at any time – and probably will collapse
within a week or a fortnight – it would indeed be risky to rent a
house for 3½ years and to have it decorated and furnished. But
I shall have to risk it."[161] In fact the only revolution that followed
the Franco-Prussian war was the rising of the workers in Paris and
the establishment of the Commune. This was quickly suppressed and
Europe subsequently enjoyed a long period of peace and stability.

On the day that Engels's last article on the war appeared, the
Commune was set up in Paris. For many years Engels had waited
for the workers of Paris to rise against Napoleon III but they never
did so. On September 1, 1870 – the day of Sedan – Marx had complained of "the miserable behaviour of Paris during the war – still
allowing itself to be ruled by the mamelukes of Louis Bonaparte
and of the Spanish adventuress Eugénie after these appalling
defeats".[162] A few days later Engels warned Marx that a premature
rising of the French workers might have fatal consequences for the
cause of revolution. Such a rising would probably be put down by
the German troops besieging the French capital. A rising should
be postponed until after peace had been signed.[163] The rising came
in March 1871 and Marx hailed it as "a new point of departure
of world-historic importance." He declared that "the struggle of
the working class against the capitalist class has entered upon a new
phase with the struggle in Paris".[164] Engels also welcomed the
establishment of the Commune with enthusiasm. He believed that
the workers were better organised than during any previous rising
and that they would be able to hold out for some time. When
Marx suggested that the Commune should fortify the northern
heights of Montmartre he may well have been passing on advice
given by Engels. After bitter street fighting, heavy loss of life, and
destruction of property the Commune collapsed at the end of May
1871. Engels's assessment of the military prospects of the Commune
had been too optimistic.[165]

The articles on the Franco-Prussian war assured Engels's
reputation as a military critic. He regarded himself as "the representative of the general staff of the party".[166] His advice on military
matters was sought not merely by socialist leaders but – somewhat
surprisingly – by Major Wachs, who was a member of the German
General Staff. Hellmut von Gerlach wrote in his memoirs:

"The first socialist whom I met was also the most famous. In 1894,
when preparing to make my first journey to study conditions in
England, I was sitting in our Social Conservative Club with Freiherr

von Ungern-Sternberg of the *Kreuzzeitung*, Rudolf von Mosch of the *Deutsches Adelsblatt*, Rudolf Stratz, J. E. Freiherr von Grotthuss and some other friends whom I met regularly in the evening. I told them of my plans and Major Wachs of the General Staff – at that time the military authority for the entire right-wing press – said: 'If you are going to London you must certainly call upon my friend Friedrich Engels'. I listened in astonishment. How could a conservative Major of the General Staff – the recognised expert on the strategic importance of Bizerta harbour – regard the last great living hero of the international socialist movement as his friend? But Wachs explained himself with growing enthusiasm for Engels. He was not interested in Engels's politics. But as a military critic – as a man of expert knowledge, objectivity and clear judgment – there was no colleague whom he held in higher esteem. So Wachs maintained a friendly correspondence with Engels. A letter of introduction from Wachs would ensure me a friendly reception if I called upon Engels."[167]

After 1871 Engels wrote less on military affairs than he had done when he lived in Manchester. Indeed there were not many campaigns to write about, except the Russo-Turkish war of 1876. Engels was particularly interested in revolutionary warfare and in 1873 he wrote a memorandum on the recent revolt in Spain which was, in his view, "a classic illustration of how *not* to organise a revolution".[168] More than once Engels drew attention to the fact that as the conscript armies on the Continent increased in size, so the number of men trained in the use of arms also increased. If the young men who had served with the colours could be converted to revolutionary socialism, they would be in the front line when the workers rose to overthrow their oppressors.

Engels frequently attacked the spirit of Prussian nationalism and militarism and he criticised the growth of the German army. In 1874 he criticised the Reich Army Law which fixed the strength of the armed forces in peacetime at 400,000 men and made financial provision for their maintenance for seven years (the *Septennat*).[169] In the following year he denounced the press campaign in Germany against France when the French National Assembly passed a law providing for an increase in the armed forces.[170] And in 1887 he warned the Germans that they would never be able to fight another war against a single adversary as they had done in 1866 and 1870. He declared that the next war would be a world war and would lead to famine and disease on a scale not known since the Thirty Years war. It would be followed by the collapse of countless European states and the disappearance of dozens of monarchies.[171]

In 1893 Engels wrote a series of articles in *Vorwärts*, which were printed as a pamphlet entitled *Can Europe Disarm?* He declared that the arms race on the Continent coupled with the existence of rival alliances could lead only to a world war or to an economic collapse due to excessive military expenditure. His remedy for this state of affairs was to reduce the length of service with the colours by international agreement. This he thought would be "the simplest and quickest method of effecting the transition from standing armies to popular militias".[172]

In 1895, shortly before his death, Engels wrote for the last time on the military aspect of a popular revolt. In particular he discussed the rôle of street fighting in towns in the future. Engels wrote: "Let us be under no illusions in this matter." "In the future it will be very unusual for revolutionaries to achieve by street fighting a decisive victory in the way in which one army can defeat another." Urban fighters behind the barricades could achieve only limited objectives. They might sap the morale of the troops opposing them. And they could abandon street fighting for passive resistance and still be a thorn in the side of their enemies.

Engels argued that in the last fifty years it had become increasingly difficult for revolutionaries to hope for success in urban street warfare. Towns had grown in size so that a large urban area had to be seized and defended by the insurgents. Urban redevelopment – such as Haussmann's reconstruction of central Paris – had cleared away slums so that broad main thoroughfares could be built. It was much more difficult for insurgents to barricade wide streets than narrow alleys. Again, over the years, the weapons used by soldiers – such as breech-loading rifles and improved artillery – had become much more efficient.

Yet Engels declared that despite these changes, which were so disadvantageous to urban insurgents, street fighting still had a rôle to play in a future revolution. He suggested that a revolt in a town should be attempted, not at the start, but at a later stage of an insurrection. And he thought that street fighting should be initiated only if large forces of insurgents were available. Finally Engels argued that the class struggle, like popular warfare, had radically changed in the last fifty years. It was no longer possible for a dedicated minority of militants to start a revolt if the vast mass of the population was apathetic to the cause of revolution. "If we aim at securing a fundamental change in the structure of society," he wrote, "we must have the masses behind us". "The masses must understand what the revolt is about and what is at stake." "The masses must appreciate why they are risking life and limb."[173]

Engels's knowledge of military affairs was also evident in writings which were primarily of a political or historical character. Thus in

1878 in his book attacking Eugen Dühring he wrote three chapters on what Dühring had called "the force theory".[174] By "force" Dühring had meant "war". Dühring had argued that the exploitation of certain groups of people – such as slaves and serfs – by others was the result of wars in the past which had created an economic and political system within which the exploitation of the weak by the strong could take place. Engels claimed that the opposite was true. It was economic factors which made it possible for the strong to make war and to enslave and exploit the weak. Engels illustrated his argument by giving a detailed account of the evolution of armies and armaments within the framework of different kinds of economies. Here he made one of his worst blunders as a military critic. He declared that, since the Franco-Prussian war, "the weapons used have reached such a stage of perfection that further progress which would have any revolutionary influence is no longer possible". "The era of evolution is, therefore, in essentials, closed in this direction."[175] In 1887–8 Engels began to write an additional chapter on "The Force Theory" which attempted to illustrate his argument by an analysis of Bismarck's unification of Germany by a policy of "blood and iron".[176] The manuscript was never completed. Here Engels summarised his views on several campaigns – from the Crimean war to the Franco-Prussian war – which he had previously described when he was writing for the press on military affairs. Meanwhile in 1884 in his book on the origin of the family, private property and the state Engels speculated upon the origin of warfare and the early organisation of armed forces. He considered that the creation of private property, the class struggle, and organised warfare all began at the same time. Wars began as soon as private property was established and as soon as rival social groups developed with different economic interests. According to Engels, the earliest armies were those organised to enable a property-owning class to protect its property and to keep its slave labour force under subjection. Warfare as practised in primitive societies was a system of organised theft and warriors set out to seize the cattle and treasure of their neighbours. War became a way of life which enabled societies to add to their store of wealth.[177] Clausewitz had argued that war was an extension of the foreign policy of rival states. In time of peace governments exchanged notes; in time of war they fought battles. Engels, on the other hand, argued that war was the climax of the struggle between rival social groups. In the class struggle of his own time the rising of armed revolutionaries took the place of workers on strike.

Engels's writings on the art of war had a profound influence upon Lenin's thinking on military problems. In her memoirs M. K. Krupskaya wrote that Lenin "had made a thorough study of the views of Marx and Engels upon revolutions and insurrections and had reflected deeply upon their writings on these subjects".[178] In an essay written in 1901 Lenin criticised those who had argued that Engels's article of 1895 had suggested that the era of armed insurrection had passed away and that socialism should be achieved by peaceful means. In 1906 Lenin discussed Engels's theory of revolutionary warfare in the light of the experience gained in the Moscow rising of December 1905. He agreed with Kautsky that those who had fought behind the barricades in Moscow had developed a new technique of street fighting but he argued that the revolutionaries had not yet fully appreciated Engels's thesis that success in urban street fighting could be achieved only by seizing the initiative at the right moment and by taking offensive action of the most vigorous kind.

During the first World War when some socialists in neutral countries advocated a policy of disarmament, Lenin replied that "Socialists cannot, without ceasing to be socialists, be opposed to all war". He declared that "Engels was perfectly right when, in a letter to Kautsky, September 12, 1882 he openly admitted that it was possible for *already victorious* Socialism to wage 'defensive wars'. What he had in mind was defence of the victorious proletariat against the bourgeois of other countries."[179]

Lenin also made a careful study of Engels's pronouncements on the organisation of armed insurrection. In 1905, for example, Lenin summarised and commented upon Engels's accounts of the Baden rising of 1849 and the Spanish revolt of 1873. On the eve of the Bolshevik revolution Lenin reprinted Engels's article of 1852 on the art of armed insurrection and summarised Engels's views in five theses of his own. Both the technique of revolution as put into practice by the Bolsheviks in 1917 and the subsequent organisation of the Red Army owed much to the ideas that Engels had put forward many years before.[180]

NOTES

1 For Engels's writings on military affairs see F. Engels, *Ausgewählte Militärische Schriften*, Vol. 1, 1958, Vol. 2, 1964. For Engels as a military critic see Max Schippel, "Die Miliz und Friedrich Engels" in *Sozialistische Monatshefte*, Vol. 30, 1914; Ernst Drahn, "Friedrich Engels als Kriegswissenschaftler" in *Kultur und Fortschritt*, 1915; S. Neumann, "Engels and Marx: Military Concepts of the Social Revolutionaries" in E. M. Earle (ed.), *Makers of Modern Strategy* (New York, 1966); S. Budkiewitsch, "Engels und das Kriegswesen" in *Friedrich Engels der Denker* (Basel, 1945: articles from the Soviet

encyclopaedia) and *Der General: Friedrich Engels als erster Militär-theoretiker der Arbeiterklasse* (Leipzig and Jena, 1957); J. L. Wallach, *Die Kriegslehre von Friedrich Engels* (Frankfurt am Main, 1968); M. E. Berger, *War, Armies and Revolution: Friedrich Engels's Military Thought* (University of Pittsburgh, 1969) and "Engels, Armies and the Tactics of Revolution" presented to the Ohio Academy of History, April 3, 1971: typescript); Heinz Hahlweg, *Friedrich Engels. Die Anfänge der proletarischen Militärtheorie, 1842–52* (1970); essays on "Engels's Kriegslehre" by W. Hahlweg, J. L. Wallach and C. D. Kernig in the *Archiv für Sozialgeschichte*, Vol. 10, 1970 and essays in *Militärwesen. Zeitschrift für Militärpolitik und Militärtheorie*, Vol. 14, Heft 10, October 1970. See also H. von Gerlach, *Von Rechts nach Links* (Zürich, 1937).

A number of memoranda by Engels on military topics are preserved in the Marx–Engels archives in Amsterdam, in the Wuppertal town library and elsewhere. They include
  (i) documents which have not been published;
 (ii) notes on topics on which Engels wrote articles;
(iii) manuscripts of published articles which may differ slightly from the printed version.
The documents include manuscripts on
  (i) preliminary studies on the use of force in history;
 (ii) mountain guerilla warfare;
(iii) notes on a future world war;
 (iv) the militia system;
  (v) organisation of the Russian army (Crimean war);
 (vi) chronological list of battles: Crimea and Italian war, 1859;
(vii) notes on how revolutionary units were armed in 1849;
(viii) notes on the Franco-Prussian war of 1870–1;
 (ix) notes on various military histories.
See W. Hahlweg's essay in the *Archiv für Sozialgeschichte*, Vol. 10, 1970.

2 Julian Harney in the *Newcastle Weekly Chronicle*, August 17, 1895.
3 F. Engels, *The Condition of the Working Class in England* (edition of 1958), p. 257.
4 F. Engels, *The Condition of the Working Class in England* (edition of 1958), p. 257.
5 F. Engels, "Zwei Reden in Elbelfeld" in the *Rheinische Jahrbücher*, 1845, reprinted in *Gesamtausgabe*, Part I, Vol. 4, p. 376.
6 *Deutsche Brüsseler Zeitung*, February 27, 1848 in F. Engels, *Ausgewählte Militärische Schriften*, Vol. 1 (1958), pp. 1–3.
7 *Neue Rheinische Zeitung*, June 28 and 29 and July 1 and 2, 1848 in F. Engels, *Ausgewählte Militärische Schriften*, Vol. 1 (1958), pp. 4–27.
8 *New York Daily Tribune*, May 18, 1852 in Karl Marx (should be F. Engels), *Revolution and Counter-Revolution or Germany in 1848* edition of 1952), p. 70.
9 Karl Marx to F. Engels, November 19, 1848 in *Gesamtausgabe*, Part III, Vol. 1, p. 104.
10 F. Engels to Karl Marx, January 7–8, 1849 in *Gesamtausgabe*, Part III, Vol. 1, p. 105.
11 *Marx–Engels Werke*, Vol. 28, p. 85.
12 *Neue Rheinische Zeitung*, May 19, 1849 in F. Engels, *Ausgewählte Militärische Schriften*, Vol. 1 (1958), pp. 152–61.
13 *New York Daily Tribune*, April 9, 1852 in Karl Marx (should be

F. Engels), *Revolution and Counter-Revolution or Germany in 1848* (edition of 1952), p. 89.

14 F. Engels to Karl Marx, July 6, 1852 in *Gesamtausgabe*, Part III, Vol. 1, p. 361.

15 Wilhelm Liebknecht in *Reminiscences of Marx and Engels* (Foreign Languages Publishing House, Moscow), p. 138.

16 *Deutsche Monatshefte für Politik, Wissenschaft, Kunst und Leben* (Stuttgart, 1850), Vol. 10 (ii), quoted in G. Zirke, *Der General* (1957), p. 8.

17 Quoted by R. Dlubek in his introduction to F. Engels, *Die Reichsverfassungskampagne* (1969), p. 8.

18 F. Engels to Joseph Weydemeyer, June 19, 1851 in Karl Marx and F. Engels, *Letters to Americans 1848–95* (1963), p. 20. For Engels's part in the campaign in Baden in 1849 see A. Happich, *Friedrich Engels als Soldat der Revolution* (1931).

19 F. Engels to Karl Marx, January 31, 1860 in *Gesamtausgabe*, Part III, Vol. 2, p. 459.

20 Karl Marx to F. Engels, August 1, 1849 in *Gesamtausgabe*, Part III, Vol. 1, pp. 110–11.

21 F. Engels (Lausanne) to J. Weydemeyer, August 23, 1849 and F. Engels to Jakob Schabelitz, August 24, 1849 in *Marx–Engels Werke*, Vol. 27, pp. 509–11.

22 F. Engels, "Die deutsche Reichsverfassungskampagne" in the *Neue Rheinische Zeitung. Politisch-Ökonomische Revue*, 1850, Heft 1, pp. 35–78; Heft 2, pp. 37–56; and Heft iii, pp. 38–50. The articles have been reprinted in F. Engels, *Ausgewählte Militärische Schriften*, Vol. 1 (1958), pp. 49–141 and in F. Engels, *Die Reichsverfassungskampagne* (edited by Rolf Dlubek, Dietz Verlag, Berlin, 1969).

23 F. Engels's obituary of P. J. Becker in the *Sozialdemokrat*, December 17, 1886: reprinted in F. Engels, *Biographische Skizzen* (1967), pp. 117–27.

24 Address drawn up on behalf of the Central Committee of the Communist League: see Wermuth and Stieber, *Die Communisten-Verschwörungen des neunzehnten Jahrhunderts* (two volumes, 1853–4 new edition, 1969), Vol. 1, Appendix 13.

25 F. Engels to J. Weydemeyer, June 19, 1851 in Karl Marx and F. Engels, *Letters to Americans 1848–95* (1963), p. 21.

26 F. Engels to Karl Marx, February 26 and March 27, 1851 in *Gesamtausgabe*, Part III, Vol. 1, p. 158 and p. 169. For Engels's assessment of Wellington as a military commander see F. Engels to Karl Marx, April 11, 1851 (*ibid.*, p. 185).

27 F. Engels to Karl Marx, February 11 and 18, 1858 in *Gesamtausgabe*, Part III, Vol. 2, p. 287 and p. 289.

28 F. Engels to F. Lassalle, March 14, 1859 in Gustav Mayer (ed.), *Ferdinand Lassalle. Nachgelassene Briefe und Schriften*, Vol. 3, *Briefwechsel zwischen Lassalle und Marx* (1922), pp. 158–9.

29 Karl Marx to F. Engels, April 2, 1851 and F. Engels to Karl Marx, April 3, 1851 in *Gesamtausgabe*, Part III, Vol. 1, p. 180 and p. 182.

30 F. Engels to J. Weydemeyer, June 19, 1851 in Karl Marx and F. Engels, *Letters to Americans 1848–95* (1963), pp. 20–2. For a later letter from Engels to Weydemeyer (August 7, 1851) on the same subject see *ibid.*, pp. 25–6.

31 F. Engels to Karl Marx, April 3, 1851 in *Gesamtausgabe*, Part III, Vol. 1, p. 183.

32 Karl Marx to F. Engels, September 23, 1851 in *Gesamtausgabe*, Part III, Vol. 1, pp. 265–9.

33 F. Engels to Karl Marx, September 26, 1851 in *Gesamtausgabe*, Part III, Vol. 1, p. 270.

34 Engels's memorandum – written between September and December 1851 – was published under the title "Betrachtungen über die Folgen eines Krieges der Heiligen Allianz gegen Frankreich im Falle einer siegreichen Revolution im Jahre 1852" in *Neue Zeit*, Jahrgang XXXIII (1914–15) and in F. Engels, *Ausgewählte Militärische Schriften*, Vol. 1 (1958), pp. 207–31.

35 F. Engels to Karl Marx, December 3, 1851 in *Gesamtausgabe*, Part III, Vol. 1, pp. 291–4.

36 F. Engels to J. Weydemeyer, January 23, 1852 in Karl Marx and F. Engels, *Letters to Americans 1848–95* (1963), p. 34.

37 *Notes to the People*, February 21, 1852, pp. 846–8.

38 Karl Marx to F. Engels, December 9, 1851 in *Gesamtausgabe*, Part III, Vol. 1, pp. 294–5.

39 F. Engels to J. Weydemeyer, January 23, 1852 in Karl Marx and F. Engels, *Letters to Americans 1848–95* (1963), pp. 33–5.

40 F. Engels to Karl Marx, January 22, 1852 in *Gesamtausgabe*, Part III, Vol. 1, p. 310.

41 *New York Daily Tribune*, August 19, 1852 in Karl Marx (should be F. Engels), *Revolution and Counter-Revolution or Germany in 1848* (edition of 1952), p. 120.

42 *New York Daily Tribune*, April 9, 1852 in Karl Marx (should be F. Engels), *Revolution and Counter-Revolution or Germany in 1848* (edition of 1952), p. 86.

43 *New York Daily Tribune*, April 17, 1852 in Karl Marx (should be F. Engels), *Revolution and Counter-Revolution or Germany in 1848* (edition of 1952), pp. 95–6.

44 This axiom appears in F. Engels to Karl Marx, September 26, 1851 in *Gesamtausgabe*, Part III, Vol. 1, p. 270.

45 On April 20, 1852 Engels told Marx that he had just settled his account with a German bookseller. On July 15, 1852 Engels wrote that Stefan Naut had made some purchases on his behalf – "obviously the library of a retired artillery officer" – from a second-hand bookseller in Cologne (*Gesamtausgabe*, Part III, Vol. 1, p. 338 and p. 365). See also F. Engels to J. Weydemeyer, April 12, 1853 in Karl Marx and F. Engels, *Letters to Americans, 1848–95* (1963), p. 53.

46 Heinz Helmert, *Friedrich Engels. Die Anfänge der proletarischen Militärtheorie* (1970), p. 102.

47 F. Engels's introduction to Sigismund Borkheim's pamphlet on *Zur Erinnerung für die deutschen Mordspatrioten 1806–7* (new edition, 1888), reprinted in F. Engels, *Biographische Skizzen* (1967), pp. 131–141.

48 F. Engels to Karl Marx, May 7, July 6 and 15, 1852 in *Gesamtausgabe*, Part III, Vol. 1, pp. 351, 361 and 365.

49 Karl Marx to F. Engels, April 30, 1852 in *Gesamtausgabe*, Part III, Vol. 1, 344.

50 Karl Marx to F. Engels, August 19, 1852 in *Gesamtausgabe*, Part III, Vol. 1, pp. 377–8.

51 F. Engels to Karl Marx, August 21, 1852 in *Gesamtausgabe*, Part III, Vol. 1, p. 383.

52 Karl Marx to F. Engels, May 7, 1861 in *Gesamtausgabe*, Part III,

Vol. 3, p. 19. In 1851 Engels had used an atlas belonging to Marx. He wrote that he was keeping it for the time being as he had "great need of it" (F. Engels to Karl Marx, February 26, 1851 in *Gesamtausgabe*, Part III, Vol. 1, p. 158.

53 F. Engels to Karl Marx, September 29, 1853 in *Gesamtausgabe*, Part Vol. 1, p. 158.

54 Karl Marx to F. Engels, September 30, 1853 in *Gesamtausgabe*, Part III, Vol. 1, pp. 505–6.

55 Karl Marx to F. Engels, November 2, 1853 in *Gesamtausgabe*, Part III, Vol. 1, p. 511.

56 Karl Marx to F. Engels, December 2, 1853 and January 5, 1854 in *Gesamtausgabe*, Part III, Vol. 1, p. 514 and Vol. 2, p. 1.

57 Karl Marx to F. Engels, December 14, 1853 in *Gesamtausgabe*, Part III, Vol. 1, p. 517.

58 F. Engels to H. J. Lincoln (draft), March 30, 1854 in Marx–Engels archives, K.350 (Amsterdam). A German translation of this letter is printed in the *Marx–Engels Werke*, Vol. 28, p. 600. See also F. Engels to Karl Marx, April 3, 1854 in *Gesamtausgabe*, Part III, Vol. 2, p. 15.

59 F. Engels to Karl Marx, April 20, 1854 in *Gesamtausgabe*, Part III, Vol. 2, pp. 18–19.

60 Karl Marx to F. Engels, May 27, 1859 in *Gesamtausgabe*, Part III, Vol. 2, p. 394.

61 F. Engels to Karl Marx, December 17, 1855 in *Gesamtausgabe*, Part III, Vol. 2, pp. 99–100.

62 F. Engels to Karl Marx, June 10, 1854 in *Gesamtausgabe*, Part III, Vol. 2, p. 36.

63 Karl Marx to F. Engels, May 3, 1854 in *Gesamtausgabe*, Part III, Vol. 2, p. 27.

64 Karl Marx to F. Engels, June 13, 1854 in *Gesamtausgabe*, Part III, Vol. 2, p. 37. Engels's article on the siege of Silistria appeared as a leading article in the *New York Daily Tribune* on July 25, 1854: reprinted in Karl Marx, *The Eastern Question* (1897, new edition, 1969), pp. 412–18. Several articles attributed by Eleanor Marx to her father (and printed in *The Eastern Question*, 1897) were actually written by Engels.

65 F. Engels, *Ausgewählte Militärische Schriften*, Vol. 1 (1958), pp. 234–396. Engels also wrote two articles on "Germany and Pan-Slavism" for the *Neue Oder Zeitung* (Breslau). Dr Max Friedländer, who was related to Lassalle, was an editor and part-owner of the *Neue Oder Zeitung*. Some of Engels's military writings on the Crimean war which appeared in the *New York Daily Tribune* were reprinted in Karl Marx (should be Karl Marx and F. Engels), *The Eastern Question. A Reprint of Letters written 1853–56 dealing with Events of the Crimean War* (edited by Eleanor Marx Aveling and Edward Aveling, 1897: new edition, 1969) and in Karl Marx and F. Engels, *The Russian Menace to Europe* (edited by P. W. Blackstock and B. F. Hoselitz, 1953).

66 *New York Daily Tribune*, November 15, 1854 in Karl Marx (should be Karl Marx and F. Engels), *The Eastern Question* (1897 and 1969), p. 493.

67 Engels wrote

The long and short of the war is this: England, and particularly France, are being dragged 'unavoidably though reluctantly', into engaging the greater part of their forces in the East and the Baltic, that is upon two advanced wings of a military position which has no centre nearer than France. Russia sacrifices her coasts, her fleets, part of her troops, to induce the Western Powers to engage themselves completely in this anti-strategical move. As soon as this is done, as soon as the necessary number of French troops are sent off to countries far from their own, Austria and Prussia will declare in favour of Russia, and march with superior numbers upon Paris. If this plan succeeds, there is no force at the disposal of Louis Napoleon to resist that shock. But there is a force which can 'mobilize' itself upon any emergency, and which can also 'mobilize' Louis Napoleon and his minions as it has mobilized many a ruler before this. That force is able to resist all these invasions; it has shown this once before to combined Europe; and that force, the Revolution, be assured, will not be wanting on the days its action is required (*New York Daily Tribune*, June 9, 1854 in Karl Marx (should be Karl Marx and F. Engels), *The Eastern Question* . . . (1897: new edition, 1969), p. 366).

68 F. Engels, *Ausgewählte Militärische Schriften*, Vol. 1 (1958), pp. 399–472 and correspondence between Marx and Engels in *Gesamtausgabe*, Part III, Vol. 2, pp. 90, 94, 95, 163, and 187.

69 *Putnam's Monthly*, August 1855.

70 F. Engels to Karl Marx, April 22, 1857 in *Gesamtausgabe*, Part III, Vol. 2, p. 185.

71 For letters exchanged between Marx and Engels on their contributions to the *New American Cyclopaedia* see *Gesamtausgabe*, Part III, Vol. 2, pp. 197–8 (list of suggested articles), 200–1, 216–24, 237, 267–8, 270, 276–8, 282–3, 300–1, 336, 418–9, and 421.

72 F. Engels to Karl Marx, April 22, 1857 in *Gesamtausgabe*, Part III, Vol. 2, p. 185.

73 Karl Marx to F. Engels, September 25, 1857 in *Gesamtausgabe*, Part III, Vol. 2, p. 228. This point of view was later elaborated by Werner Sombart in *Krieg und Kapitalismus* (1913).

74 For a list of Engels's articles in the *New American Cyclopaedia* see *Marx-Engels Verzeichnis: Werke, Schriften, Artikel* (1966), pp. 108–9.

75 F. Engels to Karl Marx, January 6, 1858 in *Gesamtausgabe*, Part III, Vol. 2, p. 268.

76 E.g. Army, Cannon, Cavalry, Fortifications, Infantry, Navy.

77 E.g. Alma, Armada, Aspern.

78 E.g. Battery, Bomb.

79 E.g. Bem, Blücher.

80 Karl Marx to F. Engels, August 15, 1857 in *Gesamtausgabe*, Part III, Vol. 2, p. 207.

81 Karl Marx to F. Engels, January 14, 1858 in *Gesamtausgabe*, Part III, Vol. 2, p. 274.

82 *New York Daily Tribune*, December 5, 1857 (leading article): reprinted in Karl Marx and F. Engels, *The first Indian War of Independence 1857–9* (Foreign Languages Publishing House, Moscow), pp. 117–123.

83 *New York Daily Tribune*, April 30, 1858 and May 25, 1858 (leading articles): reprinted in Karl Marx and F. Engels, *The first Indian War of Independence 1857–9* (Foreign Languages Publishing House, Moscow), pp. 136–49.

84 *New York Daily Tribune*, February 20, 1858 (leading article): re-

printed in Karl Marx and F. Engels, *The first Indian War of Independence 1857–9* (Foreign Languages Publishing House, Moscow), pp. 129–35.

85 F. Engels to Karl Marx, September 21, 1857 in *Gesamtausgabe*, Part III, Vol. 2, p. 220.

86 *New York Daily Tribune*, July 21, 1858 in Karl Marx and F. Engels, *The first Indian War of Independence, 1857–9* (Foreign Languages Publishing House, Moscow), p. 178.

87 Karl Marx to Ferdinand Lassalle, February 25, 1859 in H. Helmert and R. Koschulla in *Zeitschrift für Militärgeschichte*, Vol. 4, 1970, p. 397. See also F. Engels to F. Lassalle, March 14, 1859 in Gustav Mayer (ed.), *Ferdinand Lassalle. Nachgelassene Briefe und Schriften*, Vol. 3, *Briefwechsel zwischen Lassalle und Marx* (1922), pp. 158–9.

88 F. Engels, *Po und Rhein* (1859: new edition, 1915).

89 F. Engels, *Po und Rhein* (edition of 1915), p. 6.

90 F. Engels, *Po und Rhein* (edition of 1915), p. 32.

91 F. Engels to Karl Marx, May 9, 1851 in *Gesamtausgabe*, Part III, Vol. 1, p. 98. In this letter Engels summarised a conversation with an Italian businessman who had visited him in Manchester.

92 F. Engels, *Po und Rhein* (edition of 1915), p. 32.

93 Engels wrote "ein Blatt Papier" (a piece of paper). In 1914 Bethmann-Hollweg referred to the treaty which guaranteed the neutrality of Belgium as "ein Fetzchen Papier" (a scrap of paper).

94 Karl Marx, *The Civil War in France*, 1871 (Foreign Languages Publishing House, Moscow), p. 32.

95 Karl Marx wrote: "Your pamphlet has established your reputation in Germany as a military critic" (Karl Marx to F. Engels, January 11, 1860 in *Gesamtausgabe*, Part III, Vol. 2, p. 453).

96 Karl Marx to F. Engels, April 12, 1859 in *Gesamtausgabe*, Part III, Vol. 2, p. 377. Marx quoted from a letter which he had received from Ferdinand Lassalle.

97 On January 31 and February 2, 1860 Engels wrote to Marx that he was planning to write a sequel to *Po und Rhein* to be entitled *Savoyen, Nizza und der Rhein* (*Gesamtausgabe*, Part III, Vol. 2, p. 458 and p. 463).

98 F. Engels, *Savoyen, Nizza und der Rhein* (1860: new edition, 1915).

99 Engels wrote: "At this very moment we are threatened by a Franco-Russian alliance" (*Savoyen, Nizza und der Rhein*, edition of 1915), p. 46.

100 *New York Daily Tribune*, August 10, 1860 (leading article) in F. Engels, *Ausgewählte Militärische Schriften*, Vol. 2 (1964), pp. 203–7, and *New York Daily Tribune*, August 11, 1860.

101 *Allgemeine Militärzeitung* (Darmstadt), August 11, 1860.

102 For Isaac Hall's letters to Engels see the Marx–Engels archives, L.2140–2150 (Amsterdam). Isaac Hall was an attorney in the legal firm of Parker and Hall, 6 Essex Street, Manchester. His private address was Moss Grove, Withington. Hall was a Captain (later a Major) in the Volunteers.

103 Karl Marx to F. Engels, October 2, 1860 in *Gesamtausgabe*, Part III, Vol. 2, p. 514.

104 *Volunteer Journal for Lancashire and Cheshire*, September 14, 1860 in W. O. Henderson and W. H. Chaloner (eds.), *Engels as Military Critic* (1959), pp. 1–8. Fourteen of the 28 articles which Engels contributed to the *Volunteer Journal for Lancashire and Cheshire* were

reprinted by W. H. Smith as a sixpenny pamphlet entitled *Essays addressed to Volunteers* (Manchester, 1861). The preface to the pamphlet was dated March 9, 1861.

105 *Volunteer Journal for Lancashire and Cheshire*, December 6, 1861 in W. O. Henderson and W. H. Chaloner (eds.), *Engels as Military Critic* (1959), p. 112.

106 W. O. Henderson and W. H. Chaloner (eds.), *Engels as Military Critic* (1959).

107 Isaac Hall to F. Engels (no date) in the Marx–Engels archives, L.2140–2150 (Amsterdam).

108 *United Services Gazette*, March 23, 1861.

109 Karl Marx's articles in the *New York Daily Tribune* and *Die Presse* and the correspondence between Marx and Engels on the American civil war have been reprinted in Karl Marx and F. Engels, *The Civil War in the United States* (1937: new edition, 1961). A manuscript by Engels entitled "Artilleristisches aus Amerika" (September 1863) was acquired by the Wuppertal public library in 1965.

110 *Volunteer Journal of Lancashire and Cheshire*, December 6, 1861 in W. O. Henderson and W. H. Chaloner (eds.), *Engels as Military Critic* (1959), pp. 109–13.

111 *Die Presse*, March 26, 1862 in Karl Marx and F. Engels, *The Civil War in the United States* (1961), p. 164.

112 F. Engels to Karl Marx, July 30, 1862 in *Gesamtausgabe*, Part III, Vol. 3, p. 81.

113 Karl Marx to F. Engels, August 7, 1862 in *Gesamtausgabe*, Part III, Vol. 3, p. 92.

114 F. Engels to Karl Marx, September 9, 1862 in *Gesamtausgabe*, Part III, Vol. 3, p. 101.

115 Karl Marx to F. Engels, September 10, 1862 in *Gesamtausgabe*, Part III, Vol. 3, p. 102.

116 F. Engels to Karl Marx, November 5, 1862 in *Gesamtausgabe*, Part III, Vol. 2, p. 107.

117 Karl Marx to F. Engels, November 17, 1862 in *Gesamtausgabe*, Part III, Vol. 3, p. 110.

118 F. Engels to Karl Marx, May 3, 1865 in *Gesamtausgabe*, Part III, Vol. 3, p. 265.

119 *Die Presse*, March 27, 1862 in Karl Marx and F. Engels, *The Civil War in the United States* (1961), pp. 174–5. The editor of F. Engels, *Ausgewählte Militärische Schriften* regards this article as one written jointly by Marx and Engels.

120 F. Engels, *Die preussische Militärfrage und die deutsche Arbeiterpartei* (1865).

121 Engels's five articles in the *Manchester Guardian* (June 20, 25 and 28, July 3 and 6, 1866) appeared anonymously. They are attributed to Engels by Gustav Mayer (in *Friedrich Engels*, Vol. 2, pp. 150–4), by M. Rubel (in *Bibliographie des oeuvres de Karl Marx*, p. 248) and by the compiler of the *Marx–Engels Verzeichnis. Werke, Schriften, Artikel* (1966), p. 289. The articles have been reprinted W. O. Henderson and W. H. Chaloner (eds.), *Engels as Military Critic* (1959), pp. 121–40. Engels also wrote a letter (signed F. E.) to the *Manchester Guardian* (February 16, 1864) on the strength of the armies in Schleswig.

122 F. Engels to Karl Marx, July 22, 1870 in *Gesamtausgabe*, Part III, Vol. 4, p. 343.

123 Heinrich Friedjung, *The Struggle for Supremacy in Germany 1859–66* (abridged English translation, 1935), p. 213.

124 *Manchester Guardian*, July 3, 1866.

125 *Manchester Guardian*, July 6, 1866.

126 F. Engels, *Notes on the War. Sixty Articles reprinted from the "Pall Mall Gazette"* (edited by Friedrich Adler, 1923). For the *Pall Mall Gazette* see J. W. Robertson Smith, *The Life and Death of a Newspaper . . ."Pall Mall Gazette"* (1952) and *The Story of the "Pall Mall Gazette"* 1950: reference to Engels as a contributor on p. 185).

127 Karl Marx to F. Engels, July 20, 1870 in *Gesamtausgabe*, Part III, Vol. 4, p. 340.

128 Karl Marx to F. Engels, August 3, 1870 in *Gesamtausgabe*, Part III, Vol. 4, p. 355.

129 J. W. Robertson Smith, *The Story of the "Pall Mall Gazette"* 1950), p. 126.

130 F. Engels to Karl Marx, July 22, 1870 in *Gesamtausgabe*, Part III, Vol. 4, p. 343.

131 F. Engels to Karl Marx, August 3, 1870 in *Gesamtausgabe*, Part III, Vol. 4, 352.

132 Karl Marx to F. Engels, August 3, 1870 in *Gesamtausgabe*, Part III, Vol. 4, p. 356.

133 Letter from Karl Marx to the *Daily News*, January 16, 1871.

134 Karl Marx, *Enthüllungen über den Kommunistenprozess zu Köln* (1852: edition of 1952).

135 Karl Marx to F. Engels, July 28, 1870 in *Gesamtausgabe*, Part III, Vol. 4, p. 345.

136 F. Engels to Karl Marx, July 31, 1870 in *Gesamtausgabe*, Part III, Vol. 4, pp. 348–9. The article appeared in the *Pall Mall Gazette* on August 2, 1870. In it Engels wrote that "from a private source we learn that the 7th Army Corps on the 27th was on its march from Aix-la-Chapelle (Aachen), by Trèves (Trier) to the frontier".

137 Karl Marx to F. Engels, August 1, 1870 in *Gesamtausgabe*, Part III, Vol. 4, p. 350.

138 F. Engels to Karl Marx, August 5, 1870 in *Gesamtausgabe*, Part III, Vol. 4, p. 357.

139 Jenny Marx to F. Engels, August 10, 1870 in *Gesamtausgabe*, Part III, Vol. 4, p. 361.

140 *The Spectator*, August 20, 1870 and Karl Marx to Friedrich Engels, August 30, 1870 in *Gesamtausgabe*, Part III, Vol. 4, p. 374.

141 Karl Marx to F. Engels, August 3, 1870 in *Gesamtausgabe*, Part III, Vol. 4, p. 355.

142 Karl Marx to F. Engels, September 10, 1870 in *Gesamtausgabe*, Part III, Vol. 4, p. 382.

143 F. Engels to Jenny Marx, August 15, 1870 in *Gesamtausgabe*, Part III, Vol. 4, p. 368.

144 F. Engels to Karl Marx, August 3, 1870 in *Gesamtausgabe*, Part III, Vol. 4, p. 353. Marx replied that the *Pall Mall Gazette* had complained of this plagiarism.

145 Karl Marx to F. Engels, September 2, 1870 in *Gesamtausgabe*, Part III, Vol. 4, p. 374.

146 F. Engels to Karl Marx, September 4, 1870 in *Gesamtausgabe*, Part III, Vol. 4, p. 376.

147 *The General Council of the First International: Minutes*, Vol. 4, 1870–1 (Progress Publishers, Moscow), p. 231.

148 F. Engels to Wilhelm Liebknecht, June 22 and July 10, 1871 in G. Eckert (ed.), *Wilhelm Liebknecht. Briefwechsel mit Karl Marx und Friedrich Engels* (1963), p. 132 and p. 134.

149 *Pall Mall Gazette*, August 26, 1870.

150 Quoted in G. Zirke, *Der General. Friedrich Engels, der erste Militärtheoretiker der Arbeiterklasse* (1957), p. 31.

151 *Pall Mall Gazette*, November 11, 1870.

152 *Pall Mall Gazette*, November 11, 1870. *See also Engels's* article on "Prussian Francs-Tireurs" in the *Pall Mall Gazette*, December 9, 1870.

153 *Pall Mall Gazette*, November 21, 1870.

154 *The General Council of the First International: Minutes*, Vol. 4, 1870–1: meeting of January 31, 1871, p. 112.

155 Karl Marx to Dr Kugelmann, February 14, 1871 in Karl Marx, *Letters to Dr Kugelmann*, p. 119.

156 *Pall Mall Gazette*, November 26, 1870.

157 *Pall Mall Gazette*, November 26, 1870.

158 *Pall Mall Gazette*, December 8, 1870.

159 *Pall Mall Gazette*, December 17, 1870.

160 *Pall Mall Gazette*, February 8, 1871. Marx, too, thought that there was still hope for France at this time. On February 14, 1871 he wrote to Dr Kugelmann: "Despite all appearances to the contrary, Prussia's position is anything but pleasant. If France holds out, uses the armistice to reorganise her army and finally gives the war a really revolutionary character – and the artful Bismarck is doing his best to this end – the new German Borussian (Prussian) Empire may still get a quite unexpected thrashing as its baptism" (Karl Marx, *Letters to Dr Kugelmann*, p. 120).

161 F. Engels to Jenny Marx, August 15, 1870 in *Gesamtausgabe*, Part III, Vol. 4, p. 368. On August 17, 1870 Marx wrote to Engels: "I do not agree with you about renting a house for 3½ years. In view of the collapse of France, the demand for gentlemen's dwellings in London will increase and you will have no difficulty in getting rid of your house at any time" (*Gesamtausgabe*, Part III, Vol. 4, p. 370).

162 Karl Marx to F. A. Sorge, September 1, 1870 in Karl Marx and F. Engels, *Letters to Americans 1848–95* (1963), p. 80.

163 F. Engels to Karl Marx, September 7 and 12, 1870 in *Gesamtausgabe*, Part III, Vol. 4, pp. 379–81 and 383–4.

164 Karl Marx to Dr Kugelmann, April 17, 1871 in Karl Marx, *Letters to Dr Kugelmann*, p. 125.

165 See Engels's speeches to the General Council of the First International on March 21 and April 11, 1871 in *Documents of the First International. The General Council of the First International: Minutes* (Progress Publishers, Moscow), pp. 160–1 and 171–2. The speeches of Engels and Serraillier (March 21, 1871) were printed as an article in *The Eastern Post*, March 25, 1871. See also Gustav Mayer, *Friedrich Engels*, Vol. 2 (1934), p. 227.

166 F. Engels to August Bebel, December 11–12, 1884 in Werner Blumenberg (ed.), *August Bebels Briefwechsel mit Friedrich Engels* (1965), p. 205.

167 Hellmut von Gerlach, *Von Rechts nach Links* (Europa–Verlag, Zürich, 1937), p. 138. Gerlach called upon Engels in London. He wrote that "Engels did not speak quite so enthusiastically about Wachs as Wachs had spoken to me about Engels".

168 F. Engels, "Die Bakunisten an der Arbeit" (September–October 1873) in *Internationales aus dem Volksstaat* (Berlin, 1894) and *Ausgewählte Militärische Schriften*, Vol. 2 (1964), pp. 538–55.

169 F. Engels, "Das Reichs-Militärgesetz" in *Der Volkstaat*, March 8 and 11, 1874: reprinted in F. Engels, *Ausgewählte Militärische Schriften*, Vol. 2 (1964), pp. 556–64.

170 F. Engels, "Offiziöses Kriegsgeheul" in *Der Volksstaat*, April 23, 1875: reprinted in F. Engels, *Ausgewählte Militärische Schriften*, Vol. 2 (1964), pp. 570–7.

171 F. Engels's introduction to a new edition of Sigismund Borkheim's pamphlet *Zur Erinnerung für die deutschen Mordspatrioten 1806–7* (1888): reprinted in F. Engels, *Biographische Skizzen* (1967), pp. 131–41.

172 F. Engels, *Kann Europa abrüsten?* (Nürnberg, 1893), printed in Karl Marx – Friedrich Engels, Vol. 4: *Geschichte und Politik*, pp. 236–57 (Fischer Bücherei, 1966).

173 F. Engels's introduction of 1895 to Karl Marx, *Die Klassenkämpfe in Frankreich 1848 bis 1850*, quoted in J. L. Wallach, *Die Kriegslehre von Friedrich Engels* (1963), pp. 37–40.

174 F. Engels, *Anti-Dühring Herr Eugen Dühring's Revolution in Science*, 1878 (Foreign Languages Publishing House, Moscow, 1959), Part II, Chapters 2, 3 and 4. See also Engels's memorandum on "Infantry Tactics, derived from Material Causes, 1700–1870 (Appendix, pp. 495–503).

175 F. Engels, *Anti-Dühring* (1878: Foreign Languages Publishing House, Moscow, 1959), p. 235.

176 Engels's unfinished manuscript was published by Eduard Bernstein in *Neue Zeit*, Vol. 14 (i) in 1896. It was published as a book under the title *Die Rolle der Gewalt in der Geschichte* (1964) and in English translation as *The Role of Force in History* (edited by Ernst Wangermann, 1968).

177 F. Engels, *Der Ursprung der Familie, des Privateigentums und des Staats im Anschluss an Lewis H. Morgans Forschungen* (1884: fourth edition with new introduction, 1891). English translation: *The Origin of the Family, Private Property and the State* (Foreign Languages Publishing House, Moscow).

178 G. Zirke, *Der General. Friedrich Engels, der erste Militärtheoretiker der Arbeiterklasse* (1957), p. 41.

179 V. I. Lenin, "The War Programme of the Proletarian Revolution" (1916) in V. I. Lenin, *Marx–Engels–Marxism* (Foreign Languages Publishing House, Moscow, 1951), pp. 374–5.

180 J. L. Wallach, *Die Kriegslehre von Friedrich Engels* (1969), pp. 57–68.

8

ENGELS AND THE WORKING CLASSES
1850–1870

I. The Workers in Britain

When he lived in Manchester Engels followed the fortunes of the working class movements in Europe with close attention. He was not discouraged by the failure of the revolutions of 1848 for he believed that new risings of the workers would soon spread across the length and breadth of Europe. He was convinced that the next trade depression in England would spark off a revolution owing to unemployment and distress. He was confident that the reactionary governments on the Continent would soon be overthrown by popular insurrections, while in Russia the serfs would rise in a great peasant revolt to gain their freedom.

Engels dared not openly advocate revolution so long as he worked for Ermen and Engels. He could write political articles only if they appeared anonymously and, for the most part, abroad. He could take no active part in promoting the Chartist movement and he could not attend political demonstrations. He dared not offend Godfrey Ermen if he wished to keep his post in Manchester and so help to support Marx and his family. Engels kept his political opinions a secret from his colleagues in the office and on the Cotton Exchange and he acted with circumspection when he was in touch with prominent Chartists.

At this time the Chartist movement no longer commanded the popular support which it had enjoyed in the 1840s. It had never recovered the ground lost through the failure of its demonstration in London in 1848 but it was by no means dead and buried. Though many former Chartists now supported other reform movements, the hard core of the left wing of the movement remained faithful to the Chartist cause. Feargus O'Connor, Ernest Jones and Julian Harney continued to champion Chartist doctrines at public meetings and in journals such as the *Red Republican*, the *Friend of the People*, the *Democratic Review* and *Notes to the People*. The Chartists were not a united party, since the leadership was in dispute and there were sharp differences of opinion concerning future policy. As Engels had foreseen in 1845 the demand for a democratic parliamentary system – embodied in the six points of the Charter – had now been extended to include various other reforms, such as the nationalisation of landed property.

Marx and Engels believed that since England was the most advanced industrial country in the world, she would be the first to overthrow the capitalist system. They expected the Chartists to be in the forefront of the next revolution and in 1850 they resumed their contacts with Ernest Jones and Julian Harney. But relations with the Chartist leaders soon became strained. As the authors of the Communist Manifesto and as former editors of the *Neue Rheinische Zeitung* Marx and Engels expected a warmer welcome from the Chartists than that accorded to other exiles from the Continent such as Louis Blanc, Ledru Rollin, Mazzini and Kossuth. Marx and Engels were also annoyed that neither Ernest Jones nor Julian Harney would accept their own brand of socialism. So although Marx and Engels considered that the Chartists would one day be the spearhead of revolution, they soon gave up any hope of using the movement as a vehicle for spreading their own doctrines in England.

When he returned to Manchester Engels detected few signs of revolutionary fervour among the Lancashire workers. The "highly bellicose and blustery mood" of the Chartists, which he had observed a few years earlier,[1] had evaporated. Julian Harney denounced the Chartists of Manchester as "the worst lot in the country". They were, he thought, "a degraded crew of slaves and sycophants".[2] Engels visited Dr John Watts, only to discover that this former socialist had become "a completely radical philistine, who is interested only in the educational movement, supports moral force, and accepts Proudhon as his lord and master".[3] Engels's old friend James Leach[4] had – according to Harney – sunk "to the contemptible character of lacquey to O'Connor".[5] Leach was now an enthusiastic supporter of the co-operative movement. After attending a Chartist meeting in Manchester, which was addressed by Ernest Jones, Engels told Marx that – in view of his presence – "Jones had to put himself forward as a red republican and supporter of the nationalisation of landed property." Engels observed that the Chartist movement had now split up into a number of hostile factions. He considered that although Ernest Jones and Julian Harney had many friends in Manchester Feargus O'Connor's hold on the Chartist movement in the city was unlikely to be shaken. Engels added that he proposed to start a Chartist discussion group to study the Communist Manifesto.[6] Soon afterwards Feargus O'Connor came to Manchester to rally his supporters in the north of England. He was disappointed at his reception. Engels declared that the meeting had "turned out to be pure humbug". Only eight delegates, representing four towns, were present and they quarrelled bitterly among themselves.[7]

Early in February 1851 Engels was one of 13 people who met in Manchester to set up "a new Chartist locality". He reported that the proceedings had "passed off very seriously" and everyone present – except Engels himself – was elected to form a council to organise the Chartist movement in Manchester.[8] Engels's refusal to become a member of this council showed that he was giving up active participation in politics. He wrote to Marx: "We are now responsible to ourselves alone and when we are needed we shall be able to dictate our own terms." "How can people like us, who flee from official positions as from the plague, belong to a 'party'?"[9] Between March 31 and April 10, 1851 a Chartist convention met in London. This was a more successful meeting than the abortive conference in Manchester. A new radical programme was drawn up which was far wider in scope than the original charter. But the adoption of a programme of democratic reforms did little to revive the Chartist movement.

After 1851 Chartism received little support from the workers in Lancashire whose energies were now directed towards building up trade unions, co-operative stores, and friendly societies. Engels was losing interest in Chartist affairs in Manchester though he contributed occasionally to left-wing working class journals such as *Notes to the People* and *The People's Paper*.[10] In March 1852 Engels told Marx that since Feargus O'Connor had "definitely gone mad", Jones should make every effort to step into his shoes as leader of the Chartist movement. "From all I see," wrote Engels, "the Chartists are so completely disorganised and scattered, and at the same time so short of useful people, that they must either fall completely to pieces and degenerate into cliques, in which case they will for practical purposes become simply the tail of the financial reformers, or they must be reconstituted on an entirely new basis by a fellow who knows his business. Jones is quite on the right lines for this. . . ."[11] And since Julian Harney, his only rival, was fading into obscurity, Jones was able to assume O'Connor's mantle as leader of the Chartists.

Marx considered Ernest Jones to be an energetic leader of the workers. But Jones suffered from certain defects such as "his urge for publicity, his tactless fumbling after pretexts for agitation, and his restless desire to move faster than the times".[12] Marx approved of the "Parliament of Labour" which met in 1854. This marked the climax of Ernest Jones's campaign to raise funds for the powerloom weavers of Preston, who were on strike. Jones summoned "a mighty delegation from all trades" to support the strikers.[13] On Monday, March 6, 1854 – when the strike at Preston was in its 29th week – between 30 and 40 members of the Parliament of Labour met in Manchester. The delegates, mainly representatives of lower paid trades, embarked upon more ambitious schemes than Ernest Jones's plan to help the powerloom weavers of Preston and the dyers of Manchester and Salford. They prepared a project to finance strikes from a national fund to be raised by weekly subscriptions from trade unionists. The Parliament of Labour also discussed a plan to set up industrial and agricultural co-operative societies.[14] Replying to an invitation to attend the conference,[15] Marx declared that "the mere assembling of such a Parliament marks a new epoch in the history of the world".[16] In fact the Parliament of Labour was a complete fiasco.

Ernest Jones realised that there was no future for Chartism as an independent political force. He therefore attempted to secure an alliance between Chartism and other reform movements. His Labour Parliament sought to link Chartism with militant trade unionism. When this failed he supported a movement in favour of Lord John Russell's Bill of 1854 to extend the franchise even though this involved co-operating with middle-class reformers who had little sympathy with the Chartist cause. In February 1858 a Chartist conference discussed the possibility of an alliance with middle-class reformers. In the following September Ernest Jones was supporting John Bright's agitation in favour of limited parliamentary reform. Marx wrote that Jones had sold himself "to the Bright coterie", "The donkey has ruined himself politically. . . ."[17] In October Ernest Jones addressed a meeting in Manchester at which he appealed for an alliance between the Chartists and the radical reformers. Engels regarded Jones's attitude as "very disgusting". "After this affair one is really almost driven to believe that the English proletarian movement in its old traditional Chartist form must perish completely before it can develop itself into a new form, capable of life." "The English proletariat is becoming more and more bourgeois, so that this most bourgeois of all nations is apparently aiming ultimately at the possession of a bourgeois aristocracy and a bourgeois proletariat as well as a bourgeoisie. For a nation which exploits the whole world this is, of course, to a certain extent, justified."[18] In February 1859 Marx declared that he had "broken with Ernest Jones" who was persistently "trying to reach an agreement with the radical bourgeoisie".[19] The breach, however, was not a final one. Marx and Jones continued to meet from time to time though their period of political co-operation was over.

In the 1860s Chartism finally collapsed and Marx and Engels began to realise that the English workers had no appetite for revolution. Marx complained of "the sheepish attitude of the workers in Lancashire", who failed to resort to violence when they were out of work during the Cotton Famine.[20] Shortly afterwards Engels admitted that "the revolutionary energy of the English proletariat has to all intents and purposes completely evaporated and the English proletarian is in full agreement with the rule of the bourgeoisie".[21] After the victory of the Liberals at the general election of 1868 Engels declared that the proletariat had "discredited itself terribly". "Not a single working-class candidate had a ghost of a chance but my Lord Tom Noddy or any *parvenu* snob could have the workers' votes with pleasure."[22]

The energies of the workers were now devoted to building up the trade union movement. In the 1840s Engels had welcomed strikes as the first round of the class struggle that would one day overthrow the capitalist system. But in the 1860s Engels no longer believed that strikes would necessarily pave the way for the downfall of the middle classes and the triumph of socialism. He now thought that strikes were irrelevant from the point of view of the success of a future revolution. He argued that trade unionists who went on strike were acting within the framework of the capitalist system and were using industrial action merely to secure for themselves a larger share of the wealth which capitalism created. In Engels's view this was the behaviour of a "bourgeois proletariat", not a revolutionary proletariat.

In the circumstances Marx and Engels adopted a new attitude towards the English workers. While Ernest Jones attempted to secure an alliance with middle-class radicals, Marx tried to make contact with leading trade unionists such as Applegarth, Odger, George Potter and W. R. Cremer. Marx hoped to "re-electrify the political movement of the English working class"[23] through the First International which was set up in 1864. J. G. Eccarius, a former member of the Communist League and one of Marx's faithful adherents, was secretary of the International Working Men's Association between 1867 and 1871.

While Marx and Engels were disappointed that the English workers had lost their taste for revolutionary agitation, they were gratified that in Ireland the Fenians were prepared to use violence to attain their ends. In 1867, for example, a group of Fenians freed some of their fellow conspirators in Manchester by stopping a police van in broad daylight and murdering the officer in charge. Marx believed that a Fenian victory in Ireland would lead to the overthrow of the Protestant landed interest in that country. Then, deprived of "its strongly entrenched outposts in Ireland", the English landed aristocracy would be gravely weakened. If one of the pillars of capitalism in England were undermined in this way, the whole capitalist edifice would come crashing to the ground. While Marx was elaborating this interesting theory Engels visited Ireland in 1869 and began to work on a history of Ireland,[24] while Lizzie Burns was "in continual touch with the many Irishmen in Manchester, and was always well informed of their conspiracies".[25]

II. The Workers in France

In France, as in England, Marx and Engels could claim few converts before 1870. Engels had lived in Paris in 1846–7 but his propaganda among the German artisans working there had not been particularly successful. In 1852 the *Kölnische Zeitung* stated that some followers of Marx were meeting regularly at the Café de Danemarc in the rue St Honoré in Paris but Engels doubted the truth of this report.[26]

The only former member of the Communist League of any standing who was living in Paris in the 1850s was Dr A. G. Ewerbeck. Although he had resigned from the League in 1850 to devote himself to literary work,[27] his political views did not change. He contributed an article to a French journal in 1851 in which he denounced the German princes and forecast the triumph of the "communist democrats" in Germany.[28]

Marx and Engels had a poor opinion of Dr Ewerbeck, particularly when they had reason to suspect that he was on friendly terms with Proudhon.[29] In 1851 Ewerbeck sent Marx a dozen copies of his book on *L'Allemagne et les Allemands*, Marx declared that it was a worthless compilation,[30] while Engels refused to accept a copy since it was "not worth paying 6d postage for it".[31] Marx subsequently criticised "that dog Ewerbeck, who never puts any stamps on his letters and robs me of my last 10d".[32] Engels thought that Ewerbeck had declined into his second childhood.[33] In 1858 Marx told Engels that "the idiot Ewerbeck" was in financial difficulties; he was down to his last 1,200 francs and was thinking of coming to England.[34] Marx and Engels obviously did not regard Dr Ewerbeck as a useful disciple to represent their views in Paris.

There were few, if any, Marxists in France in the middle of the nineteenth century. It was Proudhon, whom Engels called "the Socialist of the small peasant and master craftsman",[35] who secured the support of the early French socialists. Marx and Engels had praised Proudhon for his attack on finance capitalism in *Qu'est-ce que la propriété?*[36] (1840) but they soon came to regard his doctrines as a serious obstacle to the progress of their own ideas in France. When they met in Paris, Marx failed to convert Proudhon to his own views, while a little later Proudhon declined to be associated with Marx's correspondence committee in Brussels.

When Proudhon's book entitled *Système des contradictions économiques, ou Philosophie de la misère* appeared in 1846, Engels dismissed the author's plan for the establishment of "labour markets" as "complete and utter nonsense".[37] Marx promptly attacked Proudhon's book in a pamphlet entitled *Misère de la Philosophie* (1847). Here he described Proudhon as "the petty bourgeois, tossed about constantly between capital and labour, between political economy and communism".[38] But Marx's pamphlet found few readers and did no harm to Proudhon's reputation in socialist circles in France. Proudhon dismissed Marx's attack as "a texture of coarseness, slander, debasement and plagiarism".[39]

In an interview with Louis Blanc in October 1847 Engels declared that Marx's pamphlet on Proudhon was an outline of the programme of "our party – that is to say, the most advanced wing of German democracy".[40] On the eve of the revolution of February 1848 in France, Engels complained that the exiled German artisans in Paris were "a lot of sleepyheads", who were more interested in the ideas of Proudhon and Weitling than in the doctrines of Karl Marx.[41] Shortly afterwards, in the Communist Manifesto, Marx and Engels again attacked Proudhon for advocating that "the proletariat should remain within the bounds of existing society, but should cast away all its hateful ideas concerning the bourgeoisie.[42] During the revolution of 1848 Proudhon advocated the establishment of a People's Bank to issue notes backed by goods (not bullion) and to grant free credit to those who produced industrial or agricultural goods.[43] Marx and Engels dismissed this "panacea for all social ills"[44] as nonsense.

There are numerous references to Proudhon in the correspondence between Marx and Engels in the 1850s and 1860s. When he returned to Manchester in 1850 Engels was dismayed to find that John Watts had "accepted Proudhon as his lord and master" and had translated some of Proudhon's writings into English. In August 1851 Marx summarised for Engels the main points in Proudhon's new book on *Idée générale de la Révolution au XIXᵉ siècle*.[45] Engels replied that "the fellow has made some progress" and that Proudhon's ideas were now more "down to earth" than they had been in the past. But Engels doubted whether Proudhon's scheme to fix the rate of interest at $\frac{1}{2}$ per cent or even $\frac{1}{4}$ per cent after a successful revolution would be a success in practice.[46] Engels thought that, on the one hand, Proudhon was making a final effort to produce a theory of socialism that would be acceptable to the middle classes while, on the other hand, he was also adopting some of Marx's ideas as his own.[47] Marx complained that Proudhon "with his customary charlatanry, has borrowed some ideas from me, as *his own* 'latest discoveries' ".[48]

Shortly afterwards, Proudhon wrote a pamphlet on Louis Napoleon's coup d'état of December 2, 1851.[49] Marx declared that Proudhon had regarded the coup d'état "as the result of an antecedent historical development". But his account of the events of December 1851 had become "a historical *apologia* for its hero".[50] In his draft of the first volume of *Das Kapital*, written in 1857–8, Marx criticised various aspects of Proudhon's doctrines, particularly the ideas on credit which he had put forward in a pamphlet of 1850 attacking Bastiat.[51] Shortly before his death in 1865 Proudhon wrote his last (and unfinished) book on *De la capacité politique des classes ouvrières* in which he looked forward to an early revival of socialism in France. And when the First International was established, Marx soon found that Proudhon's followers were strongly entrenched in the French section.

The aspect of Proudhon's teaching which had the greatest influence upon the French workers in the 1860s was what was known as "mutualism". This was Proudhon's plan to reorganise the economy in such a way that goods would be exchanged for vouchers indicating the number of hours worked to produce the goods. Production should be organised in industrial co-operative societies and not by private capitalists. With the introduction of free credit and the abolition of interest, unearned income would vanish.

Although Marx and Engels rejected Proudhon's version of socialism and did not think that his petty bourgeois followers were likely to start a revolution, they hoped that Louis Napoleon would be overthrown by a popular rising. Marx, Engels and Lassalle were confident that the great revolutionary traditions of France – the memories of the Jacobins and the Committee of Public Safety – would soon be revived. They accepted the fact that many of the peasants and petty bourgeoisie supported Louis Napoleon but they expected that the workers of Paris and the provincial towns would one day rise in revolt as they had done in 1789–92, in 1830 and in 1848. As early as the summer of 1850 Lassalle thought that there would be a revolution in France in the autumn.[52] In April 1851 Engels was hopeful that Louis Napoleon would soon be overthrown.[53] Marx and Engels were disappointed when the workers of Paris remained passive when Louis Napoleon seized power by the *coup d'état* of December 2, 1851. But they believed that Louis

Napoleon's régime was so corrupt that it would not survive for long. Just as Marx and Engels expected that the next trade slump would herald the collapse of capitalism in England, so they were convinced that Napoleon III's next failure at home or abroad would see the building of barricades in Paris. In 1858 Engels was happy to report to Marx that "all the English philistines expect war, revolution and even worse in France",[54] while in the following year Marx told Engels that Blanqui's deportation from France had infuriated the Paris workers and that he did not give Napoleon III "four months' purchase for his crown and dynasty".[55] In fact the Second Empire was not overthrown by the workers of Paris but by the German troops who defeated the French at Sedan and Metz. The rising of 1871, which led to the establishment of the Commune, was directed against the new government which was set up when Napoleon III's empire collapsed during the Franco-Prussian war.

The failure of the French craftsmen and factory workers to overthrow Napoleon III was not due to any lack of grievances. The second Empire was an autocratic and reactionary régime but the middle classes – remembering the horrors of the rising of June 1848 – supported the Emperor in his efforts to suppress the proletariat. Associations of workers – including trade unions – were declared illegal and only some harmless friendly societies and journeymen's gilds were able to survive. In the first eight years of the Second Empire nearly 4,000 workers were punished for trade union activities or for supporting a strike. The factory laws afforded the workers little protection from exploitation by their employers. The compulsory identity card (livret) was regarded by the workers as a badge of servitude which made it easy for the authorities to watch over their comings and goings.

The most discontented of the workers found a champion in Blanqui, an advocate of revolution, who spent many years in prison. He was the leader of a secret group of conspirators – numbering 2,000 or so – who were organised in cells of ten members. Blanqui aimed at the overthrow of the Second Empire and the establishment in Paris of a dictatorship run by a small band of his dedicated disciples. After a successful revolution he hoped to see the abolition of the national debt, the standing army and the judicial system, as well as the confiscation of the property of the Church – measures which would have gained the approval of Marx and Engels. Blanqui had no love for the owners of great estates but – in the hope of gaining the support of the peasants – he was prepared to allow the private ownership of smallholdings to continue.

By the 1860s the French industrial workers felt that it was safe to come out into the open. Some of the secret societies came out into the open as workers' associations of various kinds. These included some co-operative credit banks and producers' co-operative societies. In 1868, however, the central co-operative bank – the *Société du Crédit au Travail* – went bankrupt and many workers turned to political action and militant trade unionism. In that year a federation of trade unions was established in Paris. The government of the Second Empire gradually gave way to pressure from the workers. In 1864 and again in 1868 workers' associations were tolerated, though it was still very difficult to organise strikes without clashing with the civil or military authorities. By 1870 some of the French workers were adopting a militant attitude and were giving strong support to the First International. Through this organisation Marx and Engels could hope to exercise some influence over the French labour movement. In June 1871 Jules Favre sent a circular to the chancelleries of Europe demanding the suppression of the First International on the grounds that it had been largely responsible for the establishment of the Commune in Paris.

III. The Workers in Germany

Marx and Engels had few followers in England or France in the 1850s and 1860s but they did have some disciples in Germany. Even after the triumph of the reaction in Germany in 1849 the Communist League survived for three years. In the summer of 1850 it claimed that its supporters were still organised in several towns in Germany and were successfully infiltrating into some associations of peasants and gymnastic clubs.[56] The trial at Cologne of some of its leaders in 1852 led to the collapse of the Communist League. Although political associations were suppressed and many leaders of the workers were in exile or in prison, some former members of the Communist League continued their political activities as an underground movement. These little groups tried to keep in touch with each other and occasionally their representatives came to London to report to Marx on their activities.

In 1856 it was reported that small groups of workers were meeting in secret in several towns in the Rhineland to discuss plans for the next revolution. In Düsseldorf their leader was Ferdinand Lassalle. In the Wupper valley – particularly in Solingen – the supporters of revolution hoped that one day Engels would return to champion their cause. When the merchant Gustav Levy of Düsseldorf visited Marx to give him this information, Marx warned him that the workers should avoid a premature rising which was bound to fail. They should wait until a revolution broke out in Paris,

Berlin or Vienna before taking any action themselves.[57] When writing to Engels about Levy's visit Marx observed that there was "some jealousy between Cologne and Düsseldorf as to the leading of the proletarian movement" in the Rhineland.[58]

In 1860 information reached Marx that two young lawyers named Bessel and Knorsch were organising the workers in Cologne and Düsseldorf.[59] In the early 1860s Marx was in touch with Carl Klings of Solingen, a former member of the Communist League, who was described as "the secret leader" of the revolutionary workers in the Rhineland. In 1864 two Solingen workers – on the run from the police – arrived in England with a letter of introduction from Carl Klings. They saw Marx and gave him news of the progress of Lassalle's propaganda in the Rhineland.[60] In the following year Marx asked Carl Siebel to make contact with Carl Klings in Solingen and this meeting took place in February 1865.[61] In March 1865 Carl Klings left Germany for the United States and on his way there he visited Marx in London.[62] When Carl Klings emigrated, the leadership of the workers in Solingen was taken over by Carl Klein and F. W. Moll.[63]

Marx and Engels regarded the revolutionary workers of Solingen as their staunchest supporters in the Rhineland. Curious myths about Marx and Engels circulated among these faithful disciples. Engels complained in 1870 that they believed that he had once put his communist principles into practice by paying all his father's operatives equal wages on a certain pay day. Engels declared that there was no truth in the story.[64]

Marx's cause in Germany would have had little prospect of success if its future had lain in the hands of men like Levy, Klings, or Klein. But there was a leader of the workers of quite a different calibre who continued to live in Germany at a time when many revolutionaries were in gaol or abroad. This was Ferdinand Lassalle[65] who was to exercise a profound influence upon the development of the socialist movement in Germany. Even in the 1840s the ambitious young Jew from Breslau had made a great impression upon his contemporaries by his striking personality, his powers of oratory, his qualities of leadership, and his intellectual brilliance. Heinrich Heine praised Lassalle's "eminent intellectual gifts",[66] Georg Weerth considered him to be – next to Marx – the most gifted man whom he had met,[67] while Engels declared that he had "great talents".[68]

Lassalle was in the unique position of being virtually the only champion of the workers who was living in freedom in Prussia in the 1850s. He had led the workers of Düsseldorf in 1848 and had been in touch with Marx and other editors of the *Neue Rheinische*

Zeitung. He had known Wilhelm Wolff as a student in Breslau[69] and he had met Engels at a demonstration at Worringen in 1848.[70] Soon afterwards Lassalle was charged with inciting people to armed revolt. During his trial he appealed to Engels for support in the columns of the *Neue Rheinische Zeitung.*[71] Lassalle was eventually sentenced to six months imprisonment which he served between October 1850 and April 1851. While at liberty for a brief period in 1849 he helped to raise money for Marx who was virtually penniless when he fled to Paris after the *Neue Rheinische Zeitung* ceased publication. Freiligrath complained that Lassalle was so tactless in his fund raising that Marx's plight became the subject of common coffee house gossip. Lassalle for his part assured Marx that he had acted "with the utmost discretion".[72] Lassalle was out of action as a political agitator between the autumn of 1849 and the spring of 1851 and he took no part in the risings in Germany in support of the constitution drawn up by the National Assembly in Frankfurt. When many revolutionaries fled the country or languished in gaol after the insurrections, Lassalle was at liberty. And he had nothing to fear when the communist leaders were brought to trial since he had not been a member of the Communist League.

When Wermuth and Stieber compiled their list of communists in 1854 all that they could allege against Lassalle was that he had expressed willingness to join the Communist League and had actively assisted in the defence of the communist leaders during their recent trial at Cologne.[73] Fortunately for Lassalle the Cologne committee of the Communist League had rejected Marx's suggestion that Lassalle should be admitted to membership.[74] Writing on behalf of the committee in June 1850 P. G. Röser informed Marx that Lassalle "persists in maintaining aristocratic principles and is not so enthusiastic a supporter of the general welfare of the workers as he ought to be".[75] The committee clearly felt that Lassalle had placed himself in an equivocal position by working for the Countess of Hatzfeld. He was her business adviser and was helping her to secure her divorce. Many years later Engels declared that in those days Lassalle had been "interested only in the adultery and divorce case of Countess Hatzfeld and her husband". Lassalle had been "buried up to his ears in the filth which the conducting of that scandalous case required of him".[76] Lassalle's connections with the nobility cost him his admission to the Communist League but they brought him into touch with influential people and this probably explains why the Prussian authorities – while keeping a watchful eye on him – allowed him to remain at liberty. Lassalle realised that he was being spied upon and so he kept his meetings with the representatives of the workers in Düsseldorf as secret as possible.

When the Countess of Hatzfeld secured her divorce in 1854 she made Lassalle an annual allowance so that he could devote himself to his literary work. He wrote a romantic play in blank verse on Franz von Sickingen, a pamphlet on the Italian war of 1859, and scholarly books on philosophy and law.[77]

Marx's relations with Lassalle in the 1850s were of a somewhat devious nature. Marx wanted to turn Lassalle into a faithful disciple. After the Communist League had been dissolved, Marx and Engels viewed the prospects of their movement in Germany with some misgivings. In 1853 Marx wrote: "The decline of our friends is far from pleasant to contemplate."[78] "We must undoubtedly enlist new recruits for our party."[79] A few years later Engels declared: "Our best people disappear in this wretched time of peace and their successors are of very poor quality."[80] Lassalle – described by Marx in 1853 as tough, energetic and ambitious[81] – was by far the ablest leader of the revolutionary workers who was still at liberty and still living in Germany. Marx told Engels in July 1853 that Lassalle was his only associate in Germany who was able to send letters to London.[82]

Marx realised that it would strengthen his own position if he could have a reliable lieutenant in Germany who would take an active part in a rising against the reactionary rulers who were in power at that time. Lassalle continued his secret revolutionary propaganda among the workers in Düsseldorf at a time when he could take no public part in political life. He addressed groups of workers – as many as 60 on New Year's day 1856. He gave money to workers in need and he supported the families of men who were in prison for their political beliefs. He sometimes helped fugitives from justice to escape over the Dutch frontier.[83]

While Marx and Engels awaited the outbreak of a new revolution on the Continent, Lassalle was prepared to make himself useful in various ways. He occasionally gave or lent Marx small sums of money.[84] He gave Marx information concerning the political situation in the Rhineland and the attitude of the middle classes and the workers to Manteuffel's reactionary régime in Prussia. In 1850 he tried, though with little success, to secure subscribers in Düsseldorf for Marx's new journal (the *Neue Rheinische Zeitung: Poltisch-ökonomische Revue*).[85] Lassalle's contacts with the aristocracy and senior officials in Prussia enabled him to give Marx confidential information which could be used in contributions to the *New York Daily Tribune*. On the outbreak of the Crimean war he sent Marx a copy of a declaration of the Prussian government very soon after it had been despatched to London and Paris.[86] In 1853 Lassalle helped to distribute Marx's pamphlet on the trial of the Communist leaders in Cologne – a pamphlet which had been prohibited by the authorities.[87] Lassalle also secured for Marx the post of London correspondent of the *Neue Oder Zeitung*, which was edited by his cousin Dr. M. Friedländer.[88] Marx and Lassalle were in correspondence throughout the 1850s. Marx used to consult Engels before replying to Lassalle's letters so that although Engels and Lassalle were not in direct correspondence for much of the time, Engels was kept in touch with Lassalle's views and activities.

Although the correspondence between Marx and Lassalle in the 1850s suggests that they were working harmoniously together at that time,[89] the correspondence between Marx and Engels tells a different story. It is clear that they regarded Lassalle as a shallow thinker, a flashy adventurer, and a dubious colleague even when they appeared to be co-operating with him. And their doubts concerning Lassalle's integrity were shared by some of Marx's followers in Germany.

In 1856 a merchant from Düsseldorf named Gustav Levy visited Marx and recited a catalogue of complaints against Lassalle. He declared that Lassalle was dishonest in financial matters and had been engaged in speculations of a highly dubious character. He alleged that Lassalle's success in the Countess of Hatzfeld's lawsuit had been achieved by "a very low intrigue". After the Countess had secured her divorce Lassalle should have severed his connections with her. Instead he drew an annual allowance of £600 from her and lived as an *homme entretenu* "without any pretext whatever". All this, in Levy's view, was conduct unbecoming of a leader of the workers. Moreover Lasselle intended to leave provincial Düsseldorf for the fleshpots of Berlin, where he hoped to move in high society and to cut a dash in the Countess of Hatzfeld's literary salon. Levy declared that Lassalle planned to desert the workers for "a middle class party".

After consulting Freiligrath, Marx gave Engels an account of his conversation with Gustav Levy. He declared that he was prejudiced in favour of Lassalle and that he distrusted gossip. All the same he had been impressed by Levy's story. There was no smoke without fire and Marx had advised Levy and the workers of Düsseldorf to keep a sharp eye on Lassalle in the future.[90] Four years elapsed before Marx told Lassalle of the charges that had been brought against him. Lassalle replied that he had no difficulty in deducing that "a certain little Levy" had been responsible for the allegations. He denied the charges and declared that Levy had tried to make mischief because the Countess of Hatzfeld had turned down his request for a loan.[91]

Engels took a less charitable view of Levy's allegations than Marx had done. When he heard about Levy's interview with Marx he wrote:

"Lassalle: One might feel sorry for the fellow because of his great talents, but the whole affair is really too aggravating. We have always had to keep a devilish sharp eye on him. He is a real Jew from the Slav frontier and he has always been ready to exploit party affairs for his private ends. Moreover it is disgusting to see how he is always trying to push his way into the world of the upper classes. He is a greasy Jew disguised under brilliantine and flashy jewels. All this simply means that we have to watch him very carefully. But if he starts doing things directly affecting the Party, no one can blame the Düsseldorf workers for hating him."

Engels agreed with the advice that Marx had given to Levy. The workers of Düsseldorf should watch their leader. As yet Lassalle had not "overstepped the mark", but if ever he did anything "openly against the Party", strong action should be taken against him.[92] A year later Engels wrote: "We know that the fellow is useless but it is difficult to find a positive reason for breaking off relations with him, especially since we have heard nothing more from the workers of Düsseldorf."[93]

Marx, however, had no intention of breaking off relations with Lassalle at this time. Lassalle had been useful in Düsseldorf and Marx hoped that he might be even more useful in Berlin. Marx admitted that Lassalle was an abler politician than any of the leaders of the democratic parties[94] but he scoffed at Lassalle's "comical vanity"[95] and sarcastically observed that Lassalle had "actually seriously begun to make a name for himself in Berlin",[96] while Jenny Marx contemptuously dismissed Lassalle as "the little Jew from Berlin".[97]

On the other hand, in his letters to Lassalle, he continued to adopt a friendly tone. When Lassalle's study of the philosophy of Heraclitus appeared, Marx wrote to Engels that it was "a flabby botched job". It might be "an enormous exhibition of scholarship" but Marx declared that it was easy for a writer like Lassalle with time to spare and money to spend "to bring together a heap of learned notes". Lassalle could get as many books as he needed sent to his home from the University library at Bonn.[98] Yet Lassalle received a letter from Marx describing the book as a "masterly" work.[99] Marx asked Engels to give him "absolution for the praise that I have had to bestow upon Heraclitus, when writing to Lassalle".[100]

Marx's equivocal attitude towards Lassalle paid handsome dividends. In 1858 Lassalle persuaded his friend and publisher

F. G. Duncker to print Marx's *Zur Kritik der politischen Ökonomie*.[101] In 1859 he performed a similar service for Engels, whose pamphlet on *Po und Rhein* was also published by Duncker.[102] In March 1859 Engels thanked Lassalle for finding a publisher for *Po und Rhein*.[103] Lassalle replied that he was pleased to hear from Engels after so many years.[104] Shortly afterwards Engels wrote to Lassalle criticising his play on Franz von Sickingen. In a letter written to both Marx and Engels the author replied to these criticisms.[105] Next Lassalle offered to ask Duncker to publish the sequel to *Po und Rhein* but Engels had already found another publisher for *Savoyen, Nizza und der Rhein*.[106]

In 1860 the relations between Marx and Lassalle deteriorated. In the affair of Karl Vogt – who had attacked Marx – Lassalle failed to give Marx the loyal support to which Marx felt that he was entitled.[107] Marx bitterly reproached Lassalle and now told him about the accusations made against him in 1856 by Gustav Levy. The quarrel was smoothed over and in the spring of 1861 Marx visited Lassalle in Berlin. On this occasion he was able to arrange with Dr Friedländer to become a contributor to *Die Presse*, a newspaper which was published in Vienna. He approached Friedländer directly and did not use Lassalle as an intermediary.[108] On his return to London he brought with him a "beautiful military atlas" – a present from Lassalle to Engels.[109]

When Marx and Lassalle met in Berlin they discussed a plan to establish a radical newspaper in Germany. In the previous January when Lassalle had suggested reviving the *Neue Rheinische Zeitung* Marx had argued that the project "would be a miscarriage from the beginning".[110] Engels suggested that a daily paper would run into financial difficulties and favoured a less ambitious scheme to set up a weekly journal.[111] Marx continued to have his doubts about the proposed paper since he feared that he and Engels might be blamed for Lassalle's editorial follies.[112] Lassalle offered to raise between 20,000 and 30,000 thalers to start a newspaper to be edited jointly by Marx and himself. When Marx suggested that Engels should join the editorial board, Lassalle replied: "Well, if three editors are not too many, Engels can join us – but the two of you must have only one vote between you so that I shall not be permanently in a minority."[113] Marx then said that he would have to consult Engels and Wilhelm Wolff before reaching a final decision.

On his return to London Marx decided not to collaborate with Lassalle to produce a newspaper.[114] For a time their correspondence lapsed. They drifted apart and Marx's criticism of Lassalle's *Das System der erworbenen Rechte* (1861) did not help matters.[115]

Conditions in Prussia were changing and in the New Era some of the restrictions on political activities imposed during the reaction of the 1850s were relaxed. Lassalle was now able to come out into the open as a champion of the workers. In doing so he acted independently of Marx who was offended at what he regarded a failure to act in concert with the recognised leader of the revolutionary workers.

In 1862 Lassalle attempted to secure a reconciliation with Marx. In the summer of that year he came to London to visit the industrial exhibition and he stayed at Marx's house. The discussions between Marx and Lassalle during this visit were far from amicable and showed that the gulf between them could not be bridged. The visit was not a success. Marx told Engels that his guest – "the Jewish nigger Lassalle" – was "completely deranged". Jenny Marx later recalled that Lassalle had "swept through our rooms, perorating so loudly, and gesticulating and raising his voice to such a pitch that our neighbours were scared by the terrible shouting and asked what was the matter. It was the inner struggle of the 'great' man bursting forth in shrill discords".[116]

Jenny Marx visited her pawnbroker to raise a little money to maintain appearances before a guest who was spending £1 2s a day on cabs and cigars.[117] When Marx could no longer conceal his poverty, Lassalle agreed to lend him some money – a transaction which later led to bitter recriminations.[118] Engels, who first guaranteed and later repaid the loan, stayed in Manchester when Lassalle visited Marx, although Lassalle asked him to join in their discussions.[119] When he was leaving London Lassalle again suggested that he and Marx should run a newspaper together. Marx replied that, if he were well paid, he would become Lassalle's English correspondent without, however, undertaking "any other responsibility or political partnership whatever". Marx considered that co-operation between them was now impossible since they no longer agreed upon anything in politics "except for certain remote ultimate objectives".[120] Marx told Lassalle: "You cannot march with us, and we cannot march with you."[121]

If it had been in Marx's interest to collaborate with Lassalle, in the 1850s it had also been in Lassalle's interest to work in close contact with Marx. Lassalle was an ambitious politician who was determined to make a name for himself as a leader of the German workers. This would of course be possible only when the reactionary régimes allowed the resumption of political activities. While he was waiting for his opportunity it was to his advantage if the radical and revolutionary workers believed that he was Marx's right hand man. In the Rhineland there were men who had not forgotten the revolution of 1848. They remembered the days when Marx and Engels had thundered against their oppressors in the *Neue Rheinische Zeitung*. They recalled Engels's dramatic descent upon Solingen and Elberfeld in 1849 and his subsequent participation in the insurrection in Baden. They regarded Marx and Engels as their foremost champions who would one day return to lead them to victory in a new revolution. So long as Marx and Engels lived in exile these workers were prepared to accept Lassalle as a leader who – at no small personal risk – continued to live in Germany. Lassalle took full advantage of this situation. He was as anxious as Marx to keep quiet about their differences. It was to their mutual advantage to make their supporters in Germany believe that there was no rift between them.

In the 1850s Marx believed that Lassalle had accepted his doctrines and he expected Lassalle to behave as a faithful disciple should behave. Marx later told Dr Kugelmann that Lassalle had "always declared himself an adherent of the party which I represent".[122] But Lassalle was not prepared to accept a subordinate *rôle* in the next revolution. For the time being it might suit him to pose as a loyal supporter of Marx but he was confident that he was Marx's intellectual equal and that he had the ability to carve out for himself a successful political career without any help from Marx or Engels. He tried to rival Marx and Engels as a scholar and as a revolutionary agitator. If Marx could achieve distinction as an economist, then Lassalle could write on the iron law of wages, on indirect taxation, and on state-aided industrial co-operative associations. If Marx were an expert in the field of Hegelian philosophy, then he could make a critical assessment of the philosophy of Heraclitus. If Engels could write a series of articles on the Peasants' War in Germany, then he could go one better and write a romantic verse drama on the career of Franz von Sickingen. And as soon as he had found a publisher for Engels's *Po und Rhein*, Lassalle promptly wrote a pamphlet himself on the Italian question in which he argued that the war between Austria and France gave Prussia a golden opportunity to unite Germany on her own terms.[123]

The inability of Marx and Lassalle to work together after 1862 was due to various circumstances. There was a clash of powerful personalities and there was rivalry for the leadership of the workers in Germany. Moreover Marx and Lassalle held different views on the tactics to be followed to establish a socialist society. Both men were dictators at heart and neither could brook opposition from the other. Engels once observed that when Marx edited the *Neue Rheinische Zeitung* his "dictatorship was obvious, unquestioned, and freely accepted by all of us".[124] Lassalle, for his part, was – according to Marx – already behaving "like a future dictator of the workers" in 1863.[125] And Lassalle once assured Bismarck that "the workers are instinctively drawn to a dictatorship".[126] No political movement can harbour two dictators at the same time.

Marx firmly believed that he was the recognised leader of the cause of revolution and he strongly opposed Lassalle's attempt to set himself up as a rival champion of the German workers. Marx believed that capitalism would one day be replaced by communist societies all over the world. Lassalle confined his political activities to Germany and showed little interest in what happened elsewhere. Marx held that existing states and national rivalries would eventually disappear while Lassalle claimed to be a patriot who hoped to see all Germans united under a single flag. Lassalle believed that once manhood suffrage had been secured, the workers would soon gain political control in Germany and then they would be able to remould the state in their own interests. Marx saw little point in reforming a state which – according to his doctrines – was doomed to extinction when bourgeois society was replaced by a communist society. Marx advocated co-operation between his followers and left wing political parties only as a temporary expedient, since his ultimate aim was to destroy the middle classes. But Lassalle was an ambitious politician who was determined to secure power and he was prepared to make alliances with middle class parties if that suited his immediate plans.

Lassalle's political career was a short one. When the constitutional conflict broke out in Prussia on the question of financing the proposed army reforms, and the parliament (*Landtag*) was dissolved, Lassalle realised that the general election would give him the opportunity that he had long been seeking to return to public life. He did not stand for election since a maker of revolutions had better things to do than to seek a seat in parliament. Instead he discussed the political crisis in two lectures which he gave in Berlin in April 1862. In the first he discussed the nature of constitutional government[127] and in the second he examined the concept of a working class.[128] His second lecture was published as a pamphlet entitled *The Workers' Programme*. Lassalle argued that the workers were a distinct "estate" in society, with interests very different from those of the bourgeoisie. He attacked the three-class voting system in Prussia, which gave the votes of 150,000 wealthy taxpayers the same weight as those of 2,700,000 workers and peasants. He argued that in the new society which had developed after the revolution of 1848, the state would be dominated by the workers. Marx dismissed *The Workers' Programme* as "a miserable vulgarisation of the Communist Manifesto and other doctrines that we have preached often enough".[129] Many years later, however, Eduard Bernstein declared that *The Workers' Programme* was "one of the best, if not the best, of Lassalle's speeches". It was "a splendid introduction to the world of socialist thought".[130] The police in Berlin suppressed the pamphlet and charged Lassalle with "inciting the non-possessing classes to hatred and contempt of the possessing classes". Lassalle was found guilty and sent to prison for four months, but on appeal, the sentence was reduced to a fine.

In the autumn of 1862 an association of workers from Leipzig in Saxony sent a deputation to Berlin to try to make common cause with the Progressive Party which was resisting the introduction of the army reforms in Prussia. When the Progressive Party rejected these advances Dr Otto Dammer – acting on behalf of the Leipzig workers' central committee – wrote to Lassalle, praising his "Workers' Programme", and asking him for advice on the future policy of the workers in Saxony, particularly with regard to the establishment of industrial co-operative associations.[131] Lassalle replied in a pamphlet – *An Open Letter of Reply* – which summarised the programme for which he was to campaign during the next two years. He proposed that the workers should demand the establishment of state-aided industrial and retail co-operative associations which would gradually bring capitalism under the workers' control. He rejected Schulze-Delitzsch's plan to set up industrial co-operatives financed by the workers themselves for he believed that the earnings of the workers were too low to make this possible. Earnings were low because wages never rose above the level necessary to provide a bare subsistence for the worker and to maintain the labour force in the next generation. This was the so-called "iron law of wages".

Next the workers should demand electoral reform – the introduction of direct manhood suffrage in all German parliaments. Since the workers were the largest class in the country, any parliament elected by manhood suffrage would have a majority of workers' representatives. Lassalle advised the German workers to form an association, on the lines of the Anti-Corn Law League in England, to agitate in favour of electoral reform.[132] Modesty was never one of Lassalle's attributes and in March 1863 – in a letter to Gustav Levy and the workers of Düsseldorf – he actually compared the publication of his *Open Letter of Reply* to Luther's action in posting his 95 theses on the church door at Wittenberg.[133] In fact Lassalle's pamphlet heralded no new Reformation in Germany. But since his enemies vigorously criticised it in the press,

Lassalle's *Open Letter of Reply* brought its author much publicity. Lassalle's movement was now recognised as a new force in German politics with which the monarchy, the conservatives and the progressives would have to reckon.

Lassalle realised that he had no chance of pursuing a successful political career in Berlin. The authorities regarded him as a dangerous agitator and the police kept a close watch upon his movements. Moreover the city was dominated politically by the Progressive Party and many of the workers were supporters of Schulz-Delitzsch. So Lassalle left for Leipzig where in April 1863 he replied to the numerous attacks which had been made upon his *Open Letter of Reply*.[134] His views on the "iron law of wages", for example, had been sharply criticised by orthodox economists. In May 1863 Lassalle scored a personal triumph when he delivered two speeches at Frankfurt am Main reiterating his view that nearly 96 per cent of the population in Prussia belonged to families in which the head of the household earned less than thirty shillings a week. Since it was impossible to save on such wages, Lassalle urged the state to grant a subsidy of £1,500,000 to encourage the formation of industrial co-operative associations. This would be an insignificant outlay compared with the sums spent on a single military campaign.[135]

A few days later, on May 23, 1863, an association called the General German Workers' Union was established in Leipzig by delegates from eleven towns, mainly in Saxony and the Rhineland.[136] It demanded "the establishment of universal, equal, and direct suffrage by peaceful and legal means, particularly by winning over public opinion".[137] The draft of a proposed German electoral law, drawn up by Lassalle, was subsequently submitted to Bismarck.[138] Lassalle became President of the General German Workers' Union. He was elected for five years and he could not be removed from office during that time. He was granted virtually dictatorial powers. He believed that "the workers instinctively prefer a dictatorship if they are convinced that it will be exercised in their interests".[139] When it was founded, Lassalle's "empire" – as he called it in a letter to Bismarck[140] – had only about 600 members and, despite the feverish efforts of its secretary Julius Vahlteich, it still had fewer than 1,000 supporters three months later.

In June 1863 a conference of liberal working men's clubs was held at Frankfurt am Main and the Union of German Workers and Educational Societies[141] was established. This was a challenge to Lassalle's pretensions to be regarded as the sole leader of the German workers. The Frankfurt congress was a larger and more representative gathering than Lassalle's recent conference in Leipzig.

At Frankfurt 54 workers' associations from 48 cities were represented by 110 delegates. August Bebel – a future leader of the
German Social Democrat Party – was one of the delegates from
Leipzig. The conference supported the political aspirations of the
middle class progressives and concluded its deliberations by giving
three cheers for Schulze-Delitzsch, "the father of the German
working-class movement".[142] Lassalle could draw little comfort
from these proceedings.

The establishment of the General German Workers' Union was
a serious setback for Marx and Engels. For years they had planned
to lead a revolutionary socialist movement among the German
workers whenever the opportunity should arise. Now they found
that Lassalle, whom they had regarded as their supporter, was the
head of a workers' organisation which was neither revolutionary
nor socialist in character. The Communist League, which Marx
and Engels had hoped to revive, had had a democratic constitution
but the General German Workers Union was an authoritarian
organisation with Lassalle as its dictator. The Communist Manifesto
had warned the ruling classes to "tremble at a communist revolution" but no one was likely to tremble at Lassalle's association
which declared that it would work by "peaceful and legal means"
to secure its objective. The "Demands of the Communist Party in
Germany" of 1848 had called for the establishment of a republic,
the expropriation of royal property, the nationalisation of transport, and the establishment of national workshops. Lassalle in
1863 demanded only direct universal manhood suffrage and state
aid for industrial co-operative associations.

It was obvious that Marx and Engels could not support the
General German Workers Union. But they could not denounce it
either. However much they disliked Lassalle's movement, they
dared not attack it openly. A number of their faithful followers
assumed that Lassalle's agitation had the blessing of their leaders
in London and Manchester. Marx and Engels hesitated to disillusion
them for, if they did so, they might split the workers' movement
in Germany even more than it was already split between the
followers of Lassalle and Schulze-Delitzsch. Marx and Engels
normally never hesitated to pillory any black sheep in the socialist
fold who departed from the principles laid down by Marx. But
in 1863–4 they did not publicly denounce Lassalle. Moreover in
October 1864 in the inaugural address of the Working Men's
International Association Marx wrote that "co-operative Labour
ought to be developed to national dimensions, and, consequently
to be fostered by national means". This was uncommonly like
Lassalle's proposed state-aided industrial co-operative societies.

The nature of Marx's dilemma may be judged from the equivocal attitude which he adopted towards the revolutionary workers of Solingen, who were his staunchest supporters in the Rhineland. In June 1864 Marx told Engels that he had been visited by two workers from Solingen, who had "assumed as a matter of course that we have the closest ties with Itzig (Lassalle)". "Naturally I gave these chaps no indication of our real relations – or rather lack of relations – with Itzig (Lassalle)."[143] Shortly afterwards Marx declared that while he and Engels considered that it was unfortunately necessary – from motives of political expediency – to refrain from openly attacking Lassalle, they would of course refuse to be identified in any way with Lassalle's movement.[144]

But Lassalle was also in a dilemma. As Wilhelm Liebknecht observed "he forgot that he lived under a strong despotic government, which could crush him as soon as he gave the least offence". "In order not to have his movement stopped, he had to make concessions to the powers that be."[145] His concession took the form of a series of conversations with Bismarck.[146] The talks were initiated by Bismarck in May 1863[147] and it was intended that they should be confidential. It was not until 1878 that Bismarck gave an account of the conversations to the Reichstag and it was not until 1927 that the collapse of an old cupboard in a government office in Berlin brought to light the letters exchanged between Bismarck and Lassalle. But rumours about the talks soon began to circulate in Germany. Bismarck and Lassalle – however much they might have differed on other matters – were agreed in opposing the aims of the Progressive Party – Bismarck because it tried to hold up the army reforms in Prussia, Lassalle because it was the party of the middle classes which he intended to destroy. "Lassalle," Engels explained, "demanded that, in the fight between royalty and the bourgeoisie the workers should range themselves on the side of royalty".[148]

In the summer of 1864 Lassalle, in a speech to a small gathering of his followers, declared that the workers must regard the bourgeoisie as the enemy who must be fought tooth and nail. The workers should not shrink from seeking any ally in order to triumph in their struggle against the middle classes. If necessary they should support the King of Prussia and Bismarck if this would bring victory nearer. Wilhelm Liebknecht, who was present, at once denounced Lassalle for giving such advice to the workers. Reporting the incident to Marx he declared that Lassalle was "playing so complicated a game that he would never find a way out of the maze".[149]

Lassalle hoped to strike a bargain with Bismarck. He would

agree to German unification under Prussian leadership (by supporting the annexation of Schleswig and Holstein, for example)
if Bismarck would grant manhood suffrage. Bismarck made vague
promises but gave Lassalle no firm undertakings. Bismarck believed
that at some time in the future he might need the support of the
workers in his struggle with the Progressive Party and he recognised
the advantage of making contact with one of the ablest of their
leaders.

Marx and Engels denounced Lassalle's discussions with Bismarck
as a shameful betrayal of the workers. Soon after Lassalle's death,
Engels wrote:

> "It is gradually becoming clear that the worthy Lassalle was no more
> than a common rascal. We have always judged people by their
> deeds and not by their words and I see no reason why we should
> make an exception in favour of the late lamented Itzig (Lassalle).
> He may have been able to justify his actions to himself in a plausible
> fashion because he was so vain, but viewed impartially his behaviour
> was plain roguery and a betrayal of the whole working class move-
> ment to the Prussians. And what is worse the silly chump failed to
> get a quid pro quo from Bismarck. He did not get any definite
> promise and certainly no firm guarantee from Bismarck."[150]

The climax of Lassalle's career came in May 1864 when he
toured the Rhineland and aroused great enthusiasm at mass rallies
of workers by his powerful speeches. During his triumphal progress,
he basked happily in the sunshine of the workers' applause. But at
the height of his campaign some observers began to detect a decline
in his powers. He was making reckless claims and he was greatly
exaggerating his achievements.

Engels was quick to appreciate the significance of Lassalle's
sudden rise to fame as a popular agitator. He warned Marx that

> "Lassalle's agitation and the rumpus that it has caused in Germany
> is, after all, beginning to be awkward for us. It is high time that you
> finished your book if only to secure new disciples – of a different
> character from Lassalle – in the fight against the middle classes. From
> one point of view it is a good thing that we have now again secured
> a foothold in Germany, but it is most unfortunate that Itzig (Lassalle)
> should have provided us with this foothold."[151]

Lassalle's career came to a dramatic end in August 1864. He fell
in love with Helene von Dönniges and was challenged to a duel by
Count Racowitza, who was his rival for the lady's hand. Lassalle
was mortally wounded. Marx was shocked at the news of Lassalle's
death. He wrote to Engels that Lassalle had been

"one of the old guard and the enemy of our enemies. . . . It has all happened so quickly that it is hard to believe that this noisy, tumultuous, and pushing chap is now as dead as a doornail and must for ever keep his trap shut. . . . I am sorry that – through no fault of mine – our relations have been strained in recent years. But I am glad that I resisted pressure from many quarters to attack Lassalle in his 'year of triumph'."[152]

Engels was much less generous in his comments. He declared that Lassalle had been

"part Jew, part cavalier, part clown, and part sentimentalist. (Yet whatever he) may have been as a person, a writer, and a scholar, there can be no doubt that, as a politician, he was one of the most important fellows in Germany. Just now he was being a very uncertain friend and in the future he would almost certainly have been our enemy. But it comes as a shock when one realises how Germany ruins all her political extremists who have some sort of ability. What rejoicings there will be in the ranks of the factory owners and those dirty dogs of the Progressive Party. Lassalle was the only chap in Germany whom they really feared."[153]

In his will Lassalle nominated Bernhard Becker as the new President of the General German Workers' Union. Becker was utterly incompetent and he was replaced first by C. W. Tölcke and then by August Perl. In 1867 when J. B. von Schweitzer,[154] the editor of the *Social-Demokrat*, was elected President, the General German Workers' Union again had a strong hand at the helm. Schweitzer, like Lassalle, was bitterly opposed to the bourgeois Progressive Party and supported Bismarck's policy of unifying Germany under Prussian leadership. The quarrels over the leadership of the General German Workers' Union after Lassalle's death led Marx and Engels to hope that they could now establish their authority over the workers' movement in Germany. But Engels was far too optimistic when he wrote at the end of 1865 that "Lassalleanism in its official form will soon expire."[155] Marx and Engels hoped that their friend Liebknecht[156] would be able to convert the German workers to the Marxist form of socialism.

There was no doubt that Liebknecht was devoted to the socialist cause. As a youth he had organised radical German-speaking workers in Switzerland in 1847[157] and he had fought against the Prussians in Baden in 1849. Soon afterwards he had met Engels in Switzerland. Liebknecht was expelled from Switzerland and sought refuge in England where he joined the Communist League. He met Marx at a summer fête organised by the German Workers' Educational Society and he soon became a close friend of Marx and his family.[158] Marx's children called him "Library". Liebknecht attended a course of popular lectures given by Marx to members of the German Workers' Educational Society. In these lectures – and in private conversations over a number of years – Marx took great pains to give his young disciple a sound training in Marxist economics. Marx and Engels regarded Liebknecht as a thoroughly sound – if not very bright – pupil. Liebknecht returned to Germany in 1862 and settled in Berlin. In 1864, when Lassalle was at the height of his fame, Engels wrote to Marx: "It is indeed of the greatest importance to us that Liebknecht is now in Berlin. At the right moment we can spring a surprise upon Itzig (Lassalle) by letting the workers know, in confidence, just what we really think about him."[159]

Liebknecht was a member of the Berlin branch of the General German Workers' Union and achieved some success in recruiting new members. Although the ostensible aim of the Union was simply to secure electoral reform, Liebknecht was more concerned to pass on to the workers in Berlin the lessons that he had learned from Marx in London. He took every opportunity to impress upon his audiences the achievements of the Communist League and the doctrines of the Communist Manifesto. When Wilhelm Wolff died, Liebknecht delivered a eulogy of this champion of the Silesian workers and trusted friend of Marx and Engels. In the summer of 1864 Liebknecht told Marx that he had been asked by Lassalle to edit a newspaper which would support the aims of the General German Workers' Union. Liebknecht had offered to accept the post if Marx were associated with the venture. But in the end the plan fell through.[160] Lassalle then entrusted Schweitzer with the task of establishing a newspaper. After Lassalle's death, Schweitzer founded the *Social-Demokrat* and Liebknecht became an associate of the editorial board. Engels declared that it was a great step forward to have a paper in Germany in which he and Marx could express their views.[161]

The co-operation between Marx and Schweitzer was shortlived because Schweitzer was prepared to support Bismarck in his struggle against the Progressive Party. In February 1865 Marx wrote to Dr Kugelmann that the intrigues of the Countess of Hatzfeld had led to "the complete compromising of the workers' party". The Countess had tried to place the General German Workers' Union and the *Social-Demokrat* at Bismarck's disposal. Schweitzer's articles became "more and more Bismarckian". "I have found it necessary to sever all connection with the *Social-Demokrat* in a public declaration by myself and Engels."[162] Jenny Marx observed in her memoirs that Liebknecht had been duped by Schweitzer and the Countess.[163]

Shortly afterwards, in July 1865, Liebknecht was expelled from Prussia and had to leave Berlin.[164] He had come to realise – as Lassalle had realised a few years before – that the Prussian capital was no base from which to direct a revolutionary workers' movement. He was missed by his supporters in Berlin. Three of them wrote to Marx: "We lack intellectual leadership here since the departure of Liebknecht, who understood splendidly how to arouse the revolutionary spirit."[165] Marx forwarded the letter to Engels who doubted whether the writers were really workers.[166]

The breach with Schweitzer and the expulsion of Liebknecht from Berlin were grave setbacks to the hopes that Marx and Engels had entertained that they might again play an effective *rôle* in German politics. Marx now dismissed the workers' movement in Germany as "a complete fiasco"[167] and turned his attention to the Working Men's International Association which had been established in London in 1864. In the same letter in which he told Dr Kugelmann that his collaboration with Schweitzer had ended, he declared: "I prefer a hundred times over my agitation here through the International Association", which was making progress in England, France, Belgium, Switzerland and Italy.[168]

Liebknecht was not unduly discouraged by his failure in Berlin or by his chronic financial difficulties. Following Lassalle's example he moved to Leipzig where he joined the democratic Union of German Workers and Education Societies and preached Marxist doctrines to the Saxon workers. Engels gave him financial assistance from time to time. Liebknecht did not, at this stage of his career, try to found a new workers' party but instead he tried to spread the gospel of Marxist socialism among members of both the General German Workers' Union and the Union of German Workers and Educational Societies. And – at Marx's urgent request – he also tried to recruit members for the First International. By 1866 he had achieved some success in Saxony.[169] In the following year, however, the General Council of the First International reported that Germany was "in an abnormal state, not favourable to the development of our Association".[170]

Meanwhile Liebknecht had strengthened his position by securing August Bebel as an ally.[171] Bebel had been a follower of Schulze-Delitzsch and a leading member of the Union of German Workers and Educational Societies. His conversion to Marxist socialism was a triumph for Liebknecht. For many years Liebknecht and Bebel worked together as Germany's two leading socialists. One of their first essays in collaboration was the founding of the Saxon People's Party which was affiliated to the German People's Party.[172] Liebknecht's cause was also strengthened by internal dissensions within Schweitzer's party. In 1867 some members of the General German Workers' Union – incited and financed by the Countess of Hatzfeld – rejected Schweitzer's leadership and set up an independent organisation of their own. This splinter-group – known as the "female line" of the Lassallean movement – was called "Lassalle's General German Workers' Union". The two factions came together again in June 1869 but both lost some of their members in the process of reunification.[173]

In 1868, after an interval of three years, Schweitzer (now President of the General German Workers' Union and a member of the North German Reichstag) tried to re-establish good relations with Marx. He reviewed *Das Kapital* favourably in the *Social-Demokrat*. He met Liebknecht in the hope of resolving their differences. They agreed that their organisations should, at their forthcoming conference, both proclaim their support of the First International. Schweitzer invited Marx to attend the next conference of the General German Workers' Union but Marx could not do so owing to pressure of work in connection with a forthcoming conference of the First International.[174] At their conferences in 1868 the General German Workers' Union and the Union of German Workers and Educational Societies pledged their support to the First International. For the Union of German Workers and Education Societies this marked the end of its links with Schulze-Delitzsch and the Progressive Party. But some of the north German societies which belonged to the Union of German Workers and Educational Societies gave up their affiliation rather than support the First International. The brief honeymoon between Marx and Schweitzer in 1868 soon came to an end. Schweitzer's association was never actually affiliated to the First International and in 1870 Marx denounced the General German Workers' Union as an "artificial sectarian organisation" which was "opposed to the historical and spontaneous organisation of the working class". Schweitzer was attacked for his "firm resolution to preserve at all costs his autocratic power".[175]

Meanwhile Liebknecht and Bebel were making every effort to recruit more members for the First International. At the end of 1868 Liebknecht claimed that his "new societies" had a membership of 110,000.[176] But in this connection the activities of other followers of Marx and Engels – particularly Johann Philipp Becker – should not be forgotten. Becker was the editor of *Der Vorbote* which was the first German organ of the International Working Men's Association.[177]

In their correspondence Marx, Engels and Liebknecht discussed the changes that had occurred in Germany after Prussia's victories over Denmark and Austria. Marx and Engels considered that Prussia's newly won domination over Germany was a disaster but that the situation had certain compensations. They argued that it would now be possible to organise the workers on a national, instead of a local, basis and that the next revolution would take place in a united – not a divided – Germany.[178] Moreover representatives of the workers could now be returned to parliament since (although in Prussia the three-class voting system remained) the franchise had been extended in the new North German Federation to men over the age of 25. Liebknecht and Bebel were elected to the North German Reichstag in 1867. In October of that year Marx reported to the Council of the First International that "Citizen Liebknecht had been returned to the North German Parliament by the working men of Saxony. He was the only member that had dared to attack Bismarck's war policy". Shortly afterwards he read to the Council some extracts from the proceedings of the North German Reichstag. "Mr Liebknecht, a member of the Association, had delivered a speech in favour of the abolition of standing armies and the introduction of popular armaments, and subjecting Bismarck's conduct of the Luxemburg affair to a severe criticism."[179]

Liebknecht was pessimistic concerning the future prospects of the workers' movement in Germany. He had little faith in parliamentary government and he used his membership of the Reichstag simply as a vehicle for socialist propaganda. He wrote a pamphlet in which he argued that a socialist deputy was in constant danger of "sacrificing his principles" and should make a dignified exit from the chamber after making his protest. Liebknecht added that socialism would eventually be established "in the streets and on the field of battle" and not by debates in parliament.[180] Moreover Liebknecht feared that Prussia's military strength was now so great that a popular rising would be ruthlessly suppressed.[181] In October 1867 he attacked the General German Workers' Union for supporting what Schweitzer had called "the powerful Prussian heart of our German Fatherland".[182]

Marx and Engels thought that Liebknecht's judgment was becoming clouded by his detestation of Prussia. Liebknecht regarded any enemy of Prussia as a potential ally, without appreciating that the real enemy was the capitalist middle class which was just as influential in Austria or south Germany as in Prussia. Engels criticised Liebknecht for becoming infected with narrow-minded south German particularism. He wrote to Marx: "We cannot allow ourselves to be mixed up with Austrians, Guelfs and Federalists."[183]

Marx and Engels were opposed to any co-operation between

Liebknecht and Bebel on the one hand and the two People's Parties on the other.[184] They considered that a socialist movement to be successful must draw its support from the factory workers in the great urban centres of industry. But Liebknecht drew his support largely from the domestic textile workers and smallholders of Germany south of the River Main. Schweitzer, however, was gaining recruits for his General German Workers' Union in the manufacturing districts of the Rhineland[186] (where he was ably assisted by the veteran communist P. G. Röser) and he was also fostering the development of trade unions.[186] Marx and Engels feared that Liebknecht's socialist movement was developing on the wrong lines.

Liebknecht replied that, as a socialist, he was bound to oppose Bismarck who stood for militarism, autocracy, and the domination of Germany by Prussia. He was determined to attack anyone – Schweitzer included – who supported Bismarck. He was equally determined to work with anyone who was opposed to Bismarck. In 1867 Liebknecht declared, in a letter to Engels, that he could not do without the support of the petty traders and craftsmen who were strongly opposed to Bismarck, though he admitted that "politics, like misery, gives you strange bedfellows".[187]

In 1867 Liebknecht supported the demand of the People's Party for the establishment of popular militias in Germany on the Swiss model, so as to check Prussian militarism. Engels had already – in 1865 – criticised the militia system in a pamphlet addressed to the German workers[188] and now (in 1868) he wrote to Marx that, in the American civil war, the existence of "militias on both sides", had led to "terrible sacrifices of men and money".[189]

In 1870 in his preface to a new edition of his collected articles on the Peasant War in Germany,[190] Engels attacked an alliance between the German socialist movement and any middle class party. Liebknecht replied: "You do not appreciate that I have to cope with things as they are. . . . I could have plunged into the river and swum with the current or I could have stood on the bank and spouted my views on philosophy." Liebknecht claimed that he had always acted in the best interests of the German socialist movement. He had used other parties to his own advantage and he had never allowed other parties to make use of him.[191]

For five years Liebknecht and Bebel had led the Marxist wing of the workers' movement in Germany and had endeavoured to secure support from members of other organisations such as the General German Workers' Union, the German and the Saxon People's Parties, and the Union of German Workers and Educational Societies. In 1869 they were ready to launch a socialist party of their own. When Wilhelm Bracke,[192] the treasurer of the General German Workers' Union, left this party to join Liebknecht and Bebel he brought with him some influential followers of Schweitzer such as S. Spier of Wolfenbüttel and T. York, August Perl and A. Geib of Hamburg.

The offensive mounted against Schweitzer's party by Liebknecht and Bebel was aided by the action of the police in Leipzig in closing down the headquarters of the General German Workers' Union in September 1868. Shortly afterwards Schweitzer was imprisoned for some weeks. In the summer of 1869 leading members of the General German Workers' Union and the Union of German Workers and Educational Societies united to denounce Schweitzer as a traitor to the workers' cause. They called for the establishment of a new "social-democratic" party of the workers. This party was joined not only by the clubs affiliated to the Union of Workers and Educational Societies but also by some Marxist associations affiliated to the First International, some members of the German (and of the Saxon) People's Party and some defectors from the General German Workers' Union who were disgusted with Schweitzer's dictatorial leadership.[193] The Union of German Workers and Educational Societies – some 10,000 members organised in over 100 groups – was dissolved and was absorbed into the new German Social Democrat Party, which was established at a conference held at Eisenach in 1869.

The programme of the new socialist party led by Liebknecht, Bebel and Bracke reflected the divergent aims and interests of its various members.[194] The demand for state aid to establish industrial co-operative associations was a legacy of Lassalle's agitation in 1863–4. The demand that citizens' militias should replace standing armies had already been made by the People's Parties. The demand for democratic reforms – freedom of the press, free education, an independent judiciary – reflected the views of the Union of German Workers and Educational Societies. The influence of Marx and Engels was seen in the link between the new party and the First International. The German Social Democrat Party stated that it was "a branch of the International Working Men's Association." Demands for the abolition of all privileges of class, property, birth and religion, the separation of Church and State, and the removal of all schools from Church control echoed similar demands by the Communist League in 1848.

Marx and Engels regarded the new socialist party in Germany with some misgivings. Its programme made too many concessions to the Lassalleans and to the liberal supporters of the two People's Parties and the Union of German Workers and Educational

Societies. Nothing was said in the party programme about bringing capitalism under public control by nationalising the means of production. Marx and Engels regarded this as an extraordinary omission. The First International had adopted the principle of nationalisation in 1868 and of state ownership of land in 1869. But Liebknecht feared that he would lose the support of the People's Party – which had many peasants and smallholders among its members – if he agreed to the nationalisation of land. He declared that he "wanted to avoid premature trouble".[195] But before long Liebknecht and Bebel had to accept the principle of the nationalisation of the land even though it cost them the support of the petty bourgeoisie in south Germany. They also had to face the fact that the General German Workers' Union had not only survived the defection of Bracke and his friends but continued to enjoy considerable support from workers and trade unionists, particularly in the industrial centres of the Rhineland. When Schweitzer resigned as President in 1871 and was succeeded by Wilhelm Hasenclever, the membership of the General German Workers' Union – and the subscribers to its journal – was probably double that of the new socialist party led by Liebnecht and Bebel.

Thus on the eve of German unification the socialist movement was split into two rival factions, known as the "Eisenachers" and the "Lassalleans". This was a situation that Marx and Engels had long tried to avoid. A few years later Engels complained to Bebel that the "Lassallean turncoats" who came over to the Social Democrat Party from the General German Workers Union "always bring the germs of their false tendencies into the party with them". He argued that the Lassallean leaders who joined Bebel and Liebknecht were "bound by their previous public utterances – if not by their previous views – and now must prove above all things that they have not deserted their principles but that, on the contrary, the Social Democrat Workers' Party preaches *true* Lassalleanism".[196] Despite the split in the socialist ranks, the socialist movement was already powerful enough in Germany to cause Bismarck serious concern. In 1871 he told a colleague that "socialist theories and assumptions are already so widespread among the masses, that any attempt to ignore them . . . would be in vain". Bismarck feared that the socialists would soon threaten "the existing order of state and society".[197]

NOTES

1   F. Engels, *The Condition of the Working Class in England* (translated and edited by W. O. Henderson and W. H. Chaloner, 1958 and 1971), p. 260.

2   G. Julian Harney to F. Engels, December 16, 1850 in F. G. and R. M. Black (eds.), *The Harney Papers* (1969), p. 258.

3   F. Engels to Karl Marx, December 17, 1850 and February 5, 1851 in *Gesamtausgabe*, Part III, Vol. 1, p. 122 and pp. 142–3.

4   F. Engels, *The Condition of the Working Class in England* (translated and edited by W. O. Henderson and W. H. Chaloner, 1958 and 1971), pp. 151–2.

5   G. Julian Harney to F. Engels, December 16, 1850 in F. G. and R. M. Black (eds.), *The Harney Papers* (1969), p. 258.

6   F. Engels to Karl Marx, January 8, 1851 in *Gesamtausgabe*, Part III, Vol. 1, pp. 128–30: English translation in J. Saville, *Ernest Jones: Chartist* (1952), p. 232. See also the *Northern Star*, January 11, 1851.

7   F. Engels to Karl Marx, January 29, 1851 in *Gesamtausgabe*, Part III, Vol. 1, pp. 135–6: English translation in J. Saville, *Ernest Jones: Chartist* (1952), pp. 232–3.

8   F. Engels to Karl Marx, February 12, 1851 in *Gesamtausgabe*, Part III, Vol. 1, pp. 147–8. A little later (February 25, 1851) Engels referred to this group as "a new local Chartist clique" (*ibid.*, p. 156).

9   F. Engels to K. Marx, February 13, 1851 in *Gesamtausgabe*, Part III, Vol. 1, p. 148.

10 There are several references to articles contributed by Engels to the *Notes to the People* in the Marx–Engels correspondence. See *Gesamtausgabe*, Part III, Vol. 1, pp. 309, 321, 322, and 330. Engels contributed three articles to the *Notes to the People* (February 21, March 27 and April 10, 1852) on Louis Napoleon's coup d'état of December 1851.

11 F. Engels to Karl Marx, March 18, 1852 in *Gesamtausgabe*, Part III, Vol. 1, p. 330.

12 Karl Marx to F. Engels, February 13, 1855 in *Gesamtausgabe*, Part III, Vol. 2, pp. 80–1.

13 *People's Paper*, November 12, 1853 reprinted in J. Saville, *Ernest Jones: Chartist* (1952), pp. 201–8.

14 *People's Paper*, April 1, 1854 in J. Saville, *Ernest Jones: Chartist* (1952), pp. 264–73. For the Parliament of Labour see *People's Paper*, March 11, 18, and 25, 1854 and *Manchester Guardian*, November 23, 1853, March 8 and 11, 1854. A speaker at the Labour Parliament pointed out "none of the high-paid trades were directly represented in the parliament" (*Manchester Guardian*, March 11, 1854).

15 Karl Marx to F. Engels, March 9, 1854 in *Gesamtausgabe*, Part III, Vol. 2, pp. 7–8.

16 Karl Marx's letter to the Labour Parliament appeared in the *People's Paper* March 9, 1854, in J. Saville, *Ernest Jones: Chartist* (1954), pp. 274–5, and Karl Marx and F. Engels, *On Britain* (Foreign Languages Publishing House, Moscow, 1954), pp. 40–2. Marx was unable to attend the Parliament of Labour in Manchester. For the Labour Parliament of 1854 see A. E. Musson, *The Congress of 1868. The Origin and Establishment of the Trades Union Congress* (Trades Union Congress centenary edition, 1968), p. 8.

17 Karl Marx to F. Engels, September 21, 1858 in *Gesamtausgabe*, Part III, Vol. 2, p. 338.

18 F. Engels to Karl Marx, October 7, 1858 in *Gesamtausgabe*, Part III, Vol. 2, p. 340: English translation in J. Saville, *Ernest Jones: Chartist* (1952), p. 242.

19   Karl Marx to J. Weydemeyer, February 1, 1859 in *Karl Marx and F. Engels, Letters to Americans, 1848–95* (1963), pp. 60–1.

20   Karl Marx to F. Engels, November 17, 1862 in *Gesamtausgabe*, Part III, Vol. 3, p. 111.

21   F. Engels to Karl Marx, April 8, 1863 in *Gesamtausgabe*, Part III, Vol. 3, p. 135. See also Karl Marx and F. Engels, *On Britain* (Foreign Languages Publishing House, Moscow, 1953), p. 493.

22   F. Engels to Karl Marx, November 18, 1868 in *Gesamtausgabe*, Part III, Vol. 4, p. 126.

23   Karl Marx to F. Engels, May 1, 1865 in *Gesamtausgabe*, Part III, Vol. 3, p. 263.

24   F. Engels to Karl Marx, October 24, 1869 in *Gesamtausgabe*, Part III, Vol. 4, p. 231.

25   Paul Lafargue in *Reminiscences of Marx and Engels* (Foreign Languages Publishing House, Moscow), p. 88. See also R. W. Fox, *Marx, Engels and Lenin on the Irish Revolution* (1932).

26   F. Engels to Karl Marx, April 1, 1852 in *Gesamtausgabe*, Part III, Vol. 1, p. 335.

27   Address of the Central Executive Committee to the Communist League (June 1850) in Dr Wermuth and Dr Stieber, *Die Communisten-Verschwörungen des neunzehnten Jahrhunderts* (two volumes, 1853–4: reprinted in one volume, 1969), Vol. 1, p. 264.

28   *Le Republicain populaire et sociale*, November 15, 1851: see Dr Wermuth and Dr Stieber, *op. cit.*, Vol. 2, p. 45.

29   F. Engels to Karl Marx, August 21, 1851 in *Gesamtausgabe*, Part III, Vol. 1, p. 243.

30   Karl Marx to F. Engels, February 23, 1852 in *Gesamtausgabe*, Part III, Vol. 1, p. 323.

31   F. Engels to Karl Marx, March 2, 1852 in *Gesamtausgabe*, Part III, Vol. 1, p. 328.

32   Karl Marx to F. Engels, April 24, 1852 in *Gesamtausgabe*, Part III, Vol. 1, p. 340.

33   F. Engels to Karl Marx, April 25, 1852 in *Gesamtausgabe*, Part III, Vol. 1, p. 341.

34   Karl Marx to F. Engels, November 24, 1858 in *Gesamtausgabe*, Part III, Vol. 2, p. 348.

35   F. Engels's preface of 1891 to Karl Marx, *The Civil War in France* (first edition, 1871: new edition issued by the Foreign Languages Publishing House, Moscow).

36   Pierre-Joseph Proudhon, *What is Property?* (first edition, 1840; second edition, 1848) (English translation by B. R. Tucker, two volumes, 1898–1902).

37   F. Engels to Karl Marx, September 18, 1846 in *Gesamtausgabe*, Part III, Vol. 1, p. 41.

38   Karl Marx, *The Poverty of Philosophy* (translated by H. Quelch), p. 198.

39   See Samuel Bernstein, *The Beginnings of Marxian Socialism in France* (1965), p. 206.

40   F. Engels to Karl Marx, October 25–6, 1847 in *Gesamtausgabe*, Part III, Vol. 1, pp. 79–80.

41   F. Engels to Karl Marx, January 14, 1848 in *Gesamtausgabe*, Part III, Vol. 1, pp. 79–80.

42   Karl Marx and F. Engels, *The Communist Manifesto*, 1848 (Penguin Books, 1967), pp. 113–14.

43 See C. A. Dana, *Proudhon and his 'Bank of the People'* (1896).

44 F. Engels, *Socialism: Utopian and Scientific* (Chicago, 1905), p. 26.

45 Karl Marx to F. Engels, August 8, 1851 in *Gesamtausgabe*, Part III, Vol. 1, pp. 228–34.

46 F. Engels to Karl Marx, August 10 and 11, 1851 in *Gesamtausgabe*, Part III, Vol. 1, pp. 236–8.

47 F. Engels to Karl Marx, August 21, 1851 in *Gesamtausgabe*, Part III, Vol. 1, pp. 242–3.

48 Karl Marx to Adolph Cluss, December 7, 1852 in Karl Marx and F. Engels, *Letters to Americans 1848–95* (1963), p. 52.

49 Pierre-Joseph Proudhon, *La révolution sociale de montrée par le coup d'état* du 2 Decembre 1852 (1852).

50 Karl Marx, *The Eighteenth Brumaire of Louis Bonaparte* (first edition 1852; second edition 1869: new edition published by the Foreign Languages Publishing House, Moscow).

51 Karl Marx, *Grundrisse der Kritik der politischen Ökonomie (Rohentwurf,* 1857–8) (Europäische Verlagsanstalt, 1953), pp. 727–29.

52 Hermann Oncken, *Lassalle* (third edition, 1920), p. 83.

53 F. Engels to Karl Marx, April 3, 1851 in *Gesamtausgabe*, Part III, Vol. 1, p. 183.

54 F. Engels to Karl Marx, April 14, 1858 in *Gesamtausgabe*, Part III, Vol. 2, p. 316.

55 Karl Marx to F. Engels, April 22, 1859 in *Gesamtausgabe*, Part III, Vol. 2, p. 381.

56 Wermuth and Stieber, *Die Communisten-Verschwörungen des neunzehnten Jahrhunderts* (two volumes, 1853–4: new edition in one volume, 1969), Vol. 2, pp. 260–5.

57 Karl Marx to F. Engels, March 5, 1856 in *Gesamtausgabe*, Part III, Vol. 2, pp. 120–1.

58 Karl Marx to F. Engels, May 8, 1856 in *Gesamtausgabe*, Part III, Vol. 2, p. 134.

59 F. Lassalle to Karl Marx, September 3, 1860 in G. Mayer (ed.), *Der Briefwechsel zwischen Lassalle und Marx* (1922), p. 314 and Karl Marx to F. Engels, September 15, 1860 in *Gesamtausgabe*, Part III, Vol. 2, p. 506.

60 Karl Marx to F. Engels, June 3 and November 4, 1864 in *Gesamtausgabe*, Part III, Vol. 3, pp. 174–5 and p. 196.

61 Karl Marx to F. Engels, February 3, 1865 in *Gesamtausgabe*, Part III, Vol. 3, p. 223.

62 Karl Marx to F. Engels, March 18, 1865 (postscript) in *Gesamtausgabe*, Part III, Vol. 3, p. 258. Carl Klings had hoped to meet Engels in Manchester on his way to Liverpool but he failed to do so since he had been given the wrong address in Dover Street.

63 Karl Marx to F. Engels, June 3, 1864 in *Gesamtausgabe*, Part III, Vol. 3, pp. 174–5. See also Carl Klein and F. W. Moll to F. Engels, February 28, 1870 in *Marx–Engels Werke*, Vol. 32, p. 460 and Marx–Engels archives, L.2782 (Amsterdam).

64 F. Engels to Carl Klein and F. W. Moll, March 10, 1871 in *Marx–Engels Werke*, Vol. 33, pp. 188–9; Karl Marx to F. Engels, December 10, 1869 and F. Engels to Karl Marx, March 13, 1870 in *Gesamtausgabe*, Part III, Vol. 4, p. 257 and p. 291.

65 For Lassalle see E. Czóbel and P. Hajdu, "Die Lassalle-Literatur seit dem Weltkrieg" in *Marx–Engels Archiv* (ed. D. Rjazanov), Vol. 1 (1925), pp. 530–7; G. Brandes, *Ferdinand Lassalle* (1877, second

edition, 1888); W. H. Dawson, *German Socialism and Lassalle* (1888); Eduard Bernstein, *Ferdinand Lassalle* (1891, new edition, 1919: English translation, 1893); Seillière, *Études sur Lassalle* (1897); B. Harms, *Ferdinand Lassalle und seine Bedeutung für die Sozialdemokratie* (1919); Hermann Oncken, *Lassalle* (third edition, 1920); A. Schirokauer, *Lassalle. The Power of Illusion and the Illusion of Power* (1931); D. J. Footman, *The Primrose Path. A Life of Ferdinand Lassalle* (1946); H. Hümmler, *Opposition gegen Lassalle* (1963); H. J. Friederici, "Zur Einschätzung Lassalles und des Lassalleanismus in der bürgerlichen und rechtssozialdemokratischen Geschichtsschreibung" in *Beiträge zur Geschichte der deutschen Arbeiterbewegung*, Vol. 2, 1960, pp. 294–313; A. K. Worobjowa, "Aus der Geschichte der Arbeiterbewegung in Deutschland und des Kampfes von Karl Marx und Friedrich Engels gegen Lassalle und das Lassalleanertum 1862–1864" in *Aus der Geschichte des Kampfes von Marx und Engels für die proletarische Partei* (1961), pp. 235–346; C. Schmid, "Ferdinand Lassalle und die Politisierung der deutschen Arbeiterbewegung" in *Archiv für Sozialgeschichte*, Vol. 3, 1963, pp. 5–20; T. Ramm, "Lassalle und Marx" in *Marxismusstudien*, Vol. 3, pp. 185–221; Shlomo Na'aman, "Lassalle-Demokratie und Sozialdemokratie" in *Archiv für Sozialgeschichte*, Vol. 3, 1963, pp. 21–80. For the correspondence between Marx, Engels and Lassalle see Gustav Mayer (ed.), *Der Briefwechsel zwischen Lassalle und Marx* (1922: Vol. 3 of *Ferdinand Lassalle: Nachgelassene Briefe und Schriften*). A new edition of the Marx–Lassalle correspondence was published in 1967 by the Historical Commission of the Bavarian Academy of Sciences.

66　Hermann Oncken, *Lassalle* (third edition, 1920), p. 42.

67　Georg Weerth to his mother, April 11, 1849 in Georg Weerth, *Sämtliche Werke*, Vol. 5 (1857), p. 303.

68　F. Engels to Karl Marx, March 7, 1856 in *Gesamtausgabe*, Part III, Vol. 2, p. 122.

69　Hermann Oncken, *Lassalle* (third edition, 1920), p. 34.

70　Gustav Mayer, *Friedrich Engels* (second edition, 1934), Vol. 1, p. 315.

71　F. Lassalle to F. Engels, early May 1849, in Gustav Mayer (ed.), *Ferdinand Lassalle. Nachgelassene Briefe und Schriften*, Vol. 3 *Der Briefwechsel zwischen Lassalle und Marx* (1922), p. 6.

72　Franz Mehring, *Karl Marx* (edition of 1969), p. 197. See F. Lassalle to Karl Marx, July 30, 1849 in G. Mayer (ed.), *Der Briefwechsel zwischen Lassalle und Marx* (1922: Vol. 3 of *Ferdinand Lassalle; Nachgelassene Briefe und Schriften*), pp. 10–13.

73　Wermuth and Stieber, *Die Communisten-Verschwörungen des neunzehnten Jahrhunderts* (two volumes, 1853–4; reprinted in one volume, 1969), Vol. 2, p. 71.

74　Karl Marx to F. Engels, February 9, 1860 in *Gesamtausgabe*, Part 3, Vol. 2, p. 470.

75　P. G. Röser to Karl Marx, June 18, 1850 in Franz Mehring's introduction to the fourth (1914) edition of Karl Marx, *Enthüllungen über den Kommunistenprozess zu Köln* (edition of 1952), p. 163.

76　F. Engels to Paul Lafargue, May 18, 1880 in *F. Engels – Paul and Laura Lafargue: Correspondence*, Vol. 1 (1959), p. 69.

77　F. Lassalle, *Die Philosophie Herakleitos des Dunklen von Ephesos* (1857); *Franz von Sickingen: ein historisches Trauerspiel* (1859); *Der italienische Krieg und die Aufgabe Preussens* (1859); *Das System der erworbenen Rechte* (two volumes, 1861).

78 Karl Marx to F. Engels, March 12, 1853 in *Gesamtausgabe*, Part III, Vol. 1, p. 459.

79 Karl Marx to F. Engels, March 10, 1853 in *Gesamtausgabe*, Part III, Vol. 1, p. 456.

80 F. Engels to Karl Marx, February 10, 1859 in *Gesamtausgabe*, Part III, Vol. 2, p. 362.

81 Karl Marx to F. Engels, March 10 and 12, 1853 in *Gesamtausgabe*, Part III, Vol. 1, pp. 456–7.

82 Karl Marx to F. Engels, July 18, 1853 in *Gesamtausgabe*, Part III, Vol. 1, p. 491.

83 F. Lassalle to Karl Marx and F. Engels, end of February 1860 in G. Mayer (ed.), *Der Briefwechsel zwischen Lassalle und Marx* (1922), p. 265.

84 For example £3 in February 1852 and 200 Thalers in January 1855: see G. Mayer (ed.), *Der Briefwechsel zwischen Lassalle und Marx* (1922), p. 49 and p. 86. In March 1859 Lassalle offered Marx a small loan but this was refused (*ibid.*, pp. 168–9). In November 1859 Marx asked Lassalle for a loan (*ibid.*, p. 233).

85 F. Lassalle to Karl Marx, February 12, April 16 and May 16, 1850 in G. Mayer (ed.), *Der Briefwechsel zwischen Lassalle und Marx* (1922), pp. 22–5.

86 F. Lassalle to Karl Marx, February 10, 1854 in G. Mayer (ed.), *Der Briefwechsel zwischen Lassalle und Marx* (1922), pp. 67–9.

87 This was the second edition of Karl Marx's pamphlet entitled *Enthüllungen über den Kommunistenprozess zu Köln* (1852) which was published in the United States in the *Neu England Zeitung* (Boston). Engels sent 400 copies of the pamphlet to Lassalle disguised as trade circulars. The first edition, published in Switzerland, had been confiscated by the police in Baden. See F. Lassalle to Karl Marx, April 18, 1853 and to Jenny Marx, June 13, June 19, June 26 and to Marx, December 13, 1853 in G. Mayer (ed.), *Der Briefwechsel zwischen Lassalle und Marx* (1922), pp. 57–65.

88 Karl Marx to F. Engels, December 2, 1854 in *Gesamtausgabe*, Part III, Vol. 2, p. 68 and F. Lassalle to Karl Marx, January 7, 1855 in G. Mayer (ed.), *Der Briefwechsel zwischen Lassalle und Marx* (1922), p. 87.

89 The correspondence between Karl Marx and Lassalle lasted from 1848 to 1862. There is a gap in the correspondence of 18 months from November 1855 to April 1857.

90 Karl Marx to F. Engels, March 5, 1856 in *Gesamtausgabe*, Part III, Vol. 2, pp. 118–20.

91 F. Lassalle to Karl Marx and F. Engels, end of February 1860 in G. Mayer (ed.), *Der Briefwechsel zwischen Lassalle und Marx* (1922), pp. 267–8.

92 F. Engels to Karl Marx, March 7, 1856 in *Gesamtausgabe*, Part III, Vol. 2, p. 122: English translation in W. O. Henderson (ed.), *Engels: Selected Writings* (Penguin Books, 1967), pp. 129–30.

93 F. Engels to Karl Marx, May 11, 1857 in *Gesamtausgabe*, Part III, Vol. 2, p. 191.

94 Karl Marx to F. Engels, May 8, 1857 in *Gesamtausgabe*, Part III, Vol. 2, p. 190.

95 Karl Marx to F. Engels, February 25, 1859 (second letter) in *Gesamtausgabe*, Part III, Vol. 2, p. 366.

96 Karl Marx to F. Engels, December 22, 1857 in *Gesamtausgabe*, Part III, Vol. 2, p. 258.

97 Jenny Marx to F. Engels, April 9, 1858 in *Gesamtausgabe*, Part III, Vol. 2, p. 314.

98 Karl Marx to F. Engels, February 1, 1858 in *Gesamtausgabe*, Part III, Vol. 2, p. 282.

99 Karl Marx to F. Lassalle, May 31, 1858 in G. Mayer (ed), *Der Briefwechsel zwischen Lassalle und Marx* (1922), p. 123.

100 Karl Marx to F. Engels, May 31, 1848 in *Gesamtausgabe*, Part III, Vol. 2, p. 321.

101 Karl Marx to F. Engels, February 22 and 24, March 29, 1858 and Jenny Marx to F. Engels, April 9, 1858 in *Gesamtausgabe*, Part III, Vol. 2, pp. 289–90, 292, and 304. See also Karl Marx to F. Lassalle, February 22, March 11, November 12, 1858 and March 28, November 6, 1859 and September 15, 1860 in G. Mayer (ed.), *Der Briefwechsel zwischen Lassalle und Marx* (1922) and in Karl Marx–F. Engels, *Briefe über "Das Kapital"* (1954).

102 Karl Marx to F. Engels, February 25, 1859 (two letters), March 3 and 10, 1859 and F. Engels to Karl Marx, March 14, 1859 in *Gesamtausgabe*, Part III, Vol. 2, pp. 365–6 and pp. 370–1.

103 Karl Marx to F. Lassalle, February 25, 1859 in G. Mayer (ed.), *Der Briefwechsel zwischen Lassalle und Marx* (1922), p. 145; F. Lassalle to Karl Marx, end of February 1859 (*ibid.*, p. 146); F. Engels to F. Lassalle, March 14, 1859 (*ibid.*, pp. 158–9); F. Lassalle to F. Engels, March 21, 1859 (*ibid.*, p. 161).

104 F. Lassalle to F. Engels, March 21, 1859 in G. Mayer (ed.), *Der Briefwechsel zwischen Lassalle und Marx* (1922), pp. 161–2.

105 F. Engels to F. Lassalle, May 8, 1859 and F. Lassalle to Karl Marx and F. Engels in G. Mayer (ed.), *Der Briefwechsel zwischen Lassalle und Marx* (1922), p. 179 and p. 185.

106 F. Engels to F. Lassalle, end of February 1860 in G. Mayer (ed.), *Der Briefwechsel zwischen Lassalle und Marx* (1922), p. 272.

107 Karl Marx to F. Engels, February 9, 1860 in *Gesamtausgabe*, Part III, Vol. 2, p. 470.

108 Karl Marx to F. Engels, May 7 and June 10, 1861 in *Gesamtausgabe*, Part III, Vol. 3, p. 16 and p. 26.

109 Karl Marx to F. Engels, May 7, 1861 in *Gesamtausgabe*, Part III, Vol. 3, p. 19.

110 Karl Marx to F. Engels, January 29, 1861 in *Gesamtausgabe*, Part III, Vol. 3, p. 8.

111 F. Engels to Karl Marx, February 6, 1861 in *Gesamtausgabe*, Part III, Vol. 3, p. 12.

112 Karl Marx to F. Engels, February 14, 1861 in *Gesamtausgabe*, Part III, Vol. 3, p. 13.

113 Karl Marx to F. Engels, May 7, 1861 in *Gesamtausgabe*, Part III, Vol. 3, p. 18.

114 Karl Marx to F. Engels, June 9, 1861 in *Gesamtausgabe*, Part III, Vol. 3, p. 25.

115 For Engels's views on Lassalle's *Das System der erworbenen Rechte* see his letter to Karl Marx, December 2, 1861 in *Gesamtausgabe*, Part III, Vol. 3, pp. 46–7.

116 Jenny Marx, "Short Sketch of an eventful Life" in *Reminiscences of*

Marx and Engels (Foreign Languages Publishing House, Moscow), p. 234.

117   Karl Marx to F. Engels, July 30 and August 7, 1862 in *Gesamtausgabe*, Part III, Vol. 3, p. 82 and p. 91.

118   Lassalle promised to lend Marx £15 on January 1, 1863. In addition Borkheim lent Marx £40 on a bill of exchange made out by Engels in favour of Lassalle. See Karl Marx to F. Engels, August 7 and 9, September 10, November 4, 1862; F. Engels to Karl Marx, August 8, 1862; and S. L. Borkheim to F. Engels, September 10, 1862 in *Gesamtausgabe*, Part III, Vol. 3, pp. 91–106. See also the correspondence between Engels and Lassalle on these transactions in the second half of 1862 in Gustav Mayer (ed.), *Ferdinand Lassalle. Nachgelassene Briefe und Schriften*, Vol. 3: *Der Briefwechsel zwischen Lassalle und Marx* (1922), pp. 274–408.

119   F. Engels to F. Lassalle, July 23, 1862 in G. Mayer (ed.), *op. cit.*, p. 397.

120   Karl Marx to F. Engels, August 7, 1862 in *Gesamtausgabe*, Part III, Vol. 3, p. 91.

121   F. Engels to Karl Marx, April 21, 1863 in *Gesamtausgabe*, Part III, Vol. 3, p. 139.

122   Karl Marx to L. Kugelmann, February 23, 1865 in Karl Marx, *Letters to Dr Kugelmann*, p. 27.

123   F. Lassalle, *Der italienische Krieg und die Aufgaben Preussens* (1859).

124   F. Engels, "Marx und die *Neue Rheinische Zeitung*" in *Sozialdemokrat* (Zürich), March 13, 1884.

125   Karl Marx to F. Engels, April 9, 1863 in *Gesamtausgabe*, Part III, Vol. 3, p. 136.

126   Lassalle to Bismarck, June 3, 1863 in Gustav Mayer, *Bismarck und Lassalle. Ihr Briefwechsel und ihre Gespräche* (1928), p. 60.

127   F. Lassalle, *Über Verfassungswesen* (1862).

128   F. Lassalle, *Arbeiterprogramme. Über ein besonderen Zusammenhang der gegenwärtigen Geschichtsperiode mit der Idee des Arbeiterstandes* (1862).

129   Karl Marx to F. Engels, January 28, 1863 in *Gesamtausgabe*, Part III, Vol. 3, p. 125.

130   Eduard Bernstein, *Ferdinand Lassalle* (1919), pp. 160–1.

131   Dr Otto Dammer to Ferdinand Lassalle, February 11, 1863 in Eduard Bernstein, *Ferdinand Lassalle* (1919), pp. 191–3.

132   F. Lassalle, *Offenes Antwortschreiben an das Zentralkmitee zur Berufung eines allgemeinen deutschen Arbeiterkongresses zu Leipzig* (Zürich, 1963). For Marx's caustic comment on the *Open Letter of Reply* see his letter to Engels, April 9, 1863 in *Gesamtausgabe*, Part III, Vol. 3, p. 136. Eduard Bernstein declared that the *Open Letter of Reply* was a "masterpiece of propaganda" (*Ferdinand Lassalle*. 1919, p. 235).

133   Eduard Bernstein, *Ferdinand Lassalle* (1919), p. 240.

134   F. Lassalle, *Zur Arbeiter-Frage. Lassalles Rede bei der am 20, April 1863 in Leipzig gehaltenen Arbeiterversammlung* (printed by the author, 1863).

135   F. Lassalle, *Arbeiter-Lesebuch. Rede Lassalle zu Frankfurt am Main a, 17. und 19. Mai 1863* (Frankfurt am Main, 1863).

136   Hamburg, Harburg, Cologne, Düsseldorf, Mainz, Elberfeld, Barmen, Solingen, Leipzig, Dresden, Frankfurt am Main.

137   B. Harms, *Ferdinand Lassalle . . .* (1919), p. 57.

138   Lassalle to Bismarck, January 16, 1864 in Gustav Mayer, *Bismarck und Lassalle. Ihr Briefwechsel und ihre Gespräche* (1928), pp. 81–4.

139   Lassalle to Bismarck, June 8, 1863 in Gustav Mayer, *Bismarck und Lassalle . . .* (1928), p. 60. Shortly before the establishment of the General German Workers' Union, Lassalle told a worker that "whoever the president may be, the authority of his office must be as absolute as possible" (H. Oncken, *Lassalle* (third edition, 1920), p. 330). Lassalle appointed Dr Otto Dammer and Julius Vahlteich as vice-president and secretary respectively of the General German Workers Union.

140   Lassalle to Bismarck, June 8, 1863 in Gustav Mayer, *Bismarck und Lassalle . . .* (1928), p. 60.

141   *Verband deutscher Arbeiter- und Bildungsvereine.*

142   H. Oncken, *Lassalle* (third edition, 1920), pp. 331–2. An account of the congress of German Workers and Education Societies (Frankfurt am Main, June 1863) was given by August Bebel in his memoirs: see August Bebel, *Aus meinem Leben*, Vol. 1 (1911), pp. 79–97.

143   Karl Marx to F. Engels, June 3, 1864 in *Gesamtausgabe*, Part III, Vol. 3, pp. 174–5.

144   Karl Marx to F. Engels, June 7, 1864 in *Gesamtausgabe*, Part III, Vol. 3, p. 177.

145   Wilhelm Liebknecht, "Report on the Working Class Movement in Germany" (1865) in *The General Council of the First International Minutes*, Vol. 1, 1864–66 (*Documents of the First International*) (Foreign Languages Publishing House, Moscow), p. 256. Liebknecht sent this report to Marx who decided not to read it to the General Council.

146   See Gustav Mayer, *Bismarck und Lassalle. Ihr Briefwechsel und ihre Gespräche* (1928); Shlomo Na'aman, "Lassalles Beziehungen zu Bismarck – ihr Sinn und Zweck" in *Archiv für Sozialgeschichte*, Vol. 2, 1962, pp. 55–85; Wilhelm Mommsen, "Bismarck und Lassalle" in *Archiv für Sozialgeschichte*, Vol. 3, pp. 81–6.

147   Bismarck to Lassalle, May 11, 1863: "I have the honour to inform you that – in connection with an enquiry that has been undertaken concerning the condition of the working class – it is proposed to consider reports submitted by private persons who have had experience of this matter. In the circumstances I should be glad if you would give me your views on the question under discussion" (Gustav Mayer, *Bismarck und Lassalle . . .* (1928), p. 59).

148   F. Engels to Paul Lafargue, December 29, 1887 in *F. Engels–Paul and Laura Lafargue: Correspondence*, Vol. 2 (1960), p. 84.

149   Wilhelm Liebknecht to Karl Marx, June 12, 1864: Gustav Mayer, *Bismarck und Lassalle . . .* (1928), p. 53 and Wilhelm Liebknecht, *Briefwechsel mit Karl Marx und Friedrich Engels* (ed. G. Eckert, 1963), p. 37.

150   F. Engels to Karl Marx, January 27, 1865 in *Gesamtausgabe*, Part III, Vol. 3, p. 218.

151   F. Engels to Karl Marx, May 20, 1863 in *Gesamtausgabe*, Part III, Vol. 3, pp. 140–1.

152   Karl Marx to F. Engels, September 7, 1864 in *Gesamtausgabe*, Part III, Vol. 3, p. 190.

153   F. Engels to Karl Marx, September 4, 1864 in *Gesamtausgabe*, Part III, Vol. 3, p. 188. For Engels and Lassalle see H. Herkner, "Engels und Lassalle in *Preussische Jahrbücher*, July 1920.

154 See J. B. von Schweitzer, *Politische Aufsätze und Reden* (ed. by Franz Mehring, 1912); Gustav Mayer, *Johann Baptist von Schweitzer und die Sozialdemokratie. Ein Beitrag zur Geschichte der deutschen Arbeiterbewegung* (1909).

155 F. Engels to Karl Marx, December 1, 1865 in *Gesamtausgabe*, Part III, Vol. 3, p. 298.

156 For Wilhelm Liebknecht see Edward Aveling, *Wilhelm Liebknecht and the Social-Democratic Movement in Germany* (1896); Kurt Eisner, *Wilhelm Liebknecht, sein Leben und Wirken* (second edition, 1906); Paul Kampffmeyer, *Wilhelm Liebknecht. Leben und Werk* (1927); Werner Mühlbradt, *Wilhelm Liebknecht und die Gründung der deutschen Sozialdemokratie 1862–75* (University of Göttingen dissertation, 1950); Wilhelm Liebknecht, *Briefwechsel mit Karl Marx und Friedrich Engels* (ed. by G. Eckert, 1963). At the Leipzig treason trial in 1872 Wilhelm Liebknecht gave the court an account of his early life as a revolutionary socialist: see *Der Leipziger Hochverratsprozess vom Jahre 1872* (first edition with slightly different title, 1894; second edition edited by Karl-Heinz Leidigkeit, 1960). An English translation of part of Liebknecht's speech appears in Bertrand Russell, *German Social Democracy* (1896), pp. 57–9.

157 Wermuth and Stieber, *Die Communisten-Verschwörungen des neunzehnten Jahrhunderts* (two volumes, 1853–4: new edition in one volume, 1969), Vol. 2, pp. 74–5.

158 Wilhelm Liebknecht, "Reminiscences of Marx" in *Reminiscences of Marx and Engels* (Foreign Languages Publishing House, Moscow), pp. 96–100.

159 F. Engels to Karl Marx, June 9, 1864 in *Gesamtausgabe*, Part III, Vol. 3, p. 179.

160 W. Liebknecht to Karl Marx, June 3, 1864 in Wilhelm Liebknecht, *Briefwechsel mit Karl Marx und Friedrich Engels* (ed. G. Eckert, 1863), p. 33; Karl Marx to F. Engels, June 7, 1864 in *Gesamtausgabe*, Part III, Vol. 3, p. 177.

161 F. Engels to Karl Marx, November 16, 1864 in *Gesamtausgabe*, Part III, Vol. 3, p. 203.

162 Karl Marx to L. Kugelmann, February 23, 1865 in Karl Marx, *Letters to Dr Kugelmann*, pp. 27–8. See the statement by Marx and Engels in the *Social-Demokrat*, March 3, 1865 in *Marx–Engels Werke*, Vol. 16, p. 79.

163 Jenny Marx, "Short Sketch of an eventful Life" in *Reminiscences of Marx and Engels* (Moscow), p. 235.

164 W. Liebknecht to F. Engels, August 30, 1865 in Wilhelm Liebknecht, *Briefwechsel mit Karl Marx und Friedrich Engels* (ed. G. Eckert, 1963), pp. 59–62; F. Engels to Karl Marx, July 15, 1865 in *Gesamtausgabe*, Part III, Vol. 3, p. 276.

165 August Vogt, Siegfried Meyer and T. Metzer to Karl Marx, November 1865 in G. Gemkow, "Zur Tätigkeit der Berliner Sektion der I. International" in *Beiträge zur Geschichte der deutschen Arbeiterbewegung*, Vol. 1, 1959, pp. 515–31.

166 F. Engels to Karl Marx, November 17, 1865 in *Gesamtausgabe*, Part III, Vol. 3, p. 299.

167 Karl Marx to F. Engels, December 26, 1865 in *Gesamtausgabe*, Part III, Vol. 3, p. 299.

168 Karl Marx to L. Kugelmann, February 23, 1865 in Karl Marx, *Letters to Dr Kugelmann*, p. 31.

169 Karl Marx to F. Engels, June 9, 1866 in *Gesamtausgabe*, Part III, Vol. 3, p. 338.

170 R. P. Morgan, *The German Social Democratis and the First International 1864–1872* (1965), p. ix.

171 For August Bebel see his memoirs (*Aus meinem Leben*, three volumes, 1911–13); Robert Michels, "August Bebel" in *Archiv für Sozialwissenschaft und Sozialpolitik*, Vol. 37, 1913; Paul Kampffmeyer, "August Bebel" in *Biographisches Jahrbuch und deutsch-Nekrolog*, Vol. 28, 1913; Karl-Heinz Leidigkeit, *Wilhelm Liebknecht und August Bebel in der deutschen Arbeiterbewegung 1862–9* (second edition, 1958); Horst Bartel (ed.), *August Bebel: eine Biographie* (1963); E. Schraeper (ed.), *August Bebel Bibliographie* (1962); Franz Mehring, "Aus der Frühzeit der deutschen Arbeiterbewegung" in *Archiv für die Geschichte des Sozialismus und der Arbeiterbewegung (Grünbergs Archiv)*, Vol. 1, 1911, pp. 101–33; F. Engels, *Briefe an Bebel* (1958); Horst Schumacher (ed.), "Wissenschaftliches Kolloquium über August Bebel" in *Beiträge zur Geschichte der deutschen Arbeiterbewegung*, Vol. 5, 1963.

172 For the People's Party (*Volkspartei*) see Gustav Mayer, "Die Trennung der proletarischen von der bürgerlichen Demokratie in Deutschland" in *Archiv für die Geschichte des Sozialismus und der Arbeiterbewegung (Grünbergs Archiv)*, Vol. 2, 1912, pp. 1–67.

173 R. P. Morgan, *The German Social Democrats and the First International 1864–1872* (1965), pp. 21–2 and p. 28.

174 Karl Marx to F. Engels, August 26, 1868 in *Gesamtausgabe*, Part III, Vol. 4, pp. 86–7.

175 Karl Marx (January 1870) in a communication of the General Council of the First International to the Federal Council of Romance Switzerland (*The General Council of the First International, 1868–70: Minutes*) (Vol. 2 of *Documents of the First International*), p. 407.

176 Council Meeting, December 22, 1868 in *The General Council of the First International, 1868–70: Minutes* (*Documents of the First International*, Vol. 3) (Moscow), p. 55.

177 F. Engels, "Johann Philipp Becker" in *Biographische Skizzen* (1967): R. P. Morgan, *op. cit.*

178 F. Engels to Karl Marx, July 25, 1866; Karl Marx to F. Engels, July 27, 1866 in *Gesamtausgabe*, Part III, Vol. 3, pp. 349–51.

179 Council Meetings, October 8 and 22, 1867 in *The General Council of the First International 1866–68: Minutes* (*Documents of the First International*, Vol. 1) (Progress Publishers, Moscow), pp. 166–7.

180 W. Liebknecht, *On the Political Position of Social-Democracy particularly with Respect to the Reichstag* (Moscow, 1959), p. 26.

181 W. Liebknecht to F. Engels, December 11, 1867 in Wilhelm Liebknecht, *Briefwechsel mit Karl Marx und Friedrich Engels* (ed. G. Eckert, 1963), pp. 82–7.

182 R. P. Morgan, *The German Social Democrats and the First International 1864–1872* (1965), pp. 24–5.

183 F. Engels to Karl Marx, December 6, 1867 in *Gesamtausgabe*, Part III, Vol. 3, p. 458.

184 The German People's Party and the Saxon People's Party.

185 The membership of the General German Workers' Union rose from 4,610 in 1864 to 9,421 in 1865: see R. P. Morgan, *op. cit.*, p. 11.

186 Franz Mehring, *Deutsche Geschichte vom Ausgang des Mittelalters* (edition of 1952), p. 245.

187 W. Liebknecht to F. Engels, December 11, 1867 in *Wilhelm Liebknecht, Briefwechsel mit Karl Marx und Friedrich Engels* (ed. G. Eckert, 1963), p. 84.

188 F. Engels, *Die preussische Militärfrage und die deutsche Arbeiterpartei* (1865).

189 F. Engels to Karl Marx, January 1, 1868 in *Gesamtausgabe*, Part III, Vol. 4, p. 12.

190 F. Engels, *Der deutsche Bauernkrieg* (second edition, 1870).

191 W. Liebknecht to F. Engels, April 27, 1870 in *Wilhelm Liebknecht, Briefwechsel mit Karl Marx und Friedrich Engels* (ed. G. Eckert, 1963), p. 98.

192 For Wilhelm Bracke see H. Leonard, *Wilhelm Bracke. Leben und Wirken* (1930); G. Eckert, "Die Flugschriften der lassalleanischen Gemeinde in Braunschweig" in *Archiv für Sozialgeschichte*, Vol. 2, 1962, pp. 295–358; "Zur Geschichte der Braunschweiger Sektion der I. International" in *Braunschweigisches Jahrbuch*, Vol. 43, 1962, pp. 131–72; *Wilhelm Bracke und die Anfänge der Braunschweiger Arbeiterbewegung* (1959). See also Karl Marx – Friedrich Engels, *Briefwechsel mit Wilhelm Bracke 1869–1880* (1963).

193 For the founding of the German Social-Democrat Party at Eisenach in 1869 see Gunter Bensor, *Zur Herausbildung der Eisenacher Partei* (1956).

194 For the programme of the German Social-Democrat Party adopted at the Eisenach conference in August 1869 see Franz Mehring, *Die Deutsche Socialdemokratie* (1879), pp. 332–4 and Karl-Heinz Leidigkeit (ed.), *Der Leipziger Hochverratsprozess vom Jahre 1872* (1960), p. 525.

195 R. P. Morgan, *The German Social Democrats and the First International 1864–72* (1965), p. 29.

196 F. Engels to August Bebel, June 20, 1873 in F. Engels, *Briefe an Bebel* (1958), pp. 10–11: English translation: Karl Marx and F. Engels, *Selected Correspondence* (Foreign Languages Publishing House, Moscow), pp. 344–5.

197 R. P. Morgan, *The German Social Democrats and the First International 1864–72* (1965), p. 2.

9

THE FIRST INTERNATIONAL 1864–1872

I. The Founding of the First International[1]

The disappearance of the Brussels Correspondence Committee, the Fraternal Democrats and the Communist League left Marx and Engels without an organisation through which they could advocate world revolution. The collapse of the *Neue Rheinische Zeitung* and its successor deprived them of a journal under their control. Marx resumed his studies in the British Museum, while Engels embarked upon a business career. Engels was relieved that he was now "completely isolated from any sort of low party intrigues".[2]

In 1864 Marx was glad to see that at last there was "evidently a revival of the working classes taking place".[3] In England local trades councils – a new type of labour organisation – were being established and the workers were supporting an agitation aimed at promoting the extension of the franchise. A group of trade union officials, all working in London – William Allan, Robert Applegarth, Daniel Guile, Edwin Coulson and George Odger – played a dominant *rôle* in the labour movement at this time. This "Junta" had virtually gained control over the London Trades Council by 1864. In Germany Lassalle established the General German Workers' Union, while in France 60 workers in Paris signed a public declaration demanding the election of working-class representatives to the legislature. In 1864 the Working Men's International Association was founded in London and it was through this organisation that Marx hoped to "re-electrify the political movement of the working class".[4]

Ten years later, in what has been called his "Epitaph Letter", Engels discussed the achievements of the International and declared that it had been established at exactly the right time.

"It belonged to the period of the Second Empire, when the newly awakening workers' movement had every incentive owing to oppression throughout Europe – to follow the path of unity and to refrain from indulging in internal controversies. It was the moment when the common cosmopolitan interests of the proletariat came to the fore. Germany, Spain, Italy and Denmark had only just come into the movement or were just coming into it. In fact, throughout Europe in 1864 the theoretical character of the movement, among the masses, was still very dubious. German communism did not yet exist as a workers' party. Proudhonism was too weak to be able to insist upon its particular fads. Bakunin's new rubbish did not yet exist even in his own head, and even the leaders of the English trade unions thought that they could enter the movement on the basis of the programme laid down in the preamble to the statutes (of the Working Men's International Association)."[5]

Marx postponed his work on *Das Kapital* to take an active part in the affairs of the International. He hoped to influence the deliberations of its General Council and so spread his doctrines among the organised workers in England and on the Continent. As early as February 1865 he told Dr Kugelmann that the influence of the International "on the English proletariat is direct and of the greatest significance".[6] Marx's plan to use the International as an instrument of revolution in England was clearly revealed in a memorandum of January 1, 1870 in which he wrote:

"Although revolutionary *initiative* will probably come from France, England alone can serve as the *lever* for a serious *economic* revolution. It is the only country where there are no more peasants and where land property is concentrated in a few hands. It is the only country where the *capitalist form* – i.e. combined labour on a large scale under capitalist masters – embraces virtually the whole of production. It is the only country *where the great majority of the population consists of wage labourers*. It is the only country where the class struggle and organisation of the working class by *Trade Unions* have *acquired* a certain degree of maturity and universality. It is the only country where, because of its domination on the world market, every revolution in economic matters must immediately affect the whole world. If landlordism and capitalism are classical examples in England, on the other hand the *material conditions* for their destruction are the most mature here. The General Council, now being in the *happy position of having its hand directly on this great lever of proletarian revolution*, what folly – we might even say what a crime – to let this lever fall into purely English hands! The English have all the *material* necessary for the social revolution. What they lack is the spirit of *generalisation and revolutionary fervour*. Only the General Council can provide them with this (and) can thus accelerate the truly revolutionary movement here, and in consequence everywhere."[7]

For many years Marx and Engels had collaborated on various enterprises but as far as the International was concerned, Marx had to manage for six years on his own with little help from Engels who was working in Manchester. He could not serve on the General Council of the International and he could assist in its work only by correspondence. He and Lizzie Burns joined the International as individual members but he made no attempt to organise a branch in Manchester. He told Marx that – except for Samuel Moore and Dr Gumpert – he could get no local support for the International.[8] Marx had also asked Ernest Jones to form a committee in Manchester[9] but Jones was unsuccessful and returned 11 of the 12 membership cards that had been sent to him.[10] After Engels moved to London, Eugène Dupont and Edward Jones formed a Manchester branch of the International.[11] In 1864 Engels had just secured his partnership in the firm of Ermen and Engels and if he had openly supported the International, Godfrey Ermen might have accused him of neglecting his duties at the office.

Moreover when the International was established, Engels doubted whether it would survive for long. He thought that there would soon be a clash between the English trade unionists on the General Council and some of the more revolutionary supporters of the International on the Continent.[12] By the spring of 1865 he had changed his mind. He congratulated Marx on the "enormous advance of the International"[13] and he told Weydemeyer that the International was "progressing splendidly".[14] It was only after he had moved to London in 1870 that Engels was elected to a seat on the General Council of the International.

In a letter to Engels,[15] Marx explained how he had come to be involved in the affairs of the International. Some representatives of the workers in London and Paris had recently co-operated to protest against the oppression of the Poles after the failure of their rising in 1863. A deputation of workers from Paris, led by the engraver Henri-Louis Tolain – "a very decent chap" – had visited London and arrangements had been made by George Odger[16] and Randal Cremer[17] to hold a public meeting in St Martin's Hall on September 28, 1864. How little Marx knew about the trade union leaders in London may be seen from his reference to Odger as the "president" instead of the secretary of the London Trades Council and to Randal Cremer as the "secretary of the masons union", whereas he was actually a carpenter. But Marx was probably not far from the truth when he described the organisers of the meeting on September 28 as "the actual labour kings of London".[18] He was impressed by the fact that they were "the same people who had prepared such a tremendous reception for Garibaldi and who (had) thwarted Palmerston's plan for a war with the United States by 'monster meetings in St James' Hall'."[19]

Marx stated that Victor Le Lubez had asked him to recommend a speaker to address the meeting on behalf of the German workers. This young man was "an excellent intermediary between the

English and French workers" as he had been brought up in Jersey
and London. Marx recommended J. G. Eccarius to Le Lubez.
Eccarius was a German tailor who had worked in England for
many years. He had been a member of the Communist League
and had contributed an article on the tailoring trade in London to
Marx's *Neue Rheinische Zeitung: Politisch-ökonomische Revue* in
1850.[20]

It was only at the last moment that Marx was invited to attend
the meeting in St Martin's Hall on September 28, 1864.[21] He told
Engels that he usually declined such invitations but that, on this
occasion, he had accepted because many influential leaders of
English trade unions would be present and because the French
delegates (though "an insignificant lot") were genuine representatives
of the Paris workers[22] – and Marx and Engels had long looked to
Paris as the city in which a call to the barricades would one day
give the workers of Europe the signal to overthrow their oppressors.
Marx was given a seat on the platform in St Martin's Hall but he
was not asked to speak.

It was decided at the meeting on September 28 to establish the
Working Men's International Association with a General Council
which was to meet in London. This Council was not a demo-
cratically elected body. Although the original members were
elected at the meeting at which the International was founded,
those members who were subsequently appointed were co-opted by
the Council itself. Engels explained later that the Council was not
composed of members elected as representatives of branches of
the International or of affiliated societies. "The Council was
empowered to add to its numbers – and everyone so added became
an integral part of the Council. . . ."[23]

The Council – which Maltman Barry regarded as "the collective
wisdom of the Association"[24] – had two functions. First it was the
centre of a world organisation – a link between all branches of the
Association in England and elsewhere. It has been described as "a
centralised autocracy issuing mandates like a general to an army".[25]
Secondly, it was the headquarters of the English societies affiliated
to the International. The attempt to make a single body serve a
dual purpose eventually led to criticisms that the General Council
was trying to do too much by assuming a "burdensome accumulation of functions".[26]

The meeting appointed a special committee to draw up draft
statutes and a statement of policy. Marx was a member of this
committee but, owing to illness, he did not attend its earlier meetings. When the committee submitted its report on October 18, 1864
the General Council had before it some draft statutes drawn up by

Major Luigi Wolff[27] and revised by Le Lubez[28] as well as a proposed list of rules prepared by John Weston.[29] The General Council instructed its committee "to put into definite form the preamble and rules and (to) submit the same to the next meeting of the General Council".[30]

Marx attended the next meeting of the committee and promptly drew up a new policy statement which was quite different from the one previously approved by the General Council. He altered the preamble, suppressed the "Principles", and replaced 40 rules with 10 of his own. And for good measure he wrote an Inaugural Address without having been asked to do so. Marx's suggestions were accepted by the committee and by the General Council.[31]

II. Marx and the First International, 1864–70

In the Inaugural Address[32] Marx provided the International with a manifesto couched in sufficiently general terms to be acceptable to the workers' leaders in various countries, who had very different political beliefs and pursued very different aims. It has been described as "nebulous in meaning" but it was also "a model of diplomatic ingenuity".[33] The address had to reconcile such divergent views as those held by the followers of Proudhon, Lassalle, and Mazzini and also the trade unionists in England. "It had to satisfy English trade unionists, who were interested exclusively in winning strikes and cared nothing about their 'historical rôle'; French Proudhonists, who were opposed to strikes and to the collectivisation of the means of production, and who believed in co-operative societies and cheap credit; followers of the patriot Mazzini, who was chiefly interested in liberating Italy and who wanted to keep the class struggle out of it."[34]

Marx tactfully refrained from mentioning his own doctrines and the word "socialism" appeared only once. George Howell observed that the address was one which "a Gladstone or a Bright could have accepted with a good conscience".[35] Marx realised that he would first have to gain the confidence of the General Council before he could try to convert any members of the Council to his own doctrines. To do this he energetically promoted the expansion of the International. In 1866 he declared that he had "to lead the whole society".[36] Only occasionally did he neglect the International – as in the spring of 1867 when he was absent from the General Council for four months correcting the proofs of the first volume of *Das Kapital*. In 1868 Marx stated that, despite his financial difficulties, he could not leave London for Geneva (where he could live more cheaply) because, if he did so, "at this critical time, the whole labour movement, which I influence from behind the scenes, would fall into very bad hands and go the wrong way".[37] And in 1870 he complained: "My time is so taken up with the International work that I do not get to bed before three in the morning."[38]

Slowly but surely Marx strengthened his intellectual ascendancy over the General Council of the International. He was able to delay until 1871 the formation of a Federal Council in Britain of organisations affiliated to the International – a body which he could hardly hope to influence in the way that he had influenced the General Council. In the early days of the International Marx could count upon the support of five German workers – Friedrich Lessner, J. G. Eccarius, Karl Schapper,[39] Georg Löchner,[40] and Karl Pfänder – who had once been members of the Communist League. Eugène Dupont[41] and Hermann Jung[42] were also Marx's allies. And when Engels was elected a member of the General Council in 1870, Marx again had his closest friend by his side.

Marx's supporters also played an important *rôle* in the affairs of the International on the Continent and in America – Johann Philipp Becker in Switzerland and Germany, Wilhelm Liebknecht and Wilhelm Bracke in Germany, Paul Lafargue in France and Spain, and Adolf Sorge in the United States. And "at each congress of the International Association . . . there showed itself a gradually strengthening influence of the Marxian spirit. The congress imperceptibly advocated the ideas of Marx. . . ."[43] In 1867 Marx claimed that the International had become "a power in England, France, Switzerland and Belgium".[44] He boasted to Engels that "when the next revolution comes – and it may perhaps be nearer than it seems – we (that is you and I) have this powerful *engine* in our hands . . . And without any financial resources . . . We may consider ourselves very well satisfied".[45] Some years later, Engels asserted that "the International dominated ten years of one side of European history – the side on which the future lies – and can look back upon its work with pride".[46]

Marx had a facile pen which he readily placed at the disposal of the General Council. He wrote a number of policy statements for the Council which gained some publicity for the Association. They included a letter congratulating Abraham Lincoln on his re-election to the office of President of the United States,[47] two addresses on the Franco–Prussian war, and a highly controversial defence of the Paris Commune.[48] Engels declared that the address on the Commune was an outstanding example of Marx's gift "for grasping clearly the character, the import and the necessary consequences of great historical events, at a time when these events are still in progress before our eyes or have only just taken place.[49]

Engels, too, was occasionally able to help Marx by writing articles or reports. In 1866, at Marx's suggestion he contributed three articles to *The Commonwealth*[50] in which he gave advice to the workers on the question of nationalism with particular reference to the independence of Poland – a problem which was often discussed by the General Council of the International. Engels criticised the view that language should be the sole test of nationality. He considered that the German speaking cantons of Switzerland should stay in Switzerland and that the German speaking inhabitants of Alsace should remain in France. In his view the national aspirations of such peoples as the Poles, the Czechs and the Rumanians should be subordinated to the interests of the great powers. So while he advocated the establishment of an independent Poland he argued that its frontiers should be drawn in such a way as to weaken Russia – the great bastion of reaction – as much as possible, and to strengthen the states in western Europe. To achieve this a multi-racial Poland should be created which would include Lithuanians, White Russians and Little Russians as well as Poles within its frontiers. In the east the Polish frontier of 1772 should be restored but in the west the provinces of Posen and West Prussia should become part of a united Germany.

In 1869, again at Marx's request, Engels prepared a report on the miners' gilds in Saxony for the General Council of the International. These associations were financed jointly by the colliery owners and the miners.[51] Engels argued that "to be genuine workers' societies the miners' gilds must rely exclusively on workers' contributions. Only thus can they become trade unions which protect individual workers from the tyranny of individual masters". He added that "the contributions of the Saxon coalfield owners to the gild funds are an involuntary admission that capital is – up to a certain point – responsible for accidents which threaten the hired worker with mutilation or death during the execution of his duty at his place of work".

Marx also endeavoured to initiate the General Council into the mysteries of Marxian economics. An opportunity arose in connection with some articles which John Weston, a respected member of the General Council, contributed to the *Bee Hive*. Marx told Engels that Weston – "a fine old chap" – had argued that "1. a general rise in the rate of wages would be of no use to the workers, 2. that therefore . . . trade unions have a *harmful* effect".[52] Weston thought that if an employer had to pay higher wages he would raise the price of goods that he manufactured. Inflation would therefore soon reduce the real value – the purchasing power – of the increased money wages.

To refute this thesis Marx gave two lectures to the General Council in June 1865 on "Wages, Price and Profit".[53] He told Engels that "you can't compress a course of political economy into one hour. But we shall do our best".[54] He summarised his views on how "surplus value" was produced and concluded by offering some advice to the trade unionists who belonged to the General Council:

> "Trades Unions work well as centres of resistance against the encroachments of capital. They fail partially from an injudicious use of their power. They fail generally from limiting themselves to a guerilla war against the effects of the existing system, instead of simultaneously trying to change it, instead of using their organised forces as a lever for the final emancipation of the working class, that is to say, the ultimate abolition of the wages system."[55]

Six months after he had given this lecture, Marx wrote that the International had "made great progress". "We have succeeded in drawing into the movement the one really big workers' organisation, the English trade unions, which formerly concerned themselves *exclusively* with wage questions."[56] But Marx could neither convert the trade union leaders to socialism nor persuade them to adopt a militant policy aimed at overthrowing the capitalist system. He was equally unsuccessful in his efforts to induce them to set up a workers' political party. Some years later, Engels – echoing Marx's advice – appealed to the trade union movement to fight for the abolition of the wages system.[57]

III. The International in England

It is difficult to assess the support which the International received since conditions varied considerably from one country to another. In France and Germany the International was hampered by limitations to the freedom of association and freedom of speech but in England, as Robert Applegarth observed, "we have no need of creeping into holes and corners, lest a policeman should see us".[58] While later Internationals were federations of national socialist parties, the First International was largely composed of affiliated members who belonged to various types of workers' organisations.

The affiliated trade unions in England were not a representative cross-section of the labour movement.[59] Marx indulged in wishful thinking when he claimed that virtually the whole trade union movement supported the International. Indeed in 1870 he admitted that "trade unions and labour organisations held aloof from the International until they were in trouble".[60] And John Hales observed

Friedrich Engels in 1879

Karl Marx in 1871

that "the Association, though established in London . . . had made more progress abroad than here".[61]

Most of the affiliated trade unions in England were small London societies of skilled craftsmen such as tailors, shoemakers, coopers, bookbinders and cigar-makers. The Operative Bricklayers and the Carpenters and Joiners were the only large unions which joined the International. Eleven of the 27 English members of the General Council elected in 1864 belonged to the building trades.[62] Only the stonemasons held aloof. The miners, the textile operatives, and the engineers (except the malleable ironworkers) did not join the International. William Allan, the secretary of the Amalgamated Society of Engineers, told a parliamentary enquiry that his members had declined to attend a congress of the International held at Geneva. "They believed that the best thing the foreigners could do, would be to organise themselves into trade societies similar to ours and then we could begin to discuss questions with them."[63]

On the Continent, too, support for the International came from craftsmen rather than from factory workers. In 1869, for example, a National Labour Union (affiliated to the International) was established in Holland by cabinet makers, compositors, carpenters, painters, blacksmiths, masons and bricklayers.[64] In Geneva the International was supported by watchmakers, jewellers, carpenters and builders while in the Swiss Jura – Le Locle and La Chaux de Fondes – it was craftsmen who joined the International.[65]

In the early days of the International, its officials had no illusions concerning the support received from the workers in England. John Hales estimated the membership at 8,000; Hermann Jung at 14,000.[66] In July 1866 a conference of trade unionists at Sheffield, attended by 138 delegates, recommended trade unions to affiliate with the International since this organisation was "essential to the progress and prosperity of the entire working community".[67] A similar resolution was passed by a trade union congress held in Birmingham in 1869.[68] But the trade unions paid little heed to these resolutions.

In 1866, in its third annual report, the General Council gave the names of 33 affiliated trade unions (or branches).[69] At this time there were over 2,000 trade unions (or branches) in the United Kingdom.[70] The whole trade union movement probably had about 1,500,000 members in the late 1860s.[71] Perhaps 50,000 of them belonged to unions affiliated to the International. In 1867 the London Trades Council declined to become an affiliated member, though it offered to co-operate with the International.[72] "The London Trades Council declined to recognise the International even as the authorised medium of communications with trade

societies abroad and decided to communicate with these directly."[73]
The International secured very little financial support from the
trade union movement in England. By September 1867 only £73
had been obtained from this source.[74]

IV. The International in France

A French section of the International was established in Paris
in 1864. Its leaders – Tolain, Fribourg and Limousin – were disciples
of Proudhon and had little knowledge of Marx's doctrines. They
successfully warded off attacks from rival left wing groups, such
as the republicans and Blanqui's followers, and they established
several branches of the International in the provinces. At a conference held in London in 1865 the French delegates explained why
it was difficult to organise the International in France. Fribourg
observed that since there was no right of public meeting in France
the supporters of the International "could only meet in small groups
of not more than 20; if more met they were liable to be arrested".[75]
Tolain declared that "in France they could only meet by stealth
and had no means of openly propagating the principles of the
Association and therefore could not reach or inspire with confidence those to whom they were personally unknown".[76]

Some workers' "syndicates" became affiliated to the French
section of the International.[77] These associations bore little resemblance to trade unions in England. English unions were bodies of
skilled or semi-skilled workers which aimed at improving the
living standards and working conditions of their members by fighting for higher wages and reduced hours of work. A French syndi-
cate, on the other hand, might be engaged in various activities such
as those of a benefit club, a co-operative association, an educational
society, an employment agency, a political organisation and a social
club. But it might also pursue aims somewhat similar to those of
an English trade union.

Marx denounced the leaders of the Paris branch for accepting
Proudhon's doctrines in preference to his own. He rebuked Tolain
and Fribourg for putting forward these ideas at the congress of the
International held in Geneva in 1866. He complained to Dr Kugelmann that the delegates from Paris "had their heads full of the
emptiest Proudhonist phrases". "Ignorant, vain, presumptuous,
chattering, dogmatic, arrogant, they were on the point of spoiling
everything, for they came to the Congress in numbers which bore
no proportion whatever to the number of their members."[78]
Between 1864 and 1866 the French government had taken no action
against the French section of the International. But after the con-

gress at Geneva some documents relating to the transactions of the International in the possession of Jules Gottraux were confiscated by the French police. As Gottraux was a naturalised British subject the Foreign Office protested to the French government and the documents were returned.

The French government believed that the International was largely responsible for the labour unrest in France at this time. But it was probably mistaken. It has been observed that in France "the International was considerably weaker than the government suspected". "Instead of being the tightly-knit, disciplined organisation of over a million members that seemed to be on the verge of undertaking the immediate overthrow of the social order, the International in France was largely made up of a paper membership; it mainly consisted of individuals who had merely voted to affiliate with it at meetings of community and labour organisations. The process seldom went further and individual sections of the International tended to be no more than discussion groups with very little overall ideological, tactical or organisational coherence."[79] But the French government thought otherwise and in March 1868 a court dissolved the Paris branch of the International because it was an unauthorised society of over 20 members. The bookbinder Eugène Varlin promptly set up a new branch of the International in Paris. He and his followers were brought to trial in May 1868 and were sent to prison for three months.

The influence of Tolain and Fribourg declined to some extent and the Paris section of the International came under the control of rather more militant leaders, such as Eugène Varlin and it adopted a more militant policy than before. In March 1870 Varlin informed the General Council that "the Association was being resuscitated in Paris",[80] after being twice dissolved by the authorities. In May 1870 several members of the French branches of the International were arrested in Paris and Lyons but Varlin and two of his friends escaped to Brussels.[81] Despite the militancy of the leadership, the rank and file remained faithful to Proudhon's doctrines. In March 1871 a manifesto issued by the Paris branch of the International supporting the Commune contained proposals which were fully in accordance with Proudhon's views. The manifesto demanded "the organisation of credit, exchange, and co-operation to assure to the worker the entire value of his labour".[82] Engels wrote that the French adherents of the International who were members of the Commune were followers of Proudhon. "Naturally the Proudhonists were chiefly responsible for the economic decrees of the Commune, both for their praiseworthy and their unpraiseworthy aspects."[83]

V. The International in Germany

In Germany the International developed in a different way. A Prussian Law of 1850 – and similar legislation in other states – prohibited societies from joining foreign associations. In a report of 1869 Marx stated that the General German Workers Union supported "the principles of our Association, but simultaneously declared (that) the Prussian law forbade them (from) joining us".[84] German supporters of the International could, however, join as individual members.

Marx and Engels hoped that Wilhelm Liebknecht would set up branches of the International in Germany. But Liebknecht considered that his first duty was to establish a socialist party in Germany. In a report to the London conference of the International in 1865 Liebknecht took a pessimistic view of the future prospects of the International.[85] Marx urged Liebknecht *very seriously . . . to enter the Association with some men – few or many, we do not care*",[86] and sent him some paid-up membership cards.[87] But this produced no quick results and in May 1866 Marx complained to Engels that "thanks to that ass Liebknecht (good fellow as he is), it is only in Germany that we cannot make any headway".[88] Shortly afterwards, however, Marx appreciated that Liebknecht had tried to recruit German members for the International, particularly among the artisans in Saxony.[89]

Marx did not rely entirely upon Liebknecht's efforts to promote the cause of the International in Germany. He had another ally in the veteran revolutionary Johann Philipp Becker, who had fought against the Prussians in the Baden campaign of 1849.[90] Becker had attended the meeting in London at which the International had been established. From Geneva he set up many branches of the International in Switzerland and then extended his activities to Germany. His journal *Der Vorbote* became the leading German organ of the International. Becker was present at the London conference of the International in 1865 where his speech was "much applauded by those who understood the German language". He stated that the Geneva branch of the International already had 1,500 members.[91] While the conference was in session Becker "received a mandate from the workers of the Solingen factories".[92] This may have been due to Marx's contacts with Carl Klings, a leader of the workers in Solingen.[93] In 1867 the General Council reported that Becker had established some branches of the International in Germany.[94]

Unfortunately for Marx his two main allies in Germany – Becker and Liebknecht – did not work harmoniously together. Although Becker hailed the establishment of the German Social Democrat Party as a "world-historical event" he challenged its founder Liebknecht, for the leadership of the International in Germany. Engels described the rivalry between Becker and Liebknecht in a letter to T. C. Cuno:

"For a long time old man Becker has retained his own ideas of organisation, dating from the epoch *before* 1848 – little groups, whose leaders kept in touch in order to give the whole organisation a general trend, a little conspiratorial activity on occasion, and the like. Another idea, likewise dating from that period, was that the central organ of the German organisation had to be located *outside* Germany.

"When the International was founded, Becker took over the organisation of the Germans in Switzerland and other countries. He established a section in Geneva, which was gradually converted into the 'Mother Section of the Groups of German Language Sections' by organising new sections in Switzerland, Germany, and elsewhere. It then began to claim the top leadership not only of the Germans living in Switzerland, America, France, etc., but also of the Germans in Germany and Austria. All this was the old method of revolutionary agitation employed up to 1848, and as long as it was based upon the voluntary subordination of the sections, there could be no objection to it. But there was one thing the good soul Becker forgot: that the organisation of the International was too big for such methods and goals. Becker and his friends, however, *accomplished* something and always remained direct and avowed sections of the International." "In the meantime the labour movement in Germany was growing, freeing itself from the fetters of Lassalleanism, and, under the leadership of Bebel and Liebknecht, it came out *in principle* for the International. The movement became too powerful and acquired too much independent significance for it to be able to acknowledge the leadership of the Geneva Mother Section. The German workers held their own congresses and elected their own executive organs. . . ."[95]

Despite the laws which forbade societies in Germany to be linked with foreign associations the Union of German Workers and Educational Societies became affiliated to the International[96] and when the German Social Democrat Party was founded at Eisenach in 1869 it declared itself to be "a branch of the Working Men's International Association".[97] Although Liebknecht and Bebel, the leaders of the new party, were disciples of Marx and accepted his doctrines, they were more interested in building up a powerful socialist party in Germany than in promoting the growth of the International. They readily paid lip service to the ideals of the

International but they were not prepared to give it very much practical support or financial assistance. At his trial in Leipzig in 1872 Bebel told the court that the International had only about a thousand members in Germany.[98]

This situation led to vigorous exchanges between Marx and Engels and their followers in Germany. In September 1871 Marx complained to Kwasniewsky, a leading socialist in Berlin, that the German branches of the International had not sent a delegate to a recent conference in London and had not paid any subscriptions to the General Council since 1869.[99] When Liebknecht criticised Marx for communicating directly with a local branch of the International in Germany he received a sharp reply. Marx wrote that "since we are here (in London) very dissatisfied with the way in which the business of the International has been conducted (in Germany) I have – on the authority of the General Council – assumed the duty of getting into direct touch myself with the main German centres, and I have already begun to do so".[100] Liebknecht replied that "there is no prospect of securing many individual memberships in Germany and between ourselves I do not think that it matters at all".[101]

Engels now intervened in the debate. He rejected Liebknecht's attitude towards the International in Germany. On December 15, 1871 he wrote:

"Your opinion that the German members of the International should not pay dues, and that in any case it makes no difference whether the International has many or few members in Germany is the opposite of our own. If you did not collect the annual dues of one silver groschen per person per year, or if you used them up yourselves, you will have to settle this with your own conscience. I fail to understand how you can imagine that other nations should bear your share of the costs, while you are with them, like Jesus Christ, 'in the spirit', and keep your flesh and your money all to yourselves. This platonic relation must certainly come to an end, and the German workers must either *belong* to the International or *not* belong. . . ."[102]

Engels followed up this rebuke with another letter to Liebknecht in May 1872:

"Does the Social Democrat Party intend to be represented at the congress, and if so, how does it plan to be in good standing with the General Council so that its mandate cannot be challenged at the congress? For this purpose it must (a) expressly and not just *figuratively* declare itself as the German federation of the International, and (b) pay up its dues *in that capacity* before the congress. This matter is getting serious, and we have to know where we stand, or else you will compel us to go ahead on our own and consider the Social Democrat Party an alien body, indifferent to the International. We cannot allow, out of motives which are unknown to us but which are surely petty, the mandates of the German workers to be squandered or frittered away. We ask for a prompt and clear cut answer'..[103]

At the same time Engels wrote to T. C. Cuno:

"The relationship of the German workers' party to the International never was made clear, however. This relationship remained a purely platonic one: there was no actual membership for individuals (with some exceptions), while the formation of sections was forbidden by law. As a result, the following situation developed in Germany. They claimed the *rights* of membership while they brushed aside its *obligations*, and only after the London conference did we insist that henceforth they would have to comply with their obligations."[104]

VI. The International and the Labour Movement

An examination of the minutes of the General Council bears out Marx's claim that one of the main functions of the International was "to counteract the intrigues of capitalists – always ready in cases of strikes and lock outs, to misuse the foreign workman as a tool against the native workman".[105] A few years previously a strike of gas workers in London had been broken by importing bakers from Germany who were used to working in great heat.[106]

In 1866 the journeymen tailors in London struck for higher wages and the masters recruited workers on the Continent to replace those who were on strike. Marx boasted that, as a result of intervention by the International "the London masters' manoeuvre was foiled; they had to lay down their arms and meet their workers' just demands".[107] When the tailors' strike spread to Edinburgh, Engels warned Marx that 57 German tailors had arrived in that city.[108] Marx wrote to several German newspapers (on behalf of the International) to appeal to German tailors not to go to Edinburgh as strike-breakers.[109] The International also sent two emissaries to Scotland who drove a wedge between the master tailors and their foreign workers. Marx considered that "the whole affair has greatly benefited us in London".[110]

In 1871 the engineers, joiners and construction workers of Newcastle upon Tyne – organised in a Nine Hours League – stopped working for five months to secure a shorter working day. On August 8 a deputation of strikers led by John Burnett met the General Council of the International and asked for its help to prevent strike-breakers from being brought to Newcastle from

Belgium and from the royal arsenal in Denmark. Marx declared that "the misfortune was that the trade unions and labour organisations held aloof from the International until they were in trouble and then only did they come for assistance". The cigar-maker James Cohn (the International's correspondence secretary for Denmark) went to the Continent to try to stop foreign engineers from acting as strike-breakers in Newcastle. But he was not a formal delegate of the International. His expenses were paid by the Amalgamated Society of Engineers.[111] The International not only attempted to stop the flow of strike-breakers to England from the Continent. It also acted as an agent for trade unions which sent money to workers on strike in France, Belgium and Switzerland.[112]

Although Marx appreciated that the International was making its mark in the labour movement by intervening in strikes, he hoped to persuade the trade union leaders that the cause of the workers could be served equally effectively by political action. The London conference of the International (with Engels as chairman) declared in 1871 "that in the militant state of the working class, its economical movement and its political action are indisolubly united".[113]

The demand for the extension of the franchise gave Marx the opportunity for which he was seeking. The agitation in favour of a new Reform Act was being organised by the Reform League and Marx tried to secure the election of as many of his supporters as possible on to the committee of this association. In this way, he hoped to influence the reform movement from behind the scenes just as he was influencing the General Council of the International. At first his plan seemed to be succeeding. On May 1, 1865 he wrote to Engels:

"The great success of the International Association is this: the Reform League is our work. The working men on the inner Committee of Twelve (6 middle-class men and 6 working men) are all members of our Council (including Eccarius). We have baffled all attempts of the middle class to mislead the working class. The movement in the provinces is this time wholly dependent on that of London. Ernest Jones, for example, had despaired till we set the ball rolling. If we succeed in re-electrifying the political movement of the English working class, our Association, without making any fuss, will have done more for the working class of Europe than has been possible in any other way. And there is every prospect of success."[114]

A year later, when two open air meetings were held in London in support of the reform of the franchise, Marx declared that "the workers' demonstrations in London, which are marvellous compared with anything we have seen in England since 1849, are purely the work of the *International*. Mr Lucraft, for instance, the leader in Trafalgar Square, is one of our Council".[115] This was followed by a meeting in Hyde Park although it had been prohibited by the authorities. Some park railings were smashed and there was a scuffle between the constables and the demonstrators. Marx thought that this confrontation between the police and the demonstrators might lead to a rising of the workers in London. He told Engels that "if the railings – and it was touch and go – had been used offensively and defensively against the police and about twenty of the latter had been knocked out, the military would have had to 'intervene' instead of only parading. And then there would have been some fun. One thing is certain; these thick-headed John Bulls, whose brainpans seem to have been specially manufactured for the constables' bludgeons, will never get anywhere without a really bloody encounter with the ruling powers".[116] But the "really bloody encounter" never took place and Marx's hopes that the agitation for electoral reform would culminate in a popular revolt were doomed to disappointment.

In 1869 Marx wrote to Engels that the General Council of the International had been instrumental in establishing a new militant left-wing organisation called the Land and Labour League which demanded "the nationalisation of land as a starting point". The Basel congress of the International had recently approved the abolition of private ownership of land, Marx joined the Land and Labour League and his friend Eccarius became its "active secretary". Marx described the new association as a working-class party which had "broken away completely from the middle classes".[117]

Besides having a close associate of Marx as its secretary the Land and Labour League had ten members of the General Council of the International on its executive committee. The programme of the association, drawn up by Eccarius after consulting Marx, included not only the nationalisation of land but also shorter hours for workers and universal suffrage.[118] The Land and Labour League, however, made little impact on the political scene and Marx failed to secure another political organisation of workers which he could influence from behind the scenes.

VII. The International and the Irish Question

At the same time Marx used the unrest in Ireland as a means of provoking the working class in England to greater militancy in politics. In 1867 a rising in Ireland was put down while in England the Fenians failed to seize Chester castle but succeeded in freeing two of their number from a police van in Manchester. They killed a police officer in doing so. Marx told Engels that he was encouraging the English workers to support the Fenians.[119] When the murderers of the Manchester policeman were sentenced to death Marx drew up a plea for clemency which was adopted by the General Council of the International on November 20, 1867 and sent to Gathorne-Hardy. The memorial had no effect and three of the five convicted Fenians were hanged on November 23.[120] On November 30 Engels wrote to Marx about the executions. He complained that in reporting them "the English press has again behaved in a shameful manner". On the Sunday after the executions the Catholic priests in Manchester and Salford had declared from their pulpits that "these men were *murdered*".[121]

On November 26, 1867 the General Council again debated the Irish question. Marx proposed to take part in the discussion. He intended to compare "the political executions at Manchester" with "the fate of John Brown at Harper's Ferry" and to denounce the notion that "the English had a divine right to fight the Irish on their native soil, but every Irish (man) fighting against the British government in England to be treated as an outlaw".[122]

In a letter to Engels describing the debate, Marx explained that, owing to the execution of the Fenians in Manchester, he would have felt obliged "to hurl revolutionary thunderbolts instead of soberly analysing the state of affairs and the movement as I had intended". In the circumstances Peter Fox addressed the meeting instead of Marx. Fox proposed what Marx regarded as an "absurd and meaningless resolution". Marx persuaded the General Council to refer the resolution to its standing committee for further consideration.[123]

In December 1867 the Fenians tried to free two of their leaders by blowing a hole – with a cask of gunpowder – in the wall of Clerkenwell prison. The explosion caused 12 deaths, while 120 persons were injured. Marx, in a letter to Engels, denounced the Fenians for their "utter stupidity". He argued that the workers in London, who had hitherto "shown much sympathy for the Irish"[124] would be alienated by this outrage.[125] Shortly afterwards Marx gave a lecture to the German Workers' Educational Association in London on the Irish question.

In 1869 there was a fresh wave of unrest in Ireland and a campaign was mounted in England to secure an amnesty for the Fenian prisoners. Marx encouraged the International to support this campaign. A member of the General Council of the International – J. J. Merriman – was one of the speakers at a rally held in Hyde Park on October 24 to demand the release of Irish political prisoners. At a meeting of the General Council on November 16

Marx opened a debate on the Irish question. He vigorously denounced Gladstone's Irish policy and demanded an amnesty for the Fenian prisoners.[126] The discussion was resumed on November 23 and there was a heated debate. Mottershead praised Gladstone and criticised the resolutions put forward by Marx on Ireland.[127] Marx wrote to Engels that "Muddlehead" had made "a long rambling speech". In the end Marx's resolutions were accepted with only minor changes.[128] Shortly afterwards – on November 29, 1869 – Engels wrote to Marx that the election of O'Donovan Rossa, an Irish prisoner, to a seat in Parliament was "a great event". He declared that it would "make the Fenians abandon their fruitless conspiratorial tactics and staging of minor coups, in favour of practical activities which, though seemingly legal, are more revolutionary than all they have done since their unsuccessful insurrection".[129]

By 1870 Marx had come to the conclusion that the Irish question was a factor of fundamental importance for the future of the capitalist system in Britain. It was far more than the struggle of an oppressed people for independence. It was the key to the downfall of the aristocracy and the middle classes in England. In 1870 Marx drew up for the General Council of the International a memorandum on "the relation of the Irish national struggle to the emancipation of the working class". He argued that "Ireland is the bulwark of the English landed aristocracy" and that the overthrow of the great landlords in Ireland would herald their downfall in England as well. "Owing to the constantly increasing concentration of farming, Ireland steadily sends its surplus workers to the English labour market and thus forces down wages and lowers the moral and material condition of the English working class." In Britain the workers were divided into an English and an Irish proletariat and their hostility was "the secret of the impotence of the English working class, despite their organisation". "It is the secret by which the capitalist class maintains its power."[130]

In the circumstances Marx urged the International "everywhere to put the conflict between England and Ireland in the foreground and everywhere to side openly with Ireland. And it is the special task of the Central Council in London to awaken the consciousness in the English workers that for them the national emancipation of Ireland is no question of abstract justice or humanitarian sentiment but the first condition of their own social emancipation". Finally Marx claimed that the agitation in favour of an amnesty for the Fenians had forced Gladstone to agree to an enquiry into the treatment of the Irish prisoners.

VIII. Engels and the General Council, 1870–2

Of all the duties that Marx undertook on behalf of the International none gave him greater satisfaction than the composition of addresses on behalf of the General Council. The addresses, which sometimes received considerable publicity, enabled Marx to give to the world his views on the vital issues of the day, such as the Irish question, the Franco–Prussian war, and the Paris Commune. Marx saw himself as the embodiment of the international labour movement. He believed that all over the world the workers would cherish his pronouncements as coming from a leader who would one day deliver them from the oppression of the capitalists.

In 1870 Marx and Engels were able to collaborate in a way that had not been possible during the twenty years that Engels had lived in Manchester. When Engels settled in London he was elected to the General Council of the International and was able to shoulder part of the burden that Marx had hitherto carried alone. For two years Engels devoted much of his time to the International. As a military critic Engels was able to advise the General Council on the war on the Continent after the fall of Metz. As a linguist he could assist the International with its foreign correspondence. And as corresponding secretary for Spain and Italy Engels was able to give Marx valuable assistance in his efforts to resist the spread of Bakunin's influence among the workers in those countries.

In January 1871 Engels addressed the General Council on the policy that the English workers should adopt with regard to the situation on the Continent now that France had been defeated by Prussia. He declared that the opportunity for English military intervention on the side of France had passed away. He argued that England was no longer in a position to meddle in the affairs of the Continent or even to defend herself against "Continental military despotism". He appealed to the English workers to press the British government to recognise the new French Republic.[131]

Engels's appearance on the General Council exacerbated the differences between the revolutionary Marxists and the moderate trade union representatives. Engels had a poor opinion of the English workers and was exasperated by their lack of revolutionary fervour. During the general election of 1868 he had complained that the factory workers had disgraced themselves by voting for "any Lord Tom Noddy or any parvenu snob" rather than for men like Ernest Jones who had their interests at heart.[132] In 1871 Engels annoyed the trade union representatives when he criticised the English workers for failing to give financial aid to the French refugees from the Commune.[133] He quarrelled with John Hales over a request from the *Graphic* to send an artist to make sketches of the members of the General Council in session,[134] and he accused Hales of bias in writing the minutes of the Council's proceedings. This dispute led to Hales's resignation as secretary in June 1872.[135]

For their part the trade union leaders were ill at ease in the presence of a smartly dressed wealthy retired "cotton lord" who bore himself like a Prussian guardsman. Engels could run an office and keep junior clerks in their place, but he was out of his depth in dealing with working-class members of the General Council of the International. He failed to treat them as equals in debate but expected them to accept his point of view without question. Engels lacked understanding and tact when dealing with the workers and his outspoken comments gave offence to the leaders of trade unions.

IX. The International and the Paris Commune, 1871

The latent hostility on the General Council of the International between Marx and Engels on the one hand and the trade union representatives on the other came out into the open when the workers of Paris rose in revolt against the French government. They gained control of the city, and proclaimed the Commune on March 28, 1871. Engels described the events leading to the establishment of the Commune in a speech to the General Council of the International on March 21.[136] For years Marx and Engels had argued that the outbreak of the class struggle and the downfall of the capitalist system were inevitable. Now they hoped that the crisis which they had predicted had at last arrived. Before the revolutions of 1848 Marx had declared that the signal for revolution on the Continent would be "the crowing of the Gallic cock". He had not changed his mind. He and Engels still believed that a rising of the workers in Paris would spread to the rest of France and to other countries as well. While Marx hailed the Paris Commune as the work of "our heroic Party comrades",[137] Engels was more cautious and merely claimed that the Commune was "beyond doubt the child of the International intellectually".[138] Engels was particularly interested in the military aspect of the Commune's activities. His advice "to fortify the north side of the heights of Montmartre on the Prussian side" was passed on to the Commune by Marx.[139] On April 11, 1871 Engels reported to the General Council of the International that since the Commune had taken over responsibility for the defence of Paris from the central committee of the National Guard "there had been talk and no action".

"The time for action against Versailles had been when it was weak, but that opportunity had been lost and now it seemed that Versailles was getting the upper hand and driving the Parisians back." Although Engels took a gloomy view of the military prospects of the Commune at this time, he argued that "the work-people – 200,000 men – (were) far better organised than at any other insurrection".[140]

Marx, on the other hand, was more interested in the significance of the political and economic activities of the Commune. In April 1871 he wrote: "What elasticity, what historical initiative, what a capacity for sacrifice in these Parisians." "The present rising in Paris – even if it be crushed by the wolves, swine and vile curs of the old society – is the most glorious deed of our party since the June insurrection in Paris."[141] A few days later he declared: "The struggle of the working-class against the capitalist class has entered upon a new phase with the struggle in Paris. Whatever the immediate results may be, a new point of departure of world historic importance has been gained."[142] By May 23 Marx realised that the end was in sight. But he was confident that "the principles of the Commune were eternal and could not be crushed; they would assert themselves again and again until the working classes were emancipated".[143]

Marx's dream did not come true. The Commune gained little support outside Paris – risings in Lyons and Marseilles were soon put down – and the city was cut off from the outside world by a German army and the forces of the Republic. Thiers stamped out the Commune as ruthlessly as Cavaignac had crushed the workers in June 1848. The army of Versailles entered the doomed city on May 21, 1871 and between 20,000 and 25,000 people were killed in the indiscriminate slaughter that followed. The defenders of Paris made their last stand at the "Wall of the Communards" at Père Lachaise cemetery where – as Engels wrote – "the breech-loaders could no longer kill fast enough; the vanquished were shot down in hundreds by *mitrailleuse* fire".[144] The London *Times* declared on May 29 that there was no precedent for the way in which "the Versailles troops have been shooting, bayonetting, ripping up prisoners, women and children during the last six days".[145] The Communards, for their part, were responsible for the execution in cold blood of 64 hostages, including the Archbishop of Paris. The murder of the hostages horrified the civilised world and Engels's mother rebuked her son for supporting a régime which was capable of doing such a thing. Engels was quite unabashed and replied: "An enormous fuss has been made of the shooting of a few hostages in the Prussian manner and the destruction of a few palaces, again in the Prussian manner – and all other accusations are false – but nobody raises an eyebrow when 40,000 men, women and children are massacred by the Versailles troops."[146] But in an article in *Der Volksstaat* in 1874 Engels qualified his approval of the shooting of hostages and the burning of palaces by declaring that he was not prepared to defend every violent act committed by the supporters of the Commune.[147]

Marx had to make the best of a bad job and within a few days of the fall of Paris he gave the world his assessment of the achievements of the Commune. On May 30, 1871 he read to the General Council of the International his address on the subject. The Council gave its approval without any discussion and decided to print 1,000 copies. In this pamphlet – entitled *The Civil War in France* – Marx declared that although the Commune had not set the world on fire it had been a brilliant dress rehearsal for world revolution. He declared that the administration of Paris by the Commune showed how a communist state might be organised in the future. He urged socialists to profit from the experience gained from the Commune – an experience that had been dearly bought with the lives of thousands of workers who had fallen in the defence of Paris.

Marx asserted that the essential feature of the Commune – something that distinguished it from all previous forms of government – was "its essentially working class character". The men who administered Paris under the Commune had been "working men or acknowledged members of the working class". "This was the first revolution in which the working-class was openly acknowledged as the only class capable of social initiative." Councillors and public officials were expected to perform their duties on "workmen's wages" of no more than £240 a year – which was less than the allowance made by Engels to Marx. The army and the police were replaced by a popular militia. The Catholic Church in Paris was disestablished. Its endowments were confiscated. School fees were abolished. Judges and magistrates were elected to office and could be dismissed by a popular vote. A three-year moratorium on debts was proclaimed.

In Marx's view the Paris workers had established machinery of government by which "the economic emancipation of labour" could be achieved. He declared that the Commune had "intended to abolish that class-property which makes the labour of the many the wealth of the few". "It aimed at the expropriation of the expropriators." "It wanted to make individual property a truth by transforming the means of production, land and labour, now chiefly the means of enslaving and exploiting labour, into mere instruments of free and associated labour."

Marx declared that if the Commune had controlled the country districts, it would have freed the peasants from "the tyranny of the village policeman, the gendarme, and the Prefect". It would have put "enlightenment by the schoolmaster in place of stultification by the priest". It would have reversed the attempt of the middle classes "to shift on to the peasants' shoulders the chief load of the five milliards of indemnity to be paid to the Prussians".

Marx praised the Commune for being "emphatically international". A German had been appointed Minister of Labour, a Hungarian Minister of Education. "The Commune honoured the heroic sons of Poland by placing them at the head of the defenders of Paris." Marx also praised the economic and social policy of the Commune. Journeymen bakers had been protected by the abolition of night work. Employers had been forbidden to fine their workers. Factories and workshops which had been closed were to be re-opened by workers' co-operative associations. Marx claimed that the Commune had wrought a wonderful change in Paris. Crime had declined and the prostitutes had vanished.[148]

Marx's pamphlet brought him – and the International – more publicity than he had expected. Almost overnight he found himself branded as "a dangerous and even desperate advocate of revolution".[149] He declared that his address on the Commune had made "the devil of a noise, and I have the honour to be, at this moment, the best calumniated and most menaced man in London. That really does one good after a tedious twenty years' idyll in my den. The government paper – the *Observer* – threatens me with a legal prosecution. I laugh at these scoundrels".[150]

A few days later Engels wrote to Liebknecht:

"Here in London there has been an unholy row over the Address. At first it was completely ignored, but that could not last. On Wednesday, June 14, the *Evening Standard* denounced the Address. On the 15th the *Daily News* published an extract from it that was copied by most papers. Then came the *Echo* – on Saturday the *Spectator*, *Graphic*, *Pall Mall Gazette* and a leading article in the *Telegraph* and that was that. On Monday the *Times* followed suit with a really dirty leading article. The *Evening Standard* then mentioned the Address again. Yesterday the *Times* referred to the Address once more and now we – and we alone – are the talk of the whole of London."[151]

On June 6, 1871 Jules Favre, the French Foreign Minister, sent a despatch to the French ambassadors in European capitals. He instructed them to urge upon the states to which they were accredited the desirability of prohibiting the International which was a revolutionary association responsible for setting up the

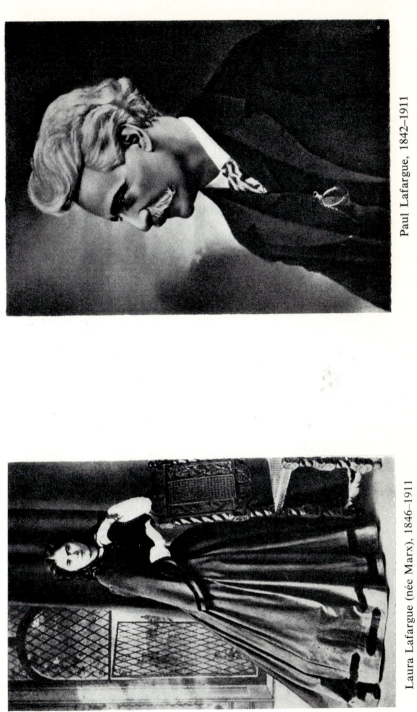

Paul Lafargue, 1842–1911

Laura Lafargue (née Marx), 1846–1911

Eleanor Marx, 1855–1898

Commune in Paris. In Britain the Foreign Office received no written representations from the French Ambassador concerning the International[152] but Henry Bruce,[153] the Home Secretary, caused enquiries to be made on the subject. His secretary approached Karl Marx who readily supplied him with copies of various addresses issued by the International.[154]

In February 1872 the Spanish government appealed to Britain to ban the International, which it described as "a powerful and formidable organisation" which "flies in the face of all the traditions of mankind" and which "effaces God from the mind". The Spanish government declared that "if the evil is to be expelled, it is necessary that all governments should unite their efforts to do so".[155] That the Spanish government was determined to stamp out the International in Spain itself was shown clearly a few months later when the congress of the Spanish section of the International, held at Saragossa, was dissolved by the authorities.[156]

The Spanish note led to a debate in the House of Commons on April 12, 1872. Opponents of the International, such as Baillie Cochrane, quoted some of the more lurid passages in Marx's pamphlet on the Commune. They asserted that it was from London that the Commune had received orders to burn Paris and murder its Archbishop. They declared that the International "desired to abolish marriage, denied God and all rights of property, and preached assassination". They appealed to the government to save the masses from being indoctrinated "with crime and treason". They demanded protection against those who aimed at the violent overthrow of existing society.

The Home Secretary replied that although the doctrines propagated by the International were mischievous, it was better that these "dangerous ideas" should be advocated openly rather than secretly by an underground movement. Freedom of expression was allowed in England and the International had kept within the law. He thought that an association which had only about 8,000 members was hardly likely to become a danger to national security.[157] The British government took no action with regard to the International in England, though in Ireland the police harassed those who tried to organise branches of the International in Dublin and Cork. The activities of the Royal Irish Constabulary doubtless pleased the Pope who regarded the leaders of the International as "the incarnation of evil".[158] The Foreign Secretary informed the Spanish government that "the revolutionary designs which form part of the Society's programme are believed to express the opinion of the foreign members rather than those of the British workmen, whose attention is turned chiefly to questions affecting wages".

Foreign refugees who incited "insurrection against the Government of their respective countries" were liable to expulsion.[159] Immediately after the debate in the House of Commons, Marx drew up a declaration on behalf of the General Council which denied the allegations made against the International by Baillie Cochrane. Marx denounced Baillie Cochrane's speech as one which exhibited "a wilful and premeditated ignorance of what he is talking about".[160]

Although the Home Office left the International alone it drew the line at admitting Marx to British citizenship. Marx was a stateless person, having given up his Prussian citizenship. In 1861 he had tried, but without success, to recover it. Now he sought British naturalisation. In 1874 two Scotland Yard detectives reported that Marx was "the notorious German agitator, the head of the International Society, and the advocate of communistic principles. This man has not been loyal to his own King and Country".[161] Marx realised that "it is very likely that the British Home Minister, who like a sultan, decides on naturalisation, will upset my plans".[162] He was right, for his application was rejected.

Soon after writing *The Civil War in France*, Marx again gave his views on the lessons to be learned from the Commune. At a banquet to celebrate the seventh anniversary of the founding of the International, Marx declared that the experience of the Commune had shown that there must be a transitional period between the downfall of capitalism and the establishment of a communist society. This phase in the development of communism would be "a dictatorship of the proletariat".[163] Engels repeated the phrase twenty years later in his introduction to a new edition of *The Civil War in France*. He wrote:

"Of late the Social Democratic philistine[164] has once more been filled with wholesome terror at the words: Dictatorship of the Proletariat. Well and good, gentlemen, do you want to know what this dictatorship looks like? Look at the Paris Commune. That was the Dictatorship of the Proletariat."[165]

Although Engels regarded *The Civil War in France* as a brilliant essay he realised that Marx had ascribed to the Commune policies which it had never carried out. He explained that Marx had "turned the *unconscious* tendencies of the Commune into more or less concrete conscious plans and, in the circumstances, this was justifiable and even necessary.[166]

On March 18, 1872 a public meeting was held in London to celebrate the first anniversary of the establishment of the Paris Commune. It was organised by "members of the International, the Democrats of London, and the Refugees of the Commune". The following resolutions, drawn up by Marx, were passed:

1. "That this meeting assembled to celebrate the anniversary of the 18th March last, declares, that it looks upon the glorious movement inaugurated upon the 18th March 1871, as the dawn of the great social revolution which will for ever free the human race from class rule.
2. "That the incapacity and the crimes of the middle classes, extended all over Europe by their hatred against the working classes, have doomed old society no matter under what form of government – Monarchial or Republican.
3. "That the crusade of all governments against the International, and the terror of the murderers of Versailles as well as of their Prussian conquerors, attest the hollowness of their successes, and the presence of the threatening army of the proletariat of the whole world gathering in the rear its heroic vanguard crushed by the combined forces of Thiers and William of Prussia."[167]

It is hardly surprising that the whole-hearted support given by Marx and Engels to the revolutionary government in Paris – and the admission of exiled members of the Commune to the General Council of the International – should have shocked the majority of the trade union leaders in England. For some years Marx and Engels had tried to work with the trade union representatives on the General Council in the hope of converting them to socialism. Now the English members of the Council were drifting away. They refused to be associated with those who advocated atheism and republicanism and who condoned the shooting of hostages and the burning of the Tuileries. Industrial output was expanding while unemployment was falling at this time so that there were fewer strikes and fewer opportunities for the General Council to intervene in industrial disputes. So while Bebel, Liebknecht, Garibaldi and Bakunin on the Continent defended the Commune, most of the English trade union leaders were not prepared to support the Commune. Odger and Lucraft repudiated Marx's address on the Commune and resigned from the General Council of the International. When he gave up his post as secretary of the General Council in the summer of 1872 – after his quarrel with Engels – Hales complained that the General Council was "filled with distrust, mistrust and suspicion, and possessed nothing of an international spirit".[168]

In January 1870 Marx had declared that it would be a crime to let the trade union movement – "this great lever of proletarian revolution"[169] fall into purely English hands. In April 1870 he had written that "to hasten the social revolution in England is the most important object of the International Working Men's Association".[170] But his hold on the "lever of proletarian revolution" – never very firm – fell from his grasp in October 1870 when an independent Federal Council for English branches of the International was set up. Marx had little influence over it and his hold over the labour movement dwindled and eventually disappeared. It is clear from a letter which Jenny Marx wrote to Wilhelm Liebknecht that Marx was under a great strain – owing to overwork and financial worries – in the summer of 1872. She wrote: "You cannot imagine what we have had to go through here in London since the fall of the Commune". She complained of the "endless sorrows and distress", which had given Marx "no rest by day or by night".[171] Friedrich Lessner later recalled that, at this time, Marx's "household expenses kept on increasing, especially after the Commune". "In his house one could always meet a number of French emigrants who had to be accommodated and maintained."[172] Shortly before Jenny Marx had written to Liebknecht, Marx had told Danielson that it was his intention to withdraw from the International in September 1872.[173] It was in that month that Marx and Engels attended the congress of the International which was held at The Hague. There he castigated the English trade union leaders who were no longer prepared to listen to his advice. "When I denounced these fellows," he declared, "I knew that I was letting myself in for unpopularity, calumny etc., but such consequences have always been a matter of indifference to me."[174]

The English workers showed little sympathy for the exiles from Paris, who sought refuge in London from the terror of the reaction in France. In July 1871 the General Council of the International set up a refugees committee to help the émigrés. Marx and Engels, who remembered their own unhappy experiences as exiles in London in 1850, did what they could to help the refugees. At that time Marx wrote that "London is overrun with refugees, whom we have to look after".[175] In August 1871 Engels complained to the General Council that "the working class of England had behaved in a disgraceful manner; though the men of Paris had risked their lives, the working men of England had made no effort to sympathise with them or to assist them".[176] In February 1872 a deputation of refugees told the General Council that "the French government was landing men on the English shores every day with scarcely any clothes to wear and absolutely penniless, and the refugees here in London were in despair. They had no funds, and did not know what to do. The Council had collected money for them and had given them from £5 to £10 per week, until a week ago and now that had fallen off".[177] In April 1872 Engels wrote to T. C. Cuno: "We have more than a hundred helpless emigrés of the Paris Commune (*literally helpless*, for no people ever feel so helpless abroad as do the French) and what they did not eat up, we sent to a fine fellow in Cork, Ireland,[178] who founded the International there and was rewarded by being excommunicated by the priests and the bourgeoisie and ultimately ruined. We have no money left just now."[179]

At the end of 1872 Engels admitted that he and Marx had lost whatever influence they might have had over the labour movement in England. He bemoaned the fact that things were "shockingly bad in the movement here – worse than they ever were, as is to be expected with such industrial prosperity".[180] At the first conference of the English branches of the International, held in Nottingham in July 1872, it was resolved that the English Federal Council should correspond directly with other federal councils and not through the General Council. At the same time that Marx's influence over the trade union movement in England declined there was a violent clash between the supporters of Marx and the followers of Bakunin on the Continent. Abandoned by both the trade unionists and the anarchists Marx realised that the days of the International were numbered.

X. Bakunin and the International

Mikhail Bakunin,[181] who was largely responsible for the fatal split in the International, had a long career of revolutionary activity behind him. He had never practised any profession or earned a regular income, but had lived the life of a revolutionary vagabond. Born in 1814, Bakunin had spent his childhood on a country estate in Russia. He had attended the artillery school at St Petersburg, and had been gazetted as an ensign. As a young man he had been strongly influenced by Hegel's philosophy. He realised that the reactionary society in which he lived was stifling his intellectual development and like some other progressive Russians – Alexander Herzen and Ivan Turgenev, for example – he preferred exile abroad to life at home under the Czar.

In 1840 Bakunin went to Berlin where he fell under the spell of the Young Hegelians. Here he met Engels for the first time. In 1842 Bakunin wrote "a brilliant essay in the popular art of turning the respectable Hegel into a philosopher of revolution".[182] In 1844 in Paris he met Marx whom he admired for "his knowledge and for his passionate and earnest devotion to the cause of the proletariat". But Bakunin added that he and Marx never became friends. "Our temperament did not allow it."[183] On a brief visit to Brussels at the end of 1847 Bakunin once more met Marx and Engels. He was scornful of their efforts to foster revolution through the Democratic Federation and the Communist League and wrote to Georg Herwegh that Marx and his followers were "plotting their usual mischief". Bakunin condemned their "vanity, malice, squabbles, theoretical intolerance and practical cowardice". The Democratic Federation he dismissed as "the greatest humbug imaginable" and he accused Marx of "ruining the workers by making theorists of them".[184]

As soon as the Orleans monarchy fell in France in February 1848 Bakunin hastened to Paris to join the National Guard. When the flames of revolution spread to central Europe he was off to Breslau in the hope of taking part in a Polish rising. But the revolt never materialised and Bakunin moved on to Prague where he attended a congress of Slavs and agitated in favour of a movement to free the various Slav peoples from Russian and Austrian domination. Once more nothing was achieved. In the autumn of 1848 Bakunin was in Berlin where he again met Marx.[185] They did not see each other again until 1864.

Having failed to stir up either a Polish or a Czech rising, Bakunin turned his attention to the revolution in Germany. Marx later declared that "the only praiseworthy thing that can be reported about his activity during the revolution is his participation in the Dresden insurrection in May 1849".[186] Bakunin – like Richard Wagner – joined the defenders of the barricades who were supporting the Frankfurt constitution against the Prussian and Saxon troops which had been sent to restore order. The rising failed and Bakunin was arrested. Eight years elapsed before he was free again. He was imprisoned in Saxony before being handed over to the Austrians who, in turn, handed him over to the Russians. Eventually he was sent to Siberia. He escaped in 1861 and reached London safely. Engels wrote to Marx that he was delighted that "the poor devil" had gained his freedom.[187] In 1862 Marx told Engels that he had not seen Bakunin, although Bakunin was living in London.[188]

Bakunin did not settle in London. He wandered from country to country looking for opportunities to stir up trouble and ever ready to foment any revolution that seemed likely to occur. When the Poles were in revolt in 1863 a small legion of Polish exiles was recruited in Paris by Colonel Lapinski – described by Marx as "undoubtedly the most gifted Pole whom I have ever met, and a man of action to boot".[189] Bakunin attached himself to Lapinski's expedition. An English vessel was chartered to take the Poles to the island of Gothland in the Baltic but the captain refused to proceed any further than Copenhagen. A Danish crew took the ship to Malmö and there the venture ended as a hopeless fiasco. After a brief stay in Stockholm – where the local radicals gave a banquet in his honour – Bakunin moved on to Italy. Here he paid his respects to Garibaldi in Caprera and settled in Florence.

In November 1864 Bakunin was in London for a brief visit and bought a suit from the German tailor Friedrich Lessner, who was one of Marx's most faithful followers. When Marx heard from Lessner that Bakunin was in London he suggested that they should meet. The International had just been established and Marx may have hoped to enrol Bakunin as a recruiting agent on the Continent for the new association. On the following day Marx wrote to Engels: "I must say that I was very pleased with him – more so than on previous occasions." "On the whole I think that he is one of the few people who has not declined after 16 years but has progressed."[190] In 1870 in a letter to Bracke and the committee of the German social democrat party in Brunswick, Marx alleged that, when he saw Bakunin in 1864, he "took him into the Association, for which Bakunin promised to work to the best of his ability".[191] If this statement is correct, it is surprising that, in his letter to Engels (written so soon after the meeting) Marx should have failed to mention that Bakunin had joined the International.

Bakunin had no intention of devoting his energies to the expansion of the International. His autocratic temperament would not permit him to play second fiddle to Marx and he aspired to lead a revolutionary movement himself. His concept of revolution differed from that of Marx and Engels. They believed that the factory workers in advanced industrial countries like England would be the spearhead of revolution, while Bakunin assigned this *rôle* to the down-trodden peasants of underdeveloped countries like Russia, Italy, and Spain. Again, Marx and Engels considered that the era of cloak and dagger conspiracies was over, and that revolution should now be openly advocated by public associations like the International. But Bakunin believed that a successful revolution could be promoted only by a handful of dedicated militants organised in an underground movement and in 1865 he established a secret society in Florence called the "Brotherhood". He does not seem to have had much success as a revolutionary in Florence and in October 1865 he moved on to Naples, where he established another underground organisation called the International Brotherhood.

The objects of the International Brotherhood were set forth in Bakunin's *Revolutionary Catechism*, which has been described as "a critical turning point in the development of his political thought".[192] He now rejected nationalism as an agent of revolution and advocated "the radical destruction of all existing institutions" throughout the world. Centralised states should be replaced by small autonomous communes; religion should be replaced by atheism; and the right to inherit property should be abolished. Bakunin proposed that all classes should be equal and that "free marriage" should be allowed.[193] This was the doctrine of anarchism and Marx and Engels had no difficulty in dismissing it as fit only for "a children's primer". Engels denounced Bakunin's plans as "a potpourri of Proudhonism and communism" and explained that their fundamental error was to regard the state, instead of capitalism, as the main social evil, which should be abolished. Marx declared that Bakunin was "a man devoid of theoretical knowledge", whose ideas on politics and economics were "a hash superficially scraped together from the Right and the Left".[194]

In the autumn of 1867 Bakunin left Italy for Switzerland. He arrived in time to attend a peace congress which opened in Geneva on September 9. Invitations had been extended on a generous scale to "all friends of free democracy" so that many different opinions were represented at the congress. Marx was deeply suspicious of any new international organisation that might rival the International and he called the organisers of the Geneva Congress "peace windbags" and "asses".[195] He told the General Council that, in his opinion, any of its members who attended the Geneva peace congress should go as private individuals and not as official representatives of the International.[196] The General Council accepted this advice but the next congress of the International – held at Lausanne – did not. The following resolution was passed at Lausanne.

"Considering that the prime and principal cause of war is pauperism and lack of economic balance, that to eliminate wars it is not sufficient to disband standing armies, but it is also necessary to change the organisation of society to bring about a more just distribution of products, this Congress adheres to the League Congress provided the latter accept the above principles."[197]

By attending the peace congress at Geneva and by delivering one of the main speeches there, Bakunin was playing a new *rôle*. For some time he had been engaged in organising secret societies like the "Brotherhoods" in Italy, but now, as an avowed anarchist, he openly advocated revolution in his speeches and writings. His new image as a public figure, however, was a little tarnished since he continued to dabble in underground movements and dark conspiracies – some of which appear to have existed only in his fertile imagination. In his address to the peace congress Bakunin denounced the existing system of "centralised states" and advocated the establishment of a federal United States of Europe, which would be made up of communes, provinces and nations.

The Geneva congress set up a League of Peace and Freedom and Bakunin served on its executive committee. It was clear from the acrimonious debates at the congress that a wide gulf separated the right wing middle class pacifist delegates and the left wing radicals, socialists and revolutionaries. Bakunin tried to convert the committee to his own way of thinking and by the middle of 1868 he had achieved some success. The committee adopted a programme demanding the elimination of religion from political institutions, the founding of a federal United States of Europe; and the reorganisation of society so as to secure an "equitable division of wealth, labour, leisure, and education".[198]

The reference in the programme to the elimination of the proletariat suggested that – as far as the social question was concerned – Bakunin was drawing closer to Marx, who had often demanded the emancipation of the workers and the abolition of class rule. In the summer of 1868 Bakunin joined the "Romance Branch" of the International in Geneva. He hoped to persuade the League of Peace and the International to amalgamate and it was his ambition to become a leader of the enlarged organisation. He endeavoured to secure the co-operation of J. P. Becker who was a friend of Marx and an influential member of the International in Switzerland. In August 1868 the committee of the League of Peace voted in favour of making an alliance with the International. But in September the congress of the International, meeting in Brussels, rejected the proposed alliance and invited members of the League of Peace to join one of the branches of the International.[199] At the second congress of the League of Peace, held shortly afterwards, Bakunin and 14 of his followers resigned when it became clear that they were in a small minority and could not hope to dominate the proceedings.

In September 1868 when Bakunin left the League of Peace, he was publicly pledged to support the International which he had recently joined. But it never occurred to him simply to serve the association as a member of its Geneva branch. He yearned to be at the heart of a revolutionary movement and he craved for a position of leadership in the International. He decided to challenge what he chose to regard as the autocratic powers of the General Council and he demanded a greater measure of autonomy for the local branches. He seems to have hoped to transfer the General

Council from England to Switzerland and to achieve a dominant position in the International for himself. On leaving the League of Peace he immediately established a new organisation called the International Social Democratic Alliance. At first its only members were a handful of Bakunin's friends. Bakunin declared that members of the Alliance would also be members of the International. He saw the Alliance as a ginger group which would train dedicated political missionaries to carry the gospel of the International to the ends of the earth. The headquarters of the Alliance was in Geneva where Bakunin co-opted five members of the local branch of the International to serve on his executive committee. The most important was J. P. Becker, an old friend of Marx and Engels and the leader of the International in Switzerland and parts of Germany. But Becker did not appreciate Bakunin's far-reaching aims.

At first Marx could not believe that the Alliance – "this shit"[200] – posed a serious threat to the International. Marx regarded Bakunin as a charlatan who was pretending to lead a powerful revolutionary organisation whereas, in fact, the only support that the Alliance enjoyed came from a tiny clique of his supporters. But Marx received a rude awakening on December 15, 1868 at a meeting of the General Council when a letter from J. P. Becker was received. Becker stated that an International Alliance of Social Democracy had been founded in Switzerland and it had joined the International.[201] The General Council asked Marx to draw up a declaration repudiating the "interloping society".[202] After the meeting Marx went home in a state of considerable agitation.[203] He worked far into the night making critical marginal notes on the programme of the Alliance,[204] which he dismissed as a "pure farce".[205] Then he wrote a letter to Engels asking for his advice. Marx denounced Bakunin for "being so condescending as to wish to take the workers' movement under *Russian* leadership". Marx claimed that he had known all about Bakunin's intrigues but had refrained from mounting a counter-attack out of consideration for his old friend Becker, who had always been a loyal supporter of the International. Marx considered that Becker, "whose propagandist zeal at times runs away with his head",[206] had been an innocent victim of Bakunin's machinations. But now that Bakunin was making a serious bid to gain for himself a position of influence in the International, Marx declared that "our association cannot commit suicide to oblige old Becker".[207]

In his reply Engels dismissed the Alliance as a "Russian intrigue" and a "swindle" with a programme that was beneath contempt. He considered that it would do more harm than good to attack Bakunin – "you must never lose your temper with a

Russian" – and he advised Marx to tell the Alliance politely that it could not join the International but that its members could belong to both organisations. In any case Engels thought that the Alliance was "stillborn" and had no hope of survival.[208] Marx agreed with this assessment of the situation and wrote that he had "handled the affair in a tactful manner – just as you advised".[209] On December 22, 1868 Marx wrote a public declaration, on behalf of the General Council, full of "thoroughly reasoned" arguments,[210] explaining why the Alliance could not be admitted to the International.[211]

There the matter rested for over two months. In that period Bakunin strengthened his position in Switzerland by securing control over the "Romance Federation", which was a union of 30 French speaking branches of the International. It published a journal called L'Égalité. At the conference in Geneva at which this federation was established Bakunin met James Guillaume, a young schoolmaster from Le Locle, who became his devoted disciple. Guillaume's propaganda among the radical workers of the Swiss Jura – and the success of his journal Progrès – gave Bakunin a firm foothold in this district. And early in 1869 Bakunin was boasting that his Alliance had gained more converts in Italy and Spain in a few weeks than the International had gained in four years.[212]

Despite these successes Bakunin was now ready to accept the ruling of the General Council and to agree to the demise of the Alliance. A new approach was made to the International at the end of February 1869. Marx sent the letter to Engels for his observations.[213] Engels replied that Bakunin had made a "complete retreat". He was glad to learn that Marx proposed to ask the Alliance for details of its membership. This, he thought, would be like pouring "a bucket of cold water over their gabbling heads".[214]

On behalf of the General Council Marx wrote to the Alliance on March 9, 1869. He noted that it was proposed to wind up the Alliance as an independent organisation and he agreed that branches of the Alliance might be enrolled as branches of the International provided that the phrase "equalisation of classes" (in the programmes of such branches) was changed to "abolition of classes".[215] In April 1869 the Geneva section of the Alliance changed its statutes to meet Marx's condition and it became a branch of the International. In June the central bureau of the Alliance formally announced its own dissolution and on July 27 the General Council admitted the Geneva branch to the International.[216] Although Bakunin and his followers had now publicly declared that the Alliance was dissolved, its organisation survived and it continued to propagate Bakunin's views in the branches of the International which it controlled. Moreover the secret "Alliance" – Bakunin's most faithful disciples – also survived as an underground movement. Marx and Engels had gained a hollow victory. They had forced the Alliance to alter its statutes and to announce its dissolution. But Bakunin now controlled an active revolutionary movement within the International which he was still determined to dominate. Engels had no illusions concerning Bakunin's ambitions at this time. Only a few days after the Geneva branch of the Alliance was admitted to the International he wrote: "It is quite clear that fatty Bakunin is behind all this." "If this damned Russian really thinks that he can secure the leadership of the workers' movement then the time has really come when he should be firmly put in his place."[217]

By September 1869 Bakunin was ready to challenge the authority of the General Council. Marx declared that Bakunin, who was "in his element as an intriguer",[218] hoped to secure "the transformation of the International into his personal instrument".[219] Bakunin attended the fourth congress of the International which was held at Basel. Since Marx was absent there was no personal confrontation between the two rivals who both aimed at controlling the General Council. Although he could count on only about a dozen votes, Bakunin was confident that his personality and powers of oratory would sway the delegates in whatever direction he chose. The clash between the General Council and Bakunin's followers came over a motion approving the abolition of the right of inheritance. Eccarius submitted a report, written by Marx on behalf of the General Council, which stated that it was more important to abolish private property than the right of inheritance. If property were nationalised – and the congress had just resolved to support state ownership in land – then the question of inheritance would not arise.[220] Bakunin's eloquent attack upon Marx's report secured its rejection. But his own resolution on inheritance was also defeated. Thus the congress failed to reach a decision on this vexed question. Bakunin however had the satisfaction of seeing the congress reject a proposal submitted by the General Council with Marx's express approval. No wonder that the unhappy Eccarius declared that "Marx will be extremely displeased".[221]

For two years after the Basel congress Marx and Bakunin were locked in a struggle for mastery over the International. When their rivalry was at its height at the end of 1871 Engels wrote to Lafargue: "I shall be very glad when this whole business is finished once and for all. You cannot imagine how much work, correspondence etc., it has involved for us. Mohr (Marx), Serraillier and I have been unable to attend to anything else for weeks."[222] A few months later he admitted that "the Bakunist rubbish cannot be cleared away in one day; it is quite enough that the process of clearing it out has at last begun in good earnest".[223] At first Bakunin delegated to his lieutenants the task of harrying Marx and the General Council. Instead of taking the initiative and following up the advantage gained at Basel, he moved to Locarno in the hope of enjoying "a year of silent, studious and lucrative retirement".[224]

Left to their own devices, Bakunin's followers in Geneva and Le Locle launched a vitriolic press campaign against the General Council. In one article after another in *L'Égalité* and *Le Progrès* the General Council was accused of "neglecting extremely important matters", such as the production of a bulletin. The General Council was attacked for failing to adopt a definite policy with regard to the rival socialist parties in Germany and for neglecting to set up a federal council for England so as to give itself more time for the important task of keeping in contact with all branches of the International. Marx rightly attributed these attacks to members of Bakunin's Alliance who still considered that it was "their special mission to usurp the supreme authority of the International Association". In January 1870 he answered the criticisms of the two newspapers in a memorandum which the General Council sent to the Federal Council of Romance Switzerland. Marx forwarded copies of this memorandum – with a covering letter entitled "Confidential Information" – to all branches of the Association.[225]

XI. The International in Spain

In 1870 Bakunin had a firm base in Geneva and in the Swiss Jura for his manoeuvres against Marx. His attempts to extend his influence elsewhere had their greatest success in Italy and Spain where, as Marx observed, "the real conditions for the workers' movement are as yet little developed".[226] These were poor backward countries in which there was a sharp contrast between the wealth of the landowners and the Church and the poverty of the peasants and the artisans. In both states the instability of the government and the corruption of its officials gave little hope that the situation would improve. Militant extremists could readily find men who were prepared to support any political movement that offered a possibility of removing the evils of poverty and oppression. And both countries had a long tradition of organising revolution through underground movements. In Italy the *carbonari* had played its part in preparing the way for the risings of 1848. In Spain in 1871 there was a secret society called *el Tiro Nacional*. Paul Lafargue, in a letter to Engels, declared that he had come across its members in all the villages that he had visited. "It is a veritable army, every member must have at his disposal a musket, a certain quantity of powder and bullets and must obey the orders of the Madrid *directorio*."[227] Bakunin's love of underground movements stood him in good stead in Italy and Spain where he could hope to infiltrate and eventually control existing secret revolutionary organisations. By appointing him corresponding secretary for these countries, the General Council gave Engels the task of stopping the advance of Bakunin's doctrines and of keeping the workers' organisations loyal to the International. Engels complained of having "to write long letters, one after another in Italian and Spanish, two languages I barely understand".[228]

When Queen Isabella of Spain was forced to abdicate in 1868, Bakunin – writing on behalf of the Geneva branches of the International – sent an address to the Spanish workers appealing to them to follow up the political revolution with an economic revolution.[229] In the autumn of 1868, after visiting Bakunin in Locarno, Guiseppi Fanelli[230] – a veteran of the rising in Lombardy in 1848 – went to Spain, where in co-operation with André Sastelica, he founded branches of the International in Barcelona and Madrid. In 1869 the Spanish branches were represented at the Basel congress of the International by G. Sentiñón and Pellicer. Bakunin took the opportunity to enrol them in the Geneva section of his Alliance and in his secret society as well. They subsequently persuaded some of their friends in the International to join them in establishing a branch of the secret Alliance in Barcelona. By July 1871 the International had expanded sufficiently in Spain to warrant the calling of a national conference in Barcelona. The conference – dominated by Bakunin's supporters – set up a Spanish Federal Council; appointed Francisco Mora as general secretary; and established a journal called *La Federacion*.

In August 1871 the Spanish Federal Council, fearing prosecution by the government, fled to Lisbon,[231] but in the following month it was found possible to hold a second conference of the Spanish branches of the International in Valencia. Anselmo Lorenzo was elected to represent the Spanish branches at a conference of the International in London. He later recalled that he had been welcomed in London by Marx who had expressed "great satisfaction with what we had achieved in Spain".[232]

Sagasta, the Spanish Minister for Home Affairs, issued a decree in January 1872 dissolving the branches of the International but the police were lax in enforcing the decree. At this time Bakunin explained to G. T. Morago, one of his staunchest supporters, how he planned to gain control over the International. By April 1870

Morago had become "the moving spirit of the Alliance in Spain".[233]

Meanwhile Paul Lafargue, forced to leave France after the fall of the Paris Commune, had been working in Spain as Marx's emissary. His letters to Engels show how – in co-operation with Francisco Mora and Pablo Iglesias – he tried to combat Morago's propaganda on behalf of the Alliance.[234] Engels and Lafargue exaggerated their achievements in Spain. In December 1871 Engels boasted that the "internal struggles of the Spanish International" had been "finally settled in our favour";[235] in February 1872 he told Becker that he was quite confident of success in Spain;[236] and in March 1872 he assured Laura Lafargue that, owing to her husband's efforts, the Marxist cause had gained "victory all along the line".[237]

Despite the ban on their activities, the Spanish branches of the International held their third conference in Saragossa in April 1872. In a message to the conference the General Council congratulated the Spanish branches on having made the International "a real force in Spain".[238] The conference was disbanded by the authorities but was left in peace when it continued to meet in private. Lafargue claimed that the Marxists had vanquished Bakunin's followers.[239] Engels also asserted that at Saragossa "our people won a victory over the Bakunists".[240] The very opposite was true. Although the conference had rejected some Bakunist resolutions it had elected a new Spanish Federal Council which was dominated by Bakunin's followers. Two leading supporters of Marx – Anselmo Lorenzo and Francisco Mora – were no longer members of the Council. Engels admitted at this time that in Catalonia – Spain's only industrial province – the Bakunists controlled the International and its journal La Federacion.[241]

In July 1872 Marx and Engels, on behalf of the General Council, wrote to the Spanish branches that the Council held proofs of the existence in Spain of "a secret society called the Alliance of Social Democracy". The activities of the Alliance were denounced as "treason against our association".[242] Marx's followers now broke away from the Spanish Federation and their new Madrid Federation was recognised by the General Council. Engels denounced the old Federal Council because many of its members belonged to "a secret society hostile to the International". Lafargue's mission had failed because when he left Spain at the end of July 1872 the International was split into hostile factions and only a small minority of the branches supported the General Council in London. The politically conscious workers had found the doctrines of Bakunin and Proudhon more palatable than those of Marx. Engels could not derive much satisfaction from the contemplation of his work as corresponding secretary for Spain.

XII. The International in Italy

Engels was equally unsuccessful in Italy, where Bakunin proved to be as dangerous an enemy as in Spain.[243] Bakunin was favourably placed to promote his revolutionary agitation, since he had lived in Florence and Naples and had "many personal friends in Italy",[244] some of whom had been enrolled in his secret societies. From the shores of Lake Maggiore he kept in touch with his followers. Engels, on the other hand, had few reliable agents in Italy. In Turin, Carlo Terzagli, the editor of *Proletariato Italiano*, turned out to be a police informer. In Milan the Austrian engineer Theodor Cuno – organiser of a workers' union and editor of *Il Martello* – was betrayed to the police by supporters of Bakunin and was expelled from Italy.[245] In Naples Engels corresponded with Carlo Cafiero, a well-to-do young man whom he had met in London.[246] Engels considered Cafiero – who had reorganised the Naples section of the International in 1871 – to be "a good fellow" but "weak". He told Laura Lafargue in March 1872 that he would cease to write to Cafiero "if he doesn't improve soon".[247] Two months later Cafiero visited Bakunin and fell completely under his spell. On June 12, 1872 he wrote to Engels that he had been converted to Bakunin's views.[248]

Numerous associations of workers had flourished in Italy in the 1850s and 1860s – trade societies, ex-servicemen's associations, political clubs, friendly societies and social clubs. Many were inspired by Mazzini and Garibaldi and supported the movement for Italian unification and independence. At first the International held few attractions for the Italian workers. In 1871, however, the rise and fall of the commune in Paris gave the supporters of the International an opportunity to launch a recruiting campaign in Italy. Engels declared that the Italian workers were deserting Mazzini who had condemned the excesses of the Commune and were now prepared to follow supporters of the Commune such as Garibaldi, Bakunin and Marx.

Although they were attacked by the Pope[249] and by Mazzini[250] – and proscribed by the government[251] – many branches of the International were set up in Italy. A police report estimated the membership of the association at nearly 32,500 in 1872. Engels told the General Council in November 1871 that the International was making "immense strides" in Italy.[252] At the same time he wrote to Carmelo Palladini that "the spontaneous movement of the proletarian masses in support of our Association has been more pronounced and more enthusiastic in Italy than anywhere else".[253]

Engels' satisfaction with the situation in Italy was shortlived. By January 1872 he realised that he was fighting a losing battle for he admitted that in Italy "the Bakunists are for the present the masters of the situation within the International".[254] At this time Vitale Regis,[255] a member of the Italian section of the International in London, visited Switzerland and Italy on behalf of the General Council. He reported that Bakunin's agents were very active in northern Italy and he warned Engels that Terzaghi was not to be trusted.[256] In March 1872 Engels complained to Laura Lafargue that "in Italy the journalists, lawyers and doctors have pushed themselves so much to the fore that up to now we have never been able to come in direct contact with the workers".[257] But he claimed that "the teachings of the pretended leaders – doctors, lawyers, journalists – had not any influence upon the real working class".[258] In May 1872 he wrote that "in Italy the attempts of the aristocracy and middle class to put themselves forward as the true representatives of the working class continued with unabated impudence".[259] In June 1872 Engels told Cuno that "the Italians must gain a little more experience and must learn how absurd it is for so backward a people of peasants to presume to tell the workers in great industrial states how to gain their freedom".[260]

Meanwhile, when Mazzini died in March 1872, many of his followers found a new leader in Bakunin, who "became the oracle of the Italian proletariat".[261] Engels's discomfiture was complete when Cafiero succeeded in uniting most of the branches of the International in Italy in a single federation. At a conference held in August 1872 at Rimini nearly all the branches broke off relations with the General Council.[262] They decided to boycott the forthcoming congress of the International at The Hague. Instead they proposed to attend a conference at Neuchâtel that was being organised by Bakunin's supporters in Switzerland. Only four Italian branches – Rome, Milan, Turin and Ferrara – remained faithful to the General Council. Bakunin was now virtually master of the International in Italy.

XIII. The Hague Congress, 1872

As Bakunin's followers gained more and more ground – particularly in Spain and Italy – Marx and Engels decided to hit back and to expel those who persistently challenged the authority of the General Council. They made their preparations well in advance

of the congress of the International which was held at The Hague
in 1872. Since the Franco–Prussian war had prevented the holding
of a public congress in 1870 or in 1871, the General Council called
a private conference of branch delegates in London instead. It
met between September 17 and 23 1871. As far as possible
Bakunin's followers – such as the Romance Federation in the Jura
district – were excluded. Firmly guided by Engels – who acted as
chairman – the London conference resolved:

> "That the existing branches and societies shall . . . no longer be
> allowed to designate themselves by sectarian names such as Positi-
> vists, Mutualists, Collectivists, Communists etc., or to form separist
> bodies under the names of sections of propaganda, Alliance of
> Democratic Socialism etc., pretending to accomplish special missions
> distinct from the common purposes of the Association."[263]

James Guillaume promptly organised a meeting of Bakunin's
followers in Switzerland as a counterblast to the recent conference
in London. This was held at Sonvillier in November 1871. The
conference demanded the immediate calling of a public congress
of the International and attacked what it regarded as the autocracy
of the General Council in London. The "Sonvillier Circular",
signed by 16 delegates, declared that:

> "If there is an undeniable fact attested a thousand times by exper-
> ience, it is the corrupting effect of authority on those in whose
> hands it is placed . . . The functions of members of the General
> Council have come to be regarded as the private property of a few
> individuals . . . They have become in their own eyes a sort of
> government; and it was natural that their own particular ideas
> should seem to them to be the official and only authorised doctrine
> of the Association, while divergent ideas expressed by other groups
> seem no longer a legitimate expression of opinion equal in value to
> their own, but a veritable heresy."

The "Sonvillier Circular" demanded that the General Council
should be stripped of the powers that it had exercised in the past
and should become "a simple office for correspondence and
statistics".[264]

Marx and Engels replied to the "Sonvillier Circular" in a
pamphlet entitled "Fictitious Splits in the International" which
was approved by the General Council on March 5, 1872 and subsequently published in Geneva. The title of the pamphlet was a
curious one since the splits in the International far from being
fictitious were very real. In this circular to branches of the International Marx and Engels gave a detailed account – from their
point of view – of Bakunin's efforts to gain control over the Inter-

national. They denounced Bakunin as an anarchist who had "taken nothing from the socialist system except a set of slogans". They concluded their attack on Bakunin's Alliance by declaring that

"All socialists see anarchy as the following programme: once the aim of the proletarian movement, i.e. abolition of classes is attained, the power of the state, which serves to keep the great majority of producers in bondage to a very small exploiter minority, disappears, and the functions of government become simple administrative functions. The Alliance draws an entirely different picture. It proclaims anarchy in proletarian ranks as the most infallible means of breaking the powerful concentration of social and political forces in the hands of the exploiters. Under this pretext, it asks the International, at a time when the old world is seeking a way of crushing it, to replace its organisation with anarchy."[265]

While this war of words was proceeding, Marx and Engels prepared their plan of campaign for the forthcoming public congress of the International at The Hague. Their object was to amass enough evidence against Bakunin to ensure his expulsion from the International. From his correspondents in Spain and Italy – particularly from Paul Lafargue – Engels obtained proofs of the activities of the Alliance through which Bakunin was plotting to undermine the authority of the General Council. Marx, for his part, sought to discredit Bakunin by laying his hands on a letter written by Sergei Nechaev to Lyubavin. Bakunin had agreed to translate the first volume of *Das Kapital* into Russian and Lyubavin had secured for him an advance of 300 roubles from a St. Petersburg publisher. Bakunin had translated only a small part of the book when he dropped the project. But he failed to return the 300 roubles. Nechaev wrote a letter to Lyubavin threatening him with all sorts of unpleasant consequences if he tried to recover the 300 roubles. Marx had recently been in correspondence with a Russian student named N. F. Danielson, who had asked to see any amendments to the first volume of *Das Kapital* which Marx proposed to make for the Russian translation. In August 1872 Marx asked Danielson to borrow Nechaev's letter from Lyubavin. Danielson succeeded in doing so and the compromising letter came into Marx's hands.

The last congress of the International met on September 2, 1872 in a "common dancing hall" – the Concordia – in the Lombardstraat at The Hague. For the first time Marx and Engels put in an appearance at a public congress of the International. They knew that the votes of the German and French delegates alone would give them a comfortable majority. Theodor Cuno, who met Engels for the first time at The Hague, described him as "a tall bony man with sharp cut features, long, sandy whiskers, ruddy complexion, and little blue eyes. His manner of moving and speaking is quick, determined and convinces the observer that the man knows exactly what he wants and what will be the consequences of his words and action. In conversation with him one learns something new with every sentence he utters".[266]

The congress appointed a committee to examine the charges brought by Marx and Engels against Bakunin and his followers. The committee reported that, on the evidence of documents procured by Lafargue, it was clear that a secret society had existed within the International in Spain. And when Marx read Nechaev's letter to Lyubavin, the committee was satisfied that "Bakunin had used fraudulent measures for the purpose of appropriating all or part of another man's wealth – which constitutes fraud – and further, in order to avoid fulfilling his engagements, had by himself or through his agents had recourse to menaces".[267] On receiving the committee's report the congress expelled Bakunin and his henchman Guillaume from the International.

Although Marx and Engels had got their way it was a hollow victory since the Congress not only banished Bakunin but it banished the General Council as well. For some time Marx had been determined to lay down the burden of trying to run the International and to keep its divergent elements together. His health was deteriorating under the strain. So he decided to secure the removal of the General Council to a place as far away from London as possible – just as in 1850 he had secured the transfer of the central committee of the Communist League from London to Cologne. The proposal to transfer the seat of the General Council from London to New York – supported by Marx, Engels and nine other members of the General Council – was accepted by the congress at The Hague on September 6, 1871 by a narrow majority. Marx hoped that the new General Council would be free from both right wing and left wing pressure. Neither the English trade union leaders nor the followers of Bakunin were likely to have any influence over a General Council meeting in New York. But the new General Council survived for only two years. When Sorge, its general secretary, resigned in 1874 – as branches of the International in America were quarrelling among themselves – Engels wrote that now "the old International is entirely wound up".[268]

For two years Engels had worked hard to relieve Marx of some of his responsibilities in connection with the International. He had regularly attended meetings of the General Council and had undertaken a heavy correspondence on its behalf. But it had not been a very successful phase of Engels's career. His tactlessness had helped to alienate Hales and other trade union leaders and he had failed to prevent Bakunin from dominating the International in Spain and Italy.

NOTES

1 For documents on Karl Marx and the First International see *Karl Marx und die Gründung der I. International. Dokumente und Materialen* (1964).

2 F. Engels to Karl Marx, February 13, 1851 in *Gesamtausgabe*, Part III, Vol. 1, p. 148.

3 Karl Marx to F. Engels, November 4, 1864 in *Gesamtausgabe*, Part III, Vol. 3, p. 196.

4 Karl Marx to F. Engels, May 1, 1865 in *Gesamtausgabe*, Part III, Vol. 3, p. 263.

5 F. Engels to A. Sorge, September 12 and 17, 1874 in Karl Marx and F. Engels, *Letters to Americans, 1848–95* (1963).

6 Karl Marx to Dr Kugelmann, February 23, 1865 in Karl Marx, *Letters to Dr Kugelmann*, p. 31.

7 Karl Marx, "The General Council of the Working Men's International Association to the Federal Council of Romance Switzerland" (January 1, 1870) in *The General Council of the First International: Minutes*, Vol. 3, 1868–70 (Progress Publishers, Moscow), pp. 401–2.

8 F. Engels to Karl Marx, May 12, 1865 in *Gesamtausgabe*, Part III, Vol. 3, p. 270.

9 Karl Marx to F. Engels, February 13, 1865 in *Gesamtausgabe*, Part III, Vol. 3, p. 237.

10 Karl Marx to F. Engels, May 9, 1865 in *Gesamtausgabe*, Part III, Vol. 3, p. 268. In 1868 P. Shorrocks wrote to the General Council of the International from Manchester that the local workers had "little faith in London". But he offered to "endeavour to get adhesion to the International" (*The General Council of the First International: Minutes*, Vol. 2, 1866–8 (February 26, 1868), p. 194).

11 Frank Hall, *A Northern Pioneer. The Story of J. R. Lancashire* (1927), p. 116 and pp. 134–5.

12 F. Engels to Karl Marx, November 7, 1864 in *Gesamtausgabe*, Part III, Vol. 3, p. 200.

13 F. Engels to Karl Marx, May 3, 1865 in *Gesamtausgabe*, Part III, Vol. 3, p. 265.

14 F. Engels to J. Weydemeyer, March 10, 1865 in Karl Marx and F. Engels, *Letters to Americans, 1848–95* (1963), p. 71.

15 Karl Marx to F. Engels, November 4, 1864 in *Gesamtausgabe*, Part III, Vol. 3, pp. 194–9.

16 For George Odger see the *Bookbinders' Trade Circular*, April 28, 1877.

17 For W. Randall Cremer see H. Evans, *Sir Randall Cremer. His Life and Work* (1909).

18 Karl Marx to J. Weydemeyer, November 29, 1864 in Karl Marx and F. Engels, *Letters to Americans, 1848–95* (1963), p. 65.

19 Karl Marx to Dr Kugelmann, November 29, 1864 in Karl Marx, *Letters to Dr Kugelmann*, p. 62.

20 J. G. Eccarius, "Die Schneiderei in London . . ." in the *Neue Rheinische Zeitung. Politisch-ökonomische Revue*, Heft 5–6 (May–October

1850): new edition with introduction by Karl Bittel, 1955, pp. 293–303.

21 W. Randall Cremer to Karl Marx, September 28, 1864 in Robert Payne, *Marx* (1968), p. 364.

22 Karl Marx to J. Weydemeyer, November 29, 1864 in Karl Marx and F. Engels, *Letters to Americans, 1848–95* (1963), p. 65.

23 *The General Council of the First International: Minutes*, Vol. 5, 1871–2 (April 16, 1872), p. 153.

24 *The General Council of the First International: Minutes*, Vol. 5, 1871–2 (July 2, 1872), p. 243.

25 S. P. Orth, *Socialism and Social Democracy in Europe* (1913), p. 68.

26 H. Collins, "The International and the British Labour Movement. Origin of the International in England" in *Labour History*. Bulletin No. 9, Autumn 1964, p. 35.

27 Major Luigi Wolff, a follower of Mazzini, had been Garibaldi's Adjutant. In 1871 he was exposed as an informer in the pay of Napoleon III.

28 Le Lubez was expelled from the General Council of the International in 1866.

29 John Weston, a carpenter, was a former disciple of Robert Owen.

30 *The General Council of the First International: Minutes*, Vol. 1, 1864–6 (October 18, 1864), p. 42.

31 Karl Marx to F. Engels, November 4, 1864 in *Gesamtausgabe*, Part III, Vol. 3, pp. 198–9 and *The General Council of the First International: Minutes*, Vol. 1, 1864–6 (November 1, 1864), pp. 43–4.

32 Karl Marx, "Inaugural Address of the Working Men's International Association in *The General Council of the First International: Minutes*, Vol. 1, 1864–6, pp. 277–89.

33 Werner Sombart, *Socialism and the Social Movement* (1909), p. 180.

34 Edmund Wilson, *To the Finland Station* (Fontana Library, 1960), p. 266.

35 G. Howell to W. Morrison, April 23, 1872 (Howell Collection: Bishopgate Institution, London). See also George Howell, "The History of the International Association" in the *Nineteenth Century*, July 1878, pp. 26–7 and F. M. Leventhal, *Respectable Radical. George Howell and Victorian Working Class Politics* (1971), p. 53.

36 Karl Marx to Dr Kugelmann, October 13, 1866 in Karl Marx, *Letters to Dr Kugelmann*, p. 42.

37 Karl Marx to Dr Kugelmann, March 6 and 17, 1868 in Karl Marx, *Letters to Dr Kugelmann*, pp. 64–5.

38 Karl Marx to Dr Kugelmann, September 14, 1870 in Karl Marx, *Letters to Dr Kugelmann*, p. 113.

39 Schapper had quarrelled with Marx and Engels in 1852 but had returned to the orthodox communist fold six years later.

40 Georg Löchner was a member of the General Council of the International between 1864 and 1867 and between 1871 and 1872.

41 Eugène Dupont moved from London to Manchester in 1870.

42 Hermann Jung ceased to support Marx's policy with regard to the International after the congress held at The Hague in 1872.

43 Werner Sombart, *Socialism and the Social Movement* (1909), p. 180.

44 Karl Marx to Siegfried Meyer, April 30, 1867 in Karl Marx and F. Engels, *Letters to Americans, 1848–95* (1963), pp. 73–6.

45 Karl Marx to F. Engels, September 11, 1867 in *Gesamtausgabe*, Part III, Vol. 3, p. 420.

46 F. Engels to Adolf Sorge, September 12 and 17, 1874 in Karl Marx and F. Engels, *Letters to Americans, 1848–95* (1963), p. 114.

47 *The General Council of the First International: Minutes*, Vol. 1, 1864–6 (Foreign Languages Publishing House, Moscow): Central Council meeting of November 29, 1864, pp. 51–4. For the reply from Charles Francis Adams (the American Ambassador in London) see pp. 68–9.

48 *The General Council of the First International: Minutes*, Vol. 4, 1870–1 (Foreign Languages Publishing House, Moscow): General Council meeting of May 30, 1871, pp. 356–412. The Address was published in London as a pamphlet (*The Civil War in France*) in 1871.

49 Karl Marx, *The Civil War in France*, 1871 (Foreign Languages Publishing House, Moscow): introduction by F. Engels to the third German edition of 1891, p. 7.

50 F. Engels, "What have the Working Classes to do with Poland?" in *The Commonwealth*, March 24 and 31, and May 5, 1866.

51 F. Engels, "Report on the Miners' Gilds in the Coalfields of Saxony" in *The General Council of the First International: Minutes*, Vol. 3, 1868–70 (Foreign Languages Publishing House, Moscow), pp. 390–7: see also the *Bee Hive*, February 27, 1869 and *Der Social Demokrat*, March 17, 1869.

52 Karl Marx to F. Engels, May 20, 1865 in *Gesamtausgabe*, Part III, Vol. 3, p. 272.

53 Karl Marx, *Wages, Price and Profit* (1898: new edition – Progress Publishers, Moscow – 1970).

54 Karl Marx to F. Engels, May 20, 1865 in *Gesamtausgabe*, Part III, Vol. 3, p. 272.

55 Karl Marx, *Wages, Price and Profit* (Progress Publishers, Moscow, 1970), p. 55.

56 Karl Marx to Dr Kugelmann, January 15, 1866 in Karl Marx, *Letters to Dr Kugelmann*, p. 33.

57 F. Engels, "Trade Unions" in *The Labour Standard*, May 28, 1881 and in F. Engels, *The British Labour Movement* (1934), p. 18.

58 Quoted by Henry Collins, "The International and the British Labour Movement. Origin of the International in England" in *Labour History*, Bulletin No. 9, Autumn 1964, p. 34.

59 For the First International in England see H. J. Collins and C. Abramsky, *Karl Marx and the British Labour Movement . . .* (1965); H. J. Collins, "The English Branches of the International" in Briggs and Saville, *Essays in Labour History* (1967); H. J. Collins, "The International and the British Labour Movement. Origin of the International in England" in *Labour History*, Bulletin No. 9, *Autumn* 1964; and R. Harrison, *Before the Socialists: Studies in Labour and Politics, 1861–81* (1965).

60 *The General Council of the First International: Minutes*, Vol. 4, 1870–1 (August 8, 1871), p. 254.

61 *The General Council of the First International: Minutes*, Vol. 3, 1868–70 (October 5, 1869), p. 166.

62 H. J. Collins, "The International and the British Labour Movement. Origin of the International in England" in *Labour History*, Bulletin No. 9, Autumn 1964, p. 27.

63 *Organisation and Rules of Trade Unions. First Report* (Parliamentary Papers, XXXII, 1867), Questions 993–6.

64 *The General Council of the First International: Minutes*, Vol. 3, 1868–70 (October 26, 1869), p. 172.

65 E. H. Carr, *Michael Bakunin* (1937), pp. 358–60.

66 Hales was referring to "bona fide members in England who have paid subscriptions": see a speech by Henry Bruce (Lord Aberdare), the Home Secretary, in the House of Commons on April 12, 1872 (*Hansard*, Vol. 210, 1872, col. 1183). For Jung's estimate see *L'Echo de Verviers*, February 20, 1866 and *The General Council of the First International: Minutes*, Vol. 1, 1864–6, p. 359.

67 *Report of the Conference of Trades Delegates of the United Kingdom held in . . . Sheffield . . . in 1866 . . .* (Sheffield, 1866), p. 72.

68 *The General Council of the First International: Minutes*, Vol. 3, 1868–70. (August 31, 1869), p. 151.

69 *The Bee Hive*, September 14, 1867 and *The General Council of the First International: Minutes*, Vol. 2, 1866–8. The non-trade union affiliated societies were the German Workers Educational Association, the French branch, the Polish Exiles; and the National Reform League.

70 *The United Kingdom First Annual Trades Union Directory* (1861: reprinted 1968) gave a list of 2,154 trade unions organisations (i.e. trade unions or branches of trade unions) in 405 towns. In 1871 the 44 principal trade unions in Great Britain had 224,000 members: see M. G. Mulhall, *The Dictionary of Statistics* (1899), p. 570.

71 In 1868 the trade unions which sent delegates to the first Trade Union Congress had a membership of 118,000 (M. G. Mulhall, *The The Dictionary of Statistics* (1899), p. 813).

72 *The Times*, January 9, 1867 and *The General Council of the First International: Minutes*, Vol. 2, 1866–8, pp. 90–1.

73 Sidney and Beatrice Webb, *The History of Trade Unionism* (1919), p. 236 (note).

74 In the financial year ending August 31, 1867 the General Council of the International had an income of £63 15s 8½d including contributions of affiliated bodies (£15 15s 10½d) and individual members (£9 18s 7d) and a loan of £2 10s 0d. The General Council had 9s 9d in hand. The balance sheet is given in *The General Council of the First International: Minutes*, Vol. 2, 1866–8, p. 311 and in *The Bee Hive*, September 21, 1867.

75 *The General Council of the First International: Minutes*, Vol. 1, 1864–6 (Foreign Languages Publishing House, Moscow): meeting of the Standing Committee with the Continental Delegates, London, September 25, 1865, p. 232.

76 *The General Council of the First International: Minutes*, Vol. 1, 1864–6, p. 234.

77 For syndicalism in France see Paul Louis, *Histoire du mouvement syndical en France* (1920).

78 Karl Marx to Dr Kugelmann, October 9, 1866 in Karl Marx, *Letters to Dr Kugelmann*, pp. 39–40.

79 E. Schulkind, *The Paris Commune of 1871* (The Historical Association, 1971), p. 12.

80 *The General Council of the First International: Minutes* (Progress Publishers, Moscow), Vol. 3, 1868–70 (March 15, 1870), p. 218.

81 Varlin was in Paris again at the time of the Commune and he was shot by the troops from Versailles on May 28, 1871.

82 S. Bernstein, *The Beginnings of Marxian Socialism in France* (1965), p. 34.

83 Introduction by F. Engels to Karl Marx, *The Civil War in France* (edition of 1891: new edition issued by the Foreign Languages Publishing House, Moscow), pp. 17–18.

84 "Report of the General Council of the fourth Annual Congress of the International Working Men's Association" in *The General Council of the First International: Minutes* (Progress Publishers, Moscow), Vol. 3, 1868–70, p. 339.

85 Wilhelm Liebknecht, "Report on the Working Class Movement in Germany" (1865) in *The General Council of the First International: Minutes* (Foreign Languages Publishing House, Moscow), Vol. 1, 1864–6, pp. 251–60. Karl Marx acknowledged the receipt of the report in a letter to Liebknecht of November 21, 1865. He wrote (in English): "As to your report, I could *not* lay it before the conference because I was too personally introduced into it" (Wilhelm Liebknecht, *Briefwechsel mit Karl Marx und Friedrich Engels* (ed. Georg Eckert, 1963), p. 66).

86 Karl Marx to Wilhelm Liebknecht, November 21, 1865 (*ibid.*, p. 67).

87 Karl Marx to Wilhelm Liebnecht, January 15, 1866 (*ibid.*, p. 70).

88 Karl Marx to F. Engels, May 17, 1866 in *Gesamtausgabe*, Part III, Vol. 3, p. 334.

89 Karl Marx to F. Engels, June 9, 1866 in *Gesamtausgabe*, Part III, Vol. 3, p. 338.

90 F. Engels, "Johann Philipp Becker" in *Der Sozialdemokrat*, December 17, 1886: reprinted in F. Engels, *Biographische Skizzen* (1967), pp. 117–26.

91 *The General Council of the First International: Minutes*, Vol. 1, 1864–6: London conference, September 25, 1865, pp. 237–8.

92 H. Jung to the editor of *L'Echo de Verviers*, February 20, 1866 in *The General Council of the First International: Minutes*, Vol. 1, 1864–6 (Appendix), p. 361.

93 Karl Marx to Carl Klings, October 4, 1864 and Karl Marx to Carl Siebel, December 22, 1864 in *Marx–Engels Werke*, Vol. 31, pp. 417–18 and p. 436.

94 "Third Annual Report of the Working Men's International Association" in *The Bee Hive*, September 14, 1867 and in *The General Council of the First International: Minutes*, Vol. 2, 1866–8, p. 302.

95 F. Engels to Theodor Cuno, May 7–8, 1872 in Karl Marx and F. Engels, *Letters to Americans, 1848–95* (1963), p. 105.

96 *The General Council of the First International: Minutes*, Vol. 3, 1868–70 (December 15, 1868), p. 53.

97 R. Morgan, *The German Social Democrats and the First International* (1965), p. 181.

98 *Der Volkstaat*, March 20, 1872.

99 Karl Marx to Kwasniewsky, September 25, 1871 in Boris Nikolajewsky, "Karl Marx und die Berliner Sektion der I. Internationale" (*Die Gesellschaft*, Vol. 3, 1933, pp. 260–1).

100 Karl Marx to Wilhelm Liebknecht, November 17, 1871 in Wilhelm Liebknecht, *Briefwechsel mit Karl Marx und Friedrich Engels* (ed. Georg Eckert, 1963), pp. 142–3.

101 Wilhelm Liebknecht to Karl Marx, December 8, 1871 in Wilhelm Liebknecht, *op. cit.*, p. 146 (note 14).

102 F. Engels to Wilhelm Liebknecht, December 15, 1871 in Wilhelm

Liebknecht, *Briefwechsel mit Karl Marx und Friedrich Engels* (ed. Georg Eckert, 1963), pp. 146–7 and M. M. Drachkowitch (ed.), *The Revolutionary Internationals, 1864–1943* (1966), p. 34.

103 F. Engels to Wilhelm Liebknecht, May 15–22, 1872 in Wilhelm Liebknecht, *Briefwechsel mit Karl Marx und Friedrich Engels* (ed. Georg Eckert, 1963), p. 167 and M. M. Drachkowitch (ed.), *The Revolutionary Internationals, 1864–1943* (1966), p. 34.

104 F. Engels to T. C. Cuno, May 7–8, 1872 in Karl Marx and F. Engels, *Letters to Americans 1848–1895* (1963), p. 105.

105 Karl Marx, "Instructions for the Delegates of the Provisional General Council" (1866) in *The General Council of the First International: Minutes*, Vol. 1, 1864–6, p. 341. For the intervention of the International in industrial disputes see an article by E. S. Beesly in *The Fortnightly Review* and an interview with Applegarth in the *New York World*, May 21, 1870.

106 H. Collins, "The International and the British Labour Movement. Origin of the International in England" in *Labour History*, Bulletin No. 9, Autumn 1864, p. 28.

107 Karl Marx, "A Warning" in the *Oberrheinischer Courier*, May 15, 1866.

108 F. Engels to Karl Marx, May 1, 1866 in *Gesamtausgabe*, Part III, Vol. 3, p. 329.

109 Karl Marx to W. Liebknecht, May 1, 1866 in Wilhelm Liebknecht, *Briefwechsel mit Karl Marx und Friedrich Engels* (ed. Georg Eckert, 1963), pp. 73–5. Marx's "A Warning" was enclosed in this letter. See also *The General Council of the First International: Minutes*, Vol. 1, 1864–6, pp. 367–8.

110 Karl Marx to F. Engels, May 10, 1866 in *Gesamtausgabe*, Part III, Vol. 3, p. 332.

111 *The General Council of the First International: Minutes*, Vol. 4, 1870–1 August 8, 1871), pp. 252–7 and Sidney and Beatrice Webb, *The History of Trade Unionism* (1919), p. 316.

112 *The General Council of the First International: Minutes*, Vol. III, 1868–71, pp. 385–6.

113 *Resolutions of the Conference of Delegates of the International Working Men's Association assembled in London from 17th to 23rd September 1871* (1871): reprinted in *The General Council of the First International:Minutes*, Vol. 4, 1870–1, pp. 440–50.

114 Karl Marx to F. Engels, May 1, 1865 in *Gesamtausgabe*, Part III, Vol. 3, p. 263: English translation in Karl Marx and F. Engels, *On Britain* (1953), p. 494.

115 Karl Marx to F. Engels, July 7, 1866 in *Gesamtausgabe*, Part III, Vol. 3, p. 343.

116 Karl Marx to F. Engels, July 27, 1866 in *Gesamtausgabe*, Part III, Vol. 3, pp. 351–2.

117 Karl Marx to F. Engels, October 30, 1869 in *Gesamtausgabe*, Part III, Vol. 3, p. 232. For the Land and Labour League see R. Harrison, "The Land and Labour League" in the *Bulletin of the Institute of Social History*, 1953, No. 3.

118 J. G. Eccarius, *Address of the Land and Labour League to the Working Men of Great Britain and Ireland* (1869): see *The General Council of the First International: Minutes*, Vol. 3, 1868–70, pp. 345–51.

119 Karl Marx to F. Engels, November 2, 1867 in *Gesamtausgabe*, Part

III, Vol. 3, p. 445. He wrote. "The trial of the Fenians in Manchester has had just the results that we desired. You will have seen what a scandal 'our people' have made in the Reform League. I have tried by every means in my power to provoke this demonstration of the English workers in favour of Fenianism."

120 Karl Marx, "The Fenian Prisoners in Manchester . . ." in *The General Council of the First International: Minutes*, Vol. 2, 1866–8, pp. 179–80 and pp. 312–13. See also Paul Rose, *The Manchester Martyrs; the story of a Fenian Tragedy* (1970).

121 F. Engels to Karl Marx, November 30, 1867 in *Gesamtausgabe*, Part III, Vol. 3, p. 455.

122 Karl Marx in *The General Council of the First International: Minutes*, Vol. 2, 1866–8, pp. 253–8.

123 Karl Marx to F. Engels, November 30, 1867 in *Gesamtausgabe*, Part III, Vol. 3, pp. 254–8.

124 Karl Marx to F. Engels, December 14, 1867 in *Gesamtausgabe*, Part III, Vol. 3, p. 463.

125 Karl Marx to F. Engels, December 17, 1867 in *Gesamtausgabe*, Part III, Vol. 3, p. 465.

126 *The General Council of the First International: Minutes*, Vol. 3, 1868–70 (meeting of November 16, 1869), pp. 178–83.

127 *The General Council of the First International: Minutes*, Vol. 3, 1868–70 (meeting of November 23, 1869 – wrongly dated November 26), pp. 186–8.

128 Karl Marx to F. Engels, November 26, 1869 in *Gesamtausgabe*, Part III, Vol. 4, p. 250.

129 F. Engels to Karl Marx, November 29, 1869 in *Gesamtausgabe*, Part III, Vol. 4, p. 251.

130 The circular was summarised by Karl Marx in a letter to S. Meyer and A. Vogt, April 9, 1870 in Karl Marx and F. Engels, *On Britain* (1953), pp. 504–8.

131 *The General Council of the First International: Minutes*, Vol. 4, 1870–1 (January 31, 1871), pp. 112–17. Engels wound up the debate at a meeting held on March 14, 1871 (pp. 154–6).

132 F. Engels to Karl Marx, November 18, 1868 in *Gesamtausgabe*, Part III, Vol. 4, p. 126: English translation in Karl Marx and F. Engels, *On Britain* (1953), pp. 499–500.

133 *The General Council of the First International: Minutes*, Vol. 4, 1870–1 (August 8, 1871), p. 256.

134 *The General Council of the First International: Minutes*, Vol. 5, 1871–2 (November 21, 1871), p. 43. Engels stated that the *Standard* and the *Scotsman* had printed accounts of the quarrel.

135 See the preface to *The General Council of the First International: Minutes*, Vol. 5, 1871–2, p. 22. For a time Engels kept his own record of the proceedings of the General Council. At a meeting of the General Council on June 11, 1872 Engels "protested against the Secretary having any power to decide what should go into the Minutes and what should be excluded" (*ibid.*, p. 218). John Hales was expelled from the International by the General Council on May 30, 1873).

136 *General Council of the First International: Minutes*, Vol. 4, 1870–1, pp. 160–1.

137 Karl Marx to Dr Kugelmann, April 12, 1871 in Karl Marx, *Letters to Dr Kugelmann*, p. 123.

138 F. Engels to A. Sorge, September 12–17, 1874 in *Marx–Engels Werke*, Vol. 33 (1966), p. 642: English translation in Karl Marx and F. Engels, *Letters to Americans, 1848–95* (1963), p. 114.

139 Gustav Mayer, *Friedrich Engels*, Vol. 2 (1934), p. 227.

140 *The General Council of the First International: Minutes*, Vol. 4, 1870–71, pp. 170–1.

141 Karl Marx to Dr Kugelmann, April 12, 1871 in Karl Marx, *Letters to Dr Kugelmann*, p. 123.

142 Karl Marx to Dr Kugelmann, April 17, 1871 in Karl Marx, *Letters to Dr Kugelmann*, p. 125.

143 *General Council of the First International: Minutes*, Vol. 4, 1870–1 (May 23, 1871), p. 200.

144 Introduction (1891) by F. Engels to Karl Marx, *The Civil War in France*, 1871 (Foreign Languages Publishing House, Moscow), p. 16.

145 E. Schulkind, *The Paris Commune of 1871* (The Historical Association, 1971), p. 34.

146 Gustav Mayer, *Friedrich Engels*, Vol. 2 (1934), p. 229. The figure "40,000" was an exaggeration.

147 F. Engels, "Programme der blanquistischen Kommuneflüchtlinge" in *Der Volksstaat*, November 73, June 26, 1874.

148 Karl Marx, *The Civil War in France*, 1871 (Foreign Languages Publishing House, Moscow).

149 H. M. Hyndman, *The Record of an Adventurous Life* (1911), p. 272.

150 Karl Marx to Dr Kugelmann, June 18, 1871 in Karl Marx, *Letters to Dr Kugelmann*, p. 126.

151 F. Engels to W. Liebknecht, June 22, 1871 in Wilhelm Liebknecht, *Briefwechsel mit Karl Marx und Friedrich Engels* (ed. by Georg Eckert, 1963), p. 131.

152 Gladstone told the House of Commons on May 21, 1872 that "no such despatch has been received at the Foreign Office" (*Hansard*, Vol. 210, 1872, col. 401). Favre's views on the International were presumably conveyed orally to the British Foreign Secretary.

153 Later Lord Aberdare.

154 Karl Marx to A. O. Rutson, July 12, 1871 in R. Payne, *Marx* (1968), pp. 427–8.

155 Señor de Blas to Señor Rances y Villanueva (Madrid, February 9, 1872): communicated to Earl Granville on February 24, 1872. See *Correspondence with the Spanish Government respecting the International Association of Workmen* (Parliamentary Papers, 1872, LXX, p. 715).

156 F. Mora to the General Council of the International, April 8, 1872 in *The General Council of the First International: Minutes*, Vol. 5, 1871–2 (April 23, 1872), p. 162.

157 *Hansard*, Vol. 210, 1872, cols. 1183–1210.

158 Statement by Karl Marx to the General Council of the International on July 25, 1871 in *The General Council of the International: Minutes*, Vol. 4, 1870–1, p. 242.

159 Earl Granville to Mr Layard in *Correspondence with the Spanish Government respecting the International Association of Workmen* (Parliamentary Papers, 1872, LXX), p. 720.

160 The declaration of the General Council of the International appeared in the *Eastern Post*, April 27, 1872 and was also published as a leaflet. See *The General Council of the First International: Minutes*, Vol. 5, 1871–2 (meeting of April 16, 1872), pp. 155–9.

161 Report by Sergeant Reimers and Superintendent Williamson of Scotland Yard, August 17, 1874 in the Public Record Office and in the Marx–Engels archives (Amsterdam), E. 85. See also R. Payne, *Marx* (1968), pp. 460–1. When Marx asked why his application had been rejected, Robert Willis replied that the Home Office was under no obligation to give any explanation for its decision.

162 Karl Marx to A. Sorge, August 4, 1874 in *Marx–Engels Werke*, Vol. 33 (1966), p. 634: English translation in Karl Marx and F. Engels, *Letters to Americans 1848–95* (1963), p. 112.

163 R. Payne, *Marx* (1968), p. 431.

164 In the German version "Social-Democrat philistine" was changed to "German philistine" by the leaders of the Social Democrat Party: see H. Hirsch (ed.), *Friedrich Engels Profile* (1970), p. 285.

165 F. Engels's introduction of 1891 to a new edition of Karl Marx, *The Civil War in France*, 1871 (Foreign Languages Publishing House, Moscow), p. 22.

166 F. Engels to Eduard Bernstein, January 1, 1884 in Helmut Hirsch (ed.), *Bernstein's Briefwechsel mit Friedrich Engels* (1970), p. 238.

167 *The International Herald*, March 30, 1872, reprinted in *The General Council of the First International: Minutes*, Vol. 5, 1871–2, p. 414. A leaflet advertising the meeting is reproduced in *The General Council of the First International: Minutes*, Vol. 5, 1871–2, p. 125.

168 *The General Council of the First International: Minutes*, Vol. 5, 1871–2 (July 9, 1872), p. 251.

169 Karl Marx, "The General Council of the Working Men's International Association to the Federal Council of Romance Switzerland" (January 1, 1870) in *The General Council of the First International: Minutes*, Vol. 3, 1868–70, pp. 401–2.

170 Karl Marx to Siegfried Meyer and August Vogt, April 9, 1870 in *Marx–Engels Werke*, Vol. 32 (1965), p. 669: English translation in Karl Marx and F. Engels, *On Britain* (1953), p. 507.

171 Jenny Marx to W. Liebknecht, May 26, 1872 in Wilhelm Liebknecht, *Briefwechsel mit Karl Marx und Friedrich Engels* (ed. by G. Eckert, 1963), pp. 168–70.

172 F. Lessner in *Reminiscences of Marx and Engels* (Foreign Languages Publishing House, Moscow), p. 162.

173 Karl Marx to N. F. Danielson, May 28, 1872 in Marx–Engels, *Briefe über "Das Kapital"* (1954), p. 217.

174 Karl Marx to Dr Kugelmann, May 18, 1874 in Karl Marx, *Letters to Dr Kugelmann*, p. 135. Marx had declared at The Hague that the "so-called leaders of the English workers" had been "more or less bought by the bourgeoisie and the government".

175 Karl Marx to Dr Kugelmann, July 27, 1871 in Karl Marx, *Letters to Dr Kugelmann*, p. 128.

176 *The General Council of the First International: Minutes*, Vol. 4, 1870–1 (August 1871), p. 251. On December 19, 1871 Hermann Jung told the General Council that "there was no money in hand for the refugees and it was necessary that something should be done as the men were starving". Charles Dilke had given him £5 for the refugees. See *The General Council of the First International: Minutes*, Vol. 5, 1871–2 (December 19, 1871), p. 65.

177 *The General Council of the First International: Minutes*, Vol. 5, 1871–2 (February 6, 1872), pp. 96–7.

178   John de Morgan. On April 9, 1872 J. Patrick McDonnell informed
the General Council of the International that De Morgan had been
"completely ruined". "Previous to his connection with the International he had a good connection as a teacher of elocution, but
every one of his pupils had been taken from him, and he had been
discharged from a situation he held in an Academy where he had
given the greatest satisfaction – solely because of the action that he
had taken." "The police were watching his house day and night, and
were warning people not to have anything to do with him. The
evident intention was to drive him out of Cork." The General Council
issued a declaration on "Police Terrorism in Ireland" which alleged
that the British government was attempting "to nip in the bud the
establishment of the International in Ireland by putting into practice
all that police chicanery which the exceptional legislation and the
practically permanent state of siege there enabled it to exercise". See
The General Council of the First International: Minutes, Vol. 5,
1871–2 (April 9, 1872), pp. 148–50.

179   F. Engels to Theodor Cuno, April 22–3, 1872 in *Marx–Engels Werke*,
Vol. 33 (1966), pp. 447: English translation in Karl Marx and F.
Engels, *Letters to Americans, 1848–95* (1963), p. 102.

180   F. Engels to A. Hepner, December 30, 1872 in *Marx–Engels Werke*,
Vol. 33 (1966), p. 553: English translation in Karl Marx and F.
Engels, *Letters to Americans, 1848–95* (1963), p. 112.

181   The Bakunin archives are in the International Institute for Social
History (Amsterdam). They were used by Max Nettlau in his manuscript biography of Bakunin. Fifty copies were duplicated and one
of them is in the British Museum. See Max Nettlau and James
Guillaume, *Michel Bakounine: Oeuvres* (six volumes, 1895–1913);
James Guillaume (ed.), *L'Internationale: documents et souvenirs* (four
volumes, 1905–10); and E. H. Carr, *Michael Bakunin* (1937).

182   E. H. Carr, *Michael Bakunin* (1937), p. 110. Bakunin's article entitled
"Reaction in Germany . . ." appeared anonymously in the *Deutsche
Jahrbücher*, October 1842.

183   Quoted in E. H. Carr, *Michael Bakunin* (1937). pp. 129–30.

184   Quoted in E. H. Carr, *Michael Bakunin* (1937), p. 146.

185   Karl Marx, who was then editing the *Neue Rheinische Zeitung*,
passed through Berlin when travelling to and from Vienna. He was
in Vienna between August 28 and September 7, 1848.

186   Karl Marx to J. P. Becker, August 2, 1870 in Karl Marx and F.
Engels, *Selected Correspondence* (Foreign Languages Publishing
House, Moscow), p. 293.

187   F. Engels to Karl Marx, November 27, 1861 in *Gesamtausgabe*,
Part III, Vol. 3, p. 46.

188   Karl Marx to F. Engels, February 25, 1862 in *Gesamtausgabe*,
Part III, Vol. 3, p. 55.

189   Karl Marx to F. Engels, September 12, 1863 in *Gesamtausgabe*,
Part III, Vol. 3, p. 155.

190   Karl Marx to F. Engels, November 4, 1864 in *Gesamtausgabe*,
Part III, Vol. 3, p. 199.

191   Karl Marx to Dr Kugelmann, March 28, 1870 (enclosure) in Karl
Marx, *Letters to Dr Kugelmann*, pp. 102–5.

192   E. H. Carr, *Michael Bakunin* (1937), p. 318.

193   E. H. Carr, *op. cit.*, pp. 318–19.

194   Karl Marx to F. Bolte, November 23, 1871 and F. Engels to Theodor

Cuno, January 24, 1872 in Karl Marx and F. Engels, *Letters to Americans, 1848–95* (1963), pp. 90–1 and p. 96.

195   Karl Marx to F. Engels, September 4, 1867 in *Gesamtausgabe*, Part III, Vol. 3, p. 417.

196   *The General Council of the First International: Minutes*, Vol. 2, 1866–8 (August 13, 1867), p. 152.

197   *The General Council of the First International: Minutes*, Vol. 2, 1866–8, p. 368 (note 198). The point of view expressed in this resolution was given to the Geneva peace congress in a speech by Eugène Dupont.

198   Quoted in E. H. Carr, *Michael Bakunin* (1937), p. 336.

199   The resolution of the congress of the International (held in Brussels in 1868) was as follows: "The delegates of the International consider that the League of Peace has, in view of the work of the International, no *raison d'être*; they invite this society to join the International, and its members to apply for admission to one of the branches of the International". See E. H. Carr, *Michael Bakunin* (1937), p. 339.

200   Karl Marx to F. Engels, December 15, 1868 (evening. after midnight) in *Gesamtausgabe*, Part III, Vol. 4, p. 141.

201   *The General Council of the First International: Minutes*, Vol. 3, 1868–70, p. 53.

202   Karl Marx to F. Engels, December 15, 1868 in *Gesamtausgabe*, Part III, Vol. 4, p. 141.

203   Karl Marx to F. Engels, December 19, 1868 in *Gesamtausgabe*, Part III, Vol. 4, p. 143.

204   Karl Marx, "Remarks to the Programme and Rules of the International Alliance of Socialist Democracy" in *The General Council of the First International: Minutes*, Vol. 3, 1868–70, pp. 379–83.

205   Karl Marx to Dr Kugelmann, March 28, 1870 (enclosure) in Karl Marx, *Letters to Dr Kugelmann*, p. 103.

206   Karl Marx to Dr Kugelmann, March 28, 1870 (enclosure) in Karl Marx, *Letters to Dr Kugelmann*, p. 103.

207   Karl Marx to F. Engels, December 15, 1868 in *Gesamtausgabe*, Part III, Vol. 4, p. 141.

208   F. Engels to Karl Marx, December 18, 1868 in *Gesamtausgabe*, Part III, Vol. 4, pp. 142–3.

209   Karl Marx to F. Engels, December 19, 1868 in *Gesamtausgabe*, Part III, Vol. 4, p. 143.

210   Karl Marx to Dr Kugelmann, March 28, 1870 in Karl Marx, *Letters to Dr Kugelmann*, p. 102.

211   Karl Marx, "The International Working Men's Association and International Alliance of Socialist Democracy": approved by the General Council on December 22, 1868: see *The General Council of the First International: Minutes*, Vol. III, 1868–70, pp. 387–9.

212   Karl Marx to F. Engels, March 14, 1869 (reference to a letter from Henri Perret to J. G. Eccarius) in *Gesamtausgabe*, Part III, Vol. 4, p. 168.

213   Karl Marx to F. Engels, March 5, 1869 in *Gesamtausgabe*, Part III, Vol. 4, pp. 164–5.

214   F. Engels to Karl Marx, March 7, 1869 in *Gesamtausgabe*, Part III, Vol. 4, p. 166.

215   Karl Marx, "The General Council of the International Working Men's Association to the International Alliance of Socialist Demo-

cracy" (March 9, 1869) in *The General Council of the First International: Minutes*, Vol. 3, 1868–70, pp. 310–11.

216 *The General Council of the First International: Minutes*, Vol. 3, 1868–70 (meeting of July 27, 1869), pp. 133–5.

217 F. Engels to Karl Marx, July 30, 1869 in *Gesamtausgabe*, Part III, Vol. 4, pp. 214–16.

218 Karl Marx to Friedrich Bolte, November 23, 1871 in Karl Marx and F. Engels. *Letters to Americans, 1848–95* (1963), p. 91.

219 Karl Marx to Dr Kugelmann, March 28, 1870 in Karl Marx, *Letters to Dr Kugelmann*, p. 104 (enclosure).

220 Karl Marx, "Report of the General Council on the Right of Inheritance" in *The General Council of the First International: Minutes*, Vol. 3, 1868–70, pp. 322–4. The report was endorsed by the General Council on August 3, 1869. See also Marx's speech to the General Council on July 20, 1869 (*ibid.*, pp. 128–32).

221 E. H. Carr, *Michael Bakunin* (1937), p. 366.

222 F. Engels to Paul Lafargue, December 9, 1871 in *F. Engels – Paul and Laura Lafargue: Correspondence*, Vol. 1, 1868–86 (1959), p. 31.

223 F. Engels to Paul Lafargue, March 11, 1872 in *F. Engels – Paul and Laura Lafargue: Correspondence*, Vol. 1, 1868–86 (1959), p. 44.

224 E. H. Carr, *Michael Bakunin* (1937), p. 373.

225 *The General Council of the First International: Minutes*, Vol. 3, 1868–70, p. 407 and Karl Marx to Dr Kugelmann, March 28, 1870 (enclosure) in Karl Marx, *Letters to Dr Kugelmann*, p. 105.

226 Karl Marx to Friedrich Bolte, November 23, 1871 in Karl Marx and F. Engels, *Letters to Americans, 1848–95* (1963), p. 91.

227 Paul Lafargue to F. Engels, October 2, 1871 in *F. Engels – Paul and Laura Lafargue: Correspondence*, Vol. 1, 1868–86 (1959), p. 26.

228 F. Engels to Paul Lafargue, December 9, 1871 in *F. Engels – Paul and Laura Lafargue: Correspondence*, Vol. 1, 1868–86 (1959), p. 31.

229 Mikhail Bakunin, *L'Association Internationale des Travailleurs de Genève aux ouvriers espagnols* (1868).

230 For Guiseppi Fanelli see Cesare Teofilato, "Guiseppi Fanelli Dalla Giovane Italia al 'Internazionale'" in *Pensiero e Volonta* (Rome), August 1, 1925 and E. Malatesta, "G. Fanelli, ricordi personali" (*ibid.*, September 16, 1925).

231 *The General Council of the First International: Minutes*, Vol. 4, 1870–1 (statement by Engels at the meeting of August 15, 1871), p. 259.

232 A. Lorenzo, *El Proletariado Militante*, Vol. 1 (1923): English translation (extract) in *Reminiscences of Marx and Engels* (Foreign Languages Publishing House, Moscow), pp. 288–91.

233 Paul Lafargue to F. Engels, April 12, 1872 in *F. Engels – Paul and Laura Lafargue: Correspondence*, Vol. 3, p. 430.

234 *F. Engels – Paul and Laura Lafargue: Correspondence*, Vol. 1, pp. 24–47 and Vol. 3, pp. 402–74.

235 F. Engels to Paul Lafargue, December 9, 1871 in *F. Engels – Paul and Laura Lafargue: Correspondence*, Vol. 1, 1868–86 (1959), p. 29.

236 Gustav Mayer, *Friedrich Engels*, Vol. 2 (1934), p. 242.

237 F. Engels to Laura Lafargue, March 11, 1872 in *F. Engels – Paul and Laura Lafargue: Correspondence*, Vol. 1, 1868–86 (1959), p. 45.

238 *The General Council of the First International: Minutes*, Vol. 5, 1871–2, pp. 415–16.

239 Paul Lafargue to F. Engels, April 12, 1872 in *F. Engels – Paul and Laura Lafargue: Correspondence*, Vol. 3, p. 428.

240 F. Engels to Theodor Cuno, April 22, 1872 in G. Del Bo (ed.), *Marx e Engels, Corrispondenza con italiani, 1848–95* (1964), p. 187: English translation in Karl Marx and F. Engels, *Letters to Americans, 1848–95* (1963), p. 102.

241 F. Engels to Theodor Cuno. April 22, 1872 in G. Del Bo, *op. cit.*, p. 187 and Karl Marx and F. Engels, *Letters to Americans, 1848–95* (1963), pp. 102–3.

242 F. Engels, "To Spanish Sections of the International Working Men's Association" (July 24, 1872) in *The General Council of the First International: Minutes*, Vol. 5, 1871–2, pp. 446–9. The address was published in *La Emancipacion*, August 17, 1872.

243 For the International in Italy see Max Nattlau, "Bakunin und die International in Italien bis zum Herbst 1872" in (*Grünberg*) *Archiv für die Geschichte des Sozialismus und der Arbeiterbewegung*, 1912, pp. 275–325; Cesare Teofilato, "Guiseppi Fanelli Dalla Giovane Italia al 'Internazionale' " in *Pensiero e Volanta* (Rome), August 1, 1925; E. Malatesta (ed.), *Bakunin e l'Internazionale in Italia dal 1864 al 1872* (1928); P. Schebert, *Von Bakunin zu Lenin* (1956); R. Hostetter, *The Italian Socialist Movement*, Vol. 1 *Origins* (New York, 1958); A. Lehning (ed.), *Michel Bakounine et l'Italie* (documents, two volumes, 1961–3); A. Romano, *L'Unita Italiana e la Prima Internazionale 1861–71* (1966); E. Ragionieri, "Engels und die italienische Arbeiterbewegung" in *Friedrich Engels, 1820–1970* (Forschungsinstitut der Friedrich-Ebert-Stiftung, Vol. 85, 1971), pp. 189–200. For the correspondence between Engels and Italian socialists see Guiseppi Del Bo (ed.), *La corrispondenza di Marx e Engels con italiani 1848–95* (Milan, 1964).

244 Carlo Cafiero to F. Engels, November 24 and December 19, 1871 in G. Del Bo (ed.), *La corrispondenza di Marx e Engels con italiani, 1848–95* (1964), pp. 93–100.

245 Theodor Cuno to F. Engels, April 17, 1872 in G. Del Bo (ed.), *op. cit.*, pp. 178–80 and Theodor Cuno, "Reminiscences" in *Reminiscences of Marx and Engels*, pp. 206–13.

246 For Carlo Cafiero see M. Cassandro, *Carlo Cafiero* (1946); A. Lucarelli, *Carlo Cafiero* . . . (1947); P. C. Masini, "Carlo Cafiero" in *Volonta*, No. 8–9, 1949, and "Engels e Cafiero" in *Tempo presente*, No. 4, 1965; C. L. Ott, "Carlo Cafiero" in *Grande Dizionario Enciclopedico*, Vol. 3.

247 F. Engels to Laura Lafargue, March 11, 1872 in *F. Engels – Paul and Laura Lafargue: Correspondence*, Vol. 1, 1868–86 (1959), p. 46.

248 Carlo Cafiero to F. Engels, June 12, 1872 (postscript, June 19) in G. Del Bo, *op. cit.*, pp. 219–25.

249 *The General Council of the First International: Minutes*, Vol. 5, 1871–2 (Report of the fifth annual Congress, September 1872), p. 460.

250 Mazzini attacked the International in *La Roma di Popolo*, November 16 and 23, 1871. For Engels's reply see his "Declaration . . . concerning Mazzini's articles about the International" (December 6, 1871) in *The General Council of the First International: Minutes*, Vol. 5, 1871–2, pp. 350–5.

251 The International in Italy was prohibited by the government on August 14, 1871. Shortly afterwards the Naples branch – the oldest and most active in the country – was disbanded by the authorities.

252 F. Engels, "The Situation in Italy" in *The General Council of the First International: Minutes*, Vol. 5, 1871–2, pp. 287–90.

253 F. Engels to Carmelo Palladino, November 23, 1871 in G. Del Bo (ed.), *La corrispondenza di Marx e Engels con italiani, 1848–95* (1964), pp. 77–9.

254 F. Engels to Theodor Cuno, January 24, 1872 in G. Del Bo (ed.), *La corrispondenza di Marx e Engels con italiani, 1848–95* (1964), p. 136 and in Karl Marx and F. Engels, *Letters to Americans, 1848–95* (1963), p. 99.

255 Regis's "Party name" was Étienne Pechard.

256 V. Regis to F. Engels, March 1, 1872 in G. Del Bo (ed.), *La corrispondenza di Marx e Engels con italiani, 1848–95* (1964), pp. 160–4. On April 22, 1872 Engels told Cuno that he had been suspicious of Terzaghi for some time (*ibid.*, p. 186).

257 F. Engels to Laura Lafargue, March 11, 1872 in *F. Engels – Paul and Laura Lafargue: Correspondence*, Vol. 1, 1868–86 (1959), p. 46.

258 *The General Council of the First International: Minutes*, Vol. 5, 1871–2 (meeting of March 5, 1872), p. 117.

259 F. Engels, "The Saragossa Congress" (report to the General Council, May 7, 1872) in *The General Council of the First International: Minutes*, Vol. 5, 1871–2, pp. 295–6.

260 F. Engels to Theodor Cuno, June 10, 1872 in G. Del Bo (ed.), *La corrispondenza di Marx e Engels con italiani, 1848–95* (1964), p. 217.

261 E. H. Carr, *Michael Bakunin* (1937), pp. 418–19.

262 For Engels's criticism of the Rimini conference see his address to the Italian sections of August 23, 1872 in *The General Council of the First International: Minutes*, Vol. 5, 1871–2, pp. 451–2.

263 "Resolutions of the Conference of Delegates of the International Working Men's Association assembled at London from 17th to 23rd September 1871" in *The General Council of the First International: Minutes*, Vol. 4, 1870–1, pp. 447–8.

264 James Guillaume, *L'Internationale: documents et souvenirs* (four volumes, 1905–10), Vol. 2, pp. 232–41.

265 Karl Marx and F. Engels, *Fictitious Splits in the International*, 1872 in *The General Council of the First International: Minutes*, Vol. 5, 1871–2, p. 407. The pamphlet was written in French and was first published in Geneva in 1872.

266 Theodor Cuno, "Reminiscences" in *Reminiscences of Marx and Engels* (Foreign Languages Publishing House, Moscow), p. 209.

267 E. H. Carr, *Michael Bakunin* (1937), p. 432.

268 F. Engels to A. Sorge, September 12–17, 1874 in Karl Marx and F. Engels, *Letters to Americans, 1848–95* (1963), p. 114. For the International in the United States see S. Bernstein, *The First International in America* (New York, 1962).

10

MARX AND ENGELS: THE LAST PHASE
1870–1883

Engels retired from business in 1869 to devote himself to the cause of socialism. He had always disliked living in Manchester and in 1870 he moved to London where he could more easily act as the military correspondent of the *Pall Mall Gazette* and where he could play a more active part in the affairs of the First International. Lizzie Burns readily agreed to the move. Engels wrote that "she has had words with her relations here and she does not want to stay in Manchester any longer".[1]

Jenny Marx helped Engels to find a house. He hesitated to take a lease of three and a half years in the autumn of 1870 because he thought that the fall of France might precipitate revolutions on the Continent requiring his personal attention. Marx assured him that he would be able to dispose of the lease of his house without difficulty if this should be necesssary.[2] Engels moved to 122 Regents Park road in September 1870[3] and lived there until November 1894 when he moved to No. 41 in the same road. He had to wait for twenty years before he could have hot running water in his bathroom and still longer for a new kitchen range.[4] In September 1890 he told Laura Lafargue that his house had "gone into the hands of other agents". "So I raised the question of a water closet and gave notice unless a new kitchen range and a new bath with hot water arrangements was put in." "Today the people have been here to look at the premises and I am informed that these demands of mine will be complied with."[5] From Regents Park Road Engels could walk to Marx's house in Maitland Park Road in a quarter of an hour.[6] Since they lived close to each other their correspondence was now limited to occasions when either Marx or Engels was away from London.

Although Marx and Engels exchanged far fewer letters between 1871 and 1883 than between 1850 and 1870 their later correspondence is not without interest. It provides evidence of Marx's continued financial dependence upon Engels. Marx no longer earned a living as a journalist by writing for the *New York Daily Tribune* or *Die Presse* and he had no regular source of income other than his allowance from Engels. The author of a great work on capital,

Marx was still incapable of balancing his own accounts or of living within his means. In 1868 Marx had complained that the high cost of living in London was "becoming more and more burdensome"[7] and two years later his wife wrote to Engels: "We live in a veritable palace which, in my view, is far too big and far too expensive."[8] But Marx did not move to a smaller house even when two of his daughters left home to get married. Marx continued to amass petty debts. At the end of 1873 he owed his pawnbroker £2 17s in interest.[9]

Engels not only sent Marx regular quarterly remittances but he readily responded to appeals for further financial aid. Indeed he sometimes encouraged Marx to ask for more. In 1873, when Marx was staying in Harrogate, Engels enquired if he was short of funds – "if so, say how much, reckoning liberally".[10] Marx asked for £12[11] and received £15.[12] In 1881 Engels wrote to Marx who was in Argenteuil: "I have some cheques here so that if you are short of cash do not feel embarassed but let me know how much you need."[13] Marx needed £30.[14] Engels told him not to worry "over a paltry £30". He promised to send a cheque to Marx's daughter Eleanor. "But if you need more, let me know and I will write a larger cheque."[15] A few days later Marx wrote that he was still short of money,[16] so Engels sent him £50 instead of £30.[17] Engels's generosity enabled Marx to take lengthy cures at fashionable spas on the Continent. He paid three visits to Carlsbad where one of the main baths has now been named after him. Marx's long visit to Algeria in 1882 and his visit to France to stay with his daughters were also paid for by Engels.

The Marx–Engels correspondence also throws light upon the deterioration of Marx's health in the 1870s.[18] In several letters he gave Engels detailed accounts of his symptoms and of the treatment prescribed by his doctors. Marx suffered from a disease of the liver, from boils and carbuncles, from chest complaints and from a nervous disorder. His visits to Carlsbad proved to be beneficial. In January 1875, for example, Eleanor Marx wrote that her father's health had much improved since he had been to Carlsbad. "He is working hard at the French translation of his book."[19] And in the following October Engels observed that Marx had been "a changed man" since returning from Carlsbad. "He is strong, fresh, cheerful and healthy, and he will soon be able to get down to serious work again."[20] But a few years later Marx wrote to Danielson: "My medical adviser has warned me to shorten my 'working day' considerably if I were not desirous to relapse into the state of 1874 and tte following years when I got giddy and unable to proceed after a few hours of serious application."[21]

In the 1870s Engels expected that Marx – in return for his allowance – would complete *Das Kapital*. But appeals from his friends and his publisher to finish his second and third volumes fell upon deaf ears. And Marx showed no concern when academic critics attacked him for failing to give the world a comprehensive survey of his theories. In 1871, for example, Dühring complained that Marx's writings on economics were a mere collection of fragments and that their author had shown himself incapable of arranging his ideas in an orderly and systematic fashion.[22]

Marx offered various excuses for failing to deliver the manuscripts of his second and third volumes to the publisher. His health was poor and this reduced the time available for working on his book. But he spent time on political activities which might have been devoted to the completion of *Das Kapital*. In the early 1870s his work on behalf of the First International left him little time for research or writing. In 1871 he complained that he was so busy that he could do no work on *Das Kapital*. "Certainly I shall one fine morning put a stop to all this, but there are circumstances, where you are in duty bound to occupy yourself with things much less attractive than theoretical study and research."[23] And in the following year Marx wrote. "I am so overworked and in fact so interfered with in my theoretical studies, that, after September I shall *withdraw* from the *commercial concern* which, at this moment, weighs principally upon my own shoulders, and which, as you know, has ramifications all over the world."[24] The "commercial concern" was, of course, the First International. In 1875 Marx wrote a strong criticism of the programme adopted by the newly united socialist party in Germany at a conference held in Gotha and two years later he contributed a chapter to Engels's book attacking Dühring's views on socialism.

When Marx did turn his attention to *Das Kapital* he gave priority to revising his first volume for the French translation which appeared in 1872.[25] According to his daughter Jenny he worked as hard on the corrections as if he – and not Joseph Le Roy – had been responsible for the translation. "Papa has rewritten it altogether . . . He works every night till two or three o'clock in the morning." A little later she wrote that "the second volume of *Das Kapital* does not progress at all, the French translation . . . takes up the whole of Mohr's time".[26] In 1872 a Russian translation of the first volume of *Das Kapital* was published[27] and a new impression of the German edition appeared.

On resuming work on the manuscripts of his second and third volumes Marx embarked upon new researches to expand what he had written in the 1860s. In 1869 he was in correspondence with

Engels concerning H. C. Carey's criticism of Ricardo's theory of rent[28] and he began to study the land legislation of Ireland. Shortly after retiring from business Engels told Marx that he had been working in the Manchester Free Library and in Chetham's Library where he had found much "valuable source material" on Irish land laws.[29]

At this time Marx undertook new researches into landownership in Belgium[30] and in Russia. He learned Russian and read Flerowski's book on the condition of the peasants, domestic workers, and factory operatives in Russia.[31] He also studied Chernyskevesky's writings on economics.[32] Engels, too, was learning Russian in the early 1870s so as to read Flerowski's book. For some years Marx devoted much of his time to studying Russian economic and social affairs and he became convinced that the future development of the village community (*mir*) would be the decisive factor in the regeneration of Russia.[33] His studies were stimulated by his conviction – shared by Engels – that "it was important that the achievement of power by Social-Democracy in the West should coincide with the political and agrarian revolution in Russia".[34] After Marx's death, Engels found that the printed Russian statistics in his friend's study filled "over two cubic metres" of bookshelf space.[35]

When not immersed in Russian statistics, Marx was engaged in research upon the latest economic developments in the United States. In 1871 he asked Julian Harney – "now Assistant Secretary of the State of Massachusetts" – for information about the way in which public lands were allocated in the United States.[36] In 1876 he asked Sorge to send him recent American book-catalogues as he wished to study works on American farming, land-ownership, finance and banking.[37] Eventually Marx built up a large collection of official American publications on these subjects.[38] In 1878 Marx wrote to Danielson:

"The most interesting field for the economist is now certainly to be found in the United States and, above all, during the period of 1873 (since the crash in September) until 1878 – the period of chronic crisis. Transformations – which to be elaborated did require in England centuries – were here realised in a few years.

"The bulk of materials, I have not only from *Russia*, but from the *United States* etc., make it pleasant for me to have a 'pretext' of continuing my studies, instead of winding them up finally for the public."[39]

And in 1880 Marx declared that he was happy that "in present circumstances", the second volume of *Das Kapital* could not be published in Germany. "At this very moment certain economic phenomena have entered into a new phase – and that means more research for me."[40]

The economic development of Russia and the United States was not Marx's only field of study at that time. In 1880 he made copious notes on a book written by Lewis H. Morgan on the primitive communism of the Iroquois Indians. And he continued to study trade fluctuations in England. In 1879 he wrote to Danielson:

"I should under no circumstances have published the second volume before the present English industrial crisis had reached its climax. The phenomena are this time singular, in many respects different from what they were in the past and this – quite apart from other modifying circumstances – is easily accounted for by the fact that never before was the English crisis preceded by tremendous (and now already five years lasting) crises in the United States, South America, Germany, Austria etc."[41]

In the 1870s Engels thought that Marx was preparing his second and third volumes for publication. In an article written in 1877 he stated that after the collapse of the First International, "Marx at last found peace and leisure again for resuming his theoretical work, and it is to be hoped that he will soon be able to have the second volume of *Das Kapital* ready for the press."[42]

When Marx died and Engels examined his papers he was astounded at the amount of work that remained to be done on them. He wrote to Bebel in August 1883 that Marx had kept quiet about his lack of progress because he knew that Engels "would have given him no peace, day or night, until the book was finished and in print".[43] Two years later Engels saw some extracts from the correspondence between Marx and Danielson between 1879 and 1881 in which Marx had made various excuses for not completing *Das Kapital*. Engels wrote to Danielson

"Alas we are so used to these excuses for the non-completion of the work! Whenever the state of his health made it impossible for him to go on with it, this impossibility preyed heavily upon his mind, and he was only too glad if he could only find some theoretical excuse why the work should not then be completed. All these arguments he had at the time made use of *vis-à-vis moi*; they seemed to ease his conscience."[44]

Engels had many other correspondents besides Marx for he exchanged letters with socialist leaders all over the world. "Every day, every post, brought to his house newspapers and letters in every European language, and it was astonishing how he found time, with all his other work, to look through, to keep in order, and remember the chief contents of them all."[45] His correspondence with Liebknecht, Bebel, Bernstein and Kautsky shows how closely Engels was identified with the fortunes of the socialist movement in Germany. A number of the letters exchanged between Engels and the Lafargues – Paul and Laura – were concerned with the socialist movement in France. And his correspondence with Laura Lafargue is particularly interesting because of the light which it throws upon Engels's private life.

In the 1870s the household at 122 Regents Park Road consisted of Engels, Lizzie Burns and her niece Ellen, nicknamed Pumps. When Lizzie Burns fell ill in September 1877 – she died a year later – Pumps kept house for him. It may be doubted whether she was a very efficient housekeeper. According to Marx she had a flighty disposition and flirted successively with Friedrich Beust, Karl Kautsky and Leo Hartmann before marrying Percy Rosher in 1882.[46] Engels insisted upon the marriage when he learned that Pumps had been seduced. Hitherto Engels had shown no great enthusiasm for the institution of marriage in a bourgeois society. In 1883 Engels told Laura Lafargue that Rosher's father had "forked out the needful"[47] to buy a partnership for his son in a firm of accountants. But the business failed and Pumps, with her husband and daughter returned to 122 Regents Park Road, where Engels supported them. In the end the black sheep of the family were packed off to Canada. Meanwhile, on Marx's death in 1883, Helene Demuth took charge of Engels's household.

The Engels–Lafargue correspondence shows that Engels lived quietly in London immersed in his scholarly researches, his literary work and his voluminous correspondence. In the 1870s he spent "the best part of eight years" studying science and mathematics[48] and he was a regular contributor to German socialist journals.[49] He wrote articles in Der Volksstaat and Vorwärts attacking those who supported doctrines which differed from those advocated by Karl Marx. After the dissolution of the First International Engels took a less active part in revolutionary politics though he occasionally emerged from his retirement. In January 1875 Engels and Marx spoke at a meeting to celebrate the twelfth anniversary of the Polish rising of 1863.[50] But on the whole Engels was content to remain behind the scenes and to advise his socialist friends in many countries. In particular he watched over the fortunes of the Social Democrat Party in Germany and was in regular correspondence with its leaders. When the socialist press in Germany was closed down by the Anti-Socialist Law of 1878 Engels was actively concerned with the establishment of a new weekly (Der Sozialdemokrat) in Switzerland.

Engels looked forward to visits from Manchester friends such as Schorlemmer and Samuel Moore. He enjoyed his holidays at the seaside in the company of Schorlemmer, the Roshers, or members of Marx's family. At week-ends he entertained his friends, many of whom were exiles living in England or foreign socialist visitors to London. Edward Aveling wrote that "a list of those who were always welcome at 122 Regents Park Road reads like a condensed epitome of the socialist movement".[51] He mentioned that Liebknecht, Bebel, Bernstein, Kautsky, Paul Singer, Victor Adler and Vera Zasulich were among those who enjoyed Engels's hospitality. In his memoirs Hellmut von Gerlach – then a member of Adolf Stöcker's Christian Socialist Workers' Party – described a "beer evening" at Engels's house. When the German socialists won a by-election, Engels broached a barrel of beer to share with his friends. Hellmut von Gerlach recalled that the company included Germans, Czechs, Magyars, and Russians. His host impressed him as a cheerful Rhinelander – "a truly fine fellow" – who made all his guests feel at home.[52]

A significant feature of the correspondence between Engels and the Lafargues was the constant appeals of Paul and Laura Lafargue for financial aid.[53] Laura's husband was as incapable as her father of earning a living and providing for his family. He was an inveterate cadger. He qualified as a doctor but practised in London for only a short time. He moved to Paris in 1868 and joined the Vaugirard branch of the First International. In 1870 when the German armies advanced upon Paris he fled to Bordeaux. He later claimed that he re-organised the First International in France "decapitated by the siege of Paris".[54] In 1871 he acted as an emissary of the Paris Commune in the provinces.

When the Commune fell, Lafargue moved on to Spain where he worked on behalf of the First International to counter Bakunin's influence over the left wing of the workers' movement. In 1872 Lafargue fled to England to avoid arrest in France owing to his activities on behalf of the Paris Commune. Here he was engaged for ten years in various unsuccessful business ventures, such as making electroplate engravings. In April 1882, when it was safe to do so, Lafargue returned to France where he secured a post with an insurance company. But he was more interested in politics than in the insurance business. He became one of Jules Guesde's most active supporters in the French Workers Party. In the 1880s he tried – with no great success – to earn a living as a free-lance journalist and popular lecturer.

Paul Lafargue considered that by marrying Laura he had become a member of the Marx family and therefore had a claim upon Engels's purse whenever he was short of money. And Engels seems to have agreed with him. Paul and Laura were married in 1868. By the end of 1874 Paul had borrowed £240 from Engels and wanted to borrow £360 more on the security of a house which he owned in New Orleans. Engels, however, declined to take a mortgage on the property. On December 28, 1874 Lafargue asked for £30 "of which I have the utmost need". In June 1875 he wrote. "It is imperative for me to have the sum of £60: I hope this will be the last time that I shall need to turn to you." Lafargue's hopes were not fulfilled. In the following August Engels gave him £70, only to be asked for a further £55 shortly afterwards. In August 1876 Lafargue wanted "a cheque for £30 as soon as you possibly can". In May 1878 Lafargue acknowledged the receipt of £15 and promptly asked for another £15.

When the Lafargues left England for France in 1882 Paul continued to ask Engels for financial assistance. On June 16, 1882, for example, he wrote that his funds were nearly exhausted. "Would you be so kind as to send me £5 by money order. Make it payable at the Tuileries post office which I pass every morning." A few days later Paul Lafargue wrote to his wife: "As you advised, I said nothing about my money affairs to Engels when I wrote. I hope you will clearly explain to him our situation which can only be put to rights with his help." So Laura wrote to Engels: "We are now seeing about getting our rooms furnished and the truth is that unless you, dear Engels, can send us some money to help us furnish them, I don't see how we are to manage." Engels sent her a cheque. In October 1882 Lafargue asked for 300 francs. In May 1883 he wrote that he had spent £20 which he had recently received and asked for another £12. In January 1884 Laura wrote to her "dear General" that the landlord "is once again about to pounce on us for his quarterly sop and our funds are once again, worse luck, at low water mark". Engels sent £15 – "which I hope will stop the landlord's cravings". These are only a few instances of demands upon Engels's purse to which reference is made in the correspondence between Engels and the Lafargues.

The main changes that occurred in Engels's private life in the 1870s were brought about by the death of his mother and his wife. Engels had a deep affection for his mother and her death in 1873 severed one of his last links with his family in Barmen. Only two years before her death Elise Engels had made a last protest against her son's political activities. She rebuked him for supporting the godless and bloodthirsty régime of the Commune in Paris. Once more she warned Engels of Marx's evil influence over him. After his mother's death Engels's visits to Germany became less frequent.

He had little in common with his brothers, though he was always grateful to Emil for coming to Manchester in 1860 to settle his future with the firm of Ermen and Engels. In his will his only bequest to his relations in Germany was that of a small picture of his father which he gave to his brother Hermann.

The death of Lizzie Burns was a more serious blow. In January 1877 Jenny Marx wrote that Engels was in excellent health and that he did not have a care in the world. This happy state of affairs came to an end in September of that year when Lizzie Burns fell ill. She died a year later on September 12, 1878. Engels married her the day before her death. He felt her loss deeply. Some years later he wrote to Julie Bebel: "My wife was a real child of the Irish proletariat and her passionate devotion to the class in which she was born was worth much more to me – and helped me more in times of stress – than all the elegance of an educated, artistic middle-class bluestocking."[55] Since Marx had offended Engels in 1863 by failing to write a proper letter of condolence when Mary Burns died it may be assumed that he did not repeat the mistake. But whatever Marx did say to Engels on this occasion it was not what he really thought about Lizzie Burns. This was reserved for a letter to one of his daughters. Marx wrote that he was present when Lizzie's effects were being examined. When a small parcel of letters was found, Engels said. "Burn them! I need not see her letters. I know she was unable to deceive me." A certain Mrs Renshaw said to Eleanor Marx afterwards. "Of course, as he had to write her letters, and to read the letters she received, he might feel quite sure that these letters contained no secrets for him – but they might do so for her."[56] It is clear that Marx was contemptuous of the illiterate Irish woman who was held in such high esteem by Engels.

By this time the health of both Karl and Jenny Marx gave Engels cause for anxiety. In an article written shortly after Marx's death Engels stated that, towards the end of his life, his friend had been "almost completely cured of a long-standing liver disease by a thrice repeated treatment at Carlsbad". But Marx also suffered from "a chronic stomach complaint and nervous exhaustion, the effect of which was headaches and mostly persisting insomnia" as well as "chronic throat ailments".[57] Meanwhile Jenny Marx suffered from cancer of the liver. In the autumn of 1881 it seemed doubtful if either had long to live. Jenny Marx died on December 2, 1881, at the age of 67 but Marx rallied, though he was unable to attend his wife's funeral. Engels delivered a eulogy at the graveside. He spoke bitterly of Jenny's sufferings in London in the early years of exile in the 1850s. He denounced "the Government and the bourgeois opposition, from the vulgar liberals to the democrats" who had "combined in a great conspiracy against her husband, and showered on him the most wretched and base calumnies; the entire press united against him; every means of defence was denied to him, so that for a time he was helpless against the enemies whom he and she could only despise". Engels ended his speech on a triumphant note. Jenny Marx, he declared, had "lived to see the calumny which had showered down upon her husband scattered like chaff before the wind, and to see his doctrines – which all reactionary parties, feudal as well as democratic, had gone to such immense pains to suppress – preached from the rooftops in all civilised countries and in all cultivated tongues".[58]

In 1882 Marx spent several months in North Africa and on the Riviera but the weather was cold and he suffered from another attack of pleurisy. On his way home he visited his daughters in France. On returning to England he went to Ventnor in the Isle of Wight. On January 10, 1883 – in the last letter of the long correspondence with Engels – he wrote that he was worried over the health of his daughter Jenny Longuet. "It is remarkable how every nervous excitement immediately affects my throat."[59] Jenny Longuet died suddenly on January 11, 1883 and her father did not survive her for long. He died peacefully at his home in London on March 14, 1883.

Engels sent letters to many of his socialist friends announcing the death of Karl Marx. To Sorge he wrote:

". . . Schorlemmer and I planned to visit Marx on New Year's day[60] when news came that it was necessary for Tussy (Eleanor Marx) to join him at once. Then Jenny's death followed and he came back with another attack of bronchitis. After all that had gone before, and at his age, this was dangerous. A number of complications set in, particularly an abscess of the lung and a terribly rapid loss of strength. Despite this the general course of the illness progressed favourably and last Friday the chief physician in attendance on him, one of the foremost young doctors in London and specially recommended to him by Ray Lankaster, gave us the most brilliant hope for his recovery. Yet anyone who has ever examined lung tissue under the microscope knows how great is the danger of a blood vessel being broken through a suppurating lung. And that is why I had a deathly fear, every morning for the past six weeks, of finding the shades down when I turned the corner of the street.

"Yesterday afternoon at 2.30, the best time for visiting him, I arrived to find the house in tears. It seemed that the end was near. I asked what had happened, tried to get to the bottom of the matter, to offer comfort. There had been a slight haemorrhage, but suddenly he had begun to sink rapidly. Our good Lenchen (Helene

Demuth), who had looked after him better than any mother cares for her child went upstairs and came down again. He was half asleep, she said and I might come in. When we entered the room he lay there asleep, but never to wake again. His pulse and breathing had stopped. In those two minutes he had passed away, peacefully and without pain. . . .

"Mankind is shorter by a head, and the greatest head of our time. The movement of the proletariat goes on, but gone is the central point to which Frenchmen, Russians, Americans and Germans spontaneously turned at decisive moments to receive always that clear incontestable counsel which only genius and perfect knowledge of the situation could give. Local lights and small talents, if not the humbugs, obtain a free hand. The final victory is certain, but the detours, the temporary and local errors – even now so unavoidable – will grow more than ever. Well we must see it through. What else are we here for? And we are far from losing courage because of it."[61]

Karl Marx was buried in Highgate cemetery in the same grave as his wife. Engels delivered a funeral oration in which he paid a tribute to the friend with whom he had collaborated so closely for nearly forty years. In the course of his speech he declared:

"Just as Darwin discovered the law of development of organic nature, so Marx discovered the law of development of human history: the simple fact, hitherto concealed by an overgrowth of ideology, that mankind must first of all eat, drink, have shelter and clothing, before it can pursue politics, science, art, religion etc.; that therefore the production of the immediate material means of subsistence and consequently the degree of economic development attained by a given epoch form the foundation upon which the state institutions, the legal conceptions, art, and even the ideas on religion, of the people concerned have been evolved, and in the light of which they must therefore be explained, instead of vice versa, as had hitherto been the case.

"But that is not all. Marx also discovered the special law of motion governing the present-day capitalist mode of production and the bourgeois society that this mode of production has created. The discovery of surplus value suddenly threw light on the problem, in trying to solve which all previous investigations of both bourgeois economists and socialist critics, had been groping in the dark.

". . . Marx was before all else a revolutionist. His real mission in life was to contribute, in one way or another, to the overthrow of capitalist society and of the state institutions which it brought into being, to contribute to the liberation of the modern proletariat, which *he* was the first to make conscious of its own position and its needs, conscious of the conditions of its emancipation. Fighting was his element. And he fought with a passion, a tenacity, and a success such as few could rival. . . .

"And, consequently, Marx was the best hated and most calumniated man of his time. Governments, both absolutist and republican, deported him from their territories. Bourgeois, whether conservative or ultra-democratic, vied with one another in heaping slanders upon him. All this he brushed aside as though it were cobweb, ignoring it, answering only when extreme necessity compelled him. And he died beloved, revered and mourned by millions of revolutionary fellow-workers – from the mines of Siberia to California, in all parts of Europe and America – and I make bold to say that though he may have many opponents he had hardly one personal enemy. His name will endure through the ages, and so also will his work."[62]

There could be no doubt that Marx's mantle would pass on to Engels who had for long been his intimate friend, his leading disciple, and his closest collaborator. "Taking up the weapons which were slipping out of the weary hand of his dying friend, Engels led the working-class movement for many years."[63] After Marx's death no one challenged Engels's position as the leader of the international socialist movement and the trusted adviser of socialists all over the world. Others might lead national Marxist parties but Engels was the uncrowned king of the international socialist movement. He alone had access to Marx's manuscripts. He alone had the experience which enabled him to give authoritative guidance on what doctrines orthodox Marxists should accept and what doctrines they should reject as heretical.

Engels was soon working on Marx's manuscripts with a view to publishing the second and third volumes of *Das Kapital*. But his labours were interrupted when he fell ill towards the end of 1883. In December of that year he wrote to Laura Lafargue that he had been in bed for eight weeks and was still unable to walk.[64] In the following June he told Kautsky that, as he could not sit at his desk, he was lying on a sofa and was dictating to a secretary.[65] In the circumstances there appears to have been no serious delay in Engels's work on Marx's manuscripts. In 1887, however, his labours were again interrupted by illness. This time he suffered from inflamation in one of his eyes. He wrote to Laura Lafargue that it was "a weakness brought on by over-exertion of the eye, especially at night time".[66]

NOTES

1 F. Engels to Karl Marx, February 22, 1870 in *Gesamtausgabe*, Part III, Vol. 4, p. 286.
2 F. Engels to Jenny Marx, August 15, 1870; Karl Marx to F. Engels, August 17, 1870 in *Gesamtausgabe*, Part III, Vol. 4, p. 368 and p. 370.

3 Jenny Marx to F. Engels, August 18, 1870; F. Engels to Karl Marx, August 20, 1870; Jenny Marx to F. Engels, September 13, 1870 in *Gesamtausgabe*, Part III, Vol. 4, pp. 370–85.

4 For the kitchen range see F. Engels to Eleanor Marx, 1894 in E. Bottigelli, "Sieben unveröffentliche Dokumente von Friedrich Engels" in *Friedrich Engels 1820–1870* (Forschungsinstitut der Friedrich Ebert Stiftung, Vol. 85, 1971), p. 325.

5 F. Engels to Laura Lafargue, September 26, 1890 in *F. Engels – Paul and Laura Lafargue: Correspondence*, Vol. 2 (1960), p. 403.

6 Formerly 1 Modena Villas: the name of the street was changed in 1868.

7 Karl Marx to Dr Kugelmann, August 10, 1868 in Karl Marx, *Letters to Dr Kugelmann*, p. 76.

8 Jenny Marx to F. Engels, September 13, 1870 in *Gesamtausgabe*, Part III, Vol. 4, p. 385.

9 Karl Marx to F. Engels, December 7, 1873 in *Gesamtausgabe*, Part III, Vol. 4, p. 411.

10 F. Engels to Karl Marx, December 5, 1873 in *Gesamtausgabe*, Part III, Vol. 4, p. 410.

11 Karl Marx to F. Engels, December 7, 1873 in *Gesamtausgabe*, Part III, Vol. 4, p. 411.

12 F. Engels to Karl Marx, December 10, 1873 in *Gesamtausgabe*, Part III, Vol. 4, p. 413.

13 F. Engels to Karl Marx, July 29, 1881 in *Gesamtausgabe*, Part III, Vol. 4, p. 504.

14 Karl Marx to F. Engels, August 3, 1881 in *Gesamtausgabe*, Part III, Vol. 4, p. 505. Marx wrote: "I very much regret having to press so hard upon your exchequer . . . I must pay £30 in London on August 15. . . ."

15 F. Engels to Karl Marx, August 6, 1881 in *Gesamtausgabe*, Part III, Vol. 4, p. 507.

16 Karl Marx to F. Engels, August 9, 1881 in *Gesamtausgabe*, Part III, Vol. 4, p. 510.

17 F. Engels to Karl Marx, August 11, 1881 in *Gesamtausgabe*, Part III, Vol. 4, p. 510.

18 See F. Regnault, "Les maladies de Karl Marx. Leur influence sur sa vie et sur ses oeuvres" in *Revue Anthropologique*, 1933, Vol. 43, pp. 293–317.

19 Eleanor Marx to Natalie Liebknecht, January 1, 1875 in Wilhelm Liebknecht, *Briefwechsel mit Karl Marx und Friedrich Engels* (ed. by G. Eckert, 1963), p. 423.

20 F. Engels to W. Bracke, October 11, 1875 in Karl Marx–F. Engels, *Briefwechsel mit Wilhelm Bracke 1869–80* (1963), p. 83.

21 Karl Marx to F. Danielson, April 10, 1879 in Marx–Engels, *Briefe über "Das Kapital"* (1954), p. 243 (letter written in English).

22 Arnold Künzli, *Karl Marx. Eine Psychographie* (1966), p. 282.

23 Karl Marx to N. F. Danielson, November 9, 1871 in Marx–Engels, *Briefe über "Das Kapital"* (1954), p. 215: this passage was written in English.

24 Karl Marx to N. F. Danielson, May 28, 1872 in Marx–Engels, *Briefe über "Das Kapital"* (1954), p. 217: except for the first two words, this passage was written in English.

25 Ten thousand copies of the French translation of Volume 1 of *Das Kapital* were printed and 58,000 were ordered before publication.

Marx met Le Roy in 1882: see Karl Marx to F. Engels, August 24, 1882 in *Gesamtausgabe*, Part III, Vol. 4, p. 554.

26 Arnold Künzli, *Karl Marx. Eine Psychographie* (1966), p. 281.

27 Translated by H. A. Lopatin and N. F. Danielson: 3,000 copies were printed and 1,000 were sold between March 27 and May 15, 1872.

28 Karl Marx to F. Engels, November 26, 1869 in *Gesamtausgabe*, Part III, Vol. 4, pp. 247–51.

29 F. Engels to Karl Marx, November 29, 1869 in *Gesamtausgabe*, Part III, Vol. 4, p. 251.

30 Karl Marx to César de Pepe, January 24, 1870 in Marx–Engels, *Briefe über "Das Kapital"* (1954), p. 206.

31 Karl Marx to L. Kugelmann, November 29, 1869 in Karl Marx, *Letters to Dr Kugelmann*, p. 95; Karl Marx to F. Engels, February 10, 1870 in *Gesamtausgabe*, Part III, Vol. 4, p. 275.

32 Karl Marx to S. Meyer, January 21, 1871 in Marx–Engels, *Briefe über "Das Kapital"* (1954), p. 212: English translation in Karl Marx and F. Engels, *Letters to Americans 1848–95* (1963), p. 82.

33 Karl Marx to Vera Zasulich, March 8, 1881 in Marx–Engels, *Briefe über "Das Kapital"* (1954), p. 262.

34 A. Voden, "Talks with Engels" in *Reminiscences of Marx and Engels* (Foreign Languages Publishing House, Moscow), p. 329. See also M. Rubel, "Gespräche über Russland mit Friedrich Engels. Nach Aufzeichnungen von Alexei M. Woden" in *Internationale Wissenschaftliche Korrespondenz zur Geschichte der Deutschen Arbeiterbewegung*, XI–XII, April 1971, pp. 11–24.

35 F. Engels to F. A. Sorge, June 29, 1883 in Karl Marx and F. Engels, *Letters to Americans 1848–95* (1963), p. 140. Among the writers whose books on the peasants in Russia at the time of the emancipation of the serfs were read by Marx were – Skaldin, Seriyevich, Skrevitsky and Golovachev: see *Marx–Engels Archiv*, Vols. 11 and 12.

36 Karl Marx to S. Meyer, January 21, 1871 in Karl Marx and F. Engels, *Letters to Americans 1848–95* (1963), p. 82.

37 Karl Marx to F. A. Sorge, April 4, 1876 in Marx–Engels, *Briefe über "Das Kapital"* (1954), p. 230.

38 F. Engels to Laura Lafargue, February 5, 1884 in *F. Engels – Paul and Laura Lafargue Correspondence*, Vol. 1 (1959), p. 169.

39 Karl Marx to N. F. Danielson, November 15, 1878 and April 10, 1879 in Marx–Engels, *Briefe über "Das Kapital"* (1954), p. 238 and p. 243: these passages were written in English.

40 Karl Marx to F. Domela-Nieuwenhuis, June 27, 1880 in Marx–Engels, *Briefe über "Das Kapital"* (1954), p. 253.

41 Karl Marx to N. F. Danielson, April 10, 1879 in Marx–Engels, *Briefe über "Das Kapital"* (1954), p. 241: the letter was written in English.

42 F. Engels in the *Volkskalender* (Brunswick, 1878): see *Reminiscences of Marx and Engels* (Foreign Languages Publishing House, Moscow), p. 23.

43 F. Engels to August Bebel, August 30, 1883 in W. Blumenberg (ed.), *August Bebels Briefwechsel mit Friedrich Engels* (1965), p. 164; Marx–Engels, *Briefe über "Das Kapital"* (1954), p. 279; and F. Engels, *Briefe an Bebel* (1958), p. 81.

44 F. Engels to N. F. Danielson, November 13, 1885 in Karl Marx and F. Engels, *Selected Correspondence* (Foreign Languages Publishing House, Moscow), p. 465.

August Bebel, 1840–1913

Wilhelm Liebknecht, 1826–1900

45 Edward Aveling in *Reminiscences of Marx and Engels* (Foreign Languages Publishing House, Moscow), p. 311.

46 B. Kautsky (ed.), *Friedrich Engels' Briefwechsel mit Karl Kautsky* (1955), pp. 33–4.

47 Engels wrote: "Percy is now partner of Garman and Rosher, chartered accountants, Walbrook House, E.C. Hope he will prosper. His father has at last forked out the needful and set him out, though with the sourest face and the unpleasantest way possible" (F. Engels to Laura Lafargue, December 13, 1883 in *F. Engels – Paul and Laura Lafargue Correspondence*, Vol. 1 (1959), p. 160).

48 Preface of September 23, 1885 to the second edition of F. Engels, *Herrn Eugen Dührings Umwälzung der Wissenschaft (Anti-Dühring)*, 1878: English translation – *Anti-Dühring: Herr Eugen Dühring's Revolution in Science* (Foreign Languages Publishing House, Moscow, 1959, p. 17).

49 Articles written by Engels for *Der Volksstaat* (Leipzig) were collected and published as a book in 1894: see F. Engels, *Internationales aus dem "Volksstaat"* (1894).

50 Engels described the meeting on Poland in an article in *Der Volksstaat*, March 24, 1875. The speeches delivered by Marx and Engels on this occasion appear in the *Marx–Engels Werke*, Vol. 18, pp. 572–5.

51 E. Aveling, "Engels at Home" in *Reminiscences of Marx and Engels* (Foreign Languages Publishing House, Moscow), p. 310.

52 Hellmut von Gerlach, *Von Rechts nach Links* (1937), p. 139. Hellmut von Gerlach's visit to London took place in 1894.

53 For Paul Lafargue see Émile Bottigelli's introduction to *F. Engels – Paul and Laura Lafargue: Correspondence*, Vol. 3, *1891–5* (Foreign Languages Publishing House, Moscow), pp. 489–542.

54 Paul Lafargue to F. Engels, November 26, 1891 in *F. Engels – Paul and Laura Lafargue: Correspondence*, Vol. 3, p. 138.

55 F. Engels to Julie Bebel, March 8, 1892 in W. Blumenberg (ed.), *August Bebel's Briefwechsel mit Friedrich Engels* (1965), p. 522 and F. Engels, *Briefe an Bebel* (1958), p. 216. See also F. Engels to Natalie Liebknecht, December 19, 1870 in Wilhelm Liebknecht, *Briefwechsel mit Karl Marx und Friedrich Engels* (ed. G. Eckert, 1963), p. 117 ("My wife is a revolutionary Irish woman").

56 Arnold Künzli, *Karl Marx* (1966), p. 388.

57 *Der Sozialdemokrat*, May 3, 1883 and *Reminiscences of Marx and Engels* (Foreign Languages Publishing House, Moscow), p. 355.

58 Robert Payne, *Karl Marx* (1968), pp. 486–7.

59 Karl Marx to F. Engels, January 10, 1883 in *Gesamtausgabe*, Part III, Vol. 4, p. 589.

60 Karl Marx had been on a visit to Ventnor in the Isle of Wight.

61 F. Engels to F. A. Sorge, March 15, 1883 in Karl Marx and F. Engels, *Letters to Americans, 1848–95* (1963), pp. 134–6 and W. O. Henderson (ed.), *Engels: Selected Writings* (Penguin Books, 1967), pp. 395–6.

62 *Der Sozialdemokrat*, March 22, 1883 and *Reminiscences of Marx and Engels* (Foreign Languages Publishing House, Moscow), pp. 348–50.

63 Franz Mehring in *Die Neue Zeit*, Vol. 2, 1904–5 and in *Reminiscences of Marx and Engels* (Foreign Languages Publishing House, Moscow), p. 362.

64 F. Engels to Laura Lafargue, December 13, 1883 in *F. Engels – Paul and Laura Lafargue: Correspondence*, Vol. 1, 1868–86 (1959), p. 159.

65 F. Engels to Karl Kautsky, June 21, 1884 in B. Kautsky (ed.),

Friedrich Engels' Briefwechsel mit Karl Kautsky (1955), p. 123. See also Paul Lafargue to F. Engels, June 20, 1884 in *F. Engels – Paul and Laura Lafargue*, Vol. 1, 1868–86 (1959), p. 209.

66 F. Engels to Laura Lafargue, March 21, 1887 in *F. Engels – Paul and Laura Lafargue: Correspondence*, Vol. 2, 1887–90 (1960), p. 29.

11

THE CHAMPION OF MARXISM 1872–1879

For many years Marx had laid aside his work on capitalism when ever he thought it necessary to refute the errors of his opponents. In the 1870s Engels assumed the mantle of defender of the Marxist faith. He explained that there was now a division of labour between Marx and himself. While Marx was writing "his great basic work", Engels was responsible for "the fight against opposing views".[1] Engels sacrificed his own researches in order to denounce the errors of Bakunin, Proudhon, Blanqui, Dühring, and Höchberg and to criticise the concessions made to the followers of Lassalle when the two German socialist parties united in 1875.

At the same time that he attacked his opponents, Engels expounded Marx's doctrines in simple language which any worker could understand. His essays in defence of Marxism appeared in letters to leading German socialists and in the columns of *Der Volksstaat* and *Vorwärts*.[2] In 1874 *Der Volksstaat* also reprinted Marx's polemic – first published anonymously over twenty years before – criticising the conduct of the Prussian authorities at the trial of the leaders of the Communist League in Cologne in 1852.[3]

I. Anti-Bakunin, 1872–3

Engels's offensive against socialist heretics opened with an attack upon Bakunin and his Alliance of Social Democracy. In a memorandum, written in collaboration with Marx, he denounced Bakunin for his intrigues against the First International. This statement was approved by the General Council of the First International and was published in May 1872.[4] Shortly afterwards Engels drew up a report on the Alliance of Social Democracy, which was submitted to the congress of the First International held at The Hague in September 1872. Engels attacked Bakunin's association for trying "to impose its sectarian programme on the whole International by means of its secret organisation".[5] In 1873 Marx and Engels wrote a report attacking the Alliance of Social Democracy and this was published anonymously as a pamphlet.[6] Shortly afterwards Engels wrote three articles for *Der Volksstaat* in which he condemned the ineptitude exhibited by Bakunin's followers when they tried to play the part of "practical revolutionaries" in Spain in the summer of 1873.

Marx and Engels had hoped that the Franco-Prussian war would spark off many revolutions on the Continent, but the only insurrections that did occur in the early 1870s were in Paris (the Commune) and in Spain. In 1873 the brief reign of King Amadeus ended with his abdication from the Spanish throne and the establishment of a republic. The re-establishment of the monarchy was not possible at this time since the monarchists were divided between supporters of Queen Isabella's son and supporters of Don Carlos. No sooner had Amadeus disappeared from the scene, than the Carlists rose in revolt in the Basque provinces. The middle class republicans were agreed that the landed estates should be divided into smallholdings but they differed on Spain's future constitution. The right wing republicans proposed to maintain a centralised form of administration, while the left wing favoured the establishment of a federal constitution to give greater autonomy to the provinces. There was also a small but active extreme left wing element in Spanish politics at this time – the revolutionary workers in the manufacturing towns. These workers – like the monarchists and the republicans – were split into rival factions, the most important of which were the Intransigents, the Marxists and the followers of Bakunin. Engels considered that the revolutionary workers should have sunk their differences and should have co-operated during the elections for the constituent assembly. Such co-operation would have ensured the return of some deputies representing the revolutionary workers in the Cortes. A small group of left-wing deputies from Barcelona and other industrial centres might have held the balance of power between rival republican groups. Engels blamed the followers of Bakunin – the Spanish section of the Alliance of Social Democracy – for the lack of unity among the revolutionary workers, which made it impossible to carry out this plan.[7]

The leaders of the Alliance of Social Democracy at first urged their followers to boycott the elections to the constituent assembly. Engels observed that to advise the workers to "abstain from politics under all circumstances, means to drive them into the arms of the priests or the bourgeois republicans".[8] The Bakunists in Spain realised their mistake and told their supporters that they should decide for themselves whether to take part in the elections or not. This abdication of leadership threw the revolutionary workers into the arms, not of any bourgeois party, but of the Intransigents.

Bakunin's followers tried to recover the initiative by calling for a general strike but this proved to be a fiasco. In Barcelona the workers refused to strike. In Alcoy the strikers gained control of the town but were soon ejected by government troops. The Intransigents were now virtually in control of the workers' revolutionary movement in Spain. They demanded the establishment of small autonomous cantons, each responsible for running its own affairs. In several provincial cities such cantons – sometimes modelled on the Paris Commune – were set up, but the republican government quickly suppressed the movement. Only Cartagena – Spain's most important naval base – held out until January 1874.

In the autumn of 1873 Engels contributed three articles to *Der Volksstaat* on recent events in Spain. He argued that Bakunin's Alliance of Social Democracy had been guilty of one blunder after another. It had been a mistake to boycott the elections. When this mistake had been realised a second mistake had been made in leaving the workers free to take part or not to take part in the elections. And it had been a mistake to try and bring about a revolution in Spain by means of a general strike. Engels declared that the followers of Bakunin had flouted every sound principle of revolutionary politics and guerilla warfare. The result of these errors of judgment had been a "senseless splitting of the revolutionary fighting forces". "This enabled the Spanish authorities, with only a handful of troops, to capture one town after another without encountering any serious opposition."[9]

II. Anti-Proudhon, 1872

In 1887 Engels declared that Proudhon had "played much too significant a *rôle* in the European working class movement for him to fall into oblivion".[10] Proudhon's doctrines had exercised a powerful influence upon French socialism in the middle of the nineteenth century and his ideas had spread beyond the frontiers of his native land. "In Belgium," wrote Engels, "Proudhonism reigned unchallenged among the Walloon workers, and in Spain and Italy, with isolated exceptions, everything in the working class movement which was not anarchist was definitely Proudhonist."[11] Proudhon's ideas had appealed to the petty bourgeoisie – craftsmen, shopkeepers, peasants, and smallholders – rather than to the industrial proletariat.

Proudhon came into prominence with his book *Qu'est ce que la propriété?* in which he denounced private property as theft and accused capitalists of exploiting the masses by appropriating the value of their labour through rent, interest and profits. During the Second Republic he put forward an abortive scheme for the establishment of a bank of exchange to grant interest-free loans to smallholders, artisans and industrialists who produced food or manufactured goods. The ideas which Proudhon put forward in his voluminous writings have been criticised as "incoherent and diffuse", abounding in "paradoxes and apparent contradictions".[12] Proudhon attacked both capitalists and communists – the former for exploiting the workers, the latter for threatening to enslave them.

Proudhon advocated a revolution which would lead to the establishment of a new type of society in which there would be no room for capitalists or landowners. The existing wage system would be abolished. Money would be replaced by vouchers representing units of labour time. Free credit from a state bank would be available to the producers of food and goods. The workers would control the administration, including the police and the law courts.[13] At the end of his life Proudhon advocated a form of anarchism, arguing that, in his utopia, mankind would attain so high a standard of social behaviour that laws and policemen would be superfluous. Bakunin, the leading anarchist on the Continent in the 1870s, hailed Proudhon as "the master of us all".[14]

In 1847, in his pamphlet on *Misère de la Philosophie*, Marx had struck what Engels regarded as "a decisive blow" against Proudhon's doctrines.[15] But the attack was a damp squib rather than a decisive blow and for the next 25 years Marx and Engels had every reason to fear Proudhon as a dangerous rival. At the time of the First International, Proudhon's followers gave Marx and Engels as much trouble as the supporters of Bakunin. Engels observed that "although the Proudhonists in France were only a small sect among the workers, they were still the only ones who had a definitely formulated programme and who were able in the Commune to take over the leadership in the economic field".[16]

In 1872 Engels was alarmed when an attempt was made to introduce Proudhon's ideas to the German workers through a series of articles on the housing shortage in the socialist journal *Der Volksstaat*.[17] The articles were written by Dr Arthur Mühlberger who was the medical officer of health in Crailsheim (Württemberg).[18] Engels wrathfully declared that Mühlberger's "undiluted Proudhonism"[19] represented "an enormous step backwards in comparison with the whole course of development of German socialism".[20] Mühlberger, in his view, was – albeit "unconsciously" – trying to "adulterate" the socialist movement in Germany.[21] Since he had made a detailed examination of the slums of Manchester, Engels regarded himself as an authority on the housing question and he wrote to Wilhelm Liebknecht that he proposed to refute "this absurd Proudhonist business".[22]

Dr Mühlberger was one of many writers who discussed the housing shortage in Germany in the early 1870s. The war against France and the unification of Germany was followed by a rapid expansion of the economy. There was a great boom in industry, particularly in coal, iron, steel, railways, and engineering. Over 900 new joint stock companies with a capital of £140 million were founded in the three years 1871–3. The erection of new factories and workshops and the construction of public works suddenly increased the labour force in the towns. The construction industry was busy erecting military installations, imposing office blocks and luxury mansions for the rich. But the construction of flats for the workers failed to keep pace with industrial expansion and the appearance of overcrowded unhealthy slums was one of the most serious social problems which the new Reich had to face. The increase in the number of homeless persons was equally alarming. In Berlin, for example, over 10,000 people were without a roof over their heads in 1871.[23] Dr Mühlberger declared that there was "no more terrible mockery of the whole culture of our lauded century than the fact that 90 per cent and more of the population have no place that they can call their own. The real key point of moral and family existence, hearth and home, is being swept away by the social whirlpool".

Dr Mühlberger, the leading disciple of Proudhon in Germany, favoured Proudhon's solution of the housing problem. This was that the workers should be transformed from tenants into house-owners. "Rent, instead of being, as previously, the tribute which the tenant must pay to the perpetual title of capital, will be – from the day when the redemption of rented dwellings is proclaimed – the exactly fixed sum paid by the tenant to provide the annual instalment for the payment of the dwelling which has passed into the possession of the tenant."[24]

Engels replied to Dr Mühlberger in three articles in *Der Volksstaat*.[25] In the first he declared that in modern industrial towns the workers – like other oppressed classes in the past – always lived in overcrowded and squalid conditions. Far from being an unusual phenomenon, as Dr Mühlberger supposed, the unsatisfactory housing situation in Germany in 1872 was a natural and normal consequence of the rapid industrial expansion of the country.

Engels dismissed Dr Mühlberger's remedies as impracticable. He thought that in England, where single family houses were common, it might be possible for some of the workers to buy their cottages and become house owners. But on the Continent many workers rented flats in large buildings containing 20 or 30 families. In such circumstances serious difficulties would arise if a worker changed his job or moved to another town. Engels argued that there would always be a housing shortage in a capitalist society. On the other hand in a socialist society there would be no difficulty in solving the problem since the state would simply take over the mansions of the rich so as to house the homeless and the overcrowded poor. "Immediately the proletariat has seized political power such a measure, dictated by the public interest, will be just as easy to carry out as other expropriations and billetings are by the existing state".[26]

Mühlberger also advocated another remedy, already recommended by Proudhon. This was the drastic reduction – and the eventual abolition – of interest on capital. Mühlberger argued that if interest on capital disappeared, the rent which had to be paid for a house would also disappear. Engels retorted that, in a capitalist society, the interest charged by a lender of capital and the rent charged by a landlord were inevitably determined solely by the law of supply and demand. In the past all attempts by governments or churches to reduce interest rates by usury enactments had failed.

III. Anti-Blanqui, 1874

In 1874 Engels wrote a series of articles in *Der Volksstaat* on the activities of the foreign exiles in London. In one of them he commented upon a manifesto signed by 33 French supporters of the Paris Commune, who advocated the doctrines preached by Blanqui.[27] The signatories demanded the overthrow of capitalist states by revolution; the establishment of a communist society; and the replacement of Christianity by atheism. The revolution which they had in mind would be led by a small group of dedicated militants organised as an underground movement. Engels rejected this conception of revolution as being out of date. He held that capitalism would never be overthrown by a small secret society of revolutionaries. It would fall only when the majority of the proletariat supported the cause of revolution. Engels also attacked those who signed the manifesto for supporting every act of violence committed by the Commune in Paris. He rejected the notion that it was possible to justify every execution and every fire for which the Paris Commune had been responsible. He declared that excesses unfortunately occurred during every revolution but that was no reason for attempting to justify them. "Eventually when the turmoil is over and one can assess calmly the events of the revolution one will have to say: 'We have done much which would have been better undone, and we have not done some things which should have been done – and so mistakes have been made.' "

Engels also criticised the view of communism held by Blanqui's supporters. "In Germany", he wrote, "communists are communists because they see clearly the goal towards which they are striving, despite all the half-way houses and compromises for which historical developments and not the communists must be held responsible. Their aim is to abolish classes and to set up a society with no private ownership of land or the means of industrial production. But the 33 followers of Blanqui are communists because they imagine that once *they* have taken the vital decision to revolt, the half-way houses and compromises can be short-circuited, and communism will be established at once. . . ." Engels dismissed this point of view as naïve and childish.

Finally the 33 signatories of the manifesto thought that religion could be abolished and atheism established by a stroke of the pen. Engels observed that "a great many things can be decreed on paper without ever being carried out" and that "to prohibit an undesirable belief by law is the surest method of encouraging its survival". Engels's comments upon the policy advocated by Blanqui's followers show that he had his feet planted firmly on the ground and that he fully recognised that those who gained power after a revolution would have to take account of human nature when trying to put their extreme policies into practice.

IV. Anti-Lassalle, 1875

In the early 1870s it might have been expected that Engels would have denounced those who advocated Lassalle's views as vigorously as he attacked the followers of Bakunin or Proudhon. But Engels's criticisms of the Lassalleans were confined to private warnings to his socialist friends in Germany and they were not made public at this time. With some reluctance Marx and Engels curbed their natural desire to attack the supporters of Lassalle's movement because they had no wish to imperil the efforts that were being made in Germany to unify the two rival socialist parties. The Social Democrat Party, established at Eisenach in 1869 had secured the support of only some German socialists. Others still belonged to the General German Workers Union which had been founded by Lassalle. Liebknecht and Bebel, the leaders of the Social Democrat Party, were Marxists while the General German Workers Union accepted Lassalle's political programme. Marx and Engels would have welcomed an opportunity to cross swords with the Lassalleans who advocated the establishment of state-aided producers' co-operatives. But Liebknecht and Bebel opposed a public denunciation of Lassalle's supporters. In May 1873 August Bebel warned Engels that it would be a grave mistake to suppose that a ruthless assault upon the Lassalleans could be made "without causing serious injury to the Party". "I quite agree that the Lassalle cult must be rooted out and that Lassalle's errors must be exposed – but only with circumspection." Bebel added that since Marx and Engels were living in London they were not in a position to make an accurate assessment of the political situation in Germany.[28]

Liebknecht and Bebel were trying to establish a single socialist party by uniting the Social Democrat Party and the General German Workers Union. As practical politicians they were prepared to compromise on matters of principle so as to secure the unification that they desired. They were ready to make concessions both to the Lassalleans and to the *Volkspartei* (People's Party). But Marx and Engels were firmly opposed to making any concessions to the Lassalleans which would involve tampering with the basic tenets of the Marxist faith.

Various circumstances paved the way for the union of the two German socialist parties in 1875. Schweitzer's retirement from politics in 1871 deprived the Lassalleans of their ablest leader. In February 1874 when the Reichstag met after a general election the 10 socialist members – seven supporters of the Social Democrat Party and three Lassalleans – agreed to form a single parliamentary group. Shortly afterwards the Prussian government deprived the Lassalleans of their party organisation by dissolving the General German Workers Union. In the circumstances they were ready to come to an understanding with Liebknecht and Bebel.

In March 1875 Marx and Engels read in *Der Volksstaat*[29] the terms of a policy statement which was to be discussed at Gotha by representatives of the two German socialist parties. This draft programme would be the basis of an agreement for unification. Engels warned Bebel against accepting a programme which made far too many concessions to the Lassalleans. He declared that Hasenclever, Hasselmann and Tölcke – supporters of Lassalle's movement – had repeatedly rejected overtures from the Social Democrat Party. "Now a babe in arms can see that these gentlemen must be in a devilish fix if they come to us of their own accord with an offer of reconciliation". Engels suggested that the Lassalleans "ought to have been received with extreme coolness and caution". "It should have been made clear to them that if they wanted unification they must drop their sectarian slogans and their demands for state aid for industrial co-operative enterprises." Engels declared that the draft programme "shows that we are a hundred times superior to the Lassalleans as far as theoretical arguments are concerned but we are much inferior to them in political cunning. Once again 'honest folk' have been thoroughly cheated by dishonest characters."

Engels denounced the proposed statement of socialist policy on various grounds. He criticised its acceptance of Lassalle's assertion that "society is divided into two groups – the working class and all other classes which are only a mass of reactionaries".[30] Engels held this to be historically inaccurate. "If the lower middle-class democrats in Germany were really a part of a 'reactionary mass' how could the Social Democrat Workers' Party co-operate for years with the People's Party? How can *Der Volksstaat* follow the political line of the lower middle class democratic *Frankfurter Zeitung*? And how can one insert in the Gotha programme seven demands which are taken word for word from the programme of the People's Party?"

Engels warned Bebel that it would be folly to include Lassalle's "iron law of wages" in the draft programme. He considered the "law" to be out of date. "Marx has shown that the laws of wages, far from being 'iron laws' are highly elastic and that Lassalle was quite wrong in imagining that his catchphrase was the solution to a complex problem." And that Lassalle's demand for state aid for industrial co-operative enterprises should be included in the draft programme was, in Engels's view, an unwarranted concession to the Lassalleans, especially since Wilhelm Bracke had recently "exposed the utter folly of the plan".[31] (Yet in 1864 in the inaugural address of the First International, Marx had written: "To save the industrial masses, co-operative labour ought to be developed to national dimensions, and consequently to be fostered by national means.")[32]

The vague reference in the draft programme to a future "international brotherhood" was, in Engels's view, a very poor substitute for the unequivocal assertion that socialism was an international movement. The Communist Manifesto had urged the workers of the world to unite against their oppressors and this was still a cardinal principle of Marx's policy. Again, Engels complained that "nothing is said in the Gotha programme about the organisation of the workers in trade unions. And this is a very important matter since the trade unions are the real class organs of the proletariat. It is trade unions which enable the workers to fight their daily battles with the capitalists. It is trade unions which are the training ground for the workers. And trade unions are so firmly entrenched that they simply cannot be destroyed even by the most powerful reaction – such as the reaction in Paris just now. In view of the strength of the trade union movement in Germany the unions should undoubtedly be mentioned in the Gotha programme and a place should be left free for them in the organisation of the Socialist Party."

Engels complained that "a lot of muddled *democratic* demands have found their way into the Gotha programme". The referendum, religious toleration, and academic freedom were "the stock in trade of every middle-class liberal programme and they look somewhat out of place in our programme". Engels also objected to the demand for the establishment of a "free state" since, in his view, "a state automatically dissolves itself and vanishes when a socialist society is established". "The state is merely a temporary phenomenon which socialists can use in the revolutionary struggle."

Finally Engels criticised the demand in the draft programme for "the removal of all social and political inequalities". He argued that it was inevitable that there should be some inequalities in the standard of life in different countries and regions. "The inhabitants of mountain districts will always live in a different sort of way from the townsman." Engels dismissed "the notion that socialist society is a society of *equals*" as an out of date idea derived from the old French revolutionary slogan: "Liberty, Equality, Fraternity."

Engels warned Bebel that if "this weak and flabby programme was adopted by a united socialist party, neither he nor Marx would be able to recognise the new party". Indeed they might "be forced to decline to accept any responsibility whatsoever for the actions of the Party".[33]

Karl Marx followed up Engels's attack upon the draft socialist programme by a detailed denunciation of his own. On May 5, 1875 he sent Wilhelm Bracke a memorandum entitled *Randglossen zum Programm der deutschen Arbeiterpartei* and in a covering letter he asked Bracke to pass on his criticisms to Liebknecht, Bebel, Geib and Auer. He stated that if the programme were adopted he and Engels would issue a public statement repudiating it.[34]

Neither Engels's letter to Bebel nor Marx's memorandum to Bracke and his colleagues were made public in 1875. Soon after Marx and Engels had written their criticisms of the draft programme, representatives of the two German socialist parties came to an agreement on the founding of a united party. In the circumstances all concerned considered that it would be in the best interests of the new party to keep silent about their differences regarding the programme adopted at the Gotha conference.[35]

Liebknecht, Bebel and Bracke were not surprised that Marx and Engels should have attacked the inclusion of some of Lassalle's proposals in the Gotha programme. This was to be expected. And after the programme had been adopted both Bebel and Bracke assured Engels that they agreed with many of his objections to it.[36] But they had kept quiet rather than endanger the success of the negotiations for the establishment of a united socialist party.

But what did surprise Liebknecht and Bebel was that Marx and Engels should have attacked not merely the policy advocated by the Lassalleans but also some of the cherished doctrines of the Social Democrat Party. The Eisenach programme of 1869, for example, had included a demand for the establishment of a democratic republic – a "free people's state". The Party's journal was called Der Volksstaat (The People's State) and August Bebel had attempted in his book Unsere Ziele to show that a socialist society could be established within the framework of a democratic republic. Now Engels had reminded Bebel that – according to Marx – the state would have only a brief life after a successful revolution and would soon disappear. Neither Liebknecht nor Bebel relished the prospect of a public controversy on the future of the state in a socialist society and this was another reason for suppressing any reference to the criticisms of the Gotha programme by Marx and Engels.

Once the Gotha programme had been accepted and the two German socialist parties had been united Marx and Engels made the best of a bad job and accepted the situation. Half a loaf was better than no bread. It was preferable for the socialists to unite under a dubious banner than for them to remain divided. Marx and Engels did not come out into the open with their criticisms of the Gotha programme and they thought better of their threats to have nothing to do with the newly-united party. In October 1875 Engels again wrote to Bebel vigorously attacking the Gotha programme as "disorganised, confused, muddled, illogical, and ridiculous". But he ended his letter on a conciliatory note. "You are quite right when you say that unification is an experiment in political education and that in these circumstances a real measure of success may be anticipated. To have achieved unity is in itself a great triumph even if it lasts for only a couple of years. But there can be no doubt that unity could have been purchased at a much lower price."[37]

V. Anti-Dühring, 1878[38]

No sooner had the Social Democrats and the Lassalleans formed a united workers' party in Germany under the banner of the Gotha programme than there was a danger of a split in the party. The new party was attracting to its ranks some trade unionists and some bourgeois intellectuals who had formerly fought shy of joining a working class organisation. There was even room in the party for a Bavarian aristocrat like Georg Heinrich von Vollmar auf Veltheim. Although Marx and Engels themselves came from middle-class families they did not extend a very warm welcome to the bourgeois converts to socialism. In 1877 Marx attacked them as a "gang of half-mature students and super-wise doctors of philosophy who want to give socialism a 'higher, ideal' turn – that is to say, to replace its materialist basis (which calls for serious objective study by anyone wanting to make use of it) by modern mythology with its godesses of justice, equality and fraternity".[39] And nine years later Engels attacked the young intellectuals – such as Max Quarck – "who hover about the boundary land between our Party and the *Katheder-Sozialismus*,[40] take jolly good care to keep clear of all the risks involved by being connected with our Party, and yet expect to reap all the benefits that may accrue from such connection".[41] Marx and Engels were particularly suspicious of wealthy recruits to the party such as Karl Höchberg[42] and Paul Singer.[43] A rich banker's son and the owner of a clothing factory might be well-meaning philanthropists but they were hardly likely to be wholehearted supporters of the principles of the Communist Manifesto. Engels was always opposed to Höchberg's form of philanthropic socialism but in later years he accepted Paul Singer as a reliable socialist colleague and welcomed him to his home.[44]

When Höchberg subsidised the publication of *Die Zukunft* Marx wrote to Bracke criticising this new socialist periodical. "Its main effort is directed towards replacing an understanding of materialism by ideological phrases such as 'Justice' etc. Its programme is a wretched one. And the review promises to indulge in phantasies of social utopias of the future. The first results of a bourgeois buying himself into the party are far from happy."[45] A little later Marx declared that Höchberg was "a 'peaceable' evolutionary and he really expects proletarian emancipation to come only from the 'educated bourgeoisie' – i.e. people like himself".[46] For his part Engels warned his socialist friends in Germany that they would be making a great mistake if they allowed "students and other ignorant know-alls to be regarded as the intellectual representatives of the

Party and to send forth into the world great quantities of utter nonsense".[47]

Some of these intellectuals found a prophet in Dr Eugen Dühring, a blind scholar who had lectured at the University of Berlin since 1863.[48] Dühring came to the fore in the early 1870s as the exponent of a new brand of socialism. His weakness as a scholar was that he imagined himself to be an expert in a wide range of academic disciplines. He had a facile pen and he wrote confidently on philosophy, history, economics, mathematics and various branches of science. He was a self-opinionated man who did not mince his words when he crossed swords with those holding views which differed from his own, even if they were scholars with established reputations in the academic world.

Marx and Engels had known about Dr Dühring since he had reviewed the first volume of *Das Kapital*.[49] Engels had found Dr Dühring's article "highly amusing" and he had dismissed the author as a "vulgar economist".[50] But Marx had adopted a more charitable attitude towards Dr Dühring. He believed that academic economists were ignoring *Das Kapital* and he encouraged Engels to make the book known in Germany by writing anonymous reviews which were sent – through his friends – to the editors of various newspapers. Marx was pleased that a University lecturer should have broken the conspiracy of academic silence over *Das Kapital*. He told Engels in January 1868 that Dr Dühring had given *Das Kapital* a "very decent" review – "particularly as I have dealt so severely with his master Carey".[51] "It says a good deal for the fellow that he virtually accepts my section on 'Original Accumulation'." Marx thought that Dr Dühring had reviewed *Das Kapital* because the book contained some "kicks in the pants" for Professor Roscher whom he cordially disliked as one who blocked "all his avenues of advancement".[52]

Two months later Marx wrote to Dr Kugelmann: "I can now understand the curiously embarrassed tone of Dr Dühring's criticism. He is ordinarily a most bumptious cheeky boy, who sets himself up as a revolutionary in political economy. He has done two things. He has published, first (proceeding from Carey) a *Kritische Grundlegung der Volkswirtschaftslehre*[53] (about 500 pages), and secondly, a new *Natürliche Dialektik*[54] (against the Hegelian dialectic). My book has buried him from both sides. He gave it a notice because of his hatred for Roscher. . . . But never mind. I must be grateful to the fellow, since he is the first expert who has said anything at all."[55]

By the early 1870s the "cheeky bumptious boy" had made a name for himself as a scholar of extreme left-wing views, who had repeatedly criticised his senior colleagues at the University. According to Engels it was about 1875 that Dr Dühring "suddenly and rather clamorously announced his conversion to socialism, and presented the German public not only with an elaborate socialist theory, but also with a complete practical plan for the reorganisation of society". "And Dr Dühring openly proceeded to form around himself a sect, the nucleus of a future separate party."[56]

That Dr Dühring should have secured the support of Johann Most was perhaps to be expected. Most held extreme left-wing views and eventually became an anarchist. Marx wrote that "every change of the wind blows him first in one direction and then in another like a weathercock".[57] But that men like Bebel, Bracke and Bernstein should (even for a time) have fallen under Dr Dühring's spell was surprising. Bebel – Liebknecht's closest ally – declared in an article in *Der Volksstaat* that one of Dr Dühring's works on economics was the best book on the subject since Marx wrote *Das Kapital*. Bracke referred to Dr Dühring as a "party comrade"[58] and declared that Dr Dühring was a scholar of great learning and reasoning powers, who had genuine sympathies for the socialist cause.[59] And Bernstein was so impressed by one of Dr Dühring's books that he distributed copies of it to the leading socialists in Germany.

As Dr Dühring gathered round him a faithful clique of enthusiastic admirers, Liebknecht became increasingly alarmed and more than once urged Marx and Engels to refute Dr Dühring's heretical doctrines. Engels wrote that Liebknecht and his colleagues "thought this absolutely necessary in order to prevent a new occasion for sectarian splitting and confusion from developing within the Party, which was still so young and had but just achieved definite unity".[60]

In May 1876 Marx told Engels that he had ignored Liebknecht's request since the correction of the errors of so insignificant a "scribbler" as Dr Dühring was only a "minor chore" unworthy of his personal attention.[61] Now he had changed his mind since he was satisfied that Dr Dühring did pose a threat to the adoption of his own doctrines by all German socialists. Marx now insisted that Dr Dühring's heretical views "must be ruthlessly exposed".[62] He himself was too busy with his researches on economics so the task of attacking Dr Dühring fell to Engels. With some reluctance Engels embarked upon a project which eventually took up much more of his time than he had originally anticipated.

Engels complained to Marx in a letter of May 1876 that "you can lie in a warm bed studying Russian agrarian conditions in general and ground rent in particular, without being interrupted,

Mikhail Alexandrovitch Bakunin, 1814–1876

Ferdinand Lassalle, 1825–1864

but I am expected to put everything else on one side immediately, to find a hard chair, to swill some cold wine, and to devote myself to going after the scalp of that dreary fellow Dühring."[63] In August 1876 Wilhelm Bracke warned Engels that if Dr Dühring were to be attacked "it will have to be done *soon* or else it will be too late".[64] A few months later Marx wrote to Liebknecht that Engels was working on his polemic against Dr Dühring. "This is a great sacrifice on his part since to do this he has had to postpone work that is much more important."[65]

Engels's first article on Dr Dühring appeared in *Vorwärts* on January 3, 1877. But it was not until April in the following year that Engels was able to tell Bracke that his articles on Dr Dühring ("what an ignorant windbag he is!") had been completed.[66] And it was only in July 1878 that the series of articles was concluded in *Vorwärts*. What began as "a minor chore" had ended as one of Engels's major works – a classic account of Marx's philosophy.

Various difficulties delayed the publication of Engels's articles attacking Dr Dühring. Engels complained that Liebknecht – who had asked Engels to refute Dr Dühring's doctrines – was not publishing the articles every week as had originally been planned. There were gaps in the dates of publication and sometimes only a part of an article was printed.[67] Moreover Dr Dühring's supporters tried to stop the publication of the articles. In 1877 at a conference of the Social Democrat Party, held at Gotha, Johann Most submitted a motion that no more of Engels's articles on Dr Dühring should appear in *Vorwärts*. But an amendment, proposed by August Bebel, was passed which allowed the articles to continue, though in future they would appear in the literary supplement of the paper.[68] Eventually on July 7, 1878 – shortly before the whole socialist press in Germany was closed down under the Anti-Socialist Law of October 21, 1878 – the last of Engels's articles appeared.

Engels's articles were soon published as a book which came to be known simply as *Anti-Dühring*. One chapter – a criticism of Dr Dühring's *Critical History of Political Economy* – was contributed by Karl Marx.[69] According to Karl Kautsky *Anti-Dühring* had little impact upon socialist opinion in Germany when it first appeared. Almost immediately after it was published in 1878 the Anti-Socialist Law came into force and members of the Social Democrat Party had other things to do than to read Engels's book.[70] But Engels later boasted that in the long run the banning of *Anti-Dühring* at the time of the Anti-Socialist Law had greatly increased its sales.[71] In 1888 the socialist journal *Der Sozialdemokrat* declared that – after Marx's work on capital – *Anti-Dühring*

was "the most important and instructive book in our party literature".[72]

Anti-Dühring was a very different type of polemic from Marx's
attacks upon his enemies. In *Herr Vogt* Marx had crushed an
opponent by the sheer virulence of his vituperation. The quarrel
between Marx and Vogt was soon forgotten and so was Marx's
book. But in *Anti-Dühring* Engels was not content to refute a
heresy. Having disposed of Dr Dühring he proceeded to give a clear
exposition of Marx's doctrines. As Engels explained in 1885 "the
'system' of Herr Dühring which is criticised in this book ranges
over a very wide theoretical domain; and I was compelled to follow
him wherever he went and to oppose my conceptions to his. As a
result, my negative criticism became positive; the polemic was
transformed into a more or less connected exposition of the
dialectical method and of the communist world outlook fought for
by Marx and myself – an exposition covering a fairly comprehensive range of subjects."[73] Engels's *Anti-Dühring* eventually exercised a powerful influence upon German speaking socialists and
especially upon the young intellectuals. Karl Kautsky later recalled
that "only after the publication of Engels's *Anti-Dühring* did we
begin to make a thorough study of Marx's doctrines and to think
and act like Marxists".[74]

It is not necessary to discuss in detail either Dr Dühring's new
philosophy of socialism or the arguments brought forward by
Engels to refute Dr Dühring's doctrines. Probably Engels was mistaken in supposing that Dr Dühring threatened the onward march
of Karl Marx's ideas in Germany. Engels's greatest success as the
champion of Marxism was achieved against one of the least important of his opponents. Dr Dühring did not rank, either as a thinker
or as an agitator, with Proudhon, Lassalle, or Bakunin. His influence
over the German socialist intellectuals would almost certainly have
declined even if *Anti-Dühring* had never been written. Dr Dühring
remained in the public eye for a time because his feud with the
University of Berlin reached its climax with his dismissal from his
lectureship. His licence to teach in a Prussian university was withdrawn. According to Liebknecht he was literally starving to death
in 1876.[75] Supporters of academic freedom such as Louis Viereck
denounced the University authorities as reactionaries. In some
quarters Dr Dühring came to be regarded as a martyr who had
been punished for daring to attack the German university system.
Engels thought that Dr Dühring had been the victim of a "despicable injustice".[76] The outcry concerning Dr Dühring's dismissal
and the controversy between Engels and Dr Dühring were soon
forgotten. Dr Dühring sank into obscurity and his name survived

only because it appeared in the title of a book which shattered his pretensions to be regarded as a serious socialist thinker.

The success of *Anti-Dühring* was followed by the still greater success of *Socialism Utopian and Scientific*. This pamphlet consisted of three chapters from *Anti-Dühring*. It appeared first in 1880 in a French translation by Paul Lafargue. In 1883 it was published in German,[77] and in 1892 there was an English translation by Edward Aveling. By this time the pamphlet was circulating in ten languages. Engels claimed that no other socialist work – "not even our Communist Manifesto or Marx's *Capital*" – had appeared in so many languages. Paul Lafargue assured Engels that his pamphlet had had "a strong influence on the theoretical development of French socialism"[78] and "a decisive effect on the direction of the socialist movement in its beginnings".[79] In Germany 20,000 copies were sold in nine years. *Socialism Utopian and Scientific* was one of the most widely read socialist pamphlets in the last two decades of the nineteenth century. This brilliant "propaganda brochure" proved to be the climax of Engels's long career as a socialist agitator.[80]

VI. Anti-Höchberg, 1879

When Engels agreed to refute Dr Dühring's views in *Vorwärts* he told Liebknecht that this was the last occasion on which he would interrupt his researches to write for the press unless exceptional circumstances made it imperative for him to do so.[81] The necessity arose sooner than he had expected Shortly after his last article on Dr Dühring appeared, the Anti-Socialist Law was passed in Germany outlawing the Social Democrat Party and banning its publications. But new socialist journals were soon established abroad. One was the *Jahrbuch für Socialwissenschaft und Socialpolitik*, launched in Zürich in 1879 and subsidised by Dr Karl Höchberg. Since Höchberg – in Kautsky's words – "rejected Marx's philosophy and had no understanding of Marx's economics"[82] his journal was hardly likely to commend itself to Marx and Engels.

In the summer of 1879 Karl Höchberg and Paul Singer visited London to seek the co-operation of Marx and Engels in publishing the journal. Both were wealthy recruits to the Social Democrat Party whom Marx and Engels regarded with considerable suspicion. Marx decided that Höchberg was "an emotional driveller" who had "bought himself into the party with his money",[83] while Singer had "a petty-bourgeois paunch".[84] At first Marx and Engels were not unfavourably disposed towards the new journal but as soon as they realised that its editorial policy would be under Höchberg's control, they hastily withdrew their support. They had had a poor opinion of *Die Zukunft* – a journal edited by Dr Höchberg – and they had no reason to suppose that his new venture would be any better. Engels warned Bebel that Höchberg was "an utterly un-political fellow who is not even a *Social Democrat* – only a social *philanthropist*". He considered that the proposed review would not support Marx's doctrines but would be a vehicle for pro-pagating the views of Höchberg and the "professional socialists".[85]

The fears of Marx and Engels were amply justified when they saw the first number of Dr Höchberg's *Jahrbuch*. This contained an anonymous article entitled "Reflections on the Social Movement in Germany".[86] There were three stars at the end of the article and it was generally assumed that this indicated that Höchberg, his secretary Bernstein, and C. A. Schramm accepted responsibility for the views expressed in it. According to Bernstein the article had been written by Dr Karl Flesch, who had been friendly with Höch-berg in his student days.[87]

The article declared that "under the pressure of the Anti-Socialist Law, the Social Democrat Party had shown that it is not prepared to follow a path leading to violent, bloodthirsty revolu-tion, but is determined – despite some breaches of the law and even acts of violence in the past – to pursue a course of peaceful reform". The image of the party in the future should not be that of "a riff raff with a mania for barricades" but of an organisation determined to secure reforms by strictly legal means. A policy of restraint would make the Social Democrat Party acceptable to many members of "the educated and property owning classes". The article recalled that Lassalle had hoped that his political pro-gramme would appeal not merely to the workers but also to democrats, intellectuals and those who believed in the brotherhood of man. The Anti-Socialist Law had given the German socialists a breathing space for reflection upon the outcome of their policy in the past. By praising the Paris Commune the leaders of the Social Democrat Party had emphasised the revolutionary character of socialism. This had been a grave mistake since it had brought the wrath of the middle classes upon the heads of the socialists and had made it impossible for well disposed members of the bour-geoisie to support the workers movement. Indeed, by unnecessarily provoking the middle classes, the socialists had encouraged Bis-marck to secure the passage of the Anti-Socialist Law through the Reichstag. The writer of the article advised the socialists to forget about establishing a utopia in the remote future and to concentrate their attention on the attainment of realistic reforms in their own day. By seeking election to local councils and by establishing co-operative societies they might hope to achieve limited reforms. The article assumed that it would be possible to transform a capitalist society into a socialist society by a series of moderate reforms.

When Engels read this article he wrote to Marx that they should state "their precise reasons for being absolutely unable to co-operate with a journal over which Höchberg exercises any influence whatsoever". He was angry that the article should actually assert that "the Germans have made a mistake in turning the socialist movement into a mere workers' movement and by aggravating the middle classes have only themselves to blame for the Anti-Socialist Law".[88] Marx realised that the "*Jahrbuch* twaddlers" must be attacked "sharply and ruthlessly".[89] And to Sorge he wrote that Karl Höchberg and his followers were "professional socialist rogues", "nonentities in theory and useless in practice", and "wretched counter-revolutionary windbags".[90] Engels agreed to write a reply to the *Jahrbuch* "three star" article[91] and this took the form of a "Circular Letter" – signed by Marx and Engels – and addressed to Liebknecht, Bebel and other socialist leaders in Germany.[92]

In the Circular Letter Engels denounced Höchberg and his friends for suggesting that the German socialists should reject revolution and advocate peaceful reform and that the proletarian character of the socialist movement should be diluted with middle-class democrats. Engels argued that Höchberg's supporters were no better than the long forgotten "true socialists" of the 1840s who had failed to appreciate the significance of the class struggle and had tried to hide their inability to produce a policy by using vague high-sounding phrases such as "a true love of humanity". While admitting that there might be a place for middle-class supporters in the Social Democrat Party, Engels argued that "to be of use to the proletarian movement these people must bring real intel-lectual elements into it". But most of the bourgeois converts to socialism in the 1870s had not advanced the movement in the slightest. They had failed to study Marx's works. Each convert tried to adapt the principles of Marx's doctrines to his own pre-conceived ideas.

"If people of this kind from other classes join the proletarian move-ment, the first condition must be that they should not bring any remnants of bourgeois, petty-bourgeois etc. prejudices with them, but should wholeheartedly adopt the proletarian outlook. But these gentlemen, as has been proved, are chock full of bourgeois and petty-bourgeois ideas. In such a petty bourgeois country as Germany these ideas certainly have their justification – but only *outside* the Social Democrat Party.

"If these gentlemen constitute themselves into a social-democratic petty bourgeoisie party they have a perfect right to do so. One could then negotiate with them and form a coalition with them according to circumstances. But in a workers' party they are an adulterating element. If reasons exist for tolerating them there for the moment it is our duty *only* to tolerate them, to allow them no influence in the Party leadership and to remain aware that a break with them is only a matter of time. That time, moreover, seems to have come. How the Party can tolerate the authors of this article in its midst is incomprehensible to us. . . .

"As for ourselves, in view of our whole past there is only one course open to us. For almost forty years we have stressed the class struggle as the immediate driving power in history, and in particular the class struggle between bourgeoisie and proletariat as the great lever of the modern social revolution. It is, therefore, impossible for us to co-operate with people who wish to expunge this class struggle from the movement. When the International was formed we expressly formulated the battle cry: 'The emancipation of the working classes themselves.' We cannot therefore co-operate with people who openly state that the workers are too uneducated to emancipate themselves and must be freed from above by philanthropic big bourgeois and petty bourgeois. If the new Party organ adopts a line that corresponds to the views of these gentlemen – that is, bourgeois and not proletarian – then nothing remains for us, much though we should regret it, but publicly to declare our opposition to it, and to dissolve the bonds of the solidarity with which we have hitherto represented the German Party abroad. But it is to be hoped that things will not come to *such* a pass. . . ."

There was no breach between Marx and Engels and the Social Democrat Party. When Engels wrote his "Circular Letter" to Liebknecht and Bebel he was preaching to the converted. Most of the party's leaders were as opposed to the views expressed in the "three star" article in Höchberg's *Jahrbuch* as Marx and Engels had been. Bebel doubted whether a couple of dozen socialists in the whole of Germany supported the policy advocated in the article. And he assured Engels that Höchberg – despite his generous gifts to the Social Democrat Party – exercised no influence over the policy of the party.[93] In December 1880 Bebel and Bernstein travelled to England – at Höchberg's expense – to visit Marx and Engels. This visit – which Bebel called his "road to Canossa" – restored the confidence of Marx and Engels in the leadership of the Social Democrat Party. Meanwhile Dr Höchberg's health was declining and he retired from his political activities in 1883. Only three numbers of his *Jahrbuch* appeared. He died in June 1885, having lavished a fortune on the socialist cause. By giving timely financial aid to Bernstein and Kautsky he had helped two exceptionally able young socialists to gain experience in politics and journalism at an early stage in their careers.[94]

NOTES

1 F. Engels, *Zur Wohnungsfrage* (first published in *Der Volksstaat* and then as two pamphlets in 1872–3: in a second edition of 1887 the two pamphlets were printed together): English translation – F. Engels, *The Housing Question*, 1872 (edited by C. P. Dutt), p. 10.

2 These were the official journals of the Social Democrat Party. Both were published in Leipzig. Wilhelm Liebknecht edited *Der Volksstaat* and was joint editor of *Vorwärts*.

3 Karl Marx, *Enthüllungen über den Kommunistenprozess zu Köln* (Basel, 1852: Boston, U.S.A., 1853): new edition with introduction by F. Engels, 1885: English translation – Karl Marx, *The Cologne Communist Trial* (ed. R. Livingstone, 1971).

4 Karl Marx and F. Engels, *Les prétendues scissions dans l'Internationale* (Geneva, 1872). English translation in *The General Council of the First International: Minutes*, Vol. 5, 1871–2 (Progress Publishers, Moscow), pp. 356–409.

5 F. Engels, *Rapport fait au Congrès de la Haye au nom du Conseil Général sur l'Alliance de la Démocratie Socialiste* (August 1872), printed in *The General Council of the First International: Minutes*, Vol. 5, 1871–2 (Progress Publishers, Moscow), pp. 461–76. English translation: *Report on the Alliance of Socialist Democracy presented in the Name of the General Council to the Congress at The Hague* (*ibid.*, pp. 505–18).

6 The pamphlet *L'Alliance de la Démocratie Socialiste et l'Association Internationale des Travailleurs* was published anonymously in London in 1873. It has been attributed (i) to Engels (by Gustav Mayer), (ii) to Marx and Engels (*Marx–Engels Verzeichnis*, Berlin 1966), and (iii) to Marx, Engels and Lafargue (by Max Nomad). German title, *Ein Komplott gegen die Internationale Arbeiterassociation (Marx–Engels Werke*, Vol. 18, p. 327.

7 For the First International in Spain see C. Marti, "La Première Internationale à Barcelona" in the *International Review of Social History*, Vol. 4, 1959. For the activities of Paul Lafargue in Madrid in 1872 on behalf of the Marxists see *F. Engels – Paul and Laura Lafargue: Correspondence*, Vol. 1, 1868–86 (1959). Lafargue helped to establish the New Madrid Federation which supported the First International and issued the socialist journal *La Emancipation*.

8 F. Engels to T. F. Cuno, January 24, 1872 in Karl Marx and F. Engels, *Letters to Americans 1848–95* (1963), p. 97.

9 F. Engels, "Die Bakunisten an der Arbeit. Denkschrift über den Aufstand in Spanien im Sommer 1873" in *Der Volksstaat*, Numbers 105, 106 and 107 (October 31, November 2 and 5, 1873): reprinted in F. Engels, *Internationales aus dem "Volksstaat" 1871–5* (Berlin, 1894), F. Engels, *Ausgewählte Militärische Schriften*, Vol. 2 (1964), pp. 536–55 and *Marx–Engels Werke*, Vol. 18, pp. 476–511. An anonymous article on Spain which appeared in *Der Volksstaat* on

March 1, 1873 has been attributed to Engels. It was entitled "Die Republik in Spanien": see *Friedrich Engels 1820–70* (Schriften des Forschungs institut der Friedrich Ebert Stiftung, Vol. 85, 1971, pp. 313–7).

10 F. Engels, *The Housing Question, 1872* (ed. C. P. Dutt), preface to the edition of 1887, p. 10.

11 F. Engels, *The Housing Question, 1872* (ed. C. P. Dutt), p. 9.

12 S. Bernstein, *The Beginnings of Marxian Socialism in France* (1965), p. 19.

13 S. Bernstein, *The Beginnings of Marxian Socialism in France* (1965), p. 25–6.

14 F. Engels, *The Housing Question, 1872* (ed. C. P. Dutt), p. 9.

15 F. Engels, *The Housing Question, 1872* (ed. C. P. Dutt), p. 21.

16 F. Engels, *The Housing Question, 1872* (ed. C. P. Dutt), p. 9.

17 Dr Arthur Mühlberger (1847–1907) wrote two books on Proudhon in the 1890s: *Studien über Proudhon* (1891) and *P. J. Proudhon. Leben und Werke* (1899).

18 A. Mühlberger, "Zur Wohnungsfrage" in *Der Volksstaat* (Leipzig), Numbers 10 to 13 (February 3 to 14, 1872), Numbers 15 (February 21, 1872) and Number 19 (March 6, 1872): subsequently reprinted as a pamphlet.

19 F. Engels, *The Housing Question, 1872* (ed. C. P. Dutt), p. 79.

20 F. Engels, *The Housing Question, 1872* (ed. C. P. Dutt), p. 21.

21 F. Engels to August Bebel, June 20, 1873 in W. Blumenberg (ed.), *August Bebels Briefwechsel mit Friedrich Engels* (1965), p. 20. English translation Karl Marx and Friedrich Engels, *Selected Correspondence* (Foreign Languages Publishing House, Moscow), p. 345.

22 F. Engels to W. Liebknecht, May 7, 1872 in Wilhelm Liebknecht, *Briefwechsel mit Karl Marx und Friedrich Engels* (ed. G. Eckert, 1963), p. 163.

23 A. Damaschke, *Die Boden reform* (1922), p. 433.

24 Quoted in F. Engels, *The Housing Question, 1872* (ed. C. P. Dutt), p. 27 and p. 32.

25 F. Engels, "Zur Wohnungsfrage" in *Der Volksstaat* (Leipzig), Number 51 to 53 (June 26–July 3, 1872), Numbers 103 and 104 (December 25–28, 1872), Numbers 2 and 3 (January 4 and 8, 1873). A second series of articles by Engels entitled "Nachtrag über Proudhon und die Wohnungsfrage" appeared in *Der Volksstaat*, Number 12 and 13 (February 8 and 12, 1873) and Numbers 15 and 16 (February 19 and 22, 1873). Both the first and the second series of articles were printed separately as pamphlets in 1872 and 1873. A second edition (both series of articles printed together) appeared in 1887. English translation: F. Engels, *The Housing Question* (ed. by C. P. Dutt).

26 F. Engels, *The Housing Question* (ed. by C. P. Dutt), p. 36.

27 F. Engels, "Programme der blanquistischen Kommuneflüchtlinge" in *Der Volksstaat*, Number 73, June 26, 1874 (in *Marx–Engels Werke*, Vol. 18, pp. 528–35).

28 August Bebel to F. Engels, May 19, 1873 in Werner Blumenberg (ed.), *August Bebels Briefwechsel mit Friedrich Engels* (1965), p. 14.

29 *Der Volksstaat*, March 7, 1875.

30 For this slogan see F. Mehring, "Zur Geschichte eines Schlagwortes" in *Neue Zeit*, Vol. 15 (ii), pp. 515 *et seq.*

31 Wilhelm Bracke, *Der Lassallesche Vorschlag* (1873).

32 "Inaugural Address of the Working Men's International Association"

(1864) in *The General Council of the First International*, Vol. 1, 1864–6 (*Documents of the First International*) (Foreign Languages Publishing House, Moscow), p. 286.

33 F. Engels to August Bebel, March 18–28, 1875 (written on March 18 and sent on March 28 to reach Bebel after he left prison on April 1) in Werner Blumenberg (ed.), *August Bebels Briefwechsel mit Friedrich Engels* (1965) pp. 27–35.

34 Karl Marx to Wilhelm Bracke, May 5, 1875 in Karl Marx–Friedrich Engels, *Briefwechsel mit Wilhelm Bracke, 1869–80* (1963), pp. 45–6 (letter) and pp. 47–70 (*Randglossen*). The memorandum (*Randglossen*) was seen by Geib, Auer and Liebknecht but not by Bebel. Bracke returned Marx's manuscript to Engels in June 1875 (see W. Bracke to F. Engels, June 28, 1875: *ibid.*, p. 77). Engels published an abbreviated version of the *Randglossen* in 1891 in *Die Neue Zeit* (Vol. 1, No. 18) under the title "Kritik des Gothaer Programms". The complete text was published in 1927: English translation – Karl Marx, *Critique of the Gotha Programme* (Progress Publishers, Moscow, 1971) which includes a translation of Marx's letter to Bracke, May 5, 1875 (pp. 9–10).

35 For the German text of the Gotha programme of 1875 see W. Mommsen (ed.), *Deutsche Parteiprogramme* (1960), pp. 313–14: English translation in V. L. Lidtke, *The Outlawed Party. Social Democracy in Germany, 1878–1890*) (1966), Appendix A, pp. 333–4.

36 August Bebel to F. Engels, September 21, 1875 (reply to Engels's letter of March 18–28, 1875): F. Engels to August Bebel, October 12, 1875 in Werner Blumenberg (ed.), *August Bebels Briefwechsel mit Friedrich Engels* (1965), pp. 35–9. Wilhelm Bracke to Karl Marx, May 10, 1875 and W. Bracke to F. Engels, May 10, May 27 and June 28 1875 in Karl Marx–F. Engels, *Briefwechsel mit Wilhelm Bracke, 1869–1880* (1963), pp. 74–80.

37 F. Engels, October 12, 1875 in Werner Blumenberg (ed.), *August Bebels Briefwechsel mit Friedrich Engels* (1965), pp. 37–9. For the unification of the two German socialist parties see F. Oelssner, *Das Kompromiss von Gotha und seine Lehren* (1955) and Erich Kundel, *Marx und Engels im Kampf um die revolutionäre Arbeitereinheit. Zur Geschichte des Gothaer Vereinigungskongresses von 1875* (1962).

38 See D. Rjasanov, "Fünfzig Jahre Anti-Dühring" in *Unter dem Banner des Marxismus*, Vol. 2 (1928). Dr Dühring was born in 1833 and died in 1921.

39 Karl Marx to Adolph Sorge, October 19, 1877 in Karl Marx and F. Engels, *Letters to Americans, 1848–95* (1963), p. 116.

40. "Academic Socialists."

41 F. Engels to Laura Lafargue, January 17, 1886 in *F. Engels – Paul and Laura Lafargue: Correspondence*, Vol. 1, 1868–86 (Foreign Languages Publishing House, Moscow, 1959), pp. 331–2.

42 For Höchberg see article by Eduard Bernstein in *Der Sozialdemokrat*, July 2, 1885.

43 For Paul Singer see article by Eduard Bernstein in *Der wahre Jacob*, February 14, 1911.

44 Karl Kautsky in B. Kautsky (ed.), *Friedrich Engels' Briefwechsel mit Karl Kautsky* (1955), p. 169.

45 Karl Marx to Wilhelm Bracke, October 23, 1877 in Karl Marx–F. Engels, *Briefwechsel mit Wilhelm Bracke, 1869–1880* (1963), p. 52.

Die Zukunft was published in Berlin between October 1877 and November 1878.

46 Karl Marx to Adolph Sorge, September 19, 1879 in Karl Marx and F. Engels, *Letters to Americans, 1848–95* (1963), p. 120.

47 F. Engels to J. P. Becker, January 11, 1878 in *Marx–Engels Werke*, Vol. 34, p. 20 and H. Hirsch (ed.), *Friedrich Engels Profile* (1970), p. 213.

48 For Dr Dühring see articles in the *Deutsches Biographisches Jahrbuch*, Vol. 3, Year 1921 (1927), p. 68 and the *Neue Deutsche Biographie*, Vol. 4 (1959), p. 157.

49 Eugen Dühring's review of *Das Kapital*, Vol. 1, appeared in the *(Hildburgerhauser) Ergänzungsblätter zur Kenntnis der Gegenwart*.

50 F. Engels to Karl Marx, January 7, 1868 in *Gesamtausgabe*, Part III, Vol. 4, p. 4.

51 Karl Marx to F. Engels, January 8, 1868 (first letter) in *Gesamtausgabe*, Part III, Vol. 4, p. 5.

52 Karl Marx to F. Engels, January 8, 1868 (second letter) in *Gesamtausgabe*, Part III, Vol. 4, p. 6.

53 *Critical Foundation of Economics.* Marx wrote *Nationalökonomie* instead of *Volkswirtschaftslehre*.

54 *Natural Dialectic.*

55 Karl Marx to Dr L. Kugelmann, March 6, 1868 in Karl Marx–F. Engels, *Briefe über "Das Kapital"* (1954): English translation – K. Marx, *Letters to Dr Kugelmann*, p. 63. In a letter to Siegfried Meyer (July 4, 1868) Marx wrote: "The only thing that has appeared in the camp of official political economy is the report by Dr Dühring (*Privatdozent* at the University of Berlin, an adherent of Carey's) printed in the *Hildburghauser Ergänzungsblätter*. The report is fainthearted, but on the whole, sympathetic" (Karl Marx and F. Engels, *Letters to Americans, 1848–95* (1963), p. 74).

56 F. Engels, *Socialism: Utopian and Scientific* (Chicago, 1905), p. v.

57 Karl Marx to A. Sorge, September 19, 1879 in Karl Marx and F. Engels, *Letters to Americans, 1848–95* (1963), p. 119.

58 Wilhelm Bracke to F. Engels, August 2, 1875 in Karl Marx–F. Engels, *Briefwechsel mit Wilhelm Bracke, 1869–80* (1963), p. 90.

59 Wilhelm Bracke to F. Engels, May 2, 1877 in Karl Marx–F. Engels, *Briefwechsel mit Wilhelm Bracke, 1869–80* (1963), p. 130.

60 F. Engels, Anti-Dühring. *Herr Eugen Dühring's Revolution in Science*, 1878 (Foreign Languages Publishing House, Moscow, 1959), preface to the first edition, p. 9.

61 Karl Marx to F. Engels, March 5, 1877 in *Gesamtausgabe*, Part III, Vol. 4, p. 405.

62 Karl Marx to F. Engels, May 25, 1876 in *Gesamtausgabe*, Part III, Vol. 4, p. 433.

63 F. Engels to Karl Marx, May 28, 1876 in *Gesamtausgabe*, Part III, Vol. 4, p. 436.

64 Wilhelm Bracke to F. Engels, August 2, 1876 in Karl Marx–F. Engels, *Briefwechsel mit Wilhelm Bracke, 1869–80* (1963), p. 169.

65 Karl Marx to W. Liebknecht, October 7, 1876 in Wilhelm Liebknecht, *Briefwechsel mit Karl Marx und Friedrich Engels* (edited by Georg Eckert, 1963), p. 204.

66 F. Engels to Wilhelm Bracke, April 30, 1878 in Karl Marx–Friedrich Engels, *Briefwechsel mit Wilhelm Bracke, 1869–80* (1963), p. 169.

67 F. Engels to W. Liebknecht, April 11, 1877 in Wilhelm Liebknecht,

Briefwechsel mit Karl Marx und Friedrich Engels (ed. Georg Eckert, 1963), p. 213. On April 11, 1877 Karl Marx wrote to Wilhelm Bracke that Engels was "highly dissatisfied with the way in which *Vorwärts* has been printing his articles against Dühring . . . Engels has sent Liebknecht a warning letter. . . ." (Karl Marx–F. Engels, *Briefwechsel mit Wilhelm Bracke*, 1869–80 (1963), pp. 118–19).

68 G. Eckert in Wilhelm Liebknecht, *Briefwechsel mit Karl Marx und Friedrich Engels* (1963), p. 199.

69 Engels printed Marx's chapter in an abridged form in the first (1878) and second (1895) editions of *Anti-Dühring* but it was published in full in the third edition (1894).

70 Benedikt Kautsky (ed.), *Friedrich Engels' Briefwechsel mit Karl Kautsky* (1955).

71 F. Engels, *Anti-Dühring*, 1878 (Foreign Languages Publishing House, Moscow, 1959); introduction to the second edition, 1885, p. 13.

72 *Der Sozialdemokrat*, December 16, 1887.

73 F. Engels, *Anti-Dühring*, 1878 (Moscow, 1959), pp. 13–14.

74 Gustav Mayer, *Friedrich Engels*, Vol. 2 (1934), p. 551. See also Karl Kautsky's comments on *Anti-Dühring* in Benedikt Kautsky (ed.), *Friedrich Engels' Briefwechsel mit Karl Kautsky* (1955), p. 4. Kautsky wrote that "no book has played a greater part in promoting an understanding of Marxism" than Engels's *Anti-Dühring.*

75 Wilhelm Liebknecht to Jenny Marx, undated letter probably written in 1876. See Wilhelm Liebknecht, *Briefwechsel mit Karl Marx und Friedrich Engels* (edited by Georg Eckert, 1963), p. 207.

76 F. Engels, *Anti-Dühring*, 1878 (Foreign Languages Publishing House, Moscow, 1959), introduction to the second edition, 1885, p. 15.

77 The German edition included an appendix ("The Mark") which, as Engels explained in his introduction to the English translation, "was written with the intention of spreading among the German socialist party some elementary knowledge of the history and development of landed property in Germany".

78 Paul Lafargue to F. Engels, July 12, 1885 in *F. Engels – Paul and Laura Lafargue: Correspondence* (Foreign Languages Publishing House, Moscow, 1959), Vol. 1, p. 297.

79 *Ibid.*, June 26, 1894, Vol. 3, p. 335.

80 *The Sozialdemokrat* (February 22, 1883) announced the forthcoming publication of Engels's *Die Entwicklung des Sozialismus von der Utopie zur Wissenschaft* in an article entitled "A new Propaganda Brochure".

81 F. Engels to Eduard Bernstein, July 26, 1879 in H. Hirsch (ed.), *Eduard Bernstein's Briefwechsel mit Friedrich Engels* (1970), p. 8.

82 Karl Kautsky's introduction of 1935 to *Friedrich Engels' Briefwechsel mit Karl Kautsky* (ed. B. Kautsky, 1955), p. 3. Karl Kautsky described Dr Höchberg as "an opponent of Marxism and the class struggle" (*ibid.*, p. 8).

83 Karl Marx to A. Sorge, September 19, 1879 in Karl Marx and F. Engels, *Letters to Americans, 1848–95* (1963), p. 119.

84 In later years Paul Singer was a welcome guest in Engels's house: see Karl Kautsky in B. Kautsky (ed.), *Friedrich Engels' Briefwechsel mit Karl Kautsky* (1955), p. 169.

85 F. Engels to August Bebel, August 4, 1879 in Werner Blumenberg (ed.), *August Bebels Briefwechsel mit Friedrich Engels* (1965), p. 45.

86 "Rückblicke auf die sozialistische Bewegung in Deutschland" in

Jahrbuch für Socialwissenschaft und Socialpolitik, edited by Dr Ludwig Richter (i.e. Karl Höchberg), Zürich, 1879, Year I, Part I, p. 75.

87   E. Bernstein in H. Hirsch (ed.), *Eduard Bernsteins Briefwechsel mit Friedrich Engels* (1970), p. 23.

88   F. Engels to Karl Marx, September 9, 1879 in *Gesamtausgabe*, Part III, Vol. 4, p. 495.

89   Karl Marx to F. Engels, September 10, 1879 in *Gesamtausgabe*, Part III, Vol. 4, p. 497.

90   Karl Marx to A. Sorge, September 19, 1879 in Karl Marx and F. Engels, *Letters to Americans, 1848–95* (1963), p. 120.

91   *Ibid.*, p. 120.

92   Marx and Engels to Bebel, Liebknecht and others (Circular Letter), September 1879: Werner Blumenberg (ed.), *August Bebels Briefwechsel mit Friedrich Engels* (1965), pp. 48–63: English translation of Part III of the Circular Letter in Karl Marx and F. Engels, *Selected Correspondence* (Foreign Languages Publishing House, Moscow), pp. 388–95.

93   August Bebel to F. Engels, October 23, 1879 (reply to the Circular Letter from Marx and Engels) in Werner Blumenberg (ed.) *August Bebels Briefwechsel mit Friedrich Engels* (1965), pp. 63–7.

94   For Karl Höchberg see articles in *Der Sozialdemokrat*, July 2, 1885 (obituary by E. Bernstein) and September 27, 1890 (last number).

12

ENGELS AS HISTORIAN[1]

Just as Engels had anticipated the Communist Manifesto in his "Principles of Communism" so he had anticipated Marx's doctrine of historical materialism in his book on the English workers. Before his partnership with Marx began, Engels had attributed to economic causes the class structure of England in the 1840s. He had explained that the bourgeoisie was the dominant class in English society and that it not only controlled the national economy in its own interests but also used every social institution to serve its own ends. Thus "the whole legal system has been devised to protect those who own property from those who do not".[2] The dominant middle classes were in constant conflict with the oppressed proletariat. Engels confidently predicted that this conflict would end in a revolution and in the triumph of the workers.

These ideas were embodied by Marx and Engels in their theory of history which they worked out in Brussels in 1846 when they were writing *The German Ideology*. They declared:

"It is quite obvious from the start that there exists a materialistic connection of men with one another, which is determined by their needs and their mode of production, and which is as old as men themselves. This connection is ever taking new forms, and thus presents a 'history' independently of the existence of any political or religious nonsense which would hold men together on its own."[3]

The German Ideology was not published at this time but in the Communist Manifesto of 1848 "the theory was applied in broad outline to the whole of modern history".[4]

The doctrine of historical materialism was based upon three propositions. First, in any society it is economic factors – the ways in which food, clothing and shelter are produced – which ultimately determine all other aspects of life such as social customs, laws, politics, philosophy, and art.

Secondly, the history of man is the history of class struggle.[5] In every society there is a dominant class which owns the means of production and a subject class which owns no property. Slaves in the ancient world, serfs in the middle ages, and factory operatives in the nineteenth century were oppressed classes. Engels declared that Marx had discovered "a great law of motion of history" which had "the same significance for history as the law of the transformation of energy has for natural science".[6] According to this "law" all the political, religious or philosophical conflicts recorded in history were really "struggles of social classes" and were brought about by conflicts of an economic nature.

Thirdly, Marx and Engels believed that history had recorded the evolution of society to a predetermined end. Hegel had seen history as the working of the Absolute Mind and as the record of progress towards the realisation of a Divine purpose. Marx and Engels accepted Hegel's view of historical progress but, since they were atheists, they did not believe that God had had any influence upon history. They thought that a succession of class struggles was bringing mankind inexorably towards a dictatorship of the proletariat and the establishment of a classless communist society.

In 1852 in a letter to Weydemeyer, Marx explained that he claimed no credit for discovering "either the existence of classes in modern society or the struggle between them". "Bourgeois historians had described the historical development of this struggle of the classes long before me, and bourgeois economists had portrayed their economic anatomy." "What I did that was new was to prove: (1) that the existence of classes is bound up only with specific historical phases in the development of production; (2) that the class struggle necessarily leads to the dictatorship of the proletariat; (3) that this dictatorship itself only constitutes the transition to the abolition of all classes and to a classless society."[7]

The doctrine of historical materialism had been worked out between 1845 and 1848. After the failure of the revolution of 1848 Marx and Engels began to write history to prove that their theory was correct. In 1850–2 Marx wrote on French history, while Engels wrote on German history. Marx discussed first the recent class struggles in France in 1848–50[8] and then Louis Napoleon's *coup d'état* of December 2, 1851.[9] Engels stated that *The Class Struggles in France* "was Marx's first attempt, with the aid of his materialist conception, to explain a phase of contemporary history from the given economic situation". Marx was able "to trace political events back to the effects of what are, in the last resort, economic causes".[10] And Marx's second pamphlet – *The Eighteenth Brumaire of Louis Bonaparte* – was, in Engels's opinion, "a work of genius". It was "a concise, epigrammatic exposition that laid bare the whole course of French history since the February days in its inner interconnection, reduced the miracle of December 2 to a natural, necessary result of this interconnection – and, in doing so, did not even need to treat the hero of the *coup d'état* otherwise than with the contempt he so well deserved".[11]

Meanwhile Engels was writing on the peasants' revolt of 1525 and the revolution of 1848 in Germany. His discussion of the peasants' revolt appeared in the same numbers of the *Neue Rheinische Zeitung: Politisch-Ökonomische Revue* as Marx's essays on class struggles in France, while his articles on events in Germany in 1848–9 were contributions to the *New York Daily Tribune*.[12] Both attempted to apply the doctrine of historical materialism to various aspects of German history.

In his account of the Peasants' War Engels analysed the complex social structure of Germany in the early sixteenth century and discussed the class interests of the nobles, the burghers, the craftsmen and the serfs. In his view Luther's breach with Rome – like the medieval heresies – could be explained by changes in the economic strength of various social groups. He believed that the Reformation represented an attempt by the urban middle class to overthrow the economic domination of the nobles and the upper clergy. But this revolt sparked off an insurrection of the serfs and the craftsmen. The former were oppressed by their feudal lords, the latter by the wealthy gild-masters. The nobles and the burghers buried the hatchet when confronted by a common danger. The princes took Luther under their wing, while Luther called upon the nobles to crush the peasants' revolt. The alliance between the feudal lords, the urban bourgeoisie, and the religious reformers put down the rebels and their leader Thomas Münzer was executed. Engels argued that there were striking resemblances between Germany in 1625 and Germany in 1848–9. On both occasions the same reactionary forces – the feudal aristocracy and the bourgeoisie – had combined to crush a popular revolutionary movement.

Engels compared the aims and characters of Luther and Münzer. He declared that "from 1517 to 1525 Luther underwent quite the same changes as the present-day German constitutionalists did between 1846 and 1849, and which are undergone by every bourgeois party which, placed for a while at the head of the movement, is overwhelmed by the plebeian proletarian party standing behind it". Engels observed that at first Luther was a revolutionary who called upon the Germans to "turn on all those evil teachers of perdition, those popes, cardinals and bishops, and the entire swarm of the Roman Sodom with arms in hand, and wash our hands in their blood". But when the peasants rose against the feudal lords, Luther changed his tune. He now declared that the Church could be reformed without resorting to violence. But no mercy should be shown to rebellious peasants. "They must be knocked to pieces, strangled and stabbed, covertly and overtly by everyone who can, just as one must kill a mad dog." Engels argued that this was "exactly what our late socialist and philanthropic bourgeoisie said when the proletariat claimed its share in the fruits of victory after the events of March 1848".

While Engels regarded Luther as a reformer who had turned into a reactionary he considered that the leader of the German peasants was a reformer who was far ahead of his time. Münzer, wrote Engels, "preached a kind of pantheism, which curiously resembles modern speculative contemplation, and at times even approaches atheism". As a revolutionary leader Münzer "went far beyond the immediate ideas and demands of the plebeians and peasants, and first organised a party of the élite of the then existing revolutionary elements, which, inasmuch as it shared his ideas and energy, always remained only a small minority of the insurgent masses".[13]

Engels wrote little history between 1850 and 1870 though he did write on the history of modern warfare in connection with his work as a military critic. In the 1870s he resumed his historical studies. In an incomplete essay (written in 1876) Engels turned his attention to pre-history and examined "the part played by labour in the transition from ape to man".[14] He argued that the decisive steps in the evolution of man were the adoption of an erect posture, the development of the hand, the ability to talk, the discovery of fire, and the domestication of animals. These advances towards civilisation were brought about by human labour. In discussing the relation between man and nature, Engels observed that the essential difference between human beings and animals was that while "the animal merely *uses* its environment and brings about changes in it simply by his presence; man by his changes makes nature serve his ends, and masters it". Engels argued that man's triumphs over nature had often had unpleasant unforeseen consequences. There were settlers who had cut down forests to secure arable land and had so decreased the rainfall as to create a desert. There were those who brought the potato to Europe and spread scrofula at the same time. "When the Arabs learned to distil spirits, it never entered their heads that by doing so they were creating one of the chief weapons for the annihilation of the aborigines of the then still undiscovered American continent." As early as 1876 Engels showed how modern industry and agriculture were polluting the environment. Engels attacked bourgeois economists for examining only those "social effects of human actions in the fields of production and exchange that are actually intended". But the consequences which were not foreseen and not intended might be of greater significance. Had Engels completed his essay he might have followed up these arguments by a plea for economic planning which would attempt to prevent the harmful effects upon the environment of man's economic activities.

In 1884 Engels again turned his attention to primitive societies and wrote a pamphlet on *The Origin of the Family, Private Property and the State*. He explained that this was "the fulfilment of a bequest". Marx had hoped to show that the American anthropologist L. H. Morgan had independently confirmed his own materialist interpretation of history. Marx had made lengthy extracts from Morgan's book on *Ancient Society* (1877) and had added some critical notes.

Engels observed that Morgan had "rediscovered, in his own way, the materialist conception of history that Marx had discovered 40 years previously".[15] His account of the Iroquois Indians substantiated the view that classless communist societies had existed among primitive peoples and that these societies had been free from the evils associated with "civilised" capitalist societies. Just as French philosophers in the eighteenth century had idealised the virtues of the "noble savage" of a bygone age, so Marx and Engels had idealised the simple village communities which had once existed in Germany, Russia and North America and which had been described by G. L. von Maurer,[16] by Freiherr von Haxthausen,[17] and by Lewis H. Morgan.[18]

In his book on the origin of the family – largely based upon Morgan's researches – Engels examined the changes in the structure of society that had occurred between the days when primitive peoples were organised in family clans and the time when states were set up by the ancient Greeks and Romans. Engels argued that two factors had influenced the development of primitive societies – first, the need to secure food, clothing, and shelter and, secondly, the need to provide for the survival of the community in the next generation. He believed that the methods by which food, clothing and shelter were provided – and the way in which family life was organised – determined the social, political, legal and religious institutions of the community.

Engels admired the way of life of the primitive classless Iroquois tribes. "Everything runs smoothly without soldiers, gendarmes or police; without nobles, kings, governors, prefects or judges; without prisons, without trials." There was no poverty since each household looked after its own sick and aged.[19] This idyllic social system had disintegrated when the efficiency of labour increased so that more goods and services could be produced. When this happened private property came into existence.

This brought the primitive social system to an end for the advent of private property – in Engels's view – abolished the former equality of wealth within the community. Private property created class antagonism between the rich and the poor. Primitive societies – with their "simple moral grandeur" – disappeared and were replaced by more sophisticated communities organised as states. The states were normally dominated by the wealthiest section of the community. Engels admitted that, in exceptional circumstances, two rival classes might be so equally balanced that neither could control the state for its own ends. Engels argued that all the political, religious and social changes recorded in history – and all the revolutions – had been caused by the rivalries of classes with different economic interests. He also believed that the early states – such as the city states of the ancient world – had suffered the same fate as primitive peoples in prehistoric times as soon as greater efficiency of production increased the wealth of the community. Engels appeared to suggest that only poor primitive communities could be happy and contented. Whenever improved methods of production were discovered – leading to greater wealth and a higher standard of living – the ideal classless society gave way to one rent asunder by the clash between the rich and the poor.

Engels's pamphlet of 1884 on the origin of the family sold well in Germany and a fourth edition appeared in 1891. But it was not one of Engels's most important books. Engels was not an expert anthropologist as he was an expert economist and military critic. Nor had he any recognised scholar to help him as he had Schorlemmer to advise him on his scientific theories. He has been criticised for his "slapdash statements and deductions" and for ignoring "the most rudimentary precepts of historical scholarship". He has been charged with "distorting and romanticising evidence to a ludicrous degree and . . . of deliberately ignoring the work of serious scholars of his own day in this field, and of basing a whole theory of family and social relationships in early and modern times alike on a single study of the Iroquois Indians".[20] As a political tract, however, Engels's pamphlet was not without importance in the 1880s. It strengthened the belief of faithful socialists – particularly in Germany – that some important aspects of Marx's doctrines had been "proved" by new evidence from prehistoric times.

In 1887–8 Engels applied Marx's ideas on historical materialism to a study of the unification of Germany. Engels's *Anti-Dühring* had been so popular that three of its chapters had appeared in France (1880) and in Germany (1883) as a pamphlet called *Socialism: Utopian and Scientific*. Next it was suggested that another three chapters – those entitled "The Force Theory" –

should be reprinted separately. Engels decided to write an additional fourth chapter for this proposed pamphlet to show the German reader "the very considerable *rôle* played by force in the history of his own country during the last thirty years".[21] Engels began to write the new chapter in which he surveyed the history of Germany between 1848 and 1871 with particular reference to Bismarck's policy of "blood and iron". But his determination to complete the editing of the later volumes of *Das Kapital* caused him to lay the manuscript aside before it was completed. The unfinished chapter was published in 1896 in the socialist periodical *Neue Zeit*. While Engels's book on the origin of the family was the work of an amateur, his essay on Bismarck's policy showed such insight that what he wrote can still be read with profit by modern students of German history in the nineteenth century.

Engels stated that his discussion concerning the *rôle* of force in history was an attempt to explain why Bismarck's use of force – his policy of blood and iron – "was bound to be successful for a time, and why it is bound to fail in the end". The first part of the essay dealt with Bismarck's success to 1871; the second with his failures after unification had been achieved. Engels argued that, after the failure of the revolution of 1848, there were three ways in which Germany might have been united. All three would involve the use of force. The question was whether force – in the form of revolution or war – would be exercised from below as a popular rising or from above as a military action by the conservative classes which wielded power in Prussia.

The first possibility was what Engels called "the open revolutionary way" which had succeeded in Italy in 1859–60 "where the Savoyard dynasty had joined forces with the revolution and thereby won the crown of Italy". But the Hohenzollerns "were absolutely incapable of such bold deeds" and there was never any hope of an alliance between the ruling house of Prussia and a popular national movement aiming at the unification of the country. Secondly, Germany might have been unified under the hegemony of Austria. Engels considered that Austria never had any chance of uniting Germany because she was "the most reactionary of all German-speaking states, the most reluctant to adapt itself to modern developments, and in addition, the only specifically Catholic Great Power". Consequently German unity, under Austria's wing, was a romantic dream.

The third way to unite Germany was for Prussia to dominate the country. She had – wrote Engels – "two good institutions – universal military service and universal compulsory education". And the German customs union,[22] founded and dominated by

Prussia, had for many years been "a great success for Prussia" and had "ranged the bourgeoisie of the small and medium-sized principalities on the side of Prussia". Bismarck made full use of these advantages. Engels described him as "a man of great practical understanding and immense cunning, a born crafty businessman, who in other circumstances would have rivalled the Vanderbilts and Jay Goulds on the New York stock exchange, and indeed most effectively steered his private ship into port".

No sooner had Bismarck been appointed Minister President than he was involved in the "constitutional conflict" with the middle class Progressive Party over the proposed Prussian army reforms. Bismarck at once showed that he was prepared to use force to attain his ends and for several years he collected taxes without the authority of parliament. He demonstrated his skill by eventually securing support for his policy of unifying Germany under Prussian leadership from both the reactionary landed gentry and the liberal bourgeoisie – rival classes with divergent economic and political interests.

The middle classes – organised in the National Union (*National-verein*) and the Progressive Party (*Fortschrittspartei*) – were demanding both unification and democratic parliamentary government. Bismarck presented them with a *fait accompli* and gave them no choice but to accept half a loaf, rather than get no bread at all. He carried out those national demands of the bourgeoisie which were in Prussia's own interests and he granted numerous reforms which facilitated the economic expansion of the country and put money into the pockets of the bourgeoisie. But effective political power remained in the hands of the reactionary forces in Prussia – the landed gentry, the army, and the civil service – and Bismarck firmly refused to allow parliamentary democracy to be established in Germany. Engels detested Bismarck but admired his immense will-power. He declared that "all the ruling classes in Germany – junkers and bourgeois alike – had so lost all traces of energy; spinelessness had become so much the custom in 'educated' Germany. that the one man amongst them who still had will-power, thereby became their greatest personality and a tyrant over them, so that they were ready to dance to his tune even against their better nature and judgment".[23]

In the second part of his pamphlet Engels discussed Bismarck's policy after the unification of Germany in 1871. He began by analysing the social structure of the Reich. The main classes were the great landowners (the junkers), the peasants, the upper and lower middle classes, and the urban and rural workers. Engels considered that although the junkers were "one of the main bulwarks of the old Prussian state", they were "in a quite weak position". "The whole junker class is always on the brink of financial disaster." The owners of the large estates east of the River Elbe were supported by state subsidies of various kinds. But they were "doomed to extinction" and when they disappeared the state of Prussia too would disappear. The peasants varied from day labourers to smallholders and tenant farmers. All were in a weak economic position. The bourgeoisie had prospered since 1848 owing to Germany's industrial expansion. From an economic point of view it was the most powerful class in the country but it had failed to secure political power. Engels considered that – since the junkers were doomed to extinction – the bourgeoisie was "the only section of the propertied classes who had any hope of the future". The petty bourgeoisie consisted largely of craftsmen and small traders. Some of the craftsmen still hoped for the re-establishment of gild privileges. Others – and also some of the petty traders – were radical in outlook. Even the socialists might hope for some recruits from the petty bourgeoisie. The workers fell into two groups. The farm labourers on the large estates in eastern Germany "still lived in semi-serfdom and were therefore politically of no account". Among the industrial workers of the towns, on the other hand, the socialists were making progress – even though they were split into two hostile factions.[24]

Engels argued that in view of the class structure of Germany in the 1870s Bismarck – once he had become the all-powerful Chancellor of the newly united Reich – should have recognised that the junkers were a declining class from an economic point of view and that the bourgeoisie was a wealthy growing class. Normally economic strength is linked with political power. Bismarck should have accepted the reality of the situation as he found it and he should have increased the political power of the middle classes at the expense of the great landowners. He should have incorporated in the new constitution of the Reich the guarantees of freedom of the press, of association and of assembly which were already embodied in the Prussian constitution. He should have established Imperial Ministers of State (at the head of government departments) responsible to the popularly elected Reichstag and he should have gradually given greater powers to the Reichstag. But Bismarck did none of these things. The Constitution provided that executive power should be exercised by the Chancellor who was responsible to the Emperor. According to Engels the Constitution of the Reich was "made to measure" for Bismarck. "It was a step further on the road to his personal rule, based on a balance of the parties in the Reichstag, and of the separate states in the

Bundesrat – a step further on the road to Bonapartism."[25] Far from adopting a policy which eventually would have transferred political power to the bourgeoisie, Bismarck bolstered the authority of the junkers and even tried to extend the traditions of Prussia over the whole of Germany. Engels argued that such a policy was ultimately doomed to failure.

Engels often wrote about the past to confirm the accuracy of Marx's interpretation of history. But sometimes he had other reasons for writing history. His accounts of campaigns, his biographies of generals, and his essays on the rifle were straightforward writings on military history which did not necessarily illustrate the doctrine of historical materialism. Engels became a military historian and critic so as to advise the workers on the science of war and the tactics of urban insurrection. Similarly his essays on the early history of the Marxist movement provided information to a new generation of socialists who had not been born in the stirring days of the revolution of 1848.

As early as 1850 Marx had suggested to Engels that he should write an account of the activities of the leading communists during the recent revolution in Germany. Engels had described the rising in Baden in the *Neue Rheinische Zeitung: Politisch-Ökonomische Revue* and had included in it a sketch of the career of the revolutionary worker Josef Moll, who had died in action in the engagement on the River Murg. Many years later Engels told Johann Philipp Becker that since young socialists wanted to know about the early days of the workers' movement in Germany, their elders should put pen to paper so that the achievements of the founders of the Communist League and the editors of the *Neue Rheinische Zeitung* should be placed on record.

In the 1880s Engels wrote several essays on the history of the Marxist movement and on the lives of some of Marx's disciples. His accounts of the Communist League[26] and the *Neue Rheinische Zeitung*[27] are a lively description of the early days of the Marxist movement. In his introductions to new editions of the Communist Manifesto, Engels drew attention to the significance of this first statement of Marx's fundamental ideas.[28] And in a little book on Ludwig Feuerbach's philosophy. Engels acknowledged the influence which this "half-way house between materialism and idealism" had exercised upon Marx and himself during their "years of storm and stress" in the 1840s when they were working out their own philosophical position.[29] Engels also wrote some biographical sketches of some of the founders of the Marxist movement.[30] The longest was an account of the life of Wilhelm Wolff who had been – next to Engels – one of Marx's closest associates. Engels's biography of Wilhelm Wolff appeared in eleven articles in *Die Neue Welt* in 1876 and a shorter version provided an introduction to a new edition of Wilhelm Wolff's pamphlet on *Die Schlesische Milliarde* ten years later.[31] Engels's other biographical essays were on his friends Georg Weerth,[32] Johann Philipp Becker,[33] Sigismund Borkheim[34] and Carl Schorlemmer.[35]

In 1890 in a letter to Joseph Bloch, the editor of the *Sozialistische Monatshefte*, Engels once more tried to explain the meaning of Marx's materialist conception of history. He claimed that economic factors were "the ultimately determining element in history". But he asserted that Marx had never pretended that economic factors were the only ones which influenced historical events. Obviously constitutions, legal systems, religious ideas, philosophical theories and tradition had helped to mould events in the past. Engels criticised those who pushed Marx's doctrine of historical materialism to absurd lengths. Thus it would be wrong to argue that the rise of Prussia to the position of a great power was "specifically determined by economic necessity". And it would be ridiculous to try to explain the existence of every small German state entirely in terms of economics. Nevertheless, in Engels's view, however varied might be the factors which influenced a particular historical event or process "the economic ones are ultimately decisive".

In conclusion, Engels admitted:

"Marx and I are ourselves to blame for the fact that the younger people sometimes lay more stress on the economic side than is due to it. We had to emphasise the main principle *vis-à-vis* our adversaries, who denied it, and we had not always the time, the place or the opportunity to give their due to the other elements involved in the interaction. But when it came to presenting a section of history, that is, to making a practical application, it was a different matter and there no error was permissible. Unfortunately, however, it happens only too often that people think they have fully understood a new theory and can apply it without more ado from the moment they have assimilated its main principles, even those not always correctly. And I cannot exempt many of the more recent "Marxists" from this reproach, for the most amazing rubbish has been produced in this quarter, too...."[36]

NOTES

1 F. Teleschnikow, "Engels als Theoretiker der historischen Materialismus" in *Friedrich Engels der Denker* (Mundus Verlag, Basel, 1945): articles from the Soviet Encyclopaedia); L. Krieger, "Marx and Engels as Historians" in *Journal of the History of Ideas*, Vol. 14 (iii), June 1953, pp. 381–403. This article discusses:
   (i) Karl Marx, *The Class Struggles in France*

    (ii) Karl Marx, *The Eighteenth Brumaire of Louis Bonaparte*

    (iii) F. Engels, *Revolution and Counter-Revolution in Germany in 1848* (1891).

2 F. Engels, *The Condition of the Working Class in England* (translated by W. O. Henderson and W. H. Chaloner, 1958: new edition 1971), p. 317.

3 Karl Marx and F. Engels, *The German Ideology* (written in 1845–6: English translation of 1965), p. 41.

4 Engels's preface of 1895 to Karl Marx, *Die Klassenkämpfe in Frankreich 1848 bis 1850* (articles written in 1850: new edition, 1895): English translation in W. O. Henderson (ed.), *Engels: Selected Writings* (Penguin Books, 1967), pp. 278–9.

5 Karl Marx and F. Engels, *The Communist Manifesto*, 1848 (Penguin Books, 1967), p. 79.

6 F. Engels, Introduction to the third (1885) edition of Karl Marx, *Der achtzehnte Brumaire des Louis Napoleon* (New York, 1852): English translation – *The Eighteenth Brumaire of Louis Bonaparte* (Foreign Languages Publishing House, Moscow).

7 Karl Marx to J. Weydemeyer, March 5, 1852 in Karl Marx and F. Engels, *Letters to Americans, 1848–95* (1963), p. 45.

8 Karl Marx's articles on the Second French Republic appeared in the *Neue Rheinische Zeitung: Politisch-ökonomische Revue,* 1850 (new edition, 1955) and were published as a pamphlet in 1895 under the title: *Die Klassenkämpfe in Frankreich 1848 bis 1850* (introduction by F. Engels.

9 Karl Marx's articles on Louis Napoleon's *coup d'état* appeared in New York in the periodical *Die Revolution* (*eine Zeitschrift in zwanglosen Heften*) (edited by J. Weydemeyer, 1852). It was published as a pamphlet entitled *Der achtzehnte Brumaire des Louis Bonaparte* in 1869 and (with an introduction by F. Engels) in 1885. A third pamphlet by Marx on French history was *The Civil War in France* (address of the General Council of the First International, 1871) (new edition with introduction by F. Engels, 1891).

10 Engels's introduction of 1895 to Karl Marx, *Die Klassenkämpfe in Frankreich, 1848 bis 1850* (English translation in W. O. Henderson (ed.)), *Engels: Selected Writings* (Penguin Books, 1967), pp. 278–9.

11 Engels's introduction to the third (1885) edition of Karl Marx, *The Eighteenth Brumaire of Louis Bonaparte* (English translation: Foreign Languages Publishing House, Moscow).

12 Engels's articles on the Peasants War in Germany appeared in the *Neue Rheinische Zeitung: Politisch-ökonomische Revue* (double number 5–6, May–October, 1850: facsimile reprint, 1955). It was printed as a book (*Der deutsche Bauernkrieg*) in 1870 and again in 1875. An English translation has been issued by the Foreign Languages Publishing House, Moscow, 1956. Engels's articles on Germany in 1848–9 appeared in the *New York Daily Tribune* in 1851–2 and were printed in 1891 (under Marx's name) as a book entitled *Revolution and Counter-Revolution in Germany in 1848* (edited by Eleanor Marx) (new edition, 1952).

13 Quotations from W. O. Henderson (ed.), *Engels: Selected Writings* (Penguin Books, 1967), pp. 243–56.

14 F. Engels, "The Part played by Labour in the Transition from Ape to Man", 1876 in *Dialectics of Nature* (Progress Publishers, Moscow, 1964), pp. 172–86 and published separately by the Foreign Languages

Publishing House, Moscow. The article appears to have been written in June 1876 and was originally intended to be the introduction to a book on *The Three Basic Forms of Slavery* (later *The Enslavement of the Worker*). But this book was never written. The essay on "The Part played by Labour in the Transition from Ape to Man" was first published in *Die Neue Zeit* (Vol. 14 (2) 1896, pp. 545–54) shortly after Engels's death.

15 F. Engels, *Der Ursprung der Familie, des Privateigentums und des Staats* (Hottingen–Zürich, 1884): quotations are from the introduction of 1884. The edition of 1952 includes an article by Engels entitled "Ein neuentdeckter Fall von Gruppeneke" (*Neue Zeit*), 1892–3, pp. 373–5. English translation: *The Origin of the Family, Private Property and the State* (Foreign Languages Publishing House, Moscow).

16 See Engels's essay on "Die Mark" – based upon Manver's researches into the village communities of Detmold – which was published as a pamphlet: *Der deutsche Bauer. Was war er? Was ist er? Was könnte er sein?* (Hottingen–Zürich, 1883).

17 August Freiherr von Haxthausen, *Die ländliche Verfassung Russlands. Ihre Entwicklung und ihre Feststellung in der Gesetzgebung von 1861* (1866). Marx's copy is listed in *Ex Libris Karl Marx und Friedrich Engels* (1967), p. 90.

18 Engels's copy of Lewis Henry Morgan, *Ancient Society or Researches in the Lines of Human Progress from Savagery through Barbarism to Civilisation* (1877) is listed in *Ex Libris Karl Marx und Friedrich Engels* (1967), p. 147. In a letter to Karl Kautsky, dated March 24, 1884, Engels stated that he had had some difficulty in getting a copy of Morgan's book and eventually secured one in a second-hand bookshop: see B. Kautsky (ed.), *Friedrich Engels' Briefwechsel mit Karl Kautsky* (1955), p. 106. Friedrich Engels wrote to F. A. Sorge on March 7, 1884: "Read Morgan (Lewis H), *Ancient Society* published in America in 1877. It discloses primeval times and their communism in masterly fashion. He independently discovered Marx's theory of history anew and closes with communist conclusions for the present day". (Karl Marx and F. Engels, *Letters to Americans, 1848–95* (1963), p. 143). On January 12, 1889 Engels complained to Mrs Wischnewetsky about the boycott "of English prehistoric old fogies against Morgan" (*ibid.*, p. 208).

19 F. Engels, *The Origin of the Family, Private Property and the State* (Foreign Languages Publishing House, Moscow), p. 159.

20 Grace Carlton, *Friedrich Engels, The Shadow Prophet* (1965), p. 218.

21 F. Engels, *Die Rolle der Gewalt in der Geschichte* (1964), p. 7 and quoted by E. Wangermann in his introduction to F. Engels, *The Rôle of Force in History* (1968), p. 11.

22 W. O. Henderson, *The Zollverein* (second edition, 1959).

23 F. Engels, *The Rôle of Force in History* (ed. E. Wangermann, 1968), pp. 29, 43, 46, 48, 56, 57.

24 F. Engels, *The Rôle of Force in History* (1968), pp. 90–4.

25 F. Engels, *The Rôle of Force in History* (1968), p. 101.

26 F. Engels, "Zur Geschichte des Bundes der Kommunisten" (1885): introduction to new edition of Karl Marx, *Enthüllungen über den Kommunistenprozess zu Köln* (edition of 1952), pp. 9–31.

27 F. Engels, "Marx und die Neue Rheinische Zeitung" in *Der Sozialdemokrat* (Zürich), March 11, 1884, reprinted in Karl Marx–

F. Engels, *Die Revolution von 1848. Auswahl aus der "Neuen Rheinischen Zeitung"* (1955).

28 Karl Marx–F. Engels, *The Communist Manifesto* (ed. by A. J. P. Taylor), pp. 53–76.

29 F. Engels, *Ludwig Feuerbach und der Ausgang der Klassischen deutschen Philosophie* (Stuttgart, 1888). The pamphlet had appeared as articles in 1886. English translation: F. Engels, *Ludwig Feuerbach and the End of Classical German Philosophy* (Foreign Languages Publishing House, Moscow, 1950). Part IV of this pamphlet appears in W. O. Henderson (ed.), *Engels. Selected Writings* (Penguin Books, 1967), pp. 315–32.

30 These biographical essays have been collected in F. Engels, *Biographische Skizzen* (1967).

31 Introduction by F. Engels to Wilhelm Wolff, *Die Schlesische Milliarde* (Hottingen–Zürich, 1886) and *Marx–Engels Werke*, Vol. 19, pp. 55–63 and pp. 83–8.

32 F. Engels, "Georg Weerth, der erste und bedeutendste Dichter des deutschen Proletariats" in *Der Sozialdemokrat*, June 7, 1883.

33 F. Engels, "Johann Philipp Becker" in *Der Sozialdemokrat*, December 17, 1886.

34 Introduction by F. Engels to Sigismund Borkheim, *Zur Erinnerung für die deutschen Mordspatrioten 1806–7* (1887).

35 F. Engels, "Carl Schorlemmer" in *Vorwärts*, July 3, 1892.

36 F. Engels to Joseph Bloch, September 21–2, 1890 in Helmut Hirsch (ed.), *Friedrich Engels Profile* (1970), pp. 272–3. English translation: Karl Marx and F. Engels, *Selected Correspondence* (Foreign Languages Publishing House, Moscow), pp. 498–500 and W. O. Henderson (ed.), *Engels: Selected Writings* (Penguin Books, 1967), pp. 333–5.

13

ENGELS AND THE GERMAN SOCIAL
DEMOCRAT PARTY, 1878–1890[1]

Engels observed that by 1870 the German socialists "had made rapid advances amongst the urban working class, and grew in the measure that largescale industry proletarianised the mass of the people and consequently exacerbated the class contradictions between capitalists and workers".[2] Eight years later the socialists had strengthened their position, having formed a united party which was now attracting support from certain trade unions and some former members of the Progressive Party and the People's Party. But in 1878 the growth of the Social Democrat Party received a dramatic setback. The Reichstag passed an "Emergency Law against the publicly dangerous Endeavours of Social Democracy" and the Social Democrat Party was outlawed as an illegal organisation.

At every general election of the Reichstag until 1877 the socialist vote had increased. Bismarck considered that the growth of the Social Democrat Party threatened Germany's unity and stability. In May 1871 he had been horrified to hear Bebel, in a speech to the Reichstag, praise the aims and policy of the Paris Commune. Bismarck declared that this was when he first realised that the socialists were the declared enemies of the state and society.[3] In October 1871 he suggested to Count Itzenplitz, the Prussian Minister of Commerce, that "any agitation which endangered the state" should be prohibited by law.[4] Nothing came of this proposal but Itzenplitz did circularise leading German industrialists and businessmen asking them not to give employment to socialists. Carl Stumm, the steel king of the Saar, barred socialists from all his mines and ironworks.[5]

Bismarck considered that it was his duty to crush the socialists because they advocated republicanism and therefore endangered the monarchy; because they supported an international workers' movement and were therefore a threat to the Fatherland; because they preached atheism and therefore flouted Christian beliefs; and because they advocated nationalisation and therefore attacked private property. He argued, too, that the threat to private property reduced the flow of investment to industry, slowed down the expansion of manufactures and increased unemployment. During the Franco–Prussian war the socialist leaders Wilhelm Liebknecht and August Bebel had opposed war credits, denounced the annexation of Alsace and Lorraine, and supported the Paris Commune. They were brought to trial – charged with "making preparations for treason" – and in 1872 they were both found guilty and sentenced to two years' imprisonment. Their trial in Leipzig – like the trial in Cologne of the leaders of the Communist League twenty years before – was given the maximum publicity and Bismarck hoped that it would serve as a warning to the German workers not to support the socialists.[6] But Bismarck's strong opposition to the socialists did not blind him to the fact that their agitation was making it imperative for the government to undertake social reforms. Some years later (in 1884) he admitted that "if some modest progress has been made towards solving the social question it is only because of the rise of socialism and the fear that socialism has inspired in certain quarters".

At first Bismarck was unable to persuade the Reichstag to strengthen the law against workers' political organisations and trade unions. In 1873 he failed to abolish the freedom of association and he was equally unsuccessful when he tried to tighten the press law by imposing heavy penalties for attacks on the family, private property and conscription. But even without new powers the German – and particularly the Prussian – authorities were able to make life difficult for the socialists. Both socialist parties were dissolved – the General German Workers' Union in 1874 and the recently united Social Democrat Party in 1876. The General German Workers' Union disappeared but the organisation of the Social Democrat Party survived in a new form. Although the party's central executive committee was dissolved a new Central Election Committee was established in Hamburg. In theory this committee had no powers outside Hamburg, but in practice its authority over other regional socialist associations was accepted throughout Germany.

Not content with dissolving the two party organisations the authorities did all in their power to hinder the activities of socialists, particularly during elections when their candidates, speakers, and supporters were harassed by the police in various ways. In 1879 Engels denounced Bismarck for pursuing a reactionary policy against the workers, involving "a return to the traditions of vilest feudalism and police authority of old Prussia".[7] The support which Bismarck received from the great industrialists in his drive against the socialists can be seen from a pamphlet which Alfred Krupp sent to his workers in 1877. Krupp treated his workers well and provided them with many welfare services but he was strongly opposed to trade unionism and to socialism. In his message to his workers he denounced the "spirit of social democracy" that was spreading among his workers. He warned them that the aims of the Social Democrat Party were neither sensible nor practical. He was, however, prepared to take the charitable view that "most people who have been won over by the Social Democrat Party continue to support it only because they fail to appreciate its criminal and ruinous aims".[8] At the same time Carl Stumm – another steel king – barred all socialists from employment in his works in the Saar and similar action was taken by many members of the Association for the Protection of the Common Economic Interests of the Rhineland and Westphalia. Stumm also founded an "Employers' Committee to fight Social Democracy".[9]

Despite the many obstacles placed in its path the socialist movement continued to grow. At the Reichstag general election of January 1877 the socialists polled 493,000 (over 9 per cent of all the votes) and gained 12 seats. Not only factory workers but craftsmen and shopkeepers – even some minor state officials such as railway porters and postmen – were now voting for the Social Democrat Party. Over 40 socialist newspapers were published, the most important being *Vorwärts*, the *Freie Presse* (Berlin), the *Volksblatt* (Hamburg–Altona), the *Neue Welt* and *Die Zukunft*. At the same time some 50,000 workers were organised in trade unions, some of which had close links with the Social Democrat Party.

The opposition between Bismarck and the socialists came to a head in 1878. On May 11 Max Hödel tried to assassinate the Emperor. But his revolver was defective and the Emperor was not hurt. Since Hödel had been a socialist agitator, it was not surprising that the Social Democrats were attacked as a party of terrorists and assassins. The police discovered that Hödel was probably as closely associated with the anarchists as with the socialists but they did not make this information public since they wished to implicate the Social Democrat Party in the attempt on the Emperor's life.[10] The socialists protested that Hödel had been expelled from their party before he tried to kill the Emperor[11] and for good measure they asserted that he was mentally unbalanced.

Bismarck acted promptly. On May 20 an Anti-Socialist Law – hastily passed by the Bundesrat – was laid before the Reichstag. Rudolf von Bennigsen, leader of the National Liberals, attacked the bill in one of his greatest speeches. He criticised the folly of trying to ban all organisations which supported "the aims of Social Democracy". The Gotha programme included demands for various democratic reforms which were also advocated by liberals who were opposed to socialism. Bennigsen argued that the legitimate activities of all democratic parties would be forbidden if the bill were passed. Liebknecht charged Bismarck – who had not troubled to attend the debate – with attempting to saddle the socialists with the "moral responsibility" for the act of a madman. The attempt on the Emperor's life was no justification for Bismarck's reactionary proposal. Liebknecht claimed that Bismarck was playing a double game. Ostensibly he was asking the Reichstag to give the government new powers to crush the socialists. But his real objective was to manœuvre the National Liberals and the Progressives into voting against the Anti-Socialist Law. Then he could attack these parties at the next elections for their lack of patriotism in failing to support a bill designed to safeguard the state from those who were planning to overthrow it by acts of violence. If this was Bismarck's plan it was successful. With the help of the two liberal parties – the National Liberals and the Progressives – the first clause of the anti-socialist bill was rejected by 243 votes to 60. The bill was then withdrawn by the government.

The opportunity to hold a general election came sooner than Bismarck had expected. On June 2 another attempt was made on the Emperor's life and this time the Emperor received serious injuries. Although Karl Nobiling, the would-be assassin, was no socialist, Bismarck now unleashed a virulent press campaign against the socialists who were accused of trying to achieve their aims by acts of violence. He also attacked the liberals for lack of patriotism in failing to support the Anti-Socialist Bill. Bismarck argued that an Anti-Socialist Law was essential to crush a party which threatened the foundations of society. The Reichstag was dissolved and a general election was held on June 30, 1878.

Bismarck's supporters tried to stampede the voters by claiming that only the conservatives could save the country from "red revolution". Count Eulenburg, the Prussian Minister of the Interior, declared that the socialists were "a mortal enemy of the state – and not only of our state but of every monarchical state".[12] The liberal parties were attacked for voting against the anti-socialist law in the last Reichstag. In his memoirs Bebel recalled that during the election virtually the whole German press – except of course the socialist papers – united to denounce the socialists as murderers and atheists who were bent upon wrecking all civilised social institutions, such as the monarchy, marriage, the family and private property. Patriotic employers vied with one another in dismissing socialist workers. Patriotic landlords gave socialist tenants notice to quit. Patriotic innkeepers asked socialists to take their custom elsewhere. From Brunswick Bracke reported that "some of our enemies have taken leave of their senses". He told Engels that "there are some people here who refuse to do business at the corn exchange because I am chairman of the company running it".[13] In Hamburg the city fathers forbade the holding of a conference of trade union delegates, while in Gotha the authorities banned a proposed congress of the Social Democrat Party.[14]

In the circumstances it was virtually certain that there would be a swing to the right at the general election. The two conservative parties gained 38 seats and the Catholic Centre Party gained one seat. The two liberal parties lost ground. Bismarck had secured a majority in the Reichstag both for an Anti-Socialist Law and for a reform of the tariff. Despite the unscrupulous tactics of their opponents – who whipped up a mass hysteria against them – the socialists did surprisingly well at the elections, gaining 437,158 votes (compared with 493,288 in 1877) and losing only three seats. During the election campaign Bracke wrote to Engels that the violent propaganda campaign against the socialists had not caused any panic among the workers. They remained calm. He thought that if an Anti-Socialist Law were passed many socialists would lose their jobs and would suffer in other ways but he was confident that in the end the Social Democrat Party would emerge from the struggle "larger, stronger, and more mature than before".[15]

The Reichstag assembled on September 9, 1878 and considered an Anti-Socialist Bill on September 16. The preamble to the bill claimed that "the socialist agitation, as carried on for years, is a continual appeal to violence, and to the passions of the multitude, for the purpose of subverting the social order. The state *can* check such a movement by depriving Social Democracy of its principal means of propaganda, and by destroying its organisation; and it *must* do so unless it is willing to surrender its existence, and unless the conviction is to spread amongst the people that either the state is impossible or the aims of Social Democracy are justifiable."[16]

On the first day of the debate Bebel attacked the bill. He asserted that socialists were peaceful reformers, not violent revolutionaries.[17] Far from advocating the wholesale confiscation of private property, they merely objected to large concentrations of capital in the hands of a few rich companies and individuals. Bebel asserted that criticisms of the unequal distribution of wealth in a capitalist society had been made by reformers who could not be described as socialists.[18] Bebel warned the Reichstag that a ban on socialist literature could not be enforced. No one could stop socialist workers and their friends from meeting in their homes, in factories, in public houses, or on country walks where politics could be discussed and forbidden literature could be passed on. Bebel also attacked Bismarck for having flirted with socialists in the past. Members of the Reichstag were astonished to learn that in 1863–4 Bismarck had held discussions with Lassalle[19] and that in 1865 Lothar Bucher, soon after being appointed by Bismarck to a post in the Prussian Ministry of Foreign Affairs, had invited Karl Marx to contribute to the official *Preussischer Anzeiger*.[20] Unfortunately for Bebel his claim that German socialists advocated reform by peaceful means was contradicted by Wilhelm Hasselmann who took two hours to inform the Reichstag that the socialists were revolutionaries who were prepared to use force to overthrow the capitalist system.

In his reply to the attacks upon the bill Bismarck reiterated his conviction that the socialist agitation in Germany in recent years had threatened the safety of the state. For the first time he gave an account of his conversations with Lassalle. He failed to mention that he had initiated the talks. Bismarck argued that his talks with Lassalle had no political significance since in 1863 Lassalle's General German Workers Union had been a small unimportant organisation. The talks had been confidential exchanges between two men who both had the welfare of the German workers at heart. Bismarck drew a sharp contrast between the German socialists of the 1860s and the socialists of the 1870s. Lassalle's organisation had largely confined its activities to campaigning in favour of manhood suffrage and this had now been granted as far as elections for the Reichstag was concerned. But during the Franco-Prussian war Liebknecht and Bebel had supported the Paris Commune and the Social Democrat Party was now, in Bismarck's view, a revolutionary organisation determined to overthrow the existing social system.

The Reichstag passed the Anti-Socialist Law on October 19, 1878 by 221 votes to 149 and its provisions came into effect two days later. The law was to remain in force until March 31, 1881. It was renewed four times – though with decling majorities – and eventually lapsed on September 30, 1890, shortly after Bismarck's fall from power.

The Anti-Socialist Law[21] prohibited all organisations which aimed at overthrowing "the existing political or social order through social-democratic, socialist or communist endeavours". A liquidator would dispose of their property in accordance with "the statutes of the organisation or general laws". Co-operative and friendly societies with socialist affiliations were to be placed under "extraordinary state control". Meetings, demonstrations and processions of socialists were banned. So were socialist books, pamphlets, periodicals and newspapers. It would be illegal to attempt to raise funds for socialist organisations. Publishers, booksellers, librarians and publicans found guilty of breaking the Anti-Socialist Law would be liable to fines or imprisonment and might also be "forbidden to continue in business". In districts where the safety of the public was deemed to be endangered by socialist agitators, stringent regulations might be enforced prohibiting meetings, demonstrations and the possession of firearms. Socialists might be forbidden to reside in such districts.

Although the Anti-Socialist Law was a stringent one there was a gap in its provisions which Bismarck later had cause to regret.[22] The law did not deprive socialists either of the right to vote at elections or of the right to be candidates at municipal or Reichstag elections. Consequently socialists continued to be elected to the Reichstag where they took part in debates which were reported in the press. During the twelve years that the Anti-Socialist Law was in force the Reichstag provided socialist deputies with a public forum. Here they could criticise the government as vigorously as they pleased. The Reichstag jealously guarded its constitutional rights and refused to allow socialist deputies to be prevented from carrying out their parliamentary duties. In 1879 it thwarted an attempt by the Prussian police to arrest two socialist deputies. In the same year it rejected a "Muzzling Bill" which threatened those who made abusive speeches in the Reichstag with suspension or expulsion. Opponents of the bill argued that any unpopular group of deputies could be silenced if the bill became law.

Although Bismarck failed to secure any extension of the powers granted to the government under the Anti-Socialist Law the enactment contained provisions which made it possible for the authorities to deal a severe blow to the Social Democrat Party. At first a number of the socialist leaders seemed to resign themselves to their fate. On October 13, 1878, when it was clear that the law would soon be passed, a meeting was held in Hamburg attended by the Central Election Committee, the socialist deputies in the Reichstag, and other party leaders. The majority of those present could see no alternative to capitulation. The majority of the leaders of the party – so often accused of planning revolution – were determined to show their respect for the law. On the very day that the Anti-Socialist Law was passed, the Central Election Committee dissolved the party organisation and soon afterwards local socialist organisations were wound up in several towns such as Breslau, Chemnitz, Magdeburg, Bremen and Brunswick. In a

speech to the Reichstag on March 17, 1879 Liebknecht insisted
that the Social Democrat Party was a party of reform, not revolution
and that its members would obey the law of the land. Engels
sharply criticised Liebknecht's "untimely meekness" on this
occasion.[23] And he later denounced those socialist leaders in Germany who had lost their nerve in 1878 "because they had moved
too long in middle class circles and were too much influenced by
bourgeois values".[24] In Engels's view the masses in Germany had
sounder political instincts than their leaders.[25]

The "untimely meekness" of some of the socialist leaders is not
difficult to understand. They hoped that the government would
regard a show of meekness as an olive branch and would reciprocate
by not applying the Anti-Socialist Law in too rigorous a fashion.
Above all they thought that it might be possible to save at least
part of the socialist press from being closed down. In 1878 nearly
50 socialist periodicals and newspapers were published in Germany.
Several prominent socialists were journalists by profession and the
printing and distribution of socialist periodicals and newspapers
gave employment to a number of party members. The wholesale
closure of the socialist press would throw many socialist printers
and distributors out of work. Before the Anti-Socialist Law was
passed Liebknecht (who earned his living as an editor of *Vorwärts*)
had written to Engels: "All our periodicals will be banned at a
single stroke. This will not destroy our party but it will destroy the
livelihood of several party members – including *mine*. In no circumstances do I want to leave Germany but I must live. Please see
if there is any chance of my securing a post as correspondent of
an English paper."[26]

Submission to the Anti-Socialist Law brought no relief to its
victims. The government had decided to stamp out the socialist
movement and the socialists suffered the full rigours of the new law.
The socialist and trade union press had to close down and all
socialist organisations were banned. Twenty-one trade unions were
dissolved and only the liberal Hirsch–Duncker unions were allowed
to survive. By June 30, 1879 the authorities had prohibited 217
organisations and had banned 127 periodicals and 278 books and
pamphlets.[27] *Vorwärts* had to cease publication although the editors
declared that they would not advocate doctrines forbidden by
law.[28] Socialist classics such as Engels's *Anti-Dühring* and Bernstein's *Die Frau und der Sozialismus* were quickly banned. Strange
to say the first volume of *Das Kapital* was not prohibited.[29] Many
adult education associations, friendly societies, social clubs and
co-operative societies – though only loosely linked with the Social
Democrat Party – were prohibited.

Before long even harsher measures were adopted. In November 1878 a minor state of siege was declared in Berlin and 67 leading socialists were expelled from the capital. They urged their followers not to be provoked by the police but to obey the law and to refrain from acts of violence. A minor state of siege was proclaimed in Hamburg and Altona in October 1880 and in Leipzig in June 1881 and many prominent members of the Social Democrat Party were expelled from these cities. These measures inflicted severe hardships upon expelled socialists and their families. But some of these exiles revenged themselves upon their persecutors by preaching socialism in rural districts in which the Social Democrat Party had formerly made little progress.

In 1879, despite the persecution of the socialists, the deputies of the Social Democrat Party in the Reichstag tried to impress the public by their moderation. They naturally criticised the establishment of a minor state of siege in Berlin and the expulsion of socialist leaders from the city – though Liebknecht went out of his way to claim that the action of the government was unnecessary since the Social Democrat Party aimed at securing reforms by strictly peaceful means. The socialist deputies naturally protested when two of their number (Fritzsche and Hasselmann) were expelled from Berlin and they insisted that the government must respect the immunity from arrest accorded to members of the Reichstag by the constitution. And it was natural that Bebel should attack a proposal that the Reichstag should be given the power to suspend a deputy who made "abusive" speeches in the house.

But when matters that had nothing to do with the Anti-Socialist Law came before the Reichstag, the socialist deputies donned the mantle of responsible legislators. One of them – Max Kayser – actually supported Bismarck's proposal to introduce a protective tariff. To many socialists it seemed strange that a socialist deputy should cast a vote in favour of a proposal sponsored by their most determined enemy. And Kayser was defended by all his socialist colleagues in the Reichstag when he was attacked by Karl Hirsch in *Die Laterne*. They pointed out that the congress of the Social Democrat Party held at Gotha in 1877 had passed a resolution stating that "the controversy concerning free trade and protection is not a matter of principle for socialists and each member of the Party is left to make his own decision on the matter". And having supported the first reading of the tariff bill Kayser voted against the third reading.

In a report on their work in the last session of the Reichstag, the socialist deputies declared in 1879 that since their party condemned war and believed in the brotherhood of man it could take no action which might lead to civil war. "We do not have to topple Bismarck's system, since it will collapse of its own accord."[30] Engels sharply attacked this report in two letters to August Bebel. In the first he declared that the socialist deputies had disgraced themselves. Not only had they quarrelled among themselves but they had quarrelled in public. Engels complained that they had made one concession after another to their enemies and had ignored the class struggle which was a fundamental doctrine of the socialist movement. "Since the German philistines are utter cowards, they respect only those who make them quake in their shoes."[31]

In a letter to Bebel of November 24, 1879 Engels again suggested how socialist deputies should act in the Reichstag. He argued that they should speak and vote on matters directly concerning the workers such as factory conditions and hours of work. But when the Reichstag discussed fiscal policy or railway nationalisation the socialist deputies should simply oppose any law that threatened to "increase the power of the government over the people". If the socialists were unable to vote together, they should not vote at all.

Engels also discussed once more the question of Kayser's conduct in the debate on the tariff. He asked if Kayser realised that by supporting the imposition of import duties on iron he had become an ally of the great ironmasters who had formed a ring to dominate the home market so as to charge German customers a high price for iron while selling surplus stocks abroad at a lower price. "Hansemann of the Dortmund Union and Bleichröder of the Royal and Laura Ironworks are laughing at this silly socialist who actually claims to have made a serious study of the subject." Engels advised Bebel to read Rudolf Meyer's *Politische Gründer und die Corruption in Deutschland* which described the recent commercial crisis and the corrupt practices of politicians. Engels observed that a study of this book was essential to an understanding of the economic and political situation in Germany. "How is it", asked Engels, "that this treasure trove of revelations was not exploited by the socialist press when the book was published"?[32] Bebel, for his part, suggested that it was difficult for Marx and Engels, who lived in England, to grasp the complexity of the practical problems that faced socialist deputies day after day in the Reichstag.[33]

At the same time that Engels wrote to Bebel to criticise the conduct of some of the socialist deputies in the Reichstag he also sent a "Circular Letter" – signed by Marx and himself – to the leading German socialists. Here he vigorously attacked the socialist policy advocated in an article in the first number of Höchberg's *Jahrbuch für Socialwissenschaft und Socialpolitik*. The writer of the article advised socialists in Germany to forget their revolutionary traditions and to seek an alliance with the bourgeois liberal parties. Engels's letters to Bebel and his "Circular Letter" show that Marx and Engels had taken up an uncompromising position with regard to the Anti-Socialist Law. They considered that a revolutionary situation existed in Germany. But it was a different type of revolution from that of 1848. Then the middle class liberals, supported by some of the workers, had taken the initiative and had attempted to overthrow the reactionary governments in Germany and Austria. Now the reactionary junkers and great industrialists had taken the initiative and had tried to wipe out the socialists before they could become the largest and most powerful political party in the country. The revolution of 1848 had developed into an armed insurrection but in 1878 Bismarck had stopped short of shooting his socialist opponents. It was, however, possible that he hoped to harass the socialists to such an extent that they would be goaded into taking up arms against the government. And the German army would have had no difficulty in putting down an armed rising of the workers. Marx and Engels urged the German socialists to recognise that a revolutionary situation had been created by the Anti-Socialist Law. Socialists should appreciate the fact that they could not survive if they submitted to Bismarck and obeyed a law which aimed at their destruction. An outlaw could not be expected to obey the law and the Social Democrat Party was now an illegal party. Marx and Engels advised their followers not to hesitate to break the law. But passive resistance – not armed insurrection – was the weapon which would eventually defeat Bismarck. Marx and Engels opposed both extremists on the left wing of the party like Johann Most, who preached anarchism and right wing socialists like Karl Höchberg who advocated an alliance with the middle classes and a compromise with Bismarck.

Although in the early days of the Anti-Socialist Law a number of socialist leaders accepted the dissolution of their party and the banning of their newspapers, it was not long before there were signs that some of Bismarck's victims were prepared to hit back at their persecutors. Public demonstrations by socialists were forbidden but the police dared not interfere with funeral processions. So the funerals of prominent leaders of the Social Democrat Party became public demonstrations of loyalty to the Party. This happened at the funerals of Reinders in Breslau, August Geib in Hamburg and Bracke in Brunswick.[34] It was legal for socialists to vote and in August 1879 Liebknecht and two other socialist candidates were, for the first time, elected to the Landtag in Saxony.[35] Auer joined them when he won a by-election in March 1880.[36] Moreover as quickly as the police closed social clubs frequented by socialists, new ones were founded. More important was the establishment of an illegal welfare committee in Leipzig by Bebel and Liebknecht in November 1878 to raise funds to support the families of socialists expelled from Berlin. Marx and Engels helped to raise money in England and in the United States for distressed German socialists.[37] In 1879 the Leipzig welfare committee shared with the socialist deputies in the Reichstag the task of acting as a substitute for the banned official executive committee of the Social Democrat Party.

Although these acts of defiance helped to restore the morale of the German socialists, Marx and Engels believed that by far the most effective method of attacking Bismarck was to establish socialist periodicals outside Germany and to smuggle them into the country. The former editors of the *Neue Rheinische Zeitung* were fully convinced of the power of the press in a revolutionary situation. The first new socialist weekly to be established at this time was *Die Laterne* (December 15, 1878). Its editor was Carl Hirsch[38] who had once been a member of Lassalle's General German Workers' Union. By 1868 he had become a supporter of Marx's First International and in 1870 he had established a local socialist paper in Crimmitschau (Saxony) called *Der Bürger und Bauernfreund*. In 1870–1 he had edited *Der Volksstaat* when Liebknecht and Hepner were in prison. Since 1874 he had worked in Paris as a journalist. *Die Laterne* was published first in Brussels and then in London. It was printed in miniature form and was sent to its readers in Germany in envelopes of normal letter size. Carl Hirsch urged his readers to defy the Anti-Socialist Law and he attacked Max Kayser for supporting the first reading of Bismarck's tariff bill in the Reichstag.

Another new socialist journal called *Freiheit* was edited by Johann Most (with the assistance of Andreas Scheu) on behalf of the German Workers' Education Society in London.[39] Marx and Engels had no very high opinion of either Most or Scheu. The former was suspected of having supported Dr Dühring while the latter was believed to have sympathised with Bakunin. Nevertheless Marx and Engels welcomed the establishment of *Freiheit*. In March 1879 Engels wrote that he and Marx wished Most's journal every success, though they could not be held responsible for its contents.[40] Most, however, soon drifted towards anarchism and began to advocate armed insurrection in Germany.

In the circumstances Marx and Engels would have nothing to do with *Freiheit*. In June 1879 Engels declined to give a lecture to the German Workers' Educational Association lest he might appear to be lending his support to the journal which it subsidised.[41] On

July 1 Engels wrote to Johann Philipp Becker that Most was advocating a revolution of "fire and slaughter".[42] In September 1879 Marx told Sorge that he and Engels had "no relationship" with *Freiheit* – "although I see Most now and then at my house".[43] Most was expelled from the Social Democrat Party in 1880. In the following year, when an article appeared in *Freiheit* approving of the assassination of Alexander II of Russia, the journal was banned and Most received a prison sentence. In 1882 Most settled in New York where he resumed the publication of *Freiheit*.[44] In 1884 Engels wrote that Most was a mere "caricature of an anarchist".[45]

By the autumn of 1879 Carl Hirsch's *Die Laterne* had ceased publication, Johann Most's *Freiheit* was virtually preaching anarchism, and Karl Höchberg's *Jahrbuch* was advocating co-operation between socialists and democrats. There were no socialist papers in neighbouring German speaking countries to fill the gap. Kautsky complained that the Austrian socialist press was in "a miserable condition".[46] So in Germany the Social Democrat Party was still without a suitable journal.

There was a lengthy correspondence between Liebknecht and Bebel in Leipzig, the German socialists in Zürich and Marx and Engels in London on the establishment of a new paper. Marx and Engels suggested that Carl Hirsch should be the editor[47] but there were influential socialists in Germany who opposed the appointment of one who had recently attacked the socialist deputies in the Reichstag so vigorously. In the end Georg von Vollmar,[48] a member of the Catholic aristocracy in Bavaria, was appointed editor of the new weekly *Der Sozialdemokrat* which was published in Zürich. The editorial board consisted of Liebknecht, Bebel and Fritzsche. Vollmar edited *Der Sozialdemokrat* from September 28, 1879 to December 1880 when he was succeeded by Bernstein, who edited the paper until the last number appeared on September 27, 1890.[49] Bernstein lived in exile for some twenty years, first in Switzerland and then in England, as he would have been arrested if he had returned to Germany.

During the fourteen months that he edited *Der Sozialdemokrat* Vollmar tried to steer a middle course between the policies advocated by the right and left wings of the Social Democrat Party. He failed to heed Bebel's warning that socialist opinion in Germany was moving decisively to the left.[50] The leading article of the first issue urged socialists to adhere strictly to the Gotha programme but also declared that the Social Democrat Party was "a revolutionary party in the true and best sense of the word".[51] Vollmar printed without comment the statement issued by the socialist deputies in defence of their actions in the recent session of the

Reichstag – a statement which roundly condemned civil insurrection.[52] And another article declared that "the assertion of our enemies that the dictatorship of the proletariat is the goal towards which socialists are striving is branded as a lie by the clear wording of our Party programme.[53]

Yet on other occasions *Der Sozialdemokrat* advocated a much more militant course of action. An article of January 4, 1880 called for "war against all the injustice, shame, and misery which is an integral part of our modern organisation of state and society". "There can be no reconciliation between the old world of class privilege and the new world of socialism. They are as incompatible as fire and water and the life of one is the death of the other."[54] And an article which appeared in February 1880 was a clarion call to German socialists to close their ranks and "to take up the military formation that the situation of today and tomorrow demands".[55]

Marx and Engels were naturally disappointed whenever *Der Sozialdemokrat* printed articles supporting the view that despite the ruthless way in which they had been persecuted the socialists should turn the other cheek and continue to behave like respectable law-abiding citizens. Soon after *Der Sozialdemokrat* was established Engels complained to Bebel that the paper was publishing articles which reflected Höchberg's brand of "petty bourgeois socialism". So long as this continued it would be impossible for Marx and Engels to be associated with the paper in any way.[56] In April 1880 Engels complained to Becker of the inconsistent editorial policy of *Der Sozialdemokrat*. One day the paper would preach revolution while on the next it would declare that an insurrection would be a great misfortune. "On the one hand the paper dreads having its hand trumped by the loud-mouthed Most, and on the other it fears that "the workers will one day take its own views seriously".[57] In November 1880 Marx wrote to Sorge that *Der Sozialdemokrat* was being run "in a miserable fashion". He and Engels had frequently written to Bebel and Liebknecht about the paper, "with sharp clashes occurring often". "Liebknecht was here a few weeks ago and 'improvement' has been promised in every respect."[58]

Meanwhile in August 1880 the Social Democrat Party had taken a decisive step in its struggle against the Anti-Socialist Law. At a secret party congress – held in the old ruined castle of Wyden in Switzerland – the 56 delegates unanimously decided to change the Gotha Programme so that in future the party pledged itself to pursue its aims "by all means" and not merely "by all legal means". By dropping one word from its programme the outlawed party gave Bismarck notice that it was back in business. The days of meek compliance with the Anti-Socialist Law was over. From now onwards the party would fight for its existence by every means in its power.

The congress established an international agency under Georg Vollmar to link the Social Democrat Party with foreign socialist parties. Fritzsche and Viereck were sent on a propaganda tour to the United States to raise money for the Social Democrat Party. The congress expelled the extremists Most and Hasselmann from the party. Members of the right wing of the party did not suffer the same fate but were let off with a caution. They were warned that in future all socialist election manifestoes must conform strictly to the Gotha Programme as modified at the Wyden congress. It was also agreed at Wyden that the socialist deputies in the Reichstag should act as the executive committee of the Social Democrat Party in place of the Hamburg Central Election Committee which had been dissolved in 1878. It was also decided that *Der Sozialdemokrat* should be recognised as the official organ of the party. Ten years later Engels declared that the calling of the Wyden congress had been a revolutionary act which had been a turning point in the history of the socialist movement in Germany. At Wyden the Social Democrat Party had "found its soul again". It had taken up the gauntlet thrown down by Bismarck and had fought back against its oppressors.[59]

After the Congress of Wyden the socialists issued a public manifesto in which they declared their determination to overthrow the existing political and social system and to replace it with a new state and a new social order. Socialists were urged to establish new local underground associations; to secure new subscribers for *Der Sozialdemokrat*; and to raise money for propaganda and for the relief of distressed party comrades.

Shortly after the Wyden congress, Marx and Engels were visited first by Liebknecht and then by Bebel and Bernstein. Liebknecht had been an intimate friend of the Marx family for thirty years and his devotion to the cause of Marxism was never in doubt. Bebel too – on his "journey to Canossa" – had little difficulty in satisfying Marx and Engels of his loyalty to Marxist principles and of his determination that in future *Der Sozialdemokrat* would advocate uncompromising opposition to the Anti-Socialist Law. Bernstein's position was rather different. He was a younger man whom Marx and Engels regarded with some suspicion, since he had – if only briefly – supported Dr Dühring and had worked for Karl Höchberg as his secretary. Moreover he was supposed to be one of the authors of the notorious "three-star" article in Karl Höchberg's *Jahrbuch* to which Marx and Engels had so strongly objected.

Eventually Marx and Engels were satisfied that Bernstein had turned over a new leaf and could safely be entrusted with the responsibility of editing the official organ of the Social Democrat Party. Georg Vollmar ceased to edit *Der Sozialdemokrat* on January 1, 1881 and now devoted himself to running the international agency established by the Wyden congress. Since Carl Hirsch had not accepted the post of editor, which he had been provisionally offered, the choice lay between Eduard Bernstein and Karl Kautsky. Although Bernstein had not had much experience as a journalist, Engels supported him – in preference to Kautsky – for the post of editor of *Der Sozialdemokrat*. On February 11, 1881 Bebel wrote two letters. One offered Bernstein the post of editor. The other informed Engels that he agreed that "Bernstein would be a better editor than Kautsky, who has all sorts of strange ideas, which are basically due to his conception and knowledge of conditions in Austria. I had a long talk with Kautsky when he was here recently and I realised that there could easily be considerable friction between him and ourselves."[60]

With Bernstein as editor, *Der Sozialdemokrat* embarked upon a new course. No support was given to those who advocated obedience to the Anti-Socialist Law. The paper adopted a policy of unrelenting opposition to Bismarck and to his henchman Robert von Puttkamer, the recently appointed reactionary Minister of the Interior in Prussia. When the Reichstag renewed the Anti-Socialist Law, when it expired on March 31, 1881, *Der Sozialdemokrat* hurled defiance at the government. Bebel wrote an article in which he declared: "Our private – that means our secret and illegal – organisation has replaced our public organisations and stands outside the law". "Only a fool or a traitor would now try to persuade us that only lawful means of resistance are available to us. In fact our only course is to strive for the violent overthrow of the existing social system."[61]

Those responsible for smuggling *Der Sozialdemokrat* into Germany were astonishingly successful. Some 10,000 subscribers received the paper every week. As Carl Schorlemmer once discovered – his belongings were searched when he was visiting relations – the police made every effort to stop the distribution of illegal newspapers and pamphlets. But they were repeatedly outwitted. Engels – "an old hand at revolutionary activities" – declared that he "often rejoiced at the quiet efficiency of the co-operation between the editors, the distributors, and the subscribers". He was "delighted at the businesslike way in which the revolutionary job was done week after week and year after year".[62] The success of *Der Sozialdemokrat* as a business venture may be seen from the fact that the paper "soon began to make a large profit for the party funds".[63] It was Julius Motteler – the "Red Postmaster" – who was largely responsible for the efficient distribution of the illegal paper.[64]

By the end of 1881 Engels was satisfied with the way in which Bernstein was editing *Der Sozialdemokrat* and, as Bebel recalled in his memoirs, he was prepared to give financial aid to the paper.[65] In Engels's view the paper was becoming "the banner of the party".[66] Engels was proud of the way in which the workers continued to support the outlawed socialist party. In July 1881, in an article in *The Labour Standard* Engels compared Bismarck's policy in Germany with Forster's policy in Ireland. He declared that "Bismarck's coercion avails him nothing; on the contrary it exasperates the people. Those to whom all legal means of asserting themselves are cut off, will one fine morning take to illegal ones and no one can blame them".[67]

At the Reichstag general election of November 1881 over 300,000 votes were cast for the Social Democrat Party. Although this represented a loss of 125,000 votes since the last general election – and although Bebel lost his seat – Engels was optimistic concerning the future of the party. He wrote to Bernstein on November 30, 1881:

"If any piece of news could have helped to put Marx to some extent on his feet again it was the result of the Reichstag election. Never has any proletariat done so well. In Germany the proletariat has suffered three years of grim repression and continual pressure. No organisation of the workers has been able to function openly. Yet our lads are standing four square in all their old self-confidence and strength. Indeed, in one respect they are more powerful than they were before because the centre of gravity of the socialist movement has moved from the semi-rural districts of Saxony to the great industrial towns. The class which naturally supports a revolution because of its economic position has become the nucleus of our movement. Moreover the movement has spread its influence uniformly over all the industrial regions of Germany. Formerly support for socialism was confined to a few local centres but now it has become a truly national movement. And that is what scares the middle classes most of all."[68]

Engels now decided to become a contributor to *Der Sozialdemokrat* and his first article – a tribute to Jenny Marx – appeared on December 8, 1881.[69]

Engels wrote articles on a variety of topics for *Der Sozialdemokrat*. He discussed the history of the communist movement in his accounts of the Communist League[70] and the *Neue Rheinische*

Zeitung,[71] as well as in articles on Bruno Bauer,[72] Karl Marx[73] Georg Weerth,[74] Johann Philipp Becker,[75] and Sigismund Borkheim.[76] He commented upon current affairs in articles on the American workers,[77] the English middle classes,[78] and the danger of German militarism.[79] Engels also reprinted in *Der Sozial-demokrat* articles which had already appeared elsewhere – for example his essay on the Mark,[80] his introductions to new editions of the Communist Manifesto[81] and the origin of the family.[83] The passages from *Socialism: Utopian and Scientific* were probably Engels's most important contribution to *Der Sozialdemokrat*. In these extracts thousands of German workers were able, for the first time, to learn about the basic principles of Marx's doctrines, expressed in clear and simple language.[84]

The year in which the Anti-Socialist Law was renewed for the first time and Bernstein became editor of *Der Sozialdemokrat* saw also the announcement of Bismarck's plan to introduce "State Socialism" in Germany. In his talks with Lassalle, nearly twenty years previously, Bismarck had shown an interest in the social problems that had arisen as a result of the industrial revolution. He now decided to try to win over the workers by introducing a far-reaching programme of social reform which included railway nationalisation, a tobacco monopoly, and compulsory state insurance against sickness, accidents, disablement and old age.

Bismarck submitted the first instalment of his welfare scheme to the Bundestag early in 1881. In a speech to the Reichstag on April 2 he declared: "For 50 years we have been speaking of a social question. Since the passing of the Anti-Socialist Law I have continually being reminded that a promise was then given that something should be done to remove the legitimate causes of socialism."[85] In a message to the newly elected Reichstag (November 17, 1881) the Emperor gave his august approval of Bismarck's plans. He observed that "the cure of social ills must not be sought exclusively in the repression of Social Democratic excesses, but simultaneously in the positive advancement of the welfare of the working classes".[86] The Health Insurance Law of 1883, the Accident Insurance Law of 1884, and the scheme for old age and disability pensions of 1889 gave effect to Bismarck's proposals. Meanwhile Albert von Maybach, the Prussian Minister of Public Works between 1878 and 1891, was engaged in nationalising some 7,500 miles of private railways in Prussia.

Bismarck's programme of social reform and nationalisation threatened to divide the German socialists. Some of the right wing members of the Social Democrat Party – such as Karl Höchberg and the deputies Kayser and Hasenclaver – were prepared to support Bismarck's proposals because they would benefit the workers. This placed Liebknecht and Bebel in a predicament. On the one hand they felt bound to reject any proposal put forward by Bismarck, so long as the socialists were outlawed. On the other hand they had to justify their stand to the workers who might secure some tangible benefits from them. To resolve the dilemma the socialist deputies in the Reichstag attacked the details of the proposed welfare schemes. They argued that the workers had to contribute too much to the health insurance and old age pensions schemes while getting too little in return. Thus a retirement pension of 191 marks a year at the age of 70 was contemptuously dismissed as a derisory reward for a lifetime of hard work. So the socialist deputies submitted amendments to Bismarck's bills, knowing that they would be defeated. They could then claim that they supported the principle of social reforms for the workers but rejected the unsatisfactory proposals actually put forward.

In articles which appeared in *Der Sozialdemokrat* attacking "State Socialism", it was argued that to tinker with capitalism by introducing welfare schemes was no substitute for the establishment of socialism. Liebknecht wrote that to hope for the success of "State Socialism" was like "expecting grapes to grow on thistles".[87] One article declared that "State Socialism" aimed at strengthening absolutism and reducing workers to "economic and political slavery".[88] Another claimed that the misery of the proletariat could only be abolished by replacing "capitalist exploitation by the establishment of a socialist state".[89]

In 1883 the publication of extracts from Engels's *Socialism: Utopian and Scientific* provided socialists with fresh ammunition to use against the supporters of "State Socialism". *Der Sozialdemokrat* also attacked Bismarck's scheme for railway nationalisation, arguing that the Chancellor's main object was to raise money for military purposes from the profits of the railways.[90] In November 1883 Wilhelm Liebknecht, writing in *Der Sozialdemokrat*, declared that "any deputy of the Reichstag, elected by socialist votes, who falls into the error of supporting Bismarck's fool's paradise of social reform, ceases at that moment to be a member of the Social Democrat Party or to represent the socialist movement in the Reichstag".[91]

The year 1883 saw also the holding of the second congress of the Social Democrat Party during the period that the Anti-Socialist Law was in force. At the Copenhagen congress of March 1883 – the month during which Marx died – the Social Democrat Party rejected Bismarck's "State Socialism" and pledged itself to support

the doctrines of Karl Marx. Both the Eisenach and the Gotha
programmes had been compromises between the ideas of Marx and
Lassalle. Now the introduction to the printed proceedings of the
Copenhagen congress declared that "German Social Democracy
proudly affirms that its aim is always to follow the principles of
its great master Marx". But the statement did not make it clear
by what means the aims of the party were to be achieved. Socialist
deputies were expected to use their membership of the Reichstag
simply to engage in propaganda activities. A seat in the Reichstag
was a forum from which socialist deputies could address the nation.
And while socialists declared that they aimed at revolutionary
goals they also protested that these goals were not to be achieved by
revolutionary means.[92]

If Bismarck hoped that parties which supported his welfare
schemes would gain votes at the expense of the socialists at the
general election of 1884 he was doomed to disappointment. Far
from losing votes the socialists more than recovered the ground
that they had lost in 1878 and in 1881. They polled 549,900 votes.
Engels was delighted. In letters to August Bebel and Karl Kautsky
he declared that "for the first time in history a strong steadfast
workers' party has emerged as a real power in politics". "The
Social Democrat Party has been aided – not hindered – by the Anti-
Socialist Law and it has given Bismarck a kick in the pants as far
as his social reforms are concerned."[93] "No working class in
Europe would have survived the challenge of the Anti-Socialist
Law so brilliantly. After being oppressed for six years no other
proletariat would have been able to build up a strong party organisation, capable of defying its persecutors by achieving such an
increase in its votes at the election."[94] "Only firm resistance has
made us a powerful party which has earned us the respect of our
opponents. Only force is respected and the philistines will respect
us just so long as we are a power in the land."[95] But Engels warned
Bebel that an unwelcome number of new socialist deputies, belonging to "the bourgeois right wing" of the party, were now
sitting in the Reichstag.[96]

The strengthening of the "bourgeois right wing" of the Social
Democrat Party in the Reichstag was one reason why German
socialists quarrelled among themselves in 1884 and 1885. One
controversy was over the Steamship Subsidy Bill[97] while another
was over the control of the editorial policy of Der Sozialdemokrat.
The government proposed to grant an annual postal subsidy of
£270,000 to German steamship lines operating in Asia, Africa and
Australia.[98] Bismarck admitted that this plan was "decisive for the
colonial policy of the government". For many years Bismarck had

rejected suggestions that Germany should establish colonies but by 1884 he had changed his mind and on April 24 the "establishments" of the German merchant Adolf Lüderitz at Angra Pequena in South West Africa were placed under Imperial protection.[99]

Marx and Engels were opponents of colonialism of long standing. They argued that capitalists in industrialised countries robbed the natives in underdeveloped regions as shamelessly as they exploited the factory workers at home. Other socialists had expressed similar views. In 1880 Karl Kautsky had strongly opposed the establishment of overseas possessions in an article entitled "Should Germany establish Colonies?"[100] When Bismarck made it clear in 1884 that he now favoured the founding of colonies it might have been expected that followers of Marx and Engels would firmly oppose him. And this was the view expressed by the writer of a leading article in *Der Sozialdemokrat* in July 1884.[101] But when the Steamship Subsidy Bill – which had been dropped in the summer of 1884 – was submitted to the newly elected Reichstag in December, the socialist deputies declared that no question of principles was involved and that individual deputies could vote as they pleased.[102] *Der Sozialdemokrat* criticised the deputies for their failure to unite in opposition to the Steamship Subsidy Bill and to Bismarck's colonial policy.

Engels gave the socialists some surprising advice. When Kayser had supported Bismarck's plan to introduce a protective tariff, Engels had criticised him vigorously. Yet when some of the socialist deputies supported the Steamship Subsidy Bill he suggested that they should negotiate with Bismarck on the matter. In letters to Liebknecht and Bebel[103] he proposed that the deputies should offer to support Bismarck provided that the royal domains in Prussia were leased to peasants' co-operative associations which should receive a government grant equivalent to the subsidy that the shipowners would obtain under the Steamship Subsidy Bill. Engels's proposal was inconsistent with policies previously advocated by Marx and Engels. First, the suggestion had something in common with Lassalle's discredited plan for the establishment of state-aided industrial co-operative associations – a plan which Bernstein had condemned in *Der Sozialdemokrat* as recently as June 1884.[104] Secondly, Engels's advice suggested that, despite the Anti-Socialist Law, the socialist deputies in the Reichstag should be prepared to bargain with Bismarck. In the past Marx and Engels had frequently condemned Lassalle for negotiating with Bismarck. Engels had called these discussions "plain roguery and a betrayal of the whole working class movement".[105]

Liebknecht summarised Engels's views in an article in *Der*

Sozialdemokrat, without mentioning Engels by name.[106] Left-wing socialists like Bebel and Bernstein were alarmed by Engels's proposal. While the Anti-Socialist Law was in force they believed that socialist deputies should always vote against the government in the Reichstag and that they should oppose a bill which might pave the way for the establishment of German colonies. In their view the fact that the Steamship Subsidy Bill might provide additional employment to German sailors and shipyard workers did not absolve socialist deputies from the duty of voting in accordance with socialist principles. Bebel's view prevailed and the socialist deputies voted against the second and third readings of the Steamship Subsidy Bill.[107]

Engels probably failed to support Bebel's uncompromising opposition to the bill because he feared that there would be a head-on collision between the two rival factions in the Social Democrat Party on this issue. And Engels was determined to do all in his power to preserve party unity. When he put forward his plan for state-aided peasants' co-operative associations on the royal domains – a proposal which he knew would not be acceptable either to Bismarck or to the Reichstag – he may have hoped that it would act as a red herring and divert attention from the arguments for and against the Steamship Subsidy Bill.

The second controversy between left-wing and right-wing socialists in Germany at this time concerned the control of the editorial policy of the official paper of the party. Early in 1885 *Der Sozialdemokrat* had attacked the attitude adopted by the socialist deputies in the Reichstag concerning the Steamship Subsidy Bill and Bismarck's colonial policy. The deputies claimed that – as the party executive – they had the right to determine the policy of *Der Sozialdemokrat*. They drew up a declaration to this effect but Bernstein refused to print it. Liebknecht went to Zürich and persuaded Bernstein to print a modified version of the declaration, but this still asserted that the deputies had the authority "to control the policy of the paper".[108] In 1890 Engels declared that "today it must seem incomprehensible to the deputies themselves that they should have done such a thing. The struggle lasted for exactly three weeks. It was on April 2, 1885 that the deputies passed their resolution. On April 30 (*sic*) a joint statement of the editors and the deputies appeared in the *Sozialdemokrat* which made it clear that the deputies had given up their claim to dictate the policy of the paper".[109] Even so the editorial committee had to accept the fact that "absolute freedom of criticism" should not be used "to hamper the party leadership in the fulfilment of its duty". Engels had warned Bebel that if the socialist deputies gained control over *Der Sozialdemokrat* he could not in future "defend the Party abroad without reservation" as he had done in the past.[110] The controversy between the party leadership and the editorial board of *Der Sozialdemokrat* ended in 1886 when the socialist deputies in the Reichstag gave up all responsibility for the contents of *Der Sozialdemokrat*. Over a year previously – in April 1885 – Engels had suggested that this should be done.[111] From November 5, 1886 onwards *Der Sozialdemokrat* ceased to be the official organ of the Social Democrat Party. This made no difference to editorial policy and there was no longer any danger that the party leadership might again attempt to influence what was printed in the paper.[112]

Der Sozialdemokrat was opposed not only to Bismarck's state socialism and to his colonial policy but also to Prussian militarism. In attacking great standing armies the paper was in agreement with Marx and Engels who had often declared that militarism – in Germany and elsewhere – was a danger to world peace. In 1867 Marx had told the General Council of the First International that "large standing armies were the necessary result of the present state of society". "They were not kept up for international warfare, but to keep down the working classes. However, as there were not always barricades to bombard, and working men to shoot, there was sometimes a possibility of international quarrels being fermented to keep the soldiery in trim."[113] Shortly afterwards Marx told the General Council that Liebknecht had spoken in the North German Reichstag "in favour of the abolition of standing armies".[114]

By the 1880s the efficiency of the German army had been improved by lengthening the period of service with the territorials (*Landwehr*), by reviving the home guard for older soldiers (*Landsturm*), by tightening up the method of enlisting conscript recruits, and by introducing the most up to date military equipment. Defence expenditure rose from £9,500,000 in 1870 to £24,000,000 in 1890. Inevitably other countries followed suit and expanded their armed forces. Moreover by annexing Alsace and Lorraine, Germany had made a permanent enemy of France and she had been able to gain a measure of security only through Bismarck's complex system of alliances.

In 1888 Engels wrote in *Der Sozialdemokrat* that the chauvinism of the German princes, nobles and middle classes was greater than ever before. The officer caste virtually dominated the country and ran it in the interests of the great landowners, industrialists and financiers. "The only war in which Prussia–Germany can now become involved", wrote Engels, "is a world war – a conflict that would be unique in extent and unprecedented in severity. From eight million to ten million men will go to war and the whole of Europe will be devoured as by a swarm of locusts."[114a]

Several articles in *Der Sozialdemokrat* attacked German militarism on similar lines – especially in 1880 and in 1887 when the seven year defence budget was being discussed in the Reichstag.[115] In April 1886 the paper argued that it was only because Bismarck had a powerful army at his beck and call – "the holy trinity of infantry, cavalry, and artillery" – that he was able to persecute the socialists.[116] In January 1887 the election manifesto of the retiring socialist deputies branded German militarism as the canker of a capitalist society. German militarism had started the arms race which would end in a great war in Europe. Only the triumph of socialism would herald the downfall of both capitalism and militarism. The manifesto called for the replacement of the existing army by a popular militia responsible to the Reichstag.[117] During the Reichstag election campaign *Der Sozialdemokrat* repeatedly denounced "the moloch of war called militarism".[118] One article described how troops had broken up a socialist election meeting in Stettin – one person was killed and several were injured – and declared that this showed "why those who rule over you want to have a larger army. They do not need more soldiers to meet a foreign foe. They need them to put down the German people."[119] At about the same time Engels wrote in *Der Sozialdemokrat* that Europe was heading for war owing to "the introduction of the Prussian military system in all the Great Powers on the Continent". He pointed out that "every expansion of the army of one state forces others to make a similar – or even a greater – increase in their armed forces". "The financial cost of all this borders on insanity." "The burden of military budgets will bankrupt the peoples of Europe and will actually soon be more costly than war, so that eventually the outbreak of hostilities – instead of being a terrible scourge – will actually appear to be a healing crisis which will put an end to an intolerable situation."[120]

In June 1887 an article appeared in *Der Sozialdemokrat* which suggested that, from one point of view, the continued growth of Germany's conscript army was actually advantageous to the socialist cause. Universal conscription meant that virtually an entire generation of young men received a basic military training. Many of them were already socialists before they joined up and others would be converted to socialism after their discharge. Thousands of young socialists were being trained to bear arms at government expense and one day they might be in the front line of a revolutionary army dedicated to the overthrow of capitalism.[121]

A few years later Engels put forward the same argument. He wrote:

"In Germany men are not eligible to vote until the age of 25 but they are liable to perform military service at the age of 20. And it is just among the younger generation that our party draws most of its recruits. Consequently the ranks of the German army are being filled with more and more supporters of the socialist cause as the years go by. Even today one soldier in five is a socialist and within a few years there will be one in three. By the end of the century the ranks of the army – once the stronghold of Prussianism in Germany – will be filled with socialists. Nothing can withstand the fateful march of events. The government in Berlin knows what is happening as well as we do but it is powerless to remedy the situation. The army is falling from its grasp."[122]

The socialists refused to be intimidated by Bismarck's repressive measures. In July 1886 nine leading socialists, including Bebel, were put on trial for being members of an illegal organisation. They were found guilty and were sentenced to terms of imprisonment varying from 6 to 9 months. In the following year the socialists gave Bismarck their reply. At the Reichstag general election of 1887 they polled 763,128 votes – 213,038 more than at the last election – but they secured only 11 seats. Nothing could have demonstrated more clearly the opposition of the workers to "State Socialism", imperialism and militarism. Bismarck had failed to crush the socialists. Engels declared that the German workers "were laughing at a Chancellor who could not do better revolutionary propaganda if he were paid to do it".[123] Moreover, Bismarck's policy was "driving the masses of workers and petty bourgeoisie into our camp in droves".[124] The German socialists held their third congress under the Anti-Socialist Law in 1887. The delegates met at Schonewegen brewery near St Gall in Switzerland and agreed to set up a committee – Bebel, Liebknecht, and Auer – to draft a revised party programme. This was a victory for the Marxist left wing of the party since no former follower of Lassalle was elected to the committee.

Faced with the continued defiance of the socialists, the German government introduced repressive measures against those who went on strike,[125] and made another attempt to muzzle the socialist press. In 1888 the Swiss authorities, under pressure from the German government, expelled Bernstein, Motteler and some other members of the staff of Der Sozialdemokrat. But this did not kill the paper since publication was transferred to offices in Kentish Town Road in London[126] and German subscribers received their copies as regularly as before. Gustav Mayer observes that in

London Bernstein edited *Der Sozialdemokrat* under Engels's watchful eye and "his ideas were firmly moulded by Engels, particularly as far as international affairs were concerned".[127]

By this time Engels was writing not only for *Der Sozialdemokrat* but also for *Die Neue Zeit*. This socialist monthly was edited by Karl Kautsky[128] and was published in Stuttgart. Kautsky had joined the Austrian socialist party in 1875 at a time when a split in the party had just occurred. The right wing "Moderates" were led by H. Oberwinder while the left wing "Radicals" were led by Andreas Scheu who later helped Most to edit *Die Freiheit* in London. Kautsky attached himself to the radicals. He soon left Austria for Switzerland where he worked for Dr Höchberg in Zürich. His conversion to Marxism came from studying Engels *Anti-Dühring* and from discussions with his friend Eduard Bernstein. Kautsky paid three visits to London, in 1881, 1883 and 1887, where he became a disciple and friend of Friedrich Engels. The relations between Engels and Kautsky became decidedly cooler after Kautsky's divorce. Engels wrote to Kautsky in 1888: "I stick to my guns and declare that you have done the most foolish thing in your life."[129] But the political collaboration between the two men continued.

Die Neue Zeit was established in January 1883. Its sales to regular subscribers rose from 2,300 copies in 1883 to 10,000 copies in 1890. It became the leading Marxist journal in Germany. It was founded at a time when the country was passing through a phase of rapid industrial expansion. In the first volume of *Das Kapital* Marx had analysed the growth of capitalism in England. Now in *Die Neue Zeit* Karl Kautsky and his collaborators examined similar developments – from a Marxist point of view – as they occurred in Germany.[130] At first Engels declined to become a contributor. He told Kautsky that he had been forced to cut down his work as a journalist owing to his other commitments – and that he was now writing only for *Der Sozialdemokrat*.[131] But Engels soon changed his mind and contributed several important articles to Kautsky's journal. They included essays on Marx and Rodbertus, England in 1845 and 1885,[132] Ludwig Feuerbach,[133] Protection and Free Trade, Russia's foreign policy, and Socialism in Germany.[134]

Discontent among the German workers was growing in the 1880s owing to low wages, long hours, poor housing, high taxes, and unemployment. The suppression of the Social Democrat Party and of many trade unions added fuel to the flames. In November 1886 Bebel told Engels that the coming winter would see much suffering among the proletariat owing to lack of work. The reduction in revenue from indirect taxes suggested that the purchasing power of the workers – and their standard of living – was declining.[135] Matters came to a head in the spring of 1889 when the workers unexpectedly showed a new spirit of militancy in relation to their employers. On May 4 production at the Hibernia colliery near Gelsenkirchen came to a halt when the miners suddenly went on strike. Within a few days 90,000 men in the Ruhr and 50,000 in other coalfields followed their example. A number of building workers also went on strike. But unrest did not spread to the steel-works in the Ruhr.[136]

The action of the miners came as a complete surprise both to the government and to the political parties. The miners had acted on the spur of the moment without making any serious preparations for a strike. If they hoped that Robert von Puttkamer's recent fall from office meant that the Prussian authorities would adopt a more lenient attitude towards the strikers, they were disappointed. Troops were called out to disperse meetings and demonstrations organised by the strikers and eleven people were killed.

Appeals to the miners to act with moderation came from Wilhelm II on the one hand and the Social Democrat Party on the other. Wilhelm II had only recently come to the throne and – as Bismarck observed – his "ideal seemed at that time to be popular absolutism".[137] He was, declared Engels, "itching to play the working man's friend"[138] and he rejected Bismarck's advice to drive the strikers down the pits by force. Wilhelm II told the cabinet that "the employers and shareholders must give way; the workers were his subjects for whom it was his place to care; if the industrial millionaires would not do as he wished he would withdraw his troops; if the villas of the wealthy mine owners and directors were then set on fire, and their gardens trampled under-foot, they would soon sing small". Bismarck retorted that "the mine owners were also subjects who had a claim to the protection of their sovereign".[139] Two days later Wilhelm II granted an audience to three representatives of the strikers (Schröder, Bunte, and Siegel) and listened sympathetically to their grievances. But he rebuked the miners for breaking their contracts and for trying to force all the workers to join in the strike. He also warned the strikers against listening to socialist agitators who were the enemies of the Fatherland. In fact the socialists were as worried as Wilhelm II about the strike. They feared that, in their present mood, the miners and other workers would try to redress their grievances by industrial action rather than by supporting the Social Democrat Party.

On May 15, 1889 an agreement was reached between Friedrich

Hammacher (chairman of the coalowners' association) and the three representatives of the miners who had recently seen Wilhelm II. This was the "Berlin protocol" which provided for a rise in pay and a reduction of hours for the workers. But the more militant leaders of the miners in the Ruhr rejected these terms and tried to prolong the strike. The government replied by arresting the whole strike committee. Only about one in five of the miners supported the militants and by the end of May all the men were back at work. The coalowners declared that, in view of the way in which the strike had ended, they were no longer bound by the "Berlin protocol" and the miners failed to achieve their objectives.[140]

The wave of strikes in 1889 brought the social question to the fore once more. Gustav Mayer – the future biographer of Engels – recalled that when he was in Berlin as a student at this time "social policy was the main interest not only of the Kaiser and his advisers, but also of the political parties, the universities and even the theatre".[141] Bismarck had submitted a bill in October 1889 to renew the Anti-Socialist Law but the Reichstag rejected the proposal in the following January. It was now obvious to all but the most bigoted reactionaries that the Chancellor had failed completely to crush the Social Democrat Party. On February 4, 1890 Wilhelm II – acting contrary to Bismarck's advice – put forward a plan for an international conference to discuss labour legislation. Even the socialists welcomed this move. *Der Sozialdemokrat* declared that it was "an event of world historical importance",[142] while Bebel wrote to Engels that Wilhelm II's "ambition is to be regarded as a great social reformer". "Far from harming us in any way this is very much to our advantage since it will put a strain upon his relations with the middle classes and will stimulate our propaganda among the masses."[143]

A general election was held on February 20, 1890. Engels was so eager to hear the results that he arranged with the central telegraph office in London for telegrams to be delivered to his home at any hour of the night.[144] On February 26 he wrote to Laura Lafargue: "When the telegrams announcing victory came raining in here thick and fast" he was "in a constant intoxication of triumph."[145] He had expected the socialists to gain 1,200,000 votes[146] and was delighted when they did even better than this. The Social Democrat Party secured 1,427,298 votes – 664,170 more than in 1887. This represented nearly 20 per cent of the votes cast as compared with 10 per cent at the last election. The socialists now sent 35 deputies to the Reichstag.[147]

In an article in *Der Sozialdemokrat* Engels declared that "February 20, 1890 marks the beginning of the end of the Bismarck era". "The German socialist workers have just won a resounding victory in their struggle. It is a triumph that they have richly deserved because of their tireless energy, grim determination, iron discipline and cheerful humour. The election results have probably surprised the socialist workers themselves as much as it surprised the rest of the world. The votes cast for socialist candidates has increased with the irresistible force of a natural process. Ruthless oppression, arbitrary police action, judicial baseness were helpless against a movement which made ever more rapid progress like an advancing column of infantry. Today the socialists are the second largest party in the Reich."[148]

At the same time Engels wrote to Wilhelm Liebknecht that the socialists in Germany were now firmly entrenched in the great centres of industry and had even done well in some rural districts such as Schleswig-Holstein, Mecklenburg, and Pomerania. "In three years we could have the farm labourers and then we have the regiments which form the core of the Prussian army." Only a coup d'état by the reactionary forces in Germany could stem a socialist landslide in the near future. Consequently the socialists should take great care to avoid presenting the junkers and the industrialists with an excuse to plunge Germany into a revolution, aimed at the overthrow of the workers. Engels urged Liebknecht to persuade his followers to act "in a peaceful and law-abiding manner *for the time being*".[149]

On March 18, 1890 Bismarck resigned as Chancellor and a few days later he was given "a first-class funeral" as he put it,[150] when he left Berlin to go into retirement. A squadron of hussars and a military band were at the station to honour the architect of German unity. But if there were any socialists in the cheering crowd they had not come to pay homage to a great statesman but to rejoice at the fall of their most implacable enemy. The departure of Bismarck and the swing to the left in the recent general election made it virtually certain that no new attempt would be made to renew the Anti-Socialist Law which was due to expire on September 30, 1890. In the last months of its existence the law was not rigorously enforced. Several provincial party congresses were held without interference from the authorities.

The leaders of the Social Democrat Party were anxious that the successes achieved in the early months of 1890 should not go to the heads of their more exuberant followers. Bebel wished to show the government and the public that the socialist leaders were responsible politicians and not irresponsible trouble makers. The clash between Bebel and the left wing of the party came over the proposal of the Second International that May 1, 1890 should be

celebrated everywhere as a "great international demonstration".
A group of militant socialists in Berlin called for a general strike
throughout the country on that day. Engels feared that militancy
on the part of the workers would lead to a violent backlash from
the reactionary forces in Germany. He wrote to Laura Lafargue
that "in Germany we shall have to keep May 1 as quiet as possible.
The military has strict orders to interfere at once and not to wait
for requisition from the civil authorities, and the secret police – on
the point of being discharged – are straining every nerve to provoke
a collision".[151] Writing to Sorge a few days later Engels dismissed
the idea of a general strike as "wholly superfluous". The socialist
workers were so elated over their success at the general election
that they needed "a certain curb in order not to make any
blunders.[152] Bebel agreed with Engels that militancy on the part
of the socialists would be fatal at this stage. He wrote to Engels:

"In Germany we find ourselves in a situation demanding the greatest
skill and tact. Consequently we must hold the masses within bounds
as regards the demonstration on May 1, so that no conflicts arise.
If the masses were given a free hand such conflicts would be
inevitable because the elections have turned the heads of the less
educated masses who think that anything can be achieved by an
act of will. . . . In view of the fact that, by and large, the state of
trade is now such that there is a demand for labour, there is a
general strike fever and the noisiest possible demonstrations on May
1 would lead at once to strikes of incredible dimensions."[153]

On April 13, the socialist deputies in the Reichstag (acting as
the executive committee of the party) rejected the proposal for a
general strike on May 1 and suggested that May Day celebrations
should take place after working hours. May Day passed off without strikes or violence and the leaders of the Social Democrat
Party could congratulate themselves on having outmanœuvred the
extremists.

No sooner had May 1 passed off quietly than there was a threat
of a new split in the Social Democrat Party. In 1890 a group of
intellectuals came to the fore in the socialist movement. They were
aged between 20 and 35 and, like the followers of Dr Dühring
twenty years before, were left-wing extremists. The "Youngsters"
(*Jungen*), as they were called, were for the most part university
graduates though Wilhelm Werner and Karl Wildberger were
craftsmen. They exercised considerable influence over some socialist newspapers, such as the *Berliner Volkstribune*, the *Volksstimme*
(Magdeburg), and the *Sächsische Arbeiterzeitung* (Dresden) and
some of them were contributors to Kautsky's *Neue Zeit*. Many of
them had studied the works of Marx and Engels and claimed to

have a thorough knowledge of socialist doctrines. The "Youngsters" had close contacts with an *avant-garde* literary circle in Berlin known as *Durch* which included Gerhard Hauptmann, whose play *Die Weber* (1892) – on the weavers' rising in Silesia in 1844 – was one of the earliest social dramas in Germany. The "Youngsters" had little to offer in the way of a new socialist policy but they found much to criticise in the conduct of the leaders of the Social Democrat Party and its representatives in the Reichstag. They declared that life in the Reichstag corrupted socialist deputies and made them think more of social advancement than of looking after the interests of the workers who had voted for them. The "Youngsters" argued that socialist deputies should use the Reichstag simply as a platform from which to expose the hypocrisy of the bourgeoisie.

Bebel had little difficulty in putting the "Youngsters" in their place. They might be able to stir up trouble by writing spiteful articles in newspapers but they were no match for so skilful a politician as Bebel when it came to putting a case before a mass meeting of workers. In August 1890 Bebel addressed meetings of socialists in Berlin, Dresden and Magdeburg and, on each occasion, he secured the adoption of a motion condemning the "Youngsters". Four of the leading "Youngsters" had to give up their posts on the staffs of socialist newspapers. And from London Engels hurled his thunderbolts at the presumptuous "Youngsters" who had dared to question the wisdom of their elders and betters in the socialist movement. Engels was an old hand when it came to dealing with socialist heretics and he did not mince his words when he denounced these new critics of the Marxist faith. He wrote to Laura Lafargue:

"There has been a students' revolt in the German Party. For the past 2–3 years, a crowd of students, literary men and other young declassed bourgeois has rushed into the Party, arriving just in time to occupy most of the editorial positions on the new journals . . . and, as usual, they regard the bourgeois universities as a socialist staff college which gives them the right to enter the ranks of the Party with an officer's, if not a general's, brevet. All these gentlemen go in for Marxism, but of the kind you were familiar with in France ten years ago, and of which Marx said: 'All I know is that I'm no Marxist!' And of these gentlemen he would probably have said what Heine said of his imitators: 'I sowed dragons, and reaped fleas'."[154]

On September 25, 1890 *Der Sozialdemokrat* (dated September 27) appeared for the last time. Engels declared that he would "miss that paper almost as much as the *Neue Rheinische Zeitung*".[155] In editing *Der Sozialdemokrat* Bernstein had been inspired by the way in which Marx had edited the *Neue Rheinische Zeitung*. Now, in the last number of *Der Sozialdemokrat*, Bernstein quoted some lines from the poem that Freiligrath had contributed to the final "red number" of the *Neue Rheinische Zeitung*. And he also quoted Marx's farewell message to his readers: "Finally, we urge you not to indulge in any armed rising in Cologne."

The two papers, however, had come to an end in very different ways. The "red number" of the *Neue Rheinische Zeitung* had hurled defiance at Marx's enemies but nothing could disguise the fact that the revolution of 1848 had failed and that the editors of the paper were fleeing from Cologne. *Der Sozialdemokrat*, on the other hand, ceased publication because the Social Democrat Party had triumphed over the "brutal authoritarian régime" which had tried to crush it by every means in its power. Bernstein declared that Bismarck's fall might appear to be due to a palace intrigue but in fact he had been given notice to quit by nearly one and a half million voters at the general election of February 20. When the Anti-Socialist Law expired on September 30 there would no longer be any need to publish a socialist paper in London and to smuggle it into Germany.[156]

In the last number of *Der Sozialdemokrat*, Engels hailed the paper as "the banner of the Social Democrat Party". He wrote: "I have twice had the honour and the good fortune to write regularly for a journal under very favourable conditions, for I have enjoyed the two greatest blessings that any contributor could desire – complete freedom of the press and the knowledge that my articles were being read by the very people I wished to influence. The first time was in 1848–9 when I was associated with the *Neue Rheinische Zeitung*. . . . The second time was when I wrote for the *Sozialdemokrat*." Engels praised the staff of *Der Sozialdemokrat* on the efficient distribution of the paper to its German readers. Yet at the very same time (in a letter to Laura Lafargue) he dismissed Motteler as an "unspeakable muddler"[157] and Motteler had been the "Red Postmaster" responsible for successfully smuggling *Der Sozialdemokrat* into the Reich. Engels congratulated Bernstein and his colleagues for courageously defying the socialist deputies in the Reichstag over the Steamship Subsidy Bill. He declared that "all the trouble and risks that had to be taken to distribute the paper were fully justified. The high standard attained by *Der Sozialdemokrat* was not merely due to the fact that it was the only socialist paper which enjoyed the advantage of complete freedom of the press. The principles of the party were stated with unusual clarity and precision and there was no deviation from them. And while the German bourgeois press is incredibly dull the *Sozialdemokrat* reflected the cheerful humour with which our

workers are accustomed to fight the chicaneries of the police".
"Now the Social Democrat Party has emerged victorious from a
struggle that has lasted for twelve years. The Anti-Socialist Law
is no more. Bismarck has fallen from power. The mighty German
Reich set all its forces in motion against us. The Party defied the
Reich and now the Reich has had to admit defeat. In future the
government of the Reich will again deal with us in accordance with
the established laws of the land. And we will now return to the
paths of legality. But let it be remembered that our victory was
won by striking hard with illegal weapons."[158]

The Anti-Socialist Law expired at midnight on September 30,
1890. Throughout Germany in beer halls and restaurants the
socialists, who had suffered so much for their political convictions,
enthusiastically celebrated their triumph over those who had hoped
to crush their movement. Divisions and rivalries within the Social
Democrat Party were forgotten for the moment as the workers
cheered the speeches of their leaders who had led them to victory.
Men who had been exiled from their homes were back with their
families. Those who had worked in the underground movement to
distribute socialist leaflets and pamphlets could openly proclaim their
faith in the socialist movement. With ever increasing support from
the electorate the Social Democrat Party could confidently look
forward to the day when it would dominate the Reichstag.

NOTES

1   See Ignaz Auer, *Nach Zehn Jahren* (1878); E. Bernstein, *Die Geschichte
    der Berliner Arbeiter-Bewegung*, Vol. 1 (1907); R. Lipinski, *Die
    Sozialdemokratie un ihren Aufängen bis zur Gegenwart*, Vol. 2
    (1928); Paul Kamffmeyer, *Unter den Sozialistengesetz* (1928);
    G. Schümer, *Die Entstehungsgeschichte des Sozialistengesetzes* (1929);
    F. Tönnies, *Der Kampf um das Sozialistengesetz, 1878* (1929);
    F. Mehring, *Deutsche Geschichte vom Ausgange des Mittelalters*
    (edition of 1952), Part VII; H. Gemkow, *Friedrich Engels' Hilfe beim
    Sieg der deutschen Sozialdemokratie über das Sozialistengesetz* (1957);
    Horst Bartel, *Marx und Engels im Kampf um ein revolutionäres
    Parteiorgan* (1961); Horst Bartel, "Die führende Rolle von Friedrich
    Engels bei der Entwicklung der Sozialdemokratie zu einer marxist-
    ischen Arbeiterpartei in der Periode des Sozialistengesetzes" in
    Geschichte in der Schule, Heft 8, pp. 468–9; Horst Bartel, "Die
    historische Rolle der Zeitung 'Der Sozialdemokrat' in der Periode
    des Sozialistengesetzes" in the *Zeitschrift für Geschichtswissenschaft*,
    1956, Heft 2, pp. 282–87; L. Stern and H. Buck (ed.), *Der Kampf der
    deutschen Sozialdemokratie in der Zeit des Sozialistengesetzes, 1878–
    90* (documents) (two volumes, 1956); A. Hellfaier, *Die deutsche
    Sozialdemokratie während des Sozialistengesetzes 1878–1890* (1958);
    E. Engelberg, *Revolutionäre Politik und Rote Feldpost, 1878–1890*
    (1959); D. Fricke, *Bismarcks Praetorianer. Die Berliner politische*

Polizei im Kampf gegen die deutsche Arbeiterbewegung, 1871–1898 (1962); V. L. Lidtke, *The Outlawed Party. Social Democracy in Germany, 1878–1890* (1966).

2   F. Engels, *The Rôle of Force in History, 1887–8* (1968), p. 93.

3   G. Brodnitz, *Bismarcks Nationalökonomische Anschauungen* (1902), pp. 124–5.

4   G. Brodnitz, *op. cit.*, p. 125. In November 1871 Bismarck wrote to Itzenplitz that the socialists threatened the existing order of society: see R. Morgan, *The German Social Democrats and the First International*, 1864–72 (1965), p. 2.

5   Fritz Hellwig, *Carl Ferdinand Freiherr von Stumm-Halberg 1836–1901* (1936), p. 231.

6   See *Der Leipziger Hochverratsprozess vom Jahre 1872* (second edition: edited by Karl Heinz Leidigkeit, 1960).

7   F. Engels in *La Plebe* (Lodi and Milan), March 30, 1879 in Karl Marx and F. Engels *Pressefreiheit und Zensur* (edited by Iring Fetscher), 1969, p. 227.

8   Alfred Krupp, *Ein Wort an die Angehörigen meiner gewerblichen Anlagen* (1877): extracts in R. Ehrenberg, *Grosse Vermögen*, Vol. 1 (1902), pp. 205–7 and W. A. Boelcke (ed.), *Krupp und die Hohenzollern in Dokumenten* (1970), p. 85.

9   F. Hellwig, *Carl Ferdinand Freiherr von Stumm-Halberg 1836–1901* (1936), pp. 231–2 and Hans Rosenberg, *Grosse Depression und Bismarckzeit* (1967), p. 206.

10 See Andrew Carlson, *Anarchism in Germany: the Early Movement* (Johns Hopkins University thesis, 1970).

11 Announcements of Hödel's expulsion from the Social Democrat Party appeared in the *Fackel*, May 12, 1878 and in *Vorwärts*, May 15, 1878.

12 E. Schraepler, *August Bebel* (1966), pp. 43–4.

13 Wilhelm Bracke to F. Engels, June 1878 in Karl Marx–F. Engels, *Briefwechsel mit Wilhelm Bracks, 1869–1880* (1963), p. 171.

14 August Bebel, *Aus meinem Leben*, Vol. 2 (1911), pp. 412–20.

15 Wilhelm Bracke to F. Engels, July 11, 1878 in Karl Marx–Friedrich Engels, *Briefwechsel mit Wilhelm Bracke, 1869–1880* (1963), pp. 64–5.

16 S. P. Orth, *Socialism and Democracy in Europe* (1913), pp. 160–1.

17 *Stenographische Berichte über die Verhandlungen des Deutschen Reichstags* (fourth legislative period: first session: September 16, 1878).

18 The "professorial socialists" (*Kathedersozialisten*) were academic economists, such as Gustav Schmoller, Lujo Brentano and Nasse, who – through the *Verein für Sozialpolitik* – advocated social reform. In his opening address to the *Verein für Sozialpolitik* Schmoller declared that he and his friends rejected "all socialist experiments".

19 Gustav Mayer, *Bismarck und Lassalle. Ihr Briefwechsel und ihre Gespräche* (1928) and Wilhelm Mommsen, "Bismarck und Lassalle" in the *Archiv für Sozialgeschichte*, Vol. 3, pp. 81–6.

20 Karl Marx to Wilhelm Liebknecht, November 21, 1865 in Wilhelm Liebknecht, *Briefwechsel mit Karl Marx und Friedrich Engels* (ed. G. Eckert, 1963), pp. 67–8. On December 10, 1864 Marx had told Engels that "Lothar Bucher – the executor of Lassalle's will, who draws an allowance of £150 a year from Lassalle's estate – has, as you probably know, deserted to Bismarck's camp" (*Gesamtausgabe*, Part III, Vol. 3, p. 213). Bucher had been a radical during the revolution of 1848–9, an exile in London in 1850–61 and a disciple of

Lassalle in 1861–4. At the end of 1864 he received an appointment in the Prussian Ministry of Foreign Affairs and became one of Bismarck's closest associates. When Bismarck retired Lothar Bucher became his private secretary and helped him to write his memoirs. See H. von Poschinger, *Ein Achtundvierziger. Lothar Bucher's Leben und Wirken* (three volumes, 1890–4) and an article in the *Neue Deutsche Biographie*, Vol. 2, pp. 698–9.

21 For the text of the Anti-Socialist Law see the *Reichs-Gesetzblatt* No. 34 of 1878, pp. 351–8 and H. Gemkow, *Friedrich Engels' Hilfe beim sieg der Deutschen Sozialdemokratie über das Sozialistengesetz* (1957), pp. 187–92: English translation in V. L. Lidtke, *The Outlawed Party. Social Democracy in Germany, 1878–1890* (1966), pp. 339–45.

22 As early as August 15, 1878 – before the Anti-Socialist Law was passed – Bismarck had written to Geheimrat Tiedemann: "Moreover I believe that, if the (Anti-Socialist) Law is effective, a time will come when it will no longer be possible to allow those citizens who are proved in law to be socialists to continue to enjoy the right to vote, the right to send for election to the Reichstag, or the right to enjoy the privileges of membership of the Reichstag" (H. Gemkow, *Friedrich Engels' Hilfe beim Sieg der Deutschen Sozialdemokratie über das Sozialistengesetz* (1957), p. 31.

23 F. Engels to J. P. Becker, July 1, 1879 in Karl Marx and F. Engels, *Selected Correspondence* (Foreign Languages Publishing House, Moscow), p. 387.

24 F. Engels to E. Bernstein, February 27–March 1, 1883 in H. Hirsch (ed.), *Eduard Bernstein's Briefwechsel mit Friedrich Engels* (1970), p. 195.

25 F. Engels to E. Bernstein, January 25–31, 1882 in H. Hirsch (ed.), *Eduard Bernstein's Briefwechsel mit Friedrich Engels* (1970), p. 70.

26 Wilhelm Liebknecht to F. Engels, June 8, 1878 in Wilhelm Liebknecht, *Briefwechsel mit Karl Marx und Friedrich Engels* (ed. G. Eckert, 1963), p. 256.

27 W. Martini, *Die Wandlungen im Parteiprogramm der Sozialdemokratie seit 1875* (Erlangen, 1908), pp. 13–17. Ignaz Auer states in his memoirs (*Nach Zehn Jahren*, p. 93) that two socialist papers in Nürnberg and Offenbach survived, having changed their names before the Anti-Socialist Law was passed.

28 *Vorwärts*, October 21, 1878.

29 Karl Kautsky in Benedikt Kautsky, *Friedrich Engels' Briefwechsel mit Karl Kautsky* (1955), p. 91.

30 *Rechenschaftsbericht der Sozialdemokratischen Mitglieder des deutschen Reichstags* (Zürich, 1879).

31 In a sentence which he crossed out, Engels wrote: "Bismarck deals with the German philistines as they deserve. He gives them a kick in the pants and they positively worship him."

32 F. Engels to August Bebel, November 14, and 24, 1879 in Werner Blumenberg (ed.), *August Bebels Briefwechsel mit Friedrich Engels* (1965), pp. 71–84. August Geib had expressed the same point of view when he wrote to Karl Höchberg on June 20, 1879 that "one cannot organise and hold the party together from abroad" (V. L. Lidtke, *The Outlawed Party. Social Democracy in Germany, 1878–1890* (1966), p. 88).

33 August Bebel to F. Engels, October 23, 1879 in Werner Blumenberg (ed.), *August Bebels Briefwechsel mit Friedrich Engels* (1965), p. 67.

34 For Bracke's funeral see *Der Sozialdemokrat*, May 9, 1880.

35 "Zur Eröffnung des sächsischen Landtages" in *Der Sozialdemokrat*, November 16, 1879. In February 1879 the socialists had done well at an election in Breslau: see F. Engels to W. Liebknecht, March 1, 1879 in Wilhelm Liebknecht, *Briefwechsel mit Karl Marx und Friedrich Engels* (ed. Georg Eckert, 1963), p. 263.

36 "Ein neuer Sieg" in *Der Sozialdemokrat*, March 7 and 14, 1880.

37 In 1880 Karl Marx wrote to Mr Swinton of the *New York Sun:* "I believe that a man of your influence might organise a subscription in the United States (Karl Marx to John Swinton, November 4, 1880 in Karl Marx and F. Engels, *Letters to Americans, 1848–95* (1963), p. 122).

38 There is a reference to *Die Laterne* in Wilhelm Liebknecht to F. Engels, December 23, 1878 in Wilhelm Liebknecht, *Briefwechsel mit Karl Marx und Friedrich Engels* (ed. Georg Eckert, 1963), p. 263.

39 During the first six months of publication *Freiheit* received a subsidy of £40 from the German Workers' Educational Association in London.

40 F. Engels to Wilhelm Liebknecht, March 1, 1879 in Wilhelm Liebknecht, *Briefwechsel mit Karl Marx und Friedrich Engels* (edited by Georg Eckert, 1963), p. 264.

41 F. Engels to F. I. Ehrhart, June 16, 1879 in H. Gemkow, *Friedrich Engels' Hilfe beim Sieg der deutschen Sozialdemokratie über das Sozialistengesetz* (1957), p. 37.

42 H. Gemkow, *op. cit.*, p. 37.

43 Karl Marx to A. Sorge, September 19, 1879 in Karl Marx and F. Engels, *Letters to Americans, 1848–95* (1963), p. 118.

44 For Most see R. Rocker, *Johann Most. Das Leben eines Rebellen* (1924) and article in the *Dictionary of American Biography*, Vol. 13, p. 282.

45 F. Engels to August Bebel, October 11, 1884 in Werner Blumenberg (ed.), *August Bebels Briefwechsel mit Friedrich Engels* (1965), p. 189.

46 Karl Kautsky to August Bebel, December 21, 1879 in Karl Kautsky (junior) (ed.), *August Bebels Briefwechsel mit Karl Kautsky* (1971), p. 4.

47 For Marx's account of these discussions see Karl Marx to A. Sorge, September 19, 1879 in Karl Marx and F. Engels, *Letters to Americans, 1848–95* (1963), pp. 118–21. Marx wrote: "After a prolonged correspondence, in which Liebknecht did not play a shining part, Hirsch withdrew. Engels wrote to Bebel that *we* are also withdrawing". See also Karl Marx to A. Sorge, November 5, 1880 (*ibid.*, p. 123).

48 Vollmar's full name was Georg Heinrich von Vollmar auf Vehtheim. For Vollmar see an article in the *Deutsches Biographisches Jahrbuch*, Vol. 4, Year 1922 (1929), pp. 276–86; Paul Kampffmeyer, *Georg von Vollmar* (1930); and R. Jansen, *Georg von Vollmar. Eine politische Biographie* (1958).

49 In 1881 Liebknecht was the nominal editor of *Der Sozialdemokrat* but since he lived in Germany and the weekly was published first in Zürich and then in London, it was Bernstein who actually acted as editor.

50 August Bebel to Georg Vollmar, November 30, 1879 in Horst Bartel, *Marx und Engels im Kampf um ein revolutionäres deutsches Parteiorgan 1879–90* (1961).

51 *Der Sozialdemokrat*, September 28, 1879.
52 "Rechenschaftsbericht der sozialdemokratischen Mitglieder des deutschen Reichstags" in *Der Sozialdemokrat*, October 12, 19 and 26, 1879.
53 "Was die Sozialdemokraten sind und was sie wollen" in *Der Sozialdemokrat*, August 29, 1880.
54 "Unsere Festtage" in *Der Sozialdemokrat*, January 4, 1880.
55 "An die deutsche Parteigenossen" in *Der Sozialdemokrat*, February 29, 1880.
56 F. Engels to August Bebel, December 16, 1879 in Werner Blumenberg (ed.), *August Bebels Briefwechsel mit Friedrich Engels* (1965), pp. 86–9.
57 F. Engels to J. P. Becker, April 1, 1880 in Horst Bartel, *Marx und Engels im Kampf um ein revolutionäres deutsches Parteiorgan, 1879–90* (1961), p. 52.
58 Karl Marx to Adolf Sorge, November 5, 1880 in Karl Marx and F. Engels, *Letters to Americans, 1848–95* (1963), p. 123.
59 *Der Sozialdemokrat*, September 27, 1890: English translation in W. O. Henderson (ed.), *Engels: Selected Writings* (Penguin Books, 1967), pp. 141–3.
60 August Bebel to F. Engels, February 11, 1881 in Werner Blumenberg (ed.), *August Bebels Briefwechsel mit Friedrich Engels* (1965), p. 102.
61 Quoted in Hans Blum, *Das Deutsche Reich zur Zeit Bismarcks* (1893), p. 375.
62 F. Engels in *Der Sozialdemokrat*, September 27, 1890: English translation in W. O. Henderson (ed.), *Engels: Selected Writings* (Penguin Books, 1967), p. 142.
63 Bertrand Russell, *German Social Democracy* (1896), p. 106.
64 For Julius Motteler see Franz Mehring, "Julius Motteler" in the *Leipziger Volkszeitung*, September 30, 1907 and in *Aufsätze zur Geschichte der Arbeiterbewegung* (1963), pp. 498–501; Joseph Belli, *Die rote Feldpost unterm Sozialistengesetz* (1912); and Ernst Engelberg, *Revolutionäre Politik und Rote Feldpost 1878–90* (1959).
65 Horst Bartel, *Marx und Engels im Kampf um ein revolutionäres Parteiorgan, 1879–90* (1961), p. 53 and August Bebel to F. Engels, January 23, 1880 in Werner Blumenberg (ed.), *August Bebels Briefwechsel mit Friedrich Engels* (1965), p. 90.
66 F. Engels in *Der Sozialdemokrat*, September 27, 1890.
67 F. Engels, "Bismarck and the German Working Men's Party" in *The Labour Standard*, July 23, 1881; reprinted in F. Engels, *The British Labour Movement* (1934), pp. 36–8.
68 F. Engels to E. Bernstein, November 30, 1881 in Helmut Hirsch (ed.), *Eduard Bernstein's Briefwechsel mit Friedrich Engels* (1970), 59–62.
69 Jenny Marx died on December 2, 1881: see F. Engels, "Jenny Marx, geb. von Westfalen" in *Der Sozialdemokrat*, December 8, 1881.
70 F. Engels, "Zur Geschichte des Bundes der Kommunisten" in *Der Sozialdemokrat*, November 12, 19 and 26, 1885: subsequently published as the introduction to Karl Marx, *Enthüllungen über den Kommunistenprozess zu Köln*, 1852 (new edition, 1885).
71 F. Engels, "Marx und die *Neue Rheinische Zeitung*, 1848–9" in *Der Sozialdemokrat*, March 13, 1884.
72 F. Engels, "Bruno Bauer und das Urchristenthum" in *Der Sozialdemokrat*, May 4 and 11, 1882.

73 F. Engels, "Das Begräbnis von Karl Marx" in *Der Sozialdemokrat*, March 22, 1883 and "Zum Tode von Karl Marx" in *Der Sozialdemokrat*, May 3 and 17, 1883.

74 F. Engels, *"Handwerksburschenlied* von Georg Weerth, 1846" in *Der Sozialdemokrat*, June 7, 1883.

75 F. Engels, "Dem Gedächtnis Johann Philipp Beckers" in *Der Sozialdemokrat*, December 17, 1886.

76 F. Engels, "Was Europa bevorsteht" in *Der Sozialdemokrat*, January 15, 1888: extract from Engels's introduction to a new edition of Sigismund Borkheim, *Zur Erinnerung für die deutschen Mordspatrioten, 1806–7* (1888).

77 F. Engels, "Die Arbeiterbewegung in Amerika" (dated January 26, 1887) in *Der Sozialdemokrat*, June 10 and 17, 1887. These articles appeared in English as the introduction to the English translation of *The Condition of the Working Class in England* which was published in the United States in 1887. See Appendix II of the new translation of this book by W. O. Henderson and W. H. Chaloner published by Basil Blackwell (Oxford) in 1958 and 1971.

78 F. Engels, "Die Abdankung der Bourgeoisie" in *Der Sozialdemokrat*, October 5, 1889.

79 F. Engels in "Sozialpolitische Rundschau" in *Der Sozialdemokrat*, March 11, 1887.

80 F. Engels, "Die Mark" in *Der Sozialdemokrat*, March 15, 22 and 29, and April 5, 12 and 19, 1883. This essay also appeared in the German (1883) and English (1892) versions of F. Engels, *Socialism: Utopian and Scientific*.

81 See *Der Sozialdemokrat*, April 13, 1882 (Russian edition), April 14, 1888 (English edition) and August 16, 1890 (German edition). Extracts from the Communist Manifesto appeared in *Der Sozialdemokrat*, April 3 and June 5, 1884.

82 F. Engels, "Zur Wohnungsfrage" in *Der Sozialdemokrat*, January 15 and 22, 1887: introduction to a new edition of Engels's pamphlet of 1872 on the housing question.

83 F. Engels in *Der Sozialdemokrat*, October 2, 1884 ("Sozialpolitische Rundschau") and October 23, 1884 ("Die neue Schrift von Friedrich Engels").

84 See "Eine neue Propagandabroschüre" and "Der Sozialismus und der Staat" in *Der Sozialdemokrat*, February 22 and December 20, 1883.

85 W. H. Dawson, *Social Insurance in Germany, 1883–1911* (1912), p. 14.

86 W. H. Dawson, *op. cit.*, p. 16.

87 Wilhelm Liebknecht, "Die Impotenz des Klassenstaates" in *Der Sozialdemokrat*, January 5, 1882.

88 "Das Erbteil der Enterbten" in *Der Sozialdemokrat*, March 9, 1882.

89 "Kathedersozialistische Weisheit" in *Der Sozialdemokrat*, October 29, 1882.

90 *Der Sozialdemokrat*, April 26, 1883.

91 Wilhelm Liebknecht, "Zur Sozialreform des Fürsten Bismarck" in *Der Sozialdemokrat*, November 8, 1883 and in Horst Bartel, *Marx und Engels im Kampf um ein revolutionäres deutsches Parteiorgan 1879–90* (1961), pp. 225–8.

92 *Protokoll über den Kongress der deutschen Sozialdemokratie in Kopenhagen: abgehalten vom 29 März bis 2 April 1883* (Hottingen-Zürich, 1883).

93 F. Engels to Karl Kautsky, November 8, 1884 in B. Kautsky (ed.), *Friedrich Engels' Briefwechsel mit Karl Kautsky* (1955), p. 154.

94 F. Engels to August Bebel, December 11–12, 1884 in Werner Blumenberg (ed.), *August Bebels Briefwechsel mit Friedrich Engels* (1965), p. 202.

95 F. Engels to August Bebel, November 18, 1884 in Werner Blumenberg (ed.), *August Bebels Briefwechsel mit Friedrich Engels* (1965), p. 196.

96 F. Engels to August Bebel, December 11–12, 1884 in Werner Blumenberg (ed.), *August Bebels Briefwechsel mit Friedrich Engels* (1965), p. 202. The deputies on the left wing of the party were Bebel, Liebknecht, Heine, Vollmar, Rödinger and Stolle. The deputies on the right wing were Auer, Blos, Dietz, Geiser, Grillenberger, Frohme, Hasenclaver, Kayser, Schumacher and Singer. See H. Gemkow, *Friedrich Engels' Hilfe beim Sieg der deutschen Sozialdemokratie über das Sozialistengesetz* (1957), p. 103.

97 R. Rothe, "Zum Streit um die Dampfersubvention" in *Archiv für Sozialgeschichte*, Vol. 1 (1961), pp. 109–118.

98 The first subsidy bill of April 1884 provided for an annual subsidy of £200,000 for lines to Australia and Asia. The second bill of November 1884 increased the subsidy to £270,000 and added a line to Africa.

99 For Bismarck's colonial policy see W. O. Henderson, *Studies in German Colonial History* (1962) and Mary Evelyn Townsend, *The Rise and Fall of Germany's Colonial Empire 1884–1918* (1930).

100 Karl Kautsky, "Soll Deutschland Kolonien gründen?" in *Staatswirtschaftliche Abhandlungen*, March 1880. See also an article by Karl Kautsky on colonies in *Die Neue Zeit*, August–September 1883.

101 "Marx über das Kolonialsystem" in *Der Sozialdemokrat*, July 10, 1884.

102 "Sozialpolitische Rundschau" in *Der Sozialdemokrat*, December 11, 1884.

103 F. Engels to August Bebel, December 30, 1884 in Werner Blumenberg (ed.), *August Bebels Briefwechsel mit Friedrich Engels* (1965), pp. 210–13 and F. Engels to W. Liebknecht, December 29, 1884 (fragment) in Wilhelm Liebknecht, *Briefwechsel mit Karl Marx und Friedrich Engels* (1963), pp. 284–5.

104 E. Bernstein, "Produktivassoziationen mit Staatskredit" in *Der Sozialdemokrat*, June 26, 1884: printed in Horst Bartel, *Marx und Engels im Kampf um ein revolutionäres deutsches Parteiorgan 1879–90* (1961), pp. 233–8.

105 F. Engels to Karl Marx, January 27, 1865 in *Gesamtausgabe*, Part III, Vol. 3, p. 218: English translation in W. O. Henderson (ed.), *Engels: Selected Writings* (Penguin Books, 1967), p. 131.

106 "Zur Dampfersubvention" in *Der Sozialdemokrat*, January 8, 1885.

107 The socialist deputies offered to support the bill on the following conditions (i) that all subsidised ships should be new and should be built by German labour in German shipyards, (ii) that the line to Africa and the branch line to Samoa (where Germany had colonial ambitions) should be excluded from the bill, and (iii) that the subsidy should be reduced to £185,000 a year. The Reichstag rejected these amendments.

108 *Der Sozialdemokrat*, April 2, 1885.

109 F. Engels in *Der Sozialdemokrat*, September 27, 1890: English trans-

lation in W. O. Henderson (ed.), *Engels: Selected Writings* (Penguin Books, 1967). The joint statement appeared in *Der Sozialdemokrat* on April 23 (not 30), 1885.

110 F. Engels to August Bebel, April 4, 1885 in Werner Blumenberg (ed.), *August Bebels Briefwechsel mit Friedrich Engels* (1965), p. 218.

111 *Ibid.*, p. 220.

112 *Der Sozialdemokrat*, October 21, 1886 and F. Engels to August Bebel, October 23 and 25, 1886 in Werner Blumenberg (ed.), *August Bebels Briefwechsel mit Friedrich Engels* (1965), p. 297.

113 *The General Council of the First International: Minutes*, Vol. 1, 1866–8 (*Documents of the First International*) (Progress Publishers, Moscow), August 13, 1867, p. 152.

114 *Ibid.*, October 22, 1867, p. 167.

114ª F. Engels in *Der Sozialdemokrat*, January 15, 1888 and introduction to a new edition of S. Borkheim, *Zur Erinnerung für die deutschen Mordspatrioten*, 1806–7 (Hottingen–Zürich, 1888).

115 Horst Bartel, *Marx und Engels im Kampf um ein revolutionäres Parteiorgan* (1961), pp. 154–64.

116 "Wie's Euch gefällt" in *Der Sozialdemokrat*, April 15, 1886.

117 "Das Wahlmanifest der sozialdemokratischen Fraktion des letzen Reichstages" in *Der Sozialdemokrat*, January 29, 1887.

118 "Was der sozialdemokratische Stimmzettel bedeutet" in *Der Sozialdemokrat*, February 11, 1887.

119 "Die neuste Schandtat der Puttkammerei" in *Der Sozialdemokrat*, February 18, 1887. Robert von Puttkamer was Minister of the Interior in Prussia between 1881 and 1888.

120 F. Engels in *Der Sozialdemokrat*, March 11, 1887. This article first appeared in French in *Le Socialiste* (Paris). For the German version see Horst Bartel, *Marx und Engels im Kampf um ein revolutionäres Parteiorgan* (1961), pp. 209–11.

121 "Die Sozialdemokratie und die Armee" in *Der Sozialdemokrat*, June 24, 1887.

122 F. Engels, "Der Sozialismus in Deutschland" in *Die Neue Zeit*, July 1892: reprinted in Iring Fetscher (ed.), *Karl Marx–Friedrich Engels*, Vol. 3, *Geschicht und Politik* (I) (Fischer Bücherei, 1966), pp. 29–41.

123 F. Engels in *Le Socialiste*, March 27, 1886: see appendix to *F. Engels – Paul and Laura Lafargue: Correspondence*, Vol. 1, 1868–86 (Moscow, 1959), pp. 406–7.

124 F. Engels to A. Sorge, January 7, 1888 in Karl Marx–F. Engels, *Letters to Americans 1848–95* (1963), p. 194.

125 Decree of April 11, 1886.

126 For an interview given by Bernstein to an English newspaper correspondent see the *Star*, September 29, 1890 ("Socialist Smugglers: Germany flooded with Papers from Kentish Town: a Talk with the Editor").

127 Gustav Mayer, *Friedrich Engels*, Vol. 2 (1934), p. 378.

128 For Kautsky see B. Kautsky (ed.), *Friedrich Engels' Briefwechsel mit Karl Kautsky* (1955).

129 F. Engels to Karl Kautsky, October 17, 1888 in B. Kautsky (ed.), *Friedrich Engels' Briefwechsel mit Karl Kautsky* (1955), p. 223.

130 Karl Kautsky to F. Engels, October 3, 1883 in B. Kautsky (ed.), *Friedrich Engels' Briefwechsel mit Karl Kautsky* (1955), p. 86.

131 F. Engels to Karl Kautsky, November 15, 1882 in B. Kautsky (ed.), *Friedrich Engels' Briefwechsel mit Karl Kautsky* (1955), p. 68.

132 *Die Neue Zeit*, June 1885. This was the German version of an article which appeared in *The Commonwealth* (London), March 1, 1885 and was subsequently incorporated in the introduction to the first English translation of F. Engels, *The Condition of the Working Class in England* (1892): see Appendix III of the translation by W. O. Henderson and W. H. Chaloner (1958 and 1971).

133 *Die Neue Zeit*, April–May, 1886: also published as a pamphlet in Stuttgart in 1888: English translation – F. Engels, *Ludwig Feuerbach and the End of Classical German Philosophy* (Foreign Languages Publishing House, 1950).

134 *Die Neue Zeit*, 1891–2: appeared originally in French in the *Almanach du Parti Ouvrier*, 1892.

135 August Bebel to F. Engels, November 2, 1886 in Werner Blumenberg (ed.), *August Bebels Briefwechsel mit Friedrich Engels* (1965), p. 301.

136 F. A. Krupp to Wilhelm II, May 9, 1890 in W. A. Buelcke (ed.), *Krupp und die Hohenzollern in Dokumente* (1970), p. 122.

137 *New Chapters of Bismarck's Autobiography* (translated by B. Miall) (1920), p. 119.

138 F. Engels to Laura Lafargue, February 26, 1890 in *F. Engels – Paul and Laura Lafargue Correspondence*, Vol. 2, 1887–90 (1960), p. 364.

139 *New Chapters of Bismarck's Autobiography* (translated by B. Miall) (1920), pp. 18–19.

140 For the miners' strike of 1889 see L. Pieper, *Die Lage der Bergarbeiter im Ruhrrevier* (1903), pp. 178–83; P. Grebe, "Bismarcks Sturz und der Bergarbeiterstreik im Mai 1889" in *Historische Zeitschrift*, Vol. 157 (1937); Max Jürgen Koch, *Die Bergarbeiterbewegung im Ruhrgebiet zur Zeit Wilhelm II* (1954), p. 33 *et seq.*; Hans Georg Kirchhof, *Die Staatliche Sozialpolitik im Ruhrbergbau 1871–1914* (1954), p. 48 *et seq.*; and an article entitled "Verrathen und Verkauft" in *Der Sozialdemokrat*, June 1, 1889. For other books and articles on the strike see H. J. Teuteberg, *Geschichte der Industriellen Mitbestimmung in Deutschland* (1961), p. 363 (note 37).

141 Gustav Mayer, *Erinnerungen. Vom Journalisten zum Historiker der deutschen Arbeiterbewegung* (1949), p. 18. See also L. Brentano, *Die Stellung der Studenten zu den sozialpolitischen Aufgaben der Zeit* (1897).

142 "Vor dem Siegeswegen der Sozialdemokratie" in *Der Sozialdemokrat*, February 15, 1890.

143 August Bebel to F. Engels, March 7, 1890 in Werner Blumenberg (ed.), *August Bebels Briefwechsel mit Friedrich Engels* (1965), p. 383.

144 F. Engels to August Bebel, February 17, 1890 in Werner Blumenberg (ed.), *August Bebels Briefwechsel mit Friedrich Engels* (1965), p. 380.

145 F. Engels to Laura Lafargue, February 26, 1890 in *F. Engels – Paul and Laura Lafargue: Correspondence*, Vol. 2, 1887–90 (1960), p. 363.

146 F. Engels to Wilhelm Liebknecht, March 9, 1890 in Wilhelm Liebknecht, *Briefwechsel mit Karl Marx und Friedrich Engels* (ed. Georg Eckert, 1963), p. 366.

147 An additional seat was gained by the socialists in 1892 bringing the total to 36: see A. Neumann-Hofer, *Die Entwicklung der Sozialdemokratie bei den Wahlen zum Deutschen Reichstage* (1898).

148 F. Engels, "Was nun?" in *Der Sozialdemokrat*, March 8, 1890 and in E. Engelberg (ed.), *Die Klassiker des wissenschaftlichen Kommunis-*

mus (1955), pp. 183–4. English translation in W. O. Henderson (ed.), *Engels: Selected Writings* (1967), pp. 141–3.

149 F. Engels to Wilhelm Liebknecht, March 9, 1890 in Wilhelm Liebknecht, *Briefwechsel mit Karl Marx und Friedrich Engels* (ed. Georg Eckert, 1963), p. 367.

150 *New Chapters of Bismarck's Autiobiography* (translated by B. Miall) (1920), p. 213.

151 F. Engels to Laura Lafargue, April 16, 1890 in *F. Engels – Paul and Laura Lafargue: Correspondence*, Vol. 2, 1887–90 (1960), p. 373. On February 26, 1890 Engels had written to Laura Lafargue that there was a danger that the German government would "provoke riot and fighting and crush us before we are too strong and then alter the constitution. That is evidently what we are drifting to, and the chief danger to be avoided. Our people, you have seen, keep excellent, wonderful discipline; but we may be forced to fight before we are fully prepared, and there is the danger" (*ibid.*, p. 365).

152 F. Engels to A. Sorge, April 19, 1890 in Karl Marx and F. Engels, *Letters to Americans 1848–90* (1963), p. 231.

153 August Bebel to F. Engels, March 31, 1890 in Werner Blumenberg (ed), *August Bebels Briefwechsel mit Friedrich Engels* (1965), pp. 384–6 and V. L. Lidtke, *The Outlawed Party. Social Democracy in Germany, 1878–90* (1966), pp. 303–4.

154 F. Engels to Laura Lafargue, August 27, 1890 in *F. Engels – Paul and Laura Lafargue: Correspondence*, Vol. 2, 1887–90 (1960), p. 386 and Engels's letter ("Eine Antwort") in *Der Sozialdemokrat*, September 13, 1890.

155 F. Engels to Laura Lafargue, September 25, 1890 in *F. Engels – Paul and Laura Lafargue: Correspondence*, Vol. 2, 1887–90 (1960), p. 401.

156 "Unser Scheidegruss" in *Der Sozialdemokrat*, September 27, 1890 in Horst Bartel, *Marx und Engels im Kampf um ein revolutionäres deutsches Parteiorgan 1879–90* (1961), pp. 269–76. Engels wrote to Laura Lafargue on September 26, 1890 that "the last number of the *Sozialdemokrat* is creating a stir here" (*F. Engels – Paul and Laura Lafargue: Correspondence*, Vol. 2 (1960), p. 402).

157 F. Engels to Laura Lafargue, September 25, 1890 in *Friedrich Engels – Paul and Laura Lafargue: Correspondence*, Vol. 2, 1887–90 (1960), p. 401.

158 F. Engels in *Der Sozialdemokrat*, September 27, 1890 and in E. Engelberg (ed.), *Die Klassiker des wissenschaftlichen Kommunismus* (1955), pp. 183–4. English translation: W. O. Henderson (ed.), *Engels: Selected Writings* (1967), pp. 141–3.

14

THE LEADER OF THE ORCHESTRA 1883–1895

I. The Legacy of Marx

On Marx's death, Engels assumed new responsibilities. He looked after Marx's family, giving financial aid to Paul and Laura Lafargue and encouraging Eleanor Marx in her work for the labour movement in England. Helene Demuth, Marx's housekeeper, found a new home in Engels's household. Engels was now accepted as the head of the international socialist movement. In 1884 he wrote to Becker:

> "All my life I have done what I was cut out for – namely to play second fiddle – and I think that I have done quite well in that capacity. And I have been glad to have had such a wonderful first violin as Marx. No one realises better than I do that I am likely to make some mistakes now that I must suddenly step into Marx's shoes as an interpreter of his theories and as leader of the orchestra."[1]

Victor Adler wrote to Engels in 1891 that if he had the money he would found a travelling scholarship to send "every able party member to spend a week with you annually in Regent's Park Road"[2] and Lenin observed later that in the 1880s and early 1890s socialists everywhere "drew on the rich store of knowledge and experience of the aged Engels".[3] Engels advised experienced politicians like Bebel and Liebknecht, and kept an eye upon a younger generation of socialists – Bernstein and Kautsky in Germany, Adler in Austria, Lafargue in France, Turati in Italy, Eleanor Marx and Aveling in England, and the Russians Plekhanov, Danielson, and Vera Zasulich.

Engels was recognised by socialists as a final court of appeal upon any doubtful point in Marx's writings. He advised the leaders of various socialist parties on problems of political strategy and tactics. Eleanor Marx declared that "at every difficulty . . . we go to Engels. And never do we appeal to him in vain. The work this single man has done in recent years would have been too much for a dozen ordinary men".[4] And Antonio Labriola wrote that "without international thinkers there can be no International, and Engels attained the rank of international thinker in the fullest measure".[5]

When Marx died, Bebel suggested that Engels might settle in Germany or Switzerland so as to be in closer touch with the German Social Democrat Party.[6] But Engels had no intention of devoting himself entirely to the affairs of the German socialists. He considered that he had responsibilities to all the socialist parties in the world and that his first duty was towards the international socialist movement. "My fifty years of service in the international socialist movement make it impossible for me to put myself forward as the representative of any one national socialist party."[7] Engels told Bebel that he would not live in a country from which he might be expelled. Since he would be safe only in England or America he would stay in London. Moreover as there was no socialist movement in England worthy of his support, he would have the time that he needed for his writing and he would be free from the distractions of political agitation. If he settled anywhere else he would be obliged to take an active part in politics in support of the socialist cause and this would take up too much of his time. He was 62 years old and he proposed to continue to enjoy his "peaceful asylum" in London where he would devote himself to editing Marx's manuscripts and to writing on Marx's career, the early history of socialism in Germany, and the achievements of the First International.[8]

As Marx's literary executor – with Eleanor Marx – Engels had to decide which of his friend's manuscripts should be printed and which of his publications should appear in new editions. He did not publish his correspondence with Marx or the early manuscripts written by Marx in 1844 – writings which scholars later found to be of absorbing interest. Engels gave priority to the preparation of the second and third volumes of *Das Kapital* for the press.

Shortly before his death Marx expressed the hope that Engels would "make something" of the manuscripts of the second volume of *Das Kapital* which dealt with the circulation of capital.[9] To do this Engels "laid aside his general philosophy of science, on which he had been working for more than ten years".[10] But he did finish his pamphlet on *The Origin of the Family*. In 1883 he saw a new German edition of the first volume of *Das Kapital* through the press. This was an onerous task since he added to the text the amendments made by Marx for the French translation.[11] At this time Engels also read some specimen chapters of the English translation of the first volume of *Das Kapital*[12] and he helped

Gabriel Deville to prepare an abridged popular version of the French translation of this volume.[13]

When Engels examined the manuscripts of Volume 2 he found that most of them had been written in the 1860s. Some were in a form suitable for publication but others were only rough drafts. As early as 1863 Marx – like Quesnay before him – had prepared a *tableau économique* to illustrate the circulation of capital[14] and four years later he told Engels that Volume 2 was on the verge of completion.[15] Yet in 1879 he wrote to Danielson that he had still not completed his researches on the circulation of capital.[16] When Marx died he left seven manuscripts on this subject and from them Engels – working from eight to ten hours a day for some months in 1884[17] – pieced together the second volume of *Das Kapital* which was published in 1885. He wrote that this volume was "a wonderful piece of research"[18] but that it analysed problems "of such a superior order that the vulgar reader will not take the trouble to fathom them and to follow them out".[19] In his preface to the second volume of *Das Kapital* Engels attacked "the Rodbertus clique" for asserting that Rodbertus[20] had thought of the theory of surplus value before Marx.

Early in 1887 Engels wrote that he hoped to start work on Marx's third volume "after clearing off some other accumulated work". He had been seeing the English translation of Volume 1 through the press.[21] In January 1888 he told Danielson that "the English translation is selling very well, indeed surprisingly well for a book of that size and class; the publisher is enchanted with his speculation. The critics, on the other hand, very very much below the average low level. Only one good article in the *Athenaeum*; the rest either merely give extracts from the preface, or – if trying to tackle the book itself – are unutterably poor". He added that "the sale of the German edition, one and two volume, goes on very well. There are a great many articles written about the book and its theories".[22]

After reading the manuscript of the third volume of *Das Kapital* Engels declared that the author's analysis of the process of capital production as a whole was "a splendid and totally unanswerable work", though it was "a mere first sketch".[23] He told Laura Lafargue that the book was "getting grander and grander the deeper I get into it". "It is almost inconceivable how a man who had such tremendous discoveries, such an entire and complete scientific revolution in his head, could keep it there for twenty years."[24] In 1888 Engels laid aside his work on this volume because of eye trouble, which sometimes reduced the time available for writing to two hours a day.[25] In this year, too, he spent over seven weeks visiting the United States. In 1889 there was a further delay since Engels's correspondence in connection with the Second International took up much of his time.[26]

Volume 3 of *Das Kapital* proved to be a harder nut to crack than Volume 2. In the summer of 1892 the revision of the text had still not been completed[27] and in the autumn of that year Engels wrote to Adler: "I am now working on the third volume of *Das Kapital*. If only I could have had three consecutive quiet months in the last four years it would have been finished long ago. But I never had such good fortune."[28] In 1893 Engels assured Danielson that he would make "a supreme effort to finish Volume 3 in this winter and spring".[29] But it was not until November 1894 that Engels at last completed the task to which he had set his hand ten years before. He realised that the preparation of a fourth volume was beyond his strength and this task had already been handed over to Karl Kautsky.[30] Eventually Marx's historical survey of the theory of surplus value appeared as a separate book entitled *Theorien über den Mehrwert*.

In the years that he spent in preparing the second and third volumes of *Das Kapital* for publication, Engels reprinted – with new introductions – several of Marx's pamphlets, such as the *Communist Manifesto*, *The Civil War in France*, *Misère de la Philosophie* (in a German translation),[31] and *Lohnarbeit und Kapital*.[32] Engels also replied to various correspondents who asked him to elucidate some of Marx's doctrines such as surplus value, historical materialism, and the class struggle.[33]

At the same time Engels commented upon the changes that were taking place in the world economy and he endeavoured to prove that Marx had correctly forecast the future development of capitalism. He considered that one of the most striking changes in the capitalist system since Marx's death had been the growth of large business enterprises and the establishment of trusts and cartels. In an addition to chapter 27 of the third volume of *Das Kapital*, Engels wrote that capitalists were setting up great combines to regulate output and that sometimes the entire production of certain goods had been monopolised by a powerful corporation. The United Alkali Trust had "brought all British alkali production into the hands of a single business firm". Engels added that in this branch of industry "competition has been replaced by monopoly in England, and the road has been paved most gratifyingly, for future expropriation by the whole of society, the nation".[34]

Engels also saw that countries, such as Russia, which had once had only domestic craft manufactures were becoming industrialised. He argued that the industrialisation of Russia was entirely in accord with Marx's predictions. He wrote to Danielson in 1892:

"A nation of 100 millions that plays an important part in the history of the world could not, under present economic and industrial conditions, continue in the state in which Russia was up to the Crimean war. The introduction of steam engines and working machinery, the attempt to manufacture textile and metal products by modern means of production, at least for home consumption, *must* have been made sooner or later, but at all events at *some* period between 1856 and 1880. Had it not been made, your patriarchal industry would have been destroyed all the same by English machine competition and the end would have been – India, a country economically subject to the great central workshop, England.[35]

"Capitalist production works its own ruin, and you may be sure it will do so in Russia too. It may, and – if it lasts long enough – it will surely produce a fundamental agrarian revolution – I mean a revolution in the condition of landed property, which will ruin both the landowners and the peasants and replace them by a new class of large landed proprietors drawn from the kulaks of the villages and the bourgeois speculators of the towns. At all events, I am sure the conservative people, who have introduced capitalism into Russia, will be one day terribly astonished at the consequences of their own doings."[36]

Engels appreciated that in the 1880s the economic and political influence of the advanced industrial states was spreading to new regions in Africa and the Pacific. Marx and Engels held that territorial expansion was an essential feature of the capitalist system. The need to control new sources of food and raw materials – coupled with the search for wider markets – made it inevitable that nothing would halt the advance of capitalism until the whole world lay within its grasp. Marx and Engels believed that the exploitation of colonial peoples by the European powers would cease only when capitalism itself was overthrown.[37]

In the 1880s and early 1890s Engels denounced the new imperialism – the scramble for Africa, the Pacific and China – as vigorously as he and Marx had condemned the activities of the English in India and the Dutch in Java in the 1850s. And the German socialists agreed with him. In 1884 *Der Sozialdemokrat* declared in a leading article: "Colonisation means the accumulation of capital and this, in turn, means mass poverty and mass misery. That, in brief, is what Marx had to say on the colonial question and that is also the view of the Social Democrat Party."[38]

After the Sino–Japanese war Engels wrote in 1894 that the opening up of China would have tragic results for the Chinese.

The links between farming and craft industries in the rural districts would be broken by the coming of railways and modern manufacturing techniques. There would be a vast migration of Chinese coolies to Europe which would then face its greatest and final economic crisis. "China is the only region left for capitalism to conquer, and in the very process of digesting it, capitalism hastens its own downfall."[39] Engels's final comment upon imperialism – written shortly before his death – was that colonisation had now become "purely a subsidiary of the stock exchange, in whose interests the European powers partitioned Africa a few years ago, and the French conquered Tunis and Tonkin".[40]

Colonial rivalry was only one aspect of the increased international tension of the early 1890s. After Bismarck's fall, Germany failed to renew her Reinsurance Treaty with Russia. France emerged from a long period of diplomatic isolation and became Russia's ally. The Continent was divided into two armed camps. Engels saw clearly the dangers to world peace inherent in this situation. He approved the strong attacks on Prussian militarism in the socialist press in Germany[41] and the refusal of the socialist deputies in the Reichstag to vote for defence budgets. Engels argued that the international arms race was involving the Great Powers in ever increasing military expenditure and was placing an intolerable burden of taxation upon the shoulders of the workers. Unless a way could be found out of the impasse a world war was inevitable. Engels feared that such a conflict would destroy the economy of Europe and halt for many years the forward march of the socialist cause.[42]

II. The Father of International Socialism

As a young man Karl Marx had declared that "philosophers have hitherto *interpreted* the world in various ways: now the time has come for them to *change* it". For many years Marx and Engels had pursued two aims. As philosophers, economists, and historians they had worked out a theory of politics which was the basis of their new form of socialism. As revolutionary agitators they had tried to change the world by putting their doctrines into practice. One aspect of their work was represented by *Das Kapital* and *Anti-Dühring*, the other by the Communist League and the First International.

After Marx's death in 1883 Engels became the leader of the international socialist movement. He carried on his own researches into "scientific socialism" – *The Origin of the Family* appeared in 1884 and *Ludwig Feuerbach and the End of Classical German*

Philosophy in 1888 – and he continued to promote the interests of the various socialist parties on the Continent. He was always ready to answer appeals for help and advice from his socialist friends. Although his literary work and the preparation of two volumes of *Das Kapital* for the press took up much of his time, he maintained a regular correspondence with the leaders of workers' parties in many countries. Until his death in 1895 Engels's house in London was a meeting place for socialists from all parts of the world.

Engels's advice to his socialist friends varied according to circumstances. In Germany, where there was a powerful Social Democrat Party, he urged his followers to gain new recruits so that the socialists would eventually dominate the political scene and take over the reins of government. In England and the United States, on the other hand – where only insignificant socialist parties existed – he advised his friends to try to infiltrate into the local labour movement. In his view such organisations as trade unions, co-operative societies, and friendly societies were a poor substitute for a socialist party since they operated within the framework of a bourgeois society and did not aim at the overthrow of the capitalist system. Again, in Russia the situation was different from either Germany or Britain since industrialisation had hardly begun and socialism was still in its infancy. Here Engels was in favour of supporting revolutionary movements – not necessarily socialist in character – which aimed at the destruction of the autocratic Czarist regime. He considered that the differences between the workers' movements in various countries could be explained partly by historical and partly by economic factors. In each case socialists should, in his view, adapt their policy to the local situation.

Germany: the Erfurt Programme

The success of the socialists at the general election of February 1890, when nearly 1,500,000 votes were gained,[43] was the climax of the "heroic age" of the Social Democrat Party. The socialists had defeated Bismarck's attempt to crush them by force. Bismarck soon resigned and the government did not seek to renew the Anti-Socialist Law when it expired at the end of September 1890. Now that the Social Democrat Party was again a legal organisation it could openly resume its propaganda among the masses. Important decisions had to be taken concerning the adoption of a new programme and the policy to be pursued by socialist deputies in the Reichstag. Engels warned the party's leaders of the dangers threatening them from the "Youngsters", from Georg von Vollmar, and from Eduard Bernstein. The "Youngsters"[44] were a left-wing group of intellectuals who declared that membership of the Reichstag was having a corrupting influence upon socialist deputies. Vollmar, as a leader of the smallholders and peasants in Bavaria, was trying to secure some co-operation between the socialists and the middle-class radicals.[45] In 1892 Engels wrote to Bebel that Vollmar was attempting to foist the "state socialism" of the *Kathedersozialisten* (the "socialist professors") on to the Social Democrat Party and that he would soon leave the socialist party.[46] Bebel was now the undisputed leader of the socialist movement in Germany. His efficiency as an organiser, his skill as a parliamentarian, his oratorial gifts and his dedication to the socialist cause were such that his position in the party could not be challenged. He had no difficulty in discrediting both the "Youngsters" and Vollmar. Two of the "Youngsters" – Werner and Wildberger – were expelled from the Social Democrat Party at the Erfurt congress of 1891.[47] And the action of the socialist deputies in voting for the budget in the Bavarian Landtag in 1894 led to a confrontation between Bebel and Vollmar at the next congress of the Social Democrat Party at Frankfurt. The congress defeated a motion which would have left socialist parties free to vote for local budgets if they wished to do so.[48]

But the threat to party unity from Bernstein was a more serious matter. In the early 1890s Engels realised that Bernstein, who had served the socialist cause so well as editor of *Der Sozialdemokrat*, could no longer be regarded as a dedicated Marxist since he was falling under the influence of right-wing socialists such as the leaders of the Fabian Society.[49] Engels warned Bebel of Bernstein's naïve enthusiasm for this society which he regarded as "nothing but a branch of the Liberal Party".[50] Engels attacked Bernstein for suggesting that the German socialists might co-operate with the Freisinnige party in elections for the Prussian Landtag.[51]

Engels's fears were amply justified for, not long after Engels's death, Bernstein began to write articles in *Die Neue Zeit* suggesting that socialist deputies in the Reichstag should co-operate with left-wing bourgeois parties to secure reforms for the workers. He argued that it would be simpler to establish socialism gradually – as advocated by the Fabians in England – rather than by the revolution which Marx and Engels had regarded as inevitable.[52] This sparked off a great controversy which shook the Social Democrat Party to its foundations.

Engels not only attacked any deviation from Marxist orthodoxy among the German socialists but he used his influence over the leaders of the Social Democrat Party to ensure the adoption of a new programme, which would eliminate all traces of Lassalle's doctrines. In 1890 at their congress in Halle an der Saale the socialists accepted Liebknecht's proposal that the Gotha programme of 1875 had outlived its usefulness and should be revised. Several drafts of a new programme were prepared, the most important being one by Liebknecht and another by Kautsky and Bernstein.[53]

Engels intervened in the debate in two ways. First he published the criticisms which Marx had made of the Gotha programme in 1875, leaving out only "a few sharp personal expressions and judgments".[54] Bebel complained that Lassalle's supporters were angry that this attack upon their leader's views had been made public. Engels vigorously defended his action in a letter to Kautsky, in which he wrote:

". . . You say that Bebel has written to you to say that Marx's treatment of Lassalle has caused bad blood among the old followers of Lassalle. That may be so. These people do not know the real story and nothing seems to have happened to enlighten them about it. It is not my fault if they do not know that Lassalle's reputation was due to the fact that for years Marx allowed Lassalle to parade the results of Marx's researches as his own. Moreover owing to his inadequate knowledge of economics Lassalle distorted Marx's views into the bargain. But I am Marx's literary executor and consequently I have a duty to perform in this matter. . . . It was my duty finally to settle accounts between Marx and Lassalle. . . ."[55]

Next Engels wrote a memorandum in which he commented upon Liebknecht's draft of a proposed new programme for the German Social Democrat Party. It was sent to leading members of the party and was not published until ten years later. Engels praised Liebknecht for dropping "the Lassallean and vulgar-socialist" aspects of the Gotha programme. He considered the theoretical part of the draft to be satisfactory and he suggested only minor amendments. But he criticised the political part of the draft programme because it left out what he considered to be an essential part of socialist policy. Engels considered that the socialists in Germany could gain effective power only if a democratic republic were established. He declared that "this is the specific form of the dictatorship of the proletariat which was seen as long ago as during the great French revolution". The founding of a republic would involve the political reconstruction of the country. The monarchies would have to be abolished and Germany would require a unitary instead of a federal constitution. Prussia should be abolished as a political unit. The tiny states – such as those in Thuringia – should be absorbed by larger neighbours. The new provinces, countries, and parishes should enjoy complete local self-government. Finally Engels suggested that the programme of the French socialists – drawn up by Marx in 1880 – should serve as a model in drawing up the economic demands to be included in the new programme of the German Social Democrat Party.[56]

The socialists did not follow Engels's advice. Bebel bluntly told Engels that "in view of the present situation in Germany it is impossible to aim at (the establishment of) a republic.[57] So when the Social Democrat Party adopted a new programme at the Erfurt congress of 1891[58] – based largely upon Kautsky's draft – there was no reference to the abolition of the monarchy, or the partition of Prussia, or the replacing of the federal constitution by a unitary constitution. On the other hand Engels was satisfied with the theoretical part of the programme. He wrote to Sorge: "We have the satisfaction of seeing the Marxian critique win all along the line. Even the last trace of Lassalleanism has been removed."[59]

Under the banner of the Erfurt programme the Social Democrat Party gained new successes at the Reichstag general election held in the summer of 1893. The socialists polled nearly a quarter of the votes cast and secured 44 seats. Five of the six deputies representing Berlin were socialists. Little wonder that the Berlin branch of the Social Democrat Party prepared a very warm welcome for Engels when he visited the city soon after the elections. He persuaded his hosts not to organise a mass meeting in his honour but to be content with a banquet in the Concordia Hall. Wilhelm Liebknecht was the main speaker.[60] In his reply[61] Engels observed that he had not been in Berlin for 51 years. Then it had been a small town with a population of 350,000 living on its court, its aristocracy and its government officials. Now it was a great industrial city with 2,000,000 inhabitants. In 1841–2 Berlin had no socialists: now the Social Democrat Party could poll 160,000 votes in the city. Engels declared that immense changes had taken place, not merely in Berlin, but throughout Germany. There had been a great expansion of industry. "When capitalists promote the growth of manufactures, they create not only surplus value for themselves but also an industrial proletariat. By destroying the petty bourgeoisie – the craftsmen and the peasants – they have aggravated the class struggle between the middle classes and the workers. Those who create industrial workers also create socialists". Engels concluded with the proud boast that the German Social Democrat Party was the largest, the most united, and the most powerful socialist organisation in the world. "It has gained one triumph after another, thanks to the patience, the discipline and the good humour with which it has fought one battle after another."

In his last years Engels's main anxiety concerning the Social Democrat Party was that the views of its right wing might have a decisive influence upon policy decisions. As the party grew it attracted more middle-class adherents and more trade union leaders who advocated a policy of moderate reform and were opposed to aims which could be achieved only by a revolution. They had no wish to see a new Anti-Socialist Law enacted. Still less did they relish the possibility of a coup d'état on the part of the upper classes, backed by the army and directed against the workers. They wanted to improve the lot of the workers by promoting social reforms which were attainable under the existing constitution. Engels forcibly reminded the socialist leaders that Marxism was a revolutionary creed which taught that the capitalist system must one day be overthrown – if necessary by force. He was disappointed that Bernstein should have fallen under the spell of the Fabians and that Liebknecht – once a stalwart supporter of Marx's ideas – should be arguing that German socialists should now follow a path of strict legality.

In the circumstances it is not surprising that a clash between Engels and Liebknecht should have occurred in 1895. Engels had written an introduction to a new edition of Marx's articles on the class struggles in France,[62] which has been called his "political testament" since he died a few months later. It proved to be his last opportunity to offer advice to the German socialists. Although Engels had agreed to make some changes in his text to meet the views of the executive committee of the Social Democrat Party,[63] Liebknecht printed carefully selected extracts from the introduction to make it appear as if Engels had ceased to advocate revolutionary action on the part of the workers.[64] Engels had every right to be angry that Liebknecht should have distorted his views and he asked Kautsky to print the introduction in full in *Die Neue Zeit*. He complained to Kautsky that Liebknecht was suggesting that he had advocated a policy of "legality at any price", which was far from being the truth.[65] To Lafargue he wrote:

"Liebknecht has just played me a fine trick. He has taken from my introduction to Marx's articles on France, 1848–51, everything that could serve his purpose in support of peaceful and anti-violent tactics at any price, which he has chosen to preach for some time now, particularly at this juncture, when coercive laws are being drawn up in Berlin. But I preach those tactics only for the *Germany of today* and even then *with many reservations*. For France, Belgium,

Italy, Austria, such tactics could not be followed as a whole and, for Germany, they could become inapplicable tomorrow."[66]

To the last Engels remained confident of the ultimate triumph of socialism in Germany. In 1893 he was asked in an interview if he expected to see a socialist government in power in Germany. He replied:

"Why not? If the growth of our Party continues at its normal rate, we shall have a majority between the years 1900 and 1910. And when we do, you may be assured we shall neither be short of ideas nor men to carry them out. You people, I suppose, about that time, will be having a government, in which Mr Sidney Webb will be growing grey in an attempt to permeate the Liberal Party. We don't believe in permeating middle-class parties. We are permeating the people."[67]

Austria: Victor Adler[68]

Engels's friendship with Victor Adler – "the witty orator and profound thinker of the Austrian Party"[69] brought him into contact with the socialist movement in the Habsburg dominions.[70] Adler, son of a prosperous Jewish merchant in Prague, had been educated in Vienna and had qualified as a doctor. In 1882 he met Kautsky and began to study socialist writings. In the following year, at the age of 31, he visited Germany, Switzerland and England to examine the working of the factory laws in those countries as he hoped to join the factory inspectorate which had just been set up in Austria. On his travels he met Engels[71] and Bebel and he returned to Vienna a convinced Marxist. He devoted the rest of his life to the socialist cause.

In 1886 Adler took the first step on the road to the leadership of the Austrian socialists when he founded the journal *Gleichheit* in Vienna.[72] The prospects of the socialists in Austria were far from bright at this time. Repressive legislation, culminating in the Anti-Socialist Law of 1884–8, enabled the authorities to ban meetings of workers and to suppress socialist publications. Adler was convicted seventeen times for his political activities and spent eighteen months in prison. Moreover the socialists were split into two rival factions – the Moderates led by Heinrich Oberwinder and the Radicals led by Andreas Scheu. The Moderates were prepared to co-operate with bourgeois progressive parties to secure reforms for the workers while the Radicals pursued a more militant revolutionary policy. In addition there were some anarchist groups in Austria at this time led by Josef Peukert[73] and their criminal activities – the murder of unpopular officials – tended to be attributed to the socialists.

For three years Adler worked hard to bring the diverse socialist groups in Austria together. By April 1889 he was able to play a leading *rôle* in organising a strike of the drivers of horse-trams in Vienna. The government banned the socialist journal *Gleichheit* and Adler was sentenced to four months' imprisonment.[74] Later in the year he went to London to discuss with Engels the final phase of the proposed establishment of a unified Austrian socialist party. Gustav Mayer writes that "a friendship developed between the aged Engels and Adler which can be compared only with the close friendship uniting Engels and Bebel". "The relationship between Engels and Adler had a special quality since the two men were on an equal intellectual level." "The young disciple honoured his 'teacher and mentor', and gave him medical advice. Engels warmly responded with a readiness to help Adler in every possible way."[75] In 1891 Engels gave half the royalties of the fourth edition of *The Origin of the Family* to the Austrian socialist party[76] and in the following year he arranged for the royalties of a new German edition of *The Condition of the Working Class in England* to be paid to Adler.[77] In 1895 Engels was responsible for raising a loan in London to assist in financing the *Arbeiter-Zeitung* (Vienna). This organ of the Austrian socialists had formerly been published twice a week and was now being turned into a daily newspaper. On January 12, 1895 Engels sent Adler a cheque for 3,500 gulden.[78]

At a conference held at Hainfeld between December 30, 1889 and January 1, 1890 Adler's efforts were crowned with success and a united Social Democrat Workers' Party was established. It accepted Marx's doctrines and its immediate demands included universal suffrage and vote by ballot. At this time Kautsky declared that "the workers' movement in Austria has reached a new peak during the past year. . . . Never before has it been so united. . . ."[79] In 1896 Adler partially achieved one of his aims when the franchise in Austria was extended by the establishment of a fifth roll of voters (*curia*). Thus a modest element of manhood suffrage was introduced into the Austrian parliamentary system.

In 1893 Engels visited Vienna and spoke at a rally of some 2,000 socialists in the Dreher Halle.[80] He wrote to Laura Lafargue: "Adler has done wonders; the tact, the constant vigilance and activity, with which he holds the party together (not an easy thing with such lively people as the Viennese), are beyond praise, and if you consider moreover the difficulties of his private position – a wife ill with nervous ailments, three children and interminable pecuniary difficulties arising therefrom – it is almost inconceivable how he can keep his head above water. And these Austrians – a mixture of all races, Celtic, Teutonic, Slavonic – are far less manageable than our North Germans."[81]

Here Engels had drawn attention to one of Adler's major problems. The Dual Monarchy was a multi-racial state in which the Germans and the Magyars ruled over various Slavonic peoples. Marx and Engels supported the independence of subject peoples, such as the Poles and the Irish – though Engels had some doubts concerning the ability of the Slavs to rule themselves. But Adler accepted the fact that Austria-Hungary was a multi-racial state. He thought that an Austrian socialist party, representing all the peoples in the country, would be in a better position to bring about the fall of capitalism than a number of smaller national parties. For a time Adler's views prevailed. But eventually the Czech population increased rapidly in some industrial towns in Bohemia which had once been inhabited almost entirely by Germans. This happened when large numbers of peasants moved into the towns from the countryside to seek work in the factories. At the congress of the socialist party held at Brünn in 1899 a "programme for national autonomy" was adopted. This programme advocated the transformation of the Habsburg dominions into a democratic federation of self-governing peoples. The unity of the socialist party was preserved for a time on the basis of the Brünn programme, but by 1911 – when the party held 83 seats in the lower house of the Reichsrat – Czech national feeling had become so strong that the Czech socialists broke away from Adler's party and formed an independent organisation of their own.

Although, in the end, Adler could not maintain the unity of the Austrian socialist party, his long period of service in the cause of the workers showed that he had taken to heart the advice that Engels had given him in his early days as a politician. His achievements placed him in the front rank of socialist leaders in the first decade of the twentieth century.

France: Paul Lafargue[82]

Engels was in close touch with the socialist movement in France through Paul and Laura Lafargue with whom he maintained a regular correspondence. His financial help made it possible for Lafargue to devote his time to the socialist cause in France.

The fall of the Paris Commune in 1871 had brought the labour movement in France to a halt since the workers' leaders were put in prison or forced to leave the country. The International was banned while the syndicates and the workers' journals were suppressed. When Thiers left office as President he boasted that socialism had been stamped out. It was true that exiled revolutionaries – the followers of Bakunin in Switzerland and of Blanqui in England – now had little influence in France but some French workers (such as many of the skilled craftsmen in Paris) remained faithful to Proudhon's form of socialism. And it soon became clear that a new workers' movement was arising from the ashes of the Commune.

The rise of a Marxist party was something new in French labour politics. In the early seventies the publication of a French translation of the first volume of *Das Kapital* brought Marx's doctrines to the notice of left-wing intellectuals. A little later Gabriel Deville's book summarising *Das Kapital* reached a wider circle of French readers.[83] One of the first French socialists to be converted to Marxism was Jules Guesde. He had been a member of the First International and had received a five-year prison sentence for his writings in support of the Commune. He escaped first to Switzerland and then to Italy. In exile he fell under Bakunin's influence. In 1876 he returned to France and began to build up a new workers' party which accepted Marx's doctrines. Guesde's propaganda was particularly successful in the industrial districts such as the Nord Department. Marx praised Guesde's journal *Egalité* and declared that it was "the first 'French' *workers' paper* in the true sense of the expression".[84] Engels thought that Guesde's writings were "the best which have appeared in the French language and he is also the best speaker in Paris". "We have certainly always found him to be straightforward and reliable."[85] In 1878 Guesde received a six months' prison sentence for organising an international workers' congress which had been banned by the authorities.

In 1880 Guesde went to London to seek the advice of Marx, Engels and Lafargue in drafting an election manifesto for the French Workers Party. In Engels's study Marx dictated the introduction (*considérants*) of the manifesto to Guesde.[86] He approved the programme except for "some trivialities which Guesde found it necessary to throw to the French workers, despite my protest, such as fixing the minimum wage and the like". Marx considered the programme to be "a tremendous step forward to pull the French workers down to earth from their fog of phraseology".[87]

Despite opposition from the anarchists, the programme was adopted in November 1880 by a workers congress held at Le Havre. But two years later Brousse and Malon broke away from Guesde, declaring that "politics is the art of the possible". They advocated co-operation with bourgeois parties in the hope of gaining seats at local elections. Engels attacked the "Possibilists", arguing that the split in the party had been unavoidable since

Guesde was taking a stand on a sound Marxist principle. In his view Guesde was the champion of the class struggle against the bourgeoisie while Brousse and Malon were mere opportunists, sacrificing socialist principles to gain seats on local councils. Engels wrote:

> "There are always internal struggles when the proletariat develops and France – where a working class party is being created for the first time – is no exception". "In Germany we have experienced the first phase of our internal struggle – against Lassalle's followers – and other conflicts await us in future." "Unity is wonderful – if it can be achieved – but there are more important things than unity . . . Since Marx and I have been fighting so-called socialists all our lives . . . we cannot complain that this conflict has broken out."[88]

The split between the Marxists and the "Possibilists" was followed by a split in the ranks of the "Possibilists" when Jean Allemane and his followers left Brousse and Malon to form a splinter group of their own.

In 1882 Paul Lafargue returned to France and became a close collaborator of Jules Guesde. He was an indefatigable writer and lecturer and he preached the Marxist gospel throughout the length and breadth of France. His translation of Engels's *Socialism: Utopian and Scientific* and his wife's translation of *Ludwig Feuerbach and the End of German Classical Philosophy* helped to popularise Marx's doctrines among French socialists. Lenin regarded Lafargue as "one of the most talented and penetrating disseminators of the ideas of Marxism".[89] Despite the efforts of Guesde and Lafargue in the 1880s and 1890s the Marxists did not make the same progress in France as in Germany and Austria. In those countries Bebel and Adler had established united socialist parties but in France the socialists were divided into hostile factions. Nevertheless the votes cast for socialist candidates at parliamentary elections rose from 47,000 in 1887 to 805,000 in 1902 and early in the twentieth century there were over 2,000 socialist municipal councillors in France.

Italy: Filippo Turati

When Engels had served as corresponding secretary for Italy, on behalf of the First International, he had been unable to check the spread of Bakunin's influence in that country. In his view the Italian workers had been led astray by "young lawyers, academics and other doctrinaires"[90] – "a few doctrinaire lawyers and newspaper writers".[91] But Engels never gave up hope of seeing a socialist party (with a Marxist programme) established in Italy.

In the 1870s Engels was in close touch with Enrico Bignami, the editor of *La Plebe*,[92] the official organ of the *Federazione dell' Alta Italia*. He contributed a few articles to this workers' journal. He did not preach the gospel of Marxism but he described the achievements of the labour movement in various countries. He wrote about the successes of the German socialists in the Reichstag elections of 1877 and he praised the courage of the German workers in resisting Bismarck's Anti-Socialist Law. He held up the German Social Democrat Party as a model which the Italian workers should copy.

Engels maintained a regular correspondence with Pasquale Martignetti, Filippo Turati, and Antonio Labriola who, in their different ways, served the cause of socialism in Italy. Martignetti was a clerk in the legal record office in Benevento, a small town near Naples. After studying the first volume of *Das Kapital* (in French translation) he decided to devote himself to the cause of international socialism. His *rôle* in the movement was to continue the work begun by Carlo Cafiero in popularising Marx's doctrines in Italy. He learned German so as to translate Engels's *Socialism: Utopian and Scientific* into Italian in 1883. This brought him into contact with the author and Engels and Martignetti exchanged letters for many years. Martignetti read the leading German socialist journals of the 1880s – *Der Sozialdemokrat* and *Die Neue Zeit* – and so kept himself informed of the most recent developments in both the German and the international workers' movements. He translated Engels's pamphlet on *The Origin of the Family*[93] into Italian, as well as numerous articles by Marx, Engels, Kautsky and Bernstein. Engels was always ready to advise him on his activities as a translator. Owing to the intrigues of his political enemies Martignetti had to face charges of misappropriation of funds in 1886. He lost his post and was involved in a lengthy lawsuit. Engels assisted him financially at this time and tried – though without success – to find a suitable post for "the poor devil" outside Italy.[94] It was largely owing to Martignetti's efforts that the leading German Marxist writers exercised a strong influence over the development of the socialist movement in Italy.[95]

While Martignetti simply translated Marxist works into Italian, Antonio Labriola was an original thinker who used the tools provided by Marx to analyse some of the social problems of his day. He was the leading exponent of Marx's doctrines in Italy.[96] He told Engels that he had become a communist because he had a thorough grounding in Hegel's philosophy.[97] This may account for the fact that when Engels met him in 1893 at the Zürich conference of the Second International he soon tired of his company and escaped from his "ponderous conversation" to seek the more congenial company of the charming young Viennese socialist Adelheid Dvorak.[98] Labriola's letters to Engels included many appeals for help in exposing the pretensions of Achille Loria,[99] who had established for himself a certain reputation as an authority on Marx's theories. Although Loria sometimes claimed to be a disciple of Marx and Engels, he criticised Marx's theory of surplus value and the doctrine of historical materialism. He asserted that Marx had failed to give the world a comprehensive survey of his ideas and actually asserted that Marx had not written anything on capital after the appearance of the first volume of his book in 1867.[100] Engels was always ready to defend Marx and to attack those who advocated socialist doctrines which differed from those of his friend. And, in old age, he had not lost his ability to crush an adversary by sheer vituperation. "Charlatan", "rogue", "plagiarist", "academic careerist", "humbug", and "windbag" were among the milder expressions which he employed to castigate the presumptuous professor who had the effrontery to suppose that there were errors in *Das Kapital*, which he was capable of correcting.

Loria might be described as Italy's Dr Dühring. Like Dühring he was an ambitious "academic socialist" who enjoyed the adulation of a group of young intellectuals. Like Dühring he was a prolific writer on a variety of topics and his disciples venerated him as a leading economist and sociologist and as an expert interpreter of Marx's theories. Their views were subsequently endorsed by the distinguished economist Luigi Einaudi, who compiled a bibliography of Loria's voluminous writings. On the other hand so eminent a philosopher as Croce attacked Loria as a shallow thinker and a superficial scholar whose nebulous theories should be allowed to fall into well deserved oblivion. And leading Italian Marxists – such as Labriola and Gramsci – denounced Loria as a pompous bourgeois provincial philistine and an academic fraud.

The controversy between Engels and Loria reached its climax in 1894 when Engels denounced his adversary in the preface to the third volume of *Das Kapital*.[101] Here Engels dealt with Loria's article on Marx in *Nuova Antologia*,[102] with his review of Conrad Schmidt's *Die Durchschnitts-profitrate auf Grundlage des Marxschen Wertgesetzes* and with his book *La Teoria Economica della Constituzione Politica*. Engels attacked Loria for claiming to have discovered in 1886 the doctrine of historical materialism already enunciated by Marx forty years before. He accused Loria of failing to understand Marx's theory of surplus value. Having first confused surplus value with profit Loria had proceeded to argue that the existence of universal rates of interest invalidated Marx's theory.[103] A few months before his death Engels again denounced Loria in a manuscript which was eventually published as a "supplement" to Volume 3 of *Das Kapital*.[104] Almost with his last breath, Engels replied vigorously to any criticism of the work of his lifelong friend.

Engels's interest in the progress of socialism in Italy – as distinct from controversies concerning Marx's doctrines – may be seen from his correspondence with Filippo Turati, the founder of the Italian Workers' Party. At first Engels regarded Turati with some suspicion since he had fallen under Loria's influence. But later Turati was converted to Marx's ideas by his Russian wife Anna Kuliscioff and he recognised that socialism could be established in Italy only by grafting those doctrines upon the existing working-class movement.[105]

The first step towards the promotion of a socialist movement among the industrial workers of northern Italy was taken in Milan early in 1877 when a federation of workers' organisations[106] adopted a programme which accepted the need for trade union and political action – it demanded universal suffrage – and firmly rejected the views of the anarchists. Engels declared that the Italian workers had at last shaken off the evil influence of Bakunin and had taken their rightful place in the ranks of the European workers.[107] Two years later Italian socialists had an opportunity of studying Marx's doctrines in a summary of the first volume of *Das Kapital*, which was brought out by Carlo Cafiero.

In the 1880s the activities of the Workers' Party of Milan,[108] in which Turati played a leading *rôle*, paved the way for the holding of a congress in Genoa in 1892 at which a national Italian Workers' Party[109] was established.[110] Its "Minimum Programme", adopted in 1895, has been described as "a mixture of Marxism and vulgar-democratic doctrines".[111] The party's demands included universal suffrage, payment of parliamentary deputies and local councillors, factory reforms, old age pensions, free school meals and a progressive income tax. These proposed reforms were similar to those advocated by liberals and radicals who were not socialists. But the programme of the Italian Workers' Party did make it clear that the ultimate goal of the socialists was to gain political power for the workers. By this time Turati had established a fortnightly socialist review called *Critica Sociale*, to which Engels occasionally contributed.[112] In 1893 at Turati's request, Engels wrote a preface for the Italian translation of the Communist Manifesto. It is surprising that in his introduction Engels made no mention of the growth of socialism in Italy in the 1880s or of the recent establishment of a workers' party with a socialist programme. It has been suggested that his failure to congratulate Turati on his achievements was due to his displeasure at the passive attitude adopted by the socialist deputies in the Italian chamber when Napoleon Colajanni uncovered the scandals connected with the affairs of the Banca Roma. Engels agreed with Labriola that the socialists had let a golden opportunity pass to denounce the iniquities of the capitalist system.[113]

Engels's last intervention in the affairs of the Italian socialists occurred in 1894 when his advice was sought in connection with a controversy in the party concerning its future tactics. There was serious unrest in Italy at this time. Successive administrations had failed to grapple with Italy's economic and social problems. Corrupt politicians lined their pockets while the economic situation rapidly deteriorated. Both farming and industry were depressed. In 1893 there was a peasant revolt in Sicily. In December of that year Crispi replaced Giolitti as prime minister. He tried to restore order by proclaiming a state of siege and by drafting troops to Sicily. He blamed the socialists for the rising and dissolved 271 socialist and workers' associations throughout the country. In February 1894 Engels wrote that in Italy "the bourgeois have maintained all the horrors of decaying feudalism, grafting on it their own infamies and oppression. The country is at the end of its resources; a change must take place, but the Socialist Party is still *very* weak and *very* confused, although there are some rather able Marxists in it."[114]

At this time there were socialists in Italy who argued that they should hold aloof from mass risings and violent demonstrations. But Turati and his wife thought that the Socialist Party should try to take over the leadership of the workers' movement, overthrow the monarchy and set up a republic. They asked Engels for his advice. In particular they wanted to know whether they should co-operate with other parties to attain their ends and whether victory could be achieved without bloodshed. This was no new problem for Engels – it has been discussed in the Communist Manifesto – and he had no hesitation in advising Turati to work with other parties to overthrow the existing régime and to replace it by a bourgeois republic. This would be the first step towards the overthrow of capitalism and the introduction of socialism. But he warned Turati that co-operation with bourgeois parties must be only of a temporary nature. Turati should never forget that he was the leader of an independent socialist party, dedicated to furthering the class interests of the workers.[115]

Britain: Eleanor Marx[116]

Marx and Engels believed that since England had been the first country to experience an industrial revolution, it would also be the first to witness the collapse of capitalism and the downfall of the middle class. Whenever there was an economic crisis in England, they thought that their hour had come and that the end of the capitalist system was in sight. They had been in contact with Chartist leaders, such as Julian Harney and Ernest Jones, in the days when – as Engels put it – "the English workmen marched at the head of the European working class".[117] Marx and Engels had been disappointed when the Chartists failed to incite the workers to revolt in 1848. And in the 1850s they had waited in vain for a revival of militant Chartism.

When the First International was established Marx – and later Engels – sat on its General Council and tried, though with little success, to persuade some of its trade union members to take a more active part in politics – on the Irish question, for example. After the collapse of the International the English workers showed little inclination towards political action and Engels complained in 1872 that "things are shockingly bad at the moment here – worse than they ever were – as is to be expected with such industrial prosperity".[118] In 1874, after the conservative victory at the general election, Engels deplored the fact that "it is particularly the big industrial cities and factory districts, where the workers are now absolutely in the majority, that send Conservatives to Parliament".[119] The organised workers promoted their interests through trade unions, benefit clubs, co-operative societies and penny banks rather than by political action. Marx wrote in disgust in 1878 that the English labour movement was politically "nothing more than the tail of the Great Liberal Party – i.e. of its *oppressors*, the capitalists".[120]

In 1879 when he received a request from Bernstein to recommend an English correspondent for the new *Jahrbuch für Socialwissenschaft*[121] Engels replied that the activities of the trade unions in England were not worth writing about and would be of no interest to German readers. He wrote:

"At the present time and for some years in the past, the labour movement in England has been involved in a hopeless cycle of strikes for higher wages and shorter hours. And industrial action has not been taken as an expedient to promote trade union propaganda or to improve the organisation of the unions. Industrial action has been the ultimate aim of the trade unions. Indeed since they specifically ban participation in politics by their rules, as a matter of principle, they cannot promote any activity in the interests of the workers as a social class. As far as politics are concerned, the workers are divided into Conservatives or Liberal-Radicals, supporting either a Disraeli (Beaconsfield) or a Gladstone government. There is in England a genuine working-class movement only in so far as strikes take place. But, successful or not, strikes fail to advance the labour movement by a single step. And in recent years when trade has been depressed, the capitalists have deliberately fomented strikes to have an excuse to close their factories. To inflate strikes into struggles of world wide significance – and this is the attitude of the London *Freiheit* – can, in my view, only do harm. There is no point in denying that at the moment, no genuine labour movement in the continental sense exists in England. So I do not think that you will miss much if, for the time being, you do not receive any reports on the activities of the English trade unions."[122]

The 1880s, however, saw the development of an agitation, supported by some left-wing intellectuals and radical trade unionists, in favour of steering the labour movement towards direct participation in politics – a movement encouraged by the success of the campaign which culminated in a new extension of the franchise in 1884. The prolonged depression of trade also stimulated the progress of socialism. Engels observed in 1884 that in England "the ten-year cycle seems to have been broken down now that, since 1870, American and German competition has been putting an end to English monopoly in the world market. In the main branches of industry a business depression has prevailed since 1868, with production slowly increasing, and now we seem both here and in America to be on the verge of a new crisis which in England has not been preceded by a period of prosperity. That is the secret of the present sudden emergence of a socialist movement here, sudden – though it has been slowly preparing for three years".[123] Engels lost no time in calling upon the workers to set up a political party of their own. He did so in 1881 in a series of anonymous leading articles in *The Labour Standard*, a radical paper edited by George Shipton, the founder of the Amalgamated Society of Housepainters and Decorators and the secretary of the London Trades Council.[124]

In these articles Engels discussed the wages system and the *rôle* of trade unions in a capitalist society. He argued that workers were swindled out of some of the produce of their labour. "The capitalist pockets the whole produce (paying the labourer out of it) because he is the owner of the means of labour." Consequently the workers should seek to own "the whole produce of its own labour" by securing the nationalisation of all the means of production.[125] Engels declared that the workers should unite to demand "the abolition of the wages system altogether".[126] And this could be done only through a workers' political party. Although the workers formed the majority of the electorate in the large towns, they had never used their votes to send "men of their own class to Parliament". "It is not in the nature of things that the working class of England should possess the power of sending 40 or 50 working men to Parliament and yet be satisfied for ever to be represented by capitalists or their clerks, such as lawyers, editors etc."[127] "For the full representation of labour in Parliament, as well as for the preparation of the abolition of the wages system, organisation will be necessary, not of separate trades, but of the working class as a body. And the sooner this is done the better."[128]

In his last article in *The Labour Standard* Engels endeavoured to answer the question: "In what degree are the different classes of society useful or even necessary?" He declared that the landed aristocracy was "economically useless in England, while in Ireland and Scotland it has become a positive nuisance by its depopulating tendencies. To send the people across the ocean or into starvation, and to replace them by sheep or deer – that is all the merit that the Irish and Scotch landlords can lay claim to". Engels argued that the capitalist middle class no longer fulfilled "its essential function as the manager and expander of social production for the benefit of society at large". By the 1880s many firms which had once been run by individual entrepreneurs had been turned into joint-stock companies "whose business is managed for them by *paid employees*, by servants whose position is, to all intents and purposes, that of superior better-paid work people". Industrial production was being concentrated "into immense establishments, which cannot any longer be managed by single capitalists". Engels considered that "in reality the capitalist owners of these immense establishments have no other function left with regard to them, but to cash the half-yearly dividend warrants". (Incidentally Engels himself – the former partner in a Manchester cotton firm – had been living on his dividend warrants since 1869.) Engels went on to explain that "another function is still left to the capitalist, whom the extent of the large undertakings in question has compelled to 'retire' from their management. And this function is to speculate with his shares on the Stock Exchange. . . . Here, indeed, the existence of the 'retired' shareholding capitalist becomes not only superfluous, but a perfect nuisance". Engels concluded by calling upon the capitalists to hand over the great industries of the country to the workers.[129]

Engels hoped that his leading articles would set the tone for the policy of *The Labour Standard* and would help to turn it into a vehicle for Marxist propaganda. But while Engels advocated socialist doctrines in his leading articles, Shipton filled the rest of the paper with much more moderate views. Engels complained that the paper was "getting worse rather than better"[130] and he wrote to Marx that his leading articles were having "absolutely no effect upon the rest of the paper or upon the public". "The paper continues to advocate a hotch-potch of views held by all possible and impossible muddleheads. In practical politics it is more or less – indeed mainly – a supporter of Gladstone's policies." "In fact the British working man is not ready for progress, so he will have to learn the hard way when Britain loses her industrial monopoly."[131] So Engels severed his connection with *The Labour Standard*.

The movement which aimed at encouraging the workers to play a more active *rôle* in English politics – stimulaed by the Reform Acts of 1884 and 1885 – led to the establishment of several left-wing organisations. Within five years the Social Democratic Federation, the Socialist League, the Fabian Society, and the Labour Electoral Committee of the Trade Union Congress were set up. (Randolph Churchill's Tory Democracy of 1883 and Joseph Chamberlain's "unauthorised radical programme" of 1885 were other signs of increasing interest in social reform at this time.) Engels did not join the Social Democratic Federation or the Socialist League, though he kept in touch with these organisations through Belfort Bax, Eleanor Marx, Edward Aveling and Friedrich Lessner.

Engels criticised the new organisations as doctrinaire sects bedevilled by "intrigues between cliques".[132] Not one had a Marxist programme. In 1881 the Democratic Federation was content to advocate adult suffrage, triennial parliaments, equal electoral districts, payment of M.P.s – demands similar to those of the Chartists – and also the abolition of corrupt practices at elections, the abolition of the legislative powers of the House of Lords, home rule for Ireland and the nationalisation of the land.

In 1882 and 1883, however, the socialist movement – as Kautsky observed – "made really remarkable progress".[133] The trade depression and rising unemployment contributed to a resurgence of militancy by the left wing of the labour movement. Intellectuals, such as William Morris and Belfort Bax, joined the Democratic Federation. Hyndman promptly jumped onto the socialist band-waggon and produced a new programme in a pamphlet entitled *Socialism made Plain*. He advocated not only the state-ownership of land but also the nationalisation of the means of production and a legal eight-hour day for industrial workers.[134] A few radical workers, such as James Macdonald and Harry Quelch – the latter "impressed Engels very favourably" – joined the Social Democratic Federation at this time. In January 1884 Hyndman established *Justice* as a weekly "organ of Social Democracy"[135] and shortly afterwards he attempted – though with no great success – to defend his new socialist faith in a public debate with Charles Bradlaugh. By 1887 Hyndman had moved still further to the left, advocating "revolutionary political change through vehement social agitation" in preference to "mere political action".[136]

In 1885 Engels denounced Hyndman's followers as "a crew of literary fellows, political careerists and adventurers" and he hoped that they would be "finished off as soon as possible".[137] In 1890 he complained that the Democratic Federation was still behaving as if "all except themselves were asses and bunglers".[138] In 1892 he condemned Hyndman's Federation for having "ossified Marxism into a dogma". It had rendered itself "incapable of ever becoming anything else but a sect".[139] And in 1894 he wrote to Sorge: "The Social Democratic Federation here shares with your German–American socialists the distinction of being the only parties that have managed to reduce the Marxian theory to a rigid orthodoxy, which the workers are not to reach themselves by their own class feeling, but which they have to gulp down as an article of faith at once. . . ."[140]

Engels was equally critical of the Socialist League, which was founded in 1884 by a group of left-wing intellectuals – led by William Morris, Belfort Bax, Eleanor Marx and Edward Aveling – who had seceded from the Social Democratic Federation. He complained that the League was run by "faddists and emotional socialists",[141] who were unable to resist the encroachments of the anarchists.[142] In May 1887 Engels told Sorge that "the anarchists must be expelled or we'll drop the whole mess".[143] Nevertheless he contributed a few articles to its organ *The Commonweal*.

The Fabian Society,[144] too, did not have a sufficiently positive programme to satisfy Engels. The Fabians declared that they were working for "the extinction of private property in land and of the consequent individual appropriation, in the form of rent, of the price paid for permission to use the earth, as well as for the advantages of superior soils and sites". The Fabians also proposed that the State should own "such industrial capital as can conveniently be managed socially". Engels denounced the Fabians as "a dilettante lot of egregiously conceited mutual admirers"[145] – well meaning middle-class reformers who believed in "the rotten vulgarised economics of Jevons, which is so vulgarised that one can make anything out of it – even socialism".[146] Indeed, from Engels's point of view, the only really sound Marxists in England

– besides himself – were his friends Schorlemmer, Samuel Moore, Lessner, Eleanor Marx and Aveling. It is not surprising that Engels felt isolated from the English socialists in the 1880s. He complained to Mrs Wischnewetzky that the socialist press had ignored the appearance of the English translation of *The Condition of the Working Class in England*. He wrote: "I am boycotted here . . . the various socialist cliques here are dissatisfied at my absolute neutrality with regard to them, and being all of them agreed as to that point, try to pay me out by not mentioning any of my writings."[147]

Engels doubted whether there was any chance of converting the English workers to socialism at this time. He wrote to Kautsky in 1882 that no workers' party existed in Britain. "There are only Conservatives and Liberal-Radicals, and the workers gaily share the feast of England's monopoly of the world market and the colonies."[148] In the following year he assured Bebel that "a really general workers' movement will come into existence here only when the workers feel that England's world monopoly is broken".[149] He admitted in 1883 that there had been a "sudden emergence of a socialist movement in England".[150] In 1885 he declared that "during the period of England's industrial monopoly, the English working class have, to a great extent, shared in the benefits of the monopoly. . . . With the breakdown of that monopoly, the English working class will lose their privileged position; it will find itself generally – the privileged and leading minority not excepted – on a level with its fellow workers abroad. And that is the reason why there will be socialism again in England".[151] And in 1888 Engels told Mrs Wischnewetzky that he had seriously offended English socialists "by saying that, so far, there is no real working-class movement here".[152] In the following year he complained to Sorge that "the most repulsive thing here is the bourgeois 'respectability' that has sunk deep into the bone of the workers".[153]

One reason why Engels failed to co-operate with any of the new left-wing organisations in the 1880s was that he distrusted their leaders. He disliked Hyndman[154] who brought together several radical and socialist clubs in London in June 1881 to form the Democratic Federation. Hyndman has been described as "a frock-coated playboy agitator with a gift for instant vituperation".[155] It has been observed that Hyndman was "quite an orthodox follower of Marx in economic theory, as he understood it, and he certainly believed in the class struggle, though he had his reservations about historical materialism. At the same time he combined this with a naively utopian idea of revolution, based on French memories and a consistent strain of jingoist, anti-German – indeed racialist – imperialism, which owed nothing to any British left-wing tradition. Unlike most other men in the British socialist movement, he originally came from Toryism and not from the Radical-Liberal or Chartist atmosphere. On practical issues he had no consistent policy at all, and hence no consistent theory".[156] Engels regarded this flamboyant, wealthy stockbroker – an old Etonian and County cricketer – as one wholly unsuited to the *rôle* of a leader of the workers. He attacked Hyndman as "an adventurer"[157] – an ex-Conservative and very chauvinist but by no means stupid careerist"[158] who combined "international phraseology" with "jingo aspirations".[159] Engels denounced Hyndman's "underhand methods"[160] and declared that he "knows his way about in crooked politics and is capable of every folly to push himself forward".[161] Hyndman, in his view, "could only overcome his personal cowardice by deafening himself with his own shouts".[162] Hyndman and his followers were "liars and swindlers".[163] Eleanor Marx shared Engels's dislike of Hyndman. She complained to Liebknecht that – although international co-operation between organised workers was a fundamental tenet of socialism – Hyndman "whenever he could do so with impunity, has endeavoured to set English workmen against 'foreigners' ".[164]

Hyndman had met Marx in 1880 and had often visited him. He wrote that he "had the advantage of very frequent conversations with the Doctor and gained a view of himself and his genius, his vast erudition, and his masterly survey of human life . . .".[165] But Marx was not impressed by Hyndman whom he described as "self-satisfied" and "garrulous"[166] and he had good reason to be offended when Hyndman failed to acknowledge that several passages in his book *England for All* had come straight out of *Das Kapital*. Hyndman had merely stated in the preface that he was "indebted to the work of a great thinker and original writer". Marx complained that Hyndman's chapters on labour and capital were "literal extracts from *Das Kapital*". "Many evenings this fellow has pilfered from me, in order to draw me out and so learn in the easiest way."[167] Hyndman explained that "this incident caused a breach between us and we did not become friends again until shortly before his lamented death".[168]

Although Marx eventually decided to overlook Hyndman's conduct, Engels was not prepared to do so. When Hyndman suggested that they should meet, he was sharply rebuffed. Engels wrote: "I shall be very happy to make your personal acquaintance as soon as you shall have set yourself right with my friend Marx."[169] Engels described Hyndman as "the most chauvinistic John Bull imaginable", who was "impatiently awaiting a chance to play the dictator"[170] and whose ambition far exceeded "either his talents or his achievements".[171] He attacked Hyndman for supporting the Lassalleans in Germany[172] and the Possibilists in France. He denounced the Social Democratic Federation for accepting money from the Conservatives[173] and accused Hyndman of damaging the socialist cause by stirring up trouble in the West End of London on Black Monday – February 8, 1886. The conduct of a crowd of hooligans on this occasion caused Queen Victoria to deplore the "momentary triumph of socialism" in her capital.[174] In 1893 Engels declared that Hyndman had provoked him "personally and politically wherever he could for ten years; I never did him the honour of answering him, in the conviction that he was man enough to ruin himself, and in the end I have been justified".[175] Engels's criticism of Hyndman's conduct were echoed by the former members of the Social Democratic Federation when they left that organisation to join the Socialist League.

Hyndman, for his part, did not conceal his antipathy towards Engels. While he revered Marx as "the Aristotle of the nineteenth century",[176] he called Engels the "Grand Llama of the Regent's Park Road" by reason of the secluded life that he led and the servile deference he exacted".[177] Hyndman deplored the "autocratic, drill-sergeant fashion in which Marx and Engels had conducted the Old International".[178] "I do not myself believe," wrote Hyndman, "that Engels, whom I never spoke to, nor even saw, was a bad man, though certainly I have no reason personally to take other than a most unfavourable view of his character; but he was exacting, suspicious, jealous and not disinclined to give full weight to the exchange value of his ready cash in his relations with those whom he helped."[179] Hyndman went out of his way to annoy Engels by referring to Eleanor Marx as "Miss Marx" when she wished to be known as "Mrs Marx-Aveling"[180] and by accusing Edward Aveling of financial malpractices.[181]

In 1891 in an article in *Justice* on "The Marxist Clique" Hyndman denounced Engels and his followers as a sectarian group whose petty intrigues were harmful to the socialist cause.[182] Twenty years later, in his memoirs, Hyndman recorded malicious gossip concerning his old enemy. He declared that Jenny Marx could not bear to think of her husband's financial dependence upon Engels.

"Not that she did not recognise Engels's services to her husband, but she resented and deplored his influence over his great friend. She spoke of him to my wife more than once as Marx's 'evil genius', and wished that she could relieve her husband from any dependence upon this able and loyal but scarcely sympathetic co-adjutor. I was myself possessed at that time of good means, and though I am quite sure that neither Marx nor Mrs Marx had the slightest idea that I either could or would take the place of Engels if need arose, I am equally certain that Engels thought I might do so, and, annoyed at the friendship and even intimacy which was growing up between Marx and myself in the winter and spring of 1880–1. made up his mind to break down what he thought might be a rival influence to his own."[183]

It may be doubted if there was a word of truth in Hyndman's allegations.

Another reason for Engels's failure to exercise much influence over the socialist movement in England in the 1880s and early 1890s was his friendship with Edward Aveling. When Marx died Engels felt obliged "to stand by his children as he would have done himself".[184] He helped Laura and Eleanor (Tussy) financially and he encouraged Eleanor in her political and trade union activities. In 1884 Eleanor Marx and Aveling began to live together. They could not marry since Aveling already had a wife. Engels accepted Eleanor's lover as one of the family. Consequently "people distrusted the Marx family and its friends". "This had fateful consequences for the young untried socialist movement in England."[185] Many socialists and trade unionists avoided Engels because they detested Aveling. Frau Gertrud Guillaume-Schack, a leader of the feminist movement in Germany, and Miss M. E. Harkness, a Salvation Army worker in the East End of London, were two ladies who refused to enter Engels's house for fear of meeting Aveling there.[186]

Few men in public life have had so unsavoury a reputation as Edward Aveling. "Startlingly and repulsively ugly",[187] he had the thieving instincts of a jackdaw and the morals of a tom cat. Frequently in debt, he bilked hotel keepers and borrowed money from friends with no intention of repaying them. In 1884 he was accused of misappropriating funds from the National Secular Society, and in 1887 he was alleged to have included Eleanor Marx's hotel bills with his own when claiming travelling expenses from the American socialists.[188] He was unscrupulous in his relations with women. He lived with Eleanor Marx for 14 years – spending much of the money which she inherited from Engels[189] – but when his wife died, he married a young actress called Eva Frye. When she discovered Aveling's infidelity Eleanor Marx took her own life by swallowing a dose of prussic acid.[190]

Hyndman described Aveling as "a man of very bad character", "untrustworthy in every relation of life";[191] Kautsky declared that he was "an evil creature";[192] Bernstein wrote that he was "a despicable rogue",[193] while Olive Schreiner could not bear to be near Aveling who inspired her with "fear and horror".[194] Ben Tillett observed that Aveling was "wayward, unstable, with darker traits in his character which spelt misery and emotional strain for the woman associated with him".[195] G. B. Shaw wrote that Aveling was "morbidly scrupulous as to his religious and political convictions, and would have gone to the gallows sooner than recant a syllable of them. But he had absolutely no conscience about money and women: he was a shameless seducer and borrower, not to say a thief. In contrast with men who were scrupulously correct in their family and business life, he seemed a blackguard, and was a blackguard; but there were occasions on which they cut a very poor figure beside him: occasions when loyalty to their convictions called for some risk and sacrifice".[196]

Shaw wrote to Ellen Terry in 1898:

"Shut up your purse, tight, or else give me all your money to keep for you. No secrecy is necessary with regard to Edward Aveling. His exploits as a borrower have grown into a Homeric legend. He has his good points, has Edward: for instance, he does not deny his faiths, and will nail his atheism and socialism to the masthead incorruptibly enough. But he is incorrigible when women or the fulfilment of his engagements (especially prepaid ones) are in question. Better write to him as follows: 'Dear Dr Aveling: You must excuse me; but I know a great many people, among them some of your old friends of the National Secularist Society and the Socialist League, and some of your pupils. Don't ask me for any money. Yours sincerely, Ellen Terry'. He will understand. If the application takes the form of a post dated cheque, don't cash it. If you would like to try a few references, consult Mrs Besant, John Mackinnon Robertson, George Standing, or the spirits of Bradlaugh and William Morris. Or come to see me, and I'll tell you all about him. Just walk into a room where we are all assembled, and say, in a cautious tentative way, 'What sort of fellow is Dr Aveling?' and you will bring down the house with a shriek of laughter, and a shout of 'How much have you lent him?'

"Did you ever see him? He is always at the Lyceum on first nights, at the back of the dress circle. His wife, Karl Marx's youngest daughter, is a clever woman. For some years past he has been behaving well, because Marx's friend Engels left Eleanor £9,000. But the other day he tried the old familiar post-dated cheque on Sidney Webb – in vain. And then, I suppose, he tried you. . . ."[197]

Retribution came in the end. Soon after this letter was written Eleanor Marx took her own life in circumstances which caused

Aveling to be "ostracised by his many friends and colleagues".[198] He died a lonely and embittered man.

Aveling enjoyed Engels's friendship because of his association with Eleanor Marx,[199] whom Engels had known since she was a child. She had inherited some of her father's intellectual gifts and had acted as his secretary for some years. She was a passionate supporter of the socialist cause. In infancy she had been so precocious that her father declared that the baby must have two brains.[200] Eleanor soon became interested in politics and at the early age of 8 she was writing letters to President Lincoln.[201] Two years later she was "a charming child with a sunny disposition"[202] who was growing into a tomboy "not afraid of fighting with boys older than herself".[203] "Marx said that his wife had made a mistake as to sex when she brought her into the world."[204]

Eleanor Marx visited Engels and Lizzie Burns in 1869 when Engels retired from business and she later recalled "the triumph with which he exclaimed: 'For the last time', as he put on his boots in the morning to go to the office . . .".[205] She considered Lizzie Burns to be "as true, as honest, and in some ways as fine-souled a woman as you could meet".[206] In the same year Eleanor accompanied Engels to Ireland and this visit stimulated her interest in the Irish question at a time when Engels and Lizzie Burns were supporters of the Fenian movement and Engels was planning to write a history of Ireland.

Ten years later Eleanor was – as Bernstein remembered her – "a charming young lady of 24 with the black hair and dark eyes of her father". "Her disposition was an extremely lively one: her voice was exceptionally melodious. She took a passionate interest in our political discussions."[207] But she was highly strung and suffered from bouts of depression. When she was 19 her father wrote that she was suffering from a "severe illness"[208] in which "hysteria played a part".[209] "This was not an isolated but rather an acute outbreak of an illness from which she has long suffered."[210] Seven years later Marx told Engels that Eleanor's doctor had diagnosed a "dangerously overwrought nervous system", which caused sleeplessness and neuralgic pains.[211] Six months later her condition had not improved.[212] And when she eventually took her own life Aveling told the coroner that Eleanor was of "a morbid disposition".[213]

Eleanor's depression was aggravated by two great disappointments – her failure to marry Lissagaray and her failure to become an actress. At the age of 19 she fell in love with Lissagaray, a French socialist refugee, who often visited the Marx household between 1873 and 1877. Franzisca Kugelmann (daughter of Dr

Kugelmann) wrote that Eleanor "considered herself engaged to Lissagaray". Franzisca described Lissagaray as "insignificant in appearance and considerably older than Tussy". "He was a count, but had given up his title and had been cast out by his whole family because of his socialist opinions."[214] Eleanor's mother appears to have recognised the engagement but her father did not.[215] Karl Marx had no great objection to counts but he did object to counts who had no money.[216] He refused to consent to the marriage and Eleanor bowed to her father's wishes. It was presumably her father's opposition to her marriage that Eleanor had in mind when she told Olive Schreiner that "for long miserable years there was a shadow between us".[217]

Having stopped Eleanor from marrying Lissagaray, Marx tried to stop her from going onto the stage. She was 27 years old when Marx wrote to Engels that his daughter was suffering from mental depression.

> "Neither travel, nor a change of climate, nor physicians can do anything in this case. All that can be done is to give way and to let her continue her drama lessons with Madame Jung. She thinks that she has ambitions to carve out for herself an independent career as an actress. And, if one accepts this, one must agree with her that, at her age, there is no more time to be lost. I am quite determined that she is not to sacrifice herself on the altar of family loyalty and devote herself to nursing an old man. In fact I am satisfied that, for the time being, Madame Jung can be her only doctor."[218]

Although in this letter Marx cast himself in the *rôle* of an indulgent father who was anxious to meet his daughter's wishes it is clear that he was strongly opposed to Eleanor's ambition to become an actress. In the end he had his way and Eleanor gave up her plans to go onto the stage.

In the following year Beatrice Potter – the future Mrs Sidney Webb – described Eleanor as "comely, dressed in a slovenly picturesque way, with curly black hair flying in all directions. Fine eyes full of life and sympathy, otherwise ugly features and expression, and complexion showing the signs of an unhealthy excited life, kept up with stimulants and tempered by narcotics. Lives alone. . . ."[219]

It may be doubted whether Eleanor was living alone at this time. Having lost Lissagaray, she consoled herself with Edward Aveling. In the summer of 1884 Engels wrote that Eleanor and Aveling had been courting "for a considerable time". Marx would never have agreed to Eleanor's liaison with a married man and Eleanor had enough sense not to bring her lover home to meet her father. But Engels – who had lived with Lizzie Burns for many years before marrying her – took a different view of such matters. Soon after Marx's death in March 1883 Eleanor decided to live with Edward Aveling. In June she told her sister Laura that she and Aveling were "going to 'set up' together".[220] And she wrote to her friend Dollie Radford that Engels and Helene Demuth approved the action that she was about to take.[221]

Engels discussed the liaison in letters to Laura Lafargue and to Bernstein. To Laura he wrote:

"Tussy and Edward are off on honeymoon No. 1, if not back already again – the grand honeymoon is to come off next Thursday. Of course Nim (Helene Demuth), Jollymeier (Schorlemmer) and I have been fully aware of what was going on for a considerable time and had a good laugh at these poor innocents who thought all the time we had no eyes, and who did not approach the *quart d'heure de Rabelais* without a certain funk. However we soon got them over that. In fact had Tussy asked my advice before she leaped, I might have considered it my duty to expatiate upon the various possible and unavoidable consequences of this step, but when it was all settled, the best thing was for them to have it out at once before other people could take advantage of its being kept in the dark. And that was one of the reasons why I was glad that we knew all about it – if any wise people had found it out and come up to us with the grand news, we should have been prepared. I hope they will continue as happy as they seem now. . . ."[222]

At the same time Engels wrote to Bernstein:

"They have been married without benefit of Registry Office and are revelling in each other's company in the Derbyshire Peak district. Please note that this should not be made public. It will be soon enough to do so if the press gets hold of the news through some reactionary fellow. The reason is that Aveling has a legal wife whom he cannot get rid of *de jure* although for years he has been rid of her *de facto*. The affair is pretty well known here and, on the whole, even the literary philistines have accepted the situation with a good grace."[223]

Edward Aveling[224] was a man of many parts. He was trained as a scientist and held the degree of D.Sc. He was a Fellow of University College, London. Between 1875 and 1881 he was Professor of Comparative Anatomy at a London hospital. He might have had a distinguished academic career but as "Alec Nelson" he sought fame as a playwright and as an actor. For a time he ran a touring theatrical company and it was their mutual interest in the stage that brought Aveling and Eleanor Marx together in about 1882. But they failed to make names for themselves on the stage. Aveling became a writer, a journalist and a popular lecturer, first as a freethinker and then as a socialist. And it was as socialist agitators that Aveling and Eleanor Marx became popular figures. Both were excellent speakers, who could hold the attention of a crowd whether in a hall or at an open air demonstration.

Engels accepted Aveling as a friend and a colleague for Eleanor's sake. He sent Aveling and Eleanor £50 to pay for their holiday in Derbyshire when they began to live together. Engels wrote to Laura Lafargue: "I like Edward very much and think that it will be a good thing for him to come more into contact with other people besides the literary and lecturing circle in which he moved; he has a good foundation of thorough studies and felt himself out of place amongst that extremely superficial lot amongst whom fate had thrown him."[225]

Engels was able to convince himself that Aveling had a future as a playwright. He wrote to Laura Lafargue:

"Of Edward's remarkable *preliminary* successes in the dramatic line you will have heard. He has sold about half a dozen or more pieces which he had quietly manufactured; some have been played in the provinces with success, some he has brought out here himself with Tussy at small entertainments, and they have taken very much with the people that are most interested in them; viz. with such actors and impressarios as will bring them out. If he has now one marked success in London, he is a made man in this line and will soon be out of all difficulties. And I don't see why he should not; he seems to have a remarkable knack of giving to London what London requires."[226]

But Aveling never found fame as a dramatist or an actor and he was never able to escape from his financial difficulties.

Despite evidence to the contrary, Engels persisted in his belief that Aveling was an honest fellow. On one occasion he gave Aveling £10 to send to Victor Adler. When the cheque bounced, Engels wrote to Adler that a bohemian like Aveling with an artistic temperament should really not be trusted with a cheque book.[227] When the American socialists complained about Aveling's inflated claims for expenses in connection with his lecture tour of 1886, Engels quickly sprang to his defence. He wrote to Mrs Wischnewetzky:

"I have known Aveling for four years; I know that he has twice sacrificed his social and economic position to his convictions, and might be – had he refrained from doing so – a professor in an English university, and a distinguished physiologist instead of an overworked journalist with a very uncertain income. I have had occasion to observe his capacities by working with him, and his character by seeing him pass through rather trying circumstances more than once, and it will take a good deal (more than mere assertions and innuendos) before I believe what some people tell about him now in New York."[228]

But to Sorge he admitted that Aveling had not been blameless in this matter. "The young man has brought all his troubles upon himself by his utter ignorance of mankind, of people, and of business. He likes to lose himself in poetic dreams. I have shaken him up and Tussy will do what is necessary. He is a very talented young fellow but he is as gushing as a teenager and always blushes when he makes a foolish mistake."[229]

Engels hoped that Aveling and Eleanor Marx would succeed where the Social Democratic Federation and the Socialist League had failed. He hoped that they would establish a working man's political party – with a Marxist programme – which would support independent labour candidates at parliamentary elections. A campaign in the East End of London, mounted by Aveling and Eleanor Marx in the spring of 1887 – in which demands for a workers' party were linked with demands for Irish home rule – suggested that Engels's dream might come true. The campaign culminated in a great meeting of workers in Hyde Park at which Aveling and Eleanor Marx were among the main speakers. An eye witness wrote that Eleanor was "enthusiastically applauded for a speech delivered with perfect self-possession".[230] Engels wrote to Laura Lafargue in March 1887:

"Aveling was making a very useful and probably successful campaign amongst the East End Radicals to engage them to cut loose from the Great Liberal Party and form a working men's party after the American fashion. If he succeeds, he will get both socialist associations into his wake; for here he gets at the heart of the working class. So far his prospects are good."[231]

A little later he wrote to Bernstein:

"Aveling and Tussy are undertaking a marvellous agitation among the radical clubs of the East End which has been stimulated by the example of the American socialists. The clubs are now seriously thinking of setting up an independent workers' party. The best of it is that these people have come to Aveling *of their own accord*. If we can establish a firm foothold in these clubs we shall be able to push both the Social Democratic Federation and the Socialist League into the background and we shall start to conquer London and gain a dozen parliamentary seats at once. Hyndman has recognised the danger that threatens him and that is why he has printed in *Justice* the libels of the New York executive against Aveling."[232]

If Engels hoped to become the power behind the scenes in guiding the fortunes of a new labour party, led by Aveling and Eleanor Marx, he was disappointed. No such party was founded. Engels was also in touch with J. L. Mahon, an energetic young agitator, who established the North of England Socialist Federation at this time. Mahon sent Engels a copy of the provisional statutes of this body for his observations. Engels offered Mahon financial assistance if he would work with Aveling in London to promote the establishment of a new workers' socialist party. But Mahon distrusted Aveling and he turned down Engels's proposal.[233]

Although they failed to set up a political party, Aveling and Eleanor Marx did make their mark in the British labour movement as organisers of trade unions of general labourers. The radical and socialist revival of the early 1880s was followed by an outburst of militancy on the part both of trade unionists and of newly organised unskilled workers. In October 1886 the Eight Hours League was established under the leadership of Tom Mann of the Amalgamated Society of Engineers.[234] (A few years later – in 1890 – Engels reported that Aveling was chairman of a central committee to organise an annual demonstration in London on May 1 in favour of an eight hours day.)[235] In 1887 there was a strike in the Northumberland coalfield, which gave Mahon, Jack Williams, and Hunter Watts an opportunity to undertake socialist propaganda among the miners and to set up the North of England Socialist Federation.

Equally significant was the rise of unions of semi-skilled and unskilled workers such as dockers, builders, stokers and general labourers. The movement was sparked off by a strike of the girls employed by the London firm of Bryant and May, which manufactured matches. The girls engaged in this dangerous occupation – many suffered from phossy-jaw – earned only from 4/- to 13/- a week, which might be reduced by arbitrary fines and deductions. The shareholders, however, enjoyed a dividend of 23 per cent. Mrs Besant and Herbert Burrows exposed the exploitation of the match girls in an article on "White Slavery in London".[236] Public sympathy was aroused, and when the girls came out on strike in July 1888, the firm agreed to abolish deductions from wages and to provide the girls with a room in which to have their meals. The Union of Women Matchmakers was established with Mrs Besant as secretary and Burrows as treasurer.

The matchgirls' strike was followed in March 1889 by a strike of men employed at the Beckton Gas Works in London – "the largest in the world"[237] in those days. The stokers and other labourers were engaged in heavy manual labour and they demanded an 8-hour instead of a 12-hour shift.[238] Output had been expanding in the gas industry for some years although there had been no appreciable changes in the technique of production or the way in which the work was organised. The men worked harder but received no extra reward for their efforts. The strike was organised by Will Thorne – whom Engels described as "a leader in battle of both courage and ability"[239] – and, within a fortnight, over 3,000 men had joined the new National Union of Gas Workers and General Labourers. The men secured the 8-hour shift for which they had been agitating.

Eleanor Marx played a leading part in setting up the National Union of Gas Workers and General Labourers. In 1889 Engels observed that she had been responsible for securing the establishment of women's branches in this union, and two years later he declared that she was "the leader of the gas workers (on the sly)".[240] Eleanor also helped to organise the labourers in some of the gasworks in the provinces. In Ireland Eleanor Marx and Aveling helped to set up a union of gasworkers in 1891. Eleanor became a close friend of Will Thorne. He was deeply moved by her tragic death a few years later and "bawled like a baby" at her funeral.[241] In his memoirs he described her as a "very brave and intelligent woman"[242] who helped him to improve his reading, writing and general knowledge.[243] It was through Eleanor that he met Engels and some of the leading socialists abroad such as Lafargue, Bebel, and Liebknecht.[244] He wrote that Aveling and Eleanor Marx "were both very earnest Internationalists". "From them I learnt much about the necessity for co-operation between the workers of the different countries; through them I met most of the leading thinkers and advocates of the working classes in the different European countries."[245]

Hard on the heels of the gasworkers came the dockers. The condition of the London dockers had long been a scandal. As a young man Engels had denounced their exploitation by the dock employers. In 1845 in *The Condition of the Working Class in England* he had quoted an account of labour conditions in the London docks from an article written by a clergyman in the East End. "At the gates of each of the docks, hundreds of poor men may be seen before daybreak waiting for the opening of the gates in the hope of obtaining a day's work; and when the youngest and most able-bodied, and those best known, have been engaged, hundreds may still be seen returning to their destitute families with that 'sickness of heart' which arises from 'hope deferred'."[246] Some twenty years later Mayhew gave a vivid description of the degrading existence of the casual labourers who earned a precarious living in the London docks – "the very focus of metropolitan wealth". He wrote that it was "a sight to sadden the most callous to see thousands of men struggling for only one day's work; the scuffle being made the fiercer by the knowledge that hundreds out of the number there assembled must be left to idle the day out in want".[247] Another twenty years passed and still conditions had not improved. In 1889 Engels wrote that the dockers were "the most miserable of all the *miserables* of the East End, the broken down ones of all trades, the lowest stratum above the *Lumpenproletariat*". He declared that they were "poor famished broken down creatures who bodily fight amongst each other every morning for admission to work".[248]

In 1889 the success of the strike of the gasworkers in London encouraged the dockers to embark upon militant industrial action to secure better conditions and higher wages. There were close links between the labourers in the gasworks and in the docks in ports like London since, in those days, it was not uncommon for men to be employed as dockers in the summer and as gasworkers in the winter. Ben Tillett had led a strike at the Tilbury docks in October 1888. Nearly a year later – in August 1889 – the dockers on the north bank of the Thames came out on strike. Engels claimed that "all this is worked and led by *our* people, by Burns and Mann, and the Hyndmanites are nowhere in it".[249] The dockers demanded higher wages and the abolition of the subcontracting system. The strike committee had its headquarters at a public house called Wade's Arms and here Eleanor Marx undertook clerical work to help the dockers. Will Thorne wrote: "John Burns' wife and Eleanor Marx-Aveling acted as correspondents for the committee: they worked long hours and walked bravely late at night, or in the early morning, to and from their distant homes."[250] And Ben Tillett recalled that Eleanor had "worked unceasingly, literally day and night, at our headquarters".[251]

The dockers held out for six weeks and eventually accepted the mediation of Cardinal Manning and the Lord Mayor of London. They dropped their demand for 8d an hour and accepted 6d an hour – the "dockers' tanner" – coupled with the abolition of the subcontracting system. They had no strike fund but were able to hold out because of support from trade unionists and from the general public. About £50,000 was raised in public subscriptions – £30,000 from trade unionists in Australia. The London dockers were supported by the Stevedores' Union and a Labour Protection League (organised by Harry Quelch) was established on the south bank of the Thames. Engels followed these events closely and

– at a critical moment in the fortunes of the dockers in the third week of the strike – he intervened (through Eleanor Marx) to offer advice to the dockers' leaders. He opposed a suggestion that a general strike of labourers should be called in London in support of the dockers. He wrote to Laura Lafargue on September 1, 1889:

". . . Now this was playing *va blanque*, staking £1,000 to win £10, it was threatening more than they could carry out: it was creating millions of hungry mouths for no reason but because they had some tens of thousands on hand which they could not feed; it was casting away wilfully all the sympathies of the shopkeepers and even of the great mass of the bourgeoisie who all hated the dock monopolists, but who would at once turn against the workmen; in fact it was such a declaration of despair and such a desperate game that I wrote to Tussy at once; if this is persisted in, the Dock Co's have only to hold out till Wednesday and they will be victorious.

"Fortunately they have thought better of it. Not only has the threat been 'provisionally' withdrawn but they have even acceded to the demands of the wharfingers (in some respects competitors of the docks), have reduced their demands for an increase of wages, *and this has again been rejected* by the Dock Companies. This I think will secure them the victory. The threat with the general strike will now have a salutary effect, and the generosity of the workmen, both in withdrawing it and in acceding to a compromise, will secure them fresh sympathy and help."[252]

When the men returned to work, Engels discussed the significance of the conflict in *Der Sozialdemokrat*.[253] He regarded the strike in a different light from most of his contemporaries. For Engels what had occurred in the East End of London was important because it showed that the middle classes in England were declining and were no longer able to fulfil the functions assigned to them by Karl Marx in his theory of the class struggle. Marx held that the *rôle* of the bourgeoisie was to abolish feudal institutions and so pave the way for the proletariat to seize power. In the past the English middle classes had generally behaved as Marx had argued that they should behave. Yet they had failed to reform the administration of the London docks which were still in 1889 an oasis of feudalism in a bourgeois society. Wharfingers, lightermen, and watermen were still organised in medieval gilds, though they had now come to be dominated by large dock companies. Enjoying a virtual monopoly, the dockowners had foolishly expanded the docks at the very time when their high charges were driving business away to more efficient provincial and continental ports. Near bankruptcy had recently forced rival companies to unite.

Engels declared that shippers and merchants, who suffered most from this state of affairs, should have insisted long ago upon a reform of the administration of the docks. When the dockers went on strike the middle classes gave them financial aid, not from humanitarian motives, but from self-interest. They realised that a defeat of the dock companies would herald a long overdue reform of the administration of the port of London. Thus Engels saw the dockers not only as underpaid workers struggling for a living wage but as men who were – perhaps without realising it – fighting on behalf of the bourgeoisie for a reform of the administration of the docks.

The London dock strike proved to be a turning point in the development of the labour movement in England. The dockers formed a union with Tom Mann as president and Ben Tillett as secretary. The establishment of unions of matchgirls, gasworkers, and dockers heralded a new phase in the history of trade unionism. Within a year of the dockers' strike a new era had dawned with the enrolment of some 200,000 unskilled workers in new unions and the establishment of a weekly socialist journal – *The People's Press* – to represent their views.[254]

The new unions of unskilled men and women were, in certain important respects, different from the old established unions of skilled workers. The older unions now favoured conciliation or arbitration rather than industrial action and preferred to spend their funds on friendly society benefits rather than on strike pay. The new unions had relatively low subscriptions and their members enjoyed few friendly society benefits. Their funds were used to support militant industrial action. And while the old unions generally held aloof from politics at this time, the new unions were closely associated with recently established socialist bodies which eventually developed into the Labour Party.

Engels commented upon the "new unionism" in 1892 in a new introduction to the English translation of *The Condition of the Working Class in England*. He observed that the revival of socialism in England was due largely to "the revival of the East End of London".

"That immense haunt of misery is no longer the stagnant pool it was six years ago. It has shaken off its torpid despair, has returned to life, and has become the home of what is called the 'New Unionism', that is to say, of the organisation of the great mass of 'unskilled' workers. This organisation may, to a great extent, adopt the form of the old unions of 'skilled' workers, but it is essentially different in character. The old unions preserve the traditions of the time when they were founded, and look upon the wages system as a once-for-all established, final fact, which they can at best modify in the interest of their members. The new unions were founded at a time when the faith in the eternity of the wages system was severely shaken; their founders and promoters were socialists, either consciously or by feeling; the masses, whose adhesion gave them strength, were rough, neglected, looked down upon by the working-class aristocracy; but they had this immense advantage, that *their minds were virgin soil*, entirely free from the inherited 'respectable' bourgeois prejudices which hampered the brains of the better situated 'old' unionists. And thus we see now these new unions taking the lead of the working-class movement generally, and more and more taking in tow the rich and proud 'old' unions. Undoubtedly, the East Enders have committed colossal blunders; so have their predecessors, and so do the doctrinaire socialists who pooh-pooh them. A large class, like a great nation, never learns better or quicker than by undergoing the consequences of its own mistakes. And for all the faults committed in past, present and future, the revival of the East End of London remains one of the greatest and most fruitful facts of this *fin du siècle*, and glad and proud I am to have lived to see it."[255]

Engels was well aware of the difficulties experienced by the new unions in the early 1890s. They quarrelled among themselves and they quarrelled with the old unions. Will Thorne's union was originally established for gasworkers but it soon adopted the motto: "One Man, One Ticket, and Every Man with a Ticket" and it threw its doors open to all unskilled labourers. But the dockers adopted a different policy. They were led by Tom Mann and Ben Tillett who were engineers with experience of a union of skilled workers. Tom Mann and Ben Tillett were opposed to the idea of a general union. It was said that they wanted "the old unionism applied to unskilled labour"[256] by putting a "ring fence" round the docks.[257]

When the new trade unions of unskilled workers appeared on the scene, they were regarded with some suspicion by the old established unions of skilled workers and by the London Trades Council. Engels complained that during the dock strike there were three engineers at the Commercial Docks who were in charge of the steam engines which operated the cranes. If they had come out on strike they could have halted the loading and unloading of ships. But the three engineers remained at their posts and the executive committee of their union took no action in the matter. Engels also observed that the strike at the Silvertown Rubber Works in 1889, which lasted for twelve weeks, eventually failed "because of the engineers, who did not join in and even did labourers' work *against* their own rules". He criticised the engineers for having a rule "that *only those who have gone through a regular period of apprenticeship* are admitted to their union".[258] Will Thorne wrote that Eleanor Marx "took a leading part" in the Silvertown strike. "She did good service both among the men and women, and formed a women's branch of the union at Silvertown of which she became secretary."[259]

In the early 1890s the militant mood of the unskilled workers rapidly spread from London to other parts of the country. Aveling and Eleanor Marx took a leading part in preaching the gospel of the new unionism in the provinces. They gained support from the workers not so much by preaching Marx's doctrines as by advocating an eight-hour day, the organisation of trade unions by unskilled labourers, and home rule for Ireland. One of their successes was gained in Leeds where a strike of gasworkers occurred in July 1890. The owners of the gasworks had recently been forced to grant an eight-hour shift and they now demanded an increase of 25 per cent in output from their workers. The men went on strike and were supported by the local branch of the Socialist League and by leaders of the socialist movement from London such as Will Thorne, Tom Mann, Cunninghame-Graham, Eleanor Marx and Aveling. The strikers and their supporters tried to stop black-legs from outside Leeds from reaching the gasworks. The police intervened and some violence followed. Most of the blacklegs took fright and left Leeds. Within a few days the employers had to withdraw their demands and the victory of the strikers was complete. Engels, on returning from a holiday in Norway with Schorlemmer, was delighted to hear "the splendid news about the two fights in Leeds"[260] and he conferred upon Will Thorne the supreme accolade – an inscribed copy of *Das Kapital* dedicated to "the victor of the battle of Leeds".[261]

Engels believed that the crucial issue in working class politics at this time was the demand for a legal eight hours day. This, in his view, was more important than the new militancy of the workers in the East End of London or the establishment of trade unions by the unskilled workers. He wrote to Kautsky in September 1890 that the question of the eight-hour day had been a "critical turning point" in the history of the British labour movement. It marked a breach in the domination of the old established conservative trade unions which operated within the existing capitalist society.[262] He had been delighted when, early in 1890, Aveling had been elected chairman of a General Committee which planned the organisation of a May Day demonstration in Hyde Park in favour of a legal eight-hour day. This committee included representatives from branches of the Socialist League, the new trade unions in the East End, and some of the radical clubs. It was decided to hold a demonstration on May 4, the first Sunday in May, rather than on May 1.

Aveling's Central Committee sought the co-operation of the London Trades Council in organising the demonstration. At first Shipton and his colleagues were unwilling to do so, but eventually – under pressure from Tom Mann[263] – they changed their minds. The Trades Council now tried to organise the demonstration in association with Hyndman's Social Democratic Federation and to push Aveling and his Central Committee into the background. The Trades Council was not above indulging in a little sharp practice to get its way. Engels explained what happened in a letter to Laura Lafargue. He wrote that "in their naïveté" Aveling and Eleanor "had called in the Trades Council without ensuring to themselves the possession of the Park first. The Trades Council, allying itself with Hyndman and Co., stole a march on them, and applied for platforms for Sunday at the Office of Works and got them, thus hoping to shut us out and being able to command; they attempted to bully us down, but Edward went to the Office of Works and got us too 7 platforms – had the Liberals been in, we should never have got them. That brought the other side down at once, and they became as amicable as you please. They have seen they have to do with different people from what they expected."[264]

Engels was present at the demonstration of May 4, 1890 and he considered that it was a great success. In an article in the *Arbeiter-Zeitung* he declared that with this demonstration "the English workers have taken their place in the great international labour movement. . . . The grandsons of the old Chartists are stepping into the front line".[265] He wrote to Laura Lafargue:

". . . I can assure you I looked a couple of inches taller when I got down from that old lumbering waggon that served as a platform – after having heard again, for the first time since 40 years, the unmistakable voice of the English proletariat. . . . The progress made in England these last 10–15 months is immense. Last May the 8 hours working day would not have brought as many *thousands* into Hyde Park as we had *hundreds of thousands*. And the best of it is that the struggle preceding the demonstration has brought to life a representative body which will serve as the nucleus for the movement, *en dehors de toute secte*; the Ceneral Committee consisting of delegates of the Gas Workers and numerous other Unions – mostly small *unskilled* Unions and therefore despised by the haughty Trades Council of the aristocracy of labour – and of the Radical clubs worked for the last two years by Tussy. Edward is chairman of this Committee. This Committee will continue to act and invite all other trade, political and socialist societies to send delegates, and gradually expand into a central body, not only for the 8 hours Bill but for all other revendications. . . ."[266]

It is clear from this letter that Engels hoped that Aveling's Central Committee would grow into a political party. Aveling thought so too. On May 9, 1890 the Central Committee met to review the position after the demonstration. Aveling urged his colleagues to keep the committee in being until a permanent organisation had been established to agitate for a legal eight-hour day.[267] Shortly afterwards he told the Bloomsbury Socialist Society that the Central Committee was destined to develop into a political party of the workers. On July 13, 1890 a number of representatives of trade unions, socialist societies, and radical clubs were brought together by Aveling's Central Committee and they established a new organisation called the Legal Eight Hours and International Labour League.

The League did not, however, develop into a political party. It was very slow to get off the ground. Its provisional executive committee did not meet until February 1891 and shortly afterwards the *Workman's Times* reported that the League was not in a healthy state.[268] In May 1891 Engels was only able to report that the League was still "in process of formation".[269] Then the League showed some signs of life by co-operating in the arrangements to hold a May Day demonstration in 1891. Once more it was not possible to hold a single demonstration. Shipton and Aveling collaborated to set up a committee to organise the event so that on this occasion there was no rivalry between the London Trades Council and Aveling's Central Committee. But the Social Democratic Federation held aloof and organised a meeting of its own in Hyde Park. Engels attended the demonstration with his old friend Sam Moore. He wrote to Laura Lafargue that "the platforms extended in an immense arc across the Park, the procession began to march in at 2.30 and had not done by 4.15; indeed fresh processions came in up to 5 o'clock. . . . The crowd was immense, about the same or more even than last year. . . . It has been almost exclusively Edward's and Tussy's work, and they had to fight it through from beginning to end. . . . The Canning Town Branch of the (Social Democrat) Federation sticks to Edward and Tussy in spite of Hyndman and marches with our people, and that is their strongest branch. . . ."[270]

Aveling and Eleanor Marx had their successes in organising May Day demonstrations and in stimulating the formation of unions of unskilled workers. But they were not able to turn the Eight Hours League into a political party. In the early 1890s the labour movement in England developed in a way that gave Aveling and Eleanor Marx little opportunity to aspire to a position to leadership among the workers. In London a new political organisation – the Progressive Party – was founded in 1889 and it put candidates up for election to the newly established London County Council and to the new London boroughs. Liberals, radicals, and Fabians rallied to the new party. The energies of reformers in the capital were concentrated on promoting the success of the new party. The Eight Hours League only survived as a propaganda organ and as a committee to organise May Day demonstrations.

At the same time the Social Democratic Federation enjoyed a new lease of life under the leadership of men like Herbert Burrows, Harry Quelch, James Macdonald, and George Lansbury. Its organ, *Justice*, edited by Quelch from 1892 to 1913, enjoyed a large circulation. And while the Social Democratic Federation and the Progressive Party were gaining strength in London the Independent Labour Party – established in 1893 – attracted the support of many workers in the provinces. In the 1880s the socialists had made little progress outside London. But in the early 1890s the workers in the manufacturing districts of the north began to show a new militancy towards their employers and began to take a new interest in labour politics. Joseph Burgess' *Yorkshire Factory Times* and Robert Blatchford's *The Clarion* encouraged the new movement in the north. The establishment of the Independent Labour Party in Bradford marked the climax of this movement. Its programme included demands for an eight-hour day, a legal minimum wage, insurance against unemployment, and the nationalisation of the land and basic industries. In 1893 Engels wrote to Sorge that the Independent Labour Party was "the most genuine expression of the present movement".[271] He thought that "Aveling was right in joining and in accepting a seat on the executive" and that the new party might "succeed in detaching the masses from the Social Democratic Federation and in the provinces from the Fabians, too, and thus force unity".[272]

Shortly before his death, Engels made some final comments upon the labour movement in England. In January 1895 he declared that

"the socialist instinct is becoming ever stronger among the *masses*, but whenever the instinctive drives here have to be converted into clear demands and ideas, the people fall asunder. Some join the Social Democratic Federation, others the Independent Labour Party, still others stay in the trades union organisation etc., etc. In short a lot of sects and no party. Almost all the leaders are unreliable, the candidates for the top leadership are very numerous but far from outstandingly fitted for the job and the two big bourgeois parties stand ready, money bag in hand to buy up whomever they can."[273]

And in March 1895 Engels wrote to Adler:

"The masses are making headway instinctively and the forward march will go on. But when it comes to giving practical expression to these instincts and tendencies one come up against the stupidity and folly of the leaders of the (socialist) sects. I feel like knocking their silly heads together. But that is the way that things are done in the Anglo-Saxon countries."[274]

The death of Engels in 1895, followed soon afterwards by the deaths of Eleanor Marx and Aveling, meant that the "Marx family party" had disappeared. Engels had been able to exercise some influence over the British labour movement through Eleanor Marx and Aveling but he never achieved his ambition to be the power behind the scenes in a political party with a Marxist programme.

Russia: Georgi Plekhanov[275]

When Marx and Engels formulated their doctrine of the class struggle they argued that just as the middle classes had once wrested power from the feudal aristocracy, so one day the industrial proletariat would triumph over the bourgeois capitalists. As modern manufacturers developed so a factory proletariat was created which grew with the expansion of the industrial sector of the economy. Eventually the workers would be strong enough to overthrow their bourgeois oppressors and establish a classless communist society which would nationalise the means of production.

Marx and Engels believed that this revolution – the culmination of the struggle between the bourgeoisie and the proletariat – would occur first in western Europe in industrialised countries such as Britain, Belgium, and Germany. There would be no similar revolution in underdeveloped agrarian countries such as Russia, Spain, Italy and the Balkans until their manufactures had developed. Marx made this clear in a letter to Vera Zasulich. He wrote that "the 'historical inevitability' of this movement is *expressly* limited to the *countries of western Europe*".[276]

Marx and Engels considered that Russia had begun to develop modern industries – though only on a very modest scale – after the emancipation of the serfs in 1861. Marx wrote in 1877 that "if Russia continues to pursue the path she has followed since 1861 she will . . . undergo all the fatal vicissitudes of the capitalist régime".[277] Fifteen years later Engels warned Danielson that "capitalist production works its own ruin, and you may be sure it will do so in Russia too".[278] Marx and Engels rejected Bakunin's assertion that the downtrodden peasants in Russia, Italy, Spain and the Balkans were potential revolutionaries. They also rejected the notion, supported by Alexander Herzen and by the Narodniks that the joint ownership of land and the communal methods of agriculture in many Russian villages could be used as the foundations upon which to build a communist society in the future. Shortly before his death Engels declared that it was "impossible to discuss things with the generation of Russians . . . which continues to believe in the spontaneously communist mission that distinguishes Russia – true Holy Russia – from the other, the profane peoples".[279]

Marx and Engels later learned Russian and studied the Russian economy after the emancipation of the serfs in the writings of Nicolai Chernyshevsky and Flerowski. They modified their views on the prospects of an early revolution in Russia. At one time they had expected that a rising of the Poles would spark off a revolution in Russia, but they now came to think that the Russian peasants and industrial workers might overthrow the autocratic régime of the czars. Marx and Engels also accepted the possibility that the village community might one day develop into a specifically Russian form of agrarian socialism. They came to believe that a revolution might break out in Russia at any time. This would obviously be different from a clash between the bourgeois capitalists and the industrial proletariat in the West but it might very well be a significant event in world history if – in addition to bringing down the reactionary régime of the czar – it also triggered off risings among the workers in the West. For some time Marx and Engels had been confident that a revolt in Paris would herald the collapse of reactionary governments all over Europe. But after the repression of the Commune in 1871 they no longer thought that the Paris workers would be in the forefront of the next revolution in Europe. A rising of the peasants and the industrial workers in Russia now seemed to them to be a more likely occurrence than a rising in the French capital. Such a revolution might be expected to topple the czar off his throne, to free the Poles, and to act as a call to arms to the workers in the West. In 1873 Engels declared that "no doubt Russia stands on the eve of a revolution"[280] and for over twenty years he waited for the revolution that did not break out until ten years after his death. In 1882 – in their introduction to the second edition of the Russian translation of the Communist Manifesto – Marx and Engels stated that Russia was now in the vanguard of the revolutionary movement. "Should the Russian revolution prove to be the signal for a great revolt of the workers in the West – so that the two revolutions complement each other – then the present Russian institution of communal landed property might serve as the starting point of a process which would culminate in the establishment of communism."[281] In 1883 Engels asserted that "Russia is the France of the present century". "To her belongs rightfully and lawfully the revolutionary initiative of a *new* social reorganisation."[282] Ten years later Engels told Voden that "it is important that the achievement of power by Social-Democracy in the West should coincide with the political and agrarian revolution in Russia".[283]

Engels was in contact with three groups of Russian revolutionaries – the exiles of the 1840s, the Narodniks, and the Marxists. First, in the 1840s, he met some members of the Russian intelligentsia – some of noble birth – who had left the repressive régime of the czar to travel or to settle in western Europe. One was P. V. Annenkov to whom Marx sent a letter containing one of his earliest criticisms of Proudhon's doctrines.[284] Another was Michael Bakunin who later became one of Engels's most determined enemies. Between 1850 and 1870, when he lived in Manchester, Engels lost touch with Russian revolutionaries but he continued to be interested in Russian affairs and he wrote several articles on the Crimean War.[285]

The second group of Russian revolutionaries whom Engels knew personally or by correspondence were intellectuals who supported the Narodnik (populist) movement.[286] The policy of the Narodniks was "to go in among the people" to spread revolutionary ideas among the Russian peasants. In 1875, shortly after the movement had been broken up by the authorities, an official report estimated that 770 persons had been members of Narodnik groups and that 265 of them were now in prison.[287] Some of the survivors of the original Narodnik movement formed a new organisation which gave up the former propaganda among the peasants and embarked upon an agitation in favour of an immediate revolt under the slogan *Zemlia i Volya* (Land and Liberty). In 1879 this movement split into an orthodox Narodnik group called *Chernyi Peredel* (the General Redivision) and a terrorist faction called *Narodnaya Volya* (People's Will).

Some exiled Narodniks had joined the Russian section of the First International in Geneva in 1870.[288] When he moved to London in that year Engels joined the General Council of the First International where he met two of the Narodniks – Herman Lopatin and Peter Lavrov – both of whom he came to hold in high esteem as dedicated revolutionaries. The Narodniks were steeped in the writings of Dobrolyubov and Chernyshevsky. Marx had a high opinion of Chernyshevsky's writings on economics. Lopatin wrote: "Marx told me several times that Chernyshevsky was the only contemporary economist who had really original ideas, while all the others were in fact only compilers; that his works were full of originality, force and depth and were the only modern works on that science which really deserved to be read and studied."[289]

Lopatin came to England in 1870 – at the age of 25 – to discuss with Marx his plan to translate the first volume of *Das Kapital* into Russian. He actually translated four chapters, the remainder of the work being undertaken by Danielson. In July 1870 Marx wrote to Engels that he had met a young Russian revolutionary called Lopatin who had recently escaped from a fortress in the Caucasus. Marx described him as "a very wide-awake fellow with a critical mind and a lively disposition who has all the stoicism of the Russian peasant".[290] In the following month Marx wrote that Lopatin was "the only 'sensible' Russian he had ever met", but that he was full of "national prejudices".[291] In September 1870 Lopatin was elected a member of the General Council of the First International[292] and he attended nine meetings between September 27 and November 22. Lopatin returned to Russia and went to Irkutsk in Siberia in the hope of organising the escape of Chernyshevsky. His attempt failed and he himself was arrested.[293] He escaped in July 1873 and succeeded in returning to England.[294] When Engels told Marx of Lopatin's arrival in London, Marx replied that Lopatin still looked upon the situation in Russia "as something unique, which is of no concern to the West".[295] A few years later, however, Marx told Engels that Lopatin had shed his jingoism.[296]

It is curious that although Lopatin knew Marx well he should have stated in a letter to a friend that he did not meet Engels until shortly after Marx's death in 1883. This is not quite correct since Lopatin had sat on the General Council of the First International on six occasions when Engels was present.[297] In his account of his meeting with Engels in 1883 he explained that their views "coincided completely". Engels told him that he did not "believe in the instant implementation of communism or anything like it" in Russia. He advised the revolutionary party in Russia "not to propagate a new socialist ideal" but to stir up "profound disturbances" and so force the czar to call an elected assembly.[298] When Lopatin returned once more to Russia he was imprisoned several times and eventually spent nine years in the fortress of Schüsselburg. He was not released until 1906. Engels praised Lopatin for rendering "great services" to the cause of revolution in Russia.[299]

Peter Lavrov[300] was one of Russia's leading sociologists and the principal philosopher of the Narodnik movement. Born in 1823 – he was three years younger than Engels – he held the rank of colonel in the army and taught mathematics for many years in the Russian college of Artillery. In the late 1850s he became more and more active in revolutionary politics and was arrested for his pains. Exiled to the Vologda region in northern Russia he made good his escape and turned up in Paris in time to see the Commune established. He actively supported the revolutionary movement in the XVIIe arrondissement. An article which he wrote on the day that the revolutionary government took office was a remarkably well-balanced appraisal of the situation[301] and the history of the events in Paris in 1871 which he wrote a few years later has been described as "one of the most informed and perceptive studies by Commune veterans".[302] In April 1871 he went to Brussels and to London on behalf of the Commune. In July he attended three meetings of the General Council of the First International by invitation.[303] In the same month Lavrov and other Russian refugees visited Marx.[304] Marx and Engels soon formed a friendship with Lavrov which lasted throughout their lives.

In 1873 Lavrov moved to Geneva, where he founded the radical journal *Vperyod* (*Forward*). He was back in London in 1874 and in January in the following year he joined Marx and Engels to attend a meeting to commemorate the Polish rising of 1863.[305] Soon after his review came to an end in 1876 Lavrov settled in Paris where he found it difficult to make ends meet. In March 1877 Marx wrote to Engels that "things are going damned badly for Lavrov"[306] and in 1885 Laura Lafargue wrote that "poor Lavrov finds it harder and harder to find remunerative work".[307] In Paris Lavrov made contact with French socialists through Marx's son-in-law Paul Lafargue. He continued to correspond regularly with Marx and Engels who sent him their books and articles and received his writings in return. In 1875 Marx sent Lavrov a copy of *Das Kapital* and the first six parts of the French edition,[308] while Lavrov sent Engels a copy of one of his articles in *Vperyod*.[309] In 1877 Lavrov praised Engels's articles in *Vorwärts* attacking Dr Dühring.[310] In 1881 Marx and Lavrov met in Paris[311] and in the following year Lavrov asked Marx and Engels to write a preface for the Russian translation of the Communist Manifesto.[312] When Marx died Lavrov wrote a tribute which Longuet read at the graveside.[313] Engels sent Lavrov the Russian books in Marx's library[314] and he kept Lavrov informed of his progress in editing the second and third volumes of *Das Kapital*.[315] It may be added that another supporter of the Narodnik movement who received regular reports from Engels on his work on *Das Kapital* was the economist N. F. Danielson – "his Russian correspondent for whom he had great respect".[316]

In one of the most important letters that Engels wrote to Lavrov, he discussed Darwin's theory of evolution. Lavrov had sent Engels a copy of an article which he had written on "Socialism and the Struggle for Existence". He had asked Engels to give his opinion on his criticism of Darwin's views. Darwin's theory of natural selection – determined by the struggle for existence – posed certain difficulties for socialists. It was not easy to apply Darwin's doctrine to human relationships since a continuous struggle for survival could hardly take place within a socialist society in which brotherly co-operation had taken the place of the sordid rivalries which characterised capitalist societies. Engels told Lavrov that he accepted Darwin's theory of evolution but that, in his view, Darwin's proof of his theory – "struggle for life, natural selection" – was only "a first, provisional, imperfect, expression of a newly discovered fact".

> "Until Darwin's time the very people who now see everywhere only *struggle* for existence . . . emphasised precisely *co-operation* in organic nature. The fact that the vegetable kingdom supplies oxygen and nutriment to the animal kingdom and that, conversely, the animal kingdom supplies plants with carbonic acid and manure was particularly stressed by Liebig. Both conceptions are justified within certain limits, but the one is as one-sided and narrow-minded as the other. The interaction of bodies in nature – inanimate as well as animate – includes both harmony and collision, struggle and co-operation."

Engels argued that Darwin's theory of the struggle for existence was "simply a transference from society to living nature of Hobbes's doctrine of 'a war of all against all', and of the bourgeois economic doctrine of competition together with Malthus's theory of population. When this conjurer's trick has been performed . . . the same theories are transferred back again from organic nature into history and it is now claimed that their validity as eternal laws of human society has been proved."

Engels held that "the essential difference between human and animal society consists in the fact that animals at most *collect*, while men *produce*. This sole but cardinal difference alone makes it impossible to transfer laws of animal societies to human societies." It was in his view ridiculous to regard Marx's doctrine of class struggles in history as similar to Darwin's theory of the struggle for existence in nature. Finally Engels criticised Lavrov for suggesting that the "war of all against all" characterised the first phase of human development. Engels, on the contrary, believed that "the social instinct was one of the most essential levers of the evolution of man from the ape".[317] Some years later Engels expanded these views in his pamphlet on *The Origin of the Family, Private Property, and the State.*

Other Russian revolutionaries known to Engels were members of the terrorist organisation *Narodnaya Volya* (People's Will) which failed to blow up a train in which Alexander II was travelling in December 1879 but succeeded in assassinating him in March 1881. The police broke up the group and some of its members fled to England. One of them – a representative of the executive committee of *Narodnaya Volya* – was Leo Hartmann,[318] who arrived in London in 1880 at the age of 30. He was welcomed by Marx[319] and by Engels, who sympathised with the "heroic nihilists".[320] Hartmann found it difficult to make a living in England and Engels complained that it was not easy to discover how Hartmann was situated owing to "his everlasting ups and downs".[321] Hartmann was a chemist with some knowledge of electricity. Engels, after consulting his friend Schorlemmer, was apparently satisfied that Hartmann was an able chemist. But he was less confident about Hartmann's abilities as a businessman. In September 1882 Engels wrote to Marx that Hartmann had patented a new type of electric battery and had sold his invention for £3,000 "to a shabby fellow under an equally shabby contract". "It is very doubtful if and when he will see his money."[322] On December 15 Engels declared that Hartmann's battery was "probably a failure for lighting", though it might perhaps work satisfactorily "to operate an electric telegraph".[323] A few days later, much to Engels's relief, Hartmann left England for the United States. Engels wrote that it was "all for the best". "I am glad that he has gone."[324]

The attitude of Marx and Engels towards the Narodnik movement – both the earlier phase of propaganda among the peasants and the later phase of terrorism – changed as time went on. Certain Narodniks, such as Lavrov, studied the works of Marx and Engels and accepted at any rate some of their theories. But they argued that Marx's doctrines were applicable only to Western Europe and not to Russia. Marx himself had clearly stated that after the collapse of feudal institutions, economic and political power must pass first into the hands of the middle classes, before the industrial proletariat, in its turn, could overthrow the bourgeoisie and establish a socialist society. The Narodniks held that Marx's theories were not relevant to Russia in the 1870s because Russia's political, social, and economic situation was quite different from that about which Marx had written in *Das Kapital*. The serfs had only recently been emancipated and Russia was still virtually a feudal society with an autocratic ruler supported by a faithful aristocracy. The middle classes were far too small to be the spearhead of a revolution.

The earliest Narodniks favoured a revolution – but it was to be a very different sort of revolution from that forecast by Marx. It would be a peasant rising – like the Peasants' War in Germany in the sixteenth century – and it would involve the transfer of land from the nobles and from the village community to the peasants. If this was socialism it was a very different sort of socialism from anything advocated by Marx and Engels. The Narodnik revolution would have led to the establishment of a new society and a new economy based upon two peculiarly Russian institutions – the *mir* and the *artel*. The *mir* was the village community which (in some parts of Russia) held land in joint-ownership and controlled the work of the peasants on their smallholdings on a communal basis. The *artels* were primitive co-operative labour organisations. Builders, fishermen and porters, for example, were men whose work was frequently organised through voluntary co-operative *artels*.

Engels rejected these arguments. In 1875 in articles on "Soziales aus Russland" in *Der Volksstaat*[325] he criticised Peter Tkachev for suggesting that "a social revolution could be started now with the greatest facility and with much less difficulty than in Western Europe". Tkachev had observed that since Russia was still a predominantly agrarian country with few modern industries, there was no capitalist organisation – no powerful bourgeoisie – to overthrow. "Our workers", declared Tkachev, "will have to fight only against the holders of *political power* – the *power of capital* is still in its early origins". Tkachev regarded the Russian peasants as "instinctive revolutionaries", who had formerly protested incessantly against serfdom and were now ready to rise at any moment to overthrow the government. Engels regarded this as wishful thinking. He asserted that the Russian peasants, far from being "instinctive revolutionaries", had never risen against the czar, "unless a false czar put himself at the helm and claimed the throne". Engels agreed that Russia stood "on the eve of revolution". But it would not be a peasant rising. The Russian revolution would be "started by the upper classes in the capital, perhaps by the government itself". Engels expected that the revolution would be "driven further by the peasants beyond the first constitutional phase". He thought that a revolution in Russia would be "of the utmost importance for all Europe, simply because it will destroy with one blow the last, until now intact, reserve of all-European reaction".[326] Nine years later Engels wrote in a postscript to this article that when the Russian revolution occurred "it would also give a new impetus to the working-class movement in the West". "It will give the workers' movement new and better opportunities for its struggle and it will therefore hasten the victory of the modern industrial proletariat. But in Russia itself the revolution cannot be expected – either through its village communities or through its capitalist institutions – to lead to the establishment of a socialist society".[327]

The third group of Russian revolutionaries with whom Engels came into contact was composed of Narodniks who eventually accepted Marx's doctrines. In 1884 Engels wrote that there had long existed in Russia revolutionaries who had shown a "sympathetic understanding of Marx's doctrines".[328] A year later he declared that he was "proud to know that there is a party among the youth of Russia which frankly and without equivocation accepts the great economic and historical theories of Marx and has decisively broken with all the anarchists and more or less Slavophil traditions of its predecessors. And Marx would have been equally proud of this had he lived a little longer. It is an advance which will be of great importance for the revolutionary development of Russia".[329]

One of these revolutionaries was Sergius Stepniak, a former army officer who had been an active leader of the workers' movement in St Petersburg in the 1870s and a dedicated terrorist. In August 1878, in broad daylight, he stabbed to death General Megentsev, the head of the Russian secret police, and thereupon left Russia for Italy. He lived in London from 1882 until his death in 1894, making his living by his pen. His books included a work on *The Russian Peasantry* and a novel entitled *Career of a Nihilist* in which the character of the hero (Andrey Kojukhov) was based upon the Russian revolutionary Andrey Jelyabov. Stepniak put in a regular appearance at May Day demonstrations.[330] He was a dedicated opponent of Russian absolutism. "No wonder," declared Kautsky, "that Engels regarded it as a privilege to be in touch with such a fighter."[331] Stepniak's wife later recalled that "one Sunday my husband and I went to Engels's with Marx's daughter Eleanor. The charming old man made a most favourable impression on me. He and my husband used to see each other and meet to talk about various political subjects".[332]

The most important group of Russian revolutionary émigrés in the 1880s were those who settled in Switzerland where they came into contact with exiled members of the German Social Democrat Party such as Bernstein. In November 1883 Bernstein wrote to Engels that "Axelrod, Plekhanov, Zasulich etc. have undertaken the task of spreading Marx's socialism among their countrymen".[333] Far from giving these new allies a warm welcome Marx accused them of deserting their posts at home. He denounced them as a "so-called party of propaganda, as opposed to the terrorists who risk their lives".[334] Eventually, however, these exiled revolutionaries played a significant *rôle* in spreading socialist ideas in Russia. In 1883 Vera Zasulich, Paul Axelrod, and Georgi Plekhanov established a party in Geneva called the Emancipation of Labour Group, which adopted a Marxist programme two years later.

Vera Zasulich – whom Peter Struve regarded as "the cleverest and subtlest woman" he had ever met[335] – had been involved in revolutionary activities since the age of sixteen. A member of the *Zemlia i Volya* movement, she was sent to prison for two years at the age of eighteen. A period of exile followed. She returned to western Russia in 1875 and resumed her career as a revolutionary agitator. In 1878 Vera Zasulich fired a shot at General Trepov, the Governor of St Petersburg, because he had ordered the flogging of a student named Bogolyubov who was in prison for taking part in a demonstration outside the Kazan Cathedral in 1876. Fortunately for her Trepov recovered. She gave herself up and was brought to trial. A sympathetic jury found her not guilty. Mackenzie Wallace, who was in the court, states that the surprising verdict was brought in partly because the jury wanted "to make a little political demonstration" and partly because the jury strongly suspected that, in flogging Bogolyubov, the prison authorities "had acted in summary fashion without observing the tedious formalities prescribed by law".[336] It may be added that after Vera Zasulich's acquittal, Trepov faced charges of peculation and was dismissed from his post. Vera Zasulich fled to Switzerland since the police intended to arrest her again.

Vera Zasulich studied the works of Marx and Engels and translated some of them in Russian. Engels congratulated her on her excellent translation of *Socialism: Utopian and Scientific*.[337] In February 1881 Vera Zasulich wrote to Marx to enquire if an underdeveloped country like Russia would have to pass through all the stages of industrialisation before its proletariat could hope to seize power. She declared that if the village commune in Russia was "fated to perish, the socialist has no alternative but to devote himself to more or less ill-founded calculations, in order to find out in how many decades the land of the Russian peasant will pass from his hands into those of the bourgeoisie, and in how many centuries capitalism will perhaps attain a development similar to that in western Europe".[338] It has been observed that "Marx's effort to reply to this question was perhaps the last vital flicker of his mind; and his several drafts of an attempt to deal with it, show the difficulty the problem gave him".[339] In the end Marx wrote quite a brief reply in which he stated that his examination of the stages of economic production in the first volume of *Das Kapital* dealt with the countries of western Europe. He explained that his analysis had not included any discussions of "the vitality of the rural community" in Russia. His subsequent researches, however, had convinced him that the village commune could be "the mainspring of Russia's social regeneration".[340]

After Marx's death Vera Zasulich asked Engels to advise her concerning works on socialist theory which she might translate into Russian. In March 1884 he replied that an abridgement of the first volume of *Das Kapital*, based perhaps upon Deville's French summary, might be "useful in a country where the book itself can be obtained only with difficulty". He went on to discuss the situation in Russia. He thought that Alexander III's reactionary régime was on the verge of collapse since the landowners and the peasants were ruined and the government was in very serious financial difficulties. Engels considered that "each month must increase the impossibility of the situation. If a constitutionally minded and hardy Grand Duke turned up, Russian 'society' itself ought to see in a palace revolution the best way out of this impasse".[341]

A year later, in another letter to Vera Zasulich, Engels gave the Russian revolutionaries some advice which was inconsistent with views that he had previously expressed. He had often declared that the days of secret societies and underground conspiracies were over and that it was no longer possible for a small dedicated group of terrorists to start a revolution with any hope of success. Now he asserted that the situation in Russia was an exceptional one and that it would be possible for the reactionary Russian autocracy to be overthrown if a handful of conspirators took action to start a revolution.

"To me the important thing is that the impulse in Russia should be given, that the revolution should break out. Whether this faction or that faction gives the signal, whether it happens under this flag or that matters little to me. If it were a palace conspiracy it would be swept away tomorrow. There – where the situation is so strained, where the revolutionary elements have accumulation to such a degree, where the economic conditions of the enormous mass of the people become daily more impossible, where every stage of social development is represented (from the primitive commune to modern large-scale industry and high finance) – and where all these contradictions are violently held in check by an unexampled despotism (a despotism which is becoming more and more unbearable to a youth in whom the dignity and intelligence of the nation are united) – there, when 1789 has once been launched, 1793 will not be long in following."[342]

In 1893 Vera Zasulich met Engels at the congress of the Second International which was held in Zürich.[343] In August 1894 Engels learned from Bebel that Vera Zasulich was being expelled from Switzerland.[344] She went to London where, according to Aveling, she was "a constant visitor at Engels's house".[345] In February 1895 Engels wrote to Plekhanov that he was concerned about Vera Zasulich's health. She had severe bronchitis. He arranged for his friend Dr Freyberger to examine her and he offered to send Plekhanov £5 to pass on to Vera Zasulich who was to be told that the money came from Plekhanov.[346] A few months later Vera Zasulich frequently visited Engels during his last illness.[347]

The leader of the Russian exiles in Switzerland in the 1880s and 1890s was Georgi Plekhanov. When Engels declared that Plekhanov was "not inferior to Lafargue or even Lassalle",[348] he did less than justice to Plekhanov's outstanding abilities as an interpreter of Marx's doctrines and as an original thinker. Aveling was nearer the truth when he described Plekhanov as "one of the most able thinkers"[349] of the socialist movement of his day.

Plekhanov was born in 1856 and entered a military school at St Petersburg at the age of seventeen. After studying there for only one term he moved to the Mining Institute. He was drawn into the revolutionary movement through his friendship with Paul Axelrod and Leo Deutsch whom he sheltered when they were hiding from the police. By 1876 Plekhanov was supporting the revolutionary cause and he was expelled from the Mining Institute for failing to attend classes regularly. He joined the *Zemlia i Volya* movement and in December 1876 he helped to organise a demonstration of students and workers in front of the Kazan Cathedral in St Petersburg. He made an inflammatory speech and the police dispersed the demonstrators. Plekhanov was now being sought by the police and, on instructions from the organisers of the *Zemlia i Volya* movement, he left Russia for Switzerland.

In Switzerland Plekhanov led a tiny group of Russian exiles – Axelrod, Deutsch, Vera Zasulich – who founded the Emancipation of Labour party in 1883. In the following year Plekhanov called upon his countrymen to organise a workers' party as soon as possible as "the only means of resolving all the economic and political contradictions of present-day Russia".[350] Plekhanov and his faithful band of associates made an intensive study of the writings of Marx and Engels and they also learned something of the achievements of the outlawed German Social Democrat Party through discussions with Bernstein and other German exiled socialists who were producing *Der Sozialdemokrat* in Zürich. When he visited Zürich early in 1884 Plekhanov made a very favourable impression upon Kautsky who wrote to Engels: "Simple, without ostentation, he is very active and he is so well read that I sometimes feel ashamed of myself." And a few years later Kautsky wrote that Plekhanov was "the most important of the younger Marxists".[351]

Plekhanov, like Vera Zasulich, translated several works of Marx and Engels into Russian. In 1882 Peter Lavrov told Marx and Engels that a new Russian translation of the Communist Manifesto had been made and that Plekhanov, the translator, was one of their "most zealous disciples".[352] Plekhanov later declared that "the reading of the Communist Manifesto constituted an epoch in my life".[353]

Plekhanov was far more than a translator and an interpreter of Marx and Engels. He made his own contributions to socialist thought. He has been described as "the author of a number of original ideas which creatively substantiated and developed certain highly important philosophical tenets of Marxism". Between 1883 when his *Socialism and the Political Struggle* appeared and 1898 when his *The Rôle of the Individual in History* was published, Plekhanov wrote numerous books, pamphlets and reviews which were "a brilliant defence, substantiation and development of Marxist theory".[354]

In the 1880s Plekhanov argued that the supporters of the revolutionary movement in Russia had been pursuing a mistaken policy. They had been convinced that the situation in Russia was entirely different from that in western Europe. They considered that Russia still had a predominantly agrarian economy and that most of her manufactured products were made by craftsmen in domestic workshops. The industrial revolution in Russia was only in its earliest phase. The Narodniks believed that once the despotism of the czar and the power of the nobles had been swept away by a successful revolution, a specifically Russian type of socialism would be established, based upon the village community and the *artel*. The Narodniks were opposed to the further development of capitalism which would, in their view, lead to the disintegration of the village community and the *artel*. Again, the Narodniks were opposed to the demand for democratic political liberties – an elected popular assembly, freedom of speech, freedom of assembly and so forth – because such reforms would benefit only the middle classes and would not be of any advantage to the workers.

Plekhanov rejected these arguments. His study of the writings of Marx and Engels had convinced him that the progress of capitalism in Russia was inevitable. The Russian economy was bound to develop in the same way as the economies of the countries of western Europe. In Russia, as in the west, the production of manufactured goods by domestic craftsmen would give way to the production of goods in factories by machines driven by steam engines. Similarly the primitive organisation of agriculture would be replaced by scientific modern methods of farming. Plekhanov argued that Marx's analysis of an advanced industrial economy in *Das Kapital* would one day be applicable to Russia. Capitalism, in his view, was an evil. But it was a necessary evil because the advent of capitalism would see the downfall of the landed aristocracy and would bring about the growth of an industrial proletariat which would, in due course, triumph over the middle classes. Plekhanov believed that the village community in Russia was doomed to extinction and that the *artels* had never played a significant *rôle* in the country's economy.

Plekhanov was expelled from Switzerland in 1889 and moved across the frontier to the Savoy district in France where he lived until 1894. He attended the first meeting of the Second International in the Salle Petrelle in Paris where he declared that "the revolutionary movement in Russia will triumph only as a revolutionary movement of the workers, or it will not triumph at all".[355] Afterwards he went to London with Axelrod and was introduced to Engels by Stepniak. Plekhanov later described his meetings with Engels as the happiest days of his life. A few years elapsed before Plekhanov ventured to write to his "greatly respected teacher" and then they corresponded until Engels's death.[356] Peter Struve has observed that by this time – the early 1890s – "the Russian social-democratic doctrine, in its main lines, had been firmly laid down in the writings of the émigré Social Democrats, namely Axelrod, Georgi Plekhanov, and Vera Zasulich. We greedily swallowed their writings, and they exercised a great influence on us". He added that the influence of Plekhanov's writings was particularly significant.[357]

In 1892 – at the time of a great famine in Russia – an attempt was made to heal the breach between the Narodniks and the Emancipation of Labour group. The initiative seems to have come from August Bebel, the leader of the German Social Democrat Party. He offered to come to London with Rusanov (representing the Narodniks) and Plekhanov (representing the Emancipation of Labour group) for a meeting and it was proposed that Engels should act as mediator. But neither Bebel nor Plekhanov arrived so that Rusanov alone discussed the problem with Engels.[358]

Plekhanov and Engels met in 1893 when Plekhanov attended the congress of the Second International at Zürich and again in the following year when he lived for a time in London after being expelled from France. On his return to Geneva he wrote to Kautsky:

"I will not find anywhere a library like the British Museum, nor anywhere will I meet a man like Friedrich Engels."[359] When Engels died, Plekhanov wrote to Kautsky: "It is needless to tell you how grieved I am. He was a great man and also an amiable man at the same time."[360]

III. The Second International[361]

The collapse of the First International may have checked but it did not halt the progress of the international labour movement. After its transfer to New York, the First International did not survive for long and the resignation of Sorge, the last secretary of its General Council, marked the end of an organisation which had for ten years embodied the socialist hopes of the brotherhood of man. Meanwhile Bakunin and his followers – ejected from the First International – held their own congress at St Imier in Switzerland. They repudiated the authority of the General Council in New York and claimed that they were the true representatives of the First International. They formed a new organisation which has been called the "Anti-Authoritarian International" because it rejected the power wielded by a single individual – Karl Marx – over the General Council of the First International. A number – though by no means all – of the leaders of this International were anarchists. At its second congress, held in Geneva in 1873, there was a lively discussion on the use of the general strike as a method of destroying the capitalist system. Like so many previous organisations with which Bakunin had been associated this "International" was "a mere handful of revolutionaries, without any following among the working classes".[362] Bakunin's powers of leadership were failing in his last years and, one by one, his disciples deserted him. Some, like Jules Guesde and Andrea Costa, became Marxists. Others, like Carlo Cafiero, remained true to their principles but transferred their allegiance to Peter Kropotkin, who came to be recognised as the new philosopher of the anarchist movement. Bakunin who had once undermined the First International lived to see his own organisation rent by disputes between the anarchists and their opponents. He died in July 1876 complaining bitterly of the ingratitude of the masses who "did not want to become impassioned for their own emancipation".[363]

In 1877 two international workers' conferences were held in Belgium. The first met at Verviers and was attended only by anarchists. It marked the end of Bakunin's "International". The second, attended by more than 40 delegates, met at Ghent in September. The organisers gave it the grandiloquent title of "World

Socialist Congress" and they hoped to revive the First International. Marx and Engels declined to attend, explaining that they
had "retired from active participation in politics".[364] Engels encouraged Wilhelm Liebknecht to go to this congress while Marx was
glad to learn that his friend Maltman Barry, a former member of
the General Council of the First International, was representing
the English workers. He regarded Maltman Barry as "our most
able and zealous party comrade" in England.[365] (Maltman Barry,
for his part, disliked Marx as a German, a Jew, and an atheist. But
he declared: "When I stood before him, listening to his words,
I forgot my idiosyncrasies and I had but one feeling – venera-
tion.")[366] At Ghent the anarchists were in a minority and resolutions were passed in favour of nationalising the means of production
and of participating in parliamentary and local elections. Marx
considered that although "the Ghent conference leaves much to be
desired in other respects, it has at least had the merit of proving
to Guillaume & Co. that they have been deserted by their former
followers".[367] Engels, too, rejoiced at the discomfiture of the anarchists, observing that they had found that "they were an insignificant
minority when brought face to face with the delegates representing
the united and unanimous large organisations of the European
workers". "Although the conference emphatically repudiated their
ridiculous doctrines and their arrogant presumption – leaving nobody
in any doubt that they were only an insignificant sect – they were
eventually treated with magnanimous tolerance. And so, after four
years of fraternal strife, complete unity of action has again been
achieved by the workers of Europe."[368]

Engels was mistaken for no unity of action was apparent in the
labour movement of the 1880s. In 1881 – as in 1877 – two rival
international conferences were held. The first was organised by the
anarchists and met in London. To the chagrin of Marx and Engels
the anarchists gained a new lease of life after Bakunin's death and
actually had the affrontery to call their organisation the "International Working Men's Association" as if they were directly
descended from the First International. They passed a resolution
that "it is absolutely necessary to exert every effort towards pro-
pagating, by deeds, the revolutionary idea and to arouse the spirit
of revolution in those sections of the popular masses who still
harbour illusions about the effectiveness of legal methods".[369] The
second congress was held at Coiré in Switzerland and it was
attended by various types of socialists. It was dominated by the
Swiss delegates. The veteran J. P. Becker, an old friend of Karl
Marx, was present. Wilhelm Liebknecht represented the German
Social Democrat Party while Malon represented the French workers.

Neither of these two conferences established a permanent workers' organisation.

Engels was opposed to any attempt to set up a new International in the 1880s. He appreciated that socialists in many lands favoured the revival of the First International. The holding of various workers' congresses – four between 1881 and 1886 – showed that the ideal of international co-operation had not been forgotten. And an occasional letter – as one from John Derbyshire of Manchester in 1883[370] – reminded Engels that the First International had not been forgotten in England. After Marx's death, Engels used his influence with socialist leaders on the Continent to pour cold water on proposals for a new workers' international. In 1886 he declared that "the International no longer has need of an organisation as such; it lives and grows by the spontaneous and ardent co-operation of the workers of Europe and America".[371] Engels even frowned upon the holding of international labour congresses. He considered them to be "unavoidable evils". He wrote to Laura Lafargue in 1889 that "people will insist on playing at congresses, and though they have their useful demonstrative side, and do good in bringing people of different countries together, it is doubtful whether the game is worth the candle when there are serious difficulties".[372]

Engels had vivid memories of his struggles against trade union leaders and anarchists when he had been a member of the General Council of the First International and had acted as corresponding secretary for Spain and Italy. In his view the rivalries between different sections of the working-class movement were still too strong to permit the formation of a new international. And Engels, of course, was determined that if a second international were established it should be run by uncompromising Marxists and should be dedicated to the class struggle and the overthrow of capitalism. In the 1880s the only socialist organisation powerful enough to take the initiative in establishing a new international was the Social Democrat Party in Germany. But this party had been banned and was an illegal body. Its leaders had their hands full with the struggle against the Anti-Socialist Law and could not be expected to devote much time to organising a new international labour association. This was another reason for delay. Engels considered that only after the disappearance of the Anti-Socialist Law would it be possible for his friends in Germany to co-operate with socialists in other countries to set up a new international workers' association.

In 1887, however, new moves were made independently by workers' organisations in Britain, Germany, and France to call an international labour congress. In England the Trade Union Congress, meeting in Swansea, proposed to convene an international congress of trade unions in 1888. In Germany the outlawed Social Democrat Party, meeting at St Gall in Switzerland, resolved to contact foreign workers' associations with a view to holding a labour conference in 1888 to discuss international action to improve working conditions in industry. In France the Possibilists proposed to celebrate the centenary of the French Revolution by holding a labour congress in Paris on July 14, 1889 (Bastille Day) to demand a universal 8-hour day in industry. This congress would coincide with the Paris industrial exhibition which was expected to attract many visitors to the French capital.

In November 1888 an international trade union conference was held in London which decided to entrust to the French Possibilists the organisation of an international labour congress in 1889.[373] In the following month the Possibilists sent out their invitations. The English Social Democratic Federation promptly accepted. Meanwhile the followers of Guesde and Lafargue had been holding workers' conferences at Bordeaux and Troyes at which it was decided to hold a rival international congress in Paris in July 1889. The attitude of the German Social Democrat Party was now of crucial importance. Although it was an illegal organisation in Germany it was the largest and best organised socialist party in Europe. No international workers' congress could hope to be regarded as successful unless it was supported by the German socialists. Despite failing eyesight,[374] Engels – who would much rather have been editing the third volume of *Das Kapital* – spent three months writing to his many socialist friends on the Continent to persuade them to support the congress organised by Guesde and Lafargue and to ignore the congress organised by Brousse and Malon.[375] At the same time – aided by Eleanor Marx and Bernstein – he attacked the English Social Democratic Federation for accepting the Possibilists' invitation and he supported the Socialist League which proposed to send delegates to Guesde's congress. He collaborated with Bernstein to write a pamphlet denouncing both the Social Democratic Federation and the French Possibilists.[376] Engels was satisfied that the pamphlet had "struck home like a thunderbolt, proving that Hyndman and Co. were liars and swindlers".[377] Engels was equally anxious to exclude from the congress both the anarchists and conservative English trade unionists such as Broadhurst and Shipton. Eventually Engels convinced Liebknecht and Bebel that they should support Guesde and Lafargue and ignore Brousse and Malon. In his view this ensured the success of the "Marxist" congress and the failure of the Possibilist congress. Paul Lafargue appreciated the services which

Engels had rendered to the Marxist cause. "It is you who have saved the congress," he wrote, "as, but for you, Bebel and Lieb-knecht would have left us in the lurch".[378]

In May 1889 Engels complained to Sorge that "the writing and running about in connection with the damned congress leave me hardly any time for anything else. It's the devil of a nuisance – nothing but misunderstandings, squabbles, and vexation on all sides, and nothing will come of the whole thing in the end".[379] But something did come of "the whole thing", though it was not quite what Engels had planned. By June Engels was more hopeful. He told Sorge that he had felt compelled to return to active politics – he had put his "shoulders to the wheel" – because he was fighting all over again "the old battle of The Hague" when he and Marx had secured the expulsion of Bakunin from the First International. "The adversaries are the same," he declared, "with the anarchist flag merely exchanged for the Possibilist one. The selling of principles to the bourgeoisie for small-scale concessions, especially in return for well-paid jobs for the leaders (city council, labour exchange etc.), and the tactics are exactly the same". Engels went on to explain that "the alliance of the Possibilists and the Social Democratic Federation was to constitute the nucleus of the new International that was to be founded in Paris". But he was satisfied that "the intriguers are beaten already, and the significance of the congress – whether it draws the other one over to its side or not – lies in the fact that the concord of the socialist parties of Europe is demonstrated to all the world, with the few sectarian representatives left out in the cold unless they submit".[380]

In March 1889 Wilhelm Liebknecht had protested that there would be an "enormous scandal" if two rival congresses were held in July in the same city. But two socialist congresses were held in the same week – July 14 to July 20, 1889 – in two halls in Paris. The meeting organised by Guesde and Lafargue met at the Salle Petrelle while the conference organised by Brousse and Malon met in the rue de Lancry. The Possibilists had boycotted a preliminary meeting at The Hague in February and now – though they were ignored by the powerful German Social Democrat Party – they insisted upon holding their own congress. Their only foreign allies were the English Social Democratic Federation and some Belgian socialists. The Possibilist congress was a predominantly French conference, representing mainly trade unions and working men's social and educational clubs. Only 91 foreign delegates attended compared with 521 French representatives. The congress organised by Guesde and Lafargue, on the other hand, had 391 delegates and was supported by the main socialist parties on the Continent and by the

English Socialist League. It was attended by many leading socialists such as Liebknecht, Bebel, Bernstein, Adler, Clara Zetkin, Guesde, Lafargue, Longuet, Niewenhuis, César de Paepe, Eleanor Marx and Aveling. Laura Lafargue suggested that Engels should come to the congress. He replied that "there are two things which I avoid visiting on principle, and only go to on compulsion: congresses and exhibitions".[381] At the same time he told Sorge: "I am not going there, of course: I can't plunge into agitation over and over again."[382]

The rival congresses were still in session when Engels confidently asserted that the Marxist conference was "a brilliant success". So many delegates had arrived that it was necessary to move from the Salle Petrelle to the Salle des Fantaisies Parisiennes in the rue Rochechouart. Engels wrote that "the intrigues of the Possibilists and the Social Democratic Federation to obtain the position of leadership in France and England by stealth have miscarried completely and their pretensions to international leadership even more so".[383] Immediately after the congress Lafargue wrote to Engels that "the most genuine fraternity prevailed at our congress. The Possibilists are thoroughly demoralised; at the last session they had but 58 people, including delegates". "I fancy that Brousse is not very eager to take part in another international congress."[384]

The congresses of July 1889 had not been an unqualified success from Engels's point of view, since the public squabbles between rival socialists were a far from edifying spectacle. Thus at the final session of the Possibilist congress Allemane had accused Bebel and Liebknecht of being Bismarck's tools. Yet Engels's optimism was not without some justification since later events proved the Marxist congress to have been the inaugural meeting of the Second International which played so important a *rôle* in the socialist movement in the next 25 years. Although no permanent organisation was established in 1889 this meeting was the first of a series of international socialist congresses which eventually grew into the Second International.

There were two aspects of the "Marxist congress" in Paris which gave Engels particular satisfaction. First, the delegates clearly believed that they were carrying on the work of the First International. Wilhelm Liebknecht told them that the First International had now "taken new shape in the mighty organisations of the workers of each country. It lives in us today. This congress here is the work of the International Working Men's Association".[385] Secondly, the congress decided that the delegates would organise demonstrations in their respective countries in favour of the eight-hour day on May 1, 1890 – a date already proposed by the American Federation of Labour. Engels considered that a world wide agitation – organised by socialists – to secure the eight-hour day would help to promote a feeling of international solidarity among the workers. The demonstrations held on May 1, 1890 – in England on the first Sunday in May – were so successful that the Second International at its second congress (held in Brussels in 1891) decided that May Day should be celebrated by the workers every year. Engels regarded May Day demonstrations as symbolic gestures of great importance and he attended May Day celebrations in London.[386] On May 1, 1890 he wrote:

> "Today . . . the proletariat of Europe and America is reviewing its forces, mobilized for the first time as a united army under one flag and for one purpose – the legal recognition of an eight hours working day – already recommended at the Geneva Congress of the International Association in 1866, and again at the Paris Labour Congress in 1889. Today's drama will bring conclusively to the notice of all the capitalists and landlords in all countries that the proletarians of all lands are really united. If only Marx were by my side to see it all with his own eyes!"[387]

But three years later he was less enthusiastic. On May 17, 1893 he wrote to Sorge:

> "The May First demonstration here was very nice; but it is already becoming somewhat of an everyday or rather an annual matter; the first fresh bloom has gone. The narrow mindedness of the Trades Council and of the Socialist sects – Fabians and the S(ocial) D(emocratic) F(ederation) – again compelled us to hold two demonstrations, but everything went off as we desired and we – the Eight Hours Committee – had many more people than the united opposition. In particular our international platform had a very good audience. . . ."[388]

The Second International might claim to carry on the traditions of the First International but there were significant differences between these two working men's associations. The First International had a varied membership – individual members, socialist societies, trade unions and other associations of workers. The Second International was a federation of national socialist parties. Other labour organisations, such as trade unions and co-operative societies, established international congresses of their own at which workers holding different political views could meet to discuss common problems. An international miners' congress was held at Jolimont in 1890 and an international textile workers congress met in Manchester in 1894. Since the Second International united socialist parties it was inevitable that the German Social Democrat

Party should play a predominant *rôle* in its affairs. It has been observed that "Engels's desire to impress the Marxist stamp" on the new International "shifted international leadership to the German Social Democrats".[389] The Second International was a larger organisation than the First International and was supported by socialists from a large number of countries. In 1869 the Basel congress of the First International had been attended by 80 delegates from nine countries but in 1893 the Zürich congress of the Second International was attended by 411 delegates from 20 countries.

Engels received a great ovation in Zürich when – on what proved to be his last visit to the Continent – he addressed the final session of the Congress of the Second International. He had been elected Honorary Chairman for the occasion and he made the following brief speech to the delegates:

"I accept the enthusiastic welcome you have given me, not in my personal capacity, but as the collaborator of the great man whose portrait you have here. It is just 50 years since Marx and I came into the movement. We were then writing our articles in the *Deutsch-Französische Jahrbücher*. Marx is dead, but, were he still alive, there would be no one – either in Europe or in America – who could look back on his life's work with so much justifiable pride. In 1872 the last congress of the International was held. It did two things: the first was to separate once and for all the cause of the International from that of the anarchists. Today it can be seen whether or not that decision was superfluous. The congresses of Paris, of Brussels, and now this one in Zürich, have had to do the same thing.

"The second resolution that it adopted was to stop the activities of the International in their previous form. That was the epoch when reaction, drunk with the blood of the glorious Commune, was at its apogee. To continue the former International would have been to demand sacrifices no longer in proportion to the results obtainable. The Congress decided to make its headquarters in America – that is to say, the International vanished from the scene.

"To the proletariat of each country was left the responsibility of organising itself in its own way. And that is what happened and today the International is stronger than in the past. It is in this spirit that we must go forward and work on common ground. We must abandon argument to avoid turning into sects, but our common principle must be preserved. This free union, this voluntary assembly, brought about by the congresses, will be enough to give us victory, and a victory that no power on earth could take from us.

"I have just been travelling through Germany and everywhere I heard our comrades complaining about the end of the Anti-Socialist Law. It was, they say, far more fun fighting the police. No police, no government could ever get the better of fights like that.

With these words I declare the congress closed: 'Long live the international proletariat!' "[390]

On leaving Zürich Engels went to Vienna and Berlin where he received an enthusiastic welcome from Austrian and German socialists. His journey – his first visit to Germany since 1876 – was a triumphal progress, and it marked the climax of Engels's career as a socialist writer and agitator.

IV. Conclusion

Death of Engels, 1895

Engels had a robust constitution and was seldom ill in his youth. When he was in Manchester there was a period of three years which he suffered from glandular fever in 1857, from piles in 1858 and from a nervous breakdown in 1860. This left him "incapable of taking a single necessary decision".[391] In about 1867 he was thrown from his horse and subsequently suffered from a hernia and had to wear a truss.[392] But he enjoyed reasonably good health in the 1860s and 1870s while several of his socialist colleagues were less fortunate. Marx was rarely free from illness; Georg Weerth died at the age of 34; Wilhelm Wolff at 55; Carl Schorlemmer at 58; and Borkheim at 60. Engels, however, was still active when he was in his sixties and seventies. Bernstein, who met him shortly after his sixtieth birthday, was surprised at his physical fitness and mental vigour.[393] When Engels was seventy, Eleanor Marx wrote: "He is vigorous in body and mind. He carries his six foot odd so lightly that one would not think he is so tall. . . . He is really the youngest man I know. As far as I can remember he has not grown any older in the last twenty hard years."[394] Engels's 70th birthday was celebrated by a party attended by Bebel, Liebknecht, Singer and four delegates from the German Workers' Educational Society – "one of whom speechless drunk". Engels wrote to Laura Lafargue: "We kept it up till half past three in the morning and drank, besides, claret, 16 bottles of champagne – in the morning we had 12 dozen oysters. So you see I did my best to show that I was still alive and kicking."[395]

In the autumn of 1883 Engels had been confined to bed for eight weeks with muscular rheumatism. When he was allowed up again he wrote to Laura Lafargue: "Although I feel considerably better, and keep in bed more for safety's sake than anything else, I am still far from able to use my legs as I ought to."[396] Six months later, in June 1884, the trouble recurred[397] and he had to engage a secretary.[398] And from about 1880 onwards, Engels had trouble with his eyes.[399] In August 1888 he was suffering from chronic conjunctivitis[400] and he could not write for more than two hours a day.[401] When he returned from a two months' holiday in America, however, he told Danielson that his eyesight had improved.[402] Early in 1892 Engels wrote to Sorge that he felt "healthier and stronger than five or six years ago".[403]

That Engels was so fit at the age of 71 was partly due to the care with which his womenfolk had looked after him. When Karl Marx died his housekeeper Helene Demuth moved into Engels's household. On her death in November 1890 Engels declared that her devotion had made it possible for him to work in peace for seven years.[404] To his friend Sorge he wrote:

"Today I have mournful tidings for you. My good faithful, dear Lenchen passed away quietly yesterday afternoon, after a brief and, for the most part, painful illness. We had lived seven happy years together in this house. We were the last two of the old pre-1848 old guard. Now I am alone again. If Marx for many years and I for the last seven years, found the quiet required for work, it was largely her doing. I do not know what will become of me now. And I shall sadly miss her tactful advice on party affairs...."[405]

Helene's place was taken by Louise Kautsky who had divorced Karl Kautsky in 1888. In December 1890 Engels wrote: "We get on capitally. She superintends the house and does my secretary's work which saves my eyes and enables me to make it worth her while to give up her profession[406] at least for the present."[407] Early in 1894 Louise Kautsky married Dr Ludwig Freyberger. He joined Engels's household, so that Engels now had a medical man on the spot to attend to him.[408] In November 1894 Engels moved from No. 122 to No. 41 Regent's Park Road.

In the summer of 1892 Engels's health deteriorated and he was confined to his armchair for six weeks.[409] He wrote to Adler that for some years there had been a recurrence of the trouble that had originally been caused by his riding accident in Manchester.[410] In May 1894 Engels wrote to Sorge:

"I had a cold during the past few days which convinces me that I am an old man at last. What I used to treat as a trifle laid me rather low for a week and kept me for fully two weeks more under medical-police supervision. Even now I am supposed to be careful for another two weeks. It was a mild bronchitis, and among the elderly this can never be taken lightly, particularly when they have tippled as freely and merrily as I have."[411]

But the old man was not finished yet. In 1893 and 1894 he was as active as ever. His articles on the urgent need for the Great Powers to halt the armaments race appeared in March 1893[412] and in the autumn he travelled for two months on the Continent and attended the congress of the Second International at Zürich. In 1894 he at last completed his work on preparing the third volume of *Das Kapital* for publication – his introduction was dated October 4 – and at the same time he contributed several articles to *Die Neue Zeit* on the history of early Christianity[413] and on the peasant question in France and Germany.[414] Early in 1895 Engels wrote an appendix to the third volume of *Das Kapital* and an introduction to a new edition of Marx's articles on the class struggles in France between 1848 and 1850.[415] In March 1895 Engels wrote to Laura Lafargue: "I am taking up Vol. 4 of the *Capital* and correcting the parts already copied out by K(arl) K(autsky) and shall then arrange with Tussy (Eleanor Marx) about her continuing the work."[416]

In May 1895 Engels told Kautsky that he had a painful swelling in his neck which had given him sleepless nights for a fortnight.[417] He had cancer of the throat. In June Dr Freyberger sent him to Eastbourne. He was accompanied by Laura Lafargue. On June 18 he wrote to Bernstein:

"I feel stronger, eat better and have an improved appetite. People say that I am looking better. So in general there is an improvement. On the other hand the illness is taking its course. I have a larger swelling, more pain and I find that it is more difficult to get some sleep. The illness is in a more acute stage and not so passive as it was in London. But that is quite normal."[418]

But a month later Dr Freyberger became seriously concerned for the patient. On July 21 Samuel Moore wrote to Eleanor Marx that he had been to Victoria Station to meet Dr Freyberger who was returning from Eastbourne after visiting Engels. Dr Freyberger warned Samuel Moore to expect the worst. "He says," wrote Samuel Moore, "that the disease has attained such a hold that, considering the General's age, his state is precarious. Apart from the diseased glands of the neck, there is danger either from weakness of the heart or from pneumonia – and in either of these two cases the end would be sudden. . . . In spite of all, however, the General is quite hopeful and is certain that he will recover, and has arranged with the two doctors to return to London."[419] Two days later Engels wrote to Laura Lafargue that he was going back to Regent's Park Road. Meanwhile Victor Adler – warned by Dr Freyberger that Engels had not long to live – travelled to Eastbourne from Austria to see his friend for the last time.[420]

By August it was clear that there could be no hope of a recovery. Towards the end Engels could not speak and communicated by writing messages on a slate. His last days were clouded by a distressing scene with Eleanor Marx. She had been led to believe that Engels was the father of Helene Demuth's illegitimate son Frederick. Shortly before his death Engels twice assured Samuel Moore that there was no truth in the story. Eleanor refused to accept the fact that Frederick Demuth was not Engels's son but the son of her own father. She was at Engels's bedside on the day before he died and questioned him about Frederick Demuth's parentage. Engels "wrote on his slate that Marx was Frederick Demuth's father". Louise Freyberger told August Bebel that "Tussy broke down when she left the room. . . . She wept bitterly on my shoulder."[421]

Engels died at 10.30 p.m. on Monday, August 5, 1895. Eleanor Marx wrote that "he had suffered much, but the end came quietly and peacefully. The loss not only to us but to the whole socialist world is beyond all words."[422] Engels had directed that his funeral should be a private one and that only his friends should attend. The funeral took place on the afternoon of Saturday, August 10 and was a purely secular affair. Engels's socialist friends – leaders of socialist parties in many countries – flocked to London to pay their tribute to Marx's lifelong ally and the veteran leader of the international socialist movement. The mourners included Samuel Moore, Friedrich Lessner, Harry Quelch, Will Thorne, Edward Aveling, August Bebel, Wilhelm Liebknecht, Eduard Bernstein, Paul Singer, Vera Zasulich and Stepniak. Engels's family was represented by his brother Hermann and by several nephews. Some 80 mourners gathered in the austere surroundings of the private station (Waterloo) of the Necropolis and National Mausoleum Company before proceeding by a special hearse train to Woking for the cremation. There were speeches by Samuel Moore, Liebknecht, Bebel, Paul Lafargue and Gustav Adolf Schlechtendahl (one of the nephews).[423] Bebel also addressed a meeting organised by the German Workers' Educational Association to honour Engels's memory.[424] In accordance with Engels's wishes his ashes were scattered in the sea off Beachy Head.

When Engels died he was worth nearly £30,000. On leaving the firm of Ermen and Engels in 1869 he had invested his money wisely and had lived in comfort in retirement for 26 years. In his will, dated July 29, 1893,[425] Engels appointed Samuel Moore, Bernstein, and Louise Kautsky (Freyberger) as his executors. Each executor was to receive £250 and Louise Freyberger was also left Engels's furniture. Engels's only bequest to a member of his family was an oil painting of his father which was left to his brother Hermann. Engels bequeathed £1,000 to Bebel and Paul Singer which was to be used to defray the election expenses of such socialist candidates for the German Reichstag as they might select. In a letter to Bebel and Singer, dated November 14, 1894 Engels had informed them of this legacy. He had written to them: "Above all see to it that you get the money and do not let it fall into the hands of the Prussians."[426] The sum of £3,000 had been left to Ellen Rosher (Pumps) under Engels's will. But in a codicil, dated July 26, 1895, Engels had revoked this bequest and had left his niece £2,230.[427]

The residue of Engels's estate (about £24,000)[428] was to be divided into eight equal parts. Three of these (£9,000) were bequeathed to each of Marx's surviving daughters – Laura and Eleanor – and two parts (£6,000) to Louise Freyberger. Much of Eleanor's share of Engels's estate quickly found its way into Aveling's pockets. Legal difficulties had prevented Engels from making any provision for the children of Marx's other daughter Jenny, who had died in 1883. In a letter to Laura and Eleanor (November 14, 1894) Engels had asked each of them to hold one third of their legacies (£3,000) in trust for Jenny's children.[429] This meant that Engels had divided the residue of his estate into four equal parts – one each to Laura Lafargue, Eleanor Marx, Louise Freyberger and Jenny Longuet's children. Louise Freyberger had been treated generously. She received as much money as Marx's daughters. In addition she received £250 as an executor and she also inherited Engels's furniture.[430]

August Bebel and Paul Singer, on behalf of the German Social Democrat Party, received Engels's library (including Marx's books), the copyright of his books and all the letters in his possession except the "family letters of Karl Marx".[431] Engels directed that "all manuscripts of a literary nature in the handwriting of my deceased friend Karl Marx and all family letters written by or addressed to him which shall be in my possession or control at the time of my death shall be given by my executors to Eleanor Marx. . . ." So while Engels's library – and the books formerly belonging to Marx which had been in his possession since 1883 – were kept together, the manuscripts were divided. Those in Marx's handwriting as well as Marx's "family letters" were given to Eleanor Marx, while the rest were left to Bebel and Bernstein.[432] Laura Lafargue complained that as Marx's eldest daughter she should have received her father's manuscripts, while Karl Kautsky complained that he – and not Bebel – should have been associated with Bernstein in having control over Engels's manuscripts.

Historians have had reason to regret the fact that in his will Engels should have provided for the splitting up of the Marx–Engels "Party archives" – a unique collection of documents from which the development of the socialist movement could be traced from the 1840s to 1895. The drawback of dividing the material soon became apparent. After Engels's death Eleanor Marx published the articles on the revolution in Germany in 1848–9 (*Revolution and Counter-Revolution*) which Engels had contributed to the *New York Daily Tribune* in 1851–2. They appeared under Marx's name. If Eleanor Marx had been able to examine the correspondence between her father and Engels she would not have made this mistake. But these letters were now in Bernstein's possession.[433]

The provisions of Engels's will concerning his own manuscripts and those of Marx were not in accordance with his earlier plans. The year before he died he told Laura Lafargue that in 1889 he had decided that "it would be useful to have one or two intelligent men of the younger generation broken in to read Mohr's handwriting". "I thought of Kautsky and Bernstein."[434] On January 28, 1889 Engels had written to Kautsky offering to teach him to decipher Marx's handwriting and to pay him £50 per annum expenses for two years to make a fair copy of the manuscript – about 750 pages – of the fourth volume of *Das Kapital*.[435] Kautsky declined Engels's offer of financial assistance but agreed to make the fair copy. But when Engels drew up his will in 1893 he did not appoint Kautsky one of his literary executors. He left the manuscripts in Marx's handwriting to Marx's daughters and his own manuscripts to Bebel and Bernstein. The reason why Engels changed his mind was because Kautsky did not complete the task of producing a fair copy of Volume 4 of *Das Kapital*. According to Engels he deciphered only "perhaps $\frac{1}{8}$ to $\frac{1}{6}$ of the whole". In a letter to Laura Lafargue of December 17, 1894 Engels made it clear that he had given up hope of persuading Kautsky to resume work on Volume 4 of *Das Kapital*. He also doubted whether Bernstein who "suffers from overwork" would be able to render much assistance.[436] A few days later Engels wrote that he would help Eleanor Marx "if she will undertake the work of writing out the original manuscript".[437]

Karl Kautsky was disappointed when he learned of the provisions of Engels's will concerning the disposal of the Marx–Engels manuscripts. He considered that he should have been entrusted with the task of editing Marx's manuscripts. Eleanor Marx did not feel able to shoulder the burden of preparing her father's manuscripts for publication. She edited some of the articles written by Marx and Engels in the 1850s but she asked Kautsky to resume his labours on the manuscript of the fourth volume of *Das Kapital*. When Eleanor Marx died in 1898 her sister Laura also encouraged Kautsky to edit this manuscript. What had originally been planned as the concluding volume of *Das Kapital* eventually appeared between 1905 and 1910 in three parts as a separate book entitled *Theorien über den Mehrwert*. Over twenty years had elapsed since Engels had first asked Kautsky to make a fair copy of Karl Marx's manuscript on the history of surplus value.

Engels's Successors

The leader of the orchestra had made his final appearance. Engels had hoped to see the twentieth century[438] but this was not to be. His death left a gap in the ranks of the socialist leaders and thinkers that could not easily be filled. Engels had promoted the socialist cause in various ways since 1883. Until the establishment of the Second International he had acted as a personal link between leaders of socialist parties all over the Continent. His lifelong connection with the socialist movement, his experience as corresponding secretary for Italy and Spain at the time of the First International, and his numerous contacts with socialists in many countries stood him in good stead. An accomplished linguist, he corresponded with socialists in several languages. Once the Second International had been established it gradually set up administrative machinery by which Engels could be relieved of the routine correspondence involved in keeping socialist leaders in touch with each other.

Engels had also filled admirably the *rôle* of an elder statesman who had placed his long experience of revolutionary politics at the disposal of the various socialist parties in Europe. His detailed knowledge of the history and politics of different countries enabled him to give sound advice not only to the powerful German Social Democrat Party but also to smaller parties in France and Italy and Austria which were still in a relatively early stage of development.[439] After Engels's death no one could assume the mantle of a veteran revolutionary campaigner whose long experience gave him the right to offer advice to a new generation of socialist leaders.

But Engels's outstanding contribution to the socialist cause after 1883 had been made as the acknowledged interpreter of Marx's doctrines. As Marx's closest friend and collaborator – who was devoting much of his time to editing the second and third volumes of *Das Kapital* – he could claim to know exactly what Marx had taught. Earnest young socialists who put their queries to Engels about surplus value or historical materialism could be confident that they would be given the right answer. In addition Engels carried on Marx's work by using his doctrines to assess economic and political changes that had occurred since Marx's death. Thus he wrote on the significance of trusts and cartels, the industrialisation of formerly underdeveloped countries such as Russia, and the exploitation of new regions in Africa and Asia by the capitalists of the West. And shortly before his death, Engels had returned to his study of history on Marxist lines by writing on the early history of Christianity.

In September 1895 Ignaz Auer wrote to Victor Adler deploring the grievous loss that the socialist movement had sustained through the loss of Engels's "experience and authority". "For the time being we shall have to manage without a 'fountain-head of wisdom' and we shall sometimes find this to be very inconvenient."[440] Auer considered that none of the younger socialists who were regarded as authorities on Marx's doctrines – Kautsky, Bernstein and Plekhanov – were men of sufficient stature to step into Engels's shoes.

At one time Engels had hoped that Bernstein[441] and Kautsky[442] would succeed him as interpreters of Marx's doctrines. He knew them both well. They had made a thorough study of the works of Marx and Engels. They were both experienced journalists who had served the socialist cause as editors of *Der Sozialdemokrat* and *Die Neue Zeit*. But eventually Engels had come to doubt whether they could fulfil the *rôle* that he had designed for them. He was alarmed at Bernstein's "comical respect for the Fabians"[443] and he thought that Bernstein's neurotic tendencies were being aggravated by overwork.[444] And Kautsky fell into Engels's bad books when he failed to keep his promise to make a fair copy of Marx's manuscript on the history of the doctrine of surplus value. In 1895 Engels was displeased with both Bernstein and Kautsky when he learned that they were planning to write a history of socialism without seeking his advice or collaboration. In his final letter to Kautsky, written during his last illness, he sharply rebuked him for his conduct.[445]

Engels could not have foreseen that soon after his death, Bernstein and Kautsky would be engaged in a bitter ideological controversy which would split the socialist movement on the Continent. In a series of articles in *Die Neue Zeit*, Bernstein declared that the time had come to revise the programme of the German Social Democrat Party. He argued that the statistical evidence provided by the Prussian industrial census of 1895 had shown conclusively that Marx had been mistaken in supposing that the continued expansion of capitalism would lead to a concentration of wealth in fewer and fewer hands and to the pauperisation of the masses. On the contrary the number of capitalists was increasing (not declining) and the condition of the workers in industrialised countries was getting better (not worse). "Instead of becoming

polarised into two opposed classes, the few extremely rich and the
multitude of poor, society was in fact more complex than before,
with an extended scale of social gradations. Middle income groups,
instead of disappearing, had grown both absolutely and relatively."[446] Bernstein also argued that Marx's forecast of a cycle of
economic crises, culminating in a revolution, had not materialised.
He suggested that, in the circumstances, the Social Democrat Party
in Germany should no longer aim at replacing capitalism by
socialism immediately by means of a revolution. Socialists in
Germany and elsewhere should work for "the peaceful transition
from capitalism to socialism" and their representatives in parliament should try to secure reforms to benefit the workers. Bernstein
asserted that a communist society was a utopian dream attainable
only in the distant future, while practical reforms – such as factory
legislation and the nationalisation of public utilities and key industries – might be achieved within a few years.[447] These arguments were very similar to those advanced nearly twenty years
before in the "three-star" article in Dr Höchberg's *Jahrbuch*
which Engels had severely criticised.

Kautsky, on the other hand, would have none of this.[448] He
argued that the increase in the number of cartels in Germany and
trusts in the United States showed that Marx had been right in
predicting that there would be an ever-greater concentration of
industry in fewer hands. He considered that Engels had given a
perfectly satisfactory explanation of the delay in the appearance of
the economic crises which – in Marx's view – would herald the
downfall of capitalism and the dawn of an era of socialism. Karl
Kautsky declared that Bernstein had not invented "revisionism"
but had taken over the ideas of Sidney Webb in England and
Jaurès in France. In these countries the existence of long established
parliamentary institutions made it possible to envisage an orderly
and gradual progress towards socialism. But in Germany, where
democracy had by no means advanced as far as in France and in
England, Bernstein's "revisionism" would not be the right policy
for the Social Democrats to pursue. And, as Bebel observed, it was
significant that "revisionism" was more popular in south Germany
than in Prussia. The south German states had more liberal traditions than Prussia. While the Kaiser denounced the socialists as "a
crew of upstarts without a fatherland", the King of Bavaria was
quite prepared to shake hands with Vollmar.

While Bernstein's ideas might be acceptable in countries with
liberal constitutions, they had no hope of success among socialists
who lived under a despotic régime such as that of the Romanovs
in Russia. In such a country a gradual progress towards social and

political reform seemed to be out of the question. It is not surprising that Plekhanov and Lenin were among the foremost
opponents of "revisionism". Lenin declared that the controversy
between Bernstein and Kautsky "resulted in as fruitful a revival
of theoretical thought in international socialism as did Engels's
controversy with Dühring twenty years earlier". Lenin asserted
that Bernstein and his friends had made the mistake of persistently
painting a "rose-coloured picture of modern small-scale production". They were guilty of making "superficial generalisations based
on facts selected one-sidedly and without reference to the system
as a whole". Lenin considered that "the position of revisionism
was even worse as regards the theory of crises and the theory of
collapse. Only for a very short time could people – and then only
the most short-sighted – think of refashioning the foundations of
Marx's theory under the influence of a few years of industrial
boom and prosperity. Realities very soon made it clear to the
revisionists that crises were not a thing of the past: prosperity was
followed by a crisis." In 1908 Lenin was confident – as Marx and
Engels had been confident so often before him – that capitalism
was "heading for a breakdown" and that Marx's predictions would
soon come true.[449]

If Kautsky could be regarded as "the principal Marxian
theoretician" after Engels's death, it was because he edited Marx's
manuscripts on the history of surplus value and not because he
made any new contributions to socialist thought. The task of
interpreting the economic and political changes that occurred
between 1895 and 1914 in accordance with Marx's doctrines was
shouldered by socialists whom Engels had never met. (Lenin had
visited Paul and Laura Lafargue in Paris in 1895 but he realised
that there was no point in going to London to see Engels who
was too ill to receive him.) But those who attempted to interpret
a new age on Marxian lines acknowledged their indebtedness to
Engels. Lenin, for example, revered Engels as "the most noteworthy scholar and teacher of the modern proletariat in all the
civilised world".[450]

Two works which would have gained Engels's approval were
Rosa Luxemburg's *The Accumulation of Capital. A Contribution
to the Economic Explanation of Imperialism* (1913)[451] – "her best
known and most important book"[452] – and Lenin's *Imperialism,
the Highest Stage of Capitalism* (1916).[453] The authors examined
various aspects of capitalism on the eve of the first World War
in the light of Marx's doctrines. Both regarded their books as a
continuation of the researches of Marx and Engels on capitalism
and imperialism.

Rosa Luxemburg examined Marx's discussion of the accumulation of capital in the second volume of *Das Kapital*. She observed that Marx had constructed a model for the maintenance of a constant stock of capital but that he had left only notes of an incomplete model for stock of capital that was not merely being maintained but was expanding. She tried to complete the unfinished model. Her main thesis was that the accumulation of capital – essential for the maintenance and expansion of the capitalist system – was the extension of capitalism to underdeveloped countries. She argued that capitalists were flooding primitive economies with cheap mass-produced consumption goods, thereby ruining local native craft industries. This had happened in India in the nineteenth century and was now taking place in many parts of Africa and Asia. In this way the capitalists in the advanced industrial countries – having saturated their markets at home – could expand their output of manufactured products by opening up new markets overseas. These arguments – foreshadowed by the attacks of Marx and Engels on the colonial ambitions of the Great Powers in the nineteenth century[454] – were illustrated by a wealth of detail from the recent history of the exploitation of underdeveloped regions by advanced industrial countries.[455]

In his essay on imperialism Lenin came to much the same conclusions as those reached by Rosa Luxemburg a few years before. He discussed two changes in the capitalist system to which Engels had already drawn attention in the early 1890s. They were, first, the rise of huge combines which monopolised the production of particular goods and commodities in the major industrial countries and, secondly, the extension of capitalism to the hitherto underdeveloped regions of the world. Lenin considered that by 1914 capitalism had reached a new phase which Marx had not described – since it did not exist in his day – but which Marx and Engels had foreseen. Imperialism, in Lenin's view, was the characteristic feature of this stage in the development of capitalism. Lenin, like Marx and Engels, believed that capitalism carried within itself the seeds of its own decay. When he republished his pamphlet in 1920 Lenin declared that "the parasitism and decay of capitalism . . . are characteristic of its highest stage of development, i.e. imperialism" and that "a handful . . . of exceptionally rich and powerful states . . . plunder the whole world simply by 'clipping coupons'."[456] These sentiments faithfully echoed the views that Engels had expressed on combines, on monopolies, and on imperialism. And they were expressed by the greatest of his disciples, the leader of the great revolution that Engels had not lived to see.

NOTES

1   F. Engels to J. P. Becker, October 15, 1884 in H. Hirsch (ed.), *Friedrich Engels: Profile* (1970), p. 270 and Eleanor Marx in *Reminiscences of Marx and Engels* (Foreign Languages Publishing House, Moscow), p. 188.

2   V. Adler to F. Engels, December 29, 1891 in *Victor Adlers Aufsätze, Reden und Briefe*, Heft 1: *Victor Adler und Friedrich Engels* (1922), p. 31.

3   E. Bottigelli in *F. Engels – Paul and Laura Lafargue: Correspondence*, Vol. 3, p. 495.

4   Antonio Labriola to Victor Adler, August 16, 1895 in *Annali Feltrinelli*, Vol. 5, 1962, p. 472.

5   Eleanor Marx in *Reminiscences of Marx and Engels* (Foreign Languages Publishing House, Moscow), p. 187.

6   August Bebel to F. Engels, March 17, 1883 in Werner Blumenberg (ed.), *August Bebels Briefwechsel mit Friedrich Engels* (1965), p. 151.

7   F. Engels, "Der Sozialismus in Deutschland" in *Die Neue Zeit*, July 1892.

8   F. Engels to August Bebel, April 30, 1883 in Werner Blumenberg (ed.), *August Bebels Briefwechsel mit Friedrich Engels* (1965), p. 152.

9   Engels's introduction to Karl Marx, *Das Kapital*, Vol. 2, 1885 (new edition, 1957), p. 6.

10   Paul Lafargue, "Reminiscences of Engels" in *Reminiscences of Marx and Engels* (Foreign Languages Publishing House, Moscow), p. 91. The unfinished manuscript was subsequently published under the title: *Dialectics of Nature* (Progress Publishers, Moscow, 1964). See also B. Kedrow, *Über Engels' Werk "Dialektik der Natur"* (1954).

11   F. Engels to F. A. Sorge, June 29, 1883 in Karl Marx and F. Engels, *Letters to Americans, 1848–95* (1963), pp. 140–1.

12   F. Engels to August Bebel, August 30, 1883 in Werner Blumenberg (ed.), *August Bebels Briefwechsel mit Friedrich Engels* (1965), p. 164.

13   Gabriel Deville, *Le Capital de Karl Marx . . .* (1883). An English edition appeared in 1905.

14   Karl Marx to F. Engels, July 6, 1863 in *Gesamtausgabe*, Part III, Vol. 3, pp. 148–52.

15   Karl Marx to F. Engels, August 24, 1867 in *Gesamtausgabe*, Part III, Vol. 3, pp. 409–11.

16   Karl Marx to N. F. Danielson, April 10, 1879 in Karl Marx and F. Engels, *Briefe über "Das Kapital"* (1954), p. 241.

17   F. Engels to Karl Kautsky, June 21, 1884 in Benedikt Kautsky (ed.), *Friedrich Engels' Briefwechsel mit Karl Kautsky* (1955), pp. 122–3.

18   F. Engels to Karl Kautsky, June 21, 1884 in Benedikt Kautsky (ed.), *Friedrich Engels' Briefwechsel mit Karl Kautsky* (1955), p. 123.

19   F. Engels to N. F. Danielson, November 13, 1885 in Karl Marx and F. Engels, *Briefe über "Das Kapital"* (1954), p. 298.

20   For Rodbertus see J. K. Rodbertus, *Overproduction and Crises* (translated by Julia Franklin, 1898).

21   F. Engels to N. F. Danielson, February 19, 1887 in Karl Marx and F. Engels, *Briefe über "Das Kapital"* (1954), p. 302.

22   F. Engels to N. F. Danielson, January 5, 1888 in Karl Marx and F. Engels, *Briefe über "Das Kapital"* (1954), pp. 304–5.

23   F. Engels to N. F. Danielson, July 4, 1889 (*ibid.*, pp. 314–15).

24 F. Engels to Laura Lafargue, March 8, 1885 in *F. Engels – Paul and Laura Lafargue: Correspondence*, Vol. 1, p. 271.

25 F. Engels to N. F. Danielson, October 15, 1888 in Karl Marx and F. Engels, *Briefe über "Das Kapital"* (1954), p. 307.

26 F. Engels to Karl Kautsky, September 15, 1889 in Benedikt Kautsky (ed.), *Friedrich Engels' Briefwechsel mit Karl Kautsky* (1955), p. 247.

27 F. Engels to N. F. Danielson, June 18, 1892 in Karl Marx and F. Engels, *Briefe über "Das Kapital"* (1954), p. 346.

28 F. Engels to V. Adler, October 23, 1892 in *Victor Adlers Aufsätze, Reden und Briefe*, Heft 1: *Victor Adler und Friedrich Engels* (1922) p. 57.

29 F. Engels to N. F. Danielson, February 24, 1893 (*ibid.*, p. 360).

30 F. Engels to Karl Kautsky, January 28, 1889 in Benedikt Kautsky (ed.), *Friedrich Engels' Briefwechsel mit Karl Kautsky* (1955), p. 227.

31 "Wie Karl Marx im Jahre 1846 über Streiks und Arbeiter Koalitionen dachte" in *Der Sozialdemokrat*, February 12 and 26, 1885.

32 F. Engels to Karl Kautsky, August 22, 1884 in Benedikt Kautsky (ed.), *Friedrich Engels' Briefwechsel mit Karl Kautsky* (1955), p. 141 and F. Engels to F. A. Sorge, March 4, 1891 in Karl Marx and F. Engels, *Briefe über "Das Kapital"* (1954), p. 324.

33 F. Engels to N. F. Danielson, October 15, 1888 (*ibid.*, p. 307); Conrad Schmidt, October 27, 1890 (*ibid.*, p. 317); Max Oppenheim, March 24, 1891 (*ibid.*, pp. 324–6); Rudolf Meyer, July 19, 1893 (*ibid.*, p. 361); Heinz Starhenberg, January 25, 1894 (*ibid.*, p. 365); J. Bloch, September 21–22 (W. O. Henderson (ed.), *Engels: Selected Writings*, 1967, pp. 333–5).

34 See *Engels on Capital* (New York International Publishers, 1937), pp. 118–19 and Jürgen Kuczynski, "Friedrich Engels und die Monopole" in *Friedrich Engels 1820–1970* (Schriftenreihe des Forschungsinstituts der Friedrich Ebert-Stiftung, Vol. 85, 1971), pp. 39–42.

35 F. Engels to N. F. Danielson, June 18, 1892 in Karl Marx and F. Engels, *Briefe über "Das Kapital"* (1954), p. 344.

36 F. Engels to N. F. Danielson, September 22, 1892 (*ibid.*, p. 355).

37 See the documents in Karl Marx and F. Engels, *On Colonialism* (Foreign Languages Publishing House, Moscow).

38 "Marx über das Kolonialsystem" in *Der Sozialdemokrat*, July 10, 1884.

39 F. Engels to Karl Kautsky, September 23, 1894 in Benedikt Kautsky (ed.), *Friedrich Engels' Briefwechsel mit Karl Kautsky* (1955), p. 411. See also F. Engels to F. A. Sorge, November 10, 1894 in Karl Marx and F. Engels, *Letters to Americans, 1848–95* (1963), p. 266.

40 F. Engels, "Supplement to *Capital*, Volume III" (1895) in L. E. Mins (ed.), *Engels on Capital* (New York, 1937), p. 117.

41 See, for example, an article in *Der Sozialdemokrat*, October 1, 1885 attacking German militarism.

42 See, for example, F. Engels, "Kann Europa abrüsten?" in *Die Neue Zeit*, March 1893.

43 F. Engels, "Was nun?" in *Der Sozialdemokrat*, March 8, 1890.

44 F. Engels, "Eine Antwort" in *Der Sozialdemokrat*, September 13, 1890.

45 For Georg von Vollmar see Reinhard Jansen, *Georg von Vollmar* (1958).

46 F. Engels to August Bebel, July 23, 1892 in Werner Blumenberg (ed.), *August Bebels Briefwechsel mit Friedrich Engels* (1965) pp. 564–5.

For Bebel's criticism of Vollmar at the Erfurt congress of the Social Democrat Party see Albrecht Langer (ed.), *August Bebel: Politik als Theorie und Praxis* (1967), p. 80.

47 F. Engels to Laura Lafargue, October 27, 1891 in *F. Engels – Paul and Laura Lafargue: Correspondence*, Vol. 3, 1891–5, p. 126 (postscript). Engels wrote: "Things at Erfurt went very well. The execution of the insolent young student and commis-voyageur (commercial traveller) lot was very necessary. They will soon disappear now, and the next lot of the same sort will be less cheeky".

48 G. Hennig, *August Bebel . . .* (1963), pp. 91–105.

49 F. Engels to August Bebel, August 14 and 20, 1892 in Werner Blumenberg (ed.), *August Bebels Briefwechsel mit Friedrich Engels* (1965), p. 572 and p. 576.

50 *Daily Chronicle*, July 1, 1893 (interview with Engels) in *F. Engels – Paul and Laura Lafargue: Correspondence*, Vol. 3, 1891–5, Appendix, p. 397. The interviewer described Engels as "a kindly, genial soul . . . and his ripe and mellow wisdom made a talk with him . . . one of the pleasantest experiences I have ever had".

51 F. Engels to Julie Bebel, October 3, 1893 in Werner Blumenberg (ed.), *August Bebels Briefwechsel mit Friedrich Engels* (1965), pp. 708–9.

52 Eduard Bernstein, *Die Voraussetzungen des Sozialismus und die Aufgaben der Sozialdemokratie* (1898). See also his articles on "Probleme der Sozialismus" in *Die Neue Zeit*, Vol. 15, 1896–7, Part I, pp. 164–71; 204–13; 303–11; 772–83 and Part II, pp. 100–7; 138–43; Vol. 16, 1897–8, Part I, 484–97; 548–57 and Part II, pp. 225–32; 388–95.

53 "Der Entwurf des neuen Parteiprogrammes" in *Die Neue Zeit*, Vol. 9, 1891: three articles were written by Kautsky and one by Bernstein.

54 F. Engels, "Kritik des Gothaer Programmes" in *Die Neue Zeit*, Vol. 9, 1891, p. 502: English translation – Karl Marx, *Critique of the Gotha Programme* (Progress Publishers, Moscow, 1871). Engels sent the manuscript of Marx's letter on the Gotha programme to Kautsky on January 7, 1891: see F. Engels to Karl Kautsky, January 7, 1891 in Benedikt Kautsky (ed.), *Friedrich Engels' Briefwechsel mit Karl Kautsky* (1955), p. 268.

55 F. Engels to Karl Kautsky, February 23, 1891 in Benedikt Kautsky (ed.), *Friedrich Engels' Briefwechsel mit Karl Kautsky* (1955), pp. 281–3.

56 F. Engels, Zur Kritik der sozialdemokratischen Programmentwurfes 1891" in *Die Neue Zeit*, Vol. 20, 1901, pp. 5–13.

57 August Bebel to F. Engels, July 12, 1891 in Werner Blumenberg (ed.), *August Bebels Briefwechsel mit Friedrich Engels* (1965), p. 424.

58 For the Erfurt programme of the Social Democrat Party see Marx–Engels, *Kritiken der sozialdemokratischen Programmentwürfe von 1875 und 1891* (1928), pp. 128–32: English translation in V. L. Lidtke, *The Outlawed Party. Social Democracy in Germany, 1878–90* (1966), Appendix B, pp. 335–8.

59 F. Engels to F. A. Sorge, October 24, 1891 in Karl Marx and F. Engels, *Letters to Americans, 1848–95* (1963), p. 237.

60 F. Engels to F. A. Sorge, October 7, 1893 in Karl Marx and F. Engels, *Letters to Americans, 1848–95* (1963), pp. 254–6. A copy of the programme is preserved in the Marx–Engels archives (Amsterdam), M 50.

61 Engels's speech at the banquet in the Concordia Hall, Berlin, on September 22, 1893 is printed in F. Engels, *Auf Reisen* (1966), pp. 235–7.

62 Karl Marx, *Klassenkampfe in Frankreich 1848–50* (Berlin, 1895).

63 Bebel wrote to Engels on March 11, 1895: " . . . We do not ask you to say something that you do not wish to say – or may not say – but we ask you *not* to say something which, if said at this time, would be embarrassing for us. . . ." (Werner Blumenberg (ed.), *August Bebels Briefwechsel mit Friedrich Engels*, 1965, p. 795).

64 "Wie man heute Revolution macht": leading article in *Vorwärts*, 1895.

65 F. Engels to Karl Kautsky, April 1, 1895 in Benedikt Kautsky (ed.), *Friedrich Engels' Briefwechsel mit Karl Kautsky* (1955), pp. 429–30. Kautsky printed Engels's introduction (though not in full) in *Die Neue Zeit*, Vol. 13, 1894–5. See also K. Kautsky, "Engels' politisches Testament" in *Der Kampf*, Vol. 18, 1925, p. 472 *et seq*, and N. Rjazanov in *Unter dem Banner des Marxismus*, Vol. 1, 1925, p. 160 *et seq*.

66 F. Engels to Paul Lafargue, April 3, 1895 in *Friedrich Engels – Paul and Laura Lafargue*, Vol. 3, 1891–5, p. 373.

67 *Daily Chronicle*, July 1, 1893 in F. *Engels – Paul and Laura Lafargue*, Vol. 3, 1891–5, Appendix, p. 400.

68 For Victor Adler see *Neue Österreichische Biographie*, Vol. 3, 1926, pp. 152–72; *Neue Deutsche Biographie*, Vol. 1, 1953, p. 72; *Österreichisches Biographisches Lexikon*, 1815–1950, Vol. 1, 1957, p. 7; Max Ermers, *Victor Adler* . . . (1932); F. Adler (ed.), *Victor Adler: Briefwechsel mit August Bebel und Karl Kautsky* (1954); *Victor Adlers Aufsätze, Reden, Brief* (11 parts, 1922–29).

69 E. Aveling, "Engels at Home" in *Reminiscences of Marx and Engels* (Foreign Languages Publishing House, Moscow), p. 312.

70 For socialism in Austria see Hans Mommsen, *Die Sozialdemokratie und die Nationalitätenfrage im habsburgischen Vielvölkerstaat*, Vol. 1, *1867–1907* (1963) and "Friedrich Engels und die politische und nationale Taktik der Sozialdemokratie in Österreich" in *Friedrich Engels, 1820–1970* (Forschungsinstitut der Friedrich Ebert Stiftung, Vol. 85, 1971, pp. 133–9); H. Steiner *Die Arbeiterbewegung Österreichs, 1867–1889* (1964); H. Steiner (ed.), *Bibliographie zur Geschichte der österreichischen Arbeiterbewegung, 1867–1918* (1962).

71 Karl Kautsky to F. Engels, July 22, 1883 and F. Engels to Karl Kautsky, September 18, 1883 in Benedikt Kautsky (ed.), *Friedrich Engels' Briefwechsel mit Karl Kautsky* (1955), pp. 76–7 and p. 84. For Leo Frankel's letter introducing Adler to Engels see *Victor Adlers Aufsätze, Reden und Briefe*, Heft 1: *Victor Adler und Friedrich Engels* (1922), p. vii.

72 *Gleichheit* was published between 1886 and 1889. When it ceased publication Adler founded a new socialist paper called *Die Arbeiter-Zeitung* (Vienna).

73 See Peukert's memoirs – Josef Peukert, *Erinnerungen eines Proletariars aus der revolutionären Arbeiterbewegung* (1913).

74 Adler did not start to serve the sentence until February 1890.

75 Gustav Mayer, *Friedrich Engels*, Vol. 2 (1934), p. 414.

76 F. Engels to V. Adler, July 22, 1891 in *Victor Adlers Aufsätze, Reden und Briefe*, Heft 1: *Victor Adler und Friedrich Engels* (1922), p. 27. The royalties amounted to 50 Marks (£2 10s) per 1,000 copies. The

publisher paid Adler 500 Marks (£25): see V. Adler to F. Engels, September 2, 1891 (*ibid.*, p. 29).

77 F. Engels to V. Adler, May 19, 1892 and V. Adler to F. Engels, May 26, 1892 in *Victor Adlers Aufsätze, Reden und Briefe*, Heft 1: *Victor Adler und Friedrich Engels* (1922), pp. 35–7. Engels stated that royalties amounting to £25 were due in the autumn of 1892 and £25 in the spring of 1893.

78 F. Engels to V. Adler, January 12, 1895 in *Victor Adlers Aufsätze, Reden und Briefe*, Heft 1: *Victor Adler und Friedrich Engels* (1922), p. 119.

79 Karl Kautsky, "Die Arbeiterbewegung in Österreich" in *Die Neue Zeit*, Vol. 8, 1890, pp. 49–56, 97–106, 154–63.

80 For the speeches by Adler and Engels at the socialist meeting in Vienna on September 11, 1893 see the *Arbeiter-Zeitung* (Vienna), September 22, 1893 and *Victor Adlers Aufsätze, Reden und Briefe*, Heft 1: *Victor Adler und Friedrich Engels* (1922), pp. 70–6.

81 F. Engels to Laura Lafargue, September 18, 1893 in *F. Engels – Paul and Laura Lafargue: Correspondence*, Vol. 3, pp. 293–4.

82 Paul Lafargue, *The Evolution of Property* (1891); *Social and Philosophical Studies* (1906); and *The Right to be Lazy* (1907); J. Varlet's introduction to *P. Lafargue: théoricien du Marxisme* (1933); G. Stolz, *Paul Lafargue, théoricien militant du socialism* (1937); Émile Bottigelli in *F. Engels – Paul and Laura Lafargue: Correspondence*, Vol. 3, pp. 489–542; S. Bernstein, *The Beginnings of Marxian Socialism in France* (1965); Georges Weil, *Histoire du mouvement socialiste en France* (1904); Claude Willard, *Le mouvement socialiste en France* (1893–1905), *Les Guesdistes* (1965).

83 G. Deville, *Le Capital de Karl Marx . . .* (1883).

84 Karl Marx to F. A. Sorge, November 5, 1880 in Karl Marx and F. Engels, *Letters to Americans, 1848–95* (1963), pp. 124–5.

85 F. Engels to E. Bernstein, October 25, 1881 in H. Hirsch (ed.), *Eduard Bernsteins Briefwechsel mit Friedrich Engels* (1970), p. 50.

86 *Ibid.*, p. 50.

87 Karl Marx to F. A. Sorge, November 5, 1880 in Karl Marx and F. Engels, *Letters to Americans, 1848–95* (1963), pp. 124–5. See also Jules Guesde and Paul Lafargue, *Le programme du Parti Ouvrier. Son histoire, ses considérants, ses articles* (1883).

88 F. Engels to August Bebel, October 28, 1882 in Werner Blumenberg (ed.), *August Bebels Briefwechsel mit Friedrich Engels* (1965), pp. 137–8.

89 Émile Bottigelli in *F. Engels – Paul and Laura Lafargue: Correspondence*, Vol. 3, p. 500.

90 F. Engels to Theodore Cuno, January 24, 1872 in G. Del Bo (ed.), *La corrispondenza di Marx e Engels con italiani 1848–95* (1964), p. 134.

91 F. Engels to J. P. Becker, February 16, 1872 in *Marx–Engels Werke*, Vol. 33, p. 404.

92 *La Plebe* was published first in Lodi and then in Milan. Engels's articles appeared in the following issues: December 12, 1871; April 24, October 5 and 8, November 17, December 14, 1872; February 26, 1877; January 22, 1878; and March 30, 1879.

93 Lafargue described this translation as "magnificent": see Paul Lafargue to F. Engels, June 15, 1885 in *F. Engels – Paul and Laura Lafargue: Correspondence*, Vol. 1, p. 294.

94   Engels wrote to Lafargue on January 28, 1887: "Martignetti has
     written to me again. It seems that he is in a tight corner. He asks me
     to try and find some way out for him and makes impossible sug-
     gestions. I have written to Hamburg and Vienna on his behalf and
     have promised him that I would write to you too: you will no doubt
     have a letter from him direct. There is nothing for him here or in
     America, since he does not know a word of English. Would there be
     any opening for him in France as a teacher of Italian? This is the
     only thing I see for him to do. Or can you think of something better?
     He is going to be dismissed from his post. Find out whether in Paris
     or in the provinces there is some opening for the poor devil"
     (*F. Engels – Paul and Laura Lafargue: Correspondence*, Vol. 3, p.
     485). See also F. Engels to Paul Lafargue, May 21, 1887 (*ibid.*, Vol. 2,
     p. 42) and F. Engels to August Bebel, August 30, 1887 in Werner
     Blumenberg (ed.), *August Bebels Briefwechsel mit Friedrich Engels*
     (1965), p. 309.

95   E. Ragionieri, *Socialdemocrazia tedesca e socialisti italiani. L'influenza
     della socialdemocrazia tedesca sulla formazione del partito socialista
     italiano, 1875–95* (Milan, 1961), pp. 192–219.

96   Antonio Labriola, *La concezione materialistica della stori* (Bari, 1965:
     edited by E. Gavin) and Antonio Labriola, *Scritti politici* (Bari, 1970:
     edited by V. Garratana).

97   Antonio Labriola to F. Engels, March 14, 1894 in G. Del Bo (ed.),
     La corrispondenza di Marx e Engels con italiani (Milan, 1964), p. 525.

98   F. Engels to Laura Lafargue, August 21, 1893 in *F. Engels – Paul and
     Laura Lafargue: Correspondence*, Vol. 3, p. 286.

99   G. M. Bravo, "Friedrich Engels und Achille Loria" in *Friedrich
     Engels, 1820–1970* (Forschungsinstitut der Friedrich Ebert Stiftung,
     Vol. 85, 1971, pp. 175–88). Loria taught at the Universities of Sienna,
     Padua and Turin.

100 F. Engels to Filippo Turati, April 12, 1894: "this charlatan announced
     to the whole world that Marx never wrote a third volume of *Das
     Kapital*" in G. Del Bo (ed.), *La corrispondenza di Marx e Engels con
     italieni* (1964), p. 531.

101 Karl Marx, *Das Kapital*, Vol. 3, 1894 (edition of 1957): introduction
     by F. Engels, pp. 17–21.

102 *Nuova Antologia*, April 1, 1883.

103 Engels's introduction to the third volume of *Das Kapital*, 1894 was
     translated into Italian by Martignetti and appeared in *Rassegna* (1895,
     No. 1) and *Critica sociale*, December 1, and 16, 1895. See also
     F. Engels to Pasquale Martignetti, January 8, 1895 in *Marx–Engels
     Werke*, Vol. 39, p. 369.

104 Loria replied to Engels's introduction to *Das Kapital*, Vol. 3 (1894) in
     Riforma Sociale, February 25, 1895. For Engels's rejoinder see his
     "supplement" to Karl Marx, *Das Kapital*, Vol. 3 (1894), (edition of
     1957), p. 27 (footnote).

105 E. Ragionieri, "Engels und die italienische Arbeiterbewegung" in
     Friedrich Engels, 1820–1970 (Forschungsinstitut der Friedrich Ebert
     Stiftung, Vol. 85), pp. 196–7.

106 *Federazione dell'Alta Italia*, The journal *La Plebe* was its official
     organ. See F. Engels to Karl Marx, February 23, 1877 in *Gesamtaus-
     gabe*, Part III, Vol. 4, p. 447.

107 F. Engels, "Aus Italien" in *Vorwärts*, March 16, 1877 and in *Marx–
     Engels Werke*, Vol. 19, pp. 91–5.

108 *Partito operaio Milano.*

109 *Partito dei Lavoratori Italiani.*

110 Three years later its name was changed to *Partito Socialista Italiano.*

111 E. Ragionieri, "Engels und die italienische Arbeiterbewegung" in *Friedrich Engels, 1820–1970* (Forschungsinstitut der Friedrich Ebert Stiftung, Vol. 85, 1971), pp. 197–8.

112 See F. Engels, "La futura Rivoluzione Italiana ed il Partito Socialista" in *Critica Sociale*, Vol. 4, No. 3, pp. 35–6: reprinted in G. Pischel, *"Critica Sociale" 1891–1926* . . . (Milan, 1945), pp. 18–22.

113 E. Ragionieri, "Engels und die italienische Arbeiterbewegung" in *Friedrich Engels, 1820–1970* (Forschungsinstitut der *Friedrich Ebert* Stiftung, Vol. 85, 1971), pp. 198–9.

114 F. Engels to F. A. Sorge, February 23, 1894 in Karl Marx and F. Engels, *Letters to Americans, 1848–95* (1963), p. 260.

115 G. Del Bo (ed.), *La corrispondenza di Marx e Engels con italieni, 1848–95* (Milan, 1964), pp. 435–7, 447–50, 458–63, 469–70.

116 For Engels and the British labour movement between 1881 and 1895 see S. Bünger, *Friedrich Engels und die britische sozialistische Bewegung von 1881–1895* (1962), M. Beer, *A History of British Socialism*, Vol. 2 (1929), and H. Pelling, *The Origins of the Labour Party, 1880–1900* (1954).

117 F. Engels, "A Fair Day's Wage for a Fair Day's Work" in *The Labour Standard*, May 7, 1881.

118 F. Engels to Adolph Hepner, December 30, 1872 in Karl Marx and F. Engels, *Letters to Americans, 1848–95* (1963), p. 112.

119 F. Engels, "Die englischen Wahlen" in *Der Volksstaat*, March 4, 1874 and in Karl Marx and F. Engels, *On Britain* (Foreign Languages Publishing House, Moscow, 1953), p. 464. Engels added that the election of two working men (Alexander MacDonald and Thomas Burt) to the House of Commons had "ushered in a new phase in English political development".

120 Karl Marx to W. Liebknecht, February 11, 1878 in Wilhelm Liebknecht, *Briefwechsel mit Karl Marx und Friedrich Engels* (ed. Georg Eckert, 1963), p. 245. English translation in Karl Max and F. Engels, *On Britain* (Foreign Languages Publishing House, Moscow, 1953), p. 509.

121 E. Bernstein to F. Engels, June 13, 1879 in Helmut Hirsch (ed.), *Eduard Bernsteins Briefwechsel mit Friedrich Engels* (1970), p. 3. This was the first letter written by Bernstein to Engels.

122 F. Engels to E. Bernstein, June 17, 1879 in Helmut Hirsch (ed.), *Eduard Bernsteins Briefwechsel mit Friedrich Engels* (1970), p. 510 and in Karl Marx and F. Engels, *On Britain* (1953), p. 510. This was the first letter written by Engels to Bernstein.

123 F. Engels to August Bebel, January 18, 1884 in Werner Blumenberg (ed.), *August Bebel Briefwechsel mit Friedrich Engels* (1965), p. 172. English translation in Karl Marx and F. Engels, *On Britain* (1953), p. 517. For the depression of 1873–96 see D. H. Aldcroft and H. W. Richardson, *The British Economy, 1870–1939* (1969), Section B(i) "Retardation in Britain's Industrial Growth, 1870–1913".

124 F. Engels, *The British Labour Movement. Articles from "The Labour Standard"* (1934).

125 *The Labour Standard*, May 21, 1881.

126 *Ibid.*, May 28, 1881.

127 *Ibid.*, April 4, 1881.

128   *Ibid.*, April 4, 1881.
129   *The Labour Standard*, August 6, 1881.
130   F. Engels to Karl Kautsky, August 27, 1881 in Benedikt Kautsky (ed.), *Friedrich Engels' Briefwechsel mit Karl Kautsky* (1955), p. 38.
131   F. Engels to Karl Marx, August 11, 1881 in *Gesamtausgabe*, Part III, Vol. 4, pp. 510–11. The circumstances of the breach between Engels and Shipton (described in this letter) were as follows. Shipton complained that two passages in an article by Kautsky on international labour legislation (which Engels had corrected) were "too strong" for his paper. Engels replied that since some of his own leading articles would be a good deal "stronger" it would be best if he ceased to contribute to *The Labour Standard*. Engels's articles had converted one future leader of the workers to socialism – James Macdonald, *How I Became a Socialist* (1896), p. 61.
132   F. Engels to Paul Lafargue, January 28, 1887 in *F. Engels – Paul and Laura Lafargue: Correspondence*, Vol. 3, p. 486.
133   Benedikt Kautsky (ed.), *Friedrich Engels' Briefwechsel mit Karl Kautsky* (1955), p. 89.
134   Edward Aveling in *Reminiscences of Marx and Engels*, p. 313.
135   Engels declined an invitation to contribute to *Justice*, explaining that he was busy editing the manuscripts of the second volume of *Das Kapital*.
136   *Justice*, January 1, 1887.
137   F. Engels to August Bebel, October 28, 1885 in Werner Blumenberg (ed.), *August Bebel Briefwechsel mit Friedrich Engels* (1965), p. 240.
138   F. Engels to F. A. Sorge, April 19, 1890 in Karl Marx and F. Engels, *Letters to Americans, 1848–95* (1963), p. 231.
139   F. Engels to Karl Kautsky, August 12, 1892 in Benedikt Kautsky (ed.), *Friedrich Engels' Briefwechsel mit Karl Kautsky* (1955), p. 359: English translation in Karl Marx and F. Engels, *On Britain* (1953), p. 528.
140   F. Engels to F. A. Sorge, May 12, 1894 in Karl Marx and F. Engels, *Letters to Americans, 1848–95* (1963), p. 263.
141   F. Engels to F. A. Sorge, September 16, 1886 in Karl Marx and F. Engels, *Letters to Americans, 1848–95* (1963), p. 162.
142   Engels wrote that "the anarchists are making rapid progress in the Socialist League" and that Morris and Belfort Bax were "wholly under their control for the present": F. Engels to F. A. Sorge, April 29, 1886 in Karl Marx and F. Engels, *Letters to Americans, 1848–95* (1963), p. 156.
143   F. Engels to F. A. Sorge, May 4, 1887 in Karl Marx and F. Engels, *Letters to Americans, 1848–95* (1963), p. 185. See also A. M. McBriar, *Fabian Socialism and English Politics* (1962).
144   For the Fabian programme of 1887 see E. R. Pease, *The History of the Fabian Society* (revised edition of 1926), p. 284.
145   F. Engels to Laura Lafargue, October 11, 1887 in *F. Engels – Paul and Laura Lafargue: Correspondence*, Vol. 2, p. 65.
146   F. Engels to F. A. Sorge, February 8, 1890 in Karl Marx and F. Engels, *Letters to Americans, 1848–95* (1963), p. 226.
147   F. Engels to Mrs Wischnewetzky, May 2, 1888 in Karl Marx and F. Engels, *Letters to Americans, 1848–95* (1963), p. 200.
148   F. Engels to Karl Kautsky, September 12, 1882 in Benedikt Kautsky (ed.), *Friedrich Engels' Briefwechsel mit Karl Kautsky* (1955), p. 63 and Karl Marx and F. Engels, *On Britain* (1953), p. 514.

149   F. Engels to August Bebel, August 30, 1883 in Werner Blumenberg (ed.), *August Bebels Briefwechsel mit Friedrich Engels* (1965), p. 166 and Karl Marx and F. Engels, *On Britain* (1953), p. 516.

150   F. Engels to August Bebel, January 18, 1884 in Werner Blumenberg (ed.), *August Bebels Briefwechsel mit Friedrich Engels* (1965), p. 172 and Karl Marx and F. Engels, *On Britain* (1953), p .517.

151   F. Engels, "England in 1845 and 1885" in *The Commonweal*, March 1, 1885; reprinted in the introduction to the English translation of F. Engels, *The Condition of the Working Class in England* (1892: new translation by W. O. Henderson and W. H. Chaloner, 1958 and 1971).

152   F. Engels to Mrs Wischnewetzky, May 2, 1888 in Karl Marx and F. Engels, *Letters to Americans, 1848–95* (1963), p. 200.

153   F. Engels to F. A. Sorge, December 7, 1889 in Karl Marx and F. Engels, *Letters to Americans, 1848–95* (1963), p. 221.

154   See H. M. Hyndman, *The Record of an Adventurous Life* (1911), and C. Tsuziki, *H. M. Hyndman and British Socialism* (1961).

155   John Barker in the *Daily Telegraph*, May 22, 1972, p. 11.

156   E. J. Hobsbawm, *Labouring Men* (edition of 1968), p. 234.

157   F. Engels to F. A. Sorge, December 31, 1884 in Karl Marx and F. Engels, *Letters to Americans, 1848–95* (1963), p. 143.

158   F. Engels to August Bebel, August 30, 1883 in Werner Blumenberg (ed.), *August Bebels Briefwechsel mit Friedrich Engels* (1965), p. 165.

159   F. Engels to Laura Lafargue, February 16, 1884 in *F. Engels – Paul and Laura Lafargue: Correspondence*, Vol. 1, p. 179.

160   F. Engels to Paul Lafargue, May 25, 1889 (*ibid.*, Vol. 2, p. 262).

161   F. Engels to Paul Lafargue, March 26, 1886 (*ibid.*, Vol. 1, p. 347).

162   F. Engels to Laura Lafargue, February 9, 1886 (*ibid.*, Vol. 1, p. 334).

163   F. Engels to F. A. Sorge, June 8, 1889 in Karl Marx and F. Engels, *Letters to Americans, 1848–95* (1963), p. 213.

164   Eleanor Marx to Wilhelm Liebknecht, January 12, 1885 in Wilhelm Liebknecht, *Briefwechsel mit Karl Marx und Friedrich Engels* (ed. Georg Eckert, 1963), p. 433.

165   H. M. Hyndman, *The Record of an Adventurous Life* (1911), p. 273.

166   Karl Marx to Jenny Longuet, April 11, 1881 in Karl Marx and F. Engels, *Correspondence, 1846–95* (1934), p. 389.

167   Karl Marx to F. A. Sorge, December 15, 1881 in Karl Marx and F. Engels, *Letters to Americans, 1848–95* (1963), p. 130.

168   H. M. Hyndman, *The Record of an Adventurous Life* (1911), p. 285.

169   F. Engels to H. M. Hyndman (no date) in C. Tsuziki, *H. M. Hyndman and British Socialism* (1961), p. 43.

170   F. Engels to Karl Kautsky, July 19, 1884 in Benedikt Kautsky (ed.), *Friedrich Engels' Briefwechsel mit Karl Kautsky* (1955), p. 138.

171   F. Engels to Karl Kautsky, June 22, 1884 in Benedikt Kautsky (ed.), *Friedrich Engels' Briefwechsel mit Karl Kautsky* (1955), p. 124.

172   H. M. Hyndman, *The Historical Basis of Socialism in England* (1883), p. 417.

173   *Pall Mall Gazette*, December 4, 1885 (letter from Hunter Watts); *Justice*, December 12, 1885 (reply from the Social Democratic Federation admitting the receipt of £340 from the Conservatives).

174   Queen Victoria to W. E. Gladstone, February 11, 1886 in *Letters of Queen Victoria, 1886–1901* (1930), Vol. 1, p. 52 and F. Engels to Laura Lafargue, February 9, 1886 in *F. Engels – Paul and Laura Lafargue: Correspondence*, Vol. 1, pp. 333–7.

175 F. Engels to F. A. Sorge, March 18, 1893 in Karl Marx and F. Engels, *Letters to Americans, 1848–95* (1963), p. 249.

176 H. M. Hyndman, *The Record of an Adventurous Life* (1911), p. 271.

177 H. M. Hyndman, *op. cit.*, p. 252.

178 H. M. Hyndman, *op. cit.*, p. 253.

179 H. M. Hyndman, *The Record of an Adventurous Life* (1911), p. 279.

180 F. Engels to Laura Lafargue, July 12, 1891 in *F. Engels – Paul and Laura Lafargue: Correspondence*, Vol. 3, p. 92.

181 H. M. Hyndman, "Dr Aveling?" in *Justice*, February 21, 1891.

182 H. M. Hyndman, "The Marxist Clique" in *Justice*, February 28, 1891.

183 H. M. Hyndman, *The Record of an Adventurous Life* (1911), p. 279.

184 F. Engels to Mrs Wischnewetzky, February 9, 1887 in Karl Marx and F. Engels, *Letters to Americans, 1848–95* (1963), p. 171.

185 Karl Kautsky in Benedikt Kautsky (ed.), *Friedrich Engels's Briefwechsel mit Karl Kautsky* (1955), p. 168.

186 Eduard Bernstein, *Aus den Jahren meines Exils* (1918), p. 218.

187 Edmund Wilson, *To the Finland Station* (1960), p. 347.

188 Hyndman revived the controversy over Aveling's expenses in an article in *Justice*, February 21, 1891.

189 Eduard Bernstein to V. Adler, April 5, 1898 in Victor Adler, *Briefwechsel mit August Bebel und Karl Kautsky* (ed. F. Adler, 1954), p. 243.

190 For the inquest on Eleanor Marx see *The Times*, April 4, 1898 and the *Forest Hill and Sydenham Examiner*, April 8, 1898. See also Eduard Bernstein, "Was Eleanor Marx in den Tod trieb" in *Die Neue Zeit*, Vol. 16 (2), 1898, p. 118 and in *Justice*, July 30, 1898. Karl Kautsky accused Aveling of driving Eleanor Marx to suicide. He wrote: "For Tussy's sake I have always been careful to judge the wretch as charitably as possible. That is now both unnecessary and impossible. According to the latest information that I have received from Ede (Eduard Bernstein) Aveling not only drove Eleanor to her death by his scandalous behaviour but he *knew* that she intended to take her own life and did nothing to stop her. Aveling was present when Eleanor sent the maid for the poison. He was present when Eleanor signed the poison book on receipt of the poison. Then Aveling – who had been behaving as if he were on his deathbed – went off for the whole day and when he came back in the evening a lady living nearby met him to prepare him for the bad news. She said: 'Oh, Mrs Aveling is very ill.' And at once he replied: 'Is she dead? Is it all over?' " (Karl Kautsky to V. Adler, April 9, 1898 in V. Adler, *Briefwechsel mit August Bebel und Karl Kautsky* (ed. F. Adler, 1954), p. 244).

191 H. M. Hyndman, *The Record of an Adventurous Life* (1911), p. 285 and p. 423.

192 "ein übles Subjekt": B. Kautsky (ed.), *Friedrich Engels's Briefwechsel mit Karl Kautsky* (1955), p. 25.

193 "Schuft", "Schurke", "Kerl": Eduard Bernstein to V. Adler, April 5, 1898 in Victor Adler, *Briefwechsel mit August Bebel und Karl Kautsky* (ed. F. Adler, 1954), p. 243.

194 Edmund Wilson, *To the Finland Station* (1960), pp. 347–8.

195 Ben Tillett, *Memories and Reflections* (1931), p. 135.

196 S. Weintraub (ed.), *Shaw. An Autobiography* (1970), p. 43. G. B. Shaw did not mention Aveling by name. He stated that he was

describing the character of "one of the several models who sat unconsciously for Dubedat" in *The Doctor's Dilemma.*

197 Christopher St John (ed.), *Ellen Terry and Bernard Shaw. A Correspondence* (1931), pp. 286–7.

198 Will Thorne, *My Life's Battles* (1926), p. 148.

199 For Eleanor Marx see Olga Worobjowa and Irma Sinelnikowa, *Die Töchter von Karl Marx* (1963); C. Tsuzuki, *The Life of Eleanor Marx. A Socialist Tragedy* (1967).

200 Karl Marx to F. Engels, April 23, 1857 in *Gesamtausgabe*, Part III, Vol. 2, p.

201 Eduard Bernstein, "Eleanor Marx" in *Die Neue Zeit*, Vol. 16 (2), 1898, p. 118 *et seq.*

202 Paul Lafargue, "Reminiscences of Marx" in *Reminiscences of Marx and Engels*, p. 82.

203 Eduard Bernstein in *Die Neue Zeit*, Vol. 16 (2), 1898, p. 118 and p. 481.

204 Paul Lafargue, "Reminiscences of Marx" in *Reminiscences of Marx and Engels*, p. 82.

205 Eleanor Marx, "Friedrich Engels" in *Reminiscences of Marx and Engels*, pp. 185–6.

206 Eleanor Marx to Karl Kautsky, March 15, 1898 in the Marx–Engels Archives (Amsterdam), D. XVI. 489.

207 E. Bernstein, *Aus den Jahren meines Exils* (1918), p. 172.

208 Karl Marx to Dr Kugelmann, August 4, 1874 in Karl Marx, *Letters to Dr Kugelmann*, p. 138.

209 Karl Marx to F. Engels, August 14, 1874 in *Gesamtausgabe*, Part III. Vol. 4, pp. 418–9.

210 Karl Marx to Dr Kugelmann, August 4, 1874 in Karl Marx, *Letters to Dr Kugelmann*, p. 138.

211 Karl Marx to F. Engels, August 18, 1881 in *Gesamtausgabe*, Part III, Vol. 4, pp. 515–16.

212 Karl Marx to F. Engels, January 5, 1882 in *Gesamtausgabe*, Part III, Vol. 4, pp. 518–19.

213 *The Times*, April 4, 1898; *Forest Hill and Sydenham Examiner*, April 8, 1898; Robert Payne, *Marx* (1968), pp. 527–8.

214 Franzisca Kugelmann in *Reminiscences of Marx and Engels* (Foreign Languages Publishing House, Moscow), p. 285.

215 Arnold Künzli, *Karl Marx. Eine Psychographie* (1966), p. 484.

216 See Karl Marx to F. Engels, May 23 and 31, 1873 in *Gesamtausgabe*, Part III, Vol. 4, p. 394 and p. 400.

217 Eleanor Marx to Olive Schreiner, June 16, 1885 in *The Modern Monthly*, Vol. 9, 1935, p. 290.

218 Karl Marx to F. Engels, January 12, 1882 in *Gesamtausgabe*, Part III, Vol. 4, p. 521.

219 Beatrice Webb, *My Apprenticeship* (1926 and 1946), pp. 258–9.

220 Eleanor Marx to Laura Lafargue, June 18, 1884 in C. Tsuzuki, *The Life of Eleanor Marx, 1855–98* (1967), p. 105.

221 Eleanor Marx to Dollie Radford, June 30, 1884 in C. Tsuzuki, *The Life of Eleanor Marx, 1855–98* (1967), pp. 105–6.

222 F. Engels to Laura Lafargue, July 22, 1884 in *F. Engels – Paul and Laura Lafargue: Correspondence*, Vol. 1, 1868–86, p. 218. On August 1, 1884 Engels wrote to Laura Lafargue that he had "still to write to 'Mrs Aveling' " (*ibid.*, p. 228).

223 F. Engels to E. Bernstein, August 6, 1884 in Helmut Hirsch (ed.),

Eduard Bernsteins Briefwechsel mit Friedrich Engels (1970), p. 289.

224 For Dr Edward Bibbins Aveling (1851–98) see F. Boase, *Modern English Biography* (1908 and 1965), Vol. 4 (supplement to Vol. 1), pp. 209–10.

225 F. Engels to Laura Lafargue, July 22, 1884 in *F. Engels – Paul and Laura Lafargue: Correspondence*, Vol. 1, 1868–86 (1959), p. 218.

226 F. Engels to Laura Lafargue, May 9, 1888 in *F. Engels – Paul and Laura Lafargue: Correspondence*, Vol. 2, pp. 121–2.

227 F. Engels to V. Adler, December 12, 1890 in *Victor Adlers Aufsätze, Reden und Briefe*, Heft 1 : *Victor Adler und Friedrich Engels* (1922), p. 22.

228 F. Engels to Mrs Wischnewetzky, February 9, 1887 in Karl Marx–F. Engels, *Letters to Americans, 1848–95* (1963), pp. 170–1. A few days later Engels wrote to Laura Lafargue: "In a day or two you will get a printed circular with Aveling's reply to the charges of the New York Executive. . . . It is nothing but the usual complaint of boorish louts against intellectuals that they live extravagantly on the pence of the working men. Fortunately we have a good reply. . . . Poor Edward had an awful shock about these ridiculous accusations. . . ." (F. Engels to Laura Lafargue, February 24, 1887 in *F. Engels – Paul and Laura Lafargue: Correspondence*, Vol. 2, p. 26).

229 S. Bünger, *Friedrich Engels und die britische sozialistische Bewegung 1881–1895* (1962), p. 124.

230 *Daily Telegraph*, April 12, 1887.

231 F. Engels to Laura Lafargue, March 21, 1887 in *F. Engels – Paul and Laura Lafargue: Correspondence*, Vol. 2, pp. 31–2.

232 F. Engels to Eduard Bernstein, May 5, 1887 in Helmut Hirsch (ed.), *Eduard Bernsteins Briefwechsel mit Friedrich Engels* (1970), p. 355.

233 F. Engels to John Lincoln Mahon, June 26, 1887 in Helmut Hirsch (ed.), *Friedrich Engels: Profile* (1970), p. 350 and Karl Marx and F. Engels, *On Britain* (1953), p. 520: J. L. Mahon to F. Engels, June 22, June 23, and July 21, 1887 in E. P. Thompson, *William Morris* (1955), pp. 863–6.

234 Tom Mann, *What A Compulsory Eight-Hour Working Day means to the Workers* (1886).

235 F. Engels to Laura Lafargue, May 10, 1890 in *F. Engels – Paul and Laura Lafargue: Correspondence*, Vol. 2, p. 377.

236 *Link*, June 23, 1888.

237 Will Thorne, *My Life's Battles* (1926), p. 137.

238 *Fifty Years of the National Union of General and Municipal Workers* (1939); Betty Grant, *Beckton Struggles* (1955); E. J. Hobsbawm, *Labouring Men* (1968), Ch. 9.

239 F. Engels to Laura Lafargue, July 30, 1890 in *F. Engels – Paul and Laura Lafargue: Correspondence*, Vol. 2, pp. 379–80. Engels was writing about Will Thorne's success in Leeds where the gas workers went on strike and gained an 8 hour day in February 1890.

240 F. Engels to F. A. Sorge, December 7, 1889 and April 19, 1890 in Karl Marx and F. Engels, *Letters to Americans, 1848–95* (1963), p. 220 and p. 230.

241 E. Bernstein to V. Adler, April 5, 1898 in Victor Adler, *Briefwechsel mit August Bebel und Karl Kautsky* (ed. Friedrich Adler, 1954), p. 244.

242 Will Thorne, *My Life's Battles* (1926), p. 125.

243 Will Thorne, *My Life's Battles* (1926), p. 117.
244 The meeting between Engels and Will Thorne occurred in 1890 on Engels's 70th birthday; see F. Engels to Laura Lafargue, December 1, 1890 in *F. Engels – Paul and Laura Lafargue: Correspondence*, Vol. 2, p. 423.
245 Will Thorne, *My Life's Battles* (1926), p. 149.
246 Rev. W. Champneys in the *Northern Star*, May 4, 1844 quoted in F. Engels, *The Condition of the Working Class in England* (ed. W. O. Henderson and W. H. Chaloner, 1971), p. 99.
247 Peter Quennell (ed.), *Mayhew's London* (1969), pp. 566–72.
248 F. Engels to Laura Lafargue, August 27, 1889 in *F. Engels – Paul and Laura Lafargue: Correspondence*, Vol. 2, p. 304.
249 *Ibid.*, p. 304.
250 Will Thorne, *My Life's Battles* (1926), p. 86.
251 Ben Tillett, *Memories and Reflections* (1931), p. 135.
252 F. Engels to Laura Lafargue, September 1, 1889 in *F. Engels – Paul and Laura Lafargue: Correspondence*, Vol. 2, p. 306.
253 F. Engels, "Die Abdankung der Bourgeoisie" in *Der Sozialdemokrat*, October 5, 1889; reprinted in Horst Bartel, *Marx und Engels im Kampf um ein revolutionäres deutsches Parteiorgan, 1879–1890* (1961), pp. 211–16. See also an article by Engels on the London dock strike in *The Labour Elector*, August 31, 1889.
254 *The Peoples Press* replaced *The Labour Elector* which ceased publication in April 1890.
255 F. Engels, *The Condition of the Working Class in England* (translated and edited by W. O. Henderson and W. H. Chaloner, 1958 and 1971), Appendix III. Preface to the English edition of 1892, pp. 370–1. See also Engels's introduction of April 20, 1892 to the English translation (by Edward Aveling) of F. Engels, *Socialism. Utopian and Scientific* (Chicago, 1905), pp. xxxviii–xxxix.
256 H. Quelch, *Trade Unionism, Co-operation, and Social Democracy* (1892).
257 Will Thorne, *My Life's Battles* (1926), pp. 90–1.
258 F. Engels to Hermann Schlüter, January 11, 1890 in Karl Marx and F. Engels, *Letters to Americans, 1848–95* (1963), pp. 222–3.
259 Will Thorne, *My Life's Battles* (1926), p. 96.
260 F. Engels to Laura Lafargue, July 30, 1890 in *F. Engels – Paul and Laura Lafargue: Correspondence*, Vol. 2, p. 379. Engels wrote that "young Will Thorne proved himself a leader in battle of both courage and ability. This mode of *lawful* resistance is very much to be approved of, especially here in England – and it succeeded".
261 Will Thorne, *My Life's Battles* (1926), p. 131.
262 F. Engels to Karl Kautsky, September 18, 1890 in Benedikt Kautsky (ed.), *Friedrich Engels' Briefwechsel mit Karl Kautsky* (1955), p. 261.
263 D. Torr, "Fifty Years of May Day" in *Labour Monthly*, Vol. 22, 1940, p. 313.
264 F. Engels to Laura Lafargue, May 10, 1890 in *F. Engels – Paul and Laura Lafargue: Correspondence*, Vol. 2, pp. 375–6.
265 F. Engels, "Der 4 Mai in London" in the *Arbeiter Zeitung* (Vienna), May 23, 1890: reprinted in *Victor Adlers Aufsätze, Reden und Briefe*, Heft 1, *Victor Adler und Friedrich Engels* (Vienna, 1922), pp. 8–15. Hyndman replied to this article by attacking Engels in *Justice*.
266 F. Engels to Laura Lafargue, May 10, 1890 in *F. Engels – Paul and*

Laura Lafargue: Correspondence, Vol. 2, pp. 375–7. For the May Day demonstration in London on May 4, 1890 see also F. Engels, "Der 4 Mai in London" in the *Arbeiter Zeitung* (Vienna), May 23, 1890, reprinted in *Victor Adlers Aufsätze, Reden und Briefe*, Heft 1 : *Victor Adler und Friedrich Engels* (1922), pp. 8–15.

267   *People's Press*, May 17, 1890.

268   *Workman's Times*, March 27, 1891.

269   F. Engels to Paul Lafargue, May 21, 1891 in *F. Engels – Paul and Laura Lafargue: Correspondence*, Vol. 3, p. 71.

270   F. Engels to Laura Lafargue, May 4, 1891 in *F. Engels – Paul and Laura Lafargue: Correspondence*, Vol. 3, pp. 56–60.

271   F. Engels to F. A. Sorge, March 18, 1893 in Karl Marx and F. Engels, *Letters to Americans, 1848–95* (1963), p. 249.

272   F. Engels to F. A. Sorge, January 18, 1893 in Karl Marx and F. Engels, *Letters to Americans, 1848–95* (1963), p. 246.

273   F. Engels to Hermann Schlüter, January 1, 1895 in Karl Marx and F. Engels, *Letters to Americans, 1848–95* (1963), p. 268.

274   F. Engels to V. Adler, March 16, 1895 in *Victor Adlers Aufsätze, Reden und Briefe*, Heft 1 : *Victor Adler und Friedrich Engels* (1922), pp. 126–7.

275   Boris Tartakowski, "Friedrich Engels und das revolutionäre Russland" and Timur Timofejaw, "Das Erbe von Engels und der Leninismus" in *Friedrich Engels, 1820–1970* (Schriftenreihe des Forschungsinstituts der Friedrich Ebert Stiftung, Vol. 85, 1971), pp. 163–8 and pp. 201–17. For Plekhanov see L. Hainson, *The Russian Marxists and the Origins of Bolshevism* (1955). S. H. Baron, *Plekhanov, The Father of Russian Marxism* (1963) and W. A. Fomina, *Die philosophischen Anschauungen G. W. Plechanows* (Berlin, 1967). See also L. Labedz (ed.), *Revisionism. Essays on the History of Marxist Ideas* (1962), Ch. 2.

276   Karl Marx to Vera Zasulich, March 8, 1881 in Karl Marx and F. Engels, *Selected Correspondence* (Foreign Languages Publishing House, Moscow), p. 412.

277   Karl Marx to the editorial board of *Fatherland Notes (Otechestvenniye Zapiski)*, November 1877 in Karl Marx and F. Engels, *Selected Correspondence* (Foreign Languages Publishing House, Moscow), pp. 376–7. Marx did not send this letter and it was not published until 1886.

278   F. Engels to N. F. Danielson, June 18, 1892 in Karl Marx and F. Engels, *Briefe über "Das Kapital"* (1954), p. 344.

279   F. Engels to G. V. Plekhanov, February 26, 1895 in Karl Marx and F. Engels, *Selected Correspondence* (Foreign Languages Publishing House, Moscow), p. 561.

280   F. Engels, "Russia and the Social Revolution (1873)" in Karl Marx and F. Engels, *The Russian Menace to Europe* (edited by P. W. Blackstock and B. F. Hoselitz, 1953), p. 215.

281   Preface by Marx and Engels to the second Russian translation of the Communist Manifesto, January 21, 1882 in Karl Marx and F. Engels, *Manifest der Kommunistischen Partei* (edition of 1957), pp. xv–xvi.

282   H. A. Lopatin to M. N. Oshanina, September 20, 1883 in *Reminiscences of Marx and Engels* (Foreign Languages Publishing House, Moscow), pp. 204–5.

283   A. M. Voden, "Talks with Engels", in *Reminiscences of Marx and Engels* (Foreign Languages Publishing House, Moscow), p. 329.

284   Karl Marx to P. V. Annenkov, December 28, 1846 in Karl Marx and

F. Engels, *Selected Correspondence* (Foreign Languages Publishing House, Moscow), pp. 39–51.

285 F. Engels, *Ausgewählte Militärische Schriften*, Vol. 1 (1958), pp. 234–396; Karl Marx (should be Karl Marx and F. Engels), *The Eastern Question* . . . (ed. by Eleanor Marx-Aveling and Edward Aveling, 1897: new edition, 1969); and Karl Marx and F. Engels, *The Russian Menace* (ed. by P. W. Blackstock and B. F. Hoselitz, 1953).

286 For the Narodniks see W. G. Simkhovitsch, "Die Ökonomische Lehre der russischen Narodniki" in *Jahrbuch für Nationalökonomie*, Vol. 69, p. 653 *et seq.*; A. I. S. Branfoot, *A Critical Survey of the Narodnik Movement* (Ph.D. thesis, University of London, 1926); and R. Kindersley, *The First Russian Revisionists* (1962), Ch. 1, "Marxism versus Narodnichestvo".

287 Report published in the *Deutsche Rundschau*, Vol. 27, 1881, p. 351.

288 See Karl Marx, "The General Council of the International Working Men's Association to committee members of the Russian section in Geneva" (March 24, 1870) in *The General Council of the First International: Minutes*, Vol. 3, 1868–70, pp. 410–11. A little later Marx wrote that "the intellectual movement now taking place in Russia testifies to the fact that deep below the surface, fermentation is going on" (Karl Marx to S. Meyer, January 21, 1871 in Karl Marx and F. Engels, *Letters to Americans, 1848–95* (1963), p. 82).

289 H. A. Lopatin to N. P. Sinelnikov, February 15, 1873 in *Reminiscences of Marx and Engels* (Foreign Languages Publishing House, Moscow), pp. 201–2.

290 Karl Marx to F. Engels, July 5, 1870 in *Gesamtausgabe*, Part III, Vol. 4, p. 403.

291 Karl Marx to F. Engels, August 3, 1870 in *Gesamtausgabe*, Part III, Vol. 4, p. 416.

292 *The General Council of the First International: Minutes*, Vol. 4, 1870–1: meetings of September 6 and 20, 1870 (p. 59 and p. 61).

293 H. A. Lopatin to N. P. Sinelnikov, February 15, 1873 in *Reminiscences of Marx and Engels* (Foreign Languages Publishing House, Moscow), pp. 201–3. This letter was published in Lopatin's autobiography in 1922.

294 F. Engels to Karl Marx, November 29, 1873 in *Gesamtausgabe*, Part III, Vol. 4, p. 406.

295 Karl Marx to F. Engels, November 30, 1873 in *Gesamtausgabe*, Part III, Vol. 4, p. 408.

296 Karl Marx to F. Engels, July 23, 1877 in *Gesamtausgabe*, Part III, Vol. 4, p. 463.

297 Engels and Lopatin were both present at meetings of the General Council of the First International held on October 11, 18 and 25, and November 1, 8 and 15, 1870.

298 H. A. Lopatin to M. N. Oshanina, September 20, 1883 in *Reminiscences of Marx and Engels* (Foreign Languages Publishing House, Moscow), pp. 204–5. This letter was first published in 1893.

299 F. Engels to Laura Lafargue, November 24, 1886 in *F. Engels – Paul and Laura Lafargue: Correspondence*, Vol. 1, p. 396.

300 For Peter Lavrov's career see an article in *L'Humanité Nouvelle* (Paris), Vol. 37 (1900), pp. 35–9. See also Peter Lavrov, *Historical Letters* (1967).

301 L. Pierre (Peter Lavrov) in *L'Internationale* (the organ of the Belgian

sections of the First International), April 2, 1871: English translation in E. Schulkind (ed.), *The Paris Commune of 1871* (1972), pp. 114–15.

302 E. Schulkind (ed.), *The Paris Commune of 1871* (1972), p. 114.

303 *The General Council of the First International: Minutes*, Vol. 4, 1870–1: Council meetings, July 4, 1871 (p. 226), July 11, 1871 (p. 231), and July 18, 1871 (p. 235).

304 *Karl Marx. Chronik seines Lebens in Einzeldaten* (Makol Verlag, 1971), p. 309.

305 *Karl Marx. Chronik seines Lebens in Einzeldaten* (Makol Verlag, 1971), p. 351 and p. 453. In December 1875 Lavrov asked Marx to attend another meeting in London in support of the Poles but Marx had to decline the invitation owing to ill-health (*ibid.*, pp. 354–5).

306 Karl Marx to F. Engels, March 3, 1877 in *Gesamtausgabe*, Part III, Vol. 4, pp. 449–50.

307 Laura Lafargue to F. Engels, April 21, 1885 in *F. Engels – Paul and Laura Lafargue: Correspondence*, Vol. 1, 1868–86, p. 282.

308 Karl Marx to Peter Lavrov, February 11, 1875 in Karl Marx and F. Engels, *Briefe über "Das Kapital"* (1954), pp. 223–5.

309 F. Engels to Peter Lavrov, November 12, 1875 in Karl Marx and F. Engels, *Briefe über "Das Kapital"* (1954), pp. 226–9: English translation in Karl Marx and F. Engels, *Selected Correspondence* (Foreign Languages Publishing House, Moscow), pp. 366–70.

310 Karl Marx to F. Engels, March 3, 1877 in *Gesamtausgabe*, Part III, Vol. 4, p. ?

311 *Karl Marx. Chronik seines Lebens in Einzeldaten* (Makol Verlag, 1971), p. 385.

312 Boris Tartakowski, "Friedrich Engels und das revolutionäre Russland" in *Friedrich Engels, 1820–1970* (Schriftenreihe der Friedrich Ebert Stiftung, Vol. 85, 1971), p. 165.

313 *Karl Marx. Chronik seines Lebens in Einzeldaten* (Makol Verlag, 1971), p. 393.

314 F. Engels to Laura Lafargue, February 5, 1884 in *F. Engels – Paul and Laura Lafargue: Correspondence*, Vol. 1, p. 169. Engels wrote "The Russian books we have promised to Lavrov: he is, I think, positively entitled to them. . . ." On March 3, 1884 Paul Lafargue told Engels that Lavrov had "received his packing case several days ago" (*ibid.*, Vol. 1, p. 184).

315 F. Engels to Peter Lavrov, April 2, 1883; January 28, February 5 and 12, 1884 in Karl Marx and F. Engels, *Briefe über "Das Kapital"* (1954), pp. 277, 281–2, 283–5, and 293–4.

316 A. Voden, "Talks with Engels" in *Reminiscences of Marx and Engels* (Modern Languages Publishing House, Moscow), p. 328. Danielson translated *Das Kapital* into Russian (Vol. 1 in collaboration with Lapotin) and was the author of *Essays on our Post-Reform Social Economy* (in Russian) (1880).

317 F. Engels to Peter Lavrov, November 12, 1875 in Karl Marx and F. Engels, *Briefe über "Das Kapital"* (1954), pp. 226–9: English translation in Karl Marx and F. Engels, *Selected Correspondence* (Foreign Languages Publishing House, Moscow), pp. 366–70.

318 For Leo Hartmann see Karl Kautsky in Benedikt Kautsky (ed.), *Friedrich Engels' Briefwechsel mit Karl Kautsky* (1955), pp. 18–19.

319 N. Morozov, "Visits to Karl Marx", in *Reminiscences of Marx and Engels* (Foreign Languages Publishing House, Moscow), p. 302.

320   F. Engels to Paul Lafargue, January 25, 1885 in *F. Engels – Paul and Laura Lafargue: Correspondence*, Vol. 1, p. 260.

321   F. Engels to Karl Marx, September 12, 1882 in *Gesamtausgabe*, Part III, Vol. 4, pp. 558–60.

322   F. Engels to Karl Marx, September 12, 1882 in *Gesamtausgabe*, Part III, Vol. 4, pp. 558–60.

323   F. Engels to Karl Marx, December 15, 1882 in *Gesamtausgabe*, Part III, Vol. 4, pp. 581–3: English translation in Karl Marx and F. Engels, *Selected Correspondence* (Foreign Languages Publishing House, Moscow), p. 429.

324   F. Engels to Karl Marx, December 22, 1882 in *Gesamtausgabe*, Part III, Vol. 4, pp. 586–7.

325   This was Engels's reply to Tkachev's pamphlet entitled *Open Letter to Mr Friedrich Engels*. . . . Marx read Tkachev's pamphlet in December 1873 and suggested that Engels should "hit back hastily": see *Karl Marx. Chronik seines Lebens in Einzeldaten* (Makol Verlag, 1971), p. 350.

326   F. Engels, "Soziales aus Russland" in *Der Volksstaat*, April 16, 18 and 21, 1875: English translation in Karl Marx and F. Engels, *The Russian Menace to Europe* (ed. by P. W. Blackstock and B. F. Hoselitz, 1953), pp. 203–15.

327   F. Engels, *Internationales aus dem "Volksstaat"*, 1871–5 (1894) and Boris Tartakowski, "Friedrich Engels und die revolutionäre Russland" in *Friedrich Engels, 1820–1970* (Schriftenreihe des Forschungsinstitut der Friedrich Ebert Stiftung, Vol. 85, 1971), p. 167.

328   F. Engels to Eugenie Papritz, June 26, 1884 in Karl Marx and F. Engels, *Selected Correspondence* (Foreign Languages Publishing House, Moscow), pp. 450–1.

329   F. Engels to Vera Zasulich, April 23, 1884 in Karl Marx and F. Engels, *Selected Correspondence* (Foreign Languages Publishing House, Moscow), p. 459.

330   F. Engels to August Bebel, May 9, 1890 in Werner Blumenberg (ed.), *August Bebels Briefwechsel mit Friedrich Engels* (1965), p. 388 and an illustration in the *Daily Graphic*, May 2, 1892 entitled: "Labour Day in London. Yesterday's Demonstration in Hyde Park. Platform No. 14."

331   Karl Kautsky in Benedikt Kautsky (ed.), *Friedrich Engels' Briefwechsel mit Karl Kautsky* (1955), p. 169.

332   F. M. Kravchinskaya in *Reminiscences of Marx and Engels* (Foreign Languages Publishing House, Moscow), pp. 335–9. Stepniak ("son of the steppes") was a nom de plume: his real name was Kravchinsky. For Stepniak see an article by Vera Zasulich in *Die Neue Zeit*, Vol. 14 (Part I), 1896, p. 490 and Eduard Bernstein, *Aus den Jahren meines Exils* (1918), pp. 231–4.

333   E. Bernstein to F. Engels, November 10, 1883 in H. Hirsch (ed.), *Eduard Bernsteins Briefwechsel mit Friedrich Engels* (1970), p. 231.

334   Karl Marx to F. A. Sorge, November 5, 1880 in Karl Marx and F. Engels, *Letters to Americans, 1848–95* (1963), p. 126.

335   S. H. Baron, *Plekhanov. The Father of Russian Marxism* (1963), p. 134.

336   Sir Donald Mackenzie Wallace, *Russia* (revised edition, 1912), pp. 599–600.

337   F. Engels to Vera Zasulich, March 6, 1884 in Karl Marx and

F. Engels, *Selected Correspondence* (Foreign Languages Publishing House, Moscow), p. 444 (postscript).

338 S. H. Baron, *Plekhanov. The Father of Russian Marxism* (1963), p. 73.

339 Edmund Wilson, *To the Finland Station* (Fontana Library, 1960), p. 351.

340 Karl Marx to Vera Zasulich, March 8, 1881 in Karl Marx and F. Engels, *Selected Correspondence* (Foreign Languages Publishing House, Moscow), pp. 411–12.

341 F. Engels to Vera Zasulich, March 6, 1884 in Karl Marx and F. Engels, *Selected Correspondence* (Foreign Languages Publishing House, Moscow), pp. 442–4.

342 F. Engels to Vera Zasulich, April 23, 1885 in Karl Marx and F. Engels, *Selected Correspondence* (Foreign Languages Publishing House, Moscow), pp. 458–61.

343 F. Engels to Laura Lafargue, August 21, 1893 in *F. Engels – Paul and Laura Lafargue: Correspondence*, Vol. 3, p. 286.

344 August Bebel to F. Engels, August 26, 1894 in Werner Blumenberg (ed.), *August Bebels Briefwechsel mit Friedrich Engels* (1965), p. 776.

345 E. Aveling, "Engels at Home" in *Reminiscences of Marx and Engels* (Foreign Languages Publishing House, Moscow), p. 312.

346 F. Engels to Georgi Plekhanov, February 26, 1895 in Helmut Hirsch (ed.), *Friedrich Engels Profile* (1970), pp. 115–16.

347 Stepniak's wife wrote that "Engels kept up his interest in all events to the very end and wrote much. Vera Zasulich often went to see him and (she) shared (her) impressions with me" (F. M. Kravchinskaya in *Reminiscences of Marx and Engels*, p. 339).

348 A. Voden, "Talks with Engels" in *Reminiscences of Marx and Engels* (Foreign Languages Publishing House, Moscow), p. 328.

349 Edward Aveling, "Engels at Home" in *The Labour Prophet*, Vol. 4, 1895, Numbers 45 and 46 and in *Reminiscences of Marx and Engels* (Foreign Languages Publishing House, Moscow), p. 312.

350 Quoted by M. Sidorov in his introduction to G. V. Plekhanov, *Utopian Socialism of the Nineteenth Century*, 1913 (Foreign Languages Publishing House, Moscow), p. 8.

351 Karl Kautsky to F. Engels, February 14, 1884 and December 12, 1891 in Benedikt Kautsky (ed.), *Friedrich Engels' Briefwechsel mit Karl Kautsky* (1955), p. 98 and p. 320.

352 Boris Tartakowski, "Friedrich Engels und das revolutionäre Russland" in *Friedrich Engels, 1820–1970* (Schriftenreihe des Forschungsinstituts der Friedrich Ebert Stiftung, Vol. 85, 1971), p. 165.

353 S. H. Baron, *Plekhanov. The Father of Russian Marxism* (1963), p. 75.

354 M. Sidorov in his introduction to G. V. Plekhanov, *Utopian Socialism of the Nineteenth Century*, 1913 (Foreign Languages Publishing House, Moscow), pp. 8–9.

355 *Reminiscences of Marx and Engels* (Foreign Languages Publishing House, Moscow), p. 329 (note 2).

356 S. H. Baron, *Plekhanov. The Father of Russian Marxism* (1963), p. 160.

357 S. H. Baron, *Plekhanov. The Father of Russian Marxism* (1963), p. 142.

358 August Bebel to F. Engels, April 11, 1892 in Werner Blumenberg (ed.), *August Bebels Briefwechsel mit Friedrich Engels* (1965), p. 531 and N. S. Rusanov, "My Acquaintance with Engels" in *Reminiscences*

of Marx and Engels (Foreign Languages Publishing House, Moscow), pp. 318–24 and in the *Arbeiter Zeitung* (Vienna), February 20, 1931.

359 G. V. Plekhanov to Karl Kautsky, December 20, 1894 in the Institute of Social History (Amsterdam).

360 S. H. Baron, *Plekhanov. The Father of Russian Marxism* (1963), p. 160 (note).

361 G. D. H. Cole, *The Second International, 1889–1914* (two volumes, 1956); James Joll, *The Second International, 1889–1914* (New York, 1956); M. M. Drachkowitch (ed.), *The Revolutionary Internationals, 1864–1943* (1966): Part II "The Second International" (by G. Niemeyer and Carl Landauer); S. Bünger, *Friedrich Engels und die britische sozialistische Bewegung, 1881–95* (1962), Ch. 7.

362 Werner Sombart, *Socialism and the Social Movement* (1909), p. 184.

363 Edmund Wilson, *To the Finland Station* (Fontana Library, 1960), p. 287.

364 F. Engels to Wilhelm Liebknecht, July 31, 1877 in Wilhelm Liebknecht, *Briefwechsel mit Karl Marx und Friedrich Engels* (ed. Georg Eckert, 1963), p. 235.

365 Karl Marx to Wilhelm Bracke, August 24, 1877 in Karl Marx–Friedrich Engels, *Briefwechsel mit Wilhelm Bracke, 1869–80* (1963), p. 148.

366 M. Beer, *A History of British Socialism*, Vol. 2 (1929), p. 265 (note).

367 Karl Marx to F. A. Sorge, September 27, 1877 in *Briefe und Auszüge von Briefen von Joh. Phil. Becker, Jos. Dietzen, Friedrich Engels, Karl Marx u. A. an F. A. Sorge und Andere* (Stuttgart, 1906), p. 156. For the Ghent socialist congress of 1877 see *Vorwärts*, Numbers 104, 110, 111, 112 and 114 of 1877.

368 F. Engels, "Die europäischen Arbeiter im Jahre 1877" in *Marx–Engels Werke*, Vol. 19, pp. 123–4.

369 Max Nettlau, *Anarchisten und Sozialrevolutionäre* (1931), p. 221 and Max Nomad, "The Anarchist Tradition" in M. M. Drachkowitch (ed.), *The Revolutionary Internationals, 1864–1943* (1966), p. 76.

370 John Derbyshire to F. Engels, October 15, 1883 in the Marx–Engels Archives (Amsterdam), L.1072.

371 F. Engels in *Le Socialiste*, March 27, 1886 and in *F. Engels – Paul and Laura Lafargue: Correspondence*, Vol. 1, pp. 406–7.

372 F. Engels to Laura Lafargue, June 11, 1889 in *F. Engels – Paul and Laura Lafargue: Correspondence*, Vol. 2, p. 276.

373 Adolphe Smith, *A Critical Essay on the International Trade Union Congress held in London, November 1888* (London, 1889).

374 In the previous autumn Engels had told Danielson that he had to be careful not to strain his eyes: F. Engels to N. F. Danielson, October 15, 1888 in Karl Marx–F. Engels, *Briefe über "Das Kapital"* (1954), pp. 307–8.

375 F. Engels to Paul Lafargue, May 11, 1889 and F. Engels to Laura Lafargue, June 11, 1889 (*F. Engels – Paul and Laura Lafargue: Correspondence*, Vol. 2, p. 241 and p. 275) and F. Engels to N. F. Danielson, July 4, 1889 (Karl Marx–F. Engels, *Briefe über "Das Kapital"* (1954), p. 314).

376 *The International Working Men's Congress of 1889. A Reply to "Justice"* (London, 1899): German translation in *Der Sozialdemokrat*, March 30 and April 6, 1889. A second pamphlet by Engels and Bernstein attacking the Social Democratic Federation was published on June 1, 1889.

377 F. Engels to F. A. Sorge, May 11, 1889 in Karl Marx and F. Engels, *Letters to Americans, 1848–95* (1963), p. 213.

378 Paul Lafargue to F. Engels, May 4, 1889 in *F. Engels – Paul and Laura Lafargue: Correspondence*, Vol. 2, p. 248. See also Paul Lafargue to F. Engels, April 14, 1889 (*ibid.*, Vol. 2, p. 220).

379 F. Engels to F. A. Sorge, May 11, 1889 in Karl Marx and F. Engels, *Letters to Americans, 1848–95* (1963), p. 212.

380 F. Engels to F. A. Sorge, June 8, 1889 in Karl Marx and F. Engels, *Letters to Americans, 1848–95* (1963), pp. 213–16.

381 F. Engels to Laura Lafargue, June 11, 1889 in *F. Engels – Paul and Laura Lafargue: Correspondence*, Vol. 2, p. 275.

382 F. Engels to F. A. Sorge, June 8, 1889 in Karl Marx and F. Engels, *Letters to Americans, 1848–95* (1963), p. 216.

383 F. Engels to F. A. Sorge, July 17, 1889 in Karl Marx and F. Engels, *Letters to Americans, 1848–95* (1963), p. 217.

384 Paul Lafargue to F. Engels, July 23, 1887 in *F. Engels – Paul and Laura Lafargue: Correspondence*, Vol. 2, pp. 293–4.

385 Werner Sombart, *Socialism and the Social Movement* (1909), p. 186.

386 F. Engels to Laura Lafargue, May 10, 1890 in *F. Engels – Paul and Laura Lafargue*, Vol. 2, pp. 375–7 and F. Engels, "Der 4.Mai in London" in the *Arbeiter-Zeitung* (Vienna), May 23, 1890, reprinted in *Victor Adlers Aufsätze, Reden und Briefe*, Heft 1: *Victor Adler und Friedrich Engels* (1922), pp. 8–15. Friedrich Lessner wrote that Engels "always attended the May celebrations in spite of his age and even climbed onto the cart that was used as a rostrum". "And who can ever forget the May parties that followed those meetings?" (F. Lessner in *Die Hütte*, 1902 and in *Reminiscences of Marx and Engels* (Modern Languages Publishing House, Moscow), p. 179.

387 Engels's introduction to a new edition of the Communist Manifesto published in 1890: see Karl Marx–Friedrich Engels, *Manifest der Kommunistischen Partei* (edition of 1957), pp. xxx–xxi.

388 F. Engels to F. A. Sorge, May 17, 1893 in Karl Marx and F. Engels, *Letters to Americans, 1848–95* (1963), p. 253.

389 G. Niemeyer in M. M. Drachkowitch (ed.), *The Revolutionary Internationals, 1864–1943* (1966), pp. 96–7.

390 For an English translation of Engels's speech to the Zürich congress of the Second International in August 1893 see *F. Engels – Paul and Laura Lafargue: Correspondence*, Vol. 3, p. 282 (note). See also F. Engels to Laura Lafargue, August 21, 1893 (*ibid.*, Vol. 3, pp. 282–7) and F. Engels to F. A. Sorge, October 7, 1893 in F. Engels, *Auf Reisen* (1966), pp. 230–4 and an English translation in Karl Marx and F. Engels, *Letters to Americans, 1848–95* (1963), pp. 254–6.

391 F. Engels to Charlotte Engels, December 1, 1884 in *Marx–Engels Werke*, Vol. 36, pp. 247–8 and Helmut Hirsch (ed.), *Friedrich Engels: Profile* (1970), p. 99.

392 F. Engels to V. Adler, September 25, 1892 and March 16, 1895 in *Victor Adlers Aufsätze, Reden und Briefe*, Heft 1: *Victor Adler und Friedrich Engels* (1922), p. 53 and p. 126.

393 E. Bernstein, "Erinnerungen an Karl Marx und Friedrich Engels" in *Mohr und General* (1965), p. 497.

394 Eleanor Marx in the *Sozialdemokratische Monatsschrift*, November 30, 1890 and in *Reminiscences of Marx and Engels* (Foreign Languages Publishing House, Moscow), p. 187.

395 F. Engels to Laura Lafargue, December 1, 1890 in *F. Engels – Paul and Laura Lafargue: Correspondence*, Vol. 2, p. 422.

396 F. Engels to Laura Lafargue, December 13, 1883 in *F. Engels – Paul and Laura Lafargue: Correspondence*, Vol. 1, p. 159.

397 Paul Lafargue to F. Engels, June 24, 1884 in *F. Engels – Paul and Laura Lafargue: Correspondence*, Vol. 1, p. 209.

398 F. Engels to Karl Kautsky, June 21, 1884 in Benedikt Kautsky (ed.), *Friedrich Engels' Briefwechsel mit Karl Kautsky* (1955), p. 123.

399 F. Engels to F. A. Sorge, May 12, 1894 in Karl Marx and F. Engels, *Letters to Americans, 1848–95* (1963), p. 262.

400 F. Engels to Laura Lafargue, August 6, 1888 in *F. Engels – Paul and Laura Lafargue: Correspondence*, Vol. 2, p. 151.

401 F. Engels to N. F. Danielson, October 15, 1888 in Karl Marx–F. Engels, *Briefe über "Das Kapital"* (1954), p. 307.

402 F. Engels to N. F. Danielson, October 15, 1888 in Karl Marx–F. Engels, *Briefe über "Das Kapital"* (1954), p. 307.

403 F. Engels to F. A. Sorge, January 6, 1892 in Karl Marx and F. Engels, *Letters to Americans, 1848–95* (1963), p. 238.

404 F. Engels to Edouard Vaillant, December 5, 1890 in *F. Engels – Paul and Laura Lafargue: Correspondence*, Vol. 2, p. 425.

405 F. Engels to F. A. Sorge, November 5, 1890 in Karl Marx and F. Engels, *Letters to Americans, 1848–95* (1963), p. 232.

406 Louise Kautsky (Freyberger) was a qualified midwife.

407 F. Engels to Laura Lafargue, December 17, 1890 in *F. Engels – Paul and Laura Lafargue: Correspondence*, Vol. 2, p. 426.

408 F. Engels to Paul Lafargue, March 6, 1894 in *F. Engels – Paul and Laura Lafargue: Correspondence*, Vol. 3, p. 326. Engels wrote: "So you were surprised by Louise's marriage? It has been brewing for some months. Freyberger has left Vienna and given up a brilliant University career because they forbade him to enlighten the workers, in his lectures, on the social causes of their ills. So he came here, and he has found very good openings in the hospitals here. Once that was settled, there was no further reason for delaying the wedding. While awaiting for his expectations to materialise he came to join his wife here. You can see that it is an entirely matriarchal marriage, the husband is his wife's boarder!"

409 On July 20, 1893 Engels wrote to Laura Lafargue: "I don't want to be laid up again lame in an armchair for six weeks" (*F. Engels – Paul and Laura Lafargue: Correspondence*, Vol. 3, p. 279.

410 F. Engels to V. Adler, September 22, 1892 in *Victor Adlers Aufsätze, Reden und Briefe*, Heft 1; *Victor Adler und Friedrich Engels* (1922), p. 51.

411 F. Engels to F. A. Sorge, May 12, 1894 in Karl Marx and F. Engels, May 21, 1895 in Benedikt Kautsky (ed.), *Friedrich Engels' Briefwechsel mit Karl Kautsky* (1955), p. 433.

412 F. Engels, "Kann Europa abrüsten? in *Vorwärts*, March 1 to March 10, 1893 and in Karl Marx–Friedrich Engels, Vol. 4: *Geschichte und Politik* (2), pp. 236–57 (Fischer Bücherei, 2966). The articles were also published as a pamplet in Nürnberg in 1893.

413 F. Engels, "Zur Geschichte des Urchristentums" in *Die Neue Zeit*, September–October, 1894 and in *Le Devoir Social*, April–May, 1895. A writer in the *Economic Journal* (Vol. 5, 1895) observed that these articles "draw out a very striking historical parallel between Christianity and Socialism. Both have been democratic and revolutionary;

both have had their periods of struggles, sects, superstitions, violence, gradual consolidation and gradual victory" (p. 492). Engels had written previously on primitive Christianity in his obituary of Bruno Bauer: see F. Engels, "Bruno Bauer und das Urchristentum" in *Der Sozialdemokrat*, Number 19 and 20, May 4 and May 11, 1882.

414 F. Engels, "Die Bauernfrage in Frankreich und Deutschland" in *Die Neue Zeit*, November 1894.

415 F. Engels's introduction to Karl Marx, *Die Klassenkämpfe in Frankreich, 1848 bis 1850* (1895).

416 F. Engels to Laura Lafargue, March 28, 1895 in *F. Engels – Paul and Laura Lafargue: Correspondence*, Vol. 3, p. 369.

417 F. Engels to Karl Kautsky, May 21, 1895 in Benedikt Kautsky (ed.), *Friedrich Engels' Briefwechsel mit Karl Kautsky* (1955), p. 433.

418 F. Engels to E. Bernstein, June 18, 1895 in Helmut Hirsch (ed.), *Eduard Bernsteins Briefwechsel mit Friedrich Engels* (1970), p. 417. Engels stayed at 4 Royal Parade, Eastbourne.

419 Samuel Moore to Eleanor Marx, July 21, 1895 (wrongly dated 1891) in the Marx–Engels archives (Amsterdam), G.161.

420 Victor Adler to F. Engels, July 13, 1895 in *Victor Adlers Aufsätze, Reden und Briefe*, Heft 1: *Victor Adler und Friedrich Engels* (1922), p. 131. Adler stayed with Engels first in Eastbourne and then in London until August 3, 1895.

421 Louise Freyberger to August Bebel, September 2 and 4, 1898 in the Bernstein papers in the International and in W. Blumenberg, *Marx* (1962), pp. 115–17 and Arnold Künzli, *Karl Marx, Eine Psychographie* (1966), pp. 325–7. Louise Freyberger wrote that "Freddy is ridiculously like Marx and only blind prejudice could see the slightest resemblance to General in the boy's typical Jewish features and blue-black hair".

422 Eleanor Marx to John Burns, August 6 and 8, 1895 in Gustav Mayer, *Friedrich Engels*, Vol. 2 (1934), p. 569 (note to p. 525).

423 Gustav Adolf Schlechtendahl (1840–1912) had married Elise Boelling, a daughter of Engels's sister Hedwig. He was a leading figure in the Reformed Evangelical Church in Barmen-Gemarke.

424 Eduard Bernstein, *Aus den Jahren meines Exils* (1918), p. 208.

425 A copy of Engels's will is preserved in the Marx–Engels archives in Amsterdam, M.53. See also E. Bernstein, "Friedrich Engels' Testament. Seine Bedeutung und sein Schicksal" in *Vorwärts (Der Abend)*, September 18, 1929 and E. Bernstein, "Geist und Ausführung des Engelsschen Testaments" in *Vorwärts (Der Abend)*, September 20, 1929.

426 F. Engels to August Bebel and Paul Singer, November 14, 1894 in Werner Blumenberg (ed.), *August Bebels Briefwechsel mit Friedrich Engels* (1965), p. 783.

427 Under the codicil Ellen Rosher (Pumps) received (in addition to her legacy of £2,230) "the reversionary interest of the said Percy White Rosher in certain monies to which he is or was entitled expectant on the death of his parents under their marriage settlement which said reversionary interest I have bought from him for the sum of £240 and which also cost me £30 for legal expenses making £270 in all".

428 Karl Kautsky in Benedikt Kautsky (ed.), *Friedrich Engels's Briefwechsel mit Karl Kautsky* (1955), p. 445.

429 F. Engels to Laura Lafargue and Eleanor Marx, November 14, 1894

in *F. Engels – Paul and Laura Lafargue: Correspondence,* Vol. 3, p. 342.

430   In a letter to his executors, dated November 14, 1894 Engels reminded them that each legacy should bear its share of death duty; that money which he had sent to Mrs Rosher, Paul and Laura Lafargue, Eleanor Marx and Edward Aveling was to be regarded as a gift and not as a loan; and that Marx's papers in his handwriting (except Marx's letters to Engels) were to be handed over to Eleanor Marx. In a postscript Engels directed that the royalties from the English edition of *The Condition of the Working Class in England* should be divided between Laura Lafargue, Eleanor Marx, Jenny Longuet's children, Samuel Moore, Edward Aveling and Mrs Wischnewetzky.

431   In a letter to Laura Lafargue and Eleanor Marx dated November 14, 1894 Engels explained why he proposed to leave to the German Social Democrat Party not only his own library but also that part of Karl Marx's library which had come into his possession on Marx's death. Engels appreciated that Marx's daughters might expect him to return their father's books. He wrote: "I have taken the liberty of disposing of all my books, including those received from you after Mohr's (Marx's) death, in favour of the German Party. The whole of these books constitute a library so unique, and so complete at the same time, for the history and the study of modern socialism and all the sciences on which it is dependent, that it would be a pity to disperse it again. To keep it together, and to place it at the same time at the disposal of those desirous to use it, has been a wish expressed to me long ago by Bebel and other leaders of the German Socialist Party, and as they do indeed seem to be the best people for that purpose, I have consented. I hope that under the circumstances you will pardon my action and give your consent too" (*F. Engels – Paul and Laura Lafargue: Correspondence,* Vol. 3, p. 342).

432   In a letter to Laura Lafargue, dated December 29, 1894 Engels wrote: "all these things I hold *in trust for you,* that you know; and consequently on my death they revert to you. In the last will I made (when Sam Moore were here last time but one) there is no special provision, but in the instructions to my executors accompanying it, there is a distinct direction to them, to hand over to Tussy, as the administrator of the will, the whole of Mohr's Mss. that are in his own handwriting, also all letters addressed to him with the sole exception of my correspondence with him. And as Tussy seems to have some doubts about the matter, I shall as soon as Sam M(oore) comes back in summer ask him to draw up a new will in which this is distinctly and unmistakably declared . . ." (F. Engels to Laura Lafargue, December 29, 1894 in *F. Engels – Paul and Laura Lafargue: Correspondence,* Vol. 3, p. 353). See also F. Engels to Laura Lafargue, January 19, 1895 (*ibid.,* p. 361).

433   Karl Kautsky in Benedikt Kautsky (ed.), *Friedrich Engels' Briefwechsel mit Karl Kautsky* (1955), p. 447.

434   F. Engels to Laura Lafargue, December 17, 1894 in *F. Engels – Paul and Laura Lafargue: Correspondence,* Vol. 3, p. 348.

435   F. Engels to Karl Kautsky, January 28, 1889 in Benedikt Kautsky (ed.), *Friedrich Engels' Briefwechsel mit Karl Kautsky* (1955), pp. 227–9.

436   F. Engels to Laura Lafargue, December 17, 1894 in *F. Engels – Paul and Laura Lafargue: Correspondence,* Vol. 3, p. 348.

437 F. Engels to Laura Lafargue, December 29, 1894 in *F. Engels – Paul and Laura Lafargue: Correspondence*, Vol. 3, pp. 352–3.

438 F. Engels to Paul Stumpf, January 3, 1895 in *Marx–Engels Werke*, Vol. 39, p. 367.

439 H. Wendel, "Friedrich Engels als politischer Mentor" in *Die Gesellschaft*, Vol. 3, 1926 (Part I), p. 70 and K. Obermann and Ursula Hermann (editors), *Friedrich Engels und die International Arbeiterbewegung* (1962).

440 Ignaz Auer to Victor Adler, September 26, 1895 in Victor Adler, *Briefwechsel mit August Bebel und Karl Kautsky* (edited by F. Adler, 1954), pp. 189–90.

441 For Eduard Bernstein see Pierre Angel, *Eduard Bernstein et l'evolution du socialisme allemande* (1961); Peter Gay, *The Dilemna of Democratic Socialism* (1952); and H. Hirsch, *Ein revisionistisches Sozialismusbild* (1966).

442 For Karl Kautsky see B. Kautsky (ed.), *Ein Leben für den Sozialismus. Erinnerungen an Karl Kautsky* (1954); Karl Kautsky, *Erinnerungen und Erörterungen* (ed. B. Kautsky, 1960); and Karl Kautsky, *Zu den Programmen der Sozialdemokratie* (documents edited by Albrecht Langer: Hegner Bücherei, 1968). For a list of Karl Kautsky's writings see Werner Blumenberg, *Karl Kautskys literarisches Werk* (1960).

443 F. Engels to August Bebel, August 14, 1892 in Werner Blumenberg (ed.), *August Bebels Briefwechsel mit Friedrich Engels* (1965), p. 572. Bebel replied on August 17, 1892 that "Ede's enthusiasm for the Fabians is simply ridiculous" (*ibid.*, p. 575). See also F. Engels to August Bebel, August 20, 1892 where he wrote about Bernstein's *Fabianschwärmerei* (*ibid.*, p. 576). Bernstein denied that his contacts with the Fabian Society had anything to do with his later policy of "revisionism": see Eduard Bernstein, *Aus den Jahren meines Exils* (1918), p. 239 *et. seq.*

444 F. Engels to Laura Lafargue, December 17, 1894 in *F. Engels – Paul and Laura Lafargue: Correspondence*, Vol. 3, p. 348.

445 F. Engels to Karl Kautsky, May 21, 1895 in Benedikt Kautsky (ed.), *Friedrich Engels' Briefwechsel mit Karl Kautsky* (1955), pp. 433–6.

446 S. H. Baron, *Plekhanov. The Father of Russian Marxism* (1963), p. 171.

447 For Bernstein's "revisionism" see E. Bernstein, *Die Voraussetzungen des Sozialismus und die Aufgaben der Sozialdemokratie* (1898); E. Bernstein, *Der Revisionismus und die Sozialdemokratie* (1909); C. Gneuss, "Um die Einklang von Theorie und Praxis. Eduard Bernstein und der Revisionismus" in *Marxismusstudien*, Vol. 2, 1957, pp. 198–226.

448 For Karl Kautsky's criticism of Bernstein's "revisionism" see Karl Kautsky, *Bernstein und die Sozialdemokratie. Eine Anti-Kritik* (1898). In the following year Rosa Luxemburg attacked Bernstein's "revisionism" in her pamphlet: *Sozialreform oder Revolution?* (1899). See also E. Matthias, "Kautsky und die Kautskyanismus. Die Funktion der Ideologie in der deutschen Sozialdemokratie vor dem ersten Weltkriege" in Marxismusstudien, Vol. 2, 1957, pp. 151–97. See also L. Labedz (ed.), *Revisionism. Essays on the History of Marxist Ideas* (1962).

449 V. I. Lenin, *Imperialism, the Highest Stage of Capitalism*, 1916 (Foreign Languages Publishing House, Moscow), p. 153.

450 V. I. Lenin, "Fredrick Engels" (1895) in V. I. Lenin, *Marx, Engels, Marxism* (Foreign Language Publishing House, Moscow, 1951), p. 56. For Engels's influence on Lenin see T. Timofejew, "Das Erbe von Engels und der Leninismus" in *Friedrich Engels 1820–1970* (Schriftenreihe des Forschungsinstituts der Friedrich Ebert Stiftung, Vol. 85, 1971), pp. 201–17.

451 Rosa Luxemburg, *Die Akkumulation des Kapitals. Ein Beitrag zur ökonomischen Erklärkung des Imperialismus* (1913: new edition, 1921): English translation – Rosa Luxemburg, *The Accumulation of Capital* (1951). For Rosa Luxemburg see J. P. Nettl, *Rosa Luxemburg* (two volumes, 1966) and H. Hirsch, Rosa Luxemburg (1969). See also D. Howard (ed.), *Selected Political Writings of Rosa Luxemburg* (1971).

452 The phrase was used by Nettl.

453 V. I. Lenin, *Imperialism, the Highest Stage of Capitalism*, 1913 (Foreign Languages Publishing House, Moscow).

454 Karl Marx and F. Engels, *On Colonialism* (collection of articles and letters) (Foreign Languages Publishing House, Moscow).

455 See Joan Robinson's introduction to Rosa Luxemburg, *The Accumulation of Capital* (1951).

456 V. I. Lenin, *Imperialism, the Highest Stage of Capitalism* (Foreign Languages Publishing House, Moscow): preface to the French and German editions, July 6, 1920 (p. 16).

Fifty years after Lenin's pamphlet was written it was still being discussed. For criticisms of Lenin's interpretation of the "new imperialism" see R. Avon, "The Leninist Myth of Imperialism" in *Partisan Review*, Vol. 18, 1951, pp. 646–62; M. Blaug, "Economic Imperialism Revisited" in *Yale Review*, 1960; D. Landes, "Some Thoughts on the Nature of Economic Imperialsm" in *Journal of Economic History*, 1961; and D. K. Fieldhouse, "'Imperialism'. An Historiographical Revision" in *Economic History Review*, 1961. For a defence of Lenin's argument (and a criticism of Fieldhouse's article) see Eric Stokes, "Late Nineteenth Century Expansion and the Attack on the Theory of Economic Imperialism" in *Historical Journal*, 1969, pp. 285–301.

DOCUMENTS

I

ADDRESS OF THE CENTRAL COMMITTEE OF THE COMMUNIST LEAGUE TO THE MEMBERS OF THE LEAGUE (BY MARX AND ENGELS), MARCH 1850[1]

Brothers!

The Communist League achieved two things during the revolution of 1848–9. First, members of the League everywhere played an active part in the revolutionary movement. In the press, on the barricades and on the battlefield they inspired the proletariat which was the only social class capable of playing a really decisive part in the revolutionary movement. Secondly, the aims of the League concerning the revolution – announced in 1847 in addresses by its congresses and central committee and in 1848 in the Communist Manifesto – have proved their value as the only correct policy for the proletariat to follow. The forecasts made in these policy statements have been proved to be absolutely correct. Views of the present state of society, once secretly propagated by the Communist League, are now universally discussed and are preached in every market place. But at the same time the former strong organisation of the Communist League was greatly weakened. Many members, personally involved in the revolutionary movement, felt that public action should now take the place of underground activities. The links between many sections and cells of the League were weakened and gradually disappeared. So while the democratic party – the organ of the petty bourgeoisie – continually improved its political organisation in Germany, the party of the proletariat lost its cohesion as an organisation. It survived only in isolated districts where it fought for local issues. As a party it came to be completely dominated by the petty bourgeois democrats. This situation must be remedied.

[1] See Wermuth and Stieber, *Die Communisten-Verschwörungen des neunzehnten Jahrhunderts* (two volumes, 1853–4; new edition, 1969), Vol. 1, Appendix 13, pp. 251–9; appendix to Karl Marx, *Enthüllungen über den Kommunistenprozess zu Köln* (new edition with introduction by F. Engels, Zürich, 1885: reprinted 1952), pp. 124–36 and Iring Fetscher (ed.), *Karl Marx-Friedrich Engels Studienausgabe*, Vol. 3 *Geschichte und Politik* (No. 1, 1966), pp. 90–9.

The central committee of the League, recognising the necessity of reasserting the independence of the proletariat as a political force, sent its emissary Joseph Moll on a tour of Germany in the winter of 1848–9 to reorganise the League in that country. Moll's mission had little result partly because the German workers still lacked political experience and partly because a new insurrection broke out in May 1849. Moll himself joined the revolutionary forces operating in Baden and the Palatinate and fell on June 29 in the action on the River Murg. The Communist League lost in Joseph Moll one of its oldest, most active and most reliable members. He had attended all our congresses and he had sat on our central committee. He had already undertaken a series of propaganda missions with great success. After the defeat of the revolutionary parties in Germany and in France in July 1849 nearly all the members of the central committee have come together again in London. They have been joined by new revolutionary forces and they are now energetically engaged in reorganising the Communist League.

The only way to achieve this reorganisation is by means of an emissary and the central committee considers that it is vital that our agent should now embark upon his task because we are on the eve of a new revolution. The party of the proletariat must take its part in this revolution as a fully organised, completely united, and absolutely independent organisation. If it fails to do this history will repeat itself and – as in 1848 – the party of the proletariat will be exploited and taken in tow by the middle classes.

We already told you, brothers, in 1848 that the German middle class would soon attain power and would then immediately use that power against the workers. You have seen that this actually happened. After the revolution of March 1848 the middle class immediately seized power and used its power to oppress the workers – their allies in the struggles – and to reduce them to their former state of servitude. And the middle class could not do this without the co-operation of the feudal party which had been overthrown in March. In the end the middle class actually had to abdicate its power in favour of the old authoritarian feudal elements in society. But the middle class abdicated its power on very favourable terms. It retained power behind the scene and protected all its interests by taking full advantage of the financial difficulties of the German governments. Consequently the revolutionary movement was able to take its course in a so-called peaceful manner. The middle class is actually in the happy position of not having to earn the hatred of the vast mass of the people by acts of violence – because the feudal counter-revolutionaries have taken all necessary steps to suppress popular movements. But one cannot expect a peaceful evolution of events. A revolution is due in the immediate future. It may come through a rising of the French workers or it may come as a reaction to an invasion of the Holy Alliance.

The *rôle* which the middle class liberals in Germany played in relation to the people in 1848 – a thoroughly treacherous *rôle* – will be taken over by the democratic petty bourgeoisie. At present the petty bourgeoisie plays the same part in opposition as the liberal middle class played before 1848. The democratic party – which is far more dangerous to the workers than the liberals ever were – is composed of three groups:

1. The progressive section of the upper middle class. This group aims at the abolition of feudalism and absolutism. It represents the former progressives of Berlin and it may be expected to refuse to pay taxes.

2. The democratic constitutional petty bourgeoisie. During the revolution of 1848 its main aim was to secure the establishment of a more or less democratic German federal state. This was the aim of its representatives who sat on the left in the Frankfurt and Stuttgart Parliaments. This was the aim of the armed rising in support of the Frankfurt Constitution.

3. The republican petty bourgeoisie. Their aim is to set up a German republic on federal lines similar to Switzerland. Today they call themselves "reds" and "social democrats" because their pious hope is to remove the pressure exerted by the great capitalists – the wealthy middle class – upon the petty bourgeoisie. In 1848 the representatives of this section of the petty bourgeoisie were members of the democratic congresses and committees. They provided the leaders of the democratic associations and the editors of the democratic newspapers.

Since the victory of the counter-revolution all these groups call themselves "republicans" or "reds" just as the French republican petty bourgeoisie now call themselves "socialists". Where – as in Württemberg, Bavaria etc. – they still have the opportunity of furthering their aims in a constitutional manner they repeat their old slogans and they show by their actions that they have not changed in the slightest. It is of course obvious that the alteration in the name of this party has not in any way changed its attitude towards the workers. The change of name simply shows that this group opposes the wealthy middle class – which is in alliance with the supporters of absolutism – and that it must therefore try to secure the support of the workers.

The party of the democratic petty bourgeoisie is very strong in

Germany. It includes not only the vast majority of the middle class inhabitants of the towns, the petty traders, and the master crafts-men, but it is also supported by smallholders and farm workers in the countryside – except in so far as these groups in the rural districts are in alliance with the urban proletariat.

The relationship between the revolutionary workers and the petty bourgeois democrats is this – the revolutionary workers sup-port the petty bourgeois democrats against the groups which they both wish to overthrow. But the revolutionary workers oppose the petty bourgeois democrats in any action which would benefit only the petty bourgeois democrats.

The petty bourgeois democrats have no intention whatever of turning society upside down to oblige the revolutionary proletariat. They aim at securing reforms which will make the present social system tolerable and satisfactory from their point of view. Above all they demand cuts in government expenditure by reducing the number of civil servants. They wish to see the great landowners and the wealthier section of the urban middle classes bear the main burden of taxation. They favour laws against usury and they desire the establishment of public credit banks to clip the wings of power-ful financiers. This would enable the petty bourgeoisie and the smallholders to borrow money on easy terms from the state and not from private capitalists. Moreover they demand the complete abolition of all feudal institutions so that property can be held in the country districts on terms acceptable to the middle classes. To secure these reforms the petty bourgeoisie need a democratic constitution – under either a republic or a constitutional monarchy – which would enable them (and their allies the smallholders) to secure a majority of seats in parliament. The petty bourgeoisie class also needs democratic institutions of local government which would enable it to control public property and to control certain functions of local administration which are at present in the hands of civil servants.

The petty bourgeoisie is opposed both to the rapid growth of the great capitalists and to any extension of their power. It there-fore favours a restriction of the right of inheritance and an ex-pansion of the public sector of the economy at the expense of the private sector. The petty bourgeois democrats definitely intend the workers to retain the status of wage-earners. But they would like the workers to enjoy high wages and greater security. They imagine that opportunities of employment could be improved if the eco-nomic activities of the state were expanded. They also favour the extension of private welfare services for the benefit of the workers. They hope to bribe the workers by what is virtually disguised charity and to crush the revolutionary enthusiasm of the workers by giving them temporary improvements in their standard of living. These demands are not made all simultaneously by the various groups which make up the petty bourgeois democratic party. Very few of these democrats would bring all these demands together as a statement of their policy. The few individual democrats – or groups of democrats – who support all these reforms are convinced that they have put forward the maximum demands which a revolution could ever hope to achieve. Such a political platform is of course quite unacceptable to the proletariat. The petty bourgeois democrats want to complete the revolution as quickly as possible by achieving the reforms that have been mentioned. It will be the task of the proletariat to further its own interests by promoting a permanent revolution. The proletariat must deprive all the propertied classes of their wealth and must seize the powers exercised by the state. Moreover the proletariat should not merely be united in one country. The workers should unite in all the leading countries in the world so that competition between them shall cease. The most important aspects of the economy should be concentrated in the hands of the workers. We are not interested in making changes in private property. We propose to destroy it. We have no desire to hide class distinctions. We wish to remove them. We do not propose to improve the existing structure of society; we seek to create a new society. It is certain that – in the course of future revolutionary developments – the petty bourgeois democrats will have a decisive influence upon German affairs for a short time.

We now have to consider the future policy of the workers – and particularly the Communist League – in relation to the petty bourgeois democrats (1) for the duration of the present position when the petty bourgeois democrats are as much oppressed as the workers, (2) during the next phase of the revolution when the petty bourgeois democrats will hold the upper hand, and (3) after the completion of the revolution when the oppressed classes and the proletariat will be in power.

1. At present the petty bourgeois democrats are everywhere oppressed and they wish to be reconciled to the workers. They hope that the workers will make common cause with the petty bourgeois democrats. They hope to establish a powerful opposition party embracing all shades of democratic opinion. They want to absorb the workers into a party dominated by the catchwords of the petty bourgeois democrats. The real class interests of the petty bourgeoisie are disguised by these hollow phrases. The petty bourgeois democrats have no intention of supporting the demands

of the proletariat. A coalition would benefit only the petty bourgeoisie and would definitely harm the proletariat. The workers would lose their political independence which they have worked so hard to secure and they would once more be tied to the apron strings of the middle class democrats. The workers should never again allow themselves to be reduced to the position of an audience which claps whenever a middle-class democrat speaks. The workers – above all the members of the Communist League – must strive to establish organisations of their own (open and underground) which will be independent of the democrats. Every group in the Communist League should be a rallying point for the local workers' associations. Here political problems can be discussed from the point of view of the proletariat, free from any middle class influence. The bourgeois democrats have no intention of forming a coalition with the workers in which the workers would have equal rights and equal powers with their middle class allies. This can be seen by examining the behaviour of the democrats in Breslau. Their organ – the *Neue Oder Zeitung* – has launched furious attacks upon the independently organised workers, whom it labels "socialists". No formal coalition between the petty bourgeoisie democrats and the working classes is necessary for the two groups to join together to fight a common enemy. As soon as an opponent has to be faced both parties – democrats and workers – will have a common interest in standing shoulder to shoulder, at any rate for the time being. As on previous occasions so in the future this co-operation will be quite brief. In the bloody conflicts that lie before us the workers – determined, courageous, self-sacrificing – will as usual bear the brunt of the fighting before victory is gained. As in the past so in the future the actions of the vast mass of the petty bourgeoisie will be characterised by sloth, hesitancy and lack of determination. As soon as victory is won the petty bourgeoisie will appeal to workers to return to their homes, to go back to work, and to avoid any so-called "excesses". The workers will not be powerful enough to stop the petty bourgeois democrats from doing this. But the armed proletariat will be strong enough to check the ambitions of the petty bourgeoisie. The workers will be strong enough to dictate terms that will ensure the eventual downfall of the petty bourgeois and will prepare the way for the future seizure of power by the proletariat. Above all – during and immediately after the revolution – the workers must do everything possible to counter any underhand moves on the part of the bourgeoisie. They must force the democrats to carry out their present terrorist threats. They must see to it that a victorious revolution is not immediately followed by a return to normality. The workers should not be frightened of so-called "excesses" – popular vengeance against detested individuals or buildings – which leave unpleasant memories in their wake. On the contrary the workers should not merely accept the fact that "excesses" occur but should try to control them. As soon as the middle classes are able to take over the administration the workers should demand guarantees for themselves. The authority of the new rulers should be restricted by every possible promise and concession. In this way the new bourgeois government will be fatally compromised. After a successful revolution – achieved by demonstrations and street fighting – the new régime will be greeted with enthusiasm. The policy of the leaders of the workers must be guided by a stern, cold-blooded assessment of the situation. They must treat new government with suspicion and reserve. They should establish their own proletarian administration through local workers' councils or clubs. In this way the middle class régime will immediately lose the backing of the workers. The new government will realise that its activities are being watched by organisations which enjoy the support of the vast mass of the workers. The policy that the workers should adopt may be summed up as follows – As soon as there are signs that the bourgeois revolution is achieving its aims the workers should cease to attack the reactionary parties and should begin to oppose the middle classes with whom they have formerly been allied. The middle classes have sought the alliance of the proletariat only in the hope of exploiting for themselves alone the fruits of the victory gained by their joint exertions.

2. In the first hour of victory the petty bourgeois democrats will begin to betray the workers. The proletariat must take energetic steps to counter this betrayal. The workers must be organised and they must be armed. They will have to get hold of flintlocks, fowling pieces, cannon and ammunition. They must, if possible, prevent the revival of the old middle class national guard which would oppose the proletariat. If this cannot be done the workers should try to set up their own militia under elected officers and an elected general staff. This militia should not obey a bourgeois government but should take its orders from revolutionary workers' councils. Those workers who are employed by the government should be organised in a special corps (under elected officers) or they could form part of the workers' militia. This militia should in no circumstances surrender its arms or ammunition. If the government should try to do this it should, if necessary, be resisted by force. During and immediately after the revolution the proletariat (and members of the Communist League) should adopt the following policy – destruction of the influence exercised by the bourgeois

democrats; immediate establishment of workers' councils; strong demands for guarantees (of a compromising nature) from the new (and unavoidable) middle class government.

3. The struggle with the workers will begin as soon as the new governments have attained a means of stability. To oppose the petty bourgeoisie effectively the workers must be organised in clubs under a central administration. When the present governments have been overthrown the central committee of the Communist League will move (from London) to Germany as soon as it is possible to do so. It will call a congress to which will be submitted plans for the establishment of an organisation to co-ordinate the activities of the workers' clubs. One of the most effective means of strengthening the party of the proletariat and of promoting its future growth will be to secure quickly the organisation of the workers' clubs at any rate on a provincial basis.

Whenever the existing governments are overthrown it will be necessary to hold elections for a national assembly. During these elections the proletariat should

(a) prevent any workers from being deprived of the vote by the chicanery of the officials of the local or central government.

(b) put forward candidates of the workers' party for all seats in opposition to middle class candidates. If possible the workers' candidates should be members of the Communist League and their election should be promoted by all means at the disposal of the proletariat. Workers' candidates should stand for election even if there is no likelihood that they will be successful. The appearance of such candidates at the election will show the public that the workers have formed an independent party of their own. The workers' candidates must put a radical and revolutionary programme before the electors. Candidates of the workers' party must not allow themselves to be blackmailed by their democratic opponents. They must not listen to the argument that to split the left wing vote by putting up working-class candidates would allow reactionary candidates to be elected. To fall for such arguments would be to prepare the way for the certain defeat of the workers. The advantages that the workers would gain by putting up independent candidates of their own would far outweigh the disadvantage of seeing some reactionary candidates elected to the assembly. And if the democratic parties stand up to present reaction in a really decisive manner – using methods of terrorism if necessary – the reaction will at once be denied any influence at the elections.

The first clash between the bourgeois democrats and the workers will be over the abolition of feudalism. What occurred during the first French revolution will occur again. The petty bourgeoisie will hand over to the peasants the land which they now cultivate under various feudal tenures. This will involve the continued existence of a landed proletariat and the creation of a class of petty bourgeois smallholders. These smallholders, like the modern French peasants, will be caught up in the vicious circle of poverty and debt.

In their own interests – and in the interests of the landed proletariat – the workers must oppose this scheme. They must demand the nationalisation of the confiscated feudal estates and their transformation into workers' farming settlements. In this way the landed proletariat will be able to cultivate the land using all the benefits to be obtained from large-scale farming. In this way the principle of nationalising the means of production can be firmly established at a time when middle class property relationships will be in a state of flux. If the democrats ally themselves to the farmers then the town workers must ally themselves to the landed proletariat. Moreover the middle class democrats will try to secure the establishment of a federal German republic. If they are forced to accept a really united German state they will try to weaken the central government by giving the provincial and other local authorities as much power as possible. The workers must aim at securing the establishment of a united German republic in which sovereignty will lie in the hands of the central authority. The proletariat must not be taken in by the fine speeches of the democrats in favour of self-government and freedom for local authorities. In Germany many local and medieval traditions and privileges still have to be swept away. In such a country it would be extremely foolish to allow every village, town and province to have enough power to check the progress of the revolution if it wished to do so. The energy of the revolution should be concentrated in the heart of a country and should not be dissipated in small localities.

The workers must insist that there should be no return after the revolution to the present situation in which the Germans must fight for the same little bit of progress in every town and in every province. Least of all should the workers allow communal property to survive in the rural parts of the country. This is an earlier form of property than modern private ownership of land and goods. Communal property must inevitably be absorbed by private property. Moreover communal property had led to quarrels between rich and poor villages and to legal actions which involve a clash between individual rights enjoyed by private citizens and communal rights enjoyed by communities. The workers have suffered from the chicanery of their opponents in such legal actions. Unless the workers offer strong resistance the establishment of a so-called "independent communal constitution" might simply perpetuate the existing state of affairs. As in France in 1793 so in Germany today the truly revolutionary party should do everything in its power to secure the establishment of a powerful central authority.[2]

We have seen how the next revolution will bring the democrats to power and how they will be compelled to introduce more or less socialist measures. One might ask what immediate reforms should be demanded by the workers. Obviously in the first stage of a revolution the workers cannot suggest the adoption of completely communist measures. But they should

1. Force the democrats to make numerous radical changes in the existing state of affairs. These reforms should effectively hamper the smooth working of the present social system and should lead to the nationalisation of many forms of economic production such as factories, railways and other transport systems. Such reforms would compromise the democrats in the eyes of the upper middle classes and the reactionaries.

2. Attack those measures proposed by the democrats which are reforms that are not of a revolutionary character. It may be possible to turn these proposed reforming measures into direct assaults upon private property. Suppose, for example, that the democrats should propose to nationalise factories and railways by purchasing them from their present owners. The workers should demand that the factories and railways should be confiscated without any compensation being paid. If the democrats should propose

---

[2] Friedrich Engels added the following note in 1885 "This statement was based upon a misconception. In 1850, thanks to the falsifications of Napoleon and liberal historians, it was assumed that the great revolution in France had introduced a powerful centralised machinery of government into France. It was thought that – particularly at the time of the Convention – the central authority had been the vitally important weapon which had enabled the revolution to overthrow royalist and federal reactionaries at home and foreign enemies abroad. But it is now known that throughout the period of the revolution until the 18e of Brumaire the country was run by autonomous Departments, arrondissements and cantons which elected their own officials and were fully responsible (within the framework of the constitution) for managing their own affairs. It is now known that this system of provincial and local autonomy (similar to the American system) provided the most powerful focus for revolutionary activities. No wonder that Napoleon – as soon as he had seized power by the coup d'état of the 18e of Brumaire – promptly abolished local autonomy and greatly increased the power of the Prefects who were from the first used to promote the reaction against the revolution. Although local and provincial autonomy prevents the establishment of a centralised administration such self-government must not be confused with the ridiculously exaggerated form of cantonal semi-independence which exists in Switzerland and which all the south German federal republicans favoured in 1848."

a reform in taxation by which everyone pays in proportion to his income, the workers should advocate progressive – as distinct from proportional – rates of taxation. And if the democrats should themselves suggest a moderate progressive income tax then the workers should insist upon rates of taxation that are so progressive as to abolish the wealth of the really large capitalists. If the democrats should propose to regulate the national debt, the workers should demand the immediate abolition of the national debt by declaring the state to be bankrupt. The precise nature of the demands of the workers should, therefore, be determined by the measures proposed – and the concessions offered – by the democrats.

It may be impossible for the (German) workers to seize power and to secure the passing of laws in their own class interests. It may require a long period of revolutionary activity before the full aims of the workers can be achieved. In such circumstances the German workers can – if they adopt the policy that we have outlined – at any rate be certain that the first act of the future revolutionary drama will coincide with the triumph of the proletariat in France. They can be sure that they have hastened the day of their own victory.

The German workers, however, will have to achieve their own triumph by their own efforts. They will have to work out for themselves the nature of their own class interests and they must never for a moment allow themselves to be deceived by the hypocritical catchwords of the petty bourgeoisie. They must hold fast to the policy of organising a workers' political party. Their battle cry must be – Forward to a victorious permanent revolution.

London, March 1850.

II

REAL CAUSES WHY THE FRENCH PROLETARIANS REMAINED COMPARATIVELY INACTIVE IN DECEMBER LAST, 1852[1]

Ever since the end of December last, the whole interest that foreign, or at least continental politics may excite, is taken up by that lucky and reckless gambler, Louis Napoleon Bonaparte. "What is he doing? Will he go to war, and with whom? Will he invade England?" These questions are sure to be put wherever continental affairs are spoken of.

And certainly there is something startling in the fact of a comparatively unknown adventurer, placed by chance at the head of the executive power of a great republic, siezing, between sunset and sunrise, upon all the important posts of the capital, driving the parliament like chaff to the winds, suppressing metropolitan insurrection in two days, provincial tumults in two weeks, forcing himself, in a sham election, down the throat of the whole people, and establishing in the same breath, a constitution which confers upon him all the powers of the state. Such a thing has not occurred, such a shame has not been borne by any nation since the praetorian legions of declining Rome put up the empire to auction and sold it to the highest bidder. And the middle-class press, from the *Times* down to the *Weekly Dispatch*, has never since the days of December, allowed any occasion to pass without venting its virtuous indignation upon the military despot, the treacherous destroyer of his country's liberties, the extinguisher of the press, and so forth.

Now, with every due contempt for Louis Napoleon, we do not think that it would become an organ of the working class to join in this chorus of high-sounding vituperation in which the respective papers of the stockjobbers, the cotton lords, and the landed aristocracy strive to out-blackguard each other. These gentlemen might as well be remembered of the real state of the question. *They* have every reason to cry out, for whatever Louis Napoleon

---

[1] *Notes to the People* (editor: Ernest Jones), February 21, 1852, pp. 846–8: appeared anonymously under the heading: "The Continental Correspondent of the *Notes.*"

took from others, he took it not from the working-classes, but from those very classes whose interests in England, the aforesaid portion of the press represents. Not that Louis Napoleon would not, quite as gladly, have robbed the working-classes of anything that might appear desirable to him, but it is a fact that in December last the working-classes could not be robbed of anything, because everything worth taking had already been taken from them during the three years and a half of middle-class parliamentary government that had followed the great defeats of June 1848. In fact, what, on the eve of the 2nd of December, remained to be taken from them? The suffrage? They had been stripped of that by the Electoral Law of May 1850. The right of meeting? That had long been confined to the "safe" and "well-disposed" classes of society. The freedom of the press? Why, the real proletarian press had been drowned in the blood of the insurgents of the great battle of June, and that shadow of it which survived for a time, had long since disappeared under the pressure of the gagging laws, revised and improved upon every succeeding session of the National Assembly. Their arms? Every pretext had been taken profit of, in order to ensure the exclusion from the National Guard of all working men, and to confine the possession of arms to the wealthier classes of society.

Thus the working-class had, at the moment of the late *coup d'état*, very little, if anything to lose in the chapter of political privileges. But, on the other hand, the middle and capitalist class were at that time in possession of political omnipotence. Theirs was the press, the right of meeting, the right to bear arms, the suffrage, the parliament. Legitimists and Orleanists, landholders and fundholders, after thirty years' struggle at last found a neutral ground in the republican form of government. And for them it was indeed a hard case to be robbed of all this, in the short space of a few hours, and to be reduced at once to the state of political nullity to which they themselves had reduced the working people. That is the reason why the English "respectable" press is so furious at Louis Napoleon's lawless indignities. As long as these indignities, either of the executive government or the parliament, were directed against the working-classes, why that, of course, was right enough; but as soon as a similar policy was extended to "the better sort of people", the "wealthy intellects of the nation", ah, that was quite different, and it behoved every lover of liberty to raise his voice in defence of "principle"!

The struggle, then, on the 2nd of December lay principally between the middle classes and Louis Napoleon, the representative of the army. That Louis Napoleon knew this, he showed by the orders given to the army during the struggle of the 4th, to fire principally upon "the gentlemen in broad-cloth". The glorious battle of the boulevards is known well enough; and a series of volleys upon closed windows and unarmed *bourgeois* was quite sufficient to stifle, in the middle class of Paris, every movement of resistance.

On the other hand, the working classes, although they could no longer be deprived of any direct political privilege, were not at all disinterested in the question. They had to lose, above all, the great chance of May 1852, when all powers of the state were to expire simultaneously, and when, for the first time since June 1848 they expected to have a fair field for a struggle; and aspiring as they were to political supremacy, they could not allow any violent change of government to occur, without being called upon to inter-pose between the contending parties as supreme umpires, and to impose to them their will as the law of the land. Thus, they could not let the occasion pass without showing the two opposing forces that there was a third power in the field, which, if momentarily removed from the theatre of official and parliamentary contentions, was yet ever ready to step in as soon as the scene was changed to its own sphere of action – to the *street*. But then, it must not be forgotten that even in this case the proletarian party laboured under great disadvantages. If they rose against the usurper, did they not virtually defend and prepare the restoration and dictatorship of that very parliament which had proved their most relentless enemy? And if they at once declared for a revolutionary government, would they not, as was actually the case in the provinces, frighten the middle class so much as to drive them to a union with Louis Napoleon and the army? Besides, it must be remembered that the very strength and flower of the revolutionary working class have been either killed during the insurrection of June, or transported and imprisoned under innumerable *different* pretences ever since that event. And finally, there was this one fact which was alone sufficient to ensure to Napoleon the neutrality of the great majority of the working classes; TRADE WAS EXCELLENT, and Englishmen know well enough, that with a fully employed and well-paid work-ing class, no agitation, much less a revolution, can be got up.

It is now very commonly said in this country that the French must be a set of old women or else they would not submit to such treatment. I very willingly grant that, as a nation, the French deserve, at the present moment, such adorning epithets. But we all know that the French are, in their opinions and actions, more dependent upon success than any other civilised nation. As soon as a certain turn is given to events in this country, they almost without resistance follow up that turn, until the last extreme in that direction has been reached. The defeat of June 1848 gave such a counter-revolutionary turn to France and, through her, to the whole continent. The present association of the Napoleonic empire is but the crowning fact of a long series of counter-revolutionary victories, that filled up the three last years; and once engaged upon the declivity, it was to be expected that France would go on falling until she reached the bottom. How near she may be to that bottom it is not easy to say; but that she is getting nearer to it very rapidly every one must see. And if the past history of France is not to be belied by future deeds of the French people, we may safely expect that the deeper the degradation, the more sudden and the more dazzling will be the result. Events, in these times of ours, are succeeding each other at a tremendously rapid rate, and what it formerly took a nation a whole century to go through, is now-a-days very easily overcome in a couple of years. The old empire lasted four years[2]; it will be exceedingly lucky for the imperial eagle if the revival, upon the most shabby scale, of the piece of performance will last out so many months. And then?

[2] The empire of Napoleon I lasted 10 years (1804 to the first abdication in 1814).

III

A FORECAST OF THE PRUSSIAN VICTORY
AT SEDAN, 1870[1]

The two latest facts of the war are these – that the Crown Prince is pushing on beyond Châlons, and that MacMahon has moved his whole army from Rheims, whither is not exactly known. Mac-Mahon, according to French reports, finds the war getting on too slowly; in order to hasten its decision he is now said to be marching from Rheims to the relief of Bazaine. This would indeed be hurrying on matters to an almost final crisis.

In our Wednesday's publication we estimated MacMahon's force at from 130,000 to 150,000 men on the assumption that all the troops from Paris had joined him. We were right in supposing that he had at Châlons the remnants of his own and of De Failly's troops; also that Douay's two divisions were at Châlons, whither we know now they went by a circuitous railway journey via Paris; also that the marines and other portions of the Baltic corps are there. But we now learn that there are still troops of the line in the forts round Paris; that a portion of MacMahon's and Frossard's men, especially cavalry, have gone back to Paris to be reorganised, and that MacMahon had only about 80,000 regular troops in camp. We may, therefore, reduce our estimate by fully 25,000 men, and set down 110,000 to 120,000 men as the maximum of Mac-Mahon's forces, one third of which would consist of raw levies.

---

[1] Engels's forecast of the defeat of the French at Sedan was written a week before the battle was fought. See "Notes on the War, XII" in the *Pall Mall Gazette*, Friday, August 26, 1870, reprinted in F. Engels, *Notes on the War* (Vienna, 1923), pp. 31–3. Engels wrote in the *Pall Mall Gazette* of September 2, 1870: "On the 26th of August, when the whole of our contemporaries, with scarcely one exception, were far too busy descanting upon the immense importance of the Crown Prince's 'resolute' march upon Paris to have any time left for MacMahon, we ventured to point out that the really important movement of the day was that which the latter general was reported to be making for the relief of Metz. We said that in case of defeat 'MacMahon's troops may have to surrender in that little strip of French territory jutting out into Belgium between Mézières and Charlemont-Givet'. What we presumed then is now almost accomplished." (F. Engels, *Notes on the War*, 1923, p. 37.)

And with this army he is said to have set out to relieve Bazaine at Metz.

Now, MacMahon's next and more immediate opponent is the army of the Crown Prince. It occupied on the 24th with its outposts the former camp of Châlons, which fact is telegraphed to us from Bar-le-Duc. From this we may conclude that at that town were then the headquarters. MacMahon's nearest road to Metz is by Verdun. From Rheims to Verdun by an almost straight country road there is fully seventy miles; by the high road via St Ménéhould, it is above eighty miles. This latter road, moreover, leads through the camp at Châlons – that is to say, through the German lines. From Bar-le-Duc to Verdun the distance is less than forty miles.

Thus not only can the army of the Crown Prince fall upon the flank of MacMahon's march if he use either of the above roads to Verdun, but it can get behind the Meuse and join the remaining two German armies between Verdun and Metz, long before Mac-Mahon can debouch from Verdun on the right bank of the Meuse. And all this would remain unaltered, even if the Crown Prince had advanced as far as Vitry-le-Français, or required an extra day to concentrate his troops from their extended front of march; so great is the difference of distance in his favour.

Under these circumstances it may be doubted whether Mac-Mahon will use either of the roads indicated; whether he will not at once withdraw from the immediate sphere of action of the Crown Prince and choose the road from Rheims by Vouziers, Grandpré, and Varennes, to Verdun, or by Vouziers to Stenay, where he would pass the Meuse, and then march south east upon Metz. But that would only be to secure a momentary advantage in order to make final defeat doubly certain. Both these routes are still more circuitous, and would allow still more time to the Crown Prince to unite his forces with those before Metz, and thus to oppose to both MacMahon and Bazaine a crushing superiority of numbers.

Thus, whichever way MacMahon chooses to get near Metz, he cannot shake off the Crown Prince, who, moreover, cannot be denied the choice of fighting him either singly or in conjunction with the other German armies. From this it is evident that Mac-Mahon's move to the relief of Bazaine would be a gross mistake, so long as he has not completely disposed of the Crown Prince. To get to Metz, his shortest, quickest, and safest road is right across the Third German army. If he were to march straight upon it, attack it wherever he finds it, defeat it, and drive it for a few days in a south easterly direction, so as to interpose his victorious army like a wedge between it and the other two German armies – in the same way as the Crown Prince has shown him how to do it – then, and not till then, would he have a chance to get to Metz and set Bazaine free. But if he felt himself strong enough to do this, we may be sure that he would have done it at once. Thus, the withdrawal from Rheims assumes a different aspect. It is not so much a move towards the relief of Bazaine from Steinmetz and Frederick Charles as a move for the relief of MacMahon from the Crown Prince. And from this point of view it is the worst that could be made. It abandons all direct communications with Paris to the mercy of the enemy. It draws off the last available forces of France away from the centre towards the periphery, and places them intentionally farther away from the centre than the enemy is already. Such a move might be excusable if undertaken with largely superior numbers; but here it is undertaken with hopelessly inferior numbers and in the face of the almost certainty of defeat. And what will that defeat bring? Wherever it occurs it will push the remnants of the beaten army away from Paris towards the northern frontier, where they may be driven upon neutral ground or forced to capitulate. MacMahon, if he really has undertaken the move in question, is deliberately placing his army in exactly the same position in which Napoleon's flank march round the southern end of the Thuringian forest in 1806 placed the Prussian army at Jena. A numerically and morally weaker army is deliberately placed in a position where, after defeat, its only line of retreat is through a narrow strip of territory leading towards neutral territory or the sea. Napoleon forced the Prussians to capitulate by reaching Stettin before them. MacMahon's troops may have to surrender in that little strip of French territory jutting out into Belgium between Mézières and Charlemont-Givet. In the very best of cases they may escape to the northern fortresses – Valenciennes, Lille, etc., where, at all events, they will be harmless. And then France will be at the mercy of the invader.

The whole plan seems so wild that it can only be explained as having arisen from political necessities. It looks more like a *coup de désespoir* than anything else. It looks as if anything must be done, anything risked, before Paris be allowed fully to understand the actual situation. It is the plan not of a strategist, but of an *Algérien*, used to fight irregulars; the plan not of a soldier, but of a political and military adventurer, such as have had it all their own way in France these last nineteen years. The language ascribed to MacMahon in justifying this resolve is quite in keeping with this. "What would they say" if he did not march to the aid of Bazaine? Yes, but "what would they say" if he got himself into a worse position than Bazaine has got himself into? It is the Second Empire all over. To keep up appearances, to hide defeat, is the thing most required. Napoleon staked all upon one card, and lost it; and now MacMahon is again going to play *va banque*, when the odds are ten to one against him. The sooner France is freed from these men the better for her. It is her only hope.

IV

PRUSSIAN FRANCS-TIREURS, 1870[1]

For some time past the reports of village-burning by the Prussians in France had pretty nearly disappeared from the press. We began to hope that the Prussian authorities had discovered their mistake and stopped such proceedings in the interests of their own troops. We were mistaken. The papers again teem with news about the shooting of prisoners and the destroying of villages. The Berlin *Börsen Courier* reports, under date Versailles, Nov. 20:

> Yesterday the first wounded and prisoners arrived from the action near Dreux on the 17th. Short work was made of the francs-tireurs, and an example was made of them; they were placed in a row, and one after another got a bullet through his head. A general order for the whole army has been published forbidding most expressly to bring them in as prisoners, and ordering to shoot them down by drumhead court-martial wherever they show themselves. Against these disgracefully cowardly brigands and ragamuffins (*Lumpenge-sindel*) such a proceeding has become absolutely necessary.

Again, the Vienna *Tagespresse* says, under the same date: "In the forest of Villeneuve you could have seen, for the last week, four francs-tireurs strung up for shooting at our Uhlans from the woods."

An official report, dated Versailles, the 26th of November, states that the country people all around Orleans, instigated to fight by the priests, who have been ordered by Bishop Dupanloup to preach a crusade, have begun a guerrilla warfare against the Germans; patrols are fired at, officers carrying orders shot down by labourers seemingly working in the field; to avenge which assassinations all non-soldiers carrying arms are immediately executed. Not a few priests are now awaiting trial – seventy-seven.

These are but a few instances, which might be multiplied almost infinitely, so that it appears a settled purpose with the Prussians to carry on these brutalities up to the end of the war. Under these

[1] F. Engels, "Prussian Francs-Tireurs" in the *Pall Mall Gazette*, Friday, December 9, 1870, reprinted in F. Engels, *Notes on the War* (Vienna, 1923), pp. 105–8.

circumstances it may be as well to call their attention once more to some facts in modern Prussian history.

The present King of Prussia can perfectly recollect the time of his country's deepest degradation, the Battle of Jena, the long flight to the Oder, the successive capitulations of almost the whole of the Prussian troops, the retreat of the remainder behind the Vistula, the complete downbreak of the whole military and political system of the country. Then it was that, under the shelter of a Pomeranian coast fortress, private initiative, private patriotism, commenced a new active resistance against the enemy. A simple cornet of dragoons, Schill, began at Colberg to form a free corps (*Gallice*, francs-tireurs), with which, assisted by the inhabitants, he surprised patrols, detachments, and field-posts, secured public moneys, provisions, war matériel, took the French General Victor prisoner, prepared a general insurrection of the country in the rear of the French and on their line of communication, and generally did all those things which are now laid to the charge of the French francs-tireurs, and which are visited on the part of the Prussians by the titles of brigands and ragamuffins, and by a "bullet through the head" of disarmed prisoners. But the father of the present King of Prussia sanctioned them expressly and promoted Schill. It is well known that this same Schill, when Prussia was at peace but Austria at war with France, led his regiment out on a campaign of his own against Napoleon, quite Garibaldi-like; that he was killed at Stralsund and his men taken prisoners. Out of these, all of whom Napoleon, according to Prussian war rules, had a perfect right to shoot, he merely had eleven officers shot at Wesel. Over the graves of these eleven francs-tireurs the father of the present King of Prussia, much against his will, had to erect a memorial in their honour.

No sooner had there been a practical beginning of freeshooting among the Prussians than they, as becomes a nation of thinkers, proceeded to bring the thing into a system and work out the theory of it. The theorist of freeshooting, the great philosophical franc-tireur among them, was no other than Anton Neithardt von Gneisenau, some time field marshal in the service of his Prussian Majesty. Gneisenau had defended Colberg in 1807; he had had some of Schill's francs-tireurs under him; he had been assisted vigorously in his defence by the inhabitants of the place, who could not even lay claim to the title of national guards, mobile or sedentary, and who therefore, according to recent Prussian notions, clearly deserved to be "immediately executed". But Gneisenau was so impressed by the greatness of the resources which an invaded country possessed in an energetic popular resistance that he made it his study for a series of years how this resistance could be best organised. The guerilla war in Spain, the rising of the Russian peasants on the line of the French retreat from Moscow, gave him fresh examples; and in 1813 he could proceed to put his theory into practice.

In August 1811, already Gneisenau had formed a plan for the preparation of a popular insurrection. A militia is to be organised which is to have no uniform but a military cap (*Gallice*, képi) and black and white belt, perhaps a military great-coat; in short, as near as can be, the uniform of the present French francs-tireurs. "If the enemy should appear in superior strength, the arms, caps and belt, are hid, and the militiamen appear as simple inhabitants of the country." The very thing which the Prussians now consider a crime to be punished by a bullet or a rope. These militia troops are to harass the enemy, to interrupt his communications, to take or destroy his convoys of supplies, to avoid regular attacks, and to retire into woods or bogs before masses of regular soldiers. "The clergy of all denominations are to be ordered, as soon as the war breaks out, to preach insurrection, to paint French aggression in the blackest colours, to remind the people of the Jews under the Maccabees, and to call upon them to follow their example. . . . Every clergyman is to administer an oath to his parishioners that they will not surrender any provisions, arms, etc., to the enemy until compelled by actual force" – in fact, they are to preach the same crusade which the Bishop of Orleans has ordered his priests to preach, and for which not a few French priests are now awaiting their trial.

Whoever will take up the second volume of Professor Pertz's "Life of Gneisenau" will find, facing the title page of the second volume, a reproduction of part of the above passage as a facsimile of Gneisenau's handwriting. Facing it is the facsimile of King Frederick William's marginal note to it – "As soon as one clergyman shall have been shot this will come to an end." Evidently the King had no great faith in the heroism of his clergy. But this did not prevent him from expressly sanctioning Gneisenau's plans; nor did it prevent, a few years later, when the very men who had driven out the French were arrested and prosecuted as "demagogues," one of the intelligent demagogue-hunters of the time, into whose hands the original document had fallen, from instituting proceedings against the unknown author of this attempt to excite people to the shooting up the clergy.

Up to 1813 Gneisenau never tired in preparing not only the regular army but also popular insurrection, as a means to shake off the French yoke. When at last the war came, it was at once accompanied by insurrection, peasant resistance, and francs-tireurs.

The country between the Weser and Elbe rose to arms in April; a little later on the people about Magdeburg rose; Gneisenau himself wrote to friends in Franconia – the letter is published by Pertz – calling on them to rise upon the enemy's line of communications. Then at last came the official recognition of this popular warfare, the Landsturm-Ordnung of the 21st of April, 1813 (published in July only), in which every able-bodied man who is not in the ranks of either line or landwehr is called upon to join his landsturm battalion, to prepare for the sacred struggle of self-defence which sanctions every means. The landsturm is to harass both the advance and the retreat of the enemy, to keep him constantly on the alert, to fall upon his trains of ammunition and provisions, his couriers, recruits, and hospitals, to surprise him at nights, to annihilate his stragglers and detachments, to lame and to bring insecurity into his every movement; on the other hand to assist the Prussian army, to escort money, provisions, ammunition, prisoners etc. In fact this law may be called a complete vademecum for the franc-tireur, and, drawn up as it is by no mean strategist, it is as applicable today as it was at that time in Germany.

Fortunately for Napoleon, it was but very imperfectly carried out. The King was frightened by his own handiwork. To allow the people to fight for themselves, without the King's command, was too anti-Prussian. Thus the landsturm was suspended until the King was to call upon it, which he never did. Gneisenau chafed, but managed finally to do without the landsturm. If he were alive now, with all his Prussian after-experience, perhaps he would see his beau-ideal of popular resistance approached, if not realised, in the French francs-tireurs. For Gneisenau was a man – and a man of genius.

V

THE MILITARY ASPECT OF AFFAIRS IN FRANCE, FEBRUARY 1871[1]

If the series of disasters to the French arms which mark the January campaign – the defeats of Faidherbe and Chanzy, the fall of Paris, the defeat and surrender to the Swiss of Bourbaki – if all these crushing events, concentrated in the short period of three weeks, may well be considered to have broken the spirit of resistance in France, it now seems not improbable that the Germans, by their extravagant demands, may rouse that spirit again. If the country is to be thoroughly ruined by peace as well as by war, why make peace at all? The propertied classes, the middle class of the towns, and the larger landed proprietors, with part of the smaller peasantry, hitherto formed the peace party; they might have been reckoned upon to elect peace deputies for the National Assembly; but if such unheard-of demands are persisted in, the cry of war to the knife may rise from their ranks as well as from those of the workmen of the large towns. At any rate, it is well not to neglect whatever chance there may be that the war may be resumed after the 19th of February; especially since the Germans themselves, if we may trust the *Daily News* of today, are not so satisfied with the prospect of affairs as to abstain from serious preparations for the resumption of hostilities. Let us, therefore, cast another glance at the military aspect of affairs.

The twenty-seven departments of France now occupied by the Prussians contain an area of 15,800,000 hectares, with a population (allowing for the fortresses still unsurrendered) of rather less than 15,500,000. The extent of all France comprises 54,240,000 hectares, and its population is 37,382,000. It thus appears that, in round numbers, thirty-eight and a half millions of hectares, with a population of 25,000,000, remain still unconquered – fully two-thirds of the people, considerably more than two-thirds of the soil. Paris and Metz, the resistance of which so long retarded further

[1] F. Engels, "The Military Aspect of Affairs in France" in the *Pall Mall Gazette*, (Wednesday, February 8, 1871) reprinted in F. Engels, *Notes on the War* (Vienna, 1923), pp. 134–6.

hostile advance, have certainly fallen. The interior of the un-conquered country contains no other entrenched camp – Lyons excepted – capable of playing the same part which these two fortresses have played. Rather less than 700,000 Frenchmen (not counting the National Guard of Paris) are prisoners of war or interned in Switzerland. But there are other circumstances which may make up for this deficiency, even if the three weeks' armistice should not be used for the creation of new camps, surrounded by field works; for which there is ample time.

The great bulk of unconquered France lies south of the line Nantes-Besançon; it forms a compact block, covered on three sides by the sea or neutral frontiers, with only its northern boundary line open to the enemy's attack. Here is the strength of the national resistance; here are to be found the men and the material to carry on the war if it is resumed. To conquer and occupy the immense rectangle of 450 miles by 250 against a desperate resistance – regular and irregular – of the inhabitants, the present forces of the Prussians would not suffice. The surrender of Paris, leaving four corps for the garrison of that capital, will set free nine divisions; Bourbaki's surrender sets free Manteuffel's six line divisions; in all, fifteen divisions, or 150,000 to 170,000 additional soldiers for operations in the field, added to Goeben's four and Frederick Charles's eight divisions. But Goeben has plenty on his hands in the north, and Frederick Charles has shown by his halt at Tours and Le Mans that his offensive powers are exhausted to the full, so that for the conquest of the South there remain not above fifteen divisions; and for some months to come no further reinforcements can arrive.

To these fifteen divisions the French will have to oppose in the beginning mostly new formations. There were about Nevers and Bourges the 15th and 25th Corps; there must have been in the same neighbourhood the 19th Corps, of which we have heard nothing since the beginning of December. Then there is the 24th Corps, escaped from Bourbaki's shipwreck, and Garibaldi's troops, recently reinforced to 50,000 men, but by what bodies and from what quarters we do not know. The whole comprises some thirteen to fourteen divisions, perhaps even sixteen, but quite insufficient as to quantity and quality to arrest the progress of the new armies which are sure to be sent against them if the armistice should expire without peace having been made. But the three weeks' armistice will not only give these French divisions time to consoli-date themselves; it will also permit the more or less raw levies now in the camps of instruction, and estimated by Gambetta at 250,000 men, to transform at least the best of their battalions into useful corps fit to meet the enemy; and thus, if the war should be renewed, the French may be in a position to ward off any serious invasion of the South, not perhaps at the boundary line of the Loire or much north of Lyons, but yet at points where the presence of the enemy will not efficiently impair their forces of resistance.

As a matter of course, the armistice gives ample time to restore the equipment, the discipline, and the morale of Faidherbe's and Chanzy's armies, as well as of all the other troops in Cherbourg, Havre etc. The question is whether the time will be so employed. While thus the strength of the French will be considerably increased, both as to numbers, and quality, that of the Germans will scarcely receive any increment at all. So far, the armistice will be a boon to the French side.

But beside the compact block of southern France, there remain unconquered the two peninsulas of the Bretagne with Brest, and of the Cotentin with Cherbourg, and, moreover, the two northern departments with their fortresses. Havre, too, forms an unconquered, well-fortified spot on the coast. Every one of these four districts is provided with at least one well-fortified place of safety on the coast for a retreating army; so that the fleet, which at this moment has nothing, absolutely nothing, else to do, can keep up the communications between the South and all of them, transport troops from one place to another, as the case may require, and thereby all of a sudden enable a beaten army to resume the offensive with superior forces. Thus while these four western and northern districts are in a measure unassailable, they form so many weak points on the flanks of the Prussians. The line of actual danger for the French extends from Angers to Besançon; for the Germans it extends, in addition to this, from Angers to Le Mans, Rouen, and Amiens to the Belgian frontier. Advantages on this latter line gained over the French can never become decisive if moderate common sense be used by them; but those gained over the Germans may, under certain conditions, become so.

Such is the strategical situation. By using the fleet to advantage the French might move their men in the West and North, so as to compel the Germans to keep largely superior forces in that neighbourhood, and to weaken the forces sent out for the conquest of the South, which it would be their chief object to prevent. By concentrating their armies more than they have hitherto done, and, on the other hand by sending out more numerous small partisan bands, they might increase the effect to be obtained by the forces on hand. There appear to have been many more troops at Cherbourg and Havre than were necessary for the defence; and the well-executed destruction of the bridge of Fontenoy, near Toul, in the centre of the country occupied by the conquerors, shows what may be done by bold partisans. For, if the war is to be resumed at all after the 19th of February, it must be in reality a war to the knife, a war like that of Spain against Napoleon; a war in which no amount of shootings and burnings will prove sufficient to break the spirit of resistance.

VI

LETTERS ON HISTORICAL MATERIALISM,
1890–1894

Engels to C. Schmidt[1]   August 5, 1890

Many young German writers are now using the term "materialism" as a convenient phrase to cover anything and everything without giving the matter any further thought. They stick this label onto something that they have written and then they think that they have finished with it. But for us (socialists) history is above all a guide to our studies. It is not the foundation of any Helegian philosophical system. All history must be approached from a new angle. We must examine the basic factors which underlie the existence of one after another of the various aspects of society. This is an essential preliminary to the discovery of the political, legal, aesthetic, philosophical and religious aspects of different types of society. Hitherto little has been achieved since so few scholars have seriously tackled the problem from this point of view. We need all the help that we can get and anyone who is prepared to undertake research on these lines can achieve a great deal and can add to his reputation. What has happened is that the catchphrase "historical materialism" – and everything is turned into a catchphrase nowadays – is used by many of the younger Germans merely to organise their scanty knowledge of the past as quickly as possible into a "philosophy of history" and to march on majestically from there. And if their knowledge of history in general is pretty meagre their knowledge of economic history is more meagre still! Then someone like Barth can come along and attack the idea which has in fact – in his own circle – already been degraded to a mere catchphrase.

But all this will work itself out in time. We socialists are strong enough in Germany to survive a great deal. One of the greatest services which the Anti-Socialist Law performed for us was to free us from any pressure from academic pseudo-socialists. Now we are

[1] *Karl Marx–Friedrich Engels*, Vol. 1 *Philosophie* (Fischer Bücherei, 1966), pp. 225–6.

strong enough to swallow even the German academics who are once more throwing their weight about. Someone like yourself who has really achieved something must have noticed how few of the young literary gentlemen who have attached themselves to the Socialist Party take the trouble to master the science of economics, or the history of the structure of society, or such important aspects of economic history as the evolution of trade, industry and agriculture. How many of them know anything about Maurer except his name? What should be studied thoroughly by scholars is left to the ephemeral efforts of mere journalists. It seems to me that these academic people think that anything is good enough for the workers. If only they realised that Marx himself considered that even his best writings were not really good enough for the workers. He thought that it would be a positive crime to offer the workers anything less than the very best!

Engels to J. Bloch[2]   September 21–22, 1890

. . . According to the materialist conception of history, the *ultimately* determining element in history is the production and reproduction of real life. More than this neither Marx nor I have ever asserted. Hence if somebody twists this into saying that the economic element is the *only* determining one, he transforms that proposition into a meaningless, abstract, senseless phrase. The economic situation is the basis, but the various elements of the superstructure – political forms of the class structure and its results, namely: constitutions established by the victorious class after a successful battle etc., juridical forms, and even the reflexes of all these actual struggles in the brains of the participants, political, juristic, philosophical theories, religious views and their further development into systems of dogmas – also exercise their influence upon the course of the historical struggles and in many cases preponderate in determining their *form*. There is an interaction of all these elements in which, amid all the endless host of accidents (that is, of things and events whose inner interconnexion is so remote or so impossible of proof that we can regard it as non-existent, as negligible) the economic movement finally asserts itself as necessary. Otherwise the application of the theory to any period of history would be easier than the solution of a simple equation of the first degree.

We make our history ourselves, but, in the first place, under very definite assumptions and conditions. Among these the economic

² From Marx to Engels, *Selected Correspondence* (Foreign Language Publishing House, Moscow), pp. 498–500 and W. O. Henderson (ed.), *Engels: Selected Writings* (Penguin Books, 1967), pp. 333–5.

ones are ultimately decisive. But the political ones etc. – and indeed even the traditions which haunt human minds – also play a part, although not the decisive one. The Prussian state also arose and developed from historical, ultimately economic, causes. But it could scarcely be maintained without pedantry that among the many small states of North Germany, Brandenburg was specifically determined by economic necessity to become the great power embodying the economic, linguistic and, after the Reformation, also the religious differences between North and South, and not by other elements as well (above all by its entanglement with Poland, owing to the possession of Prussia, and hence with international political relations – which were indeed also decisive in the formation of the Austrian dynastic power). Without making oneself ridiculous it would be difficult to explain in terms of economics the existence of every small state in Germany, past and present, or the origin of the High German consonant permutations, which widened the geographical partition wall formed by the mountains from the Sudeten range to the Taunus to form a regular fissure across all Germany.

In the second place, however, history is made in such a way that the final result always arises from conflicts between many individual wills, of which each in turn has been made what it is by a host of particular conditions of life. Thus there are innumerable intersecting forces, an infinite series of parallelograms of forces which give rise to one result – the historical event. This may again itself be viewed as the product of a power which works as a whole *unconsciously* and without volition. For what each individual wills is obstructed by everyone else, and what emerges is something that no one willed. Thus history has proceeded hitherto in the manner of a natural process and is essentially subject to the same laws of motion. But since the wills of individuals – each of whom desires what he is impelled to by his physical constitution and external, in the last resort economic, circumstances (either his own personal circumstances or those of society in general) – do not attain what they want but are merged into an aggregate mean, a common result, it must not be concluded that they are equal to zero. On the contrary each contributes to the result and is – to this extent – included in it.

Moreover I would ask you to study this theory from its original sources and not at second hand; it is really much easier. Marx hardly wrote anything in which it did not play a part. But especially *The Eighteenth Brumaire of Louis Bonaparte* is a most excellent example of its application. There are also many allusions to it in *Capital*. Then may I also direct you to my writings: *Herr Eugen*

Dühring's Revolution in Science and *Ludwig Feuerbach and the End of Classical German Philosophy*, in which I have given the most detailed account of historical materialism which, as far as I know, exists.

Marx and I are ourselves partly to blame for the fact that younger people sometimes lay more stress on the economic side than is due to it. We had to emphasise the main principle *vis-à-vis* our adversaries, who denied it, and we had not always the time, the place or the opportunity to give their due to the other elements involved in the interaction. But when it came to presenting a section of history – that is, to making a practical application – it was a different matter and there no error was permissible. Unfortunately, however, it happens only too often that people think they have fully understood a new theory and can apply it without more ado from the moment they have assimilated its main principles, and even those not always correctly. And I cannot exempt many of the more recent "Marxists" from this reproach, for the most amazing rubbish has been produced in this quarter too. . . .

Engels to H. Starkenberg   January 25, 1894

Here are the answers to your questions.

1. The economic factors which Marx and I considered to be fundamental influences upon society include the way in which people in a particular society produce what they require in order to live as well as the methods which they employ to exchange these products – assuming of course that there is a division of labour. Among the basic economic factors, therefore, we include the whole technique of production and transport. We consider that the technique of production is responsible for the way in which output is divided among consumers and also – after the dissolution of the primitive *gens* society – the division of society into classes. The relationship between master and serf, the nature of the state, politics and the law are all included in our examination of the class structure of society. Economic factors include the geographical environment of society – an environment upon which economic development depends – as well as the residue of former economic systems which often survive only in the form of traditions or *vis inertiae* within the framework of the new economic system.

Although, as you say, the level of technological attainment in any society depends upon the level of scientific achievement there is much greater truth in the statement that the level of scientific achievement is dependent upon the *level* and the *needs* of technology. If society requires a certain technical advance then this will encourage scientific progress more than the efforts of ten universities put together. Progress in water engineering in Italy in the sixteenth and seventeenth centuries by men like Torricelli were brought about by the needs of the rulers of the mountain streams. We have come to learn something about the science of electricity only after electricity has been put to practical use. Unfortunately in Germany it has become customary to write histories of science as if scientific discoveries fell from heaven.

2. We (socialists) believe that economic factors are the fundamental cause of historical developments. Race, too, is an economic factor. In this connection, however, there are two points to remember.

(a) Political, legal, philosophical, religious, literary, and artistic developments depend upon economic factors. But these aspects of human life react upon each other and upon the economic factor which is fundamental to all of them. It would not be true to say that the economic factor is the *sole* cause – the *only* active impulse – influencing social developments. On the contrary the various factors that we have mentioned influence each other but *in the final analysis* they are all determined by economic necessities. The state, for example, influences the development of society through protection, free trade, a good or a bad fiscal policy. In Germany the long period of economic stagnation between 1648 and 1830 was responsible for the complete exhaustion and impotence of the lower middle classes. This state of affairs resulted first in Pietism, secondly in sentimentality, and finally in a miserable toadying to the princes and nobles. Yet even this was by no means without economic consequences. It was a major obstacle to Germany's economic recovery and it was only swept aside when the revolutionary and Napoleonic wars still further aggravated social distress. Some people put forward the easy and convenient theory that events follow automatically upon economic causes. But this is an over simplification of what really happens. People make their own history – but they make it within a given framework. And this framework is based upon actual facts. However important political and ideological factors may be it is in the last instance the economic factor which is decisive. The economic factor is the scarlet thread that we must follow to arrive at an understanding of the true causes of historical events.

(b) People make their own history. But hitherto they have not made history with a common will in accordance with a common plan. Not even closely knit societies have been able to achieve this. Their efforts clashed and in all such societies there is therefore a *need* for change which has hitherto worked itself by *chance*. And this necessity – which achieves its purpose by chance – is an economic necessity. It is at this point that the so-called "great man of history" appears in a particular society at a particular time and this of course purely a matter of chance. But supposing that the "great man" had not appeared. In that case there would still be a need for change and the problems of the day would in the end have to be solved without him *tant bien que mal*. It was a pure chance that the Corsican military dictator Napoleon solved the problems left by a French Republic exhausted by its own wars. But if Napoleon had not existed someone else would have taken his place and done the job. The "great man" always turns up when he is needed. This assertion can be proved by considering the appearance of men like Julius Caesar, the Emperor Augustus and Oliver Cromwell on the stage of history. Karl Marx discovered the materialist conception of history. But French writers such as Thierry, Mignet and Guizot and all the English historians who wrote before 1850 paved the way for this idea. And Morgan discovered it independently at about the same time as Marx. This shows that the idea *had* to be discovered by somebody.

This argument also holds good for all other chance – or apparently chance – occurrences. The further removed that the field of study upon which we are engaged is removed from economics – the closer that it approaches abstract ideological thought – the more likely we are to come across developments that are due to chance. Progress is made not in a straight line but in a zig-zag curve. But once you discover the axis of the curve you will find that – the longer the period that you study and the wider the field of your investigations – this axis runs more or less parallel to the axis of economic development.

In Germany the greatest obstacle to a correct understanding of all this is the irresponsible neglect of economic history by scholars. It is very difficult to forget the "history" that has been thumped into us at school. It is still more difficult to master all the material that has to be examined in order to appreciate the significance of economic history. Who, for example, reads old G. von Gümeln nowadays? Yet his collection of documents – dull though it may be – includes a great deal of material that throws light upon countless aspects of political history. . . .

Please do not regard every word that I have written as gospel truth. Read my letter as a whole. I regret that I have not the time to work out the argument as precisely as I would have to do if I were writing for publication.

VII

SOCIALISM IN GERMANY, 1891–1892[1]

The following article is a translation of one that I wrote at the invitation of our Paris friends for the *Almanach du Parti Ouvrier pour 1892*. I feel that I have a duty both to French and to German socialists to publish the article again in Germany. I am under an obligation to the French socialists to make it clear to the Germans that it is possible to discuss frankly with the French in what circumstances German socialists would undoubtedly take up arms against France. And I must make it clear to the Germans how free the French socialists are from the chauvinism and thirst for revenge that is shared by all the French middle-class parties from the monarchists to the radicals. And I have a duty to the German socialists to repeat to them what I have said about them to the French.

It should be self-evident – but I repeat it yet again – that this article represents only my own personal views. I am not writing in the name of the German Social Democrat Party. Only the Party's elected representatives, officials and committees have any authority to do that. My fifty years of service to the international socialist movement make it impossible for me to put myself forward as the representative of any one national socialist party. On the other hand I cannot forget that I am a German by birth and that I am proud of the achievements of the German workers in the socialist movement – achievements which are greater than those of socialists anywhere else.

Part I

The German socialist movement had its origin in events that occurred long before 1848. It began with two independent movements. The first was a purely working class movement which

[1] The first version of this article was written in French for the *Almanach du Parti Ouvrier pour 1892*. A second – and longer – article subsequently appeared in German. This is a translation of the German article. See *Marx–Engels III Geschichte und Politik I* (Fischer Bücherei, 1966), pp. 29–41.

derived its inspiration from the early communist agitation of the French workers. One aspect of this German movement was Weitling's utopian communism. The second was a purely intellectual movement which developed as a result of the collapse of Hegel's philosophical system and this type of socialism was from the first dominated by Karl Marx. The Communist Manifesto of January 1848 represented the fusion of these two early German socialist movements. This union was finally forged in the fiery furnace of the revolution of 1848 when all socialists – workers and intellectuals alike – stood shoulder to shoulder on the barricades.

After the collapse of the European revolutions in 1849 socialism in Germany had to go underground. It was not until 1862 that Lassalle – one of Marx's disciples – raised the   socialist banner again. Lassalle's type of socialism, however, was not the bold courageous socialism of the Communist Manifesto. Lassalle merely demanded the establishment of state-subsidised industrial co-operative factories for the benefit of the workers. This was just a revival of the programme put forward by a group of Paris workers who had – prior to 1848 – supported Marrast's republican newspaper, the *National*. Marrast had been opposed by the republicans who supported the views expressed by Louis Blanc in his *Organisation du Travail*. Lassalle's demands were obviously only a very meagre socialist programme. Nevertheless his agitation represented the second phase in the development of the socialist movement in Germany. Lassalle's talents, fiery zeal and irrepressible energy called into existence a new working class movement. And everything that the German workers achieved on their own in ten years was ultimately derived from Lassalle's movement in one way or another. The links may have been forged by his opponents. They may have represented positive or negative attitudes to Lassalle's policy. But there can be no doubt of the reality of Lassalle's contribution to the socialist cause in Germany.

Could Lassalle's doctrines, as preached in their pristine purity in the 1860s, satisfy the socialist hopes of the people that had been aroused by the Communist Manifesto? Of course not. And so – thanks above all to the efforts of Bebel and Liebknecht – there arose in Germany a working class party which openly supported the principles of the manifesto of 1848. Next, three years after Lassalle's death (the first volume of) Karl Marx's *Das Kapital* appeared in 1867. It is from the day of the publication of this work that the decline and fall of Lassalle's brand of socialism may be dated. The doctrines laid down in *Das Kapital* rapidly became the common heritage of all German socialists. And in due course even the followers of Lassalle were numbered among the converted. From time to time entire groups of Lassalle's adherents came over – with banners flying and drums beating – to the party of Liebknecht and Bebel which had accepted the Eisenach programme. The Eisenach party steadily gained in strength and there was soon open hostility between the two socialist parties in Germany. The enmity between them became most serious – even leading to physical violence – at the very time when they were no longer divided on any question of principle. The arguments and even the weapons employed by the two factions were on all important points identical!

The rivalry between the two socialist parties became positively ridiculous when Lassallean and Eisenach deputies sat side by side in the Reichstag and the need for united action was becoming daily more and more obvious. The situation became absolutely impossible. At last in 1875 the two factions united and from that time onwards the former rivals have acted together harmoniously as a completely united family. Even if there had been the slightest chance of the party again falling into rival factions Bismarck very kindly made this quite impossible when his notorious Emergency Law of 1878 declared the German Socialist Party to be an illegal organisation. Bismarck's hammer blows fell impartially upon Lassalleans and Eisenachers alike with the result that the two groups have been finally forged into a single homogeneous political party. Today a standard edition of Lassalle's collected works is being published under the auspices of the German Social Democratic Party at the very time that – with the aid of former followers of Lassalle – the last vestiges of Lassalle's doctrines are being expunged from the party programme.

Shall I describe in detail all the vicissitudes, the struggles, the reverses, and the triumphs experienced by our party since its establishment? When manhood franchise was introduced and the doors of the Reichstag were opened to the socialists we were supported by a hundred thousand voters and gained two seats.[2] Today the party polls a million and a half votes and sends 35 deputies to the Reichstag. The Social Democrat Party secured more votes than any other party in the general election of 1890. After eleven years of the Anti-Socialist Exceptional Law the strength of the party – measured in votes – has increased fourfold and it is now the strongest party in the country. In 1867 the middle-class deputies looked upon their socialist colleagues as strange creatures from another planet. Today, whether they like it or not, they have to accept Socialist deputies as representatives of a powerful popular force to which the future belongs. The Social Democrat Party has toppled Bismarck from power and – after a struggle which lasted

[2] i.e. those held by Bebel and Liebknecht.

for eleven years – it crushed the Exceptional Law which crumbled into fragments. Our party is like a great flood which is bursting all the dams that hold it in check and which is flooding both urban and rural districts and penetrating even the most reactionary agrarian regions. Today the growth of the party enables us to predict with almost mathematic certainty the date on which it will achieve power.

The votes cast for socialist candidates at Reichstag elections have been as follows:

1871	...	101,927	1884	...	549,990
1874	...	351,670	1887	...	763,128
1877	...	493,447	1890	...	1,427,298

Ever since the last election the government has moved heaven and earth to wean the mass of the workers from socialism. It has clamped down upon unions and strikes. Despite the rise in the cost of living the government has maintained the bread and meat taxes and has increased the price of food at the expense of the poor for the benefit of the great landowners. At the next Reichstag elections – to be held in 1895 – we can confidently hope to poll at least 2,250,000 votes. In 1900 we can expect to secure between 3,500,000 and 4,000,000 votes. What a fine *fin du siècle* gift that will be for our middle classes!

The united and growing mass of popular support for the Social Democrat Party is opposed only by rival middle class parties which are divided among themselves. At the elections of 1890 the two Conservative parties together secured 1,377,417 votes, the National Liberals 1,177,807, the Radicals 1,159,915, and the Roman Catholic Centre 1,342,113. In these circumstances a united socialist party supported by over 2,500,000 voters is in a position to triumph over any government.

The main strength of German socialism, however, does not by any means lie solely in the number of voters who support the Social Democrat Party at Reichstag elections. In Germany men are not eligible to vote until the age of 25 but they are liable to perform military service at the age of 20. And it is just among the younger generation that our party draws most of its recruits. Consequently the ranks of the German army are being filled with more and more supporters of the socialist cause as the years go by. Even today one soldier in five is a socialist and within a few years there will be one in three. By the end of the century the ranks of the army – once the stronghold of Prussianism in Germany – will be filled with socialists. Nothing can withstand the fateful march of events. The government in Berlin knows what is happening just as well as we

do but it is powerless to remedy the situation. The army is falling
from its grasp.

Time and time again the middle classes have urged us to confine
ourselves to propaganda, to keep within the law, and to abstain
under any circumstances from employing revolutionary means to
further our cause. They now argue that the repeal of the Exceptional
Law has restored to all German citizens – including the socialists –
the protection afforded by the rule of law. But we cannot accept
such advice from the middle classes. At the moment, however, it is
not the socialists who are defying the rule of law. This is because
the rule of law at present operates very much to our advantage.
So long as this situation lasts we should indeed be fools to defy
the law. Much more pertinent is the question whether it is not the
middle classes and the government who are more likely to defy
the law if, by so doing, they could wipe out their socialist enemies.
We shall see. Meanwhile let us say to the middle classes: "You fire
first, gentlemen, if you please!"

There can be no doubt that it is the middle classes who will be
the first to open fire. One fine day they – and the government which
they support – will tire of sitting with folded arms while the tide
of socialism overwhelms them. And they will seek refuge in the
overthrow of the rule of law. They will try to retain power by a
coup d'état. And what good will that do? Force of arms can
suppress a minor movement operating in a limited area but it
cannot wipe out a party supported by two or three million voters
spread all over the territories of the German Reich. A counter-
revolutionary coup d'état might achieve some temporary success
and might perhaps delay the triumph of socialism for a few years.
But this would be achieved only at the cost of making the ultimate
victory of socialism more certain, more complete, and more
permanent.

Part II

The arguments that have been advanced so far have been based
upon the assumption that the blessings of peace will continue and
that the economic and political development of Germany can
proceed undisturbed. In the event of war the whole situation would
be radically changed. And war can break out any time.

When one refers to "the war" everyone knows what is involved.
The war will be between France and Russia in opposition to
Germany and Austria–Hungary – perhaps also Italy. Should war
break out the socialists of all countries will have to fight against
fellow socialists whether they like it or not. What would the

German Social Democrat Party do in those circumstances? And
how would a world war affect the fortunes of the Party?

Although Germany is ruled by a semi-feudal monarchy its
policy is ultimately determined by the economic interests of the
middle classes. Thanks to Bismarck the government has made
colossal blunders. Its conduct of domestic affairs has been characterised by a mean petty policy enforced by police misconduct
unworthy of a great nation. All middle class states under liberal
governments despise this policy. The foreign policy of Germany
has earned the distrust – indeed the detestation – of its neighbours.
By forcibly annexing Alsace-Lorraine the German government has
made any reconciliation with France impossible for very many
years and – without gaining any advantage for itself – it has made
Russia the arbiter of Europe. This has long been self-evident.
Indeed on the very day that Sedan fell, the General Council of
the First International accurately forecast the present international
situation. In its address of September 9, 1870 the General Council
declared: "Do the Teutonic patriots really think that they can
ensure peace and freedom by driving France into the arms of
Russia? If Germany – inflamed by the over-confidence engendered
by military successes – allows dynastic intrigues to despoil France
of any of her territories then one of two things will follow. France
will either become the tool of Russia's expansionist policy or she
will embark upon a new 'war of defence'. This will not be the
sort of 'local war' that has recently become fashionable. It will be
a racial war in which the Germans will be fighting the allied Slavs
and French."

There can be no doubt that as compared with *this* German Reich
even the French Republic of the present day represents a revolutionary force – only a middle-class revolution but a revolution all the
same. The situation would, of course, be radically changed if the
French Republic were to accept orders from Czarist Russia. The
Czarist régime in Russia is the enemy of all the western nations.
It is the enemy even of the middle classes in those countries.
Should the Russian hordes overrun Germany they would not bring
freedom with them but slavery, not progress but barbarism. In
alliance with the Czars France could not offer Germany an iota
of freedom. Any French general who talked about the "German
Republic" would be laughed out of court throughout Europe and
America. France would deny its entire historical revolutionary *rôle*
in such circumstances and it would enable Bismarck's empire to
claim that it represented western progress as against oriental
barbarism.

But while official Germany holds the stage there is another

Germany – a socialist Germany – waiting in the wings. The future – the very near future – belongs to the Social Democrat Party. As soon as this party assumes office it would be unable to govern the country or to maintain its authority unless it reversed the injustices done to other nations by its predecessors. A socialist German government would prepare the way for the restoration of the independence of Poland – a country so shabbily betrayed by the French middle classes. It would give North Schleswig and Alsace-Lorraine the chance to decide their own political future. All such territorial questions could easily be solved in the near future so long as Germany is left in peace. No dispute concerning Alsace-Lorraine would endanger the relations between a socialist Germany and a socialist France. The whole question could be settled in a minute. All that we have to do is to wait patiently for ten years or so for the solution of these territorial problems. The whole proletariat of England, France and Germany is waiting for its freedom. Cannot the patriots of Alsace-Lorraine wait a little longer? Is it right that their impatience should lead to the destruction of a whole continent and its eventual delivery into the hands of the Russians? Is such a game really worth the candle?

On the outbreak of hostilities the chief campaigns will be fought in Germany and in France. Those two countries will bear the brunt of the cost and the devastation of the war. From the very first day such a war would be characterised by a degree of treachery among states bound by solemn treaties of alliance such as even international diplomacy – that arch-begetter of treachery – has never seen before. And France and Germany would be the first to suffer from such treachery. In the light of these circumstances it is obviously not in the interests of either France or Germany to provoke a war. Russia, however, is in a different position. She is protected by her geographical and economic situation from the worst destructive consequences of a series of military defeats. Only Czarist Russia has an interest in provoking so frightful a conflict. Anyhow, in the present international situation, the betting is ten to one in favour of the French marching on the Rhine as soon as a shot is fired on the Vistula.

If that happened the Reich would be fighting for survival. If Germany were to win such a war there is no territory for her to annex since both in the east and in the west she is already trying to digest provinces inhabited by people who are not German. On the other hand if the Reich were crushed between the French hammer and the Russian anvil, East Prussia and Germany's Polish provinces would be seized by Russia, Schleswig by Denmark, and the whole of the left bank of the Rhine by France. Even should

France hesitate to annex the left bank of the Rhine she would be forced to do so under pressure from Russia. This is because it is in Russia's interests that there should always be a bone of contention between France and Germany so as to maintain a permanent enmity between those two countries. But if France and Germany were reconciled Russia could not dominate Europe. Should Germany be greatly reduced in size after a lost war she could no longer fulfil her historic mission of furthering Europe's mission as a civilising influence in the world. If Germany were again reduced to the frontiers once forced upon her by Napoleon at the Peace of Tilsit she would have to prepare for a new war to recover the territory that she needs for survival. Meanwhile Germany would be a mere satellite state – always at the beck and call of the Czar who would, if necessary, not hesitate to use her against France.

What would be the fate of the German Social Democrat Party in such circumstances? It is certain that the Czar, the middle-class republicans of France, and the German government would all take full advantage of such a heaven-sent opportunity to crush the one party which all three consider to be their deadly enemy. We have seen how Thiers and Bismarck embraced each other over the ruins of the Paris Commune. We would see the Czar, Constans and Caprivi – or their successors – clasping hands over the dead body of German Socialism.

Thanks to thirty years of continuous struggle and sacrifice the German Social Democrat Party has won for itself a unique position among the Socialist parties of the world. It has gained for itself a position which makes it certain that it will achieve power within a very short time. If Germany were ruled by the Social Democrat Party it would hold the most honourable and responsible place in the international working class movement. The Social Democrat Party is bound to defend this position to the last man against any assault mounted against it.

What is the duty of German socialists when faced with the fact that a Russian victory over Germany would inevitably be followed by the suppression of their party? Should they passively stand by and let events that would lead to their destruction take their course? Should they surrender without a struggle the honourable position which they have a responsibility to the working classes of the world to maintain?

Certainly not. To further the European revolution the German socialists must defend what they have won. They must not surrender either to the enemy at home or to the enemy abroad. To defend their gains they will have to fight the Russians to the last man. And they will also have to fight Russia's allies whoever they may be. If the French Republic takes service under His Majesty the Czar and autocrat of all the Russias the German socialists would take up arms and would throw themselves enthusiastically into battle. It would in certain circumstances be possible for the French Republic to act as the representative of a bourgeois revolution in opposition to the Kaiser's Germany. On the other hand it is the German socialists who undoubtedly carry the banner of the revolution of the working classes in opposition to the French Republic of Constans, Rouvier and even Clemenceau.

Germany would be engaged in a life and death struggle if she were invaded by the Russians and the French at the same time. Only by revolutionary means could she survive as a nation. It is certain that in those circumstances the present German government would not foster the revolution unless it were forced to do so. But we have a powerful Social Democrat Party which will force it to do so. Alternatively the Social Democrat Party will take over the reins of government.

We have not forgotten the wonderful example which France gave us in 1793. The centenary of 1793 is approaching. If the Czar's lust for conquest and the chauvinism of the French middle classes combine to halt the victorious peaceful progress of the Social Democrat Party then – make no mistake about it – the German socialists will prove to the world that the German workers of today are no unworthy successors of the French sansculottes of 1793 and that 1893 could have as worthy a place in history as 1793. Should M. Constans's troops invade Germany they will be greeted with the words of the Marseillaise:

> Quoi, ces cohortes étrangères
> Feraient la loi dans nos foyers!

A period of peace will bring the Social Democrat Party to power within about ten years. But a war would either bring the German socialists to power within two or three years or it would lead to their utter ruin for at least fifteen or twenty years. It would be sheer folly for the German socialists to desire a war which would place their future in jeopardy when they have only to wait patiently for certain victory if peace is maintained. No socialist, whatever his nationality, desires a military triumph by the present German government, by the French middle class Republic – and least of all by the Russian Czar – which would lead to the subjugation of the whole continent. That is why socialists of all countries want peace. But if war did come it would involve from fifteen to twenty million combatants and the continent would be devastated as never before. Such a conflict would either bring immediate victory to the socialists or it would lead to so complete a collapse of the existing order of things and to such enormous destruction that it would be quite impossible for capitalist society to survive. Social revolution would be postponed for ten or fifteen years but its cuccess then would be as rapid and as complete as one could wish.

So much for the article that I wrote for the *Almanach du Parti Ouvrier pour 1892*. It was written in the late summer of 1892 at a time when the excitement caused by the French naval visit to Kronstadt had raised the martial spirits of the French middle classes. At the same time the great French manœuvres between the Seine and the Marne – the old battlefields of 1814 – had brought French patriotic feelings to fever heat. At that time the France whose views are expressed in the national press and the speeches of members of the majority parties in the Chamber of Deputies was prepared to perpetrate almost any folly to oblige the Russians. In those circumstances there was a very real danger that war might break out. So that there should be no last-minute misunderstandings between French and German socialists I felt it necessary to make it clear to the French socialists what – in my view – the attitude of the German socialists would be should war break out.

Then the Russian warmongers received a severe check. First the harvest failed and there was a danger of famine. Next the French loan failed and that represented the final collapse of the credit of the Russian government. It was claimed that the £20 million loan had been heavily over-subscribed but when the Paris bankers tried to unload the bonds on the public they could not get rid of them. The bankers had to sell good securities to raise money to buy unsound Russian bonds. This was done on such a scale on the big European stock exchanges that there was a general fall in the value of shares. And the new Russian bonds fell well below the price at which they had been issued. There was a financial crisis and the Russian government had to buy back £8 million worth of bonds and eventually secured only £10 million on the loan instead of £20 million. The Russians cheerfully tried to borrow another £40 million from abroad and this loan, too, was a complete failure. This showed that the policy of French capitalists was not influenced in any way by "patriotism" but that it *was* influenced by a healthy fear of war.

Since that time the failure of the harvest has indeed been followed by a famine – and one on a scale which has been unknown in Western Europe for a long time. Famines of such severity rarely occur even in India which is the typical country which suffers from such calamities. Indeed Holy Russia itself in former times, before the days of railways, very seldom experienced a famine of such severity. How has this come about?

The explanation is quite simple. The Russian famine is not due merely to a failure of the harvest. It is part and parcel of a gigantic social revolution that has taken place in Russia since the Crimean war. The poor harvest has simply thrown a glaring light upon the acute disorders brought by this social revolution. Old Russia sank into its grave for ever on the day when Czar Nicholas – despairing of himself and of old Russia – took poison. On its ruins has been built the Russia of the bourgeoisie. In those days an incipient middle class already existed in Russia. It consisted partly of bankers and import merchants (mostly Germans, German Russians or their descendants) and partly of Russians in the interior of the country who had come up in the world. The latter were largely army contractors and suppliers of spirits who made money at the expense of the state and of the man in the street. The early middle class in Russia also included some factory owners. From that time onwards the growth of the middle classes – particularly the manufacturers – has been artificially promoted by state aid on a massive scale, by subventions and premiums, and finally by a fiscal policy of very high protection. The idea was to turn the huge Russian empire into a self-sufficient economic unit which could do without (or virtually do without) imports from abroad. It was anticipated that the home market would grow continuously. The Russian government also hoped that even the products of the more temperate zones could be grown in Russia and this explains Russia's continuous efforts to extend her territories in the Balkans and in Asia. The final aim of the Russians has been to seize Constantinople on the one hand and India on the other. This is the secret – this is the underlying economic cause – of the tremendous expansionist zeal of the Russian middle classes. The expansion to the south west we call Pan-Slavism.

Serfdom, of course, was quite incompatible with such plans for the promotion of industrial growth. The serfs were emancipated in 1861. But what an emancipation it was! Russia followed the example of Prussia where the serfs had been very gradually freed from their various feudal obligations between 1810 and 1851. Russia, however, tried to accomplish emancipation in only a few years. Consequently in order to overcome their opposition far greater concessions had to be made to the great landowners who possessed serfs than had been made by the Prussian government and its corrupt officials to the gracious nobles. And when it comes to bribery Prussian civil servants are mere babes in arms when compared with Russian bureaucrats. Consequently when the

Russian estates were broken up the nobles secured land which had generally been made fertile by the labour of many generations of peasants. On the other hand the peasants secured a minimum amount of land on which to try to make a living and even this was generally poor heath land. The lords secured the communal woods and meadows and if the peasant wanted to use them – and he had to use them to survive – he had to pay a rent for them to the landowner.

To be certain that both parties – lords and peasants alike – should be ruined with the greatest possible speed, the government paid the nobles for lands surrendered to the peasants in the form of state bonds while the peasants had to pay off their debts to the state in the form of annual payments spread over a long period. As was to be expected the nobles dissipated their bonds in a glorious spending spree. The peasant, on the other hand, was faced with annual payments that were positively enormous for a person in his position. At the same time he was suddenly thrown out of a natural economy into a money economy.

The Russian peasant who formerly – except for the payment of relatively small taxes – did not have occasion to pay for things in money is now expected not only to make ends meet but also to pay higher taxes and his annual redemption payments – and to pay in hard cash. He has to do this despite the fact that he is now working on a smaller and poorer plot of land than before and no longer enjoys free wood or any rights of free pasturage. This has put him in a position in which he can neither live nor die. To make matters worse the manufactured products made by peasant-craftsmen at home now have to compete with the articles made by the factories that have recently been established. At one time domestic industry was the peasants' chief method of making money. And where village domestic industry was not totally destroyed it fell under the domination of merchants and middle men. As a part-time domestic craftsman the Russian peasant has become the slave of a capitalist – generally a merchant from Saxony or a sweater[3] from England. Anyone who wants to know about the fate of the Russian peasant in the last fifty years should read the chapter on "the establishment of the home market" in the first volume of Karl Marx's *Das Kapital*.[4]

The transition from a natural to a money economy is the main method by which industrial capital captures the home market. When this happens the peasant economy is completely shattered. Boisguillebert and Vauban have given a classic description of this

[3] "Sweater" in English in the original.

[4] Marx–Engels, *Gesamwelte Werke*, Vol. 23, pp. 773–6.

process as it took place in France in Louis XIV's reign. But what happened in those days was mere child's play to what is happening in Russia at this moment. In Russia the process is taking place on a scale three or four times greater than in France. Moreover, the changes in methods of industrial production – to which the life and work of the peasant have to be adapted – are much more rapid and decisive than they were in France. The French peasant was drawn step by step into the new manufacturing system while the Russian peasant has been plunged overnight into the rough and tumble of large scale industrial production. The flintlocks of the rural craftsman have suddenly been replaced by the repeating rifles of the modern factory.

It was this state of affairs that was abruptly brought to light when the harvest failed in 1891. The transition from a domestic to an industrial economy has been going on quietly in Russia for many years and has hardly been noticed by the philistine middle classes of Western Europe. A situation developed in which the first harvest failure was bound to lead to an international crisis. The crisis duly arrived and many years will pass before it is over. Any government would be helpless in face of a famine on this scale – and especially a Russian government which has deliberately trained its officials to be thieves. Since 1861 the old communal economy and traditions of the Russian peasants have been systematically destroyed, partly by economic forces and partly by the deliberate policy of the government. The old village community (mir) has collapsed or is disappearing. Yet at the very time when the individual peasant is expected to stand on his own feet the ground has been cut away from beneath him. No wonder that last autumn the winter seed was sown in only a few districts. And where it was sown it was generally soon destroyed by bad weather. No wonder that the peasant has been unable to find fodder for his working beasts and has eventually eaten the animals himself. No wonder that the peasant is deserting his homestead and is fleeing to the towns where he seeks employment in vain and in the end succumbs to hunger-typhus.

This is a great economic and social crisis which is quite different from any ordinary famine. The background of the crisis has been a long period of change that amounts to an economic revolution. All that the famine has done is to reveal in an acute form the social evils that were there already. This crisis is chronic in character and it will last for many years. The crisis may be expected to have significant economic consequences. The traditional village community (mir) will disappear. The village usurers (kulaks) will become richer and will establish themselves as great landlords.

In a word the crisis will enable the new middle class to take over land and power from both the nobles and the peasants. Owing to the economic crisis there will be no war in Europe just now. The Russian warmongers have had their wings clipped for some years to come. Instead of millions of soldiers dying on the field of battle millions of Russian peasants are perishing of hunger. We must wait and see how all this will affect the future of the despotic régime in Russia.

VIII

CAN EUROPE DISARM? (1893)[1]

Introduction

The articles which are now printed as a pamphlet originally appeared in the Berlin newspaper *Vorwärts* in March 1893 when the Reichstag was debating the army estimates.

It is generally agreed – and I wrote on this assumption – that the continued growth of standing armies in Europe has now reached a point where the choice lies between bankruptcy caused by excessive military expenditure or a world war of devastating destructiveness. One of these catastrophes will occur unless standing armies are replaced by popular militias while there is still time.

My purpose is to show that such a change is possible at this moment. It can be done by existing governments in the present political situation. I proceed on this assumption and simply suggest the measures which could be adopted by every existing government without endangering national security in any way. From a purely military point of view there is absolutely no reason why modern standing armies should not be disbanded. If they are allowed to survive their continued existence will be for political and not for military reasons. They will be used as a defence against opposition at home rather than against a foreign enemy.

The suggestion that the length of service with the colours should be gradually reduced by international agreement lies at the heart of my thesis. I regard this as the simplest and quickest method of effecting the transition from standing armies to popular militias. The necessary treaties would naturally vary according to the type of government involved as well as the political situation at the time of the signing of each agreement. It would be impossible to think of a better time than the present for taking the action that I am advocating. Today it is possible to argue in favour of making a start with a *maximum* of two years' military service. Then in a

[1] Published as a series of articles in *Vorwärts* between March 1 and 10, 1893 and subsequently reprinted as a pamphlet: *Kann Europa abrüsten?* (Nürnberg, 1893). See Karl Marx–Friedrich Engels, Vol. 4, *Geschichte und Politik* 2, pp. 236–57 (Fischer Bücherei, 1966).

few years it might be possible to agree upon a much shorter period
of service with the colours.

I

For the past twenty-five years the whole of Europe has been
arming on a scale that has never been known before. All the great
powers are competing in armaments and in preparations for war.
Germany, France and Russia are becoming exhausted by their
determination to take the lead in the armaments race. At this very
moment the German government has announced to the people its
plans for such an increase in armaments that even the present
docile Reichstag is aghast at the prospect. In the circumstances it
might be thought to be mere foolishness to talk about disarmament.

Yet in all countries there are demands for disarmament from the
common people who supply nearly all the recruits and pay nearly
all the taxes. And the piling up of armaments has everywhere led
to such a state of exhaustion that countries are finding that they
simply have not got the means to go on arming any more. One
country runs out of recruits, another is short of money, while a
third can find neither new troops nor the additional funds that it
requires. Is there no way out of this impasse, other than a war of
destruction such as the world has never seen before?

I am prepared to assert that disarmament, which would guaran-
tee peace for the future, is not only possible but is relatively easy
to achieve. I believe that Germany – more than any other advanced
country – has both the duty and the ability to take the lead in
reducing her armaments.

After the Franco–Prussian war of 1870–1 the system of raising
armies by (limited) conscription – with the possibility of a man
avoiding service if he provided a substitute – finally gave way to the
system of universal service first in the army, then in the reserve,
and finally in the territorials (*Landwehr*). It is true that in 1870–1
the system in Germany was still in its original somewhat underdeveloped Prussian form. Virtually all continental states adopted
the German system of military service in one form or another.
There might have been no great harm in this since under the new
system the bulk of the men under arms were middle aged married
men who were naturally less aggressive than Napoleon III's army
which contained a strong element of substitutes who were professional soldiers.

Then came the annexation of Alsace and Lorraine. The result
of this annexation was that France regarded the Treaty of Frankfurt as a mere armistice – just as Prussia had once regarded the

Peace of Tilsit as a mere armistice. After the Franco–Prussian war there was a feverish armaments race between Germany and France into which Russia, Austria and Italy were gradually drawn. At first the length of service in the territorials (*Landwehr*) was extended. In France a new reserve of older men was added to the existing territorial army. In Germany two periods of service with the territorials was required and there was even a revival of the *Landsturm* for the older soldiers. And so it went on until men were being recalled to the colours at – even after – the age at which nature puts a term to a man's ability to perform military service.

The next step was to tighten up the method of calling up recruits with the object of increasing the size of the army still further. Here too the limit has been reached – or very nearly reached. Last year's recruits to the French army already include quite a number of young men who are barely able – or are wholly unable – to perform their military duties effectively. English officers were present at the great manœuvres in the Champagne as independent observers. They were lavish in their praise of the general efficiency of the modern French army but they reported that a surprising number of the younger soldiers were exhausted by the long marches and exercises. It is true that in Germany we have not yet completely come to the end of our reserves of young men but the new military estimates will see to that! From this point of view too we are reaching the limits of our resources.

The modern revolutionary principle of the Prussian military system lies in the obligation of every able bodied man of military age to serve with the colours in the defence of his country. And the only really revolutionary aspect of all the changes in military affairs that have occurred since 1871 lies in the fact that this principle – once a mere fantasy of the chauvinists – has (though often reluctantly) been increasingly put into actual practice. Nothing can now change either the length of time that a man is liable to serve in the army or the calling up of all young men to the colours – certainly not in Germany and least of all by the Social Democrat Party which alone is capable of applying the principle in its most complete form.

There is only one way in which an approach can be made towards solving the problem of disarmament – by shortening the length of service with the colours. Progress towards disarmament could be achieved by means of an international agreement between the Great Powers to limit to two years (in the first instance) the actual service performed by men in all branches of the services. Agreement might also be reached on a further reduction of this period as soon as the states concerned are satisfied that this can be done. The agreement should also provide for the eventual universal adoption of the militia system. I am certain that Germany, above all, should take the lead in putting forward a proposal on these lines. I believe that Germany, more than any other country, would gain an advantage through making such a suggestion – even if the idea should be rejected.

II

If the maximum period of service with the colours were fixed by international agreement all states would be equally affected. It is generally accepted that when an army, which has not been under fire before, is engaged in its first campaign its efficiency as an offensive force (both from a strategic and a tactical point of view) depends – within certain limits – upon the length of time previously devoted to the training of its recruits. In 1870 our troops gained experience at Wörth and Sedan of the wild fury of the bayonet attacks of the long service Imperial infantry and the charges of the French cavalry. But in the first days of the campaign at Spichern the German forces showed that they were able – even when outnumbered – to dislodge the French infantry from strongly held positions. It is generally accepted that – within certain limits which may vary from one country to another – the general efficiency of troops under fire for the first time and their ability to take the offensive depends upon the length of their previous training.

If an attempt to fix the maximum length of the period of military service were successful, the relative efficiency of the various armies would remain much the same as they are today. If one army were to lose something of its efficiency in the early stages of a campaign then other armies would also suffer a similar loss of efficiency. The possibility of one army defeating another will be the same in the future as it is now. Let us take France and Germany as an example. Any difference between the length of service in those countries is so small as to be of little consequence. If the time devoted to training the troops were shortened the relative efficiency of the two armies would depend – as it does now – upon the way in which the time for training was used. Moreover the relation between the size of the two armies would depend upon the relation between the size of the population of the two countries. Once universal military service has been effectively introduced the size of an army must always depend upon the size of the population in countries of approximately equal economic development – for the proportion of men unfit for military service depends upon the degree of economic development. The way in which a new Prussian army was created in 1813 can never be repeated again.

Much depends upon the use that is made of the time devoted to the training of a soldier. In all armies there are people who could – if they were allowed to do so – let the cat out of the bag and let us all know that, owing to the need for economy, some recruits have been "trained" in only a few months. In such circumstances the instructors have to concentrate upon essentials and there is no time for any silly parade ground nonsense. And they are astonished to discover how short a time it takes to turn an average young man into a soldier. Bebel has told the Reichstag that the officers were astonished at the efficiency of the German substitute-reserve forces. Plenty of officers in the Austrian army are prepared to testify that their territorials (*Landwehr*) are better troops than the regiments of the line. And the time taken to train the Austrian territorials is much the same as that given to training the German substitute-reserve forces. There is nothing surprising in this. In training territorials there is simply no time to waste on the parade ground follies of the regiments of the line.

The German infantry training manual of 1888 has reduced to an absolute minimum the time spent on tactical formations for the offensive. The manual contains nothing new. After the war of 1858 the Austrians introduced the principle that formations in reverse must be capable of immediate offensive action. At about the same time Hesse-Darmstadt introduced the system of forming a battalion-column by simply joining four company-columns together. But after 1866, under pressure from Prussia, Hesse-Darmstadt had to give up this sensible arrangement. The new manual at last abolishes a mass of old Frankish tribal ceremonies which were as useless as they were revered. I should be the last person to complain about the manual. After the Franco–Prussian war I indulged myself in the luxury of drawing up a scheme – suited to modern warfare – for closed and open formations at company and battalion level and I was surprised to find that my ideas had been adopted almost verbatim in the relevant parts of the manual.

To put a manual into practice is a very different thing from drawing it up. The knights of the parade ground, who always come to their own in peacetime in the Prussian army, have found a back-door method of wasting time despite the recommendations contained in the manual. These officers claim that the "true discipline" gained by marching up and down the parade ground is absolutely essential to counteract the effects of fighting in loose order. Consequently completely useless exercises are still being practised on the parade ground. The abolition of the goose-step alone would enable many more weeks to be spent on sensible exercises. An additional advantage would be that we could invite foreign officers to watch German military manœuvres without splitting their sides with laughter.

Sentry duty is also quite out of date. The traditional view is that sentry duty develops the intelligence and the power of self-expression. This is done by training soldiers – in case they have not learned it already – to think about nothing at all when doing sentry duty for two hours at a time. Nowadays training in sentry duty takes place in the open. The use of sentries in towns – where we have adequate police forces – has become an anomaly. If sentry duty were abolished at least 20 per cent more time could be made available for proper military duties – and the maintenance of order in the streets of our cities could be handed over entirely to the civil authorities.

There are moreover plenty of soldiers who for one reason or another are excused most military duties – craftsmen, officers' servants and so on. There is room for much improvement here.

Next we may consider the cavalry. Surely the training of the cavalry requires as much time as possible. Although one would wish for adequate time to train recruits who have never before ridden or looked after a horse nevertheless the time taken to train a cavalryman could be reduced in various ways. For example there should be less economy in the provision of fodder. If horses are to be strong enough to take part in manœuvres they must be fed properly beforehand. It would be desirable for every squadron to have a number of extra horses on its strength so that cavalrymen could have more practice on horseback. In short what is needed is a determination to introduce a more intensive training and to cut out inessentials so that the time spent by a cavalryman with the colours could be reduced. Of course I agree that there is an imperative need to train remount riders but even here it would be possible to find ways and means to reduce the time spent with the colours. Moreover the system of three or four year volunteers for the cavalry could be kept – and extended – with appropriate subsequent reduction of service for such volunteers in the territorials and the reserve. Lacking such an incentive it would be difficult to secure volunteers.

Of course if you consult the "military authorities" you will hear a very different tale. They say that all my suggestions are worthless. They argue that if anything is changed then the whole military system will collapse. But in the last fifty years I have seen so many military institutions that were once regarded as holy and untouchable consigned to the rubbish heap – by the same "military authorities". What is more I have seen things praised to the skies by the "military authorities" of one country discarded as useless by "military authorities" in another country. How often have I seen treasured and beloved traditions proved to be useless when put to the test under conditions of actual warfare. Moreover I know that every army has – for the benefit of the common soldier and the man in the street – a sort of conventional tradition which is sedulously cultivated by senior officers. But this sort of tradition is scorned by officers who are capable of thinking for themselves and in any case it disappears as soon as the troops are involved in an actual campaign. In short I have had enough experience of what has happened in the past to advise everybody never to put their trust in "military authorities".

III

It is a remarkable fact that although senior army officers are very conservative people from a professional point of view there have been greater and more revolutionary changes in military practices in recent years than those which have occurred in any other department of human activity. Centuries seem to separate the old six and seven pounders and the primitive rifles that I once handled on the parade ground in Berlin with the modern breech loaders and five millimetre rifles with magazine breech loaders. And this is by no means the end of progress in the field of military affairs. Every day technology produces some new invention which consigns to the rubbish heap some weapon that has only recently been adopted. And now even the old romantic gunpowder is being superseded and future campaigns will be quite different – and quite unpredictable – as compared with those of the past. In view of these continual fundamental changes in military techniques it is increasingly difficult to forecast the course of future campaigns.

Only forty years ago the effective range of rifle fire was limited to 300 paces. At that distance an individual soldier could face a salvo from a whole battalion and survive unharmed – assuming of course that all the enemy soldiers really aimed at him. In those days the range attained by the field artillery was, for practical purposes, no more than 1,500 to 1,800 paces. In the Franco–Prussian war the maximum effective range of the rifle was 600 to 1,000 paces and the artillery 3,000 to 4,000 paces. Now the new small calibre rifles – admittedly not yet tested in actual warfare – have a range nearly equal to that of the artillery. And their bullets have a power of penetration which is from four to six times greater than that of older types of rifle. Today a section armed with modern rifles has a fire power equal to that of an entire company armed with old-fashioned rifles. Although the artillery has not made progress comparable to that of the rifle – as far as the range of fire is concerned – the new explosives used by the artillery have a destructive power that would formerly have been regarded as impossible. But it is not yet certain who will have to survive the blast of the new explosive – the soldier who fires the gun or the soldier at whom the shell is fired!

Yet in the midst of these continuous and rapidly increasing changes in the technique of warfare there are military authorities who – only five years ago – were capable of putting their troops through the conventional ballet dancing associated with Frederick the Great's troops although no one would dream of using such tactics on the field of battle. The same authorities still practised formations guaranteed to lead to defeat because the troops had marched to the right and there was no room to march to the left. And these military authorities do not even dare to remove from the uniforms of their men the buttons and other bright metal objects which are such good targets for five millimetre bore rifles. They send the lancers (Uhlans) into battle with broad red breastplates while the dragoons – admittedly without their breastplates – face enemy fire in white coats. It was only with the greatest reluctance that the military authorities brought themselves to sacrifice on the altar of the fatherland the beloved epaulettes (beloved because they were so utterly lacking in taste) rather than the soldiers who wore them!

I should have thought that it was in the interest neither of the German people nor of the German army that conservative superstition should dominate military thinking and practice in the midst of a technical revolution. We need more independent and bolder military leaders and – unless I am very much mistaken – there are plenty of them to be found among our ablest officers. These are officers who yearn for freedom from mere routine and drill which have dominated military training during twenty years of peace. But until these officers have the opportunity and the courage to put their ideas into practice those of us who are on the outside must step into the breach and do our best to prove that we too learned something when we were in the army.

I have tried to show that a two year period of training with the colours could be introduced now in all branches of the services. In two years it would be possible to give recruits an adequate training for service in time of war. And I have made it clear that a reduction of the training to two years would be only a beginning. My proposal for an international treaty limiting military training to two years would be only the first step towards gradual further reductions in the period of service – to eighteen months (two summers and a winter), then to a year, and finally to. . . ? Here we come to the future when a genuine system of militias would be introduced. A discussion on the militia had better wait until a start has been made by cutting down the present period of service with the colours.

It is vitally necessary to make a start. First, it must be recognised that a reduction in the period of military service is essential for the economic welfare of all countries and the maintenance of peace in Europe. Next it must be appreciated that part of a young man's military training should take place at a much earlier age than at present.

When I returned to the Rhineland after an absence of ten years I was agreeably surprised to see that horizontal and parallel bars had been set up in the playgrounds of the village schools. So far so good – but not good enough. The apparatus has been correctly installed in the usual efficient Prussian manner but it has never been used properly. Is it too much to ask that gymnastics should be properly taught? Is it too much to ask that every class should be given adequate exercises on the apparatus and in free gymnastics? This should be done at an age when boys' limbs are still supple and it should not be delayed until lads are twenty years of age. At the moment one can see these young conscripts perspiring all over as they try in vain to get some elasticity into their stiff joints, muscles and ligaments. Any doctor will tell you that owing to the division of labour in modern industry every worker is crippled because entire sets of muscles are overdeveloped at the expense of others. The type of injury suffered by industrial workers varies from one type of job to another. Special physical defects are characteristic of every type of industrial work. It is surely the height of folly first to allow youths to acquire physical defects and then – when they are in the army – to try and cure those defects. Surely civil servants can be expected to have enough sense to realise that the army would get recruits in three times better physical condition if boys at schools and youths in trade schools were prevented from acquiring physical defects.

That, however, is only a beginning. At school a boy can easily be taught about the drill and movement of troops in formation. It is natural for a schoolboy who has practised gymnastics to hold himself erect at attention or on the march. Everyone who has served in the army knows what our recruits look like on parade and knows too how difficult it is to get them to stand up straight or to march properly. The movement of troops in line – at company level – can also be learned much more easily at school than in the army. What the recruit looks upon as a detestable exercise – and one which he often finds impossible to perform – is regarded by schoolboys as an enjoyable game. It is difficult for adult recruits to master the art of marching forwards and turning in line but schoolboys can learn this as if it were a game if they are regularly exercised. If most of the summer months were devoted to route marches and to exercises in the open the boys would benefit both physically and mentally. Moreover the army would save money since it would be able to reduce the time devoted to the early training of recruits. The results achieved by my old friend Beust, a former Prussian officer, in his school in Zürich, show conclusively that military exercises enable boys to learn successfully how to cope with army life in the open air. Beust's experience also shows that such exercises develop the intelligence of the scholars and provide a basic military training in a relatively short time. Modern warfare is a highly complicated business and, without a basic training at school, it is impossible to envisage a smooth transition from the conscript armies of today to the militias of the future. From this point of view Beust's experiments are of great significance.

I would now like to strike a specific Prussian note. The future of non-commissioned officers who have completed their service raises serious problems. As civilians they have been turned into policemen, customs officials, porters, clerks and minor civil servants of all kinds. They are bundled into all sorts of unsatisfactory corners of the Prussian bureaucratic machine. The authorities have tried hard to find posts for retired non-commissioned officers. But these non-commissioned officers have all too often ended up in jobs for which they have no qualifications and they are being asked to perform tasks without any previous experience of the work. Surely the time has come when these men should be given jobs for which they are qualified because of their army experience. As schoolmasters they could perform a useful service for the community. They would give boys instruction in gymnastics and military exercises – not in reading or writing. This would be good for them and for their pupils. And our rebellious youths might exercise a civilising influence upon the non-commissioned officers when they emerge from the dark privacy of barracks and military discipline into the light of a school playground and civil law.

IV

We shall discuss later the prospect of securing acceptance of our proposal that an international treaty should be concluded to provide for the universal and simultaneous reduction of the length of military service in stages. But let it be assumed for the moment that such an agreement will be signed. In that case the question would arise: "Would the agreement actually be put into practice and would all the signatories faithfully honour their obligations?"

On the whole I have little doubt that the agreement would be carried out. Any attempt at evasion (on such a scale as to be worth while) could not be concealed for long. Moreover, the people themselves would insist upon the agreement being carried out. No conscript would stay in the army of his own accord once his legal period of service had been completed.

The treaty would be welcomed by Austria and Italy and also by all the second and third rate powers which have introduced universal conscription. They would adhere strictly to the terms of the treaty. We shall consider the position of Russia in our next article. But what about France? The attitude of the French towards the treaty will be of decisive importance.

There can be no doubt that once the French government has signed and ratified such a treaty it will, to all intent and purpose, fulfil its engagements. It is true that just now the desire for revenge against Germany has gained the upper hand among the French property owning classes and among those sections of the workers who have not been converted to socialism. In these circumstances there might be open or concealed attempts to evade the obligations of a treaty designed to reduce the period of military service. But such infringements of the agreement would be of no great consequence. If the French government really felt unable to carry out its obligations it would simply denounce the treaty. Germany is in the fortunate position of being able to turn a blind eye to minor infringements of the treaty. While the efforts made by the French to render impossible any repetition of the defeat of 1870 must command our respect the fact remains that if war did break out Germany's prospects of victory are even better than they might appear at first sight. There are several reasons for this. First, the population of the Reich is increasing every year and Germany now has over twelve million more people than France. Secondly, Prussia's military system has been in existence for over seventy years and the inhabitants of the country have got used to it. The Prussian army has frequently been mobilised and has gained so much experience that all the problems associated with preparing for active service have been solved. These advantages are shared by the armies of other German states. France, on the other hand, has a more complicated military organisation than Germany and she has not yet undertaken a general mobilisation. Thirdly, the undemocratic system of one-year voluntary service with the colours has run into insuperable difficulties since the soldiers who have to serve for three years have used sharp practices to force the privileged one year volunteers out of the army. This shows that the political conscience of the Germans – and the political institutions tolerated by the Germans – cannot be compared with those of the French. But what is a drawback from a political point of view is, in this instance, an advantage from a military point of view. There is no doubt that no country has so many young people in grammar and middle schools in relation to its population as Germany. This makes it possible to work the system of one-year volunteers however undemocratic and politically objectionable it may be. From a military point of view it is an excellent method of securing reasonably well educated men who can be trained as officers. The success of the one-year volunteer system was first seen in the campaign of 1866. Since the Franco–Prussian war this aspect of Germany's military power has been fostered almost to excess. Even if in recent years some German officers have done their level best to bring the one-year volunteer system into disrepute, there can be no doubt that, on the whole, man for man, these officers are superior to their French rivals from a military point of view. The main point to remember is that Germany has in the ranks of its reserves and territorials a far higher proportion of men qualified to be officers than any other country.

Since Germany has an unusually large number of officers at her disposal she is able on mobilisation to put into the field more new formations (already trained in peacetime) than any other country. Richter has stated that on mobilisation every German infantry regiment will be joined by a mobile reserve regiment, two territorial battalions and two substitute battalions. As far as I know his assertion has not been contradicted either in the Reichstag or the Military Commission. In other words there will be ten wartime battalions to three peacetime battalions. The 519 battalions of 173 peacetime regiments will in wartime become 1,730 battalions, not counting the fusiliers and the sharpshooters. This expansion of the armed forces on mobilisation will take place far more quickly in Germany than in any other country.

I have it on the authority of a French reserve officer that France has far fewer trained reserve officers than Germany. But, according to an official statement, there are enough of them to lead the new formations required upon mobilisation. My informant, however, admitted that half of these officers were not very competent. It is questionable whether all the proposed new French formations could be created if war broke out and even if they were there would not be anything like as many as Germany could put into the field. And France would immediately have to use all her available officers if she mobilised her armies while Germany would have some in reserve for future use.

In former wars there has been a lack of officers after the first few months. This is still true of all countries other than Germany. Only Germany has an inexhaustible supply of officers. So Germany is quite strong enough to turn a blind eye to minor French infringements of a treaty reducing the period of service with the colours. It would be a matter of indifference to Germany if the French trained some of their men for two or three weeks longer than they should have done under the treaty.

V

It would be a matter of indifference whether Russia were prepared to discuss a treaty for the reduction of the period of military service or not. And it would not matter very much whether she signed such a treaty. Russia can virtually be ignored in any discussion of this problem.

Russia's population of over 100 millions is more than double that of Germany but, in the event of war, Russia cannot mobilise an army of anything like the size of the German army. Germany's population of 50 millions live in a restricted region of 540,000 square kilometres while the 90 to 100 million Russians (those who have to be considered from a military point of view) are scattered over an area of at least three and a half million square kilometres. Germany has a significant military advantage since she has a much greater density of population than that of Russia. This advantage is accentuated by the fact that Germany's railway network is immeasurably superior to that of Russia. But the fact remains that in the long run a population of 100 millions can produce more soldiers than one of 50 millions. It will take time for these troops to arrive but they must arrive one day. What then?

An army needs officers as well as men. And from that point of view the Russians face very real problems. It is only the nobles and the urban middle classes who can supply the officers that the army needs. The aristocracy is limited in numbers and the urban middle class is still more limited. In Russia only one in ten of the population live in towns and few of these towns are worthy of the name. The number of middle schools – and the number of their pupils – is very small. So where can Russia get the officers that she needs?

What suits one country does not suit another. The system of universal conscription can be introduced successfully only in countries that have attained a certain level of economic and cultural development. Where this level has not been reached universal conscription can do more harm than good. This has obviously happened in Russia.

It takes a relatively long time to turn the average Russian recruit into a trained soldier. No one doubts the courage of the Russian soldier. So long as tactical decisions were reached by the infantry attacking in close formation the Russian soldier was in his element. All his experience of life has taught him to work in close association with his fellow men. If he lives in a village he is brought up in a semi-communist society (the *mir*) and if he lives in a town he is accustomed to work as a member of a co-operative association (the *artel*). Both provide for the mutual liability of all members. Russian society is based upon a system of mutual dependence but this means that the individual is lost if he is expected to act on his own initiative. And this applies also to the Russian when he is in the army. A Russian battalion cannot be scattered. The greater the danger the more tightly are the men packed together. The instinct to herd together was of immense value as late as the Napoleonic wars when it counter-balanced some of the weaknesses of Russian troops in other respects. Today it is a serious drawback, for mass infantry attacks have disappeared in modern warfare. Troops now advance in scattered columns – and different units may be mixed up together. It can easily happen that an officer has to assume command of men whom he has never seen before. Today every soldier must be prepared to act on his own initiative and to do what has to be done – without, however, losing touch with his comrades. This kind of co-operation is hardly compatible with the primitive herd instinct of the Russians. It can be acquired only if the individual soldier has intelligence and exercises initiative. The soldiers who can be taught to use initiative are men who have reached the level of culture which can be attained in the industrialised countries of Western Europe. The small calibre breechloader and smokeless powder have turned what was once the great merit of the Russian soldier into a great defect. Today it will take much longer than formerly to turn a Russian recruit into a competent soldier. And even when he is fully trained he will still be no match when faced with troops from West European countries.

Where are the officers coming from who will take charge of all the new formations that would be called up if war broke out? If it is difficult for France to find enough officers for her requirements how much more difficult will it be for Russia to secure the necessary officers! In Russia the educated part of the population – from which alone competent officers can be drawn – forms a relatively tiny proportion of the population. Moreover in Russia even the fully trained soldiers require more officers to each unit than is necessary in other armies.

Moreover the mobilisation of the Russian army will be hampered by the fact that Russian civil servants – and even army officers – are notoriously corrupt and dishonest. In all former wars in which Russia has been engaged it immediately became apparent that even parts of the peace time army and their equipment existed only on paper. What will happen when the reserves and the territorials are called up and have to be provided with uniforms, arms and munitions? When an army is mobilised everything should go smoothly and everything should be available at the right place and at the right time. Any failure in this respect would cause utter confusion. How can things be expected to go smoothly when a mobilisation is controlled by dishonest corrupt Russian officials? A Russian mobilisation – that will indeed be a sight for the gods!

So what it all amounts to is that – on purely military grounds – we can let the Czar call up as many men as he pleases and he can help them with the colours for as long as he likes. Apart from the troops already under arms it will be very difficult for him to call up many more and it will be even more difficult for him to make them available at the right time. To experiment with universal conscription might well prove to be an expensive luxury for the Russians.

If Russia were involved in a war her army would stand on the frontiers from Kovno (Kaunas) to Kamieniec in her own territory yet in enemy country inhabited by Poles and Jews – for the Czar's government has managed to turn the Jews into deadly enemies. A few defeats would force the Russians back from the Vistula to the Dwina and the Dnieper. Then an army of Polish allies would be set up behind the German lines advancing into Russia. Prussia would receive a just punishment for her treatment of the Poles in the past if she were forced, in the interest of her own security, to re-establish a powerful Polish state.

So far we have discussed only the purely military factors and we have come to the conclusion that Russia can safely be ignored as far as a treaty for limiting the length of military service is concerned. Our arguments will be strengthened by examining Russia's present economic condition and particularly the state of her finances.

VI

Russia's present internal situation is a desperate one. Russia was once a very stable country but now this European China is undergoing an economic and social revolution which is pursuing a truly relentless course. This is due to the emancipation of the serfs in 1861 and the growth of industrial capitalism. At the moment the revolution in Russia is cataclysmic in character.

When serfdom was abolished the landowners received state bonds in compensation and they squandered the money as quickly as possible. When these funds were exhausted the construction of new railways opened up a new market for timber from the great estates. The nobles sold their trees and again enjoyed a carefree existence on the proceeds. But they failed to farm their estates properly with labour which had to be paid. No wonder that the Russian land-owners fell head over heels into debt – if they were not completely insolvent. No wonder that the output of their estates failed to expand and actually declined.

The peasants received less land – and generally land of poorer quality – than the land which they had farmed in the days of serf-dom. They lost access to woods as well as the right to make use of the common land. Taxes were increased. Peasants who once paid for wheat they needed in kind now had to pay in cash for their purchases. Moreover they had to make cash redemption payments as well as payment to cover interest and amortisation in respect of the loans made by the state to pay compensation to the nobles for the land allocated to the peasants when serfdom was abolished. The peasant economy suffered a sharp decline at the very time when a money economy was replacing the former natural economy – a change which in itself is sufficient to ruin the peasants. The peasants have been grossly exploited by the wealthy land-lords, by the rich farmers and publicans, and by the moneylenders. And as if that were not enough those peasants who combined farming with some form of domestic industry have been faced with competition from the new factories run by capitalists. This has completed the downfall of the peasants. The competition from the new factories in the towns has not only undermined the livelihood of the village craftsman who makes things for his own family but it has also ruined the village craftsman who sells his products in the open market. If he has not been actually driven out of business the village craftsman has fallen under the domination of a capitalist middleman (*Verleger*) or – worse still – of his agent. The Russian peasant has been accustomed to farm a smallholding that was originally established by clearing a forest. He lived within the framework of an established communal society (the village *mir*). Now he has suddenly had to adapt himself to a modern capitalist society in a highly developed form – an economy incidentally which had to dispose of its products on the home market. This situation has ruined the peasant who is also a village craftsman. Nine-tenths of the population are peasants. Consequently if the peasants are ruined the state is ruined.

These changes have been going on for twenty years or so. Now further consequences are coming to light. Reckless cutting down of timber has ruined the capacity of the soil to retain water. In the winter great floods occur when rain or melting snow flows quickly into ponds and streams. In the summer the streams are sluggish and the soil is dry. There are reports from many of the most fertile districts in the country that the water level has sunk by as much as a metre. When the roots of cereal plants are no longer able to reach the water they fail to germinate. It is not only human beings who have been ruined. The very soil has been destroyed in many districts – at least for a generation to come.

The famine of 1891 has marked the climax of this chronic economic and social decline. Now the whole world has appreciated what has taken place. Russia has not been able to recover since the great famine. That tragic event has robbed the peasants of their cattle – their last asset. Now they have sunk still further into debt and their will to live must soon break down.

In such a catastrophic situation Russia is in no position to wage a war – except a war of desperation. Nobles and peasants – the very state itself – are all ruined by debts. We know that Russia's foreign debts amount to over £200 millions. Nobody knows the extent of the internal debt. We have no information concerning the value of the state bonds that have been bought by the public. We do not know how much paper money is in circulation because the value of Russian notes fluctuates from day to day. It is certain that Russia's credit abroad is exhausted. The Russian state bonds of £200 millions have completely saturated the money market of western Europe. England has long ago rid herself of Russian bonds and Germany has recently got rid of most of hers too. That France and Holland have had their fill of Russian bonds can be seen by the fate of the last Russian loan in Paris. The loan was for 500 million francs. Bonds worth only 300 million francs were purchased by the public. The Russian Minister of Finance had to take the remaining 200 million francs off the hands of the underwriters. This shows that even in France there is absolutely no prospect of launching a new Russian loan in the immediate future.

That is the condition of the country that is supposed to be a military threat to Germany. In fact Russia cannot wage even a "war of despair" – unless of course we were so stupid as to supply Russia with the funds that she would need to wage war!

It is very difficult to understand either the foolish policy of the French government which supports Russia or the equally stupid

views held by the "public opinion" of the French middle classes
who are backing the present régime. France has no need of Russia.
It is Russia that needs France. Lacking French support the Czar –
and his policy – would be isolated in Europe. The Czar would have
no influence over events either in the West or in the Balkans. By
using a little common sense the French could get anything that
they want from Russia. In fact the French government is crawling
on its belly in front of the Czar.

Russia's wheat exports have already been ruined by competition
from cheaper American wheat. Rye is now Russia's main export
and most of it is sent to Germany. Whenever the Germans decide
to eat wheaten bread instead of rye bread the present Czarist-
upper middle-class Russia is finished for good.

VII

Enough criticism of our peaceful neighbours and potential
enemies! We will now turn to the home front.

In Germany we shall derive an advantage from a gradual reduction in the period of service in the army only if we can stop,
once and for all, the brutal treatment of soldiers which has become
notorious in recent years and is much more prevalent than people
care to admit. On the one hand we have spit and polish and parade
ground drill: on the other hand we have shameful brutality. Both
have always been characteristic of the Prussian army in times of
peace and inactivity. From Prussia these evils have spread to
Saxony, Bavaria and other German states. This state of affairs has
been inherited from the days of "old Prussia" when the conscripts
were either rogues or the sons of serfs, and accustomed to accept
without complaint the harsh treatment they received at the hands
of their junker-officers. Officers from districts east of the Elbe –
particularly members of families whose fortunes have declined – are
still to be found in the Prussian army. They are the harshest officers
from the men's point of view. The only officers who can compete
with them in this respect are the sons of up-and-coming middle-
class families who are trying to ape their social superiors.

The brutal treatment of soldiers never quite died out in the
Prussian army and it has now become more frequent and more
serious than in former times. Soldiers have more to learn than
before but time has not been made available for extra instruction
by getting rid of old-fashioned tactical exercises which have now
become quite pointless. In the circumstances the practice has grown
up of giving more and more authority to non-commissioned officers
and they have been allowed to use what methods they please so long

as they teach the recruits what has to be learned. The non-commissioned officers are virtually forced to employ drastic measures to give the troops all the instruction that is necessary in a limited time. It is true that on paper a soldier has the right to complain of ill treatment. This however is a farce in practice. Old-fashioned Prussian techniques are readily employed to silence a soldier who dares to complain. I am sure that regiments from west of the Elbe and regiments composed largely of recruits from big cities are less subject to these evils than regiments of peasants recruited from the east.

At one time the Prussian soldier had a remedy. In the days of the muzzle loader it was quite easy to drop a pebble down the muzzle of a gun and "accidentally" shoot a detested officer on manœuvres. I knew a young man from Cologne in 1849 who was killed in this way by a shot intended for his captain. It is less easy to do this with the modern breech loader without being seen. It may be added that army suicide statistics provide a fairly accurate guide to the degree of ill treatment suffered by soldiers at the hands of their officers. Should officers go too far the old type of revenge may be revived – and indeed there were reports that it had been revived in the last wars in which Prussia was involved. But this is not the way to ensure the defeat of the enemy!

English officers who were present at the manœuvres in the Champagne district in 1891 unanimously praised the good relations between officers and men in the French army. Here the scandals reported in the press about incidents in Germany army barracks would be impossible. Even before the revolution of 1789 it was found to be impossible to introduce corporal punishment, as practised in the Prussian army, into the French army. Not even in the worst period of the campaign in Algeria – not even in the days of the Second Empire – would a French officer have dared to indulge in a tenth of the brutalities that we know take place in the German army. Now that universal conscription has been introduced I would like to see the French non-commissioned officer who would sink so low as to order his men to box each other's ears or to spit in each other's faces. What a low opinion the French soldiers must have of their future enemy when they hear and read of the things that German soldiers are prepared to suffer at the hands of their officers without a murmur. And you may be certain that steps are taken to ensure that soldiers in every French barracks are told about such incidents.

The morale of the French army and the relationship between French officers, non-commissioned officers and men is the same as that which inspired the Prussian army between 1813 and 1815 and twice took our soldiers to Paris. But in Germany we are reverting to the state of affairs in 1806 when a soldier was hardly regarded as a human being and was cursed and treated with shameful brutality. There was a yawning chasm between officers and men. That state of affairs led to the catastrophic defeat of the Prussians at the battle of Jena and their internment in French prison camps.

There is much talk about morale as the decisive factor in war. Yet when we are at peace we are systematically undermining the morale of the German army.

VIII

So far we have assumed that the proposal for the simultaneous gradual reduction of the period of military service – leading eventually to a transition to a militia system – will be universally adopted. But will it be accepted?

Let us suppose that Germany takes the initiative and puts forward the suggestion to Austria, Italy and France. Austria would jump at the chance of securing a maximum period of service of two years and would probably cut down the length of service still further. It seems that Austrian officers are saying – far more openly than German officers – that successful results can be achieved in training at any rate some of the troops for a shorter period than is now employed. Many Austrian officers actually assert that the territorials (*Landwehr*) who train for only a few months are more efficient than regiments of the line. I have been assured that a territorial battalion can be mobilised in 24 hours as compared with several days for a battalion of the line. This is not surprising since the line regiments are hampered by old habits of humdrum routine while the territorials are modern units whose officers have had the courage to reject out of date traditions. The Austrian government and people yearn for a reduction of the military expenses that they have to bear. Austria's experience will encourage her to favour a plan to reduce the time spent with the colours.

Italy will also eagerly accept the proposal because she is suffering financially from the burden of heavy military expenditure. The situation in Italy is so serious that some action must be taken quickly. The reduction of the maximum time during which men serve in the army would obviously be the simplest way to secure financial economies. Either the Triple Alliance (Germany, Austria, Italy) goes bankrupt or it must adopt some such remedy as the one that we are advocating.

Should Germany – having gained the support of Austria and Italy – approach France with a proposal that the length of military service should be reduced by international agreement the French government would be placed in an awkward position. If France were to accept the proposal she would not impair her relative military strength in the slightest. In fact she would actually improve her military position in relation to Germany. The fact that the French only introduced universal compulsory service 20 years ago is in many respects a drawback. But it has one compensating advantage. It means that the French military organisation is up to date, that old traditions have been swept aside, and that further improvements can easily be introduced without having to overcome the opposition of those who hold fast to old-fashioned methods. In general it may be said that after a great defeat any army is ready for great improvements. France, more than any other country, would be in a position to make the best possible use of the proposed shorter period of military service. Moreover France is at the moment engaged in reforming her educational system so that it will be easier for her – than for other countries – to adapt the physical education and pre-military training of her schoolboys to the future needs of the army without delay. This would improve France's military strength in relation to that of Germany. Nevertheless it is possible, indeed, even likely, that the protests of the chauvinists in France would be strong enough to bring about the fall of any government that accepted the proposal which we have made, especially if the proposal came from Germany. The French patriots are just as foolish as the German patriots.

If this happened Germany – as the initiator of the idea – would gain a great advantage. After 27 years of Bismarck's rule Germany is hated everywhere abroad. And there is some justification for this. Germany has annexed the Danes of north Schleswig and has ignored the relevant article of the Treaty of Prague concerning the holding of a plebiscite in Schleswig. Germany has annexed Alsace and Lorraine and has employed methods of petty oppression in Prussia's Polish provinces. These annexations have had nothing to do with the achievement of national unity. We have to thank Bismarck for the fact that Germany is feared as a potential aggressor who is planning to make further annexations in the future. The chauvinist German middle classes have turned the German Austrians out of Germany but talk glibly about Germany still stretching from the Etsch to the Memel and they continue to expect Germans and Austrians to be linked by bonds of brotherly love. They want to annex Holland, Flanders, Switzerland and what they call the "German" Baltic provinces of Russia. Bismarck has been supported by these super-patriots with such success that nobody in Europe trusts the "honest Germans" any more. Wherever you go you will find sympathy for France and distrust of Germany. And Germany is held responsible for the present danger of war. Germany could put an end to all this if she were to support the proposal that I have put forward. She would be the champion of peace and all the doubts of her detractors would vanish. The very country responsible for starting the arms race would now take the lead in reducing armaments. Europe's distrust of Germany would disappear while fear of Germany would give way to sympathy for her new aims. The catch phrase that the Triple Alliance is an alliance for peace would become a reality. And the Triple Alliance which now exists only on paper would become a genuine alliance. Germany would be supported by public opinion throughout Europe and America. This would be a great moral victory which would more than outweigh any possible military objections that might be made with regard to our proposal.

On the other hand should France reject the disarmament proposal she would find herself isolated and regarded with the very suspicion that now hangs over Germany. The middle class of Europe – and their "public opinion" is of vital significance – would say: "Now we can all see who wants war and who wants peace!" And then if by chance a government took office in France which really wanted war it would be faced with a situation in which it would be impossible to embark upon hostilities. In those circumstances France would stand before the world as an aggressor. England and the smaller countries on the Continent would not support her. France would not even be sure of Russia's support – that traditional support which consists of encouraging one's ally to go to war only to leave him in the lurch at a critical moment.

It must be remembered that England will play the most decisive rôle in the next war. Should hostilities break out between the Triple Alliance and the Franco–Russian alliance both sides would need to import large quantities of wheat by sea. France would be separated from her ally by enemy territory and would not be able to secure any wheat from Russia. England has complete command over the sea routes to the Continent. If England's navy were placed at the disposal of one of the rival alliances the other would face a famine because it would be cut off from supplies of wheat. Just as Paris had to surrender owing to a shortage of food so the alliance which lacked wheat would suffer from famine on a much larger scale and would have to surrender. It is as simple as the two times table.

At the moment the Liberals have the upper hand in England and they are decidedly sympathetic to France. Old Gladstone himself is a friend of the Russians. If war breaks out upon the Continent England will stay neutral as long as she can but even her "benevolent neutrality" might, in certain circumstances, be of great advantage to one side or the other. If Germany puts forward our proposal for a shortening of the period of military service we may be sure that England's sympathy for the French would disappear. In such circumstances Germany would have gained the benevolent neutrality of England. Germany would have made it virtually impossible for England to join Germany's enemies.

If France accepts our proposal the danger of war – brought about by the continual growth of armaments – would disappear. Countries will all be able to look forward to peace and Germany would have the honour of having brought this about. But if France were to reject our proposal she would damage her own position in Europe and she would improve Germany's position to such an extent that Germany would not fear that she might be attacked at some time in the future. Without any danger to herself Germany would be able – in association with her Triple Alliance partners who would now really be true allies – to begin gradually to reduce her own period of military service without troubling herself about the policy of other countries in this respect. Germany could also work towards the transition to a militia system. Will Germany have the courage to take the step that would be her salvation? Or will Germany wait until France at last appreciates the true position of Russia and decides to take the decisive step herself – and so gain the respect and sympathy of all Europe?

Since I take the view that the gymnastic and military training of all young men should be an essential feature of the transition to the proposed new system I should make it clear that the militia which I am suggesting bears no resemblance to any existing militia such as the Swiss militia.

London, March 28, 1893

                                                           F. Engels

IX

FREDERICK DEMUTH, 1898

Louise Freyberger to August Bebel, London, September 2 & 4, 1898.[1]

My dear August,

. . . General himself[2] told me that Freddy Demuth was Marx's son. At Tussy's[3] insistence I asked the General straight out. He was very surprised that Tussy should stick to her point of view so obstinately[4] and even at that time he authorised me – should the occasion arise – to deny any rumour that he had disowned his own son. You will remember that I told you about this long before General's death.

Moreover a few days before he died General told Mr Moore[5] that Frederick Demuth was Karl Marx's son. Thereupon Mr Moore went to Orpington to tell Tussy. She replied that General was lying since he had always said that he was the father. Moore returned from Orpington and once more asked the General as a matter of urgency to clear the matter up. The old man repeated his assertion that Freddy was Marx's son. He told Moore: "Tussy wants to make an idol of her father."

On Sunday,[6] the very day before he died, General himself wrote on his slate[7] that Marx was Frederick Demuth's father. Tussy broke down when she left the room. All her hatred of me was forgotten and she wept bitterly on my shoulder.

General authorised us (Mr Moore, Ludwig and myself) to reveal the facts only if he were accused of having treated Freddy badly.

[1] A copy of this letter is in the Bernstein papers in the International Institute for Social History (Amsterdam). It has been printed in W. Blumenberg, *Marx* (1962), pp. 115–17 and in Arnold Künzli, *Karl Marx. Eine Psychographie* (1966), pp. 325–7.

[2] i.e. Friedrich Engels.

[3] i.e. Eleanor Marx.

[4] Eleanor Marx believed that Engels was the father of Frederick Demuth.

[5] Samuel Moore, who – with Aveling – translated into English the first volume of *Das Kapital*.

[6] August 4, 1895. Engels died on August 5.

[7] Engels was suffering from cancer of the throat and could not speak.

He was not going to have his name dragged in the mud – especially as it would do nobody any good. He had agreed to take Marx's place in order to save Marx from serious domestic difficulties. The existence of Marx's son was known to us,[8] to Mr Moore, to Lessner,[9] and to Pfänder.[10] I think that Laura[11] guessed the truth even although she may have had no positive information on the subject. When the letters to Freddy were published[12] Lessner said to me: "Freddy must be Tussy's brother. Of course we knew about it but we could never find out where the boy was brought up."

Freddy is ridiculously like Marx and only blind prejudice could see the slightest resemblance to General in the boy's typical Jewish features and blue-black hair. I have seen the letter that Marx wrote to Engels in Manchester at the time.[13] General had not yet moved to London. I believe that General destroyed this letter as he destroyed so many others in the Marx–Engels correspondence.

That is all that I know about the affair. Neither his mother[14] nor General ever told Freddy the name of his father. I got to know Freddy on the occasion of my first visit to London. Old Nimm[15] introduced him to me as her admirer and he came to visit her regularly once a week. It is curious that he never entered the house by the front door but always came to the kitchen through the tradesman's entrance. Freddy's visits continued after I had taken charge of General's household and I saw to it that he had the full rights of a guest.

I have just read again what you wrote about the affair. Since his wife was dreadfully jealous Marx was always afraid that she would leave him. He had no affection for the boy. To acknowledge him would precipitate too great a scandal. I think that Freddy was boarded with a certain Mrs Louis and he took the name of his foster mother. It was only after Nimm's death that he called himself Demuth.

[8] i.e. Louise Freyberger and Bebel.

[9] Friedrich Lessner (1825–1910), a member of the Communist League in the 1840s and a close friend of Marx and Engels.

[10] Karl Pfänder (1818–76), a member of the Communist League and a friend of Marx and Engels.

[11] Laura Marx.

[12] i.e. Eleanor Marx's letters to Frederick Demuth (written shortly before her suicide). The letters were published by Eduard Bernstein in "Was Eleanor Marx in den Tod trieb" (*Die Neue Zeit*, XVI, ii, 1897–8, p. 481 et. seq.)

[13] i.e. the time of Frederick Demuth's birth.

[14] Helene Demuth.

[15] Helene Demuth.

BIBLIOGRAPHY

Printed Documents

WRITINGS OF MARX AND ENGELS

Karl Marx and F. Engels, *Werke* (40 volumes in 43 books)
Karl Marx and F. Engels, *Studienausgabe* (ed. Iring Fetscher, four volumes, 1966)

MARX–ENGELS CORRESPONDENCE

Karl Marx and F. Engels, *Historisch-kritische Gesamtausgabe: Werke, Schrigten, Briefe:* Part I, Vols 1 to 4, edited by D. Rjazanov, 1929–35: popular edition, 1949
The Selected Correspondence of Karl Marx and F. Engels, 1846–95 (1942)
Karl Marx and F. Engels, *Selected Correspondence* (Foreign Languages Publishing House, Moscow)

VICTOR ADLER

Victor Adlers Aufsätze, Reden und Briefe, Part I *Victor Adler und Friedrich Engels* (1922)
F. Adler (ed.), *Victor Adler: Briefwechsel mit August Bebel und Karl Kautsky* (1954)

AUGUST BEBEL

F. Engels, *Briefe an Bebel* (1958)
W. Blumenberg (ed.), *August Bebels Briefwechsel mit Friedrich Engels* (1965)
Karl Kautsky Jnr (ed.), *August Bebels Briefwechsel mit Karl Kautsky* (1971)

J. P. BECKER

E. Eichorn (ed.), *Vergessene Briefe* (1920)

EDUARD BERNSTEIN

E. Bernstein (ed.), *Die Briefe von Friedrich Engels an Eduard Bernstein* (1925)
H. Hirsch (ed.), *Eduard Bernstein: Briefwechsel mit Friedrich Engels* (1970)

WILHELM BRACKE

Karl Marx–Friedrich Engels, *Briefwechsel mit Wilhelm Bracke, 1869–80* (1963)

N. F. DANIELSON

K. Mandelbaum (ed.), *Die Briefe von Karl Marx und Friedrich Engels an Danielson* (1929)

FERDINAND FREILIGRATH

F. Mehring, *Freiligrath und Marx in ihrem Briefwechsel* (Supplement No. 12 to *Die Neue Zeit*, 1912)

JULIAN HARNEY

F. G. and R. M. Black (eds.), *The Harney Papers* (1969)

ERNEST JONES

J. Saville (ed.), *Ernest Jones: Chartist* (1952)

KARL KAUTSKY

B. Kautsky (ed.), *Friedrich Engels Briefwechsel mit Karl Kautsky* (1955)
F. Adler (ed.), *Victor Adler: Briefwechsel mit August Bebel und Karl Kautsky* (1954)
Karl Kautsky, Jnr (ed.), *August Bebels Briefwechsel mit Karl Kautsky* (1971)

L. KUGELMANN

Karl Marx, *Letters to Dr Kugelmann* (1934)

FERDINAND LASSALLE

Gustav Mayer (ed.), *Ferdinand Lassalle: Nachgelassene Briefe und Schriften*, Vol. 3 *Der Briefwechsel zwischen Lassalle und Marx* (1922)
Gustav Mayer, *Bismarck und Lassalle. Ihr Briefwechsel und ihre Gespräche* (1928)

PAUL AND LAURA LAFARGUE

F. *Engels – Paul and Laura Lafargue: Correspondence* (Foreign Languages Publishing House, Moscow, three volumes, 1959–60)

WILHELM LIEBKNECHT

G. Eckert (ed.), *Wilhelm Liebknecht: Briefwechsel mit Karl Marx und Friedrich Engels* (1963)

CONRAD SCHMIDT

"Engels Briefe an Conrad Schmidt" in *Sozialistische Monatshefte*, 1920

F. A. SORGE

Briefe und Auszüge aus Briefen von Joh. Phil. Becker, Jos. Dietzgen, Friedrich Engels, Karl Marx u.A. an F. A. Sorge und Andere (1906)
Karl Marx and F. Engels, *Letters to Americans, 1848–95* (1963)

GEORG WEERTH

Georg Weerth, *Sämtliche Werke*, Vol. 5 *Briefe* (1959)

J. WEYDEMEYER

"Aus der Flüchtlingszeit von Marx und Engels" in *Die Neue Zeit*, Vol. 25, 1906–7
Karl Marx and F. Engels, *Letters to Americans, 1848–95* (1963)

1838–45

Zwischen 18 und 25: Jugendbriefe von Friedrich Engels (1965)

Miscellaneous

Karl Marx–F. Engels, *Kritiken der sozial-demokratischen Programm-Entwürfe von 1875 und 1891* (1928)

Karl Marx and F. Engels, *On Britain* (Foreign Languages Publishing House, Moscow, 1953): includes articles, letters and F. Engels, *The Condition of the Working Class in England*

Karl Marx and F. Engels, *The Civil War in the United States* (1961): articles and letters

Karl Marx, *The Eastern Question* (ed. Eleanor Marx and E. Aveling, 1897: new edition 1969): includes articles by Engels

Karl Marx and F. Engels, *The Russian Menace to Europe* (ed. P. W. Blackstock and B. F. Hoselitz, 1953)

Karl Marx and F. Engels, *Briefe über "Das Kapital"* (1954)

L. E. Mins, *Engels on Capital* (1937)

Karl Marx and F. Engels, *On Colonialism* (Foreign Languages Publishing House, Moscow): articles and letters

W. O. Henderson (ed.), *Engels: Selected Writings* (Penguin Books, 1967)

H. Hirsch (ed.), *Friedrich Engels Profile* (1970)

The General Council of the First International: Minutes 1864–72 (Foreign Languages Publishing House, Moscow, five volumes)

Die Internationale in Deutschland (1864–72): Dokumente und Materialen (1964)

L. Stern (ed.), *Der Kampf der deutschen Sozialdemokratie in der Zeit des Sozialistengesetzes 1878–90: die Tätigkeit der Reichs-Commission* (two volumes, 1956)

Books and Pamphlets by Engels

1845

Die Lage der arbeitenden Klasse in England (first edition 1845: new edition 1892: printed in 1932 in *Gesamtausgabe*, Part I, Vol. 4 with notes by V. Adoratskij: new edition with introduction by W. O. Henderson, 1965: English translation by Mrs Wischnewetzky, 1887 (U.S.A.) and 1892 (England): new translation by W. O. Henderson and W. H. Chaloner, 1958 and 1971)

1859

Po und Rhein (new edition, 1915)

1860

Savoyen, Nizza und der Rhein (new edition, 1915): sequel to *Po und Rhein*.

1865

Die Preussische Militärfrage und die Deutsche Arbeiterpartei

1872

Zur Wohnungsfrage (1872: new edition 1887): English translation – *The Housing Question* (1935)

1878

Herrn Eugen Dührings Umwälzung der Wissenschaft (1878): English translation – *Anti-Dühring* (1959)

1882

Die Entwicklung des Sozialismus von der Utopie zur Wissenschaft (three chapters from *Anti-Dühring* with an appendix on "The Mark") 1882: English translation – *Socialism, Utopian and Scientific* (1892)

1884

Der Ursprung der Familie, des Privateigentums und des Staates (1884): English translation – *The Origin of the Family, Private Property and the State.*

1891

In Sachen Brentano contra Marx wegen angeblicher Zitatsfälschung (1891)

PUBLISHED AFTER ENGELS'S DEATH

Dialektik der Natur: German text first published in full in 1925: English translation – *Dialectics of Nature* (Progress Publishers, Moscow, 1964)
Die Rolle der Gewalt in der Geschichte: German text first published in 1964: English translation – *The Rôle of Force in History* (1968)
The Part played by Labour in the Transition from Ape to Man, 1876: German text first published in *Die Neue Zeit* in 1896: English translation issued by the Foreign Languages Publishing House, Moscow.

Collections of Articles by Engels

1850

Neue Rheinische Zeitung. Politisch-Ökonomische Revue, 1850: reprinted in 1955 (ed. Karl Bittel): articles on the Baden campaign of 1849, the Ten Hours Bill and the Peasants War in Germany

1851–2

Revolution and Counter Revolution or Germany in 1848 (ed. Eleanor Marx, 1896 and wrongly attributed to Marx): articles in the *New York Daily Tribune,* 1851–2

1853–6

The Eastern Question . . . 1853–6 (ed. Eleanor Marx and E. Aveling, 1897: published under Marx's name, though some of the articles – as stated in the introduction – had been written by Engels: articles in the *New York Daily Tribune* and *The People's Paper*. See also Karl Marx and F. Engels, *The Russian Menace to Europe* (ed. P. W. Blackstock and B. F. Hoselitz, 1953)

1860–6

Engels as Military Critic (ed. W. O. Henderson and W. H. Chaloner, 1959): articles on the volunteer movement in England, the history of the rifle, the French army and the American civil war in the *Volunteer Journal*, 1860–1: articles on the war in Schleswig-Holstein and the Seven Weeks War in the *Manchester Guardian*, 1864 and 1866

1870–1

Notes on the War (ed. F. Adler, 1923): articles on the Franco-Prussian war in the *Pall Mall Gazette*, 1870–1

1872

The Housing Question (ed. C. P. Dutt): articles in *Der Volksstaat*, 1872

1870–6

Internationales aus dem "Volksstaat" (1894): articles on international affairs contributed to *Der Volksstaat* between 1870 and 1876

1881

The British Labour Movement (1934): articles in *The Labour Standard*, 1881

MILITARY AFFAIRS

Ausgewählte Militärische Schriften (two volumes and index: Verlag des Ministeriums für Nationale Verteidigung, Berlin, 1958)

BIOGRAPHIES

Biographische Skizzen (1967): articles and obituaries written between 1878 and 1892 on Karl Marx, Jenny Marx, Jenny Longuet, Wilhelm Wolff, Georg Weerth, J. P. Becker, S. Borkheim and Carl Schorlemmer

TRAVEL

Friedrich Engels, *Auf Reisen* (1966)

Biographies of Engels

Karl Kautsky, *Friedrich Engels: sein Leben, sein Wirken, seine Schriften* (1895): first appeared in the *Oesterreichische Arbeitskalender*, 1888

Max Adler, *Engels als Denker: zum 100. Geburtstag Friedrich Engels* (1920)

D. Rjazanov, *Marx und Engels* (1927)

Gustav Mayer, *Friedrich Engels. Eine Biographie* (two volumes, 1934) Abridged English translation in one volume 1936

E. Czóbel etc., *Friedrich Engels, der Denker und Revolutionär* (1935)

August Cornu, *Karl Marx und Friedrich Engels. Leben und Werk*, Vol. 1, 1818–44 (1954), Vol. 2, 1844–5 (1962)

Grace Carlton, *Friedrich Engels. The Shadow Prophet* (1965)

H. Ullrich, *Der junge Engels*, Vol. 1 (1961), Vol. 2 (1966)

H. Hirsch, *Friedrich Engels* (1968)

H. Gemkow (ed.), *Friedrich Engels. Eine Biographie* (1970)
H. Pelger (ed.), *Friedrich Engels, 1820–1970. Referate, Diskussionen, Dokumente* (Schriftenreihe des Forschungsinstituts der Friedrich Ebert Stiftung, Vol. 85, 1971)
E. A. Stepanowa, *Friedrich Engels. Sein Leben und Werk* (1958)
O. J. Hammon, *Die Roten 48er. Karl Marx und Friedrich Engels* (1972)

Bibliographies

Maximilien Rubel, *Bibliographie des oeuvres de Karl Marx avec, en appendice, un repertoire des oeuvres de Friedrich Engels* (1956)
M. Kliem, H. Merbach, R. Sperl, *Marx Engels Verzeichnis. Werke, Schriften, Artikel* (1966)

Essays on Engels

Hans Pelger (ed.), *Friedrich Engels Referate, Diskussionen, Dokumente* (Schriftenreihe des Forschungsinstituts der Friedrich-Ebert-Stiftung, Band 85, 1971): papers read at an international conference held in Wuppertal May 25–29, 1970.
Friedrich Engels – Denker und Revolutionär (Frankfurt am Main, 1971): proceedings of a conference at Wuppertal organised by the German Communist Party, November 28–29, 1970.

Index

(Marx and Engels omitted)